WORDS AND PLACES

WORDS AND PLACES

OR

ETYMOLOGICAL ILLUSTRATIONS

OF

HISTORY ETHNOLOGY AND GEOGRAPHY

BY THE

Rev. ISAAC TAYLOR, M.A.

EDITED WITH CORRECTIONS AND ADDITIONS

BY

A. SMYTHE PALMER, D. D

LONDON
GEORGE ROUTLEDGE & SONS LTD
1909
REPUBLISHED BY GALE RESEARCH COMPANY, BOOK TOWER, DETROIT, 1968

Library of Congress Catalog Card
Number 68-26608

PREFATORY NOTE

IT may be doubted whether it is within the compass of any one man to write a book such as Dr. Isaac Taylor had the hardihood to essay in his *Words and Places*. It was a pioneer effort and worthy of all praise at the time when it was made. In order to give a trustworthy account of the place-names of all countries, the investigator must not only have a competent knowledge of the languages of all peoples, of their ethnology and development from the earliest times, as traceable in charters, chronicles and institutional documents, of their folk-lore, superstitions and religious beliefs, but, along with all this, have some first-hand acquaintance with the topographical and geographical features of the places about which he has undertaken to write. Thus local etymology is a science of encyclopœdic requirements, and casts its roots deeply into a past that is often prehistoric. Theorizing on the origin and meaning of a place-name in its modern form, without tracing its historical descent back to its oldest, and, if possible, primitive source, has over and over again proved a pitfall to engulf the light-hearted etymologer. What so eminent an authority as Professor Skeat has said of

English place-names may be extended *à fortiori* to those
of more remote and less known regions : ' There is no
subject of study that is, generally speaking, in so neglected
a state. The wild and ignorant guess-work of the eighteenth
century, and some of the nineteenth, has filled our books
of antiquities and our county histories with many mis-
leading theories ; and the results of these unconscionable
inventions have not unfrequently found their way even into
the ordnance-maps ' (*Place-names of Cambridgeshire*, p. I.)
We should take caution from what Wordsworth has so
well said upon the mutability of language and the monu-
mental antiquity of the names which cling to places :

> Mark ! how all things swerve
> From their known course, or vanish like a dream ;
> Another language speaks from coast to coast ;
> Only perchance some melancholy stream
> And some indignant hills old names preserve,
> When laws, and creeds, and people all are lost !

Dr. Taylor was not unconscious of the difficulty of the
herculean task which he had undertaken. His ample
footnotes attest that he made a strenuous effort to acquaint
himself with the literature of the subject so far as it came
within his ken. It was his misfortune, not his fault, that
he wrote when philological science was tentative and
immature, and in half a century since then it has made
huge strides. We cannot be surprised then that many
of his etymological speculations, which were pardonable

at the time, have now to be revised and amended, or sometimes even dismissed as impossible. The work of an editor is exposed to the same difficulties and dangers as those of the original writer, and he cannot hope that he has obelized or corrected every error made in a field that is literally world-wide in its extent. The more obvious ones he has to the best of his ability briefly commented on or corrected, and these additions are printed [thus] within square brackets. In cases of doubtful derivation he has been content with appending a simple query [?], which is intended to put the reader on his guard against accepting that particular statement as an ascertained result.

The abiding value of this book will probably be found to consist especially in the careful analytical grouping which it supplies of statistical details as to the distribution of place-names, and the sections, as it were, which it gives of the ethnical stratification of nomenclature produced by the historical deposits of the centuries.

The following are some of the chief works on Local Names which have appeared since the first publication of the present volume :—

C. R. Beazley, *The Dawn of Modern Geography*, 1897.

C Blackie, *Etymological Geography* (with introduction by Professor J. S. Blackie), 1875.

H. Bradley, ' English Place-Names,' in *Gentleman's Magazine*, N.S., No. 28, pp. 228 *seq.*

W.P.

Cocheris, *Origine et Formation des Noms de Lieux.*

G. S. Davies, *Surrey Local Names.*

Dr. Dawson, *Geography of Canada.*

W. H. Duignan, *Staffordshire Place Names,* 1902 ; *Worcestershire Place Names,* 1905.

Egli, *Nomina Geographica.*

Austin Farmar, *Place-Name Synonyms Classified.*

H. C. Gillies, *Place-Names of Argyll.*

F. H. Habben, *London Street Names : their Origin, Signification and Historic Value.*

Alexander Knox, *Glossary of Geographical and Topographical Terms.*

' The Interest of Place-Names ' in *The Guardian,* August 14, 1907, p. 1,322.

H. Harrison, *Place-Names of the Liverpool District,* 1898.

Houzé, *Noms de Lieux en France.*

J. Jacobsen, *Old Shetland Dialect and Place-Names of Sheffield.*

J. B. Johnston, *Place-Names of Scotland,* 1903 ; *Place-Names of Stirlingshire,* 1904.

P. W. Joyce, *Irish Names of Places, First Series,* 1869, *Second Series,* 1875.

Sir Herbert Maxwell, *Scottish Land Names : Their Origin and Meaning,* 1894.

J. Macdonald, *Place-Names of Strathbogie.*

A. W. Moore, *Manx Names,* 1890 ; revised edition, 1906.

' The Orthography of Geographical Names ' in *The Standard*,
  December 24, 1891.

Professor W. W. Skeat, *Place-Names of Bedfordshire*, 1906 ;
  Place-Names of Cambridgeshire, 1901 ; *Place-Names
  of Hertfordshire*, 1904 ; *Place-Names of Huntingdonshire (Cam. Antiquarian Soc.)*.

B. E. Smith, *The Century Cyclopædia of Names in Geography, etc.*

G. S. Streatfield, *Lincolnshire and the Danes*, 1884.

Isaac Taylor, *Names and Their Histories*, 1896.

W. J. Watson, *Place-Names of Ross-shire and Cromarty*.

                              A. SMYTHE PALMER.

PREFACE TO THE SECOND EDITION
[1865]

THE FIRST EDITION of this book having been rapidly exhausted, I have been encouraged by its favourable reception to spare no labour which might make this Second Edition more complete and trustworthy.

Various errors have been detected, and while new matter to the extent of more than sixty pages has been introduced, a slight typographical re-arrangement has prevented any increase in the absolute bulk of the volume. In endeavouring to secure increased accuracy and completeness, I have derived much valuable aid from the suggestions of many hitherto unknown correspondents, as well as from the able and careful reviews which have appeared in the literary journals.

PREFACE TO THE FIRST EDITION
[1864]

NEARLY two years have passed since this volume was first announced as ready for the press. At that time it did not seem premature to make such an announcement, inasmuch as ten years had been devoted, more or less, to the collection of materials, and the several chapters of the work had been written, and in great part re-written.

The delay that has occurred in the publication will easily be understood and accounted for by those who have been engaged on fields of research where new and untrodden paths are continually inviting exploration, and where many commonly-received opinions require to be examined anew, and perhaps to be corrected in accordance with later or more exact investigation. Some limit, however, must be assigned to such inquiries, which might otherwise be pursued endlessly. In truth, the volume has already far exceeded the size that was at first intended for it, and therefore, such as it has become, it is now put into the reader's hand.

The design of the work, and an outline of its contents, are sufficiently set forth in the Introductory Chapter, and need not therefore be spoken of in this place.

It may appear strange that a subject so fertile in suggestive materials should not already have received due attention from any competent English student. Since the publication, two centuries ago, of Verstegan's *Restitution of Decayed Intelligence in Antiquities*,[1] no work has appeared in England bearing any great resemblance to the present one. There are, it is true, a few alphabetical lists of geographical etymologies :—such are Baxter's crude collection of ingenious conjectures and wild etymological dreams, and Skinner's *Etymologicon Onomasticon*, a far more safe and sober guide. Of more recent date are Mr. Charnock's *Local Etymology*, a book exhibiting some research, but no critical faculty whatever, and a few small school-books, of greater or less value, by Messrs. Sullivan, Gibson, Morris, Hughes, Boardman, and Adams. These, however, being all arranged on the alphabetical plan, are as unreadable as they are, for the most part, untrustworthy.

On the Continent, in Germany especially, subjects allied to that of this volume have been copiously and eruditely treated by such men as Jacob Grimm, Pott, Zeuss, Förstemann, Wilhelm Von Humboldt, Diefenbach, Knobel, Renan, and Pictet. It will be obvious that the author has derived great aid in the accomplishment of his

---

[1] [A book to be included among the untrustworthy, the data being manipulated or invented to suit the author's theories.]

task from the labours of these distinguished scholars, whose acknowledged learning, accuracy, ingenuity, and caution need no commendation from him. Leo, Glück, Buttmann, and De Belloguet, though lesser stars abroad, would in England be luminaries of the first magnitude. There are also numerous monographs of great value hidden in the transactions of foreign academies :—such are the essays of Vilmar, Piderit, Massmann, Petersen, and Meyer, with which the English monographs of Ferguson, Hartshorne, and Monkhouse are worthy to rank. The somewhat dangerous works of Dr. Donaldson and Dr. Latham have been used with caution, and have contributed useful materials and suggestions.

The author cannot allow himself to suppose that, in writing upon a subject which ranges over so wide and various a field, he has always been successful in his endeavour to avoid errors. He can only make this statement —that he has laboriously aimed at accuracy, both in advancing general statements, and in making references to the authorities which he cites. It is, perhaps, unnecessary to state that the common but objectionable practice of quoting at second hand has in no case been adopted without the reader's attention being expressly drawn to the fact. For the convenience of those who may feel inclined to pursue any of the lines of research which are indicated in the notes, a Bibliographical List has been compiled, enumerating the exact titles and editions of the books consulted.

In conclusion, the author has the agreeable task of acknowledging his obligations to those who have given him the benefit of their special acquaintance with certain departments of his subject. The chapters relating to the Semitic languages have been kindly revised by the Venerable Archdeacon Tattam, D.D., LL.D. ; by the Rev. H. G. Williams, B.D., Professor of Arabic at Cambridge ; and by E. Stanley Poole, Esq. The chapter on Celtic names has been annotated by the Rev. John Davies, M.A., while Professor Donkin, of Queen's College, Liverpool, has given the benefit of his acquaintance with the Sanskrit and the Romance languages. G. P. Marsh, Esq., the United States Minister at Turin, has contributed most useful bibliographic information, and has also communicated observations of his own upon the ethnology of Northern Italy ; and the Rev. S. A. Brooke, Chaplain to the British Embassy at Berlin, has given constant literary aid, and has made numerous valuable suggestions during the progress of the work. Lastly, the Author's thanks are due to the authorities at the Topographic Department of the Royal Engineers, and at the library of the Royal Geographical Society, who have afforded every facility for the consultation of their extensive collections of ancient and modern maps.

CONTENTS

CHAPTER I

THE SIGNIFICANCY OF LOCAL NAMES

CHAPTER II

NAMES OF RECENT ORIGIN

CHAPTER III

THE ETHNOLOGICAL VALUE OF LOCAL NAMES

CHAPTER IV

THE NAMES OF NATIONS

xvii

CHAPTER IX

THE CELTS

CHAPTER X

THE HISTORIC VALUE OF LOCAL NAMES

CHAPTER XI

THE STREET-NAMES OF LONDON

Contents

Contents

BIBLIOGRAPHICAL LIST OF BOOKS CONSULTED

Abela, F. Giovanfrancesco :—*Malta Illustrata, ovvero descrizione di Malta, Isola del Mare Siciliano e Adriatico, con sue antichità ed altre notizie,* etc. 2 vols. fol. Malta, 1772.

Adami, M. Canonici Bremensi— *Libellus de situ Daniæ.* (Elzevir.) 24 mo Lugduni Batavorum, 1629.

Adelung, Johann Christoph, und Vater :—*Mithridates : oder allgemeine Sprachenkunde.* 4 vols. 8vo. Berl. 1806, 1809, 1817.

Alcock, Sir Rutherford :—*The Capital of the Tycoon : a Narrative of a Three Years' Residence in Japan.* 2 vols. 8vo. Lond. 1863.

Amari, Michele :—*Storia dei Musulmani di Sicilia.* 2 vols. 8vo. Firenze, 1854–1858.

Ammiani Marcellini—*Quæ supersunt.* 3 vols. 8vo. Lipsiæ, 1808.

Ansted, Prof. D. T. :—*A Short Trip to Hungary and Transylvania.* 8vo. Lond. 1862.

Ansted, Prof. D. T., and Latham, Dr. R. G. :—*The Channel Islands.* 8vo. Lond. 1862.

Astruc, Jean :—*Mémoires pour l' Histoire Naturelle de la Province de Languedoc.* 4to. Paris, 1737.

Archæological Association, Journal of the. 8vo. Lond.

Archæological Institute, Proceedings of the. 8vo. Lond.

Arndt, Christian Gottlieb von :— *Ueber den Ursprung und die verschiedenartige Verwandtschaft der Europäischen Sprachen.* 8vo. Frankfurt am Main, 1818.

Arnold, Thomas, D.D. :—*History of Rome.* 3 vols. 8vo. Lond. 1838–43.

Bancroft, George :—*History of the United States, from the Discovery of the American Continent.* Tenth Thousand. 5 vols. 12mo. Lond. 1854–5.

Baring-Gould, Sabine, M.A. :— *Iceland, its Scenes and Sagas.* 8vo. Lond. 1863.

Barry, Rev. John :—*History of the Orkney Islands.* Second Edition. 4to. Lond. 1808.

Barth, Dr. :—*Travels in North and Central Africa in* 1849–55. 5 vols. 8vo. Lond. 1857.

Barth, C. Karl :—*Ueber die Druiden der Kelten, und die Priester der Alten Teutschen.* 8vo. Erlangen, 1826.

Baxter, William :—*Glossarium Antiquitatum Britannicarum.* Second Edition. 8vo. Lond. 1773.

Beardmore, Nathaniel :—*Manual of Hydrology.* 8vo. Lond. 1862.

Beaufort, Emily A. :—*Egyptian Sepulchres and Syrian Shrines, including some stay in the Lebanon, at Palmyra, and in Western Turkey.* 2 vols. 8vo. Lond. 1861.

Becker, W. A. :—*Charicles : Illustrations of the Private Life of the Ancient Greeks.* Translated. Second Edition. 8vo. Lond. 1854.

Beckmann, J. :—*History of Inventions, Discoveries, and Origins.* Translated by Johnson. Fourth Edition. 2 vols. 8vo. Lond. 1846.

Bender, Dr. Joseph :—*Die Deutschen Ortsnamen, in geographischer. historischer, besonders in sprachlicher Hinsicht.* 8vo. Siegen, 1846.

Bergmann, Frédéric Guillaume :— *Les Gètes ; ou la filiation Généalogique des Scythes aux Gètes.* 8vo. Strasbourg, 1859.

Betham, Sir William :—*The Gael and the Cymbri.* 8vo. Dublin, 1834.

Bianchi-Giovini, A. :—*Sulla Dominazione degli Arabi in Italia.* 8vo. Milano, 1846.

Biondelli, B. :—*Studii Linguistici.* 8vo. Milano, 1856.

Blomefield, Francis :—*An Essay towards a Topographical History of Norfolk.* 5 vols. fol. Fersfield, 1739–1775.

Bocharti, Samuelis—*Opera Omnia.* Editio Tertia. 3 vols. fol. Lugduni Batavorum, 1582.

Booth, Rev. John, B.A. :—*Epigrams, Ancient and Modern.* 12mo. Lond. 1863.

Borring, Étienne :—*Sur la Limite Méridionale de la Monarchie Danoise.* 8vo. Paris, 1849.

Borrow, George :—*Wild Wales ; its People, Language, and Scenery.* 3 vols. 8vo. Lond. 1862.

Bosworth, Rev. Joseph, D.D. :— *The Origin of the English, Germanic, and Scandinavian Languages and nations.* 8vo. Lond. 1848.

Bouche, Charles-François :—*Essai sur l'Histoire de Provence.* 2 vols. 4to. Marseille, 1785.

Boudard, P. A. :—*Sur l'Origine des Premiers Habitants des Iles Baléares,* in the Revue Archéologique, vol. xii. pp. 248–250.

Boudard, P. A. :—*Numismatique Ibérienne.* 4to. Béziers.

Bowditch, N. I. :—*Suffolk Surnames.* Second Edition. 8vo. Boston, 1858.

Brace, Charles L. :—*The Races of the Old World.* 8vo. Lond. 1863.

Brandes :—*Das Ethnographische Verhältniss der Kelten und Germanen.* 8vo. Leipsig, 1857.

British Association, Reports of the. 8vo. Lond.

Brown, Charles Philip :—*Carnatic Chronology.* 4to. Lond. 1863.

Bruce, Rev. John Collingwood :— *The Roman Wall : an Historical, Topographical, and Descriptive Account of the Barrier of the Lower Isthmus.* 4to. Lond. 1851.

Buchanan, William :—*An Inquiry into the Genealogy and Present State of the Ancient Scottish Surnames.* 8vo. Glasgow, 1820.

Buckingham and Chandos, Richard, Duke of—*The Private Diary of.* 3 vols. 8vo. Lond. 1862.

Buckingham, James Silk—*Autobiography of.* 2 vols. 8vo. Lond. 1855.

Buckle, H. T. :—*History of Civilization in England.* 2 vols. 8vo. Lond. 1857, 1861.

Bunsen, Christian Charles Josias :— *Outlines of the Philosophy of Universal History.* 2 vols. 8vo. Lond. 1854.

Bunsen, C. C. J. :—*On the Results of Recent Egyptian Researches in reference to Asiatic and African Ethnology,* in the British Association Reports for 1847.

Burgon, Rev. John William :— *Letters from Rome to Friends in England.* 8vo. Lond. 1862.

Burn, Robert Scott :—*Notes of an Agricultural Tour in Belgium, Holland, and the Rhine.* 8vo. Lond. 1862.

Burton, R. F. :—*Abeokuta and the Camaroons Mountains.* 2 vols. 8vo. Lond. 1863.

Burton, R. F. :—*A Mission to Gelele, King of Dahome.* 2 vols. 8vo. Lond. 1864.

Butler, Rev. Alban :—*The Lives of the Fathers, Martyrs, and other principal Saints, compiled from Original Monuments and other authentic Records.* Stereotype Edition. 12 vols. 8vo. London and Dublin, 1824.

Buttmann, Al. :—*Die Deutschen Ortsnamen, mit besondere Berücksichtigung der Ursprünglich Wendischen, in der Mittelmark und Niederlausitz.* 8vo. Berlin, 1856.

Buttmann, Philipp :—*Mythologus, oder gesammelte Abhandlungen über die Sagen des Alterthums.* 2 vols. 8vo. Berlin, 1828–9.

Buyers, Rev. William :—*Recollections of Northern India.* 8vo. London, 1848.

Calendar of State Papers. 8vo. Lond. 1856–1863.

Cambro-Briton and General Celtic Repository. 3 vols. 8vo. Lond. 1819–22.

Camden, W. :—*Britannia.* Second Edition. Edited by R. Gough. 4 vols. fol. Lond. 1806.

Caswall, Rev. Henry, M.A. :—*The American Church and the American Union.* 8vo. Lond. 1861.

Caussin de Perceval, A. P. :— *Essai sur l'Histoire des Arabes.* 3 vols. 8vo. Paris, 1847–8.

Chalmers, George :—*Caledonia ; an Account, Historical and Topographic, of North Britain.* 3 vols. 4to. Lond. 1810–1824.

Chambers, Robert :—*Ancient Sea Margins, Memorials of Changes.* 8vo. Lond. 1848.

Charnock, Richard Stephen :— *Local Etymology ; a Derivative Dictionary of Geographical Names.* 8vo. Lond. 1859.

Codex Diplomaticus, see Kemble.

Conde, José Antonio :—*Historia de la Dominacion de los Arabes en España.* 8vo. Paris, 1840.

Conybeare, Rev. W. J., and Howson, Rev. J. S. :—*The Life and Epistles of St. Paul.* Third Edition. 2 vols. 8vo. Lond. 1857.

[Cooley, W. D.] :—*The History of Maritime and Inland Discovery.* (Lardner's Cabinet Cyclopædia.) 3 vols. 12mo. Lond. 1830–1831.

Contzen :—*Die Wanderungen der Kelten.* 8vo. Leipsig, 1861.

Courson, Aurélien de :—*Histoire des Peuples Bretons.* 2 vols. 4to. Paris.

Court de Gebelin :—*Le Monde Primitif.* 5 vols. 4to. Paris, 1773 –1778.

Cowel :—*A Law Dictionary.* Fol. Lond. 1727.

Crichton, Dr. Andrew, and Wheaton, Dr. Henry :—*Scandinavia, Ancient and Modern.* 2 vols. 12mo. Edin. 1838.

Cunningham, Peter :—*A Handbook for London, Past and Present.* 2 vols. 8vo. Lond. 1849.

Curtius, Ernst :—*Griechische Geschichte.* 2 vols. 8vo. Berlin, 1857, 1861.

Curtius, Ernst :—*Die Ionier vor der Ionischer Wanderung.* 8vo. Berlin, 1855.

Curtius, Georg :—*Grundzüge der Griechischer Etymologie.* Vol. i. 8vo. Leipsig, 1858.

Darwin, Charles :—*On the Origin of Species by means of Natural Selection.* Fifth Thousand. 8vo. Lond. 1860.

Dasent, George Webbe, D.C.L. :— *The Story of Burnt Njal.* 2 vol. 8vo. Lond. 1861.

Dasent, G. W. :—*The Norsemen in Iceland.* In Oxford Essays for 1858.

Davies, Edward :—*Celtic Researches on the Origin, Traditions, and Language of the Ancient Britons.* 8vo. Lond. 1804.

Davies, Rev. John. Various Papers in the Transactions of the Philological Society.

De Belloguet, Roget, B^on. :—*Ethnogénie Gauloise, ou Mémoires Critiques sur l'Origine et la Parenté des Cimmériens, des Cimbres, des Ombres, des Belges, des Ligures, et des Anciens Celtes.* Vol. i. 8vo. Paris, 1858.

Dennis, George :—*The Cities and Cemeteries of Etruria.* 2 vols. 8vo. London, 1848.

Depping, E. B. :—*Histoire des Expéditions Maritimes des Normands.* 2 vols. 8vo. Paris, 1826.

De Smet :—*Essai sur les noms de la Flandre orientale et occidentale.* In the Mémoires de l'Academie Royale de la Belgique, vol. xxiv. and vol. xxix. Bruxelles, 1820, 1825.

Diefenbach, Dr. Lorenz :—*Lexicon Comparativum Linguarum Indo-Germanicarum. Vergleichen des Wörterbuch der Gothischen Sprache.* 2 vols. 8vo. Frankfort am Main, 1847–1851.

Diefenbach, Dr. Lorenz :—*Celtica. I. Sprachliche Dokumenta zur Geschichte der Kelten.* 8vo. Stuttgart, 1839.

Diefenbach, Dr. Lorenz :—*Celtica. II. Versuch einer genealogische Geschichte der Kelten.* 2 vols. 8vo. Stuttgart, 1840.

Diefenbach, Dr. Lorenz :—*Origines Europææ. Die alten Völker Europas, mit ihren Sippen und Nachbarn.* 8vo. Frankfurt am Main, 1861.

Diez, Friedrich :—*Lexicon Etymologicon Linguarum Romanorum. Etymologisches Wörterbuch der Romanischen Sprachen.* 8vo. Bonn, 1853.

Diez, Friedrich :—*Grammatik der Romanischen Sprachen.* 3 vols. 8vo. Bonn, 1836–44.

Dixon, B. Homer :—*Surnames.* 8vo. Boston, 1857.

Dixon, Rev. W. H., M.A., and Raine, Rev. James, M.A. :—*Fasti Eboracenses* ; *Lives of the Archbishops of York.* 2 vols. 8vo. Lond. 1863.

Domesday Book, see Ellis.

Donaldson, John William, D.D. :—*The New Cratylus* ; *or Contributions towards a more accurate Knowledge of the Greek Language.* Second Edition. 8vo. Lond. 1850.

Donaldson, John William, D.D. :—*Varronianus* ; *a Critical and Historical Introduction to the Ethnography of Ancient Italy,* etc. Second Edition. 8vo. Lond. 1852.

Donaldson, John William, D.D. :—*On English Ethnography.* In Cambridge Essays, Vol. ii. 8vo. Lond. 1856.

Dorow, Dr. :—*Denkmäler alter Sprache und Kunst.* 2 vols. 8vo. Berlin and Bonn, 1823–27.

Drake, Nathan :—*Shakespeare and his Times.* 2 vols. 4to. Lond. 1817.

Drake, Samuel G. :—*The Book of the Indians.* Eighth Edition. 8vo. Boston, 1841.

Ducange, Car. Dufresne :—*Glossarium Mediæ et Infimæ Latinitatis—cum Supplementis Carpenterii et aliorum, disgessit Henschel.* 7 vols. 4to. Paris, 1840-4.

Dudo :—*De Moribus et actis Primorum Normanniæ Ducum.* In Andreas Duchesne's Historiæ Normannorum Scriptores Antiqui. Fol. Lutetiæ Parisiorum, 1819.

Duff, M. E. G., M.A. :—*Sicily.* In Oxford Essays for 1857.

Dufferin, Lord :—*Letters from High Latitudes.* 8vo. Lond. 1857.

Duncker, Maximilian Wolfgang :—

Origines Germanicæ. 4to. Berlin, 1840.

Dyer, George :—Vulgar Errors, Ancient and Modern. 8vo. Exeter, 1816.

Ellis, Sir Henry :—Domesday Book, with General Introduction. 4 vols. folio. Lond. 1783–1816.

Engelhardt :—Das Monte Rosa und Matterhorn Gebirg. 8vo. Strasburg, 1852.

Engelmann, Dr. W. H. :—Glossaire des Mots Espagnols et Portugais dérivés de l'Arabe. 8vo. Leyde, 1861.

Ersch and Gruber :—Allgemeine Encyklopädie der Wissenschaften und Künste. 122 vols. 4to. Leipsig, 1818, etc.

Esquiros, Alphonse :—The Dutch at Home. Translated by Lascelles Wraxall. 2 vols. 8vo. Lond. 1861.

Ethnology and Topography, in The Church of England Quarterly Review, No. lxxv. 8vo. Lond. 1855.

Eustace, Rev. John Chetwoode :— A Classical Tour through Italy. 4 vols. 8vo. Lond. 1815.

Ewald, Heinrich :—Geschichte des Volkes Israel. 3 vols. 8vo. Göttingen, 1843.

Fairholt, Frederick William :—Up the Nile and Home Again. A Handbook for Travellers. 8vo. Lond. 1862.

Farrar, Frederick W., M.A. :— Essay on the Origin of Language. 12mo. Lond. 1860.

Ferguson, Robert :—The Northmen in Cumberland and Westmoreland. 12mo. Lond. 1856.

Ferguson, Robert :—The River-Names of Europe. 12 mo. Lond. 1862.

Finnson, Hans :—Islands Landnamabok. 4to. Havniæ, 1774.

Fleming, George :—Travels on Horseback in Mantchu Tartary. Royal 8vo. Lond. 1863.

Forbes, Duncan :—The History of Chess. 8vo. Lond. 1860.

Forbes, James D. :—Travels through the Alps of Savoy, with Observations on Glaciers. 4to. Edinburgh, 1843.

Forbiger, Albert :—Handbuch der Alten Geographie, aus den Quellen bearbeitet. 3 vols. 8vo. Leipsig, 1842–4.

Ford, Richard :—Gatherings from Spain. 8vo. Lond. 1847.

Förstemann, Ernst. :—Die Deutschen Ortsnamen. 8vo. Nordhausen, 1863.

Förstemann, Ernst :—Altdeutsches Namenbuch. 2 vols. 4to. Nordhausen, 1854.

Förstemann, Ernst : — Deutsche Volksetymologie. In Kuhn's Zeitschrift. Vol. i.

Frontier Lands of the Christian and the Turk. 2 vols. 8vo. Lond. 1853.

Gardner, George :—Travels in the Interior of Brazil, 1836–1841. Second Edition, 8vo. Lond. 1849.

Garnett, Rev. Richard :—The Philological Essays of. Edited by his Son. 8vo. London and Leipsig, 1859.

Gayangos, Pascual de :—History of the Mohammedan Dynasties in Spain, by Ahmed Ibn Mohammed Al-Makkuri. Translated with Notes. 2 vols. 4to. Lond. 1840–1843.

Gentleman's Magazine.

Germania ; Viertel-Jahrsschrift für Deutsche Alterthumskunde. Stuttgart und Wien, 1856, etc.

Gerville, M. de :—Recherches sur les Anciens Noms de lieu en Normandie. In the Mémoires de la Société Royal des Antiquaires de France, vol. vi. 8vo. Paris, 1824.

Gesenius, Dr. W. :—*Versuch über die Maltesische Sprache, zur Beurtheilung der neulich Wiederholten Behauptung dass sie ein Ueberrest der Altpunischen sey.* 4to. Leipsig, 1810.

Gesenius, Dr. W. :—*Scripturæ Linguæque Phœniciæ Monumenta.* 4to. Leipsig, 1837.

Gibbon, Edward :—*The History of the Decline and Fall of the Roman Empire.* New Edition. 8 vols. 8vo. Lond. 1821.

Gibson, T. A., and Gibson, G. M. : —*Etymological Geography : being a Classified List of Terms and Epithets of most frequent occurrence entering as Prefixes or Postfixes into the Composition of Geographical Names.* Second Edition. 8vo. Edinburgh, 1840.

Gilbert, Josiah, and Churchill, G. C. :—*The Dolomite Mountains.* 8vo. London, 1864.

Gladstone, Rt. Hon. W. E. :— *Studies on Homer and the Homeric Age.* Vol. i. 8vo. Oxford, 1858.

Glück, Christian Wilhelm :—*Die bei Caius Julius Cæsar vorkommenden Keltischen Namen, in ihrer Echtheit gestellt und erläutert.* 8vo. München, 1857.

Gough, R. *see* Camden.

Grimm, Jacob :—*Geschichte der Deutschen Sprache.* 2 vols. 8vo. Leipsig, 1848.

Grimm, Jacob :—*Deutsche Grammatik.* 4 vols. 8vo. Göttingen, 1822–1837.

Grimm, Jacob :—*Deutsche Mythologie.* Second Edition. 8vo. Göttingen, 1843–46.

Grimm, Wilhelm :—*Die Deutsche Heldensage.* 8vo. Göttingen, 1829.

Grote, Harriet :—*Collected Papers, original and reprinted, in prose and verse.* 8vo. Lond. 1862.

Guest, Dr. E. :—*On Gentile Names.* In the Philological Proceedings, vol. i.

Haigh, Daniel H. :—*The Conquest of Britain by the Saxons.* 8vo. Lond. 1861.

Hakluyt, Richard :—*The Principal Navigators, Voyages, Traffiques, and Discoveries of the English Nation.* 3 vols. fol. London, 1599–1600.

Haldorsen, Biorn :—*Islandske Lexicon.* 2 vols. 4to. Havniæ, 1814.

Hall's *Chronicle, collated with the Editions of 1548 and 1550.* 4to. Lond. 1809.

Hallam, Henry :—*View of the State of Europe During the Middle Ages.* Fifth Edition. 3 vols. 8vo. Lond. 1829.

Halliwell, J. O., F.R.S. :—*Rambles in Western Cornwall by the Footsteps of the Giants.* 8vo. Lond. 1861.

Hartshorne, Rev. Charles Henry, M.A. :—*Salopia Antiqua, with Observations upon the Names of Places.* Royal 8vo. Lond. 1841.

Hartwig, Dr. G. :—*The Tropical World.* 8vo. Lond. 1863.

Haupt, Moriz :—*Zeitschrift für Deutsches Alterthum.* 12 vols. 8vo. Leipsig, 1841, etc.

Hinchliff, Thomas Woodbine :— *South American Sketches.* 8vo. Lond. 1863.

Hoeck, Karl :—*Kreta.* 3 vols. 8vo. Göttingen, 1823–9.

Hofer, Albert :—*Zeitschrift für die Wissenschaft der Sprache.* 8vo. Greifswald, 1845, etc.

Holtzmann, Adolf :—*Kelten und Germanen : Eine Historische Untersuchung.* 4to. Stuttgart, 1855.

Horsley, John :—*Brittania Romana ; or, the Roman Antiquities of Britain.* Folio. London, 1732.

[Hotten, J. C.] :—*The Slang Dictionary ; or the Vulgar Words, Street Phrases, and Fast Expressions of High and Low Society.* 8vo. Lond. 1864.

Hoveden, Roger de, apud Saville's Scriptores.

Huc, l'Abbé :—*The Chinese Empire.* 2 vols. 8vo. London, 1852.

Humboldt, Alexander von : — *Cosmos : Sketch of a Physical Description of the Universe.* Seventh Edition. 2 vols. 8vo. Lond. 1849.

Humboldt, Wilhelm von :—*Prüfung der Untersuchungen über die Urbewohner Hispaniens.* 4to. Berlin, 1821. Reprinted in vol. ii. of the Collected Works.

Hume, Dr. A. :—*Geographical Terms considered as tending to enrich the English Language.* Reprinted from Vol. xi. of the Transactions of the Historic Society of Lancashire and Cheshire. 8vo. Liverpool, 1859.

Ihre, Johannes :—*Glossarium Suio-Gothicum.* 2 vols. Folio, Upsal, 1769.

Innes, Cosmo :—*Origines Parochiales Scotiæ.* 2 vols. 4to. Edinb. 1850–55.

Ingram, Rev. J., B.D. :—*The Saxon Chronicle, with an English Translation.* 4to. London, 1823.

Islands Landnamabok :—See Finnson.

Jacobi, Victor :—*Die Bedeutung der böhmischen Dorfnamen für Sprach- und Weltgeschichte.* 8vo. Leipsig, 1856.

Jephson, Rev. J. M. : *Narrative of a Walking Tour in Brittany.* 8vo. Lond. 1859.

Kausler :— *Wirtembergisches Urkundenbuch. Herausgegeben von dem Königlichen-Staatsarchiv in Stuttgart.* 2 vols. 4to. Stuttgart, 1849 and 1858.

Keferstein, Chr. :—*Ansichten über die Keltischen Alterthumer.* 2 vols. Halle, 1846–1848.

Kelly, W. :—*Curiosities of Indo-European Folk Lore and Tradition.* 8vo. Lond. 1864.

Kemble, John Mitchell :—*The Saxons in England ; a History of the English Commonwealth till the Period of the Norman Conquest.* 2 vols. Lond. 1849.

Kemble, John M. :—*Codex Diplomaticus Ævi Saxonici.* 5 vols. 8vo. Lond. 1845–1848.

Kennett, Rev. W. :—*Parochial Antiquities.* 2 vols. 4to. Oxford, 1818.

Kenrick, John, M.A. :—*Essay on Primæval History.* 8vo. Lond. 1846.

Kenrick, John, M.A. :—*Phœnicia.* 8vo. Lond. 1855.

Kenrick, John, M.A. :—*Ancient Egypt under the Pharaohs.* 2 vols. 8vo. Lond. 1850.

Kenrick, John, M.A. :—*The Egypt of Herodotus.* 8vo. Lond. 1841.

K[enrick], J. :—*On the Names of the Antehellenic Inhabitants of Greece,* in vol. i. of the Philological Museum. 8vo. Cambridge, 1832.

King, Rev. Samuel William :—*The Italian Valleys of the Pennine Alps.* 8vo. Lond. 1858.

Knapp, J. A. :—*English Roots and Ramifications.* 8vo. Lond. 1857.

Knobel, August :—*Die Völkertafel der Genesis. Ethnographische Untersuchungen.* 8vo. Giessen, 1850.

Kuhn, Dr. A. :—*Zur ältesten Geschichte der indo-germanischen Völker.* 4to. Berlin, 1845.

Kuhn, Dr. A. :—See *Zeitschrift für Vergleichende Sprachforschung.*

Laing, Samuel :—*The Heimskringla, or Chronicle of the Kings of Norway. Translated from the Icelandic of Snorro Sturleson.* 3 vols. 8vo. Lond. 1844.

Landnamabok :—See Finnson.

Lappenberg, J. M. :—*History of England under the Anglo-Saxon Kings.* Translated by Thorpe. 2 vols. 8vo. Lond. 1846.

Lappenberg, J. M. :—*History of England under the Anglo-Norman Kings.* Translated by Thorpe, 8vo. Lond. 1857.

La Roquette :—*Recherches.* *See* Petersen.

Lassen, Christian :—*Indische Alterthumskunde.* Vol. i. Bonn, 1847.

Latham, Dr. Robert Gordon :—*The English Language.* Fourth Edition. 2 vols. 8vo. 1855.

Latham, Dr. R. G. :—*Man and his Migrations.* 12mo. Lond. 1851.

Latham, Dr. R. G. :—*The Nationalities of Europe.* 2 vols. 8vo. Lond. 1863.

Latham, Dr. R. G. :—*The Germania of Tacitus, with Ethnological Dissertations and Notes.* 8vo. Lond. 1851.

Latham, Dr. R. G. :—*The Ethnology of the British Islands.* 12mo. Lond. 1852.

Latham, Dr. R. G. :—*Opuscula : Essays, chiefly Philological and Critical.* 8vo. Lond. and Leipsig, 1860.

Latham, Dr. R. G. :—*Channel Islands.* *See* Ansted.

Latham, Dr. R. G. :—*The Eastern Origin of the Celtic Nations.* *See* Prichard.

Leake, William Martin :—*Travels in Northern Greece.* 4 vols. 8vo. Lond. 1835.

Lechner, Dr. Ernst, Pfarrer in Celerina St. Moritz :—*Piz Languard.* 8vo. Leipsig, 1858.

Leo, Dr. Heinrich :—*Vorlesungen über die Geschichte des Deutschen Volkes und Reiches.* 3 vols. 8vo. Halle, 1854, 57, and 61.

Leo, Dr. Heinrich :—*Rectitudines Singularum Personarum.* 8vo. Halle, 1842.

Leo, Dr. Heinrich :—*Treatise on the Local Nomenclature of the Anglo-Saxons, as exhibited in the Codex Diplomaticus Ævi Saxonici.* Translated by Williams. (A translation of a portion of the preceding work.) 8vo. Lond. 1852.

Leo, H. :—*Feriengeschriften. Ver-mischte Abhandlungen zur Geschichte der Deutschen und Keltischen.* 8vo. Halle, 1847-1852.

Leo, H. :—*Walhen und Deutsche-* In Kuhn's Zeitschrift für Vergleichende Sprachforschung, vol. ii. 1853.

Le Prevost : — *Recherches.* *See* Petersen.

Lewis, Sir George Cornewall :—*Essay on the Origin and Formation of the Romance Languages.* Second Edition, 8vo. Lond. 1862.

Lewis, Sir George Cornewall :—*An Inquiry into the Credibility of the Early Roman History.* 2 vols. 8vo. 1855.

Liddell, Henry G. :—*History of Rome.* 2 vols. 8vo. 1855.

Lindsay, Lord :—*Progression by Antagonism.* 8vo. Lond. 1846.

Lingard, John :—*History of England.* Fifth Edition, 10 vols. Lond. 1849.

Lluyd, Edward : — *Adversaria.* Appended to Second Edition of Baxter's Glossarium Antiquit. Britann. q. v.

Loudon, J. C. :—*Encyclopædia of Plants, comprising the description of all the Plants indigenous to, or cultivated in, Britain.* 8vo. Lond. 1829.

Louth :—*The Wanderer in Western France.* 8vo. Lond. 1863.

Lucas, Samuel :—*Secularia.* 8vo. Lond. 1862.

Lyell, Sir Charles :—*Principles of Geology : or, the Modern Changes of the Earth and its Inhabitants, considered in illustration of Geology.* Ninth Edition. 8vo. Lond. 1853.

Lyell, Sir Charles, M.A. :—*The Geological Evidences of the Antiquity of Man.* 8vo. Lond. 1863.

Macaulay, Lord :—*History of England.* 8vo. Lond. 1856.

Mackay, Charles :—*A History of London.* 8vo. Lond. 1838.

Maclear, George Frederick, M.A. :— A History of Christian Missions during the Middle Ages. 8vo. Cambridge, 1863.

Mahn, Dr. C. A. F. :—Ueber den Ursprung und die Bedeutung des Namens Preussen. 8vo. Berlin, 1850.

Mahn, Dr. C. A. F. :—Ueber die Bedeutung des Namens der Städte Berlin und Köln. 8vo. Berlin, 1848.

Mannhardt, Dr. Wilhelm :—Die Götterwelt der deutschen und nordischen Völker. Vol. i. 8vo. Berlin, 1860.

Mannhardt, Dr. Wilhelm :—Germanische Mythen. 8vo. Berlin, 1858.

Marsh, George P. :—Lectures on the English Language. Edited by Dr. W. Smith. 12mo. Lond. 1862.

Marsh, George P. :—The Origin and History of the English Language. 8vo. Lond. 1862.

Marsh, George P. :—Man and Nature ; or, Physical Geography as modified by Human Action. Lond. 8vo. 1864.

Matthæi Paris :—Historia Major. Ed. Will. Wats. Folio. Lond. 1640.

Maury, L. F. Alfred :—Histoire des Grandes Forêts de la Gaule, êt de l'ancienne France. 8vo. Paris, 1850.

Mayhew, Henry :—German Life and Manners as seen in Saxony at the present day. 2 vols. 8vo. Lond. 1864.

Ménage :—Les Origines de la Langue Françoise. 4to. Paris, 1650.

Meyer, Dr. Charles :—On the Importance of the Study of the Celtic Language. In the Reports of the British Association for 1847.

Meyer, Dr. H. :—Die Ortsnamen des Kantons Zürich. In the Mittheilungen der Antiquarischen Gesellschaft in Zürich, vol. vi. 4to. 1848.

Michel, Francisque :—Histoire des Races Maudites de la France et de l'Espagne. 2 vols. 8vo. Paris, 1847.

Miller, Hugh :—Sketch-Book of Popular Geology ; being a series of Lectures delivered before the Philosophical Institution of Edinburgh. 8vo. Edinburgh, 1859.

Milman, Henry Hart, Dean of St. Paul's :—History of Latin Christianity. Second Edition, 6 vols. 8vo. 1857.

Mommsen, Theodore :—The History of Rome. Translated by the Rev. W. P. Dickson. 2 vols. 8vo. Lond. 1862.

Mommsen, Theodore :—The Earliest Inhabitants of Italy. Translated by George Robertson. 8vo. Lond. 1858.

Monkhouse, Rev. W., B. D. :— Etymologies of Bedfordshire. 8vo. Bedford, 1857.

Mone, Franz Joseph :—Geschichte des Heidenthums im nördlichen Europa. 2 vols. 8vo. Leipsig und Darmstadt, 1822, 1823.

Mone, Franz Joseph :—Celtische Forschungen zur Geschichte Mitteleuropas, 8vo. Freiburg in Breisgau, 1857.

Morris, R. :—The Etymology of Local Names, with a short Introduction to the Relationship of Languages. 12mo. Lond. 1857.

Motley, John Lothrop :—The Rise of the Dutch Republic. 3 vols. 12mo. Lond. 1861.

Movers, F. C. :—Die Phönizier. 3 vols. 8vo. Berlin und Bonn, 1841, 49, 50.

Movers, F. C. :—Phönizien. In Ersch und Gruber's Allgemeine Encyklopädie. Part iii. vol. xxiv. pp. 319-443.

Müller, Ferd. H. :—Der Ugrische Volksstamm. 2 vols. 8vo. Berlin, 1837, 1839.

Müller, Hermann :—Die Marken des Vaterlandes. Vol. i. 8vo. Bonn, 1837.

Müller, Karl Otfried :—*Prolegomena zu einer Wissenschaftlichen Mythologie.* 8vo. Göttingen, 1825.

Müller, C. O. :—*History and Antiquities of the Doric Race.* Translated by H. Tufnell and G. C. Lewis. Second Edition. 2 vols. 8vo. 1839.

Müller, Max, M.A. :—*Lectures on the Science of Language.* Second Edition. 8vo. Lond. 1862. Second Series, 1864.

Müller, Max :—*On Comparative Mythology.* In Oxford Essays for 1856. 8vo. Lond.

Müller, Wilhelm :—*Geschichte und System der altdeutschen Religion.* 8vo. Göttingen, 1844.

Murphy, J. C. :—*The History of the Mahometan Empire in Spain.* 4to. Lond. 1816.

Murray, John :—*A Handbook for Travellers in Switzerland and the Alps of Savoy and Piedmont.* Eighth Edition. 8vo. Lond. 1854.

Murray, John :—*Handbook of Devon and Cornwall.* 8vo. Lond. 1859.

Newman, Francis W. :—*Regal Rome* 12mo. Lond. 1852.

Nicholls, Rev. H. G., M.A. :—*The Forest of Dean, an Historical and Descriptive Account.* Sq. 8vo. Lond. 1858.

Niebuhr, B. G. :—*Lectures on Ancient Ethnography and Geography.* Translated by Dr. L. Schmitz. 2 vols. 8vo. Lond. 1853.

Niebuhr, B. G. :—*Lectures on the History of Rome.* Edited by Dr. L. Schmitz. 3 vols. 8vo. Lond. 1844–1849.

Niebuhr, B. G. :—*The History of Rome.* Translated by J. C. Hare, and Connop Thirlwall. Fourth Edition. 3 vols. 8vo. Lond. 1847–1851.

Olshausen, J. :—*Ueber phönicische Ortsnamen ausserhalb des semi-tischen Sprachgebiets.* In vol. viii. of the Rheinisches Museum für Philologie. 8vo. Frankfurt am Maine, 1853.

Ormerod, George :—*History of the County Palatine and City of Chester,* 3 vols. fol. Lond. 1819.

Palgrave, Sir Francis :—*History of Normandy and England.* 4 vols. 8vo. Lond. 1851, 1857, 1864.

Palgrave, Sir Francis :—*History of the Rise and Progress of the English Commonwealth during the Anglo-Saxon Period.* 2 vols. 4to. Lond. 1832.

Panzer, Friederich :—*Beitrag zur Deutschen Mythologie.* 8vo. München, 1848.

Papon :—*Histoire Générale de Provence.* 4 vols. 4to. Paris, 1777 —1786.

Pauli, Dr. Reinold :—*Pictures of Old England.* Translated by E. C. Otté. 8vo. Lond, 1861.

Pennant, Thomas :—*A Tour in Wales.* 2 vols. 4to. Lond. 1778–1784.

Pennant, Thomas :—*Some Account of London.* Third Edition. 4to. London, 1793.

Pertz, G. H :—*Monumenta Germaniæ Historica, ab anno Christi 500 usque ad annum 1500.* 12 vols. fol Hannov. 1826–1848.

Petersen, N. M., and Le Prevost : —*Recherches sur l'origine, l'étymologie, et le signification primitive de quelques noms de lieux en Normandie.* *Traduites au danois par M. de La Roquette.* In the Bulletin de la Société de Géographie, Jan. 1835. 8vo. Paris, 1835.

Philological Museum. 2 vols. 8vo. Cambridge, 1832, 1833.

Philological Society, Proceedings of the. 6 vols. 8vo. Lond. 1842—1853.

Philological Society, Transactions of the. 8vo. Lond. 1854–1861.

Philology, Comparative :—In the Edinburgh Review, vol. xci. Oct. 1851.

Philosophical Transactions of the Royal Society of London. 4to. Lond.

Pictet, Adolphe :—*Les Origines Indo-Européennes, ou les Aryas Primitifs.* 2 vols. 8vo. Paris, 1859, 1863.

Piderit, Dr. F. C. H. :—*Die Orts-namen in der Provinz Nieder-hessen.* In the Zeitschrift des Vereins für hessische Geschichte und Landeskunde, vol. i. pp. 283–316. Kassel, 1837.

Piers Ploughman. The Vision and the Creed of. 2 vols. 12mo. Lond. 1832.

Pihan, A. P. :—*Glossaire des Mots Français tirés de l'Arabe, du Persan, et du Turc, etc.* 8vo. Paris, 1847.

Planta, Joseph :—*An Account of the Romansch Language.* In the Philosophical Transactions of the Royal Society, vol. lxvi. 4to. 1776.

Porter, Major Whitworth, R. E. :—*History of the Knights of Malta,* 2 vols. 8vo. Lond. 1858.

Poste, Rev. Beale :—*Britannic Researches.* 8vo. Lond. 1853.

Pott, Dr. A. F. :—*Etymologische Forschungen auf dem Gebiete der 2 vols. 8vo. Indo-Germanischen Sprachen.* Lengo, 1883.

Pott, Dr. August Friedrich :—*Die Personen-namen, insbesondere die Familien-namen und ihre Entstehungsarten, auch unter Berücksichtigung der ortsnamen.* 8vo. Leipsig, 1853.

Pott, Dr. A. F. :—*Die Zigeuner in Europa und Asien.* 2 vols. 8vo. Halle, 1844, 1845.

Pott, Dr. A. F.:—*Mytho-Etymologie.* In Kuhn's Zeitschrift. Vol. ix.

Pott, Dr. A. F. :—*Etymologische Spahne.* In Kuhn's Zeitschrift. Vol. v.

Pott, Dr. A. F. :—*Indo-Germanischer Sprachstamm.* In Ersch und Gruber's Allgemeine Encyklopädie. Second Section. Vol. xviii. pp. 1–112.

Poulson, George :—*The History and Antiquities of the Seignory of Holderness.* 2 vols. 4to. Hull, 1840, 1841.

Preller, C. :—*Griechische Mythologie.* 2 vols. 8vo. Leipsig, 1854.

Prescott, W. H. :—*History of Ferdinand and Isabella.* 3 vols. 12mo. Lond. 1850.

Prescott, W. H. :—*History of the Conquest of Peru.* Fourth Edition. 3 vols. 12mo. Lond, 1850.

Prichard, Dr. James C. :—*Researches into the Physical History of Mankind.* Third Edition. 4 vols. 8vo. 1841–1847.

Prichard, Dr. James C. :—*The Eastern Origin of the Celtic Nations.* Edited by Dr. Latham. 8vo. Lond. 1857.

Prichard, Dr. J. C. :—*On the Various Methods of Research which Contribute to the Advancement of Ethnology.* In the Reports of the Seventeenth Meeting of the British Association, for 1847.

Pryce, William, M. D. :—*Archæologia Cornu-Britannica ; or an Essay to Preserve the Ancient Cornish Language.* 4to. Sherbourne, 1790.

Purchas :—*His Pilgrimes.* 5 vols. Folio. Lond. 1625.

Quarterly Journal of Education. 10 vols. 8vo. Lond. 1831–1835.

Quarterly Journal of the Geological Society. 8vo. Lond.

Radlof, Dr. I. G. :—*Neue Untersuchungen des Keltenthumes.* 8vo. Bonn, 1822.

Rawlinson, Rev. George, M.A., Sir Henry Rawlinson, K.C.B., and Sir J. G. Wilkinson, F.R.S. :

—*The History of Herodotus. A New English Version, with copious Notes and Appendices, etc.* 4 vols. 8vo. Lond. 1858.

Redding, Cyrus :—*History and Description of Modern Wines.* Third Edition. 8vo. Lond. 1851.

Rees, Rev. W. J. :—*Lives of the Cambro-British Saints.* 4to. Llandovery, 1853.

Rees, Prof. Rev. Rice, M.A. :— *An Essay on the Welsh Saints, or the Primitive Christians usually considered to have been the founders of Churches in Wales.* 8vo. Lond. 1836.

Reinaud, L'Abbé Joseph-Toussaint : —*Invasions des Sarazins en France, et de France en Savoie ; en Piémont et dans la Suisse, pendant les 8ᵉ, 9ᵉ, et 10ᵉ Siècles de notre ère.* 8vo. Paris, 1836.

Renan, Ernest :—*De l'Origine du Langage.* Second Edition. 8vo. Paris, 1858.

Renan, Ernest :—*Histoire Générale et Système Comparé des Langues Sémitiques.* Pt. i. Third Edition. 8vo. Paris, 1863.

Revue Archéologique. 8vo. Paris.

Robertson, E. William :—*Scotland under her Early Kings ; a History of the Kingdom to the Close of the Thirteenth Century.* 2 vols. 8vo. Edinburgh, 1862.

Robinson, Edward, D.D. :—*Biblical Researches in Palestine, Mount Sinai, and Arabia Petræa.* 3 vols. 8vo. Lond. 1841.

Robinson, Edward, D.D., LL.D. : —*Later Biblical Researches in Palestine and the adjacent Regions.* 8vo. Lond. 1856.

Russell, W. H. :—*My Diary, North and South.* 2 vols. 8vo. Lond. 1863.

Saint Fargeau, A. Girault de :— *Dictionnaire des toutes les Communes de la France.* 3 vols. 4to. Paris, 1844-1846.

St. John, James Augustus :—*History of the Four Conquests of England.* 2 vols. 8vo. Lond. 1862.

Salverte, Eusèbe :—*Essai Historique et Philosophique sur les Noms d'Hommes, de Peuples, et des Lieux.* 2 vols. 8vo. Paris, 1824.

Sankey, William S. :—*The Portefeuille of Science and Art.* 8vo. Edinburgh, 1838.

Saxon Chronicle. See Ingram.

Sayer, Captain :—*The History of Gibraltar.* 8vo. Lond, 1862.

Schafarik, Paul Joseph :—*Slawische Alterthümer. Deutsch von M. von Aehrenfeld.* 2 vols. 8vo. Leipsig, 1843, 1844.

Schleicher, A. :—*Die Sprachen Europas.* 8vo. Bonn, 1850.

Schleicher, A. :—*Zur Vergleichenden Sprachengeschichte.* Bonn, 1848.

Schmeller, J. A. :—*Ueber die sogenannten Cimbern der VII. und XIII. Communen auf den Venedischen Alpen, und ihre Sprache.* In the Abhandlungen der Philosophisch - Philologe - Classe der Königlich Bayerisch Akademie der Wissenschaften, vol. ii. pt. 3, pp. 559–708. 4to. München, 1834.

Schott, Albert :—*Die Deutschen Colonien in Piémont.* 8vo. Stuttgart und Tübingen, 1842.

Schott, Albert :—*Die Deutschen am Monte Rosa, mit ihren Stammenosser in Wallis und Uechtland.* 4to. Zürich, 1840.

Sheppard, Dr. John G. :—*The Fall of Rome, and the Rise of the New Nationalities.* 8vo. Lond. 1861.

Singer, S. W. :—*Wayland Smith, a Dissertation on a Tradition of the Middle Ages ; from the French of G. B. Depping and Francisque Michel, with additions.* 12mo. Lond. 1847.

Skene, William, F. :—*The Highlanders of Scotland ; their Origin, History, and Antiquities.* 2 vols. 12mo. 1837.

Smiles, Samuel :—*Lives of the Engineers.* 2 vols. 8vo. Lond. 1861.

Smith, George, LL.D. :—*The Cassiterides ; an Inquiry into the Commercial Operations of the Phœnicians in Western Europe.* 8vo. Lond. 1863.

Smith, Goldwin :—*Irish History and Irish Character.* 8vo. Oxford and Lond. 1861.

Smith, J. T. :—*Antiquarian Rambles through the Streets of London.* 2 vols. 8vo. Lond. 1846.

Smith, Captain John :—*The Generall Historie of Virginia, New England, and the Summer Isles.* 4to. Lond. 1627.

Smith, Captaine John :—*The True Travels, Adventures and Observations of in Europe, Asia, Africke, and America.* 4to. Lond. 1630.

Smith, Dr. W. :—*Dictionary of Greek and Roman Geography.* 2 vols. 8vo. Lond. 1856, 1857.

Sousa, Fr. Joao de :—*Vestigios da Lingua Arabica em Portugal.* 8vo. Lisboa, 1789.

Souvestre, Emile :—*Les Derniers Britons.* 2 vols. 12mo. Paris, 1854.

Sparschuh, Dr. N. :—*Berichtigungen und Beitrage zu Grimm's Geschichte der Deutschen Sprache.* 8vo. Maintz, 1850.

Stalder, Franz Joseph :—*Die Landessprachen der Schweiz, oder Schweizerische Dialektologie* 12mo. Aarau, 1819.

Stanley, Rev. A. P. (Dean of Westminster) :—*Historical Memorials of Canterbury.* Second Edition. 8vo. Lond. 1855.

Stanley, Rev. A. P. :—*The Study of Modern History in London. A Lecture.* 8vo. Lond. 1854.

Stanley, Dr. Arthur Penrhyn :—*Sinai and Palestine : in Connexion with their History.* Twelfth Thousand. 8vo. Lond. 1862.

Stanley, Dr. A. P. :—*Lectures on the History of the Jewish Church.* 8vo. Lond. 1863.

Steub, Ludwig :—*Ueber die Urbewohner Rätiens, und ihrer Zusammenhang mit den Etruskern.* 8vo. München, 1843.

Steub, Ludwig :—*Zur Rhätischen Ethnologie.* 8vo. Stuttgart, 1854.

Stow, John :—*Survey of the Citiee of London and Westminster.* 2 vols. Folio. Lond. 1720.

Strinnholm, A. M. :—*Vikingzüge der alten Skandinavier. Aus dem Schwedischen, von Dr. C. F. Frisch.* 8vo. Hamburg, 1839.

Sullivan, Robert, LL.D. :—*A Dictionary of Derivations ; or, an Introduction to Etymology on a new plan.* Seventh Edition. 12mo. Dublin, 1855.

Symington, Andrew James :—*Pen and Pencil Sketches of Faröe and Iceland.* 8vo. Lond. 1862.

Talbot, H. Fox :—*English Etymologies.* 8vo. Lond. 1847.

Tallack, William :—*Malta under the Phenicians, Knights, and English.* 8vo. Lond. 1861.

Taylor, Joseph :—*Antiquitates Curiosæ : the Etymology of many Remarkable Old Sayings, Proverbs, and Singular Customs Explained.* 12mo. Lond. 1818.

Thierry, Amédée :—*Histoire des Gaulois.* Second Edition. 3 vols. 8vo. Paris, 1835.

Thierry, Augustin : — *Historical Works of, containing the Conquest of England by the Normans, and Narrative of the Merovingian Era.* 8vo. Lond. 1851.

Thirlwall, Connop, Bishop of St. David's :—*The History of Greece.* 8vo. Lond. 1845.

Thornbury, G. W. :—*The Monarchs of the Main ; or, Adventures of the Buccaneers.* 3 vols. 8vo. Lond. 1855.

Thorpe, Benjamin :—*Northern Mythology ; comprising the principal*

Popular traditions and superstitions of Scandinavia, North Germany, and the Netherlands. 3 vols. 8vo. Lond. 1851.

Thrupp, John :—*The Anglo-Saxon Home, a History of the Domestic Institutions and Customs of land from the Fifth to the Eleventh Century.* 8vo. Lond. 1862.

Timbs, John :—*Curiosities of London.* 12mo. Lond. 1855.

Tooke, John Horne : — ΕΠΕΑ ΠΤΕΡΟΕΝΤΑ : *or, the Diversions of Purley.* Second Edition. (First Edition of part ii.) 4to. Lond. 1798–1805.

Train, Joseph :—*An Historical and Statistical Account of the Isle of Man.* 2 vols. 8vo. Douglas, 1845.

Trench, Richard Chenevix, D.D. (Archbishop of Dublin) :—*On the Study of Words.* Fifth Edition. 12mo. Lond. 1853.

Trench, Dr. R. C. :—*English Past and Present.* Five Lectures. Fourth Edition. 12mo. Lond. 1859.

Trench, Dr. R. C. :—*A Select Glossary of English Words used formerly in senses different from their present.* Second Edition. Lond. 12mo. 1859.

Trollope, Adolphus :—*A Lenten Journey in Umbria and the Marches.* 8vo. Lond. 1862.

Tschudi :—*Haupt-Schlüssel zu verschiedenen Alterthumen.* Fol. Constantz, 1758.

Turner, Sharon :—*The History of the Anglo-Saxons.* Fifth Edition. 3 vols. 8vo. Lond. 1828.

Ungrisches Magazin. 4 vols. 8vo. Pressburg, 1781–1787.

Verstegan, Richard :—*Restitution of Decayed Intelligence in Antiquities.* 12mo. Lond. 1673.

Vilmar, Dr. :—*Die Ortsnamen in Kurhessen.* In the Zeitschrift des Vereins für hessische Geschichte und Landeskunde. Vol. i. pp. 237–282. 8vo. Kassel, 1837.

Warnkönig, Leopold August :— *Flandrische Staats- und Rechtsgeschichte, bes zum Jahr, 1305.* 3 vols. 8vo. Tübingen, 1835–1842.

Warter, Rev. John Wood :—*The Seaboard and the Down ; or, My Parish in the South.* 2 vols. 8vo. Lond. 1860.

Weber, Albrecht :—*Indische Skizzen.* 8vo. Berlin, 1857.

Wedgwood, Hensleigh :—*A Dictionary of English Etymology.* Vols. i. and ii. 8vo. Lond. 1859, etc.

Welsford, Henry :—*On the Origin and Ramifications of the English Language.* 8vo. Lond. 1845.

Wenrich, Joannes Georgius :— *Rerum ab Arabibus in Italia insulisque adjacentibus, Sicilia maxime, Sardinia atque Corsica gestarum Commentarii.* 8vo. Lipsiæ, 1845.

Weston, Stephen, B.D. :—*Remains of Arabic in the Spanish and Portuguese Languages.* 12mo. Lond. 1818.

Wheeler, J. Talboys :—*The Geography of Herodotus.* 8vo. Lond. 1854.

Whitaker, John :—*The History of Manchester.* 2 vols. 4to. Lond. 1775.

Whitaker, Thomas Dunham :—*An History of the Original Parish of Whalley, and Honor of Clitheroe.* Third Edition. Folio. Lond. 1818.

Wilkinson, Sir J. G. :—*Manners and Customs of the Ancient Egyptians.* 6 vols. 8vo. Lond. First Series, 1837 ; Second Series, 1841.

Williams, Archdeacon John :— *Essays on Various Subjects.* 8vo. Lond. 1858.

Williams, Roger :—*A Key into the Languages of America.* 16mo. Lond. 1643.

Wilson, Daniel :—*The Archæology and Pre-historic Annals of Scotland.* Royal 8vo. Edin. 1851.

Wilson, Daniel, F.S.A. :—*Prehistoric Man ; Researches into the Origin of Civilization in the Old and the New World.* 2 vols. 8vo. Cambridge, 1862.

Wilton, Rev. Edward, M.A. :—*The Negeb, or " South Country " of Scripture,* 12mo. Lond. 1863.

Witte, J. H. F. Carl :—*Alpinisches und Transalpinisches. Neuen Vorträge.* 16mo. Berlin, 1858.

Worsaae, J. J. A. :—*An Account of the Danes and Norwegians in England, Scotland, and Ireland.* 8vo. Lond. 1852.

Wright, Thomas, M.A. :—*Essays on Archæological Subjects.* 2 vols. 8vo. Lond. 1861.

Wright, Thomas, M.A. :—*Wanderings of an Antiquary, chiefly upon the Traces of the Romans in Britain.* 12mo. Lond. 1854.

Wright, Thomas, M.A. :—*The Celt, the Roman, and the Saxon.* 8vo. Lond. 1861.

Wright, Thomas, M.A. :—*On Wayland Smith.* In the Journal of the Archæological Association, vol. xvi. pp. 50–58.

[Yonge, C. M.] :—*History of Christian Names.* 2 vols. 8vo. Lond. 1863.

Zeitschrift für Vergleichende Sprachforschung auf dem Gebiete des Deutschen, Griechischen und Lateinischen. Herausgegeben von Dr. T. Aufrecht und Dr. A. Kuhn. 10 vols. 8vo. Berlin, 1852, etc.

Zeitschrift der Morgenlandische Gesellschaft.

Zeitschrift für Deutsche Mythologie, und Sittenkunde. 4 vols. 8vo. Göttingen, 1853–1859.

Zeitschrift für Deutsches Alterthum. See Haupt.

Zeitschrift für die Wissenschaft der Sprache. 8vo. Greifswald, 1845, etc. See Höfer.

Zeuss, J. C. :—*Grammatica Celtica.* 2 vols. (paged continuously) 8vo. Leipsig, 1853.

Zeuss, Kaspar :—*Die Herkunft der Baiern von den Markomannen gegen die bisherigen Muthmassungen bewiesen.* 8vo. München, 1839.

Zeuss, Kaspar :—*Die Deutschen und die Nachbarstämme.* 8vo. München, 1837.

Classical writers, such as Pliny, Tacitus, Josephus, Juvenal, Jerome, Beda, Gregory the Great, etc., are cited by the chapter and verse. The same has been done with the English classics—such as Shakespeare, Chaucer, Wicliffe, Milton, Scott, and Blackstone.

The titles of the German Philological Journals quoted are given at full length in the preceding list. This has not seemed to be necessary with well-known English periodicals—such as the *Quarterly, Edinburgh, North British,* and *Saturday Reviews, The Times, The Guardian, Notes and Queries.*

Great use has been made of Richardson's *New Dictionary of the English Language,* 2 vols. 4to [altogether obsolete in its etymologies] ; as well as the useful *Imperial Dictionary.* I have constantly consulted K. von Spruner's *Historisch-Geographisches Hand-Atlas ;* the Maps of the Useful Knowledge Society ; the Ordnance Survey of Great Britain ; and the convenient reduction published by Crutchley. I have also used the large Government Surveys of France, Switzerland, Belgium, Würtemberg, Bavaria, etc., and other ancient and modern maps too numerous to mention.

WORDS AND PLACES

CHAPTER I

THE SIGNIFICANCY OF LOCAL NAMES

Local Names always significant, and possessed of great vitality—Some descriptive—Geological value of such names—Others conserve ethnological and historical facts, or illustrate the state of civilization or religion in past times.

LOCAL names, whether they belong to provinces, cities, and villages, or are the designations of rivers and mountains, are never mere arbitrary sounds, devoid of meaning. They may always be regarded as records of the past, inviting and rewarding a careful historical interpretation.

In many instances the original import of such names has faded away, or has become disguised in the lapse of ages ; nevertheless, the primeval meaning may be recoverable, and whenever it is recovered we have gained a symbol that may prove itself to be full-fraught with instruction ; for it may indicate—emigrations—immigrations—the commingling of races by war and conquest, or by the peaceful processes of commerce :—the name of a district or of a town may speak to us of events which written history has failed to commemorate. A local name may often be adduced as evidence determinative of controversies that otherwise could never be brought to a conclusion.

The names of places are conservative of the more archaic forms of a living language, or they embalm for us the guise and fashion of speech in eras the most remote. These topographic words, which float down upon the parlance of successive generations of men, are subject in their course to less phonetic abrasion than the other elements of a people's speech. Such words, it is true, are subject to special perils, arising from attempts at accommodating their forms to the requirements of popular etymological speculation ; but, on the other hand, they are more secure than other words from the modifying influences of grammatical inflexion.

The name of many an ancient city seems as if it were endowed with a sort of inherent and indestructible vitality : it is still uttered, unchanged in a single letter—*monumentum ære perennius*—while fragments of marble columns, or of sculptures in porphyry or granite, are seen strewing the site confusedly.[1]

What has been affirmed by the botanist as to the floras of limited districts, may be said, with little abatement, concerning local names—that they survive the catastrophes which overthrow empires, and that they outlive devastations which are fatal to almost everything besides. Wars may trample down or extirpate whatever grows upon a soil, excepting only its wild flowers, and the names of those sites upon which man has found a home. Seldom is a people utterly exterminated,[2] for the proud conqueror leaves ' of the poor of the land ' to till the glebe anew ; and these enslaved outcasts, though they may hand down no memory of the splendid deeds of the nation's heroes, yet retain a most tenacious recollection of the names of the hamlets which their own ignoble progenitors inhabited, and near to which their fathers were interred.

Nineteen-twentieths of the vocabulary of any people lives only in the literature and the speech of the cultured classes.[3] But the remainder—the twentieth part—has a robust life in the daily usage of the sons of toil : and this limited portion of the national speech never fails to include the names of those objects which are the most familiar and the most beloved. A few score of ' household words ' have thus been retained as the common inheritance of the whole of the Indo-European nations ;[4] and the same causes have secured the local preservation of local names.

---

[1] As in the case of Tadmor, Sidon, or Hamath.

[2] Thus in the historical books of the Old Testament, we have, incidentally, a proof of the large Canaanite element remaining after the Israelitish conquest of Palestine. We see the old Canaanite names struggling for existence with those imposed by the conquerors :—Kirjath Arba with Hebron ; Kirjath Sepher with Debir ; Keneth with Nobar ; Luz with Bethel ; Ephrath with Bethlehem.—See Stanley's *Lectures on the Jewish Church*, [vol. i], p. 275.

[3] Of the 50,000 words in the English language, some 10,000 constitute the vocabulary of an educated Englishman, and certainly not 1,000, perhaps not more than 500, are heard in the mouths of the labouring classes.—See Marsh, *Lectures on the English Language*, pp. 125, 126 ; Max Müller, *Lectures on the Science of Language*, p. 268 ; *Saturday Review*, November 2, 1861.

[4] The names of the numerals, of father, mother, and brother, of the parts of the body, of two or three of the commoner metals, tools, cereals, and domesticated animals, such

These appellations, which have thus been floated forward from age to age, have often, or they had at first, a *descriptive import ;*—they tell us something of the physical features of the land. Thus it is that they may either give aid to the philologist when the aspect of the country remains the same—its visible forms standing in view as a sort of material lexicon or a tongue that has ceased to be vernacular ; or, on the other hand, where the face of nature has undergone extensive changes—where there were formerly, it may be, forests that have been cleared, marshes that have been drained coast-lines that have advanced seaward, rivers that have extended their deltas or found new channels, estuaries that have been converted into alluvial soil, lakes that have been silted up, islands that have become gentle inland slopes surrounded by waving corn-flats ;—in all such cases, instances of which will be adduced hereafter, these pertinacious names have a geological significance—they come into use as a record of a class of events, as to which, for the most part, written history is silent. In this manner—and the instances are many—the names of places become available as the beacon-lights of geologic history. In truth, there are instances in which local names, conserved in places where little or nothing else that is human has endured, may be adduced as evidence of vast physical mutations, side by side with the stone hatchets and the spear-heads of the drift of Abbeville, the canoes and anchors found in the alluvium of the Carse of Falkirk and Strathclyde, the gnawed bones of the Kirkdale Cavern, the glaciated rocks of Wales, the rain-dinted slabs of Sussex, and other massive vouchers in the physical history of the globe.

The picturesque or descriptive character of local names is, as might be anticipated, prominently exemplified in the appellations bestowed on the most striking feature in landscape—

---

as the cat, the mouse, and the goose, as well as the names of the plough, of grist, of fire, of the house, as well as some of the personal pronouns and numerals, come within this category. The analysis of words of this class enables us to speculate upon the relative epochs at which the Celtic, Romance, Sclavonic, and Teutonic families separated from the parent stock, or from each other, and also to detect what progress had been made in the arts of life at the periods when each of these separations took place. See Grimm's *Geschichte der Deutschen Sprache*, pp. 9–113 ; Max Müller, *On Comparative Mythology*, in the *Oxford Essays* for 1856, pp. 14–26 ; Leo, *Vorlesungen*, vol. i. p. 11 ; Wilson, *Prehistoric Annals of Scotland*, p. 350 ; Weber, *Indische Skizzen*, *pp.* 9, 10 ; Gladstone, *Homer*, vol. i. p. 299 ; Pritchard, *Reports of Brit. Assoc.* for 1847, p. 240 ; Mommsen, *Inhabitants of Italy*, pp. 11–14 ; Pictet, *Origines Indo-Europ.* pt. i. pp. 149–530 ; pt. ii. pp. 739–751 ; Bunsen, *Philosophy of Universal History*, vol. i. pp. 75, 76 ; Mannhardt, *Götterwelt*, vol. i. p. 47 ; Kuhn, *Zur älteste Geschichte*.

mountain peaks and ranges. Thus it is easy to perceive that, in every region of the world, the loftier mountains have been designated by names which describe that natural phenomenon, which would be most certain to impress the imagination of a rude people. The names of Snowdon, Ben Nevis, Mont Blanc, the Sierra Nevada in Spain, Snafell in Iceland, the Sneeuw Bergen at the Cape of Good Hope, the Sneehätten in Norway, Sneekoppe in Bohemia, and the Weisshorn, the Weissmies, and the Tête Blanche in Switzerland, as well as the more archaic or more obscure names of Lebanon, of Caucasus, of Haemus, of the Himalaya, of Dwajalagiri, and of Djebel-es-Sheikh, are appellations descriptive, in various languages, of the characteristic snowy covering of these lofty summits.

But there are many names which conjoin historical and physical information. Thus, when we learn that the highest summit in the Isle of Man is called SNAFELL, we recognize at once the descriptive character of the name, and we might be satisfied with simply placing it in the foregoing list. But when we discover that the name Snafell is a true Norse word, and that it serves moreover for the name of a mountain in Norway, and of another in Iceland, we find ourselves in presence of the historical fact that the Isle of Man was, for centuries, a dependency of the Scandinavian Crown—having been conquered and colonized by the Norwegian Vikings, who also peopled Iceland.

This is an instance of what we may call the ethnological import of names. The chief value of the science of geographical etymology consists in the aid which it is thus able to give us in the determination of obscure ethnological questions. There are many nations which have left no written records, and whose history would be a blank volume—or nearly so—were it not that in the places where they have sojourned they have left traces of their migrations, sufficient to enable us to reconstruct the main outline of their history. The hills, the valleys, and the rivers are, in fact, the only writing-tablets on which unlettered nations have been able to inscribe their annals. It may be affirmed that, with hardly an exception, the great advances in ethnological knowledge which have recently taken place are due to the decipherment of the obscure and time-worn records thus conserved in local names. The Celtic, the Iberic, the Teutonic, the Scandinavian, and the Sclavonian races have thus, and for the most part, thus only, made known to us their migrations, their conquests, and their defeats.

To this subject—Etymology in its relations to Ethnology —several of the succeeding chapters will be devoted.

But we sometimes derive historical information in a still more explicit form from local names. They often preserve the memory of historic sites, and even enable us to assign approximate dates to certain memorable events. Thus there is a meadow, near Stamford Bridge,[1] which still goes by the name of BATTLE FLATS. For eight centuries, this name has kept in its tenacious grasp the memory of the precise locality of the famous territorial concession which Harald, son of Godwine, made to Harald Hardráda, King of Norway, 'seven feet of English ground, or as much more as he may be taller than other men'.[2] And at the other extremity of the kingdom the name of the town of BATTLE, in Sussex, is the epitaph which marks the spot where, in less than a month, the Saxon king lost his kingdom and his life.

The names of MESSINA in Sicily, of CARTHAGENA in Spain, and of MILETUS in Ionia, repeat the names of the mother-cities which sent out these colonies ; and the name of TRIPOLI reminds us that there were three cities—Tyre, Sidon, and Aradus—which joined in establishing the new settlement.

The name of the PHILIPPINE Islands tells us of the reign in which the Spanish galleons steered from Peru across the Southern Sea. The name of LOUISIANA reminds us that, in the days of the *Grand Monarque*, France was the rival of England in the colonization of the Western World ; and the names of VIRGINIA, of the CAROLINAS, and of GEORGIA give us the dates of the first foundation of England's colonial empire, and of some of the chief successive stages in its progress. The word LONDONDERRY speaks to us of the resettlement of the desolated city of Derry by the London guilds ; while the names KING'S COUNTY and QUEEN'S COUNTY, PHILIPSTOWN, and MARYBOROUGH, commemorate the fact that it was in the days of King Philip and Queen Mary that the O'Mores were exterminated, and two new counties added to the English Pale.

There are materials of yet another class which may be col-

---

[1] Stamford Bridge was long known as Battle Bridge—*Pons Belli.*—Lappenberg, *Anglo-Saxon Kings*, vol. ii. p. 281.

[2] Saga of Harald Hardráda, in Laing's *Heimskringla*, vol. iii. p. 89.

lected from the study of ancient names. From them we may decipher facts that have a bearing on the history of ancient civilization. With regard, for example, to Saxon England, we may from local names draw many inferences as to the amount of cultivated land, the state of agriculture, the progress of the arts of construction, and even as to the density of the population, and its relative distribution. In the same records we may discover vestiges of various local franchises and privileges, and may investigate certain social differences which must have characterized the districts settled respectively by the Saxons and the Danes. And we may collect enchorial vestiges of the heathenism of our forefathers, and illustrate the process by which it was gradually effaced by the efforts of Christian teachers.

We thus perceive how many branches of scientific, historical, and archaeological research are capable of being elucidated by the study of names ; and it is manifest that, upon many grounds, the work of their Historical Interpretation is called for. The almost virgin soil of a rich field, which has never yet been systematically cultivated, presents itself before the labourer ; and an industrious criticism, bringing into combination the resources of Geography, of Physical Description, of Geology, of Archaeology, of Ethnology, of Philology, and of History, may hope to reach results, more or less important, in each of these departments of knowledge ; or, at all events, it cannot fail to indicate, for future exploration, some of the sites where lie buried the hidden treasures of the past.

CHAPTER II

THE peopling of the Eastern Hemisphere is an event of the distant past. The names upon the map of Europe have remained there, most of them for ten, many of them for twenty, centuries. To study them is a task full of difficulties ; for they are mostly derived from obscure or unknown languages, and they have suffered more or less from the phonetic changes of so many years. But with the New World the case is different. The colonization of America has been effected during the modern historic period, the process of name-giving is illustrated by numerous authentic documents, and the names are derived from living languages. Just as the best introduction to the study of geology is the investigation of recent formations, abounding in the remains of still existing organisms, so we may fitly commence our present task by an examination of what we may call the tertiary deposits of America and Australia, which are still in process of formation ; and we shall then be better prepared to explore the Wealden and other secondary formations of the Teutonic Period, and the still older primary Celtic strata—Silurian, Cambrian, and Devonian. We shall find that the study of the more recent names throws much light on those natural laws which have regulated the nomenclature of Europe : and the investigation is, moreover, full of interest, from the numerous associations with the names of the bold conquistadors and the daring seamen whose enterprise has added another continent to the known world.

By means of the names upon the map, we may trace the whole history of the successive stages by which the white men have spread themselves over the Western World. We may discover the dates at which the several settlements were founded, we may assign to each of the nations of Europe its proper share in the work of colonization, and, lastly, we may recover the names of the adventurous captains who led their little bands of daring followers to conquer the wilderness from nature, or from savage tribes.

The name of GREENLAND is the only one which is left to remind us of the Scandinavian settlements which were made in America during the tenth century. The discoveries of Leif, son of Eric the Red, have been forgotten, and the Norse names of Vinland (Massachusetts), Markland (Nova Scotia), Helluland it mikla (Labrador), and Litla Helluland (Newfoundland), have been superseded, and now survive only in the memory of the curious.[1]

Without disparagement of the claims of Leif Ericson to the discovery of the New World, we may regret that the names of the city of COLOMBUS and of the district of COLUMBIA form the only memorials of the bold Genoese adventurer; and we may wish that the name of the entire continent had been such as to remind us, day by day, of the exploits of Christopher Columbus rather than of those of Amerigo Vespucci.[2] Alexander von Humboldt[3] has, indeed, vindicated Vespucci from the charge of trickery or forgery which Las Casas attempted to fasten upon him; and we must, therefore, regard the name of AMERICA as an unfortunate mistake rather than as an inglorious and successful fraud.[4]

The deep religious feeling of the earlier voyagers is well illustrated by the names which they bestowed upon their discoveries. The first land descried by Columbus was the

[1 For the settlements of Norsemen in America see E. J. Payne, *History of the New World*, 1892, vol. i. pp. 69–74; C. F. Keary, *The Vikings*, 1891, pp. 186–7; J. Toulmin Smith, *The Discovery of America by the Northmen*, 1839; T. Stephens, *Madoc*, 1893; *The World's History*, ed. H. F. Helmolt, vol. i., 1901.]

2 *Cosmos*, vol. ii. note 457.

3 The error obtained currency from a work on Geography, published in the year 1507.

4 [But ' the New World named from Americo Vespucci of Florence ' occurs on the title-page of voyages published at Vicenza in 1507. See E. J. Payne, *Hist. of the New World*, i. 189, and H. Vignaud's *critique* on Toscanelli's connexion with Columbus.]

island of SAN SALVADOR. From day to day he held on, in spite of the threats of his mutinous crew, who threatened to throw the crazy visionary into the sea. With what vividness does this name of San Salvador disclose the feelings with which, on the seventieth night of the dreary voyage, the brave Genoese caught sight of what seemed to be a light gleaming on some distant shore ; how vividly does that name enable us to realize the scene when, on the next day, with a humble and grateful pride, he set foot upon that NEW WORLD of which he had dreamed from his boyhood, and, having erected the symbol of the Christian faith and knelt before it, he rose from his knees and proclaimed, in a broken voice, that the land should henceforth bear the name of San Salvador—the Holy Saviour, who had preserved him through so many perils !

We cannot but reverence the romantic piety which chequers the story of the violence and avarice of the conquistadors. On the discovery of unknown shores, the first thought of those fierce soldiers was to claim the lands as new kingdoms of their Lord and Master, and to erect forthwith His symbol, the SANTA CRUZ, the VERA CRUZ, the name of which marks upon our maps so many of the earliest settlements of the Spaniards and Portuguese.

The name of SAN SEBASTIAN, the first Spanish colony founded on the continent of South America, forms a touching memorial of the perils which beset the earlier colonists. On disembarking from the ships, seventy of the Spaniards were killed by the poisoned arrows of the Indians ; on which account the dangerous spot was put under the special protection of the martyr, who, by reason of the circumstances of his death, might be supposed to feel a personal and peculiar sympathy with those who were exposed to the like sufferings. [1]

As in the case of many great men, there seems to have been a sort of mysticism underlying the piety of Columbus. On his third voyage he discerned three mountain-peaks rising from the waters, and supposed that three new islands had been discovered. On a nearer approach, it was found that the three summits formed one united land—a fact which the admiral recognized as a mysterious emblem of the Holy Trinity, and

[1] So too the name of the LADRONES, or ' Robbers' Islands ', commemorates the losses of Magelhaen's crew from the thievish propensities of the natives. The name SIERRA LEONE, The Lion's range, records the terrors of the Portuguese discoverers at the nightly roaring of the lions in the mountains which fringe the coast.

therefore bestowed upon the island the name of LA TRINIDAD, which it still retains.

The Spaniards were devout observers of the festivals of the Church, and this circumstance often enables us to fix the precise day on which great discoveries were made. Thus FLORIDA, with its dreary swamps, is not the ' Flowery Land ', as it is sometimes thought to be ; but its name records the fact that it was discovered by Juan Ponce de Leon on Easter Sunday—a festival which the Spaniards call Pascua Florida, from the flowers with which the churches are then decked. The island of DOMINICA was discovered on a Sunday—*dies Dominica*. NATAL was discovered by Vasco de Gama on Christmas-day—*dies Natalis*. Alfonso de Sousa founded the first Portuguese colony in the Brazils, and its name JANEIRO, recalls the fact that he landed on the Feast of St. Januarius. The town of ST. AUGUSTINE, the oldest in the United States, was founded on St. Augustine's-day by Melendez, who was sent by Philip II of Spain on the pious mission of exterminating a feeble colony of Huguenot refugees, who were seeking, on the coast of Florida, that religious liberty which was denied them in their native land.

The islands of ASCENSION and ST. HELENA, the River ST. LAWRENCE, and other places too numerous to mention, thus date the day of their discovery by their names.

A religious feeling equally intense with that which dictated the names bestowed by the Spanish discoverers, but very different in character, is evinced by the names which mark the sites of the earlier Puritan colonies in North America.

SALEM was intended to be the earthly realization of the New Jerusalem, where a ' New Reformation ', of the sternest Calvinistic type, was to inaugurate a fresh era in the history of the world, and a strict discipline was to eradicate every frailty of our human nature from this City of the Saints. From the laws of the neighbouring town of Newhaven,[1] as given by Hutchinson, we may gather some notion of Life in this Puritan Utopia. Among other things, it was there enacted, under severe penalties :—

[1] Caswall, *The American Church and the American Union*, p. 35. Lucas, *Secularia* pp. 219, 227. Since the first Edition of *Words and Places* was published I have received a letter from an American correspondent in which he informs me that these so-called ' Blue Laws ' are a forgery. My correspondent assigns no reasons, but I sincerely hope his statement is correct.

' That no one shall be a freeman unless he be converted.

' That no one shall run on the Sabbath, or walk in his garden.

' That no one shall make beds, cut hair, or shave, and no woman shall kiss her children on the Sabbath.

' That no one shall make mince-pies, or play any instrument, except the trumpet, drum, and jews'-harp.

' That no food or lodging shall be given to any Quaker or other heretic '.

The laws of Massachusetts assigned the penalty of death to all Quakers, as well as to ' stubborn and rebellious sons ', and to all ' children, above sixteen, who curse or smite their natural father or mother ', and to persons guilty of idolatry, witchcraft, or blasphemy.

These laws, breathing the spirit of Christianity as understood by the Puritan exiles for conscience' sake, quickly bore their fruit. Roger Williams, a noble-hearted man, who, strange to say, had been chosen to be minister at Salem, dared to affirm the heresy that ' the doctrine of persecution for cause of conscience is most evidently and lamentably contrary to the doctrine of Christ Jesus ', and that ' no man should be bound to worship against his own consent '. For maintaining these heterodox opinions, which struck at the root of the New England system of polity, Williams had sentence of exile pronounced against him. He wandered forth into the snows of a New England winter : ' for fourteen weeks ', he says, ' he often, in the stormy night, had neither fire nor food, and had no house but a hollow tree '.

The savages showed him the mercy which his fellow-Christians had refused him, an Indian chief gave him food and shelter ; but that wigwam in the far forest was soon pronounced to be within the jurisdiction of the Puritan colony, and the Apostle of Toleration, hunted even from the wilderness, embarked with five companions in a canoe, and landed in Rhode Island. With simple piety he called the spot where the canoe first touched the land, by the name of PROVIDENCE —a place which still remains the capital of Rhode Island, the State which Williams founded as ' a shelter for persons distressed for conscience '.[1]

---

[1] Bancroft, *History of the United States*, vol. i. pp. 276-286.

The name of CONCORD, the capital of the State of New
Hampshire, shows that some at least of the Puritans were actuated by feelings more in harmony with the spirit of the religion
they professed ; while PHILADELPHIA, the City of Brotherly
Love, tells a touching tale of the unbrotherly persecutions
which filled the gaols of England with 60,000 Quakers—persecutions from which they fled, in the hope of inaugurating a
Utopian era of peace and harmony.

All readers of Pepys' amusing Diary are familiar with the
name of his colleague at the Admiralty, Sir William Penn.
The funds which should have found their way into the naval
chest were diverted to purposes more agreeable to the ' merry
monarch ' than the purchase of tar and timber ; and, in consequence, the fortune which the Comptroller of the Navy bequeathed to his Quaker son, was a claim on the royal purse for
the sum of £16,000.   The money not being forthcoming, young
Penn—who, much to the annoyance of his family, had em-
braced the tenets of the Quakers—obtained, in satisfaction of
his claims, a large grant of forest-land in North America, and
led forth a colony of Quakers to found the new colony, called,
after himself, PENNSYLVANIA.

The name of BOSTON reminds us of the part of England
from which the first Puritan settlers emigrated.   They had,
with much difficulty, escaped from the Lincolnshire coast—
some of them having been apprehended on the beach for the
crime of attempting to reach a country where they might
worship according to their consciences.   Their first refuge
was in Holland, from whence the *Mayflower* carried them to
the shores of New England, and on December 11, 1620,
landed them on a desolate spot, five hundred miles from the
nearest settlement of white men.   To this spot they gave the
name of PLYMOUTH—a reminiscence of the last English land
which they had seen as they passed down the Channel.[1]

HOBOKEN (an Indian word, meaning the ' smoke pipe ') was
the name of a spot in New Jersey, at which the settlers met
the Indian chiefs in council, and smoked the pipe of peace,
while they formed a league of amity—too soon, alas ! to be
broken by the massacre of BLOODY BROOK, where so many of

---

[1] The Puritan emigration lasted twenty years—from 1620 to 1640. During thi[s]
period, 21,000 emigrants crossed the Atlantic.   The population of the six New England
States is now [1864] upwards of three millions.

the colonists were treacherously slain. Hoboken is one of the many Indian names which we find scattered over the map of the American continent, and which are frequently used to designate the great natural features of the country, the lakes, the rivers, the mountain ranges, and the chief natural territorial divisions.[1] Such are the names of the NIAGARA, the POTOMAC, the OTTAWA, the RAPPAHANNOCK, the SUSQUE-HANNA, the MISSISSIPPI, the MISSOURI, the MINNESOTA, CANADA, MASSACHUSETTS, CONNECTICUT, ARKANSAS, WISCONSIN, MICHI-GAN. The name of MEXICO is derived from Mexitli, the Aztec war-god. TLASCALA means ' the place of bread '. HAYTI is the ' mountainous country '. The ANDES take their name from the Peruvian word *anta*—copper. Local names are the only memorial of many once powerful tribes which have become extinct. The names of the ALLEGHANY Range, the MOHAWK Valley, Lake HURON, Lake ERIE, Lake NIPISSING, the City of NATCHEZ, CHEROKEE County, the River OTTAWA, and the States of KANSAZ, OHIO,[2] and ILLINOIS are all derived from the names of tribes already extinct or rapidly becoming so. Centuries hence, the historian of the New World will point to these names as great ethnological landmarks : they will have, in his eyes, a value of the same kind as that which is now attached to the names of Hesse, Devonshire, The Solway, Paris, or Turin.[3]

The name of VIRGINIA carries us back to the reign of the Virgin Queen, and gives us the date of the exploits of those hardy sailors, who cast into the shade the deeds even of the Spanish conquistadors. Not far from the scene of one of his ruinous enterprises [4] the most chivalrous, the most adventurous, the most farsighted, and the most unfortunate of Englishmen, has recently had a tardy tribute paid to him, in the adoption, by the Legislature of North Carolina, of the name of RALEIGH as the designation of the capital of the State in which Raleigh's colony was planted. On RALEIGH ISLAND, at the entrance of Roanoke Sound, may still be discerned the

[1] The rivers and mountains receive their names from the earliest races, villages and towns from later colonists. Many illustrations of the principle will be adduced in Chapter IX.

[2] [Ohio is said to be from the nation *Ohionh-iio*, ' river-beautiful ', like Ontario from *Oniatar-iio*, ' lake-beautiful ' (E. J. Payne, *Hist. of New World*, i. 369), the termination being an exclamation of admiration. We may compare our *Westward-ho*.]

[3] See Chapter IV. and Appendix A.

[4] CAPE FEAR commemorates the narrow escape from destruction of one of the expeditions sent out by Raleigh.

traces of the fort around which the adventurers built the CITY OF RALEIGH, a place which has now vanished from the map. Of Raleigh's other enterprises, more especially of his quixotic ascent of the Orinoco for four hundred miles in small open boats, no local name remains as a memorial.

The names of other heroes of the Elizabethan era are to be sought elsewhere. In the Northern Seas we find a record of the achievements of four brave Englishmen—Frobisher, Davis, Baffin, and Hudson. The adventurous spirit which actuated this band of naval worthies is shown in the declaration of Martin Frobisher, who deemed the discovery of the North-West Passage ' the only thing of the world that was yet left undone by which a notable minde might be made famous and fortunate '. In command of two little barks, respectively of 25 and 20 tons, and accompanied by a small pinnace, FROBISHER steered for the unknown seas of ice, and, undaunted by the loss of the pinnace and the mutinous defection of one of his crews, he persevered in his enterprise, and discovered the strait which bears his name.[1]

John Davis, with two ships respectively of 50 and 35 tons, followed up the discoveries which Frobisher had made. With a brave heart he kept up the courage of his sickly sailors, who were struck with terror at the strange sight of huge floating icebergs towering overhead, and at the fearful crash of the icefloes as they ground one against the other, and threatened the ships with instant destruction. When, at length, the wished-for land came in sight, it was found to be so utterly barren and inhospitable that the disappointed seamen gave it the name which it still bears—CAPE DESOLATION. But Davis persevered, and was rewarded by the discovery of an open passage leading to the North-West, to which the name of DAVIS' STRAITS has been rightfully assigned.[2]

Bylot and Baffin, with one small vessel, and a crew of fourteen men and two boys, eclipsed all that Davis had done, and ventured into unknown seas, where, for the next two hundred years, none dared to follow them. They discovered the magnificent expanse of water which is known by the name of BAFFIN'S BAY, and they coasted round its shores in hopes of

[1] Hakluyt, *Navigations*, vol. iii. pp. 29–96. Cf. *Calendar of State Papers, Dom. Ser.* 1577–9.
[2] Hakluyt, *Navigations*, vol. iii. pp. 98–120.

finding some outlet towards the North or West. Three channels were discovered, to which they gave the names of Sir James LANCASTER, Sir Thomas SMITH, and Alderman JONES, by whose countenance and pecuniary assistance they had been enabled to equip the expedition.

The adventurous life and tragic fate of Henry Hudson would make an admirable subject for an historical romance. The narration is quaintly given in *Purchas His Pilgrimes* ; [1] but, fortunately or unfortunately, it has not, so far as I am aware, been selected as a theme by any modern writer. Hudson's first voyage was an attempt to discover the North-East Passage to India. With ten men and a boy, he had succeeded in attaining the coast of Spitzbergen, when the approach of winter compelled him to return. In a second voyage he reached Nova Zembla. The next year he traced the unknown coast-line of New England, and entered the great river which bears his name. His last expedition was rewarded by still greater discoveries than any he had hitherto effected. In a bark of 55 tons he attempted the North-West Passage, and, penetrating through HUDSON'S STRAIT, he reached HUDSON'S BAY. where his ship was frozen up among the icefloes. Patiently he waited for the approach of spring, although, before the ship was released, the crew had been reduced to feed on moss and frogs. After awhile, they fortunately succeeded in catching a supply of fish, and prepared to return home, with provisions for only fourteen days. Dismayed at this prospect of starvation, the crew mutinied, and, with the object of diminishing the number of mouths to be fed, they treacherously seized their brave captain ; and having placed in a small boat a little meal, a musket, and an iron pot, they cast Hudson adrift, with eight sick men, to find a grave in the vast inland sea, the name of which is the worthy epitaph of one of the most daring of England's seamen. The names of these four men— Frobisher, Davis, Baffin, and Hudson—the world will not willingly let die.

The naval triumphs of the Elizabethan era are also associated, in the minds of Englishmen, with the exploits of Drake and Gilbert, although they have not been fortunate enough to give their names to seas or cities. Drake's almost fabulous adventures—his passage of the Straits of Magalhaens—his

---

[1] Purchas, *Pilgrimes,* vol. iii. pp. 567–609.

capture of huge treasure-ships with his one small bark—his voyage of 1,400 miles across the Pacific, which he was the first Englishman to navigate—his discovery of the western coast of North America, and his successful circumnavigation of the globe, form the subject of a romantic chapter in the history of maritime adventure.

But a still higher tribute of admiration is due to the brave and pious Sir Humphrey Gylberte, who, on his return from his expedition to NEWFOUNDLAND, attempted to cross the Atlantic in his ' Frigat ', the *Squirrel*, a little vessel of 10 tons. Near the Azores, a storm arose, in which he perished.   The touching account of his death as given in Hakluyt, is well known, but it can hardly be repeated too often : ' The Generall, sitting abaft with a booke in his hand, cried out to us in the Hind, so oft as we did approach within hearing, " We are as neere to heaven by sea as by land ", —relterating the same speech, well beseeming a souldier resolute in Jesus Christ, as I can testifie he was.   The same Monday night, about twelve of the clocke, or not long after, the Frigat being ahead of us in the Golden Hinde, suddenly her lights were out, whereof, as in a moment, we lost the sight, and withall our watch cryed the Generall was cast away, which was too true ; for in that moment the Frigat was devoured and swallowed up of the sea '.[1]

Such were the gallant gentlemen and ' soldiers resolute in Jesus Christ ' who made the reign of Elizabeth illustrious.

The records of the progress of English colonization during the next reign are to be sought on the banks of the JAMES River.   On either side, at the entrance of this river, are Cape HENRY and Cape CHARLES.   Cape Charles was called after ' Baby Charles', and Cape Henry bears the name of the hopeful prince whose accession to the throne might probably have changed the whole course of English history.   ELIZABETH County, which formed M'Clellan's base of operations in the late campaign, and in which stands Fortress Monroe, was so called in honour of the sister of these princes—the hapless Winter Queen, the mother of Prince Rupert.   SMITH'S ISLES, near Cape Charles, and SMITHFIELD, on the opposite side of the James River, are memorials of Captain John Smith, a man of rare genius and enterprise, to whom, even more than to

[1] Hakluyt, *Navigations*, vol. iii. p. 159.

Raleigh, the ultimate establishment of the English colony in Virginia is due.

Even in those days of wild adventure, Smith's career had been such as distinguished him above all his fellow-colonists in Virginia. When almost a boy he had fought, under Leicester, in that Dutch campaign, the incredible mismanagement of which has been so ably detailed by Mr. Motley. His mind, as he tells us, ' being set upon brave adventures ', he had roamed over France, Italy, and Egypt, doing a little piracy, as it would now be called, in the Levant. Coming to Hungary, he took service for the war with the Turks, against whom he devised many ' excellent stratagems ', and performed prodigies of valour in various single combats with Turkish champions, slaying the ' Lord Turbashaw ', also ' one Grualgo, the vowed friend of Turbashaw ', as well as ' Bonny Mulgro ', who tried to avenge the death of the other two.

After numerous adventures, for which the reader must be referred to his amusing autobiography, a general engagement took place, and Captain Smith was left for dead upon the field of battle. Here he was made prisoner, and sold into slavery at Constantinople. Being regarded with too much favour by his ' fair mistresse ', who ' tooke much compassion on him ', he was sent into the Crimea, where he was ' no more regarded than a beast '. Driven to madness by this usage, he killed his taskmaster, the Tymor, whose clothes he put on, and whose horse he appropriated, and thus succeeded in escaping across the steppes ; and, after overcoming many perils, he at last reached a Christian land. ' Being thus satisfied with Europe and Asia ', and hearing of the ' warres in Barbarie ', he forthwith proceeded to the interior of Morocco, in search of new adventures. We next hear of him ' trying some conclusions at sea ' with the Spaniards ; and at last, at thirty years of age, he found himself in Virginia, at a time when a great portion of the hundred colonists had perished, and the survivors were meditating the abandonment of what seemed a hopeless enterprise. Before long, Smith's force of character placed him at the head of affairs, which soon began to improve under the influence of his resolute and hopeful genius. But the position of responsibility in which he was placed could not put a stop to the execution of his adventurous projects. In an open boat he made a coasting voyage of

some three thousand miles, in the course of which he discovered and explored the Potomac. On the occasion of one
of these expeditions, his companions were all cut off by the
Indians, and he himself, ' beset with 200 salvages ', was taken
prisoner and condemned to die. Brought before the King
of Pamaunkee, ' the salvages ' had fastened him to a tree, and
were about to make him a target for the exhibition of their
skill in archery, when he obtained his release by the adroit
display of the great medicine of a pocket-compass. ' A
bagge of gunpowder ', which had come into the possession of
the salvages, ' they carefully preserved till the next spring, to
plant as they did their corne, because they would be acquainted
with the nature of that seede '. Taken at length before ' Pow-
hattan, their Emperor ', for the second time Smith had sentence of death passed upon him. ' Two great stones were
brought ; as many as could, layd hands on him, dragged him
to them, and thereon laid his head, being ready with their
clubs to beate out his braines '. At this juncture ' Pocahontas,
the king's dearest daughter ', a beautiful girl, the ' nonpareil of
the country ', was touched with pity for the white-skinned
stranger ; and, ' when no intreaty could prevaile ', she rushed
forward and ' got his head in her armes, and laid her owne
upon his to save him from death ', and thus succeeded, at the
risk of her life, in obtaining the pardon of the prisoner. Pocahontas was afterwards married to John Rolfe, ' an honest
and discreet ' young Englishman, and from her some of the
first families of the Old Dominion are proud to trace their
descent.[1]

The State of FLORIDA, as the name imports, was originally
a Spanish colony. LOUISIANA, NEW ORLEANS, MOBILE, and
many other names, remind us that, in the reign of Louis XIV,
France held firm possession of the Valley of the Mississippi,

---

[1] This account is abridged from *The True Travels, Adventures, and Observations of
Captain John Smith in Europe, Asia, Africke, and America*, London, 1629 ; and *The
Generall Historie of Virginia, New England, and the Sommer Isles*, London, 1627—two
most quaint and delightful works, of which a well-edited reprint would be opportune.
A brief narrative of Smith's adventures will be found in Bancroft, *History of the United
States*, vol. i. pp. 94–112 ; Drake, *Book of the Indians*, bk. iv. pp. 7–18 ; and Cooley,
History of Maritime and Inland Discovery, vol. ii. pp. 212–215. See also *Calendar of
State Papers, Colonial Series*, 1614. Smith, of Virginia, bore for arms a chevron, between
the three Turks' heads, which he had cut off. He is the hero of the Blackletter Ballad
in the British Museum, entitled—' The Honor of a London Prentice ; being an account
of his matchless manhood and boyhood.—Smith's *Antiquarian Ramble in the Streets
of London*, vol. ii. p. 133.

and stretched a chain of forts, by ST. LOUIS, ST. CHARLES, and the State of Illinois, to FOND DU LAC and LAC SUPERIEUR, the 'Upper Lake' of the great chain of lakes, as far as DETROIT, the 'narrow passage' between the LAC ST. CLAIR and Lake Erie. In Canada we are surrounded by French names. QUEBEC is a name transferred from Brittany,[1] and MONTREAL is the 'Royal Mount', so named by the Frenchman Cartier in 1535. Lake CHAMPLAIN takes its name from Champlain, a bold Normand adventurer 'delighting marvellously in these enterprises', who joined an Indian war-party, and was the first to explore the upper waters of the St. Lawrence and the Mississippi. The *Habitans* (as the French Canadians of the Lower Province are called) still retain the characteristics of the Normand peasantry in the time of Louis XIV. Cape BRETON was discovered, by mariners from Brittany, as early as the lifetime of Columbus. The name of the State of VERMONT shows that it came within the great French dominion, and the State of MAINE repeats in the New World the name of one of the maritime provinces of France. But the genius of Lord Chatham wrested the empire of the New World from France ; and Fort Du Quesne, the key of the French position in the Valley of the Ohio, under its new name of PITTSBURGH, commemorates the triumphs of the great war-minister, and is now one of the largest cities in the United States.

The State of DELAWARE was 'planted' in 1610 by Lord De la Warr, under a patent granted by James I. The further progress of colonization in this region is commemorated by the Roman Catholic colony of MARYLAND, named after Henrietta Maria, Queen of Charles I ; and BALTIMORE, the capital of the State, takes its name from Lord Baltimore, the patentee of the new colony,[2] who thus transferred to the New World the Celtic name of the little Irish village from which he derived his title.

NEW JERSEY, in like manner, was founded under a patent granted, in the reign of Charles II, to George Carteret, Lord Jersey ; while NOVA SCOTIA was a concession to Sir William Alexander, a Scotchman, who, with a band of his compatriots, settled there in the time of James II. Its recolonization in the

---

[1] The etymology of Lamartinière from *Quel bec!* What a cape! is too absurd to need refutation.
[2] *Calendar of State Papers, Colonial Series,* 1632.

reign of George II is marked by the name of HALIFAX, given in honour of Lord Halifax, the president of the Board of Trade.

The city of CHARLESTON, ALBEMARLE Sound, the rivers ASHLEY and COOPER, and the States of North and South CAROLINA,[1] date from the time of the Restoration ; and the people are justly proud of the historical associations which attach to many of the local names.[2] ANNAPOLIS, the capital of Maryland, as well as the RAPIDAN and NORTH ANNA Rivers, bring us to the reign of Queen Anne ; and GEORGIA, the last of the thirteen colonies, dates from the reign of George II. NEW INVERNESS, in Georgia, was settled by Highlanders implicated in the rebellion of 1745. FREDERICKSBURG, the scene of the recent bloody repulse of the Federals, and FREDERICK CITY, in Maryland, bear the name of the weak and worthless son of George II. As has been observed by the Southern correspondent of the *Times*, ' It is safe to observe that Virginia has done more than the mother country to keep alive the memory of a prince, who lives for Englishmen only as he is gibbeted in the Memoirs of Lord Harvey '.[3]

The Scandinavian colony of NEW SWEDEN has been absorbed by the States of Pennsylvania, Delaware, and New Jersey ; but a few names, like SWEDESBORO' and DONA,[4] still remain as evidences of a fact now almost forgotten.

The map of the State of NEW YORK takes us back to the reign of Charles II. The King's brother, James, Duke of York and Albany, had a grant made to him of the as yet unconquered Dutch colony of the NEW NETHERLANDS, the two chief cities of which, NEW AMSTERDAM and FORT ORANGE, were rechristened, after the Dutch had been dispossessed, by the names of NEW YORK and ALBANY, from the titles of the royal patentee. The names of the KATSKILL Mountains, STATEN Island, BROOKLYN (Breukelen), WALLABOUT Bay, YONKER'S Island, the HAARLEM River, and the villages of FLUSHING, STUYVESANT, and BLAUVELT,[5] are among the local memorials which still remind us of the Dutch dominion in North America.[6]

---

[1] The name of the Carolinas seems to have been revived at this period, having been originally given at the time of the first colonization by the Huguenots in the reign of Charles IX of France.   [2] Russell, *Diary North and South*, vol. i. p. 171.

[3] *Times*, December 27, 1862.   [4] [Swed. *dona* is trapping.]

[5] We may add the names of Kinderhook, Haverstraw, Spuyten Duyvel, Watervliet, Roosefelt, Roseboom, Rosendale, Staatsburg, and Claverack.

[6] The word creek, which often appears in American river-names, appears to be a vestige of the Dutch dominion. Kreek is a common suffix in the Netherlands. Förstemann, *Ortsnamen*, p. 35.

The Dutch colony in South America has had a greater permanence. NEW AMSTERDAM, FREDENBERG, BLAUWBERG, and many other Dutch names in the same neighbourhood, surrounded as they are by Portuguese and Spanish names, are an exhibition of the results of intrusive colonization, and are instructive analogues of obscure phenomena, which we shall hereafter find exhibited on the Continent of Europe.

CAPE HORN, or rather CAPE HOORN, as it should properly be written, is also a vestige of the early enterprise of Holland. The name is derived from Hoorn, a village on the Zuyder Zee, which was the birthplace of Schouten,[1] the first seaman who succeeded in doubling the Cape. Before the time of Schouten's voyage, the Pacific had been entered by the STRAITS OF MAGALHAENS, a passage between Tierra del Fuego and the mainland, which had been discovered by a man who, for genius, fertility of resource, and undaunted courage, deserves a place on the roll of fame beside Columbus, Cortez, Smith, and Hudson. Fernando Magalhaens was a Portuguese, engaged in the Spanish service, and was sent out to wrest from his fellow-countrymen the possession of the Moluccas, which, under the terms of the famous Papal Bull, were conceived to be included in the Spanish moiety of the world. Threading his way through the straits which bear his name, Magalhaens held on his way, in spite of the mutiny of his crews, the loss of one ship, and the desertion of another, and at last reached the Philippine Islands, where, during an attack by the natives, he fell beneath a shower of spears. TORRES' STRAITS bear the name of one of Magalhaens' lieutenants.

The PHILIPPINES and the CAROLINES bear the names of two Spanish monarchs, Philip II and Charles II, under whose respective auspices the first were colonized and the second were discovered.

The MARQUESAS received their name in honour of the Marquis Mendoza de Cañete, who, from his Viceroyalty of Peru, equipped the expedition which led to the discovery. But these were not the only results of Spanish enterprise in the Pacific. JUAN FERNANDEZ, a bold Spanish sailor, chanced upon the solitary isle which bears his name—an island which is chiefly memorable to Englishmen from having been, for four years, the abode of one of Dampier's comrades—Alexander Selkirk,

---

[1] Esquiros, *The Dutch at Home*, vol. i. p. 255.

whose adventures suggested to De Foe the inimitable fiction of *Robinson Crusoe*. The BERMUDAS, ' the still-vexed Bermoothes', alluded to in Shakespeare's *Tempest*, were discovered, at an earlier period, by another Spaniard, Juan Bermudez : they took the name of the SOMERS ISLANDS, by which they were long known, from the shipwreck of Sir George Somers, one of the deputy-governors of Virginia.[1]

We cannot complete the list of Spanish explorers without a mention of the name of ORELLANA, which, according to some maps, is borne by the largest river of the world. There are few more romantic narratives of adventure than the history of Orellana's voyage down the Amazons. In the company of Gonzales Pizarro he left Peru, and having penetrated through the trackless Andes, he came upon the head waters of a great river. The provisions brought by the explorers have at length become exhausted, their shoes and their saddles were boiled and eaten, to serve as a condiment to such roots as could be procured by digging. Meanwhile the energies of the whole party were engaged in the construction of a small bark, in which Orellana and fifty men committed themselves to the mighty stream, which, in seven long months, floated them down to the Atlantic, through the midst of lands utterly unknown, clad to the water's edge with gigantic forest-trees, and peopled by savage and hostile tribes. Not content, however, with describing the real perils of the voyage, or, perhaps, half-crazed by the hardships which he had undergone, Orellana, on his return to Spain, gave the reins to his imagination, and related wild travellers' tales concerning a nation of female warriors who had opposed his passage ; and posterity has punished his untruthfulness by enshrining, in a memorial name, the story of the fabled AMAZONS, and letting the remembrance of the daring explorer fade away.[2]

We find the records of Portuguese adventure in BAHIA, PERNAMBUCO, BRAGANÇA, and a host of other names in the Brazils, which were accidentally discovered by Cabral, who was sailing with an expedition destined for the East Indies. But the great field of Portuguese enterprise lay in the East, where the names BOMBAY, MACAO, and FORMOSA, attest the wide-

---

[1] See *Calendar of State Papers, Colonial Series*, 1610.
[2] See Cooley, *Hist. of Maritime and Inland Discovery*, vol. ii. p. 84 ; Prescott, *Conquest of Peru*, vol. ii. pp. 320–323.

spread nature of the commerce which the newly found sea-route to India threw into the hands of its discoverers. Their track is marked by such names as SALDANHA BAY, CAPE AGULHAS, ALGOA BAY, and CAPE DELGADO, which we find scattered along the southern coasts of Africa. The name of the Cape itself reveals the spirit of hopeful enterprise which enabled the Portuguese to achieve so much. Bartholomew Diaz, baffled by tempests, was unable, on his first expedition, to weather the cape which he had discovered, and he, therefore, named it CABO TORMENTOSO—the Cape of Storms—a name which John, the sanguine and enterprising king, changed to the CABO DE BONA ESPERANZA, arguing the GOOD HOPE which existed of the speedy discovery of the long-wished-for route to the realms of ' Ormus and of Ind '.[1]

The Eastern route found by the Portuguese was soon followed by the Dutch. The names of the MAURITIUS and the ORANGE RIVER were bestowed by them at the time when, under the Stadtholder Maurice, Prince of Orange, they were heroically striving against the colossal power of Spain. This death-struggle for freedom did not prevent them pursuing their discoveries in the Eastern seas : and at the lowest point of their fortunes, when all seemed likely to be lost, it was soberly proposed to cut the dykes and leave the Spaniards the task of once more reclaiming Holland from the waves, and for themselves to embark their families and their wealth, and seek in BATAVIA, a new eastern home for the Batavian nation.

From their colonies of Ceylon and Java, the Dutch fitted out numerous expeditions to explore the then unknown southern Seas. Carpenter, a Dutch captain, was the first to discover the northern portion of the Australian continent. His name is attached to the Gulf of CARPENTARIA ; and the ' great island ' in the gulf bears the Dutch name of GROOTE EYLANDT, which he gave to it. The earliest circumnavigation of the new southern continent was achieved by means of two vessels of discovery, which were equipped by Antony VAN DIEMEN, the Governor of Batavia, and entrusted to the command of Abel Jansen TASMAN. NEW ZEALAND and NEW HOLLAND, the chief fruits of this expedition, had conferred upon them the names of two of the United Provinces ; and on the discovery of a third large island, an attachment as romantic as a Dutchman

[1] Cooley, *History of Discovery*, vol. i. p. 374.

may be supposed capable of feeling, caused the rough sailor, if tradition speaks the truth, to inscribe upon our maps the name of the beautiful daughter of the Batavian governor, Maria Van Diemen.[1]

We may here briefly enumerate a few remaining discoverers, whose names are found scattered over our maps. DAMPIER'S Archipelago and WAFER Inlet bear the names of William Dampier and Lionel Wafer, the leaders of a band of West Indian buccaneers who marched across the Isthmus of Darien (each man provided only with four cakes of bread, a fusil, a pistol, and a hanger), and who, having seized a Spanish ship, continued for a long time to be the terror of the Pacific. Kerguellen was an officer in the French service, who, in the reign of Louis XV, discovered the island called KERGUELLEN'S LAND ; while JAN MEYEN, a Dutch whaling captain, has handed down his obscure name by his re-discovery of that snow-clad island cone, which forms such a striking frontispiece to Lord Dufferin's amusing volume [*Letters from High Latitudes*, 1857.].

BEHRING, a Dane by birth, was sent by Peter the Great to explore the eastern shores of Asia. He crossed Siberia, and having constructed a small vessel on the coast of Kamtschatka, he discovered the strait which separates Asia from America. On his return from a second expedition, his ship was wrecked, and the hardy sailor, surrounded by the snows and ice of an Arctic winter, perished miserably of cold, hunger, and fatigue, on an island which bears his name.

At the instance of the British Government, Captain VANCOUVER succeeded in surveying 9,000 miles of the unknown western coast-line of America. His name stands side by side with those of Hudson, Behring, Franklin, and Cook—the martyrs of geographical science ; for the exposure and the toil which he underwent proved fatal.

Mr. Bass, a naval surgeon, in an open whale-boat manned by a crew of six men, made a voyage of 600 miles, which resulted in the discovery of BASS'S STRAITS, which separate Van Diemen's Land from the Australian Continent.

The discoveries of Captain Cook are so well known, that a

---

[1] In consequence of an ignorant prejudice, which was supposed to deter intending colonists, the name of Van Diemen's Land, or Demon's Land, as it was called, has after the lapse of two centuries, been changed to TASMANIA, in honour of the sailor who preferred the fame of his mistress to his own.

brief reference to the names which he added to our maps may here suffice. He was despatched to observe the Transit of Venus in 1769. In this expedition he discovered the SOCIETY ISLANDS, so named from the Royal Society, at whose instigation the expedition had been undertaken ; as well as the SANDWICH ISLANDS, called after Lord Sandwich, the First Lord of the Admiralty, who had consented to send it out. In his second voyage, Captain Cook explored and named the coast of NEW SOUTH WALES, the NEW HEBRIDES, NEW CALEDONIA, NORFOLK ISLAND, and SANDWICH LAND.

We must not forget those Arctic explorers who, within the last half-century, have added so largely to our geographical knowledge. The names of MACKENZIE, ROSS, PARRY, FRANKLIN, BACK, HOOD, RICHARDSON, DEASE, SIMPSON, CROZIER, MACLURE, M'CLINTOCK, and KANE, perpetually remind those who examine the map of the Arctic regions, of the skill, the courage, and the endurance of the brave men who have, at last, solved the problem of three hundred years—' the only thing of the world yet left undone by which a notable minde might be made famous '.[1] Such names as REPULSE BAY, POINT TURNAGAIN, RETURN REEF, POINT ANXIETY, the BAY OF MERCY, FORT ENTERPRIZE, FORT PROVIDENCE, FURY BEACH, and WINTER HARBOUR recall to the memory of the readers of Arctic adventure some of the most thrilling passages in those narratives ; and, at the same time, they form a melancholy record of the difficulties, the hardships, the disappointments, and the failures, which seemed only to braven the resolution and to nerve the courage of men whom all Englishmen are proud to be able to call their fellow-countrymen.

Mention has already been made of the Sandwich Islands and the Marquesas, as commemorating the names of statesmen who have been instrumental in furthering the progress of geographical discovery. Other names of this class—primeministers, eminent statesmen, lords of the admiralty, and secretaries of the navy—are to be found in great profusion in the regions which have most recently been explored. We may instance the names of MELVILLE, DUNDAS, MELBOURNE, AUCKLAND, BARING, BARROW, CROKER, BATHURST, PEEL, WELLINGTON, and SYDNEY.[2] Port PHILIP, BRISBANE, the River

[1] See p. 14.
[2] CHATHAM Island does not belong to this class : it bears the name of the brig *Chatham*, by which it was discovered. Cf. Mt. EREBUS, FURY Beach, etc.

DARLING, and MACQUARIE take their names from governors of the Australian Colonies, and Lake SIMCOE from a governor of Canada. BOOTHIA FELIX, GRINNELL LAND, SMITH'S SOUND, and JONES' SOUND commemorate merchant-princes who fitted out exploring expeditions from their private resources ; while the names of KING GEORGE, QUEEN CHARLOTTE, the PRINCE REGENT, KING WILLIAM, QUEEN ADELAIDE, VICTORIA, and ALBERT are scattered so lavishly over our maps, as to prove a serious source of embarrassment to the young student of geography ; while, at the same time, their English origin testifies to the energy and success with which, during the last hundred years, every corner of the globe has been explored by English-men.

CHAPTER III

Local names are the beacon-lights of primeval History—The method of research illustrated by American Names—Recent progress of Ethnology—The Celts, Anglo-Saxons, and Northmen—Retrocession of the Sclaves—Arabic Names—Ethnology of mountain districts—The Alps.

ETHNOLOGY is the science which derives the greatest aid from geographical etymology. The names which still remain upon our maps are able to supply us with traces of the history of nations that have left us no other memorials. Egypt has bequeathed to us her pyramids, her temples, and her tombs ; Nineveh her palaces ; Judæa her people and her sacred book ; Mexico her temple-mounds ; Arabia her science ; India her institutions ; Greece her deathless literature ; and Rome has left us her roads, her aqueducts, her laws, and the languages which still live on the lips of half the civilized world. But there are other nations which once played a prominent part in the world's history, but which have bequeathed no written annals, which have constructed no monuments, whose language is dying or is dead, whose blood is becoming mingled with that of other races. The knowledge of the history and the migrations of such tribes must be recovered from the study of the names of the places which they once inhabited, but which now know them no more—from the names of the hills which they fortified, of the rivers by which they dwelt, of the distant mountains upon which they gazed. As an eloquent writer has observed, ' Mountains and rivers still murmur the voices of nations long denationalized or extirpated '.[1] Language adheres to the soil when the race by which it was spoken has been swept from off the earth, or when its remnants have been driven from the plains which they once peopled into the fastnesses of the surrounding mountains.

It is mainly from the study of local names that we must re-

[1] Palgrave, *Normandy and England*, vol. i. p. 701.

construct the history of the Sclaves, the Celts, and the Basques, as well as the earlier chronicles of the Scandinavian and Teutonic races ; while from the same source we are able to throw great light upon the more or less obscure records of the conquests and colonizations of the Phoenicians, the Greeks, the Romans, and the Arabs. In many instances, we can thus convert dubious surmises into the clearest historical certainties.

The nomenclature of America, the nature of which has been indicated in the preceding chapter, may serve to explain the method by which etymological considerations become available in ethnological inquiries. Here we have a simple case, where we possess documentary evidence as to the facts which we might expect to be disclosed by etymological investigations, and where we can thus exhibit the method of research, and at the same time test the value of the results to which it leads.

If we examine a map of America, we find names derived from a dozen languages. We first notice a few scattered Indian names, such as the POTOMAC, the RAPPAHANOCK, or NIAGARA. These names are sparsely distributed over large areas, some of them filled almost exclusively with English names, while in others, the names are mostly of Spanish or Portuguese origin—the boundary between the regions of the English and Spanish, or of the Spanish and Portuguese names being easily traceable. In Louisiana and Lower Canada we find a predominance of French names, many of them exhibiting Normand and Breton peculiarities. In New York we find, here and there, a few Dutch names, as well as patches of German names in Michigan and Brazil. We find that the Indian, Dutch, and French names have more frequently been corrupted than those derived either from the English or from the Spanish languages. In New England we find names like SALEM and PROVIDENCE ; in Virginia we find such names as JAMES River, Cape CHARLES, and ELIZABETH County. In many places the names of the Old World are repeated : we find a NEW ORLEANS, a NEW BRUNSWICK, a NEW HAMPSHIRE, and the like.

If we were entirely destitute of any historical records of the actual course of American colonization, it is evident that, with the aid of the map alone, we might recover many most important facts, and put together an outline, by no means to be despised, of the early history of the continent ;—we might successfully investigate the retrocession and extinction of the Indian tribes—we might discover the positions in which the colonies of the several European nations were planted—we might show, from the character of the names, how the gradually increasing supremacy of the Anglo-American stock must have enabled it to incorporate, and overlay with a layer of English names, the colonies of other nations, such as the Spanish settlements in Florida and Texas, the Dutch colony in the neighbourhood of New York, and the French settlements on the St. Lawrence and the Mississippi. We might even go further, and attempt to discriminate between the colonies founded by Puritans and by Cavaliers ; and if we possessed a knowledge of English and French history, we might assign approximate dates for the original foundation of a large number of the several settlements. In some cases we might be able to form probable conjectures as to the causes and methods of the migration, and the condition of the early colonists. Our investigations would be much facilitated if we also possessed a full knowledge of the *present* circumstances of the country— if, for example, we knew that the English language now forms the universal medium of communication throughout large districts, which nevertheless, are filled with Spanish or French names ; or if we learned that in the State of New York the Indian and Dutch languages are no longer spoken, while many old families bear Dutch, but none of them Indian surnames. The study of the local names, illustrated by the knowledge of such facts, would enable us to reconstruct, in great part, the history of the country, and would prove that successive bands of immigrants may forget their mother-tongue, and abandon all distinctive national peculiarities, but that the names which, on their first arrival, they bestowed upon the places of their abode, are sure to remain upon the map as a permanent record of the nature and extent of the original colonizations.

Centuries hence, when Macaulay's New Zealander shall have succeeded in escaping from his perilous position on the broken arch of London Bridge, and has taken up his stand among certain fallen columns which mark the supposed site of the British Museum, there to lament the destruction of the literary treasures which might have enabled him to investigate the

early history of the land of his ancestors, he will do well to
devote himself to a comparison of the local names of New
Zealand with those of the United States ; and he will find
it easy to prove that the two countries must have been peopled
from the same source, and under circumstances not very
dissimilar, and he might succeed in recovering, from a comparison and analysis of English and New Zealand names,
many of those facts which he fancied had been lost for ever.

We shall hereafter investigate classes of names which
present a perfect parallelism to those in America. In the
case of Spain, the Celtic, Phœnician, Arabic, and Spanish
names answer in many points to the strata of Indian, Dutch,
French, and English names which we find superimposed in the
United States ; while an isolated name like Swedesboro',
in New Jersey, may be compared with that of the town of
ROZAS, which stands upon the Gulf of RHODA—names which
have handed down the memory of the ancient Rhodian colony
in North-eastern Spain. Again, the Scandinavian names
scattered over a wide area throughout England, Ireland,
Scotland, France, Flanders, Iceland, and Greenland, present a
parallel to the names in the English colonies of North America,
Australia, and New Zealand.[1] The phenomena of the Old
World are similar to those presented in the New. In either
case, from similar phenomena we may draw similar inferences.

This method of research—the application of which has
been exhibited in the familiar instance of the United States,
where the results attained can be compared with well known
facts—has of late years been repeatedly applied, and often
with great success, to cases in which local names are the only
records which exist.

Wilhelm Von Humboldt was one of the pioneers in this new
science of etymological ethnology. On the maps of Spain,
France, and Italy he has marked out,[2] by the evidence of
names alone, the precise regions which, before the period of the
Roman conquest, were inhabited by those Euskarian or Iberic
races who are now represented by the Basques—the moun-

---

[1] In Norway, as in England, a strict law of primogeniture has dispersed the cadets
of a fully-peopled country over a wide geographical area. In the guards of Norway
are to be found peasant proprietors, clad in homespun, who are the lineal representatives
of the elder line of the chief royal and noble families of Western Europe.—See Laing,
Heimskringla, vol. i. p. 109.

[2] *Prüfung der Untersuchungen über die Urbewohner Hispaniens.*

taineers of the Asturias and the Pyrenees. He has also shown that large portions of Spain were anciently Celtic, and that there was a central zone inhabited by a mixed population of Euskarians and Celts.

Archdeacon Williams,[1] in like manner, has indicated the limits of the Celtic region in Northern Italy, and has pointed out detached Celtic colonies in the central portion of that peninsula. Mone,[2] Diefenbach,[3] Duncker,[4] Brandes,[5] and other industrious explorers have followed the wanderings of this ancient people through Switzerland, Germany, and France, and have shown that, in those countries, the Celtic speech still lives upon the map, though it has vanished from the glossary.

From the evidence of local names alone, Prichard[6] has demonstrated that the ancient Belgæ were of Celtic, and not of Teutonic race, as had previously been supposed. So cogent is the evidence supplied by these names, that ethnologists are agreed in setting aside the direct testimony of such a good authority as Cæsar, who asserts that the Belgæ were of German blood.[7]

In our own country, this method has afforded results of peculiar interest and value. It has enabled us to detect the successive tides of immigration that have flowed in ; just as the ripple-marked slabs of sandstone record the tidal flow of the primeval ocean, so wave after wave of population—Gaelic, Cymric, Roman, Saxon, Anglian, Norwegian, Danish, Norman, Frisian, and Flemish—has left its mark upon the once shifting, but now indurated sands of language.

Baxter and Lhuyd,[8] Chalmers,[9] Whitaker,[10] Skene,[11] Robertson,[12] Garnett,[13] Davies,[13] Latham,[14] and other writers have investigated the Celtic names of our own islands. Not only have they shown that the whole of England was once Celtic, but they have made it probable that the Scottish lowlands were peopled by tribes belonging to the Welsh and not to the

---

[1] *Transactions of the Royal Society of Edinburgh,* vol. xiii.
[2] *Celtische Forschungen zur Geschichte Mitteleuropas.*   [3] *Celtica.*
[4] *Origines Germanicæ.*
[5] *Das Ethnographische Verhältniss der Kelten und Germanen.*
[6] *Researches into the Physical History of Mankind,* vol. iii.
[7] Latham, *English Language,* vol. i. p. 12.
[8] *Glossarium Antiquitatum Britannicarum.* Appendix by Edward Lhuyd.   [9] *Caledonia.*   [10] *History of Manchester.*   [11] *History of the Highlanders.*   [12] *Scotland under her early Kings.*   [13] Papers in the *Proceedings and Transactions of Philological Society,* and in the *Quarterly Review.*
[14] *English Language,* vol. i. pp. 363-367 ; *Ethnology of the British Isles.*

Gaelic stock, thus clearing up some of the disputed questions as to the affinities and distribution of the Picts and Scots.

The study of Anglo-Saxon and Scandinavian names has been prosecuted by Leo,[1] Ingram,[2] Kemble, [3] Worsaae,[4] Ferguson,[5] Borring,[6] Depping,[7] Palgrave,[8] and Lappenberg.[9] They have shown how we may draw the line between the Anglian and the Saxon kingdoms—how, from the study of the names of the villages of Lincolnshire, of Leicestershire, of Caithness, of Cumberland, of Pembrokeshire, of Iceland and of Normandy, we may learn the almost-forgotten story of the fierce Vikings, who left the fiords of Norways and the vics of Denmark, to plunder and to conquer the coasts and kingdoms of Western Europe.

By the use of the same method, Buttmann,[10] Bender,[10] and Zeuss [11] have shown how we may investigate the obscure relations of the tribes of Eastern Europe, and mark the oscillations of the boundaries of the Sclaves and Germans, and even detect the alternate encroachments and retrocessions of either race. Thus in Eastern Bavaria, which is now a purely German district, we find scattered Sclavonic names, more especially in the Valley of the Naab.[12] From the number and character of these names, we may infer that, at some remote period [13] the Sclavonians must have extended themselves westward much beyond the present frontier of Bohemia,[14] even as far as Darmstadt, where the River WESCHNITZ marks the extreme western limit of Sclavonic occupancy. For several centuries, however, the German language has been encroaching towards the east ; and the process is now going on with accelerated speed. In Bohemia, where almost every local name is Scla-

---

[1] *Rectitudines Singularum Personarum.*   [2] *Appendix to Saxon Chronicle.*   [3] *Codex Diplomaticus,* vol. iii. ; *Saxons in England.* [4] *The Danes and Norwegians.*   [5] *The Northmen in Cumberland.* [6] *Sur la limite Méridionale de lo Monarchie Danoise.* [7] *Histoire des Expeditions Maritimes des Normands.* [8] *England and Normandy.* [9] *Anglo-Norman Kings.* [10] *Die Deutschen Ortsnamen.* [11] *Die Deutschen und die Nachbarstämme.*

[12] In the Aischthal, the presence of the Wends is denoted by names like Brodswinden, Ratzenwinden, Poppenwind, Reinhardswind, etc. In Würtemberg, we find Windischgrätz and Winnenden ; in Baden, Windischbuch ; in Saxony, Wendischhayn ; in Brunswick, Wenden and Wendhausen ; in Westphalia, Windheim and Wenden.—Schafarik, *Slaw. Alterth.* vol. i. p. 85 ;] Bender, *Deutschen Ortsnamen,* p. 31 ; Zeuss, *Die Deutschen* ; Latham, *Nat. of Europe,* vol. ii. pp. 321, 309.

[13] It is probable that, in the fifth and sixth centuries, the Sclaves took possession of the regions left vacant by the inroads of the Teutonic nations toward the west and south ; while in the seventh and eighth centuries the Germans began to recover the lost ground, and to drive the Sclaves to the eastward.

[14] See Latham, *English Language,* vol. i. p. 106 ; *Nat. of Europe,* vol. ii. p. 357 ; vol. i. p. 4 ; *Germania,* p. 151 ; *Philological Proceedings,* vol. iv. p. 187. For a list of Sclavonic names in the Valley of the Mayn, see Zeuss, *Die Deutschen,* pp. 649, 650.

vonic, and where five-and-twenty years ago few of the elder people knew any language but their Bohemian speech, we find that the adults are now universally able to speak German ; and in half a century, there is every likelihood that the Bohemian language will be extinct.[1]

Farther to the north a similar process has only taken place. Proceeding from west to east, the River BOMLITZ, near Verden in Hanover, is the first Sclavonic name we meet with. In Holstein, Mecklenburg, Luneburg, and Saxony—in East and West Prussia—in Brandenburg and Pomerania—we find numerous Sclavonic names,[2] such as POTSDAM,[3] LEIPSIG, LOBAU, or KULM, scattered over an area which is now purely German. These names gradually increase in frequency as we proceed eastward, till, at length, in Silesia, we find that the local names are all Sclavonic, although the people universally speak German, except on the eastern rim of the Silesian basin, where the ancient speech still feebly lingers.[4]

It will be manifest that this distribution of Sclavonic names will greatly guide us in interpreting the obscure historical notices which relate to the great struggle by which, in the ninth and tenth centuries, Mecklenburg, Pomerania, Brandenburg, Silesia, Saxony, and part of Courland were wrested by the Germans from the Sarmatians.[5]

The names in Eastern Europe illustrate the maxim that Ethnology must always be studied with due reference to Hydrography. In rude times, the rivers form the great highways. The Rhine, the Danube, and the Elbe seem to have regulated the directions of the early movements of nations. And the distribution of Sclavonic names proves that the Sclaves must, originally, have descended by the valleys of the Elbe and the Mayn, just as the Germans descended by the valley of the Danube, where we find a wedge or elbow of German names protruding eastward into the Sclavonic region. So, again, in Hungary we find that the central plains are occupied by the Magyar shepherds from the steppes of the Volga, while the original Sclavonic population has been driven to the mountain

---

[1] Ansted, *Trip to Hungary*, p. 79.
[2] Zeuss, *Die Deutschen und die Nachbarstämme*, p. 676 ; Bender, *Ortsnamen*, p. 90.
[3] Potsdam is a Germanized form of the Sclavonic Potsdupimi. Förstemann, in Kuhn's *Zeitschrift*, vol. i. p. 15.
[4] The phenomena, in fact, are analogous to those which are exhibited as we proceed from Somersetshire, through Devonshire, to Cornwall.
[5] Latham, *Man and his Migrations*, p. 165.

region on either side.[1]   Still farther to the east we find the isolated Saxon colony of Siebenbürgen (Transylvania), where, surrounded on all sides by Sclavonic, Magyar, and Wallachian names, we find cities called Kronstadt, Hermannstadt, Klaussenburg, Elisabethstadt, and Mühlenbach, which are inhabited by a population that has been transferred from the Lower Rhine to the Lower Danube.   For seven centuries this little colony has retained, unchanged, its own peculiar laws, language, institutions, and customs.   Siebenbürgen, in fact, presents a well-conserved museum of mediaeval peculiarities—a living picture of Ancient Germany, just as in Iceland we find the language and customs of our Scandinavian ancestors still subsisting without any material change.[2]

We find similar phenomena in the west and south.   Franche Comté, Burgundy, and Lombardy contain many disguised German names—evidences of ancient conquests by Germanic tribes, which have now lost their ancient speech, and have completely merged their nationality in that of the conquered races.[3]   In Alsace, which has now become thoroughly French in feeling and in language, the German names of the villages have suffered no corruption during the short period which has elapsed since the conquest under Louis XIV.

The Arabic names which we find in Asia, in Africa, in Spain, in Sicily, in Southern Italy, in Provence, and even in some valleys of the Alps, tell us of the triumphs of the Crescent from the Indus to the Loire.   In some instances, these names even disclose the manner in which the Mahometan hosts were recruited for the conquest of Europe from the valley of the Euphrates and the borders of the Sahara ; and we can trace the settlement of these far-travelled conquerors in special valleys of Spain or Sicily.

In mountainous regions, the etymological method of ethnological research is of special value, and yields results more definite than elsewhere.   Among the mountains the botanist and the ethnologist meet with analogous phenomena.   The lowland flora of the glacial epoch has retreated to the Gram-

---

[1] The Sclavonic inroad into Greece is well marked by local names, such as WALIGOST which extend even into the Peloponnesus.—Zeuss, *Die Deutschen*, p. 634 ; Arndt, *Europ Spr.* p. 105 ; Schafarik, *Slawische Alterthümer*, vol. ii. p. 226 ; Keferstein, *Kelt. Alterth* vol. ii. p. 436.

[2] Ansted, *Trip to Hungary and Transylvania*, pp. 30, 31.

[3] See Latham's *Germania of Tacitus*, Epilegomena, pp. xxxix. and lv. ; *Nationalities of Europe*, vol. ii. p. 283 ; Lewis, *On the Romance Languages*, p. 18.

pians, the Carpathians, the Alps, and the Pyrenees ; [1] and in like manner we find that the hills contains the ethnological sweepings of the plains. Mountain fastnesses have always formed a providential refuge for conquered tribes. The narrow valleys which penetrate into the great chains are well adapted to preserve for a time the isolation of unrelated tribes of refugees, to hinder the intermixture of race, and thus preserve from extermination or absorption those who should afterwards, at the right time, blend gradually with the conquerors of the plains, and supplement their moral and intellectual deficiencies.[2]

Instances of this peculiar ethnological character of mountain districts will occur to every one. The Bengalees, though they are in geographical contact with the hill tribes of India, are yet, in blood, further removed from them than from ourselves. Strabo informs us that in his day no less than seventy languages were spoken in the Caucasus, and the number of distinct dialects is probably, at the present time, quite as large. Here, in close juxtaposition, we find archaic forms of various Georgian, Mongolian, Persian, Semitic, and Tatarian languages, as well as anomalous forms of speech which bear no affinity to any known tongue of Asia or of Europe.[3]

In the Pyrenees we find the descendants of the Euskarians, who have been driven from the lowlands of France and Spain. The fastnesses of Wales and of the Scotch Highlands have enabled the Celts of our own island to maintain their ancient speech and a separate existence. An inspection of the map of the British Isles will show that The Peak of Derbyshire and the mountains of Cumberland retain a greater number of Celtic names than the adjacent districts ; and the hills of Devonshire have served as a barrier to protect the Celts of Cornwall from the Anglo-Saxon conquerors.

But Switzerland is the most notable instance of the ethnological interest attaching to a mountainous district. In a country only twice the size of Wales, the local names [4] are derived from half a dozen separate languages, three or four of which are still spoken by the people, while in some dis-

---

1 See Darwin, *On the Origin of Species*, pp. 365-369.
2 Goldwin Smith, *Irish History and Irish Character*, p. 14.
3 Lyell, *Antiquity of Man*, p. 460 ; Max Müller, *Lectures*, p. 52 ; Knobel, *Völkertafel*, p. 14 ; Pott, *Ungleichheit d. menschlicher Rassen*, p. 238, apud Renan, *Orig. du Langage*, p. 176 ; Latham, *Nationalities of Europe*, vol. i. p. 294.
4 An admirable monograph on the local names in Canton Zurich, by Dr. Meyer, will be found in the *Mittheilungen der Antiq. Gesellschaft in Zurich*, vol. vi. pt. i,

tricts almost every village preserves its separate dialect.[1] Thus, in the Cantons of Neufchâtel, Vaud, Geneva, and in the western part of the Valais, French is the prevailing language. In the northern and central cantons, which were divided among Burgundian, Alemannic, and Suevic tribes, various high German dialects are spoken ;[2] while in Canton Ticino, and in portions of the Grisons, Italian is the only language understood. The Romansch language, spoken in the upper valley of the Rhine, is a debased Latin, with a few Celtic, German, and, possibly, some Iberic and Etruscan elements.[3] In the Upper Engadine we find the Ladino, another Latin dialect,[4] distinct from the Romansch ; while throughout the whole of Switzerland, numerous Celtic names[5] show traces of a still earlier wave of population, of which no other evidence remains. Not only has the region of the Alps been the immemorial abode of Celts, but there also we find indications of fragments of intrusive races—the meteoric stones of Ethnology. Thus, in the Valley of Evolena, there are traces of the former presence of a race of doubtful origin—possibly Huns or Alans, who long retained their heathenism.[6]   In some valleys of the Grisons there are names which suggest colonies from Southern Italy ; for example, LAVIN, which is apparently a reproduction of Lavinium, and ARDETZ, of Ardea.[7]   Mommsen, a high authority, believes the Rhoetians of the Grisons and the Tyrol to be the descendants of an Ancient Etruscan stock ;[8] while other valleys

---

[1] Planta, *Romansch Language,* p. 144 ; Adelung, *Mithridates,* vol. ii. p. 602 ; Lewis, *Romance Languages,* p. 46. Stalder, *Die Landes-sprachen der Schweiz,* pp. 273-418, gives specimens of thirty-five dialects of German, sixteen of French, five of Romansch, and eight of Italian, which are spoken in the several Swiss cantons.

[2] German Switzerland is mainly Alemannic, French Switzerland is mainly Burgundian. In Berne, however, as well as in portions of Freiburg, Lutzern, and Argau, the Burgundians have retained their German speech. Grimm, *Gesch. d. Deut. Spr.* p. 703.

[3] For instance, in the dialect of Groeden. Niebuhr, *Hist. Rome,* vol. i. p. 113. A list of Romansch words which are possibly Etruscan, will be found in Tschudi, *Hauptsch-lüssel,* pp. 289, 290. See also Steub's works [and R. Martineau in the Philolog. Soc. Transactions].

[4] See Lechner, *Piz Languard,* p. 28.

[5] An analysis of the names in Canton Zurich shows the following proportions :—

Celtic { 2 cities. 100 important rivers, mountains, and villages.   Alemannic { 3,000 homesteads. 100 hamlets. 20 villages.

The other names are of modern German origin.—Meyer, *Ortsnamen,* p. 75.

[6] Forbes, *Alps,* p. 289 ; Diefenbach, *Celtica,* i. p. 238.

[7] Witte, *Alpinisches und Transalpinisches,* p. 124 ; Planta, *Romansch Language,* p. 134.

[8] The village-names of Tilisuna, Blisadona, Trins, Vels, Tschars, Naturns, Velthurns, Schluderns, Villanders, Gufidaun, Altrans, Sistrans, Axams, and others, bear a remarkable resemblance to those Etruscan names with which we are acquainted. Compare also the names Tusis and Tuscany, Rhoetia and Rasenna. This subject is discussed at great length in two works of Ludwig Steub,· *Ueber die Urbewohner Rätiens, und ihren zusam-*

in the Valais and the Grisons astound us by the phenomenon of Arabic names, for whose presence we shall presently endeavour to account.

On the Italian side of the Alps we find valleys filled with Sclavonic names, besides many isolated villages of Teutonic colonists,[1] who still keep themselves distinct from their Italian neighbours, and who speak a German dialect more or less corrupt. The German-speaking villages are often surrounded by a penumbra of German local names, which prove that the little settlement must formerly have occupied a more extensive area than at present.[2] It is difficult to say whether these intrusive populations did, at some remote period, cross the passes and take possession of the unoccupied Italian valleys, or whether they are fragments thrown off at the time of either the Burgundian or the Lombardic invasions, and which the isolation of the mountain-valleys has prevented from being Italianized. In the case of the valleys of Macugnaga, Gressonay, Alagna, Sermenta, Pommat, and Sappada, we may, perhaps, incline to the former supposition ; while with regard to the Sette Comuni, near Vicenza, and the Tredici Comuni, near Verona, which still retain their Lombard-German speech, the latter hypothesis may be the more probable.[3]

menhang mit den Etruskern, and Zur Rätischen Ethnologie. Cf. Tschudi, Hauptschlüssel zu verschiedenen Alterthümern, p. 290 ; Adelung, Mithridates, vol. ii. p. 598 ; Mommsen, Hist. Rome, vol. i. p. 108 ; Inhabitants of Italy, p. 56 ; Newman, Regal Rome, p. 101 Note by Latham in Prichard's Eastern Origin of Celtic Nations, pp. 87–90 ; Niebuhr Hist. Rome, vol. i. p. 113, and vol. ii. p. 525 ; Dennis, Etruria, vol. i. pp. xxxiv. xlv. Pott, Indo-Germ. Spr. p. 25 ; Planta, Romansch Language, p. 132.

1 Thus in the valley of the Tagliamento, north of Venice, we find the Sclavonic village-names, GNIVA, STOLVIZZA, and others, and the mountains POSGOST, STOLAC, and ZLEBAC. Zeuss, Die Deutschen, p. 617 ; Latham, Nat. of Europe, vol. ii. p. 283 ; Biondelli, Studii Linguistici, p. 55.

2 In some valleys the German language has become entirely extinct. In Ornavasco, north of the Lago Maggiore, this has taken place within the memory of persons now living. Latham, Nat. of Eur. vol. ii. p. 283. The upper part of the Val d'Ayas is called Canton des Allemands, though no German is now spoken there.—See Schott, Die Deutschen am Monte Rosa.

3 See Forbes, Alps, p. 330 ; Tour of Mont Blanc, p. 266 ; King, Italian Valleys, p. 449 ; Latham, Nationalities of Europe, vol. ii. p. 282 ; Germania, p. xl. ; Lewis, Romance Languages, p. 97 ; Biondelli, Studii Linguistici, pp. 47–54 ; Gilbert and Churchill, Dolomite Mountains, p. 379 ; Steub, Zur Rätischen Ethnol, pp. 56–65. On the valleys of Macugnaga, etc., see two capital monographs by Schott, Die Deutschen am Monte Rosa, and Die Deutschen Colonien in Piedmont. The best account of the Sette and Tredici Comuni is by Schmeller, Ueber die sogenannten Cimbern auf den Venedischen Alpen. Till the beginning of the present century they formed an independent republic. Schmeller, p. 563. They speak a Platt-deutsch dialect, and call themselves Cimbri. A peasant, if asked, will tell you, ' Ich pin an Cimbro'. Schmeller, p. 565. Eustace, Classical Tour, vol. i. p. 142, and Crichton, Scandinavia, vol. i. p. 69, accept the local tradition which makes them the remains of the Cimbrian horde which was overthrown by Marius in the neighbourhood of Verona. See Notes and Queries, vol. i. p. 176 ; Biondelli, Studii Linguistici, p. 53 ; Arndt, Eur. Spr. p. 105. J. K. [enrick ?], in Journal of Education, vol. vi. p. 353, thinks they are the remains of German mercenaries.

We shall proceed to fill up some portions of the outline which has just been traced, and endeavour to decipher from the map of Europe the history of the conquests and immigrations of some of the chief races that have succeeded one another upon the stage.

CHAPTER IV

THE NAMES OF NATIONS

Ethnic Names are of obscure origin—Name of Britain—Many nations bear duplicate names—Deutsche and Germans—' Barbarians '—Welsh— Gaels—Aryans—Names of conquering Tribes—Ancient Ethnic Names conserved in those of modern cities—Ethnic Names from rulers—From geographical position—Europe—Asia—Africa—Ethnographic Names —' Warriors '—' Mountaineers '—' Lowlanders '—' Foresters '—' Coast-landers '—Greeks.

THE names borne by nations and countries are naturally of prime importance in all ethnological investigations. They are not lightly changed, they are often cherished for ages as a most precious patrimony, and therefore they stretch back far into the dim Past, thus affording a clue which may enable us to discover the obscure beginnings of separate national existence. But, fortunately, few departments of etymology are beset with more difficulties, or are subject to greater uncertainties. Some of those ethnic names which have gained a wide application had at first a very restricted meaning, as in the case of ITALY or ASIA;[1] others, like that of the ROMANS, may have arisen from special local circumstances, of which we can have only a conjectural or accidental knowledge ;[2] others again, as in the case of LORRAINE,[3] may be due to causes which, if history be silent, the utmost etymological ingenuity is powerless to recover. It is only here and there, as in the case of the UNITED STATES, LIBERIA, ECUADOR, the BANDA ORIENTAL, or the ARGENTINE REPUBLIC,[4] that we find countries

---

[1] See pp. 55, 62, *infra* ; and Newman, *Regal Rome*, p. 6.
[2] The name of Roma is perhaps from the *Groma*, or four cross-roads at the Forum, which formed the nucleus of the city. See Donaldson, *Varronianus*, pp. 60, 270. Other plausible conjectures will be found in Curtius, *Grundzüge*, vol. ii. p. 261 ; Mommsen, *Hist. of Rome*, vol. i. p. 44 ; and Pott, *Etym. Forsch.* vol. ii. p. 284.
[3] See p. 53, *infra*.
[4] Ecuador is the republic of the ' Equator ' ; the Banda Oriental occupies the ' eastern bank ', and the Argentine Republic the western bank of the Rio de la Plata, or River of the ' Silver '.

bearing names which have originated within the historic era, and the meaning of which is obvious. But the greater number of ethnic names are of great antiquity, and their elucidation has often to be sought in languages with which we possess only a fragmentary acquaintance. Frequently, indeed, it is very difficult—sometimes impossible—to discover even the language from which any given ethnic name has been derived.

It is not needful to travel far for an illustration of the mode in which this difficulty presents itself—the name of our own country will supply us with an instance. The BRITISH people, the inhabitants of GREAT BRITAIN, are, we know, mainly of Teutonic blood, and they speak one of the Teutonic languages. None of these, however, affords any assistance in the explanation of the name. We conclude, therefore, that the Teutonic colonists must have adopted an ethnic appellation belonging to the former inhabitants of the country. But the Celtic aborigines do not seem to have called themselves by the name of Britons, nor can any complete and satisfactory explanation of the name be discovered in any of the Celtic dialects. We turn next to the classic languages, for we find, if we trace the literary history of the name, that its earliest occurrence is in the pages of Greek, and afterwards of Latin writers. The word, however, is utterly foreign both to the Greek and to the Latin speech. Finally, having vainly searched through all the languages spoken by the diverse races which, from time to time, have found a home upon these shores—having exhausted all the resources of Indo-European philology without the discovery of any available Aryan root, we turn, in despair, to the one remaining ancient language of western Europe. We then discover how great is the real historical significance of our inquiry, for the result shows that the first chapter of the history of our island is in reality written in its name—we find that this name is derived from that family of languages of which the Lapp and the Basque are the sole living representatives ; and hence, we reasonably infer that the earliest knowledge of the island, which was possessed by any of the civilized inhabitants of Europe, must have been derived from the Iberic mariners of Spain,[1] who either in their own ships, or in those of their Punic masters, coasted along to Brittany, and thence crossed to Britain, at some dim pre-historic period. The

[1] Niebuhr, *Hist. Rome*, vol. ii. p. 522 ; Arnold, *Hist. Rome*, vol. i. p. 489.

name Br-*itan*-ia contains, it would seem, the Euskarian suffix *etan*, which is used to signify a district or country.[1] We find this suffix in the names of many of the districts known to, or occupied by the Iberic race. It occurs in Aqu-*itan*-ia or Aquitaine, in Lus-*itan*-ia, the ancient name of Portugal, in Maur-*etan*-ia, the ' country of the Moors ', as well as in the names of very many of the tribes of ancient Spain, such as the Cerr-*etan*-i, Aus-*etan*-i, Lal-*etan*-i, Cos-*etan*-i, Vesc-*itan*-i, Lac-*etan*-i, Carp-*etan*-i, Or-*etan*-i, Bast-*itan*-i, Turd-*etan*-i, Suess-*etan*-i, Ed-*etan*-i, and others.

This illustration not only indicates the value of the results which may accrue from the investigation of ethnic names, but it will also serve to show how difficult it may often be to determine even the language from which the explanation must be sought.

In attempting to lay down general principles to guide us in our investigations, we have in the first place to deal with the remarkable phenomenon—an instance of which has just presented itself—that the greater number of ethnic names are only to be explained from languages which are not spoken by the people to whom the name applies. Most nations have, in fact, two, or even a greater number of appellations.[2] One name, by which the nation calls itself, is used only within the limits of the country itself ; the other, or cosmopolitan name, is that by which it is known to neighbouring tribes.

Thus, the people of England call themselves the English, while the Welsh, the Bretons, the Gaels of Scotland, the Irish, and the Manxmen, respectively, call us Saeson, Saoz, Sasunnaich, and Sagsonach.[3] The natives of Wales do not call themselves the Welsh, but the Cymry. The people to the east of the Rhine call themselves Deutsche, the French call them Allemands, we call them Germans, the Sclavonians call them Niemiec,

---

[1] This is the explanation usually given, but it would be more correct to say that *etan* is the plural of *an*, the suffixed locative preposition, or sign of the locative case. See Boudard, *Numatis. Ibér.* pp. 92, 93 ; and a tract by the same writer *Sur un suffixe Ibérien*, in the *Revue Archéologique*, xi. pp. 562–567 ; Adelung's *Mithridates*, vol. ii. p. 26. The first syllable, *bro, bri, orbrit*, is possibly Iberic, or more probably it may be a Celtic gloss (Brezonec, *bro*, a country, which appears in the name of the Allo-*bro*-ges), to which the Iberic *etan* was appended. Humboldt, *Prüfung der Untersuchungen*, pp. 62, 63, 143 ; Prichard, *Researches*, vol. iii. p. 28 ; *Philolog. Transactions*, vol. i. p. 176 ; Pott, *Etymol. Forschung.* vol. ii. pp. 42, 582 ; Renan, *Lang. Sémit.* p. 203 ; Smith, *Diction-ary of Greek and Roman Geogr.* s. v. Britannicae Insulae, vol. i. p. 434. Cf. Diefenbach, *Celtica*, ii. pp. 59–63 ; De Belloguet, *Ethnog.* vol. i. p. 251. [Old Celt. *Britto*, a Briton.]

[2] See Mahn, *Nam. Preuss.* pp. 4, 8 ; Verstegan, *Restitution*, p. 46.

[3] See Grimm, *Geschichte der Deut. Sprache*, vol. ii. p. 658 ; Souvestre, *Derniers Britons*, vol. i. p. 219.

the Magyars call them Schwabe, the Fins call them Saksalainen, the Gipsies call them Ssasso.[1] The people whom we call the Dutch call themselves Nederlanders, while the Germans call them Holländers. The Lapps call themselves Sabme, the Fins call themselves Quains. Those whom we call Bohemians call themselves Czechs. The Germans call the Sclavonians, Wends, but no Sclavonian knows himself by this name.[2]

The origin of these double names is often to be explained by means of a very simple consideration. Among kindred tribes, in a rude state of civilization, the conception of national Unity, is of late growth. But it would be natural for all those who were able to make themselves mutually intelligible, to call themselves collectively ' The Speakers ', or ' The People ', while they would call those neighbouring races, whose language they could not understand, by some word meaning in their own language ' The Jabberers ', or ' The Strangers '.[3]

A very large number of ethnic names can be thus explained.

The Sclavonians call themselves [4] either SLOWJANE, ' the intelligible men ', or else SRB, which means ' Kinsmen ', while the Germans call them WENDS, which means ' Wanderers ', or ' Strangers '.

The Basques call themselves the EUSCALDUNAC,[5] ' Those who have speech '. The LELEGES are ' The Speakers ' [6], the SABAEANS are the ' Men ', and the name of SHEBA or SEBA is referable to the same root.[7] All the Sclavonic nations call the Germans NIEMIEC,[8] ' the dumb men '. The earliest name

---

[1] This name affords a curious piece of evidence as to the road by which the gipsies entered Europe. It would seem that the first German people which became known to them must have been the Saxon colony in Transylvania. See Pott, *Die Zigeuner in Europa und Asien*, vol. i. p. 53. Another indication that the gipsies immigrated by the valley of the Danube, is the name Romani, by which they call themselves. This is the enchorial appellation of the Wallachians, among whom, therefore, it would appear that the gipsies must have been domiciled. See, however, Pott, *Indo-Germ. Sprach.* p. 42; Adelung, *Mithridates*, vol. i. p. 237.

[2] Adelung, *Mithridates*, vol. ii. p. 655.

[3] See a paper by J. K. [enrick], *On the Names of the Ante-Hellenic Inhabitants of Greece*, in the *Philolog. Museum*, vol. i. pp. 609–627; Arndt, *Eur. Spr.* pp. 251, 303 ; Strinnholm, *Wikingzüge*, p. 284 ; Renan, *Origine du Langage*, p. 180.

[4] Schafarik, *Slawische Alterthümer*, vol. i. p. 180; vol. ii. p. 42; Arndt, *Eur. Spr.* p. 93; Zeuss, *Deutschen*, p. 68; Pott, *Etym. Forsch.* vol. ii. p. 521; *Indo-Germ. Spr.* p. 107; Adelung, *Directorio für Sud-Sach. Spr.* quoted in *Mithridates*, vol. ii p. 612.

[5] From *euscara*, speech ; *dunac*, those who have. Mahn, *Namen Preuss.* p. 9 ; Adelung, *Mithridates*, vol. ii. p. 12; Humboldt, *Prüfung*, p. 57.

[6] *Philological Museum*, vol. i. p. 616.

[7] The Getes or Goths are, perhaps, the 'kinsmen'. Pictet, *Orig. Indo-Eur.* pt.i. p.84. The names of the Achaeans, the Sacae, and the Saxons may be of kindred meaning. See Gladstone, *Homer*, vol. i. p. 558. Glück thinks the Cymry are the ' people '. *Kelt. Namen*, p. 26. The Samojedes call themselves Chasowo, the ' men '. Müller, *Ugr. Volks.* vol. i. p. 313 ; Arndt, *Eur. Spr.* pp. 247, 326.

[8] Strictly speaking, they are called Niemiec by the Poles, Nemec by the Bohemians

by which the Germans designated themselves seems to have been TUNGRI,[1] ' Those who have tongues ', the ' Speakers '. This name was succeeded by the term DEUTSCHE,[2] ' the People ', ' the Nation ', a name which still holds its ground.   We have borrowed this national appellation of the Germans, but curiously enough we have limited its use to that portion of the Teutonic race on which the Germans themselves have bestowed another name.[3]

But while the Germans call themselves ' The People ', the name given to them by the French means ' The Foreigners ', The French word ALLEMAND is modernized from the name of the Alemanni, the ancient frontier tribe between Germania and Gaul.   The Alemanni seem to have been a mixed race— partly Celtic, partly Teutonic, in blood.   The name is itself Teutonic, and probably means ' Other Men ' or ' Foreigners '' and thus, curiously enough, the French name for the whole German people has been derived from a tribe whose very name indicates that its claims to Teutonic blood were disowned by the rest of the German Tribes.[4]

The English name for the same nation has been adopted from the Latin term, GERMANIA.   It must have been from

and Bulgarians, Njemc by the Lusatians, and Njemetz by the Russians. Grimm, *Gesch. der Deut. Spr.* p. 780 ; Leo, in Kuhn's *Zeitschrift*, vol. ii. p. 258 ; Max Müller, *Lectures* p. 83 ; Pott, *Etym. Forsch.* vol. ii. p. 521 ; Schafarik, *Slaw. Alt.* vol. i. p. 443 ; Zeuss. *Deutschen,* p. 68. The Gipsies call the Lithuanians, Lalerri, ' The dumb'. Pott, art, *Indo-Germanischer Sprachstamm,* in Ersch und Gruber, p. 44.

[1] Tacitus, *Germania,* cap. 2 : Grimm, *Gesch. der Deut. Spr.* p. 788 ; Donaldson, *English Ethnog.* p. 38 ; Mahn, *Namen Preuss.* p. 9. The QUADI are the speakers. Cf. the Sanskrit, *wad* [rather *gad*], to speak, and the Anglo-Saxon *cwede* [*cwedhan*], and Welsh *chwed* [?], speech. So the JAZYGES derived their name from the Sclavonic word *jazik,* the tongue.

[2] The form in which this name first appears suggested to Von Hammer the possibility that it might have been formed by the conjunction of the definite article and the root of the German word *Leute,* people—the Roman *laeti.* This Pott rightly pronounces to be ' völlig unhaltbar ', *Etym. Forsch.* vol. ii. p. 518. Dr. Donaldson derives the name of the Letts, Lithuanians, and even of the Latins from the same root. Donaldson, *Varronianus,* p. 62. See, however, p. 99,101 *infra*. On the etymology of the word Deutsche, see Grimm, *Gesch. der Deut. Spr.* pp. 789, *seq.*; Leo, in Kuhn's *Zeitschrift,* vol. ii. pp. 255–257: Leo, *Vorlesungen,* vol. i. p. 192 ; Leo, *Rectitudines,* p. 137 ; Diefenbach, *Vergleich. Wörterb.* vol. ii. pp. 705–708 ; Zeuss, *Die Deutschen,* pp. 63, 64 ; Latham, *English Language,* vol. i. pp. 289–297 ; Müller, *Marken,* pp. 218–230 ; Pott, *Etym. Forsch.* vol. ii. p. 521 ; *Indo-Germ. Spr.* p. 95 ; Bergmann, *Les Gètes,* pp. 74, 75.

[3] It seems to have been only in the seventeenth century that the application of the word DUTCH was restricted to the Low Germans. See Archbishop Trench, *Glossary,* p. 65. [p. 66, ed. Routledge.]

[4] The *al* in Alemanni is probably, the *al* in *al*ius and *Al*satia, or the *el* in *el*se and *El*sass, not the *al* in *all*. Thus the Alemanni are the ' other men ', not the ' all men ' or ' mixed men ', as is usually supposed. Compare the *al* in Allobroges. Latham, *Germania,* Epileg. p. liii. ; Pott, *Etymolog. Forsch.* vol. ii. pp. 523–526 ; Zeuss, *Die Deutschen,* p. 318 ; Förstemann, *Orisnamen,* p. 132 ; Ménage, *Origines,* pp. 27, 31 ; Diefenbach, *Celtica,* i. p. 17 ; *Orig. Eur.* p. 224 ; Glück, *Kelt.* Namen, p. 26 ; Smith, *Dict. of Geography,* art. Germania ; Latham, *Nationalities of Europe,* vol. ii. p. 322 ; Leo, *Vorlesungen,* vol. i. p. 245 ; Müller, *Marken,* pp. 213, 216 ; Bosworth, *Origin,* p. 120. [Zeuss thinks Germania=hill-folk ', Aryan *gara,* a hill].

the Celts of Gaul that the Romans obtained this word, which seems foreign to all the Teutonic languages. The etymology has been fiercely battled over ; the most reasonable derivation is, perhaps, that suggested by Professor Leo, from the Gaelic *gairmean*, one who cries out,[1] and the name either alludes to the fierce war-cry of the Teutonic hordes, or more probably it expresses the wonder with which the Celts of Gaul listened to the unintelligible clash of the harsh German gutturals.

The Russians call the contiguous Ugrian tribes by the name TSCHUDES, a Sclavonic word which means ' Strangers ' or ' Barbarians '.[2] The PHILISTINES are, probably, the ' Strangers '[3] and if this be the true meaning of the name, it strengthens the supposition that this warlike people arrived in Palestine by sea, probably from Crete,[4] during the anarchic period which succeeded to the Israelitish conquest under Joshua. The names of the African and Asiatic KAFFIRS, of the PERIZZITES, of the IONIANS,[5] and of the FLEMINGS are also nearly identical in meaning with those of the Philistines, Allemands, and Tschudes.[6] The word Barbarian was applied by the Egyptians, and afterwards by the Greeks and Romans, to all who did not speak their own language.[7] The root *barbar* may be traced to the Sanskrit *varvara*, ' a foreigner ', or ' one who speaks confusedly ', and, according to the opinion of the

---

[1] See Leo, in Haupt's *Zeitschrift*, vol. v. p. 514 ; Smith, *Diction. of Geogr.* vol. i. p. 993 ; Grimm, *Gesch. der Deut. Spr.* pp. 785–788 ; Gladstone, *Homer*, vol. i. p. 554 ; Latham, *English Language*, vol. i. pp. 286–289 ; Bosworth, *Origin*, p. 12 ; Bergmann, *Gètes*, pp. 76–79 ; Mahn, *Nam. 'Preuss.* p. 1 ; Forbiger, *Alt. Geogr.* vol. iii. pp. 314, 315 ; Keferstein, *Kelt. Alt.* vol. i. pp. xxii., 293 ; vol. ii. p. 366 ; Radlof, *Neue Untersuch*, pp. 241–255 ; Arndt, *Eur. Spr.* p. 114. Dr. Latham refers the word German to the Turkish *Kerman*, a castle ! *Nat. of Europe*, vol. ii. p. 215.

[2] Prichard, *Researches*, vol. iii. p. 273 ; Müller, *Marken des Vaterl.* vol. i. p. 219 ; Latham, *Nat. of Europe*, vol. i. p. 161 ; Arndt, *Eur. Spr.* p. 323.

[3] Knobel, *Völkertafel*, p. 218 ; Stanley, *Sinai and Palest.* p. 256 ; Movers, *Phönizien*, in Ersch und Gruber, p. 327.

[4] I am inclined to regard this emigration from Crete as a result of the Dorian conquest of that island. The two events seem to have been synchronous, or nearly so. Compare Bochart, vol. iii. p. 422, with Müller's *Dorians*, vol. i. p. 494 ; Hoeck, *Kreta*, vol. ii. pp. 16, 368, 417, *seq.* ; Stanley, *Jewish Church*, p. 287 ; Movers, *Die Phönizier*, part. i. pp. 4, 27 ; and part ii. vol. ii. p. 254 ; Renan, *Lang. Sémit.* p. 54 ; Ewald, *Volk. Isr.* vol. i. p. 292 [and now Hastings, *Bib. Dict.* iii. 846]. [The Philistines (*Purusati*) first came from the southern region of Asia Minor, i.e. Caphtor (Eg. Keftō), whence they migrated into Palestine in the twelfth century, B.C.—G. F. Moore, *Eneycl. Bib.* 3716–18.]

[5] See p. 62, *infra*.

[6] Pott, *Etymol. Forschungen*, vol. ii. p. 527 ; Renan, *Langues Sémitiques*, pt. i. pp. 30, 110 ; Müller, *Marken*, vol. i. pp. 159, 210 ; Knobel, *Völkerstafel*, pp. 169, 177 ; Movers, *Phönizier*, vol. ii. pt. i. p. 12 ; *Phönizien*, in Ersch und Gruber, p. 328. *Flemd*, the root of Fleming, means fugitive. De Smet, *Noms*, p. 10.

[7] Holzapfel, in Höfer's *Zeitschrift*, vol. iv. p. 240 ; Kenrick, *Ancient Egypt*, vol. ii. p. 248.

best scholars, it is undoubtedly onomatopoeian.[1] So also in the case of the HOTT-EN-TOTS we find a name which is supposed to have been given by the Dutch in imitation of the characteristic click of the Hottentot language, which sounds like a repetition of the sounds *hot* and *tot*.[2]

Few Ethnic names are more interesting than that of the WELSH. The root enters into a very large number of the Ethnic names of Europe, and is, perhaps, ultimately onomatopoeian. It has been referred to the Sanskrit *mlêch*, which denotes ' a person who talks indistinctly ',—' a jabberer '.[3] The root appears in German, in the form wal, which means anything that is ' Foreign ' or ' strange '. Hence we obtain the German words waller[4] a stranger or pilgrim, and wallen to wander, or to move about. [A mistake ; see Kluge, *s. v.v.*] A walnut is the ' foreign nut ', and in German a turkey is called Wälsche hahn, ' the foreign fowl ', and a French bean is Wälsche bohne, the ' foreign bean '. All nations of Teutonic blood have called the bordering tribes by the name of Wälsche, that is, Welshmen, or ' foreigners '. We trace this name around the whole circuit of the region of Teutonic occupancy. Wälschland, the German name of Italy, has occasioned certain incomprehensible historical statements relating to Wales, in a recent translation of a German work on mediaeval history. The Bernese Oberlander calls the French-speaking district to the south of him, by the name of Canton WALLIS, or Wales. WALLENSTADT and the WALLENSEE are on the frontier of the Romansch district of the Chur-*walchen*, or men of the Grisons.[5] The Sclaves and Germans called the Bulgarians Wlochi or

---

[1] Pictet, *Origines Indo-Européennes*, pt. i. pp. 57, 55 ; Curtius, *Grundzüge der Griech. Etym.* vol. i. p. 255 ; Weber, *Indische Skizzen*, p. 9 ; Renan, *Langues Sémitiques*, pt. i. p. 35 ; *Orig. du Lang.* p. 178 ; Lassen, *Ind. Alt.* vol. i, p. 855 ; Müller, *Marken*, p. 185 ; *Philolog. Museum*, vol. i. p. 611 ; Max Müller, in Kuhn's *Zeitschrift*, vol. v. pp. 141, 142.

[2] Farrar, *Origin of Language*, p. 76. Compare the onomatopoeian name of the ZAM-ZUMMIN, the Aborigines of Palestine. Renan, *Lang. Sém.* p. 35 ; *Orig. du Lang.* p. 117.

[3] The Sanskrit *m* often becomes *w* in Gothic ; thus, from *mlai*, to fade, we have *vlacian*, to flag, *welken*, to wither, and the name of the soft mollusk called a *whelk* [?]. According to this phonetic law, from the Sanskrit *mlêch* we obtain the German *wlack*, *walach*, and *Walch*. See an Essay on *Walhen und Deutsche*, by Professor Leo, in Kuhn's *Zeitschrift*, vol. ii. pp. 252–255 ; Pictet, *Orig. Indo-Euro.* pt. i. p. 57 ; Renan, *Lang. Sémit.* part i. p. 35 ; *Orig. du Lang.* pp. 178, 179 ; Lassen, *Ind. Alt.* vol. i. p. 855 ; Leo, *Vorlesungen*, vol. i. p. 43.

[4] The word *waller*, a pilgrim, no longer survives in English except as a surname ; but we retain the derivative [?] *wallet*, a pilgrim's equipage. It may be noted that *peri-grinare* and *pilgrim* are filially connected in the same way as *wallen* and *waller*. With *wallen*, to wander, are connected the words to *walk*, and to *valze* or *waltz* [?]. Diefenbach, *Vergl. Wörterb.* vol. i. pp. 189, 181.

[5] They are called Walisenses in the Chronicles. Schott, *Deut. Col.* p. 206.

Wolochi,[1] and the district which they occupied WALLACHIA ; and the Celts of Flanders, and of the Isle of WALCHEREN, were called WALLOONS [2] by their Teutonic neighbours. North-western France is called VALLAND in the Sagas,[3] and in the Saxon Chronicle WEALAND denotes the Celtic district of Armorica. The Anglo-Saxons called their Celtic neighbours the WELSH, and the country by the name of WALES.[4] Corn*wall* was formerly written Cornwales, the country inhabited by the Welsh of the Horn. The chroniclers uniformly speak of North-Wales and Corn-Wales. In the charters of the Scoto-Saxon kings the Celtic Picts of Strath Clyde are called Walenses.

Entangled with this root *wal*, we have the root *gal*. The Teutonic *w* and the Celtic and Romance *g* are convertible letters. Thus the French Gualtier and Guillaume are the same as the English Walter and William. So also guerre and war, garde and warde, guise and wise, guile and wile, gaif and waif, gaude and woad, gaufre and wafer, garenne and warren, gault and weald, guarantee and warranty, are severally the French and English forms of the same words.[5] By a similar change the root *wal* is transformed to *gal*. The Prince of Wales is called in French ' le Prince de Galles '. Wales is the ' pays de Galles ', and Cornwall is Cornuailles, a name which was also given to the opposite peninsula of Brittany. CALAIS was anciently written indifferently Galeys or Waleys ; and the name, as will be shown elsewhere, most appropriately indicates the existence of the remnant of a Celtic people surrounded by a cordon of Teutonic settlers.

This convertibility of the roots *gal* and *wal* is a source of much confusion and difficulty ; for it appears probable that *gal* may also be an independent Celtic root,[6] entirely uncon-

[1] Compare the Polish *Wloch*, an Italian, and the Slowenian *Vlah*, a Wallachian. From the same Sanskrit root we have the name of the BELOOCHS or *Welsh* of India. Pott, *Indo-Germ. Spr.* p. 48 ; Adelung, *Mithridates*, vol. ii. p. 641 ; Leo, in Kuhn's *Zeitschrift*, vol. ii. p. 255.
[2] The name of the Belgae, a Cymric tribe, seems to have been given them by the Gaels, whom they displaced. Cf. the Erse, *Fir-bolg*, ' intruding men '.
[3] Laing, *Heimskringla*, vol. i. p. 293.
[4] Strictly speaking, Wales is a corruption of *Wealhas*, the plural of *wealh*, a Welshman or foreigner.
[5] Cf. *Philolog. Proceed.* vol. i. p. 108 ; Knapp, *English Roots*, p. 8 ; Verstegan, *Restitution*, pp. 166, 363 ; Max Müller, *Lectures*, 2nd series, p. 265.
[6] No satisfactory explanation from Celtic sources has, I believe, been offered. Possibly it may mean the ' west '. See Mone, *Celtische Forschungen*, p. 326. Pott derives it from *gwâl*, the ' cultivated country '. *Etym. Forsch.* vol. ii. p. 531. Zeuss thinks it means the ' warriors '. *Die Deutschen*, p. 65. Dr. Meyer prefers the cognate significa-tion of ' clansmen'. *Report, Brit. Assoc.* for 1847, p. 301 ; Bunsen, *Phil. of Univ. Hist.* vol. i. p. 145. CELT is of course only the Greek form of *gael* or *gallus*.

nected with the Teutonic *wal*; for while the Welsh of Wales or Italy never called themselves by this name, it appears to have been used as a national appellation by the GAELS of *Cale*donia [1] and the GAULS of *Galli*a. *Gal*way, Done*gal*, *Gallo*-way, and Ar*gyle* are all Gaelic districts; and GOELLO is one of the most thoroughly Celtic portions of Brittany. The inhabitants of *Gal*licia and Portu*gal* possess more Celtic blood than those who inhabit any other portion of the Peninsula. The Austrian province of *Gal*itz or *Gal*icia is now Sclavonic, and the name, as well as that of Wallachia, is probably to be referred to the German root *wal*, foreign; though it is far from impossible that one or both of these names may indicate settlements of the fragments of the Gaelic horde which in the third century before Christ pillaged Rome and Delphi, and finally, crossing into Asia, settled in and gave a name to that district of *Gala*tia, whose inhabitants, even in the time of St. Paul, retained so many characteristic features of their Celtic origin.[2]

So interlaced are these primeval roots that it is almost hopeless to attempt to disentangle them.[3]

Another root which is very frequently found in the names of nations is *ar*. This ancient word, which enters very extensively into the vocabularies of all the Indo-Germanic races,

---

[1] This word possibly contains the root *gael*. If so, the Caledonians would be the Gaels of the duns or hills. The usual etymology is from *coildooine*, the ' men of the woods '. See Diefenbach, *Celtica*, ii. part i. p. 14; *Cambro-Briton*, vol. i. pp. 48, 373; vol. iii. pp. 397, 399; Thierry, *Hist. Gaul.* vol. i. pp. xxix. xxxv; Chalmers, *Caledonia*, vol. i. p. 200.

[2] [See Dr. J. B. Lightfoot, *Ep. to the Galatians*, Dissert. I.] GALATA, near Constantinople, is regarded by Diefenbach as a vestige of the passage of the Galatian horde. *Celtica*, ii. part i. p. 7. It seems more probable that this name is Semitic, and should be classed with KELAT in Beloochistan, ALCALA in Spain, and CALATA in Sicily. See Chapter VI.

[3] On the roots *gal* and *wal*, see Zeuss, *Die Deutschen und die Nachbarstämme*, pp. 66, 576; Diefenbach, *Celtica*, ii. part ii. pp. 127, 128; Diefenbach, *Vergleich. Wörterb.* vol. i. pp. 180, 181; Guest, on *Gentile Names*, in *Philolog. Proc.* vol. i. p. 105; Müller *Die Marken des Vaterl.* vol. i. pp. 194–203; Prichard, *Eastern Origin of the Celtic Nations*, pp. 104–110; Latham, *English Language*, vol. i. p. cv; Latham, *Germania*, pp. 83, 98; *Nat. of Europe*, vol. ii. pp. 192, 387; Conybeare and Howson, *Life of St. Paul*, vol. i. p. 284; Arnold, *Hist. of Rome*, vol. i. p. 520; Yonge, *Christian Names*, vol. ii. p. 9; Charnock, *Local Etymol.* p. 291; Basil Jones, in *Archaeologia Cambrensis*, 3rd series, vol. iv. pp. 127–132; Lord Lindsay, *Progression by Antagonism*, p. 62; Rawlinson, *Herodotus*, vol. iii. p. 190; Verstegan, *Restitution*, pp. 46, 166, 167; Pott, *Etym. Forsch.* vol. ii. p. 529; *Indo-Germ. Spr.* p. 91; *Saturday Review*, April 11, 1863; Arndt, *Eur. Spr.* p. 253; Schafarik, *Slaw. Alt.* vol. i. p. 377; Bp. Thirlwall, in *Philolog. Trans.* for 1860–1, pp. 199–203; and Holzapfel, in Höfer's *Zeitschrift*, vol. iv. p. 240, who quotes a work which I have not been able to procure—Massmann, *Deutsch und Welsch*. München, 1843. Niebuhr, in his *Lectures on Ethnology and Geography*, vol. ii. p. 308, holds the untenable opinion that the Celtic national appellation is the root of the German *wal*, and that the Germans took the name of some contiguous Gaelic tribe as a general term for foreigner. See p. 45, *supra*.

seems primarily to have referred to the occupation of agriculture. The verb used to express the operation of ploughing is in Greek ἀρόω, in Latin *aro*, in Gothic *ar*jan, in Polish *orac*, in old High German *aran*, in Irish *araim*, and in Old English *ear*. Thus we read in our version of the Bible, ' The oxen . . . that *ear* the ground shall eat clean provender '.[1] A plough is ἄροτρον in Greek, *aratrum* in Latin, *ardr* in Norse, and *arad* in Welsh ; and the English *har*row [2] was originally a rude instrument of the same kind. The Greek ἄρουρα the Latin *arvum*, and the Polish *oracz* mean a field, or *arable* ground. *Aroma* was the *aromatic* smell of freshly ploughed land ; while ἄρτος [2] and *har*vest [2] reward the ploughman's labour. The Sanscrit *irâ*, the Greek ἔρα, the Gothic *air*tha, and their English representative, *earth*,[2] is that which is *eared* or ploughed.[3]

The Sanskrit word *arya* means an agriculturist, a possessor of land, or a householder generally ; hence it came to denote any one belonging to the dominant race [4]—the aristocracy of landowners—as distinguished from the subject tribes ; and at length it began to be used as an ethnic designation, corresponding to some extent with the word deutſch, as used by the Germans.[5]

The name of this conquering ARYAN race, which has gone forth to till the earth and to subdue it, is probably to be found

---

[1] Isaiah xxx. 24. So the two great operations of ploughing and reaping are called ' earing and harvest '. Gen. xlv. 6 ; Ex. xxxiv. 21.

[2] [These words (and probably *earth*) have no connexion with *ar*, to plough.]

[3] Scores of related words might be collected from the Romance, Celtic, Sclavonic, and Gothic languages. Tilled land being the chief kind of property, we have the Gothic *arbi*, an inheritance. Since ploughing was the chief *earnest* occupation practised at an early stage of civilization, the root comes to take the general signification of any kind of work. Hence the Greek ἔργον the Latin *ars*, the German *arbeit*, the English *errand* ; all of which deserve *earnings* and *earnest* money. It would not be difficult to trace the connexion of the Greek ἐρ-ετμὸς, τρι-ήρ-ης and ὑπ-ηρ-έης, the Latin *remus*, the English *oar*, the Sanskrit *aritra*, a ship, as well as of *urbs* and *orbis*. [All the words in this and the following note affiliated to the root *ar*, to plough, have another origin.] On the meaning and ramifications of the root *ar*, see Diefenbach, *Vergleich. Wörterb.* vol. i. pp. 65, 70 ; Diefenbach, *Celtica*, i. pp. 11–13 ; Grimm, *Gesch. der Deut. Spr.* vol. i. pp. 54, 55, 68 ; Kuhn, *Zur älteste Gesch*, pp. 12, 13 ; Pictet, *Origines Indo-Europ*. part ii. pp. 28–31, 67, 75, 78, 88, 123, 183–185 ; Curtius, *Gründzège der Griech. Etym.* vol. i. pp. 306–308 ; Prichard, *Rep. Brit. Assoc.* for 1847, p. 242 ; Lassen, *Ind. Alt.* vol. i. pp. 5–8 ; Pott, *Ueber alt-persische Eigennamen* in the *Zeitschrift der Morgenl. Gesellschaft*, vol. xiii. p. 374 ; *Church of England Quarterly*, no. 73, p. 139 ; Mommsen, *Inhabitants of Italy*, pp. 16, 17 ; Renan, *Lang. Sémit*. p. 14 ; Pott, *Indo-Germ. Sprach.* p. 46 ; Max Müller, *Lectures on Science of Language*, pp. 237–257 ; Arndt, *Eur. Spr.* p. 158 ; *Phil. Trans.* for 1857, p. 55 ; *Edinburgh Review*, vol. xciv. pp. 315, 316 ; *Zeitschrift d. Morgenl. Gesellschaft*, vol. iii. p. 284.

[4] The profession of *arms* being engrossed by the ruling race has caused the root, if indeed it be the same, to enter into a number of military terms—army, armour, arms, harness, hero, Ἄρης. Curtius and Pictet, however, think these words are of independent origin.

[5] Leo, in Kuhn's *Zeitschrift*, vol. ii. p. 257.

in the names of IRAN,[1] HERAT, ARAL, ARMENIA, and, perhaps, of IB-ER-IA, IRELAND, and ERIN.   In languages which belong to the Teutonic branch of the Aryan stock, we find the root in the form *ware*,[2] inhabitants.   Burghers are those who inhabit towns, and a skipper[3] is one who lives in a ship, as may be seen by tracing the words back to the Anglo-Saxon *burh-vare*, citizens, and the old Norse *skipveri*, a sailor.[4]   The word *ware* enters into the names of a great number of German tribes. It is Latinized into the forms *uari*, *oari*, and *bari* ; and the *w* is sometimes changed into a *g*, in accordance with a phonetic law which has been already illustrated.   Among the peoples of Central Europe are found the Ing-*uari*-i, the Rip-*uari*-i, the Chas-*uari*-i, the Chatt-*uari*-i, the Att-*uari*-i, the Angri-*vari*-i, and the Ansi-*bari*-i.   The name of the Boio-*ari*-i is preserved in the modern name of BA-VARI-A, the land of the Boii.   The BULG-ARI-ANS were the men from the Bolg, or Volga, on the banks of which river there is another, or Great Bulgaria.[5] King Alfred speaks of the Moravians under the name Marv*aro*, the dwellers on the river Marus or Morava.[6]   Hun-*gar*-a, or HUNGARY, is the land formerly peopled by the Huns ; and the name survives, though the Huns have been long dispossessed by Magyars and Sclavonians.   WO-*r*-CESTER is a corruption of Hwic-*wara*-ceaster, the castle of the inhabitants of the country of the Huiccii.   The men of Kent were the Cant-*ware* ; and though this term is obsolete, it survives in the name of their chief town, Cant-*wara*-byrig, or CANT-*er*-BURY, ' the burgh of the men of the headland ', while the ordinary signature of the primate, Cant-*uar*,[7] exhibits the Saxon root *ware* in a

---

[1] In the cuneiform inscriptions the Medes and Persians claim proudly to be Aryans, and Darius styles himself an Arya of the Aryans. The Ossetes in the Caucasus call themselves IRON.   The name German may perhaps be referred to this root. [See p. 43, note 4.]   Compare the names Ar-iovistus, Ar-minius, Her-mann.

[2] On the root *ware*, see Zeuss, *Die Deutschen*, p. 367 ; *Herkunft der Baiern*, pp. 5–11 ; Förstemann, *Ortsnamen*, pp. 184, 197 ; Grimm, *Gesch. der Deut. Spr.* p. 781 ; Mone, *Celt. Forsch.* p. 245 ; Müller, *Marken des Vaterlandes*, vol. i. p. 108 ; *Philological Proceedings*, vol. i. p. 10 ; Schafarik, *Slaw. Alt.* vol. i. p. 367. Compare the Sanskrit *vira*, the Latin *vir*, the Celtic *gwr* and *fir*, the Gothic *vairs*, and the Spanish *varon*, all which denote a man. From the low Latin, *baro*, a male, comes *baron*, and perhaps the Scotch *bairn*. Pictet, *Or. Indo-Euro.* part ii. p. 196 ; Diez. *Gram. Rom. Spr.* vol. i. p. 26 ; Glück, *Kelt. Namen*, p. 100. .

[3] [' Skipper ' comes direct from the Dutch *schipper*, a shipper or shipman.]

[4] Grimm, *Gesch. der Deut. Spr.* p. 781 ; Müller, *Marken*, vol. i. p. 192. The Prussian land*wehr* is the levy *en masse* of the whole population, and not the *landguard*, as is commonly supposed.

[5] Adelung, *Mithridates*, vol. ii. p. 641 ; Prichard, *Researches*, vol. iv. p. 32.

[6] Zeuss, *Die Deutschen*, p. 639.

[7] That is, Episcopus Cantuarensis. See Latham, *Eng. Lan.* vol. i. p. 143 ; Müller, *Marken*, vol. i. p. 192 ; Wright, *Wanderings*, p. 72 ; Guest, in *Philolog. Proceed*, vol. i. p. 10.

prominent form. CAR-ISBROOK, in the Isle of Wight, is a name closely analogous to Canterbury. Asser writes the word Gwiti-*gara*-burg, ' the burgh of the men of Wight '. [Also found in the form *Wiht-gares-burh*.] It will easily be seen how the omission of the first part of the name, and the corruption of the last part, have reduced it to its present form.

Another of these widely diffused roots is *saetan*, *set*tlers, or inhabitants, and *saete* or *setna*, the *seat* or place inhabited.[1]

Als*at*ia, ALSACE, or ELSASS, is the ' other seat ', the abode of the German *set*tlers west of the Rhine, a district where, as we have seen, the names of places are still purely German. HOL-STEIN is a corruption of the dative case of Holt-sati, the ' forest abode '.[2] From the same root we get Somer*set* and Dor*set*. It would appear that the *t* in Wil-*t*-shire is also due to this root, since the men of Wiltshire are called in the Saxon chronicle Wil-saetan, just as the men of Somerset and Dorset are called Sumor-saetan and Dornsaetan.[3] We have also Pecsaetan, men of the Peak (Derbyshire) ; Scrobsaetan, the men of Shropshire or Scrubland ; Cilternstaean, the men of the Chilterns ; and Wocensaetan, the people of the Wrekin or hill-country of Ex-moor.[4]

Conquering tribes, numerically insignificant, when compared with the other elements of the population, have not unfre-quently bestowed their names upon extensive regions. ENG-LAND, for instance, takes its name from the Angles, who only colonized a small portion of the country. In the case of SCOTLAND, we may believe that the Angles, the Norwegians, and the Cymric Celts severally constituted a larger element in the population than the Scots, yet this conquering Irish sept, which appears to have actually colonized only a portion of Argyle, has succeeded in bestowing its name upon the whole country. FRANCE takes its name from the Franks, a small German tribe [5] which effected a very imperfect colonization

---

[1] Cf. the verbs to *sit*, *sitzen*, *sedere*. See Leo, *Rectitudines*, p. 48. On *set*, see Guest on *Gentile Names*, in *Phil. Proc.* vol. i. pp. 105, 107.

[2] Förstemann, in Kuhn's *Zeitschrift*, vol. i. p. 10 ; *Ortsnamen*, p. 105 ; Müller, *Marken des Vaterl.* vol. i. p. 121.

[3] Kemble, *Saxons in England*, vol. i. p. 78 ; *Saxon Chron.* A.D. 800 and 878.

[4] Kemble, *Saxons*, vol. i. p. 83.

[5] The mixed multitude of Greeks, Italians, Maltese, English, Germans, French, and other western Europeans who are found in the streets of Cairo and other eastern cities, all go by the name of Franks to this day : parturiunt mures, et nascitur mons. The cause of the supremacy of the Frank name in the Levant is probably due to the prominent position taken at the time of the crusades by Godfrey of Boulogne, and the Franks of Northern France. See Purchas, *His Pilgrimes*, vol. i. p. 305 ; Trench, *Study*

of a portion of central France : the whole of Picardy, Normandy, Brittany, Burgundy, Languedoc, Guienne, and Gascony being excluded from their influence. Even so late as the time of Philippe Auguste, the term FRANCE did not comprehend either Aquitaine or Languedoc.[1] Several of the old French provinces—BURGUNDY, NORMANDY, FRANCHE COMTÉ, and the ISLE OF FRANCE—preserve the names of the German tribes which conquered them. The eastern division of the Frank nation has left its name in the Bavarian province of FRANKEN, or Franconia, as we call it. We find the name of the Suevi preserved in SUABIA ; of the Rugii in the Isle of RUGEN ; [2] of the Chatti in HESSE ; of the Saxons in SAXONY ; of the Lombards in LOMBARDY ; of the Huns in HUNGARY ; of the Atrebates in ARTOIS ; of the Pictones in POITOU ; of the Cymry in CUMBERLAND, CAMBRIA, and the CUMBRAY Islands at the mouth of the Clyde ; [3] of the Goths or Jutes in CATALONIA, JUTLAND, the Isle of GOTHLAND, and the Isle of WIGHT ; [4] and that of the Vandals possibly in ANDAL-USIA.[5]

The Celtic Boii, who left their ancient ' home ' in BOHEMIA [6] (Boi-hem-ia, or Boi-heim) to Sclavonic occupants, have also given their name to *Bai*-ern, or BAVARIA. [7] So the Sclavonic and Hellenic districts under Moslem rule are called TURKEY, from the Turkomans or Turks, who constitute only a small

of Words, p.72, [ed. Routledge, p.107]. Grimm, *Gesch. der Deut. Spr.* p. 789, attributes this diffusion of the Frank name to the repute of the Carlovingian empire. Latham ascribes it to the exploits of Robert Guiscard and his Normans ! *Nat. of Europe*, vol. ii. p. 23.

1 Palgrave, *Normandy and England*, vol. ii. p. 147. The ' languages ' or ' nations ' into which the Hospitallers were divided (A.D. 1322) were :—Provence, Auvergne, France, Italy, Aragon, England, Germany, and Castile.

2 Knobel, *Völkertafel*, p. 38.

3 Knobel, *Völkertafel*, p. 29 ; Kennedy, in *Philolog. Trans.* for 1855, p. 164. To this list we may perhaps add the names of CAMBRAI, COIMBRA, CAMBRILLA, and QUIMPER. Archdeacon Williams refers MONTGOMERI in France, and the mountain refuge of Monte Comero (anciently Cumerium Promontorium) in Italy, to the same people. *Edinburgh Trans.* vol. xiii. p. 526.

4 In the laws of Edward the Confessor the men of the Isle of Wight are called Guti, i.e. Jutes or Goths. We have also the intermediate forms Geat, Gwit, Wiht, and Wight. G and W are convertible. See p. 50. On the identity of the names Geat and Goth, see Grimm, *Gesch. der Deut. Spr.* p. 439.

5 See p. 54, *infra*, for another etymology.

6 The Boii broke into Italy, and perhaps gave their name to Bononia, now BOLOGNA, and to BOVANIUM, another town in Italy. It has been thought that BORDEAUX and BOURBON also bear the name of the Boii. See Diefenbach, *Celtica*, ii. part i. pp. 261, 316 ; Grimm, *Gesch. der Deut. Spr.* vol. i. pp. 166, 502 ; Prichard, *Researches*, vol. iii. p. 89 ; Prichard, *Eastern Origin of Celtic Nations*, pp. 133–136 ; Tschudi, *Hauptschlüssel*, p. 179 ; Knobel, *Völkertafel*, pp. 47, 48 ; Mommsen, *Hist. of Rome*, vol. i. p. 338 ; Latham, *Germania*, p. 92 ; Latham, *Nationalities of Europe*, vol. ii. p. 326 ; Zeuss, *Die Deutschen*, p. 641 ; Liddell, *Hist. Rome*, vol. i. p. 165 ; Schafarik, *Slaw. Alt.* vol. i. p. 382.

7 See p. 49, *supra*.

governing class ; [1] and it is singular that the Philistines, the 'strangers' from Crete, who merely occupied a narrow strip of the sea-coast, should, through their contact with the western world, have given their name to the whole of the land of PALESTINE, in which they never succeeded in gaining any lasting supremacy. [2]

The names of ancient tribes are also very frequently preserved in the names of modern cities. The process by which this has taken place is exemplified in the case of the Taurini, whose chief city, called by the Romans Augusta Taurinorum, is now Torino, or TURIN ; while the capital of the Parisii, Lutetia Parisiorum, is now PARIS ; and that of the Treviri, Augusta Trevirorum, has become Trier or TREVES. [3] We have the name of the Damnonii in DEVON, and a portion of the name of the *Duro*triges is preserved in *Dor*chester, of the Huiccii in *W*orcester, of the Iceni in *Iken* and *Ick*borough, of the Selgovae in the *Sol*way, of the Bibroci in *Bra*y hundred, near Windsor, of the Regni in *Regne*wood or *Ring*wood in Hants, and of the Cassii of Caesar in the hundred of *Cashio*, [4] Hertfordshire, and in *Cashio*bury Park, which probably occupies the site of the chief town of the tribe. Many of these names have a certain ethnological value, inasmuch as they enable us to localize ancient tribes ; and therefore a list of such probable identifications is subjoined in the appendix. [5]

The world-famous name of imperial Rome has been retained by various insignificant fragments of the Roman empire. The Wallachians, the descendants of the Roman colonists on the Danube, proudly call themselves ROMANI, and their country ROMANIA. The language of modern Greece is called the ROMAIC ; that of Southern France is the ROMANCE ; and that of the Rhaetian Alps the ROMANSCH. The ROMAGNA of Italy preserves

---

[1] The word Turk had a still wider signification in the sixteenth and seventeenth centuries, when it was used to denote all Mahomedans, as the word Saracen was in the twelfth century. Trench, *Glossary*, p. 222. [Ed. Routledge, p. 214.] Compare the collect for Good Friday—'All Jews, Turks, infidels, and heretics'.

[2] Renan, *Langues Sémitiques*, p. 57 ; Stanley, *Sinai and Palestine*, pp. 256, 257 ; *Jewish Church*, p. 362.

[3] Of course, in cases of this kind it is impossible to say that the name of the city is not more ancient than the name of the tribe. The names Parisi or Taurini, for instance, may not be true ethnic names, but may have been derived from the name of their capital, the original name of which can only be dimly discerned through its Latin garb. See Ansted and Latham, *Channel Islands*, p. 311.

[4] [Cashio, formerly spelt *Caysho, Kaysho*, is the A. Sax. *Cæges-ho* (Charter dated, 793) i.e. Cæga's (or Kay's) hoe or hill-spur. It is identical with the Bedfordshire name Keysoe. See Prof. Skeat, *Place Names of Bedfordshire*, p. 30.]

[5] Appendix A. [p. 439].

the memory of the bastard empire which had its seat at Ravenna ; and the name of the Asiatic pashalics of ROUM and ERZEROUM are witnesses to the fact that in the mountain fastnesses of Armenia the croed and the traditions of the Eastern Empire of Rome continued to exist long after the surrounding provinces had fallen under the dominion of the Turks ; while for the European province of ROUMELIA was reserved the privilege of being the last morsel to be swallowed by the Moslem Cyclops.

Conversely the name of a city has often become attached to the surrounding region. The ROMAN EMPIRE must ever remain the chief instance of such an extension of meaning. This has also been the case with the kingdom of CABOOL, with the State of NEW YORK, with BERNE, ZÜRICH, and others of the Swiss cantons, with several German States, such as HANOVER, BADEN, BRUNSWICK, and MECKLENBURG, and with a large number of the English counties, as YORKSHIRE, LANCASHIRE, and SALOP.

A few countries have taken their names from some ruler of renown. LODOMIRIA, which is the English form of the Sclavonic Vlodomierz, is so called from St. Vladimar, the first Christian Tzar.[1] The two Lothairs, the son and the grandson of Louis le Débonnaire, received, as their share of the Carlovingian inheritance, a kingdom which comprised Switzerland, Alsace, Franche Comté, Luxembourg, Hainault, Juliers, Liége, Cologne, Trèves, the Netherlands, Oldenburg, and Friezland. This territory went by the name of the Regnum Lotharii, Lotharingia, or Lothier-regne ; but by the incapacity or misfortune of its rulers the outlying provinces were gradually lost, so that in the course of centuries the ample ' realm of Lothair ' has dwindled down into the contracted limits of the modern province of LORRAINE.[2]

The most recent instance of a state called from the name of its founder is BOLIVIA ; a name which remains as a perpetual reproach to the Bolivians, proclaiming the discords and jealousies which drove Bolivar, the liberator and dictator, to die in obscure exile on the banks of the Mississippi. *Stet nominis umbra.*

The name by which we know CHINA belongs, in all probability, to the same category. It was during the reign of the

[1] *Across the Carpathians*, p. 206.
[2] Palgrave, *Normandy and England*, vol. i. p. 363 ; Yonge, *Christian Names*, vol. ii. p. 391.

dynasty of Thsin, in the third century before Christ, that the
first knowledge of the Celestial Empire was conveyed to the
West.   That the form of the name should be China, rather
than Tsin or SINA,[1] seems to prove that our first acquaintance
with the Chinese empire must have been derived from the
nation in whose hands was the commerce with the far East—
the Malays—who pronounce Thsina as China.[2]

The names of America, Tasmania, Georgia, Carolina, and
others of this class have already been discussed.[3]

Another class of names of countries is derived from their
geographical position.   Such are ECUADOR, the republic under
the Equator, and PIEDMONT, the land at the foot of the great
mountain chain of Europe.   Names of this class very frequently enable us to discover the relative position of the nation
by which the name has been bestowed.   Thus SUTHERLAND,
which occupies almost the extreme northern extremity of our
island, must evidently have obtained its name from a people
inhabiting regions still further to the North—the Norwegian
settlers in Orkney.   [Compare Sodor, *infra* p. 120.]   We may
reasonably attribute to the Genoese and Venetians the name
of the LEVANT,[4] for to the Italians alone would the eastern
shores of the Mediterranean be the ' land of the sunrise '.   In
like manner the Greeks of Constantinople, who watched the sun
rise over the mountains of Asia Minor, called the land ANA-
TOLIA (the rising), a name which is preserved in that of the
Turkish province of NATOLIA.   The name of JAPAN or Jehpun
is evidently of Chinese, and not of native origin, for it means
the ' source of day '.[5]   The AMALEKITES,[6] as well perhaps as
the SARACENS,[7] are the ' Orientals ' ; BACTRIA comes from
a Persian word *bakhtar*, the east ;[8] the Portuguese province
of the ALGARBE is ' the west ' ; and some scholars are of opinion
that the name of ANDALUSIA is also from an Arabic source, and
that it signifies Hesperia, or the ' region of the evening '.[9]

---

[1] The ancient form SINA indicates transmission through the Arabs.   Strinnholm
Wikingzüge, p. 284.   [A. H. Keane thinks that Sinae, Arab and Pers. *Sin* stands for the
Chinese *Jin*, men, people (*Man, Past and Present*, p. 214).]
[2] Huc, *China*, vol. i. p. 347; Cooley, *History of Maritime and Inland Discovery*,
vol. i. p. 120; Fleming, *Travels*, p. 336.
[3] See Chapter II.   [4] Compare the use of the word Orient.
[5] Kenrick, *Phœnicia*, p. 85 ; Alcock, *Capital of the Tycoon*, vol. ii. p. 88.   [Otherwise
Nipon, from Chinese *nit* and *pon* ' sun origin '—Keane, *Man, Past and Present*,
p. 308.]   [6] Renan, *Lang. Sémit.* p. 109.
[7] Welsford, *English Language*, p. 27.   [8] *Ibid.*
[9] See Gibbon, note, chap. 51, vol. vi. p. 429.   It is more probable, however, that
Andalusia is Vandalusia, the country of the Vandals.   See p. 51, *supra*; Keferstein,
Kelt. Alt. vol. ii. p. 313 ; Gayangos, *Moham. Dynasties*, vol. i. pp. 23, 322.

The name of the DEKKAN is a Sanskrit word, which means the ' South '. The etymology of this word gives us a curious glimpse into the daily life of the earliest Aryan races. The Sanskrit *dakshina* (cf, the Latin *dextera*) means the right hand, and to those who daily worshipped the rising sun, the south would, of course, be the *dakkhina,* or *dekkan,* 'that which is to the right '.[1]

Hesychius tells us that EUROPE means χώρα τῆς δύσεως, the land of the setting sun, and the etymology is supported by Kenrick[2] and Rawlinson,[3] who think that we have in this case a Semitic root applied by the Phœnicians to the countries which lay to the west of them. Dean Trench, on the other hand, supports the common explanation that the term εὐρ-ώπη is descriptive of the ' broad face ' or profile, which the coast, near Mount Athos, would present to the Asiatic Greek.[4]

The origin of the name of ASIA is also in dispute. Pott[5] refers it to the Sanskrit *ushas,*[6] and thinks that it means the ' land of the dawn ', and is, therefore, to be classed with such names as Levant, Anatolia, and Japan. On the other hand, much may be said in favour of the view that the word Asia was originally only the designation of the marshy plain of the Cayster[7]—the Asian plain on which EPHESUS (ἔφ-εσ-ος) was built ; and the root *as* or *es* may, perhaps, be referred to that widely-diffused word for water which enters into the names of so many rivers and marshes throughout the Indo-European region.[8] As the dominion and the importance of the city of Ephesus increased, the name of this Asian district would naturally be extended to the surrounding region, and the Romans afterwards transferred to the whole country east of

---

1 Pictet, *Orig. Indo-Eur.* vol. ii. p. 495 ; Prichard, *Researches*, vol. iv. p. 93 ; Brown, *Carnatic Chronology*, p. 83. Lassen, however, *Ind. Alt.* vol. i. p. 46, derives the name from the Sanskrit *deggân*, peasants. ES SHAM, the local name of Syria, means ' the left '.

2 *Phœnicia*, p. 85. [Ass. *ereb*, ' the dark ' region, the west ; whence also Erebus

3 *Herodotus*, vol. iii. p. 40. [Appendix C. p. 368.]

4 *English, Past and Present*, p. 226. Grimm makes the application of the root refer rather to the broad face of the earth, than to the broad outline of the coast. *Deut. Myth.* p. 631. It is curious that the same etymological connexion which appears to exist between the εὐρεῖα, Europe, and the mythological Europa, is found between the Norse words *rinta*, the earth, *Rindr*, the spouse of Odin, and *rind*, cattle. *Deut. Myth.* p. 230 Cf. Karl Müller, *Mythologie*, p. 133.

5 *Etymol. Forsch.* vol. ii. p. 190.

6 Cf. the Greek ἕως.

7 Ἀσίω ἐν λειμῶνι, Καϋστρίου ἀμφὶ ῥέεθρα Homer, *Iliad*, b. ii. l. 461. See For-biger, *Alt. Geogr.* vol. ii. p. 38. [Appendix C, p. 368].

8 See Chapter IX.

the Ægean the name which they found attaching to that Asiatic province with which they first became acquainted.[1]

The earliest name for the African continent was LIBYA. The root is, perhaps, the Greek word λίβα moisture—an etymology which, inappropriate as it may seem, would indicate the fact that Africa was first known to the Greeks as the region from which blew the Libyan or 'rain-bringing' south-west wind.[2] [Λίψ.]

The meaning of the word AFRICA, the Roman name of Libya, is very doubtful. The name seems to have originated in the neighbourhood of Carthage, and is probably Punic, at all events Semitic. It has been conjectured, with some show of probability, that it is derived from the ethnic designation of some tribe in the neighbourhood of Carthage, and whose name signified 'The Wanderers',[3] in the same way that the NUMIDIANS were the νομάδες—Nomad, or wandering shepherd tribes, ancestors of the Berbers and Kabyles—and as the Suevi or Swabians,[4] and probably also the Vandals and the Wends,[5] were the roving border tribes of ancient Germany.[6]

A few names of races are descriptive of personal appearance, or physical characteristics; and they therefore possess a peculiar value in the eyes of ethnographers.

---

[1] The name of Asia Minor seems to have been invented by Orosius in the fifth century, when a wider geographical knowledge required the name of Asia for all the regions to the east of the Mediterranean. See Trench, *Study of Words*, p. 96.

[2] Rawlinson, *Herodotus*, vol. iii. p. 40.

[3] See Movers, *Die Phönizier*, pt. ii. vol. ii. p. 204 ; Rawlinson, *Herodotus*, vol. ii. p. 40 ; and Mommsen, *Hist. Rome*. Ahrens, in Kuhn's *Zeitschrift*, vol. iii. p. 171, thinks Africa is the 'south land'. Cf. Förstemann, *Ib.* vol. i. p. 15. [Appendix D.]

[4] From *schweben*, to move. See Zeuss, *Die Deutschen*, p. 57 ; Müller, *Marken*, vol. i. pp. 164–168. Grimm thinks the root is a Sclavonic word meaning free. *Gesch. der Deut. Spr.* p. 322. Leo, *Vorlesungen*, vol. i. p. 96, prefers a Sanskrit root meaning 'offerers', and he believes that the practice of human sacrifice lingered long in the tribe. On human sacrifice among the Germans, see Milman, *Hist. Latin Christianity*, vol. i. p. 244 ; Mone, *Gesch. Heidenthums*, vol. ii. pp. 20, 136 ; Turner, *Anglo-Saxons*, vol. i. p. 222.

[5] The root of these two names appears in the German word *wandeln*, and its English equivalents, to *wander* or *wend*. To this root may also be attributed the name of FLANDERS ; as well, perhaps, as those of VINDELICIA, VINDOBONUM, VENETIA, and others. See Zeuss, *Die Deutschen und die Nachbarstämme*, p. 57 ; Grimm, *Gesch. der Deut. Spr.* pp. 322, 475, 476 ; Latham, *Germania*, Epileg. p. xc. ; Arndt, *Eur. Spr.* p. 89.

[6] The name of the SCOTS has been deduced from an Erse word, *scuite*, meaning 'wanderers', which is preserved in [quite distinct from] the English word *scout*. Meyer, *Brit. Assoc. Reports* for 1847, p. 305 ; Bunsen, *Phil. of Univ. Hist.* vol. i. p. 151 ; Wilson, *Prehist. Annals of Scotland*, p. 477 ; Betham, *Gael*, pp. xi. xii. [Prof. Rhys connects Scotti with the Welsh *ysgythru*, to cut, as if 'the scarred' or tattooed, *Celtic Britain* 237.] The name of the Scythians may possibly be allied to that of the Scots. The PARTHIANS are the 'wanderers' or strangers. Pott, *Indo-Germ Spr.* p. 52 ; Bergmann, *Les Gètes*, pp. 24, 28. On Ethnic names of this class, see Bergmann, *Peuples Primitifs de la Race de Jafète*, pp. 42, 45, 52, 53, quoted by Renan, *Lang. Sémit.* p. 39.

The EDOMITES were the 'red' men,[1] the MOORS [2] and the PHŒNICIANS [3] probably the 'dark' men, and of still darker hue are the NEGROES of NEGROLAND, and the ETHIOPIANS, or 'burnt-faced men',[4] quos India torret—and we may compare the name of the Du-gall and Fin-gall, the 'black' and 'white' strangers from Scandinavia, who plundered the coasts of Scotland, with that of the 'Pale faces', who have encroached on the hunting-grounds of the 'Red men' of North America, and of the 'Blacks' of the Australian continent. The Gipsies term themselves the ZINCALI or 'black men'.[5]

Professor Leo, with a great deal of learning, traces the name of the GOTHS or GETÆ to the Sanskrit word *gata*, which denoted a special mode of dressing the hair in the form of a half moon, which was practised by the devotees of Siva.[6] The same writer thinks that the BOII are the 'trim' or 'neat' men.[7]

The name of the Britons has been conjectured, rightly or wrongly, to be from the Celtic *brith*, paint; [8] and till rather recent times Claudian was supposed to be correct in his etymology of the name of the painted Picts—nec falso nomine Picti. It is, however, far more probable that the PICTS, as well as the PICTONES of Gaul, are the 'fighters', the name being traceable to the Gaelic *peicta*, or the Welsh *peith*, a

---

[1] Knobel, *Völkertafel*, pp. 12, 135 ; Renan, *Lang. Sémit.* p. 39.

[2] Movers, *Phönizier*, part ii. vol. ii. p. 372.

[3] From φοῖνιξ, reddish-brown. See Knobel, *Völkertafel*, pp. 12, 317 ; Kenrick, *Phœnicia*, p. 68 ; Forbiger, *Alt. Geogr.* vol. ii. p. 659 ; Mommsen, *Hist. Rome*, vol. ii. p. i. Movers inclines to the opinion that Phœnicia is the 'land of palms'. *Die Phönizier*, p. ii. vol. i. pp. 2–9. Cf. Stanley, *Sinai and Pal.* p. 267.

[4] Αἰθίοψ, from αἴθω, to burn. Cf. Πέλοψ, the swarthy-faced. Curtius, *Grundzüge Gr. Etym.* vol. i. p. 215 ; Donaldson, *New Cratylus*, p. 138 ; *Varronianus*, p. 30 ; J. K. [enrick], in *Phil. Mus.* vol. i. p. 353. So the native name of Egypt, Chêmi (Ham), means black. Kenrick, *Egypt of Herodotus*, p. 22 ; Knobel, *Völkertafel*, pp. 13, 239, 240 ; Renan, *Lang. Sémit.* p. 42 ; Wilkinson, *Anc. Egypt*, vol. ii. p. 47 ; Bunsen, Report on Ethnology in *Brit. Assoc. Reports* for 1847, p. 254. The name EGYPT denotes the country which the Nile overflows. The root αιγ, which means 'water', [?] appears in the name of the Ægean Sea. Kenrick, *Ancient Egypt*, vol. ii. p. 116 ; Curtius, *Die Ionier vor der Ionischer Wanderung*, p. 18. Mizraim, the Biblical name, means 'the two' banks, or more probably 'the two' districts of Upper and Lower Egypt. Knobel, *Völkertafel*, p. 273 ; Wilkinson, *Anc. Egypt*, 2d series, vol. i. p. 261 ; Forbiger, *Alt. Geogr.* vol. ii. p. 767. So INDIA and SINDE are each the 'land of the river'. Pictet, *Or. Indo-Euro*, vol. i. pp. 119, 144.

[5] Pott, *Zigeuner*, vol. i. p. 27.

[6] Leo, *Vorlesungen*, vol. i. pp. 83–85 and 258. Cf. Buyers, *Northern India*, p. 449 ; Bergmann, *Les Gètes*, pp. 43, 47. So the Hastings or Astingi, the noblest race of the Goths, are the 'men with well-ordered hair'. Leo, *Vorlesungen*, vol. i. p. 86.

[7] From the Gaelic word *boigh*, pronounced *boi*. Leo, *Vorlesungen*, vol. i. p. 247. Thierry makes them 'the terrible'. *Hist. d. Gaulois*, vol i. p. liv. Cf. Keferstein, *Kelt. Atl.* vol. ii. p. 293.

[8] No nation would have called themselves by such a name. The peculiarity might have struck a foreigner, but not a native. See p. 41, note. [Prof. Rhys connects Brython with the old Welsh *brith*, cloth, as if the clothed or cloth-clad people.—*Celtic Britain*, 207–209.]

'fighting man '.[1] It has been thought that the SCYTHIANS [2]
are either the ' shooters ', or the ' shield men ' ; and that the
men of the BALEARIC Isles are the ' slingers '.[3] The TURKS
are the 'men with helmets ',[4] and the TATARS probably
derive their name from a Turanian root, meaning primarily
to stretch, and hence ' to draw the bow ', and ' to pitch
tents [5] ' The name of the COSSACKS is also Turanian, and
means ' mounted warriors '.[6]

The hatred and trembling contempt felt by the Hindoos
for those fierce, lowborn freebooters who carved so many
kingdoms out of the falling Mogul empire, is expressed by the
name MAHRATTA, which signifies ' pariahs ' or ' outcasts '.
There are two similar ethnic names in India.   The CANNADI
are ' rubbish ', and the TULAVA are ' vile '.[7]

With regard to the SAXONS, the old etymology of Verstegan,[8] broached two hundred years ago, has recently been
revived and supported by competent scholars.   It would seem
that the name did not refer to any particular tribe, but was the
designation of a military confederation composed of adventurers from various low-German peoples, who were all distinguished by their use of the *seax*, a short knife-like sword.[9]
Dr. Latham, indeed, is of opinion[10] that the names Angle and
Saxon related to the same people—the names, perhaps, not

---

[1] Compare the Latin word *pugna.* Pictet, *Orig. Indo-Eur.* vol. ii. p. 208 ; Meyer,
in *Brit. Assoc. Reports* for 1847, p. 305 ; Wilson, *Prehistoric Annals of Scotland,*
p.470. See, however, Pott, *Etym. Forsch.* vol. ii. p. 531 ; Gladstone, *Homer,* p. 347. [But
Picti is very probably a translation of their name in Irish, viz. *Cruithne* (Adamnan),
which means ' painted ', coloured, from *cruith,* colour. (Joyce, *Irish Names of Places,*
1st. Ser. p. 95.). See also Lord Strangford, *Letters and Papers,* 162 ; Rhys, *Celtic Britain,*
235 ; and Trench, *Study of Words* (ed. Routledge), 124.]
[2] More probably, however, the name Σκύθης is a corruption of TSCHUD, barbarian
(see p. 44) ; a name which the Greek colonists on the Euxine heard applied by their
Sclavonic neighbours to the barbarous tribes further to the north. See Schafarik, *Slaw.
Alterth.* vol. i. pp. 285, 286 ; Arndt, *Eur. Spr.* pp. 138, 323.
[3] Movers, *Die Phönizier,* pt. ii. vol. ii. p. 584 ; Bergmann, *Les Gètes,* pp. 31, 32 ;
Diefenbach, *Orig. Eur.* p. 239 ; Boudard, *Sur l'Origine des Premiers Habitants des Iles
Baléares,* in the *Revue Archéologique,* xii. pp. 248–250.
[4] Gabelentz, in the *Zeitschrift d. Morgenl.* vol. ii. p. 72.
[5] See an admirable article on *Comparative Philology* in the *Edinburgh Review,* vol.
xciv. p. 308. Arndt, *Eur. Spr.* pp. 317, 326 327, derives the name of the Tatars from
the Chinese *Ta-ta,* a barbarian. This would probably be onomatopœian, like *mléch,*
and *varvara.* See pp. 44, 45, *supra.*
[6] Latham, *Nationalities of Europe,* vol. i. p. 376.
[7] Brown, *Carnatic Chronology,* p. 84.
[8] *Restitution of Decayed Intelligence,* p. 24.
[9] Leo, *Vorlesungen,* vol. i. pp. 236 and 288. The *seax* was originally a stone knife,
or celt, the name being derived from *saihs,* a stone. Cf. the Latin *saxum.*
[10] Latham, *Eth. Brit. Is.* pp. 191–195 ; *Eng. Lang.* vol. i. pp. 162–165. Cf.Arndt,
Eur. Spr. p. 250. Grimm, *Gesch. der Deut. Spr.* pp. 228, 609, Donaldson, *English Ethnography,* p. 44, and Turner, *Anglo-Saxons,* vol. i. p. 100, connect the Saxons with the
Asiatic Sacæ. Pictet rejects this. *Orig. Indo-Europ,* vol. i. p. 87 ; Cf. Bergmann
Les Gètes, p. 22.

being co-extensive ; all Angles were probably Saxons, though all Saxons were not Angles. Or Angle may have been the native name, and Saxon that bestowed by Franks or Celts.

It has been supposed that the FRANKS were distinguished by the use of the *france, franca,* or *framea,* a kind of javelin ; and the Langobards or LOMBARDS, by a long *parti*san or hal*berd*.[1] These etymologies are plausible, but by no means indisputable. They may, however, be supported by the analogous fact in the history of names that the Red men of North America called the early European settlers by words signifying ' sword men ' and ' coat men '.[2]

The name of DAUPHINY is unique. Its origin is to be traced to the Dolphin, which was the heraldic bearing of the Counts of Albon, the feudal lords of the district. The name of this cetacean, if traced to its source, proves, curiously enough, to be derived from a local name. The chief shrine of Apollo was at Delphi, and the animal, δελφίς, was sacred to ·the Delphian God [3] [i.e. the dolphin, or fish with the great belly, δελφύς].

The natural features of the country have supplied many ethnic names. From the Greek τράχύς we obtain the name of THRACE,[4] the rugged country, as well as of TRACHONITIS,[5] a sort of basaltic island in the Syrian desert—a scene of grand rocky desolation, where vast fissures, and lines of craggy battlement call to mind the lunar landscape, as viewed through a powerful telescope, rather than any scene on the surface of the earth.[6] PETRA takes its name from the long sandstone parapets which gird the Wady Mousa ; ALBION is the ' hilly land ' of Scotland,[7] and ALBANIA is so called from the snowy range, whose peaks are seen, from the Ionian islands, glistening

[1] Similarly the name of the ANGLES has been derived from *angol,* a hook, that of the GERMANS from the javelin called a *gar,* and those of the HERULI and the CHERUSCI from the Gothic *heru,* a sword. Kemble, *Saxons,* vol. i. p. 41; Grimm, *Gesch. der Deut. Spr.* pp. 81, 512; Leo, *Vorlesungen,* vol. i. p. 255; Wackernagel, in Haupt's *Zeitschrift,* vol. vi. p. 16. Cf. Müller, *Marken,* pp. 176–180; Latham, *Eng. Lang.* vol. i. p. 216; Bosworth, *Origin,* p. 122; and Mone, *Gesch. Heidenth,* vol. ii. p. 124; who quotes, Leo, *Othins Verehrung,* a work which I have not been able to procure. [According to others the Longobardi were those who dwelt ' *along the border*' of the Elbe (Gibbon, *Rise and Fall,* ed. Smith, v. 165 note).]
[2] Roger Williams, *Key into the Languages of N. America,* p. 39.
[3] C. O. Müller, *Dorians,* vol. i. p. 325; Ménage, *Origines,* pp. 250, 698; Yonge, *Christian Names,* vol. i. p. 157; see, however, Curtius, *Grundzuge,* vol. ii. p. 65; Kuhn, *Zeitschrift,* vol. ii. p. 129.
[4] Gladstone, *Homer,* vol. i. pp. 158, 347, 382; Grimm thinks the root is θρασύς rather than τραχύς. *Gesch. der Deut. Spr.* p. 195.
[5] Trachonitis is the Greek translation of Argob, the Hebrew name.
[6] See Stanley, *Jewish Church,* p. 213; Graham, in *Cambridge Essays* for 1858, p. 145.
[7] Pictet, *Orig. Indo-Euro.* vol. i. p. 70. Cf. Meyer, in *Reports of Brit. Assoc.* for 1847, p. 303.

brilliantly in the evening sun. Cambria and Cumberland are the lands of the Cymry—the mountaineers,[1] and the CROATS or Chorwats,[2] as well as the KABYLES,[3] the MALAYS,[4] the CHAUCI,[5] the ARCADIANS,[6] the GREEKS, the DORIANS,[7] the THURINGIANS, and the TYROLESE are the 'Highlanders', while ATTICA is the 'Promontory'.[8]

The CANAANITES are the 'lowlanders', [9] as distinguished from the AVITES and the AMORITES, or 'dwellers on the hills', and from the HITTITES and the HIVITES, who were respectively the 'men of the valleys', and the 'men of the towns'.[10] The POLES or Polacs are the 'men of the plain',[11] VOLHYNIA is the 'level country', WESTPHALIA the great 'western field',[12] HOLLAND is the 'fen',[13] BATAVIA (Bet-au), the 'good land',[14] BRABANT the 'ploughed land',[15] and EUBŒA is the 'well tilled'.[16] The ARGIVES lived in the 'tilled' plain of Argos,[17]

---

[1] The Cymry are probably the 'men of the combes', or mountaineers. Mone, *Celtische Forschungen*, p. 329. Cf. Donaldson, *Varron*, p. 63; Wright, *Essays*, vol. i. p. 101. Glück, *Kelt. Namen*, p. 26, thinks they are 'the people.' See p. 57, *supra*. [More probably *com-brog*, the united people.]

[2] From the Sclavonic word *Chorwat*, a mountain. The root is found in the name of Carinthia, and also of the Carpathians, which were anciently called Chorwat or Chrbat. See Adelung, *Mithridates*, vol. ii. p. 647; Knobel, *Völkertafel*, p. 44; Schafarik, *Slaw, Alterth.* vol. i. p. 49; vol. ii. p. 305; Buttmann, *Ortsnamen*, p. 72; *Church of England Quarterly*, No. 73, p. 144; Bronisch, in *Neues Lausitzisches Magazin*, vol. xxxii. p. 274. [3] Brace, *Races*, p. 173.

[4] Malaja means a mountain in the Turanian languages of India. Lassen, *Ind. Alt.* vol. i. p. 57.

[5] Haupt, in Haupt's *Zeitschrift*, vol. iii. p. 190.

[6] The root is seen in the Latin *arx*, and the Greek ἄκρον. See *Church of England Quarterly*, No. 73, p. 147.

[7] The same root is found in the Latin *turris*, and in the Tors of Devonshire and Derbyshire. The Tyrol, however, may take its name from a castle near Meran.

[8] The root is found in ἀκτή and ATHOS. *Phil. Mus.* vol. ii. p. 366.

[9] Curtius, *Grundzüge der Gr. Ety.* vol. i. p. 32; Knobel, *Völkertafel*, p. 309; Renan, *Lang. Sémit.* p. 182; Stanley, *Sinai and Pal.* pp. 133, 267; Ewald, *Gesch. d. Volkes Isr.* vol. i. p. 281; Movers, *Phönizier*, pt. ii. vol. i. p. 6.

[10] Movers, *Phönizier*, pt. ii. vol. i. p. 80; Ewald, *Gesch. d. Volkes Isr.* vol. i. pp. 279–282; Movers, Art. *Phönizier*, in Ersch und Gruber, pp. 319, 327, 331; Wilton, *Negeb.* p. 159.

[11] Schafarik, *Slaw. Alt.* vol. i. p. 49; vol. ii. p. 399; Arndt, *Europ. Spr.* p. 249.

[12] Zeuss, *Die Deutschen*, p. 390.

[13] From *ollant*, marshy ground. Bosworth, *Origin*, p. 21.

[14] *Bet*, the first part of this name, is the obsolete positive degree of better and best. The second syllable *au*, land, is seen in the word fall-ow, the bad or *failing* land. [Quite wrong. 'Fallow', M. Eng. *falwe*, is properly 'harrowed land' from O. Eng. *fealgian*, to harrow, *fealga*, a harrow (See *Old Eng. Glosses*, ed. Napier, p. 64; Kluge *s.v. felge*; Skeat, *Notes on Eng. Etymology*, p. 87), and has nothing to do with *fail*.] Bosworth, *Origin*, p. 92; Motley, *Dutch Republic*, vol. i. p. 4. Cf. Thierry, *Hist. Gaul*, vol. ii. p. 43.

[15] Brabant, anciently Brach-bant, is from the old high German *prácha*, ploughing. *Bant* means a district, as in the names of the Subantes, Tribantes, and Bucinobantes Grimm, *Gesch. der Deut. Spr.* p. 593; Förstemann, *Ortsnamen*, p. 102.

[16] Gladstone, *Homer*, p. 102.

[17] The root is seen in ἔργον. Gladstone, *Homer*, pp. 384–402; Thirlwall, *Greece*, vol. i. p. 38; Curtius, *Die Ionier*, p. 17; Movers, *Die Phönizier*, pt. i. p. 8. The PELASGIANS are, perhaps, the 'men of the plain'. Gladstone, *Homer*, p. 214. Other conjectures will be found in Marsh, *Horæ, Pelasgicæ*, p. 17; Thirlwall, *Greece*, vol. i. p. 45; Donaldson, *Varronianus*, p. 30; *New Crat.* p. 138.

and the LATINS are the men of the ' broad plain ' of Latium.[1]
The KURDS are the ' shepherds ', the SARMATIANS are the ' men
of the steppe ',[2] and the ARABS as well as the BEDOUIN [3] are the
' men of the desert ', as contrasted with the FELLAHS or
FELLAHIN, the ' men of the cultivated ground '.

The BURGUNDIANS were the dwellers in burghs or fortified
towns.[4] The TYRRHENIANS, or ETRUSCANS, were the tower-
builders.[5] The SPARTANS were the dwellers in Sparta, the
town of ' scattered houses ', more loosely built than other Grecian cities, because unconfined by a wall '.[6] The RAMNES
as Mommsen thinks,[7] were the ' Foresters ', a meaning which,
according to Wilhelm von Humboldt, attaches to the name
of the BASQUES, the BISCAYANS, and the GASCONS. The
CALEDONIANS are, probably, the ' men of the woods ',[8] FIFE is
the ' forest ', LYCIA [9] and CORSICA [10] the ' wooded '.

PONTUS was the province on the Black ' Sea '. POMER-
ANIA[11] is a Sclavonic term, meaning ' by the sea'. The Celtic
names of the MORINI,[12] of ARMORICA,[13] of MORHIBAN, of MORAY or
MURRAY, and of GLAMORGAN or Morgant,[14] have the same signification. The Salian Franks, to whom is attributed the Salic
law of succession, lived by the salt water at the mouth of the

---

1 Mommsen, *Hist. of Rome*, vol. i. p. 36 ; Forbiger, *Alt. Geogr.* vol. iii. p. 649.

2 From *sara*, a desert or steppe, and *mat*, a tribe or race. This root is seen in the names of the Jaxa-matæ, Thisa-matæ, Aga-matæ, Chari-matæ, and other Asiatic tribes. Schafarik, *Slaw. Alterth.* vol. i. p. 367.

3 From *arabah*, a desert, and *badiya*, a desert.

4 Grimm, *Gesch. der Deut. Spr.* p. 700.

5 See Knobel, *Völkertafel*, p. 90 ; Donaldson, *New Crat.* p. 133 ; Donaldson, *Varron.* p. 13.

6 Pott, *Etymologische Spahne*, in Kuhn's *Zeitschrift*, vol. v. p. 252.

7 *History of Rome*, vol. i. p. 44.

8 See p. 47, *supra*.

9 A word akin to *lucus* must have once existed in the Greek language. See Gladstone's *Homer*, vol. i. p. 186. The LACEDÆMONIANS are either the dwellers in the forest, or, more probably, the dwellers in the hollow or marsh.

10 Bochart, vol. iii. p. 570.

11 From *po*, by, and *mere*, the sea. So the Prusi, or PRUSSIANS are, probably the Po-Rusi, the men near the Rusi, or Russians, or perhaps near the Russe, a branch of the river Niemen. See Friedrich the Great, *Mem. Hist. Brand.* and Voigt, *Gesch. Preussens*, vol. i. p. 668, quoted by Mahn, *Nam. Preussens*, p. 3. Compare Donaldson, *Varron*, p. 70 ; Pictet, *Orig. Indo-Eur.* vol. i. p. 110 ; Latham, *Ethnology of Brit. Is.* p. 73 ; Arndt. *Eur. Spr.* pp. 250, 293.

12 And of the Morgetes, on the coast of Sicily, according to Archdeacon Williams, *Essays*, p. 89.

13 The preposition *ar*, on, by, or at, is that found in the names of Argyle, Arles, Armagh, etc. [But Ar-gyle (*Arre-gaithel*) is the ' District of the Gaels ' (Johnston, 17), and Armagh (Ard-Macha) is ' Macha's height ' (Joyce, i. 73).] See Adelung, *Mithridates*, vol. ii. pp. 43, 44 ; Davies, *Celtic Researches*, p. 221 ; Pott, *Etymols. Forsch.* vol. ii. p. 42 ; Deifenbach, *Celtica*, vol. i. pp. 62, 80 ; *Orig. Eur.* p. 231 ; Glück, *Kelt. Namen.*, pp. 31–36 ; Ménage, *Origines*, pp. 61, 680 ; Thierry, *Hist. d. Gaul.* vol. i. pp. xxxix., 5.

14 From *mor*, the sea, and *gant*, side.

Maas.[1] Dr. Donaldson follows Mr. Kenrick[2] in thinking that the IONIANS are the ' coast-men ' :[3] they were called also the Αἰγιαλεῖς, or the ' Beachmen '.[4] The ACHÆANS[5] may be the ' Seamen ', and the ÆOLIANS the ' mixed men '.[6] The HELLENES, if not ' hillmen ', may be the ' warriors ', whose martial prowess caused their name to be extended to the whole of the people whom we know by the name of GREEKS. This last name is a curious misnomer. Just as the name of Italy originally designated only the extreme southern portion of the Peninsula,[7] so the name of GREECE was derived from a small and unimportant Epirote tribe of ' mountaineers '—the Græci, who, in blood, were probably not Hellenes at all, but Illyrians. By the accident of geographical proximity[8] the Romans became first acquainted with this tribe, and applied their name to the whole of Hellas ; and the modern world has adopted this unfortunate blunder from the Roman, and stamped it with the approval of its usage.

[1] Leo, *Vorlesungen*, vol. i. p. 257.

[2] Donaldson, *New Crat.* pp. 134, 143 ; Kenrick, *Egypt of Herodotus*, and a paper *On the Early Kings of Attica*, by J. K[enrick], in the *Philolog. Museum*, vol. ii. pp. 366, 367.

[3] From ἠιών, the coast. More probably they are the ' wanderers ', from the Sanskrit root *jâ*, which we find in the names of Ion, Hyperion, and Amphion. Curtius, *Ionier*, pp. 7, 8 ; Curtius, *Grundzüge*, vol. i. p. 37. Lassen and Pott think the root is the Sanskrit *juwan*, young. This, however, seems too abstract. Knobel, *Völkertafel*, p. 79.

[4] Gladstone, *Homer*, p. 382 ; Thirlwall, *Hist. Greece*, vol. i. p. 43.

[5] Conjecturally from an obsolete Greek root, allied to the Latin *aqua*, and found in the names of the Achelous and the Acheron. See note 4, p. 57, *supra* ; and *Church of England Quarterly*, No. 73, p. 155.

[6] Donaldson, *New Crat.* p. 142. Adelung thinks that the names of the VENETI and of the WENDS mean shore-dwellers. *Mithridates*, vol. ii. pp. 451 and 655 ; Schafarik, *Slaw. Alterth.* vol. i. pp. 159, 164. See, however, p. 56, *supra*.

[7] In Aristotle the word Italy denotes only a portion of Calabria. In the time of Augustus it came to mean the whole peninsula. Niebuhr, *Hist. Rome*, vol. i. p. 17 ; Liddell, *Hist. Rome*, vol. i. p. 16 ; Lewis, *Credibility Rom. Hist.* vol. i. p. 272. So Tyre seems to have given its name to the whole of SYRIA, and the names of PERSIAN and PARSEE are traceable to the small province of Fars, or Pars. Gladstone, *Homer*, vol. i. p. 549. Compare the case of Asia, p. 55, and see Kenrick, *Egypt of Herodotus*, p. 81 ; Buttmann, *Mythologus*, vol. ii. p. 172. ITALY is, perhaps, the ' land of cattle '. [ἰταλός, Lat. *vitulus*, Mommsen ; Curtius, i. 257.] Curtius, *Grundzüge*, vol. i. p. 177 ; Forbiger, *Alt. Geogr.* vol. iii. p. 488 ; Bunsen, *Phil. of Univ. Hist.* vol. i. p. 103. Niebuhr, however, ridicules this etymology [but it is confirmed by the Oscan form *Viteliu*].

[8] See Latham, *Germania*, p. 28 ; *Eng. Lang.* vol. i. p. 166 ; Mommsen, *Hist. of Rome*, vol. i. p. 141 ; Thirlwall, *Hist. Greece*, vol. i. p. 39. Compare the case of Palestine, p. 52, and of the Alemanni, p. 43. So the gipsies call the Germans, Saxons (see p. 42), and the Magyars call them Schwabe, the Suabians being the German tribe with which they first became acquainted.

CHAPTER V

THE PHŒNICIANS

Physical character of Phœnician sites—Tyre—Sidon—Phœenice—Phœnician colonies in Crete, Cyprus, Sardinia, Corsica, Italy, Sicily, Malta, Africa, Spain, and Britain.

THE Phœnicians established a vast colonial empire. The Mediterranean coast-line of three continents was thickly dotted over with their settlements, which extended beyond the pillars of Hercules, as far as the River Senegal[1] to the south, and as far as Britain to the north. The causes of this development of colonial dominion must be sought, firstly, in the over-population of their narrow strip of Syrian coast, shut in between the mountains and the sea, and, secondly, in the spirit of mercantile enterprise with which the whole nation was imbued.[2] As in the case of the Venetians, the Dutch, and afterwards still more notably of the English, the factories, which were established for commercial purposes alone, rose gradually to be separate centres of dominion.[3] To protect themselves from the lawless violence of the barbarous tribes with whom they traded, the merchant princes of Tyre found themselves unwillingly compelled to assume sovereignty over the surrounding districts. The origin of the colonial empire of the Tyrians is curiously indicated by a physical characteristic which marks the sites of many of their settlements. These were placed, almost invariably, on some rocky island near the coast, or on some promontory connected with the mainland by a low isthmus. A position of this kind would usually afford the advantage of a natural harbour, in which vessels might find safe anchorage, while the trading settlement would be secured from the attacks of the barbarous

---

1 As evidenced by the Phœnician names of Rysadion (Cape Blanco), Soloeis (Cape Cantin), Soloentia (Cape Bojador), and Bambotus (the river Senegal). Movers, *Phönizier* part ii. vol. ii. p. 534 ; Renan, *Lang. Sémit.* p. 200. [See also Prof. G. Rawlinson, *Hist of Phœnicia,* 1889.]
2 Movers, *Die Phönizier,* part ii. vol. ii. p. 5.
3 Renan, *Langues Sémitiques,* p. 44.

tribes which occupied the mainland. Tyre itself was probably at first only a trading colony sent forth from the mother city at the entrance of the Persian Gulf. The name TZUR[1] or TYRE, which means a 'rock', characterizes the natural features of the site—a rocky island near the coast—well suited to the requirements of a band of mercantile adventurers. The neighbouring city of Aradus stood also upon a littoral island. SIDON occupies a somewhat similar position, being built on a low reef running out to sea, and the name, which denotes a 'fishing-station',[2] suggests to us what must have been the aspect of the place in those prehistoric times when the first settlement was made. Not unfrequently the names of the Phœnician settlements thus indicate the circumstances of their foundation. Sometimes, as in the case of Spain, Malaga, or Pachynus, the names refer to the nature of the traffic that was carried on—more frequently, as in the case of Cadiz, Hippo, or Lisbon, we have a reference to the fortifications which were found necessary to protect the wealthy but isolated factory.

We find the name of the nation repeated in Cape PHINEKE[3] in Lycia, also in PHŒNICE in Epirus, a place which now bears the name of Finiki,[4] and in five places called PHŒNICUS, severally in Cythera, in Messenia, in Marmarica, in Ionia, and in Lycira. Pliny also states[5] that the island of Tenedos, as well as a small island near the mouth of the Rhone, was called PHŒNICE. The latter may probably be identified with one of the Hieres islands, which would satisfy the conditions which the Phœnicians sought in their trading stations. One of the Lipari islands, anciently called Phœnicodes, now goes by the name of FELICUDI.

But the most interesting spot on which the Phœnicians have left their name, is a rocky promontory on the southern coast of Crete, which possesses good harbours on either side. This place is still called PHŒNIKI, and has been identified[6] with the

[1] Movers, *Phönizier*, part ii. vol. i. p. 174 ; Ersch und Gruber, sect. iii. vol. xxiv. p. 436; Stanley, *Sinai and Pal*. pp. 270, 498. The name of SYRIA is probably derived from that of Tzur, its chief city. *Ib*. p. 270.

[2] Movers, *Phönizier*, part ii. vol. i. pp. 34, 868. Compare the name of BETH-SAIDA, the 'house of fish'.

[3] Kenrick, *Phœnicia*, p. 87.

[4] Leake, *Northern Greece*, vol. i. p. 66. It is possible that some of these places may be named from the palm-trees 'φοῖνιξ' growing on them. Olshausen, *Phön. Ortsnamen*, p. 335.   [5] Pliny, *Hist. Nat.* iii. 11, and v. 39.

[6] Conybeare and Howson, *Life and Epistles of St. Paul*, vol. ii. pp. 395–400 ; Movers, *Phönizier*, pt. ii. vol. ii. p. 260.

haven of Phœnice mentioned in the Acts of the Apostles. St. Luke says, ' We sailed under Crete . . . and came into a place which is called the Fair Havens . . . and because the haven was not commodious to winter in, the more part advised to depart thence also, if by any means they might attain to Phenice, which is an haven of Crete, and there to winter '. With true commercial instinct the Phœnicians seem to have selected for the centre of their Cretan trade this sea-washed promontory, with its double harbour, now, as in the time of St. Paul, the best haven along the southern coast of the island.

LEBENA, another harbour on the Cretan coast, is the ' Lion promontory '.[1]   There is a Cretan JORDAN flowing from a Cretan LEBANON.[2]   IDALIA in Cyprus, now Dalin, is the ' sacred grove '.[3]   SAMOS is the ' lofty ', and the name of SAMOTHRACE contains the same root.[4]   From the Phœnician word *sela*, a rock, we derive the name of SELINUS, now Selenti, in Cilicia—a town which stands on a steep rock almost surrounded by the sea.[5]   TARSUS, the birthplace of St. Paul, is ' the strong '.[6]   LAMPSACUS, now Lamsaki, near Gallipoli, is the ' passage ',[7] and seems to have been the ferry across the Hellespont.

Sardinia is full of Phœnician names. CAGLIARI, the chief town, was a Tyrian colony, and its Phœnician name Caralis, or Cararis, has suffered little change. BOSA still bears its ancient Tyrian name unaltered. MACOPSISA, now Macomer, is the ' town '; OTHOCA seems to be a corruption of Utica, the ' old ' town, and NORA, like so many other Phœnician settlements, was built upon a little island off the coast.[8]

The name of CORSICA, according to Bochart, means the ' wooded '.[9]   The desolate forest-clad mountains of this island seem, however, to have had few attractions for the Phœnician merchants, since none of the towns bear names which, in their language, are significant.[10]

1 Kenrick, *Phœnicia*, p. 83 ; Movers, *Phönizier*, pt. ii. vol. ii. p. 260.
2 Olshausen, *Phönicische Örtsnamen*, p. 324.
3 Bochart, vol. iii. p. 356 ; Engel, *Kypros*, vol. i. p. 153, apud Smith, *Dict. Geogr.* vol. ii. p. 13.
4 Bochart, vol. iii. p. 378 ; Renan, *Lang. Sémit.* p. 44.
5 Movers, *Phönizier*, pt. ii. vol. ii. p. 174.
6 Gesenius, *Monumenta*, p. 427.
7 Movers, *Phönizier*, pt. ii. vol. ii. p. 296.
8 Other Phœnician names found in Sardinia, are Cornus, Carbia, Olbia, Buccina, Cunusi, Charmis, and Sulchi. Movers, *Phönizier*, part ii. vol. ii. pp. 558, 572, 576–578 ; Bochart vol. iii. p. 576.
9 Bochart, vol. iii. p. 579.   10 Movers, pt. ii. vol. ii. p. 578.

At Cære, in Italy, there was a Tyrian settlement, which anciently bore the Phœnician name of AGYLLA, the ' round town '[1] and in lower Italy we find the Phœnician names of Malaca, Sybaris, Crathis, Tempsa, Medma, and Hippo.[2]

Cape PACHYNUS in Sicily, was the ' station' for the boats engaged in the tunny fishery.[3] Catana, now CATANIA, is the ' little ' town.[4] MAZARA, which still preserves its ancient name, is the ' castle '[5] and the familiar name of ETNA is a corruption of *attuna*, the ' furnace '.[6] Many other ancient names attest the long duration of the Phœnician rule in this island.[7]

Diodorus informs us that the Island of MALTA was a Phœnician settlement ; and we find that not only does the name of the island bear out this assertion,[8] but at HAGIAR CHEM —' the stones of veneration '—we have extensive remains of a Phœnician Temple. The site was explored by Sir H. F. Bouverie about twenty years ago [i.e. about 1840], when the outlines of the seven courts of the temple were traced, and the statues of the seven presiding planetary deities were disinterred.[9]

The Phœnician capital was, probably, near the south-eastern extremity of the island. Here is a deep bay, on the shores of which stand the ruins of a temple of Melcarth, the ' city king '.[10] This word *cartha*, a city, appears in the Old Testament in the names of twelve places called Kirjath, as well as in that of CARTHAGE, the great Tyrian Colony in Northern Africa.[11]

[1] Mommsen, *Hist. of Rome*, vol. i. p. 136 ; Olshausen, *Phönicische Orts namen*, p. 333. Cf. Gesenius, *Monum.* p. 419.

[2] Movers, pt. ii. vol. ii. p. 344.   [3] *Ib.* p. 325.   [4] *Ib.* p. 329.

[5] *Ib.* p. 332, Gesenius, p. 425.

[6] Bochart, vol. iii. p. 526.   The name cannot be derived from the Greek αἴθω, as Pictet shows. It may possibly be Oscan, according to Benfey, in Höfer's *Zeitschrift*, vol. ii. p. 117 ; Curtius, *Grundzüge*, vol. i. p. 215.   Cf. *Church of England Quarterly*, No. 73, p. 147.

[7] e.g. Arbela, which also occurs in Palestine ; Thapsus, the ' passage ', Anesel, the ' river head ', Amathe, the ' castle ', Adana, Tabæ, Motuca, Mactorium, Ameselum, Bidis, Cabala, Inycon, and many more. Movers, pp. 329, 339-342 ; Gesenius, pp. 419, 428.

[8] Melita means a ' place of refuge ', Gesenius, p. 92 ; Bochart, vol. iii. p. 500 ; Movers, in Ersch und Gruber, § iii. vol. xxiv. p. 349.

[9] Kenrick, *Phœnicia*, p. 110 ; Tallack, *Malta*, pp. 115-127 ; Movers, *Phönizier*, part ii. vol. ii. p. 351.

[10] The word Melek, a king, is found in all the Semitic languages. It is seen in the names of Melchisedek, Melchior, Abdu-l-malek, etc.

[11] It appears also in the names of Cirta, Ta-carata, Cartili, Cartenna, Caralis, Carpie, Carepula, Mediccara, Cura, Curum, Rusucurum, Ascurum, Ausocurro, Curubis, Garra, Medugarra, Tagara, Tagarata, etc. Gesenius, *Scrip. Ling. Ph. Mon.* p. 417 ; Wilton, *Negeb*, p. 99. A suburb of Palermo anciently bore the name of Karthada. Movers, pt. ii. vol. ii. p. 30.

CARTHAGE—Kart-hada, or Kartha hadtha—the 'New Town'[1] soon eclipsed in splendour and importance the older settlement of UTICA, 'the ancient';[2] and before long she began to rival even the mother city of Tyre, and to lay the foundations of a colonial empire of her own.

SPAIN seems to have been first known to the Phœnicians as the land where the skins of martens[3] were procured, and the name Hispania or Spain appears to be derived from a Phœnician word *sapan* [*shaphan*], or *span*, which denotes the abundance of these animals.[4] Many of the Phœnician colonies in Spain were Tyrian rather than Carthaginian. ESCALONA is, probably, the same word as Ascalon; and MAGUEDA is, perhaps, identical with Megiddo. Asido, now MEDINA SIDONIA, was, as the name denotes, a colony of the Sidonians.[5]

Cadiz, as we learn from Velleius Paterculus, was founded before Utica, and consequently long before Carthage. The name CADIZ is a corruption of the ancient name Gadeira, and is referable to the Phœnician word *gadir*, an inclosure.[6] The site presents the features of other Tyrian settlements—an island separated by a narrow channel from the main land. The same is the case at Carthagena, which is built on a small island in a sheltered bay. The name of CARTHAGENA is a corruption of Carthago Nova or new Carthage; and we may, therefore, assign to it a Carthaginian rather than a Tyrian origin. Near Gibraltar there is another town named CARTEJA, anciently Carteia.[7] The name of MALAGA is derived from the Phœnician word *malaca*, salt.[8] Hispalis, now SEVILLA, was also a Carthaginian colony, and the name is deducible from

1 Movers, p. 139; Gesenius, p. 421; Bochart, vol. iii. p. 468. [Assyrian *Qart-had-shat*, 'New city', on the monuments *Karti-Khadashti*—Maspero, *Passing of the Empires*, 283.]

2 Bochart, vol. iii. p. 474; Gesenius, p. 429. Movers (p. 512) doubts this etymology.

3 Γαλῆ Ταρτήσιαι—martens, or perhaps rabbits [Heb. *Shâphân*, Ps. civ., 18]—see the passages from Herodotus, iv. 192; Strabo, iii. 2, 6; Schol. in Aristoph. Ran. 475; Ælian. V. H. xii. 4, and other writers which are quoted by Movers, part ii. vol. ii. p. 606. Compare Charnock, *Local Etymology*, p. 254.

4 Bochart, vol. iii. p. 631; Niebuhr, *Lectures on Ethnol. and Geograph.* vol. ii. p. 279.

5 Movers, part ii. vol. ii. p. 641.

6 Movers, p. 621; Gesenius, p. 304; Kenrick, p. 126. Compare the names of the Ægades Islands near Sicily, of Geder (Joshua xii. 13); Gedera (Josh. xv. 36); Gedor (Josh. xv. 38); and Gadara, the city of the Gadarenes (Josephus, *Jewish War*, iv. 3; St. Mark v. 1). See Bochart, vol. iii. p. 608; Movers, pp. 139, 549.

7 Perhaps identical with Tartessus. Duke of Buckingham, *Diary*, vol. i. p. 70; Bochart, vol. iii. p. 615; Olshausen, *Phön. Ortsnamen*, p. 328; Smith, *Dictionary*, vol. i. p. 528; Movers, pp. 632—635.

8 Bochart, vol. iii. p. 616; Movers, p. 632. Cf. Gesenius, p. 312; Prescott, *Ferd. and Isabella*, vol. ii; p. 13.

a Phœnician word meaning a ' plain '.[1]   The TAGUS is the river
of fish.[2]   The name of Olisippo, which has been corrupted
into LISBON, contains the word *hippo*, the ' walled ' town, which
occurs so frequently in Phœnician names.   There were three
cities called HIPPO in Africa, one of them celebrated as the
See of the great Augustine, and two of the same name in
Spain.[3]

Tarraco, now TARRAGONA, is the ' palace '.[4]   The name of
CORDOVA, anciently Cortuba, may be derived either from
coteba, the ' olive press ', or from *Kartha Baal*, the ' city of
Baal '.[5]   BELON, now Belonia, near Tarifa ; [6] as well, perhaps,
as the BALEARIC [7] Isles, contain the name of Bel or Baal, the
deity whose name enters into the composition of so many
Tyrian and Carthaginian names, such as Hannibal, Asdrubal,
Maherbal, Ethbaal, Agbalos, Jezebel, Belshazzar, and Baalbec.[8]   There are many other places in Spain which seem
originally to have been Carthaginian colonies, since their names
can be explained from Punic sources.   Such as Abdera, now
ADRA ;   Barcino, now BARCELONA ; [9] Ebora, now EVORA,
the ' ford ' ;[10] Arci, now ARKOS ; the River Anas, now the
GUADIANA ;   TOLEDO, and others.[11]

Whether the Carthaginians reached the shores of Britain
is uncertain.   We have already seen that the Euskarian
origin of the name makes it probable that the earliest knowledge of the island was obtained from Iberic traders ; and
it certainly is not improbable that the Carthaginians followed
in the track discovered by their Spanish subjects.   It is a

[1] Bochart, p. 603 ; Gesenius, p. 423 ; Movers, p. 641.
[2] Ford, *Gatherings*, p. 28.   The root appears in the name of the god Dagon.
[3] We have also Orippo, Belippo, Baesippo, Irippo, and Lacippo, all on the Spanish coast. Humboldt, *Prüfung*, p. 64 ; Movers, *Phön*. pt. ii. vol. ii. pp. 144, 640 ; Cf. Bochart, vol. iii. pp. 475, 627 ; Gesenius, *Monum* p. 423.   [Lisbon was sometimes called Ulissippo, to bring it into connexion with Ulysses ; Ulis-bona in H. Howard, *Defensative against supposed Prophecies*, 1620, p. 15.]
[4] Bochart, vol, iii. p. 623.
[5] Bochart, vol. iii. p. 602.
[6] Movers, p. 639.
[7] Bochart, vol. iii. p. 634.   See, however, p. 58 *supra*. *Ebusus*, now IVIÇA, means the ' pine island ', and the Greek name Pitusæ is merely a translation of the earlier Phœnician appellation. Movers, *Die Phönizier*, p. 545 ; art. *Phönizien* in Ersch und Gruber, p. 349.   The Balearic Islands present many Phœnician names, such as Cinici, Cunici Bocchorum, Jamna, Mago, and Sanifera. Movers, pp. 584, 585.
[8] Kenrick, *Phœnicia*, pp. 129, 300 ; Renan, *Langues Sémitiques*, p. 44 ; Bochart, vol. iii. p. 634.
[9] Movers, p. 636.
[10] *Ib.* p. 640. Cf. Gesenius, p. 422.
[11] e.g. Murgis, Urci, Certima, Saborra, Suel, Salduba, Ucia, Castalo, and Nebrissa. Movers, pp. 633–643. Gesenius, *Scr. Ling. Ph. Mon.* vol. i. pp. 340, 422.

noteworthy circumstance that the almost unique physical characteristics of St. Michael's Mount, in Cornwall, conform precisely to the account given by Diodorus Siculus of the trading station from which the Phœnicians obtained their tin. We may mention, though we can hardly maintain the supposition, that the names of MARAZION,[1] the 'hill by the sea', and POLGARTH (root *Kartha*) are of Phœnician origin, and are records of the first intercourse of our savage ancestors with the civilized world.[2]

---

[1] Marazion seems to have been a Jewish settlement at a later time, and it is possible that the name may be Hebrew, rather than Phœnician. It can, however, be explained from Cornish sources. See Halliwell, *Cornwall*, pp. 47–52 ; Pryce, *Archœologia Cornu-Brit*. s. v. On the Phœnicians in Cornwall, see Wilson, *Prehist. Ann. of Scotland*, p. 196 ; Bochart, vol. iii. pp. 648–654 ; Turner, *Anglo-Saxons*, vol. i. pp. 51–55 ; Smith's *Cassiterides* ; and a tract on the Phœnician Tin Trade, recently published by Colonel James. [Also *Life of Chas. Kingsley*, vol. ii. p. 238 ; M. Müller, *Chips*, iii. 299.]

[2] On Tyrian and Carthaginian names, see the erudite work of Bochart, *Geographiæ Sacræ pars posterior, Chanaan, seu de Coloniis et sermone Phœnicum*, and the more trustworthy works of Movers, *Die Phönizier*, and the Article *Phönizien* in Ersch und Gruber's *Allgemeine Encyklopädie*, sect. iii. vol. xxiv. See also Kenrick's *Phœnicia* ; and the valuable treatise of Gesenius, *Scripturæ Linguæque Phœniciæ Monumenta*. Gesenius discusses the etymologies of more than 400 names, collected from modern maps, the ancient itineraries, coins, inscriptions, and the ancient Geographers, Ptolemy, Strabo, etc. [Also M. A. Levy, *Phönizische Studien*, 1856–70 ; Dr. W. Cunningham, *Essay on Western Civilization*, 1898 ; A. S. Wilkins, *Phœnicia and Israel*, 1871. The Hebrew origin of Mara-zion, analysed as Mara-Zion, ' Bitter (i.e. afflicted) Zion ', was supposed to be corroborated by its later name Market Jew (C. Kingsley, *Yeast*, 1851, p. 255). But it really stands for the Cornish *Marhas*, market, and *ian*, insular, ' the island market ', so called from its vicinity to St. Michael's Mount. Market Jew is merely a corrupt Anglicization of the Cornish *marhas-gow* (or—*diow*), ' Thursday Market ' (*Mercatus Iovis diet*), later forms of which were *Marcajewe* and *Marcasju*. But Mr. J. Jacobs has shown that there were Jews in Cornwall temp. Richard I (*The Jews of Angevin England*, p. 187).]

CHAPTER VI

THE ARABS IN EUROPE

*The Empire of the Cailiphs—Arabic Names in Southern Italy and Sicily—
Tribes by which the conquest of Sicily was effected—Conquest of Spain—
Tarifa and Gibraltar—Arabic article—River-names of Spain—Arabs in
Southern France—They hold the passes of the Alps—The Monte Moro
pass and its Arabic Names—The Muretto pass and Pontresina.*

THE Arab conquests in the seventh and eighth centuries
form one of the most remarkable episodes in the history of
the world. At the time of its greatest extension, the empire
of the Cailiphs extended from the Indus to the Loire. In
the course of a single century they overran Persia, Syria,
Egypt, Northern Africa, Spain, and the south of France.

We find Arabic names scattered over the whole of this
vast region ; and it will be an interesting and profitable task
to investigate these linguistic monuments of Moslem Empire,
confining our attention more especially to those districts
where Christianity has long resumed its sway.

In Southern Italy the dominion of the Arabs lasted hardly
half a century, and consequently we cannot expect to find
many Arabic names. Their chief conquests lay in the neighbourhood of the cities of Benevento and Bari, not far from
which we find the doubtful Arabic names of ALIFE, ALFIDENA,
and the river ALMARO.[1]

In Sicily, where the Arab colonization was more extensive,
and where their empire was more enduring than in Italy,
we naturally find more abundant and less doubtful traces of
their presence. The well known name of MARSALA means,
in Arabic, the ' Port of God '. *Gebel*, the Arabic name for a
mountain, is still retained in the *patois* of the Sicilian peasantry,
who prefer the mongrel term MONGIBELLO to the ancient

[1] See Wenrich, *Rerum ab Arabibus gestarum Commentarii*, p. 140.

70

Phœnician name of Etna.[1] From the same root comes the name of the GIBELLINA—a mountain ridge of the Province of Trapani.

It would appear that the Arabs kept down by military rule a considerable subject population, for the island is covered with fortresses of their erection. The position of these we can often discover by means of the Arabic word *kal'ah*, or *kal'at*,[2] a castle on a rock—a root which enters into the names of many Sicilian towns, such as CALOTABALOTTA (Kal'at-a-bellotta, oak-tree castle [3]), CALATAGIRONE, or Caltagirone (Kal'at-a-Girun), CALASCIBETTA (Kal'at-a-xibetta), CALATA-FIMI (Kal'at-a-fieni), CALATAMISETTA (castle of the women), CALATAVUTURA, CALTANISETTA, CALATABIANO, CALAMONACI, and CATALAMITA.[4]

There are also in this island many Arabic names of villages and farms.[5] The word *menzil*, a 'station', or 'hut', is found in MISILMERI (Menzil-Emîr), and in MEZZOJUSO (Menzil-Yusuf). The most common of these Arabic prefixes is *rahl*, a 'house', which appears in the names of REGALMUTO and RE-SULTANA. It occurs no less than one hundred and seven times, while Kal'at is only found in twenty names, and Menzil in eighteen.[6] We have *ras*, a cape, in the names of RASICANZIR, the cape of swine, RASICALBO, the dog's cape, RASACARAMI, the cape of vineyards, and RASICORNO, or Cape Horn.[7] In Palermo the two chief streets bear the Arabic names of the CASSARO, or 'Castle Street', and the MACCHEDA, or 'New Street',[8] and we find many other Arabic names scattered here and there over the island, such as GODRANO, the 'marsh';

---

1 Duff, in *Oxford Essays* for 1857, p. 93 ; Wenrich, *Rer. ab Ar. gest.* p. 309 ; Pihan *Glossaire*, p. 136.
2 This word is not confined to the Semitic languages. We have the Persian *Kálat* or *Kalátah*, a 'hill castle', and the Sanskrit *Kalatra* (?*Kataka*), a 'fortress'. Pictet, *Orig. Indo-Eur.* vol. ii. p. 194.
3 Gayangos, *Mohammedan Dynasties*, vol. i. p. 450 ; Wenrich, p. 308.
4 Compare the names of KHELAT, the capital of Beloochistan, and of GALATA, a walled suburb of Constantinople. YENIKALE in the Crimea is Yeni Kal'ah, the ' new fortress ' —a name half Turkish, and half Arabic.
5 As Abela says, the Arabs have left in Sicily ' un gran novero di nomi di città, di terre, e di luoghi particolari '. *Malta Illustrata*, vol. i. p. 682. There are many Arabic words in the Sicilian *patois*, as *saliare*, to wonder, *chamarru*, an ass, *hannaca*, a necklace. The few Arabic words in Italian, such as *alcova*, a chamber, *ammiraglio*, an admiral, *arsenale*, an arsenal, and the vessels called *carraca* and *feluca*, were probably introduced through the Spanish. See Bianchi-Giovini, *Dominazione degli Arabi in Italia*, pp. 55, 56 ; Diez, *Gram. Rom. Spr.* vol. i. pp. 59, 70 ; Duff, in *Oxford Essays* for 1857, p. 91 ; Wenrich, pp. 309–312, 323.
6 Amari, *Storia dei Musulmani*, vol. ii. p. 434.
7 Bianchi-Giovini, *Dominazione degli Arabi*, p. 56 ; Wenrich, p. 308 ; Amari, *Storia dei Musulmani*, vol. ii. p. 435. 8 Bianchi-Giovini, *Domin. d. Arabi*, p. 57.

CHADRA, and CADARA, the 'green'; ALCARA, MISTRETTA, MUSSOMELI, GAZZÌ, MONTE MERINO; and a few personal names, such as ABDELALI and ZYET.[1] Altogether there are in Sicily some 328 local names of Arabic origin, and the distribution of these is remarkable, as showing the relative amount of Arab influence in different portions of the island. In the Val di Mazara there are 209 Arabic names, in the Val di Noto 100, and the Val Demone only 19.[2]

The mediæval and modern names of Sicilian villages supply us with curious information as to the countries out of which was gathered the motley host that fought under the standard of the Prophet. In Sicily alone we find traces of tribes from Scinde, Mesopotamia, Egypt, Syria, and Spain.[3] Thus, a fountain near Palermo, now called DENNISINNI, was anciently *Ain es-Sindi*, the fountain of Scinde. But the conquest of Sicily seems to have been effected, for the most part, by troops levied from the neighbouring continent of Africa. There are more than a dozen indisputable names of Berber tribes to be found in Sicily, chiefly in the neighbourhood of the Val di Mazara.[4]

In the islands of Sardinia and Corsica the Arab rule was brief, and we find no Arabic names, except AJACCIO, and, perhaps, ALGHERO and ORISTAN. But Malta is full of Arabic names. The word *mirsah*, a port, which is found in the name of Marsala, in Sicily, appears in Malta in the names of numerous bays and inlets, such as MARSA SCIROCCO, MARSA SCALA, MARSA MUSCETTO, and MARSA FORNO. The ravines commonly go by the name of *vyed*, or *wied*, a corruption of the Arabic word *wadî*.[5] The hills have the prefix *gebel*, the fountains *aayn*, the wells *bir*, the castles *cala*, the houses *deyr*, the caves *ghar*, the villages *rahal*, the capes *ras*. From the map of the island it would be easy to collect scores of such names as AAYN IL KEBIRA, the great fountain; AAYN TAIBA, the good fountain; GEBEL OOMAR, the mountain of Omar; RAS EL TAFAL, Chalk Cape. In the neighbouring isle of Gozo we find the

---

[1] Amari, *Storia dei Musulmani,* vol. ii. p. 435.
[2] Amari, *Storia dei Musulmani,* vol. ii. p. 435.
[3] The local names of Sicily, as illustrating the *nationality of the tribes* by which the conquest was effected, have been investigated by Amari, *Storia dei Musulmani di Sicilia,* vol. ii. pp. 31–36.
[4] Amari, *Musulmani,* vol. ii. p. 35.
[5] An exhaustive enumeration and explanation of the names in Malta is to be found in a work called *Malta Illustrata, Ovvero descrizione di Malta con sue antichità, ed altre notizie,* by F. Giovanfrancesco Abela, vol. i. pp. 231–369.

Arabic village-names of NADUR, ZEBBEY, GARBO, SANNAT, and XEUCHIA. Among the peasants of Malta and Gozo a corrupt Arabic *patois* still holds its ground against the Lingua Franca, the Italian, and the English which threaten to supplant it.[1]

Of the island of Pantellaria the Duke of Buckingham says, 'the language spoken is a bad Italian, mixed up with a bastard Arabic. All the names of places, headlands, and points are pure Arabic, and every hill is called ghibel something'. [2]

In no part of Europe do we find such abundant vestiges of the Arab conquest as in Spain and Portugal. The long duration of the Arab rule—nearly eight centuries—is attested by the immense number of Arabic local names, as compared with the dozen or half-dozen that we find in Italy, France, or Sardinia, whence they were soon expelled.

The very names of the first invaders are conserved in local memorials. In September, A.D. 710, Tarif-Abú-Zar'ah, a Berber freed-man, effected a landing at a place which has ever since been called after him—TARIFA. He was quickly followed by Tarik-Ibn-Zeyad,[3] a liberated Persian slave, who, at the head of a body of light horsemen, advanced, in a few weeks, some seven hundred miles across the peninsula, as far as the Bay of Biscay. This bold chieftain landed in the Bay of Algeziras,[4] and he has left his name on the neighbouring rock of GIBRALTAR, which is a corruption of the Arabic name Gebel-al-Tarik, the 'Mountain of Tarik'.

The accompanying sketch-map will serve to give a rough notion of the distribution of the Arabic names upon the map

---

[1] See Tallack's *Malta*, p. 246. It has been asserted by Michaelis, Majus, and other writers, that the Maltese dialect contains many punic words, and contains traces of Punic grammar. This is denied by Gesenius. See his *Versuch über die Maltesische Sprache zur Beurtheilung der neulich wiederhohlten Behauptung dass sie ein Ueberrest der Altpunischen scy.* He allows that there are many Berber or *Moorish* words mingled with the Arabic, but none clearly to be referred to the time of the Carthaginian conquest. The same conclusion, substantially, is arrived at by Kosegarten, in Höfer's *Zeitschrift*, vol. ii. pp. 1, 30, and by Renan, *Langues Sémitiques*, pt. i. p. 413.

[2] *Private Diary*, vol. ii. p. 139.

[3] Mariana and Conde assert the identity of these two chieftains, but the latest and best authority on the subject, Reinaud, in his *Invasion des Sarazins*, pp. 432, 433, has vindicated the accuracy of Gibbon, and has conclusively shown that Tarif and Tarik were separate personages. See also Gayangos, vol. i. pp. 264–289, 318, 517 ; Sayer, *Hist. of Gibraltar*, pp. 5, 6 ; Murphy, *Mahometan Empire*, pp. 53–59 ; Conde, *Dominacion*, pp. 14, 15 ; Pihan, *Glossaire*, p. 137.

[4] ALGEZIRAS means 'the island'. By the Arabic chroniclers it is called Jezirah al-Khadhra, 'the green island'. Gayangos, vol. i. pp. 317, 517 ; Prescott, *Ferdinand and Isabella*, vol. i. p. 398 ; Sayer, *Hist. of Gibraltar*, p. 8. ALGIERS is a corruption of the same name, Al Jezirah, a name which has also been given to Mesopotamia—the peninsula between the Tigris and the Euphrates.

of Spain. Unfortunately, owing to the smallness of the scale, it has been impossible to indicate the position of more than a proportion of the names.

These local linguistic monuments make it easy for us to distinguish those districts where the Arab population was most dense. The Arabic names are seen to cluster thickly

DISTRIBUTION OF ARABIC NAMES IN SPAIN AND PORTUGAL.

round Lisbon and Valentia; and in the neighbourhood of Seville, Malaga, and Granada,[1] the last strongholds of the

[1] Contrary to what might have been supposed, we find that the Arabic names in the immediate vicinity of Granada are relatively less numerous than in some other places, as the neighbourhoods of Valencia and Seville. This is probably due to the forced eviction of the inhabitants of Granada under Ferdinand and Isabella, and the wholesale substitution of a large Christian population; whereas in the case of earlier conquests, the Arab population, being allowed to remain till gradually absorbed, succeeded in transmitting the great number of the local names.

Moslem kingdom, they are also very numerous ; but as we approach the Pyrenees, and the mountains of Galicia and the Asturias, these vestiges of Moslem rule entirely disappear, and are replaced by names derived from the Basque, Celtic, and Spanish languages.

An obvious feature which characterizes the local nomenclature of Spain and Portugal, is the prevalence of the Arabic definite article *al*, which is prefixed to a very large proportion of names, such as Alicant, Albuera, Almanza, Alcala, Almarez, Almeida, Alhambra, and Algoa. On the maps of the Peninsula published by the Useful Knowledge Society, there appear about two hundred and fifty names containing this prefix. Of these sixty-four per cent. are found to the south of the Tagus, and only thirty-six per cent. to the north of that river.

The Spanish river-names beginning with Guad are very numerous. In Palestine and Arabia this word appears in the form *wadî*,[1] a ' ravine', and hence a ' river '. The name of the GUADALQUIVIR is a corruption of Wadi-l-Kebîr, the great river—a name which is found also in Arabia. We have also the river-names GUADALCAZAR, which is Wadi-l-Kasr, the river of the palace ; GUADALHORRA, from Wadi-lghar, the river of the cave ; GUADARRANKE, from Wadi-lramak, the mare's river ; GUADALQUITON, from Wadi-l-kitt, the cat river,[2] GUADALAXARA, from Wadi-l-hajarah, the river of the stones ; GUAROMAN, from Wadi-r-roman, the river of the pomegranate-trees ; GUADALAVIAR, from Wadi-labyadh, the white river ; GUADALUPE, the river of the bay ; GUALBACAR, the ox river ; GUADALIMAR, the red river ; GUADARAMA, the sandy river ; GUADALADIAR, the river of houses ; and the more doubtful names of GUADAIRA, the river of mills ; GUADALERTIN, the muddy river ; and GUADALBANAR, the river of the battle-field. We have also the GUADIANA and the GUADALETE, which embody the ancient names of the Anas [3] and the Lethe.[4]

---

[1] This word appears to have been adopted by the Greeks, and corrupted into the form ὄασις. [No—it is the Coptic *ouahe*.] Renan, *Lang. Sémit.* pt. i. p. 205. Cf. Peyron, *Lexicon Copt.*, p. 160.

[2] [More probably ' the little river '.]

[3] The name of the Anas is Phœnician according to Bochart, vol. iii. p. 627, but it is capable of a Celtic etymon.

[4] We find also the rivers Guadafion, Guadehenar, Guadajor, Guadalbarro, Guadalbullon, Guadalcana, Guadalerce, Guadalertin, Guadaleste, Guadalmallete, Guadalmedina, Guadalmelera, Guaderriza, Guedaxira, Guadazamon, Guadazelete, Guadacenas, Guadetefra, Guadarmena, Guadalfeo, Guadalmez, Guadalcalon, and others, the names of which are elucidated with more or less success by Gayangos, Weston, and De Sousa.

The name of MEDINA, which means ' city', appears not only
in Arabia [1] and Senegambia, but also five times in Spain.[2]
The word *kal'ah*, a castle, which we have traced in Sicily and
Malta, is found in CALATAYUD, ' Job's castle', [3] in Aragon ;
CALAHORRA, the ' fort of stones ',[4] in Old Castile ; and CALA-
TRAVA, the ' Castle of Rabah', [5] in New Castile. There are
also half a dozen places called ALCALA, which is the same word
with the definite article prefixed.

Such names as BENAVITES, BENIAJAR, BENARRABA, BENI-
CALAF, BENIAUX, BENTARIQUE, and BENADADID, may embody
curious information as to the names of the original Arab settlers,
for the first syllable of such names is the patronymic Beni,
' sons', and the remainder is a personal or tribal appellation.[6]

But the great mass of Hispano-Arabic names are descriptive
terms, relating to the artificial or natural features of the country. Such are the names ALBORGE, the turret ; ALBUFEIRA,
the lake ; [7] ALMEIDA, the table ; ALCACOVA, the fortress (a common name) ; ALMANZA, the plain ; [8] ALPUXARRAS, the ' grassy '
mountains ; [9] ALMENA,[10] the battlemented tower ; ALMAZEN,
the storehouse ;[11] ALMADEN,[12] the mine ; ALHAMBRA, the red,[13]
ALGARBE, the west ; [14] ARRECIFE, the causeway ;[15] ALMAZARA
the mill ; [16] ALCAZAR, the palace ; ALDEA, the village ; ALCANA,
the exchange ; [17] ALCANTARA, the bridge ; [18] ALQUERIA, or

---

[1] Yathrib, the city to which Mohammed fled from Mecca, bore thenceforward the
name of Medinet-ennabi, the city of the prophet. Caussin de Perceval, *Histoire des
Arabes*, vol. iii. p. 21.
[2] Medinaceli, Medina Sidonia, etc. Pihan, p. 200 ; Prescott, *Ferd. and Isab.* vol. i.
p. 398.
[3] Built by the chieftain Ayub, or Job, who took a foremost part in the conquest,
and was afterwards Governor of Spain. Conde, *Dominacion*, pp. 30–33 ; Gayangos,
vol. i. p. 373 ; Weston, *Remains of Arabic in the Spanish and Portuguese Languages*,
p. 143 ; De Sousa, *Vestigios da Lingua Arabica em Portugal*, p. 4.
[4] Weston, p. 145.
[5] Gayangos, vol. ii. p. 356. Cf. Weston, p. 146.
[6] On the inferences to be drawn from Spanish names as to the nationalities of the
Moslem settlers, see Gayangos, vol. i. p. 356 ; vol. ii. pp. 20–29, 402, 403, 442. On the
prefix *Beni*, see Wilton, *Negeb*, p. 140.
[7] A corruption of *Al-buheyrah*. Gayangos, vol. i. p. 374.
[8] Gayangos, vol. i. p. 354 ; vol. ii. p. 515 ; Charnock, *Loc. Etym.* p. 28.
[9] Prescott, *Ferd. and Isab.* p. 398.
[10] From the same root comes the word *minaret*. Weston, p. 61.
[11] From the same root comes the word *magazine*. De Sousa, p. 45 ; Charnock, *Loc.
Etym.* p. 8 ; Weston, p. 60 ; Engelmann, *Glossaire*, p. 52.
[12] The greatest quicksilver mine in Europe. Engelmann, p. 47.
[13] De Sousa, p. 38 ; Weston, p. 54 ; Pihan, p. 31 ; Murphy, *Mahometan Empire in
Spain*, p. 191.
[14] De Sousa, p. 35 ; Weston, p. 53 ; Pihan, p. 29 ; Conde, *Dominacion*, p. 671.
[15] Prescott, *Ferd. and Isab.* p. 398 ; Engelmann, p. 62.
[16] Gayangos, vol. ii. p. 541.
[17] From the same root come *dogana* and *douane*. Pihan, p. 113 ; Weston, p. 45.
[18] Pihan, p. 24 ; De Sousa, p. 22 ; Gayangos, vol. i. pp. 61, 370 ; Weston, p. 44.

ALCARRIA, the farm ; [1] and TRAFALGAR (*Taraf al-ghar*), the promontory of the cave.[2]

A large number of Hispano-Arabic names are illustrated in Weston's ' Remains of Arabic in the Spanish and Portuguese languages', and in Pihan's ' Glossaire des Mots Français tirés de l'Arabe, du Persan, et du Turc'. A competent and exhaustive investigation of these names has, as far as I am aware, never been attempted ; and it would, undoubtedly, supply materials of great value to the historian of the conquest. The Arabic names in Portugal have been well discussed by Fr. Joaõ de Sousa, in a work entitled, ' Vestigios da Lingua Arabica em Portugal '.[3]

Flushed by the ease and rapidity of their Spanish conquest, the Arabs crossed the Pyrenees, and spread their locust swarms over the southern and central regions of France, as far as Tours. In the neighbourhood of this city, in the year 732, Charles Martel gained one of the great decisive battles which have changed the current of the world's history, and the almost total destruction of the Moslem host rescued western Christianity from the ruin which seemed to be impending. After this event the fugitives seem to have retired into Provence, where they maintained a precarious sovereignty for some thirty years.

In the Department of the Basses Pyrénées we find some vestiges of these refugees. At Oloron, a town not far from Pau, is a fountain called LA HOUN (*ain*) DEOUS MOUROUS, or the fountain of the Moors ; and in a neighbouring village, which bears the name of MOUMOUR, or Mons Mauri, there stands a ruined tower called LA TOUR DES MAURES.[4]

FONTARABIE, in the Department of the Charente Inférieure, marks a kind of oasis in the sandy desert of the Landes, and, like Fontarabia on the Bidassoa, may have been a station of the Arabs.[5]

In the *patois* of south-eastern France there are several

---

[1] Gayangos, vol. i. p. 353 ; Conde, p. 671 ; Engelmann, p. 23.

[2] See p. 72, *supra* ; and Gayangos, vol. i. p. 320.

[3] On Spanish words of Arabic origin, see Diez, *Gram. d. Rom. Spr.* vol. i. pp. 70. 333 ; Gayangos, *History of the Mohammedan Dynasties in Spain*, vol. ii. pp. xxxvi. clxix. clxx. ; and vol. i. p. 487 ; and Engelmann, *Glossaire des Mots Espagnols et Portaugis dérivés de l'Arabe*, whose lists contain about 400 Spanish and Portuguese words derived from the Arabic.

[4] Michel, *Hist. des Races Maudites*, vol. ii. p. 98.

[5] In this latter case much may be said in favour of the etymology Fuente Rabia —Fons Rabidus, or rapidus. Salverte, *Essai sur les Noms*, vol. ii. p. 264.

words of Arabic origin,[1] while down to the seventeenth century, many families of Languedoc, descended from these Moors, bore the name of 'Marranes'. In Auvergne also there is a pariah race called Marrons, whose conversion to Christianity has given the French language the term *marrane*, 'a renegade'.[2]

After an interval of more than a century, the Moorish pirates, who had long infested the coast of Provence, established themselves in the stronghold of Fraxinet, near Frejus (A.D. 889), and held in subjection a large part of Provence and Dauphiny. The FORÊT DES MAURES, near Frejus, is called after them ; and the names of PUY MAURE and MONT MAURE, near Gap, of the COL DE MAURE, near Château Dauphin, and of the whole county of the MAURIENNE, in Savoy, are witnesses of the rule in France [3] of these Moorish conquerors.

In the tenth century the Moors still held the Maurienne, and in the year 911, by a convention with Count Hugo of Provence, they crossed the Cottian Alps, and took possession of the passes of the Pennine chain, which they guarded for Count Hugo's benefit, while they levied blackmail on travellers for their own. In the years 921 and 923, and again in 929, the chroniclers record that English pilgrims, proceeding to Rome, were attacked by Saracens while crossing the Alps. The bishops of York, Winchester, Hereford, and Wells were among those who thus suffered.[4] In the year 973 St. Majolus, Abbot of Cluny, was taken prisoner by these marauders at Orsières, on the pass of the Great St. Bernard, and he could only obtain his freedom by the payment of a ransom, which consisted of a thousand pounds' weight of the church plate of Cluny.[5]

Such are the few meagre historical facts relating to the Arabs in the Alps which we are able to glean from mediaeval chroniclers ; fortunately, it is possible to supplement our knowledge by the information which has been conserved in

---

[1] A list will be found in Astruc, *Hist. Nat. de Languedoc*, pp. 494–497.
[2] Michel, *Races Maudites*, vol. ii. pp. 45, 96.
[3] On the subject of the Moors in France, see Reinaud, *Invasion des Sarazins en France*, passim ; Bouche, *Histoire de Provence*, vol. i. pp. 101, 204 ; Palgrave, *Normandy and England*, vol. i. p. 416 ; Bianchi-Giovini, *Dominazione degli Arabi*, pp. 25, 26 ; Gayangos, vol. i. p. 228 ; Wenrich, *Rer. ab Arab. gest.* pp. 123, 144–146 ; Papon, *Histoire de Provence*, vol. ii. pp. 77, 146, 165.
[4] The capture of S. Elphege is related by Osbern, *Vit. S. Elpheg.* apud Thrupp, *Anglo-Saxon Home*, p. 247. Cf. St. John, *Four Conquests of England*, vol. i. p. 326.
[5] Reinaud, *Invasion des Sarazins en France*, p. 166 ; Wenrich, *Rer. Arab.* p. 147.

local names. The mountain to the east of the hospice on the Great St. Bernard bears the name of MONT MORT, which there is reason for believing to be a corruption of Mont Maure. If this name stood alone, we might hardly feel ourselves justified in connecting it with the local traditions which refer to the Arabs in the Alps. We find, however, that the name MONTE MORO, the ' Moor's Mountain', is attached to another pass which was much frequented in early times,[1] before the great roads of the St. Gothard, the Simplon, and the Splügen had been constructed. Though no direct historical evidence of the fact exists, it seems impossible not to believe that this pass of the Monte Moro must have been held by these ' Saracens', or ' Moors '.

In the first place, we find that a strong position, which commands the passage up the Val Anzasca on the Italian side of the pass, is called CALASCA—a name which is apparently derived from the Arabic *kal'ah*, a castle, which occurs in the Alcalas and Calatas of Spain and Sicily. The peak opposite Calasca is called PIZ DEL MORO. On the other side of the valley is the CIMA DEL MORO, beneath which lies the hamlet of MORGHEN. Crossing the Moro pass, the first hamlet we arrive at is placed on a mountain spur or terrace, which commands the view both up and down the valley. This place is called ALMAGEL, which, on the hypothesis of an Arab occupation, would be a most appropriate name, since *al mahal* denotes in Arabic ' the station ', or ' the halting-place '. A high grassy mound, probably the terminal moraine of an ancient glacier, is called the TELLIBODEN, the first syllable of which name seems to be the Arabic word *tell*, a round hill. The neighbouring pasture goes by the name of the MATMARK, the ancient form of which was Matmar, or the ' Moor's Meadow'. Close by is another pasture called the EYEN—a name which is pronounced in exactly the same way as the Arabic *aïn*, a ' fountain', or ' source of waters '—a very opposite description, as will be admitted by all those Alpine tourists who, before the recent construction of a road, have splashed across it, ankle deep, for some hundred yards.

---

[1] A paved Roman road exists beneath the snows of the Monte Moro. In the sixteenth and seventeenth centuries a great permanent extension of the Nevé took place in the neighbourhood of Monte Rosa, which has brought the summit of the Moro above the summer snow-line, and rendered the Moro impassable for mules. Lyell, *Antiq. of Man*, p. 292 ; Murray, *Handbook for Switzerland*, p. 290.

Passing the DISTEL Alp—a doubtful Arabic name—we find the valley completely barred by an enormous glacier. This is called the ALALEIN Glacier, and the Arabic interpretation of the name, *Alâ'l aïn*, or 'Over the source', gives a most graphic picture of the precipitous wall of ice, with the torrent of the Visp rushing from the vast cavern in its side.

Opposite Almagel, and a little to the north of the Alalein Glacier, are the MISCHABEL HÖRNER, three peaks, the midmost of which, the Dom, is the loftiest summit in Switzerland.[1] The latter part of the name Mi-schabel is pronounced almost exactly in the same way as the Arabic *gebel*, a mountain. The genius of the Arabic language would, however, require *gebel* to be a prefix rather than a suffix, but it is quite possible that Mischabel may be a hybrid formation, akin to Mongibello in Sicily.[2] Or we may derive the name from the Arabic word, *migbâl*, which means, according to Freytag, 'crassus, ut mons'. The conquerors of the East, we may well believe, brought with them the word dome, which Jerome tells us was, in Palestine and Egypt, the universal designation of a house roof.[3]

The northern outlier of the Mischabel range is called the BALFRAIN, a name whose Arabic interpretation—'the peak with two river sources'—describes the twin glaciers which hang from the flanks of the mountain, and send their tributary streams to join the Visp.[4]

It is probable that the etymologies assigned to some of these names may be fallacious, but the cases are too numerous, and the accordances with the physical features of the spot are too precise, to allow us to explain them away altogether by any hypothesis of accidental coincidence of sound ; and, therefore, though we may not be able to find any historical evidence whatever that the Moro was one of those passes which were occupied by Count Hugo's Moors, yet it seems impossible not to believe, on the evidence of the names alone, that the present inhabitants of the Saas Valley are descended from the marauders from the Maurienne.

The third of the passes which in ancient times formed the

---

[1] Mont Blanc is in France—Monte Rosa partly in Italy.
[2] See p. 70, *supra*.
[3] See Ducange sub voc. Vol. ii. p. 901. [But it is merely from the Latin *domus*.]
[4] In the neighbourhood we find the names Jazi, Fee, Saas, Balen, and others, which may possibly be traceable to Arabic roots.

chief communication between Italy and the North, was that which connects the Lake of Como with the Engadine. This, also, if would seem, was occupied by the Arabs. Near the summits of the St. Bernard and of the Moro we have the Mont Mort and the Piz del Moro ; and so, near the summit of the Maloja and MURETTO passes we have the PIZ MURETTO, the PIZ MORTIRATSCH, and the PIZ MORTER. Descending the pass on the northern side, we come to a very ancient stone bridge of one arch, springing from rock to rock across a narrow chasm. This place is called PONTRESINA, which seems to be a corruption of Ponte Saracina, the Saracens' bridge. The village of Pontresina is composed of solid stone houses, Spanish rather than Swiss in their appearance. Five minutes' walk from the village, we come to an ancient five-sided stone tower called SPANIOLA. In documents of the twelfth and fourteenth centuries we find mention of families inhabiting this valley bearing the names De Ponte Sarisino, Sarracino, Sarazeno, and the like. Saratz is still a very common surname in the district, and those bearing it claim descent from the Saracens, and possess a marked oriental type of feature.[1] A Herr Saratz is now [1865] president of the Gotthaus Bund, Eastern division of the Grisons.

In the neighbourhood of Pontresina there are several names apparently of Arabic origin, such as SAMADEN, ALVENEN, ALBIGNA, TARASP, AL-VASCHEIN, MAD-UL-EIN, and the Val AIN-AS. The river which flows from the Maloja on the Italian side is called the MAIRA. Near the Swiss frontier a barrier of *roches moutonées* blocks up this valley so completely that it has been necessary to excavate a considerable tunnel through the rock to admit of the passage of the road. On the summit of this admirable defensive position stands a ruined castle, which goes by the name of Castel MURO, and an ancient building by the side of the castle exhibits certain Saracenic features which are in striking contrast with the Italian architecture around.[2]

To the west of Pontresina is the SCALETTA pass, which leads to the valley of the Upper Rhine. A local tradition affirms that the Scaletta owes its name to the bleaching *skeletons*

---

[1] Lechner, *Piz Languard,* pp. 12, 13. There are also at Bergamo families called Saratz.

[2] In the summer of 1862 I made diligent inquiries of the peasantry in the neighbourhood of Castel Muro, but could discover no traditions of Saracenic occupation resembling those which are current at Pontresina.

W.P.   G

of a band of marauding Moors from Pontresina, who were defeated by the men of Chur, and whose corpses were left strewn over the mountain side where they fell in the attempted flight across the pass. The encounter is supposed to have taken place at the foot of the pass, on the western side, where there is a pasture which still goes by the name of KRIEGS-MATTEN, the 'battle field'. Whether there be truth in this tradition or not,[1] it testifies to the popular belief in the existence of a Moorish colony in the valleys of the Bernina, and it harmonizes well with the curious evidence supplied by the still existing local names.[2]

[1] More probably the Scaletta is the 'Staircase' pass.
[2] On the subject of the Moors in Switzerland, see Engelhardt, *Das Monte Rosa und Matterhorn Gebirg* ; Lechner, *Piz Languard*, pp. 12, 13 ; Reinaud, *Invasion des Sarazins* ; Wenrich, *Rerum ab Arabibus gestarum Commentarii* ; Stanley, *Sinai and Palestine*, p. 15.

CHAPTER VII

THE ANGLO-SAXONS

England is the land of inclosures—This denoted by the character of Anglo-Saxon Names which end in ' ton', ' yard', ' worth', ' fold', ' hay,' and ' bury '—Ham, the home—The Patronymic 'ing'—Teutonic clans —Saxon colony near Boulogne—Saxon settlement in England began before the departure of the Romans—Early Frisian settlement in Yorkshire —Litus Saxonicum near Caen—German village-names in France and in Italy—Patronymics in Westphalia, Franconia, and Swabia—Seat of the ' Old-Saxons '

ENGLAND is pre-eminently the land of hedges and inclosures. On a visit to the Continent almost the first thing the tourist notices is the absence of the hedgerows in England. The fields, nay even the farms, are bounded only by a furrow. The bare shoulders of the hills offend an eye familiar with the picturesque wooded skyline of English landscape, the rectangular strips of cultivation are intolerable, and the interminable monotony of the plains, varied only by the straight rows of formal poplars which stretch for miles and miles by the side of the *chaussée*, is inexpressibly wearisome to those who have been accustomed to quaint, irregular crofts, and tall, straggling hedgerows, twined with clematis and honeysuckle—

' *Little lines of sportive wood run wild*',

overshadowed here and there by gnarled oaks and giant elms.

And if we compare the local names in England with those on the Continent, we shall find that for more than a thousand years England has been distinctively and pre-eminently the land of inclosures. The suffixes which occur most frequently in Anglo-Saxon names denote an inclosure of some kind— something hedged, walled in, or protected. An examination of these names shows us that the love of privacy, and the seclusiveness of character which is so often laid to the charge of Englishmen, prevailed in full force among the races which imposed names upon our English villages.[1] Those universally recurring terminations *ton, ham,*[2] *worth, stoke, fold, garth, park, burgh, bury, brough, borrow,* all convey the notion of inclosure or protection. The prevalence of these suffixes in English names proves also how intensely the nation was imbued with the principle of the sacred nature of property,[3] and how eager every man was to possess some spot which he could call his own, and guard from the intrusion of every other man. Even among those portions of the Teutonic race which remained on the Continent, we do not find that this idea of private right has been manifested in local names to the same extent as in England. The feeling, seems, indeed, to have been more or less enchorial, for we find strong indications of it even in the pure Celtic names of Britain. Probably more than one half of the Celtic names in Wales and Ireland contain the roots *llan, kil* or *bally,* all of which originally denoted an inclosure of some kind. The Teutonic suffixes which do not denote inclosures, such as *gau, dorf, leben, hausen, stadt,* and *stein,* all so numerous in Germany, are not reproduced in England to anything like the same extent as on the Continent. It would seem, therefore, that the love of inclosure is due more or less to the Celts who were gradually absorbed among the Saxon colonists.

The suffix *ton* constitutes a sort of test-word by which we are enabled to discriminate the Anglo-Saxon settlements. It is the most common termination of English local names ; and although it is a true Teutonic word, yet there is scarcely a single instance of its occurrence throughout the whole of Germany.[4] It appears in two small Anglo-Saxon settlements on the French coast,[5] and it is found not unfrequently in Sweden[6]—a fact which may lead to the establishment of a

---

[1] This characteristic of the Teutonic race did not escape the acute observation of Tacitus. Colunt discreti ac diversi, ut fons, ut campus, ut nemus placuit. Vicos locant, non in nostrum morem connexis et cohærentibus ædificiis : suam quisque domum spatio circumdat. *Germania,* t, 16.

[2] The overwhelming number of surnames derived from these local suffixes is witnessed by the saw preserved by Verstegan :—
     In Foord, in Ham, in Ley, in Tun,
     The most of English surnames run.
           Restitution of Decayed Intelligence, p. 326.

[3] See Leo, *Anglo-Saxon Names,* p. 71.

[4] We have, however, Altona, near Hamburg, and Ost- and West-tönne in Westphalia.

[5] e.g. Colincthun, Alencthun, and Todincthun. See p. 93 ; and Appendix B.

[6] e.g. Eskilstuna, Sollentuna, Wallentuna, Sigtuna, and Frotuna. See Bender, *Ortsnamen,* pp. 54, 13ᵉ ; Förstemann, *Altdeutsches Namenbuch,* vol. ii. p. 1414 ; Pott, *Personen-Namen,* p. 76.

connexion, hitherto unsuspected, between the Anglo-Saxon Colonists of England and the tribes which peopled eastern Scandinavia.[1]

The primary meaning of the suffix *ton* is to be sought in the Gothic *tains*,[2] the old Norse *teinn*, and the Frisian *têne*, all of which mean a twig—a radical signification which survives in the prase ' the *tine* of a fork'. We speak also of the *tines* of a stag's horns. In modern German we find the word Zaun, a hedge, and in Anglo-Saxon we have the verb *tynan*, to hedge. Hence a *tun*, or *ton*, was a place surrounded by a hedge, or rudely fortified by a palisade.[3] Originally it meant only a single croft, homestead, or farm, and the word retained this restricted meaning in the time of Wicliffe. He translates Matt. xxii. 5, ' But thei dispiseden, and wenten forth, oon into his toun (ἀγρός), another to his marchaundise'. This usage is retained in Scotland, where a solitary farmstead still goes by the name of the *toun*; and in Iceland, where the homestead, with its girding wall, is called a *tùn*.[4] In many parts of England the rickyard is called the bar*ton* [5]—that is, the inclosure for the *bear*, or crop which the land bears. There are lone farmhouses in Kent called Shottington, Wingleton, Godington, and Appleton. But in most cases the isolated *ton* became the nucleus of a village, and the village grew into a *town*, and, last stage of all, the word TOWN has come to denote, not the one small croft inclosed from the forest by the Saxon settler, but the dwelling-place of a vast population, twice as great as that which the whole of Saxon England could boast.[6]

The Anglo-Saxon *yard*, and the Norse equivalent *garth*, contain nearly the same idea as *ton*. Both denote some place

[1] Sweden takes its name from the Suiones who peopled it. The Suiones are probably identical with the Suevi or Swabians who, as will be shown, contributed largely to the Teutonic colonization of England.

[2] [Rather in the old Keltic *dun*, a strong-hold; no connexion with the words here suggested.] The root is widely diffused through the Aryan languages. Compare the Sclavonic *tuin*, a hedge, and even the Armenian *tun*, a house. See Diefenbach, *Vergleichendes Wörterbuch*, vol. ii. pp. 653, 654 ; Monkhouse, *Etymologies*, p. 13 ; Kemble, *Codex Diplom.* vol. iii. p. xxxix.; Leo, *Anglo-Saxon Names*, pp. 31–37; Mone, *Geschichte Heidenthums*, vol. ii. p. 95.

[3] The phrase ' hedging and tining ', for hedging and ditching, was current two hundred years ago. Verstegan, *Restitution*, p. 326. Brushwood, used for hedging, is called *tineium* in law Latin. Cowel, *Law Dictionary*, sub voce *Tinet*; Bailey, *Dictionary*, sub voce *Tinetum*.

[4] Dufferin, *Letters from High Latitudes*, p. 46 ; Dasent, in *Oxford Essays* for 1858, p. 203.

[5] In Iceland the *bærtun*. There are some sixty villages in England called Barton or Burton ; these must have originally been only outlying rickyards. [An enclosure for *bere* or barley.]

[6] It appears from Domesday that the population of Saxon England was about a m llion and a half. Turner, *Anglo-Saxons*, vol. iii. p. 256.

girded round, or guarded. The word *tains*, a twig, stands in the same etymological relation to *ton* as the old English word *yerde*,[1] a switch or rod, does to *yard, garth*, and *garden*.[2] The inclosure is named from the nature of the surrounding fence.

The same may be said respecting *stoke*, another common suffix, which we find in BASINGSTOKE and ALVERSTOKE. A *stoke* is a place *stock*aded, surrounded with *stocks* or piles. A somewhat similar inclosure is denoted by the suffix *fold*.[3] This was a stall or place constructed of *felled* trees, for the protection of cattle or sheep. [These words are not connected. See *infra*, p.112.]

The Anglo-Saxon *weorthig*, which appears in English names in the form of *worth*, bears a meaning nearly the same as that of *ton* or *garth*. It denotes a place *warded*, or protected.[4] It was, probably, an inclosed homestead for the churls, subordinate to the *tun*. We find this suffix in the names of BOSWORTH, TAMWORTH, KENILWORTH, WALWORTH, WANDSWORTH, and many other places. [*Worth* is properly a holding or property, akin to A.S. *weorth*, value—Skeat, *Place Names of Cambridge*, 25.]

A *haigh*, or *hay*, is a place surrounded by a hedge, and appears to have been usually an inclosure for the purposes of the chase. We find it in ROTHWELL HAIGH, near Leeds; HAYE PARK, at Knaresborough; and HORSEHAY, near Colebrookdale.[5] The word *park*, which is of kindred meaning, seems to have

---

[1] In old English a *yerde* means a rod. ' Yet under the yerde was the maide '.—Chaucer, *Shipmannes Tale*. A yard measure is a wand of a fixed length. The yards of a ship are the poles on which the sails are extended. Cf. the German *gerte*, and the Anglo-Saxon *gerd*. The Goths and Franks seem to have introduced the word *jardin* into the French, Spanish, and Italian languages. Of cognate origin are the Albanian *gërdine*, the Servian *gràdena*, the Russian *gorod* and *grad*, and the Persian *gird*, a city or fortified town. Diez, *Etymolog. Wörterb.* p. 173; Diefenbach, *Vergleichendes Wörterb.* vol. ii. p. 376; Sparschuh, *Berichtigungen*, p. 53; Pictet, *Orig. Indo-Europ.* part ii. p. 265.

[2] [Neither of these pairs are etymologically connected, see Skeat, *s.v.v*, notwithstanding the analogies of *rod, pole, perch* and *virgate* (from L. *virga*, a rod).]

[3] Anglo-Saxon *falod*. [i.e. ' planked ' (enclosure) from A. S. *fala*, a plank.]

[4] From the Anglo-Saxon *warian*, to ward or defend. Kemble, *Codex Diplom.* vol. iii. p. xli.; Leo, *Anglo-Saxon Names*, p. 59. A *weir*, which wards off the waters of a river, is from the same root. Wedgwood derives *worth* from the Welsh *gwyrdd*, green. *Philolog. Proc.* vol. iv. p. 260. But more probably both *gwyrdd* and *worth* are sister words, coming from a common Aryan source. Compare the Sanskrit *vri*, to protect, and the Zend *vara*, a place hedged round. Pictet, *Orig. Indo-Europ.* part ii. p. 80.

[5] The HAGUE (correctly Gravenhage, the count's hedge) was originally a hunting-seat of the Orange princes. Cf. the Dutch *haag*, an inclosure; the old High German *hag*, a town; the German *hagen*, to hedge; the French *haie*, a hedge; and the English *ha-ha*, and *haw*-thorn, or hedge-thorn. Haia is a term often used in Domesday. The source seems to be the Sanskrit *kakscha*, which means ' bush ' and also a ' fence '. See

been adopted by the Saxons from the Celtic *parwg*, an inclosed field.[1]

Related to the Anglo-Saxon verb *beorgan*, and the German *bergen*, to shelter or hide, [2] are the suffixes *bury, borough, burgh, brough*, and *barrow*. Sometimes these words denote the funeral mound which gave shelter to the remains of the dead, but more frequently they mean the walled inclosure which afforded refuge to the living. Since such walled places were often on the crests of hills, the word came to mean a hill-fortress, corresponding to the Celtic *dun*. In Anglo-Saxon a distinction was made between *beorh*, which answers to the German *berg*, a hill, and *buruh*, which is the equivalent of the German *burg*, a town. This distinctive usage is lost in modern English. The word *Barrow*, [3] however, is generally confined to funeral mounds. *Burgh*, and *Brough*,[4] are Anglian and Norse, as are, probably, four-fifths of the *boroughs*,[5] while *bury* is the distinctively Saxon form.[6]

The suffix, *ham*, which is very frequent in English names, appears in two forms in Anglo-Saxon documents. One of these, *hăm*,[7] signifies an inclosure, that which hems in [8] —a meaning not very different from that of *ton* or *worth*. These words express the feeling of reverence for private right, but *hām* involves a notion more mystical, more holy.

Diez, *Etym. Wörterb*, p. 656, Leo, *Rectitudines*, p. 54 ; Förstemann, *Ortsnamen*, p. 57 ; Ellis, *Introduction to Domesday*, p. xxxvi. The suffixes *hagen* and *hain* are common in Hesse. Vilmar, *Ortsnamen*, p. 269.

[1] The word *park* is common to all the Celtic and Romance languages. See Diez, *Etym. Wörterb*. p. 252 ; Kemble, *Codex Diplom*. vol. iii. p. xxxv. ; Diefenbach, *Celtica*, p. 167 ; and Diefenbach, *Vergleichendes Wörterbuch*, vol. i. p. 265, where the etymological affinities of *park* and *borough* are discussed.

[2] Compare the phrases to burrow in the earth ; to borrow, i.e. to obtain goods on security ; to bury, i.e. to hide in the earth ; the bark of a tree is that which hides or covers the trunk [?]. The etymology of borough may be compared with that of the Latin *oppidum*, the work [?]. Mommsen, *Hist. of Rome*, vol. i. p. 39.

[3] e.g. Inglebarrow.   [4] e.g. Jedburgh, Broughton, Brough.

[5] e.g. Peterborough, Scarborough, Marlborough.

[6] This widely diffused Aryan root appears to have been introduced from the Teutonic into the Romance languages. To it we may refer Burgos, Bergamo, Cherbourg, Luxembourg, Perga, Pergamos, and scores of other names spread over Europe and Asia. Gothic *baurgs*, Greek πύργος, Macedonian βύργος. Even the Arabs borrowed *burg*, a fortress, from the Goths. See Diefenbach, *Verg. Wört*. vol. i. pp. 262–265 ; Diez, *Rom. Gram*. vol. i. p. 9 ; Pictet, *Orig. Indo-Eur*, vol. ii. p. 194 ; Kemble, *Codex Diplom*. vol. iii. p. xix. ; Hartshorne, *Salopia Antiqua*, pp. 245–247 ; Sparschuh, *Bericht*. pp. 40, 52.

[7] This is, for the most part, the source of the Frisian suffix *um*, which fringes the coast-line of Hanover and Oldenburgh. In Brunswick and Wolfenbüttel we find Born-*um*, *Eilum*, etc. It occurs in Holstein and part of Sleswic, in the Danish islands Sylt and Föhr, and in the Frisian colony in Yorkshire. See p. 98, *infra*. Latham, *English Lang*. vol. i. pp. 125–130 ; *Ethnol. Brit. Is.* p. 182. The suffix *um* is sometimes only the sign of the dative plural.

[8] Several Bedfordshire villages, as Felmersham, Biddenham, and Blunham, which are almost surrounded by the serpentine windings of the Ouse, exhibit this suffix. See Monkhouse, *Etymologies*, pp. 8–11.

It expresses the sanctity of the family bond ; it is the HOME,[1] the one secret (geheim) and sacred place.[2]   In the Anglo-Saxon charters we frequently find this suffix united with the names of families—never with those of individuals .[3]   This word, as well as the feeling of which it is the symbol, was brought across the ocean by the Teutonic colonists, and it is the sign of the most precious of all the gifts for which we thank them. It may indeed be said, without exaggeration, that the universal prevalence throughout England of names containing this word HOME, gives us the clue to the real strength of the national character of the Anglo-Saxons.   It has been well observed that it was this supreme reverence for the sanctities of domestic life which gave to the Teutonic nations the power of breathing a new life into the dead bones of Roman civilization.[4]

The most important element which enters into Anglo-Saxon names yet remains to be considered.   This is the syllable *ing*.[5]   It occurs in the names of a multitude [6] of English villages and hamlets, often as a simple suffix, as in the case of BARKING, BRADING, DORKING, HASTINGS, KETTERING, TRING, or WOKING ; but more frequently we find that it forms the medial syllable of the name, as in the case of BUCKINGHAM, BIRMINGHAM,   KENSINGTON,   ISLINGTON,   HADDINGTON,   or WELLINGTON.[7]

[1] Cf. the German *heim*, home, which enters so largely into the names of Southern Germany.   What a world of inner difference there is between the English word *home*, and the French phrase *chez nous*.

[2] [These late and evolved ideas are, of course, not the radical ones.]

[3] Leo, *Anglo-Saxon Names*, p. 37.

[4] Kemble, *Anglo-Saxons*, vol. i. p. 231 ; Turner, *Anglo-Saxons*, vol. i. p. 189.   On the suffixes *hăm* and *hām* see Kemble, *Codex Diplom.* vol. iii. pp. xxviii. xxvii. ; Leo, *Rectitudines*, pp. 30–33 ; Diefenbach, *Vergleich. Wörterb.* vol. ii. pp. 499–501 ; Pictet, *Orig. Indo-Europ.* part ii. pp. 290, 291.   With *hăm* compare the Gothic *haims*, the Lithuanian *kaimas*, and the Greek κώμη, a village.   The ultimate root seems to be the Sanskrit *çî*, to repose.   Cf. κεῖμαι and κοιμάω.

[5] On the root *ing* see Förstemann, *Alt-deutsches Namenbuch*, vol. ii. p. 835 ; Förstemann, *Ortsnamen*, pp. 178, 204, 245 ; Grimm, *Gesch. d. Deut. Spr.* p. 775 ; *Deut. Gram.* vol. ii. pp. 349–352 ; Kemble, *Saxons in England*, vol. i. pp. 56–63, and 445–480 ; Kemble, in *Philolog. Proceedings*, vol. iv. pp. 1–9 ; Guest, in *ib.* vol. i. p. 117 ; Pott, *Personen-Namen*, pp. 169, 247, 553 ; Crichton, *Scandinavia*, vol. i. p. 160 ; Zeuss, *Herkunft der Baiern*, pp. xii. xxiii. xxxv. ; Massmann, in Dorow's *Denkmäler alter Sprache und Kunst*, vol. i. pp. 185–187 ; Schott, *Deut. Col.* p. 211 ; Max Müller, *Lectures on Language*, 2nd Series, p. 16 ; Latham, *Ethnol. Brit. Is.* p. 241, seq. ; Latham, *Eng-Lang.* vol. i. p. 111 ; Meyer, *Ortsnamen*, p. 139 ; Bender, *Ortsnamen*, pp. 103, 104 ; Vilmar, *Ortsnamen*, pp. 264, 265 ; Buttmann, *Ortsnamen*, p. 2 ; Wright, *Celt. Roman, and Saxon*, pp. 438–441 ; *Edinburgh Review*, vol. cxi. pp. 374–376 ; Donaldson, *English Ethnography*, p. 61.   [6] In about one-tenth of the whole number.

[7] Mr. Kemble has compiled a list of 1,329 English names which contain this root. To ascertain the completeness of the enumeration, the Ordnance Maps of three counties —Kent, Sussex, and Essex—were carefully searched, and it was discovered that Mr. Kemble had overlooked no less than forty-seven names in Kent, thirty-eight in Sussex

This syllable *ing* was the usual Anglo-Saxon patronymic. Thus we read in the Saxon Chronicle (A.D. 547) :—

Ida wæs Eopping,	Ida was Eoppa's son,
Eoppa wæs Esing,	Eoppa was Esa's son,
Esa wæs Inguing,	Esa was Ingwy's son,
Ingui, Angenwiting.	Ingwy, Angenwit's son.

In fact the suffix *ing* in the names of persons had very much the same significance as the prefix Mac in Scotland, O' in Ireland, Ap in Wales, or Beni among the Arabs. A whole clan or tribe, claiming to be descended from a real or mythic progenitor, or a body of adventurers attaching themselves to the standard of some chief, were thus distinguished by a common patronymic or *clan* [1] name.

The family bond, which, as we have seen, was so deeply reverenced by the Anglo-Saxon race, was the ruling power which directed the Teutonic colonization of this island. The Saxon immigration was, doubtless, an immigration of clans. The head of the family built or bought a ship, and embarked in it with his children, his freedmen, and his neighbours, and established a family colony on any shore to which the winds might carry him.[2] The subsequent Scandinavian colonization was, on the other hand, wholly or mainly effected by soldiers of fortune, who abandoned domestic ties at home, and, after a few years of piracy, settled down with the slave women whom they had carried off from the shores of France, Spain, or Italy, or else roughly wooed the daughters of the soil which their swords had conquered.[3] Thus the Scandinavian adventurers Grim, Orm, Hacon, or Asgar, left their names at GRIMSBY, ORMSBY, HACONBY, and ASGARBY ; whereas in the Saxon districts of the Island we find the names, not of individuals, but of clans. It is these family settlements which are denoted by the syllable *ing*. Hence we perceive the value of this word as an instrument of historical research. In a great number of cases [4] it enables us to assign to each of the

and thirty-four in Essex. If the omissions in other counties are in the same ratio, the total number of these names would be about 2,200. Large additions might also be made from Domesday Book. The Exon and Ely Domesdays alone contain thirty-six names not given by Mr. Kemble.

[1] It may be observed that the etymology of the word *clan* proves the patriarchal nature of the Scottish clans. It is derived from the Gaelic [*clann*] *cluin*, children. Pictet, *Orig. Indo-Europ.* pt. ii. p. 386 ; Newman, *Regal Rome*, p. 49.

[2] See Thrupp, *Anglo-Saxon Home*, p. 178.

[3] See Thrupp, *Anglo-Saxon Home*, p. 319 ; St. John, *Four Conquests*, vol. i. p. 306.

[4] The syllable *ing* has sometimes a topographic rather than a patronymic signification. Thus, in the Chronicle and the Charters, mention is made of the Centings, or men of

chief German clans its precise share in the colonization of the several portions of our island.

In investigating the local topography of England, we constantly meet with the names of families whose deeds are celebrated in the mythic or legendary history of the Teutonic races.[1] Thus members of a Frankish clan—the Myrgings, or Maurings, of whom we read in the ' Traveller's Song ', and who, at a later time, are familiar to us as the Merovingian dynasty of France—seem to have settled in England at MERRING in Nottinghamshire, and at MERRINGTON in Durham and Shropshire.[2] The family of the Harlings, whose deeds are also chronicled in the ' Traveller's Song ', are met with at HARLING, in Norfolk and in Kent, and at HARLINGTON, in Bedfordshire and Middlesex. The families of the Brentings, the Scylfings[3] (a Swabian race), the Banings, the Hælsings, the Hôcings,[4] and the Scærings, which are all mentioned in Beowulf or in the ' Traveller's Song ',[5] are found at BRENTINGLEY, SHILVINGTON, BANNINGHAM, HELSINGTON, HUCKING, WOKING, and SHERRINGHAM ; and the Scyldings[6]—a Danish family, to which Beowulf himself belonged—are found at SKELDING in Yorkshire. In the Edda and in Beowulf we read of the Wælsings,[7] whom we find settled at WOLSINGHAM in Norfolk, WOOLSINGHAM in Durham, and WOLSINGHAM in Northumberland. The Thurings, a Visigothic clan,[8] mentioned by Marcellinus, Jornandes, and Sidonius Apollonaris, are found at THORINGTON in Suffolk and THORRINGTON in Essex. The Silings, a Vandal tribe, mentioned by Ptolemy, are found at SELLING in Kent. The Icelings, the noblest

Kent, the Brytfordings, or men of Bradford, and the Bromleagings, or men of Bromley. Sometimes, as Mr. Kemble and Dr. Massmann think, the suffix *ing* has simply the force of the genitive singular. Kemble, in *Philolog. Proc.* vol. iv. pp. 1–9 ; Massmann, in Dorow's *Denkmäler*, vol. i. p. 186 ; Förstemann, *Ortsnamen*, p. 178. Occasionally it denotes a meadow.

[1] The same patronymics which occur in local names were borne by persons mentioned in ancient German charters and other documents. Förstemann collects 270 such names from documents of the eighth, ninth, tenth, and eleventh centuries. *Alt-Deutsches Namenbuch*, vol. i. p. 782.

[2] Müllenhoff, in Haupt's *Zeitschrift*, vol. vi. pp. 430–435 ; Kemble, *Saxons*, vol. i. p. 469 ; Zeuss, *Herkunft der Baiern*, p. xxxv. ; Latham, *English Lang.* vol. i. p. 221. See Mone, *Geschichte Heidenthums*, vol. ii. p. 133, for the Merovingian traditions. The Meringas are also mentioned in a charter. *Cod. Dipl.* No. 809.

[3] Müllenhoff, in Haupt's *Zeitschrift*, vol. vi. p. 431.

[4] The Hôcings are probably the same as the Chauci of Tacitus—the interchange of *h* to *ch* or *w* often takes place, as in the case of the *Ch*atti and *H*esse. The Wokings were probably the same as the Hôcings. Grimm, *Gesch. der Deut. Spr.*, p. 674.

[5] Kemble, *Saxons*, vol. i. pp. 59–63, and 456–478.

[6] Müllenhoff, in Haupt's *Zeitschrift*, vol. vi. p. 431.

[7] The Wælsings were probably Franks. Latham, *Eng. Lang.* vol. i. p. 226.

[8] Müller, *Marken*, p. 175 ; Latham, *Nationalities*, vol. ii. p. 312.

family of Mercia, are found at ICKLINGHAM in Suffolk. The Hastings, the noblest race of the Goths, are found at HASTING-LEIGH in Kent, and HASTINGS in Sussex. The Ardings, the royal race of the Vandals, are found at ARDINGTON in Berkshire, and ARDINGLEY in Sussex; and a branch of the royal Visigothic family is found at BELTING in Kent. The Irings, the royal family of the Avars,[1] are found at ERRINGHAM in Sussex, and at ERRINGTON in Yorkshire. The Varini, who are placed by Tacitus in juxtaposition with the Angli, are found at WARRINGTON in Lancashire and Bucks, and at WARRINGTON in Devon and Northamptonshire. The Billings, who were the royal race of the Varini,[2] seem, as might have been anticipated, to have profited extensively by the conquest of England, for we find their name is no less than thirteen places, as BILLINGE, BILLINGHAM, BILLINGLEY, BILLINGTON, and BILLINGSHURST. The Æscings, the royal race of Kent, are likewise found in thirteen places. Some families seem to have spread much more widely than others. Of many only an isolated local name bears witness, some are confined to a single county, while the names of others, as the Æscings and the Billings, are spread far and wide throughout the island.[3]

Where the patronymic stands without any suffix, as in the case of MALLING, BASING, or HASTINGS, Mr. Kemble thinks that we have the original settlement of the clan, and that the names to which the suffixes *ham* or *ton* are applied mark the filial colonies sent out from this parent settlement. This theory is not, perhaps, altogether carried out by a study of the names, but it certainly derives considerable support from the way in which these patronymics are distributed throughout the English counties. By a reference to the subjoined table, it will be seen that the names of the former class are chiefly to be found in the south-eastern districts of the

[1] Piderit, *Ortsnamen,* p. 311.

[2] Lappenberg, *Anglo-Saxon Kings,* vol. i. p. 213. In the earliest records, however, the Billings are mythological rather than historical. The first undoubtedly historical Billing died in the year 967. The root *bil* signifies gentleness. Billich is Equity personified. Cf. the modern German *billig,* cheap. The name Billingsgate may perhaps be thus explained. Grimm, *Deut. Mythol.* p. 347.

[3] The Cyllings and the Wealings are found in twelve places; the Dodings, the Wittings, and the Willings, in eleven; the Ofings in ten; the Donings and the Sillings in nine; the Edings, the Ellings, the Hardings, and the Lings in eight; the Fearings, the Hemings, the Herrings, the Holings, the Hornings, the Newings, the Serings, and the Wasings in seven; the Cannings, the Cerrings, the Hastings, the Lullings, the Hannings, the Stannings, the Teddings, the Tarings, and the Withings, in six; the Bennings, the Bings, the Bobbings, the Cædings, the Collings, the Gillings, and the Stellings, in five, and the remaining 400 or 500 patronymics in four or a smaller number of places.

island, where the earliest Teutonic settlements were formed, namely, in Kent, Sussex, Essex, Middlesex, Norfolk, Suffolk, and the adjacent counties, and that they gradually diminish in frequency as we proceed towards the northern and western counties. Still farther to the west, as in Gloucestershire and Warwickshire, the names of the former class are very rare ; those of the second abound. In the semi-Celtic districts of Derbyshire, Devonshire, and Lancashire names of either class become scarce, while in Cumberland, Westmoreland, Cornwall, and Monmouth they are wholly or almost wholly wanting. On Mr. Kemble's hypothesis this remarkable distribution of these names would accord with the supposition that the Saxon rule was gradually extended over the western and central districts by the cadets of families already settled in the island, and not by fresh immigrants arriving from abroad.

From the lists given by Mr. Kemble the following table has been compiled, so as to represent the proportion of names of these two classes to the acreage of the several counties. The absolute numbers are not given, since the varying sizes of the counties would vitiate the results :—

	Original Settlements.	Filial Colonies.		Original Settlements.	Filial Colonies.
Kent	22	29	Derbyshire . .	3	15
Sussex	21	41	Gloucestershire .	2	46
Middlesex . . .	18	38	Northumberland	2	32
Essex	18	24	Leicestershire .	2	29
Norfolk . . .	15	46	Buckinghamshire	2	28
Suffolk	13	36	Warwickshire .	1	44
Bedfordshire . .	12	51	Somerset . . .	1	35
Huntingdonshire .	11	46	Salop	1	33
Berkshire . . .	9	29	Wiltshire . . .	1	23
Surrey	9	22	Devonshire . .	½	12
Hertfordshire . .	6	14	Rutland . . .	0	36
Northamptonshire	5	41	Cheshire . . .	0	31
Oxfordshire . .	4	51	Worcestershire .	0	24
Nottinghamshire .	4	31	Herefordshire .	0	23
Hampshire . .	4	23	Staffordshire . .	0	22
Lincolnshire . .	3	34	Durham . . .	0	21
Cambridgeshire .	3	29	Cumberland . .	0	5
Yorkshire . . .	3	26	Westmoreland .	0	3
Dorsetshire . .	3	25	Cornwall . .	0	2
Lancashire . .	3	16	Monmouth . .	0	0

For the preceding results no great amount of novelty can be claimed, since they are based mainly on the researches of Mr. Kemble, and of Professor Leo of Halle.

But, having occasion, for another purpose, to make a minute examination of the sheets of the large Government survey of France, I was startled by a remarkable phenomenon, which, so far as I can ascertain, seems hitherto to have escaped the notice which it deserves. In the old French provinces of Picardy and Artois, there is a small well-defined district, about the size of Middlesex, lying between Calais, Boulogne, and St. Omer, and fronting the English coast, in which the name of almost every village and hamlet is of the pure Anglo-Saxon type ; and not only so, but the names are, most of them, identically the same with village-names to be found in England. To exhibit graphically the distribution of these Saxon villages the accompanying sketch-map has been constructed. Each dot represents the position of one of the Saxon names.

SAXON NAMES IN PICARDY AND ARTOIS.

Thus we have in the

French District.	Corresponding English Names.
Warhem	Warham, *Norfolk.*
Rattekot	Radcot, *Oxon.*
Le Wast	Wast, *Gloucestershire, Northumberland.*
Frethun	Freton, *Norfolk.*
Cohen, Cuhem, and Cuhen	Cougham, *Norfolk.*
Hollebeque	Holbeck, *Notts., Yorks., Lincoln.*
Ham, Hame, Hames . .	Ham, *Kent, Surrey, Essex, Somerset.*
Werwick	Warwick, *Warwick, Cumberland.*
Appegarbe	Applegarth, *Dumfries.*
Sangatte	Sandgate, *Kent.*
Guindal	Windle, *Lancashire.*
Inghem	Ingham, *Lincoln, Norfolk, Middlesex.*
Oye	Eye, *Suffolk, Hereford, Northamptonsh., Oxon.*
Wimille[1]	Windmill, *Kent.*
Grisendale	Grisdale, *Cumberland, Lancashire.*

We have also such familiar English forms as Graywick-the River Slack, Bruquedal, Marbecq, Longfosse, Dalle, Vendal, Salperwick, Fordebecques, Staple, Crehem, Pihem, Dohem, Roqueton, Hazelbrouck, and Roebeck. Twenty-two of the names have the characteristic suffix -*ton*, which is scarcely to be found elsewhere upon the Continent,[2] and upwards of one hundred end in *ham, hem,* or *hen*. There are also more than one hundred patronymics ending in *ing*. A comparison of these patronymics with those found in England proves, beyond a doubt, that the colonization of this part of France must have been effected by men bearing the clan-names which belonged to the Teutonic families which settled on the opposite coast.[3] More than eighty per cent. of these French patronymics are also found in England.

Thus we have

---

[1] Sankey, *Portefeuille*, p. 53, refers this very remarkable name to the time of the occupation of Boulogne by the English in the sixteenth century. I cannot doubt that it is an evidence of a much earlier connexion.

[2] See p. 84, *supra.*

[3] A few phonetic changes are worthy of notice. We find *ham* once or twice close to the coast—the usual form, however, is *hem*—and further inland it changes to *hen*; while *ing* is sometimes changed into *eng* or *inc*, and *gay* into *gue*. The suffix *gay* which we find in Framlingay, Gamlingay, etc., is found abundantly in those parts of Germany from whence the Saxons emigrated. It there takes the form *gau*. This word orginally denoted a forest clearing, hence afterwards it came to mean the primary settlement with independent jurisdicton, like the Cymric *tref*. Palgrave, *English Commonwealth*, vol. i. p. 88 ; Förstemann, *Ortsnamen*, p. 63.

In France.		In England.
Alencthun	. . . .	Allington, *Kent.*
Bazingham	. . . .	Bassingham, *Linc.*
Balinghem	. . . .	Ballingham, *Hereford.*
Berlinghen	. . . .	Birlingham, *Worcester.*
Colincthun	. . . .	Collington, *Sussex.*
Elingehen	. . . .	Ellingham, *Hants.*
Eringhem .	. . . .	Erringham, *Sussex.*
Hardinghem	. . . .	Hardingham, *Norfolk.*
Linghem .	. . . .	Lingham, *Cheshire.*
Lozinghem	. . . .	Lossingham, *Kent.*
Maninghem	. . . .	Manningham, *Yorks.*
Masinghen	. . . .	Massingham, *Norfolk.*
Pelincthun	. . . .	Pallington, *Dorset.*
Todincthun	. . . .	Toddington, *Bedford.*
Velinghen	. . . .	Wellingham, *Norfolk.*

A more detailed comparison of these patronymics will be found in the appendix,[1] and to this the attention of the student is specially requested. It is confidently believed that such a comparison will render it impossible not to admit that the same families which gave their names to our English villages must have also made a settlement on that part of the French coast which lies within sight of the English shore.

The question now arises whether the Saxons, as they coasted along from the mouths of the Rhine, made the Boulogne colony a sort of halting-place or stepping-stone on their way to England, or whether the French settlement was effected by cadets belonging to families which had already established themselves in this island.

In favour of the latter view we may adduce the entire absence of Saxon names from that part of the coast which lies to the north-east of Cape Grisnez. Why should the intending settlers have passed along this stretch of coast, and have left it entirely untouched ? The map [2] shows conclusively that the colonists did not arrive from the east, but from the west—the Saxon names radiate, so to speak, from that part of the coast which fronts England. And the names are arranged exactly as they would have been if.the invaders had set sail from Hythe for the cliffs on the horizon. The district about St. Omer was evidently colonized by men who landed, not in the neighbourhood of Dunkerque, but in

[1] Appendix B.   [2] See p. 93, *supra.*

the neighbourhood of Boulogne. [1] Again, if any importance is to be attached to Mr. Kemble's theory of original and final settlements, [2] the Saxon villages in France must all have been *filial settlements*. We find that *ing* is never a mere suffix ; in every case it forms the medial syllable of the name.

On the other hand, it may be said that these names mark the position of the ' Litus Saxonicum in Belgica Secunda '— the coast settlement of the Saxons in Flanders—which is mentioned in the Notitia Imperii. This Litus Saxonicum existed as early as the third century, and therefore, it may be urged, its foundation must have been long anterior in date to the Saxon colonization of Britain, which, according to the chroniclers, commenced in the fifth century, with the arrival of Hengist and Horsa. Eutropius informs us that the Emperors Diocetian and Maximian appointed Carausius, ' apud Bononiam ", (Boulogne) to protect the Flemish coast and the adjoining sea, ' quod Saxones infestabant '. Carausius was a Menapian, that is, a native of the islands near the mouth of the Rhine.[3] He was probably one of those pirates whose incursions he was appointed to suppress. Carausius, it would seem, entered into a compact with his Saxon kinsmen, and promoted their settlement, as subsidized naval colonists, in the neighbourhood of his fortress at Boulogne.[4]

It may be said, in reply, that the date ordinarily assigned for the commencement of the Saxon colonization of Britain is too late by at least a couple of centuries. Even in the time of Agricola the Saxon piracy had begun.[5] In the south-east of England a Saxon immigration seems to have been going on in silence during the period of the Roman rule.[6] Without supposing, as some inquirers have done, that the Belgæ, whom Cæsar found in Britain, were Low Germans in blood

---

[1] As if to preclude all doubt, at some distance inland, on the northern border of the Saxon colony, we find the village of Marck, a name which always indicated an ethnological frontier. See Chapter X.

[2] See p. 92, *supra*.

[3] Palgrave, *English Commonwealth*, vol. i. p. 375.

[4] Lappenberg, *England under the Anglo-Saxon Kings*, vol. i. pp. 44–47 ; Zeuss, *Die Deutschen*, pp. 381, 384 ; Gough's *Camden*, vol. i. p. 308 ; Leo, *Vorlesungen*, vol. i. p. 267 ; Turner, *Anglo-Saxons*, vol. i. p. 145 ; Depping, *Expéditions Maritimes*, vol. i. p. 84 ; Warnkönig, *Flandrische Staatsgeschichte*, vol. i. p. 91.

[5] Poste, *Britannic Researches*, p. 20.

[6] Haigh, *Conquest of Britain* pp 61–166. The Roman Legions stationed in Britain, were composed mainly of Germans. This must have introduced a considerable German element into the population. Leo, *Vorlesungen*, vol. i. p. 268 ; Wright, ' On the Ethnology of South Britain at the extinction of the Roman Government '. *Essays*, vol. i. pp. 70, 71.

and speech, we may suppose that, after the extermination
of the Iceni, the desolated lands of Eastern Britain were
occupied by German colonists.   In Essex and Suffolk there
is a smaller proportion of Celtic names than in any other district of the island, and this would indicate that the Germanization of those counties is of very ancient date.   Gildas, Nennius,
and Beda, among all their lamentations over the ' destruction
of Britain ' by the Jutish and Saxon invaders, are strangely
silent as to any settlements on the eastern coast, where,
from geographical considerations, we might have expected
that the first brunt of invasion would be felt.   While we
can trace the progress of the Saxons in the western and central
districts of England, with respect to the east both the British
bards and the Saxon chroniclers are dumb.   They tell us of
no conquests, no defeats.[1]   Descents had, however, been
made, for we learn that Ammianus Macellinus that, nearly
a century before the date assigned by Beda for the landing
of Hengist and Horsa, London was taken by Saxon invaders,
who slew the Duke of Britain and the Count of the Saxon
shore.

This name alone might suffice to set the question at rest.
Even before the time of Constantine, there was in England,
as well as in Flanders, Litus Saxonicum, or Saxon coast
settlement, which extended from Brancaster in Norfolk as
far as Shoreham in Sussex.[2]   The Roman names of the place
in this district seem in some cases to be referable to Teutonic
rather than Celtic roots.   The modern name of RECULVERS
probably approximates very closely to the original word which
was Latinized into Regulbium, and it suggests the settlement
of a Teuton named Raculf.[3]   The name of DOVER,[4] Latinized
into Dubris, reminds us of DOUVRES in the Saxon shore near
Bayeux, and of DOVERCOURT in the intensely Teutonized
district near Harwich, as well as of the Dovrefjeld in Norway,
and THANET, also a Teutonic name, appears in the pages of

1 Palgrave, *English Commonwealth*, vol. i. p. 413.
2 Grimm, *Gesch. d. Deut. Spr.* p. 625 ; Palgrave, *English Commonwealth*, vol. i.
pp. 389, 412 ; St. John, *Four Conquests*, vol. i. p. 44 ; Latham, *Ethnology of Brit. Is.*
p. 199 ; Donaldson, *English Ethnog*, p. 45.
3 The name of the British usurper, Tetricus, whose date is about 270 A.D. appears
to be only the German name Dietrich in a Latinized form. Haigh, *Conquest of Britain*,
p. 162.
4 The root may be the Anglo-Saxon *Ofer*, shore, with a preposition, or the definite
article prefixed [?].   The usual derivation is from the Celtic *dufr*, water. Glück,
Kelt. Namen, p. 35 ; Zeuss, *Die Deutschen*, p. 575.

W.P.   H

Solinus, an author certainly not later than the fourth century.

There are several concurrent indications that the district of Holderness was occupied by Teutonic settlers before the close of the Roman rule. Holderness is a fertile tract of some 250 square miles, bounded on the north, east, and south by the sea and the Humber, and on the west by the Wolds, which were probably a frontier of wooded and impenetrable hills.[1] In this district Ptolemy places a people whom he calls the Παρίσοι. Grimm has shown that the old German *p* is interchangeable in Latin with *f*, the aspirated form of the same letter.[2] This would lead us to identify the Παρίσοι with the F-risii or Frisians.[3] In the same district Ptolemy places PETUARIA, a name which cannot be explained from Celtic sources, but which points undoubtedly to the German root *wǽre*—inhabitants, which appears in Cantware, Wihtware, and so many other names.[4] Nor is this all, for Ptolemy gives us a third name in the district of Holderness, Gabranto*vic*orum Sinus, which must be either Filey Bay or Bridlington Bay. Now this word contains the root *vic*, which was the appellation of a bay in the language of the *vik*ings or Bay-men who, at a later period, descended in such numbers from the Frisian region.[5]

There seems therefore to be good ground for asigning for the commencement of the Saxon settlements in Britain a date anterior to the time of Carausius,[6] and we may believe that the Saxon settlement in Flanders may be partly due to the energetic measures by which he compelled or induced the Saxon pirates, who were establishing themselves on the British coast, to seek a new home beyond the channel.

There was also a third Litus Saxonicum, in the neighbour-

---

[1] The name Holderness means a wooded promontory. The Wolds are ' the woods '. Cf. the German *wald*.

[2] *Gesch. d. Deut. Spr.* p. 394.

[3] The Frisian form of *ham* is *um*. See p. 87, *supra*. Holderness is the only part of England where this form occurs. Here we find the village names Arg-a*m*, News-o*m*, Holl-*ym*, Arr-*am*, Rys-*om* Garth, and Ulro*me*, as well as Owstwick, another Frisian form. The village of FRISMERSK is now washed away. Poulson, *Hist. of Holderness*, vol. ii. p. 528.

[4] See p. 49, *supra*. Ptolemy also gives us a Vand-*uar*-ia, near the wall, apparently a settlement of some tribe of Vandals or Wends.

[5] Cf. Wright, ' On the remains of a primitive people in the south-east of Yorkshire '. *Essays*, vol. i. p. 1 ; Latham, *English Lang.* vol. i. pp. 5, 6 ; Poulson, *Hist. of Holderness*, vol. i. pp. 4-9.

[6] The date usually assigned to the landing of Hengist and Horsa is 449 A.D. The Saxons took London in 367. Carausius was appointed in 287. The latest writer on the subject places the commencement of the Saxon colonization ' three or four centuries ' before 449. Thrupp, *Anglo-Saxon Home*, p. 4.

hood of Caen, and which extended as far as the islands at the mouth of the Loire,[1] where the population still retains the distinctive outward marks of Saxon blood.[2] The Swabian *læti* who, as we learn from the Notitia, were settled at Bajoccas (Bayeux) may have formed the nucleus of this settlement. In the year 843 the annalists mention the existence of a district in this neighbourhood called Otlinga [3] Saxonica, and Gregory of Tours speaks of the Saxones bajocassini. This Saxon settlement dates from the third century, and its formation was probably contemporaneous with that of the colony in Picardy. By the aid of local names we can still trace its sharply defined boundaries.[4] It will be seen that in the departments of the Eure and of the Seine Inférieure, where the Danish names of a later period are so thickly clustered, hardly a single Saxon name is to be found, while in the department of the Calvados, and in the central portion of La Manche, where the Danish names are comparatively scarce, their place is occupied by names of the Saxon type. The Northmen seem to have respected the tenure of their Teutonic kinsmen, and to have dispossessed only the Celtic tribes who dwelt to the east and north-west of the Saxon colony. The artificial landscape in this Saxon district is of a thoroughly English type. The sketcher might image himself in Devonshire or Kent. The country is divided by thick hedgerows into small irregular crofts, and the cottages are unmistakably English rather than French in structure and appearance.[5]

In this neighbourhood we find the village names of SASSETOT (Saxons'-field), HERMANVILLE, ETREHAM, or OUISTREHAM [6] (Westerham), HAMBYE,[7] LE HAM, LE HAMELET, COTTUN (cows yard), ETAINHUS, HEULAND (highland), PLUMETOT (Blomfield

[1] Zeuss, *Die Deutschen*, p. 386 ; Lappenberg, *Anglo-Saxon Kings*, vol. i. pp. 44, 46 ; *Anglo-Norman Kings*, p. 23 ; Latham, *Channel Is.* p. 313 ; *Ethnol. Brit. Is.* p. 197 ; *Nationalities of Europe*, vol. ii. pp. 21, 292 ; Depping, *Expéditions Maritimes*, vol. i. pp. 84, 85 ; Petersen, *Recherches*, p. 44.

[2] Louth, *Wanderer in Western France*, p. 292.

[3] This phrase, which has elicited so many ingenious etymological guesses, does not mean the district where the Saxon language was spoken, but, as Grimm has suggested, it was the abode of Saxon nobles, *Adalings* or *Æthelings.—Gesch. der Deut. Sprach.* p. 626. See Donaldson, *English Ethnog.* p. 45 ; Depping, *Expéditions*, vol. i. p. 85 ; and compare the name of Athelney, which in the Saxon Chronicle (A.D. 878) is written *Æthelinga-igge*, the isle of the Æthelings.

[4] See the coloured map, and the sketch map of Normandy in the next chapter.

[5] These two characteristic features of Saxon colonization are also to be noted in the Litus, Saxonicum near Boulogne.

[6] La Roquette, *Noms en Normandie*, p. 56.

[7] This mongrel growth is apparently a Danish graft on a Saxon stock.

or Flowerfield), DOUVRES, on 'the shore', which reminds us of our own Dover, and CAEN, which was anciently written Cathem and Catheim.[1] There are also about thirty Saxon patronymics. It is curious to observe in how many cases we find the same families on the opposite coast of Hants, Dorset, Devon, and Cornwall. In the whole of Cornwall there are only two patronymic names, and both of these are also found among the thirty on the opposite coast.

We have the

Families of the	Near Bayeux at	In England at
Berrings	Berengeville	Berrington, *Dur.*, *Glouc.*,
	Berigny	Salop, *Worcester.*
Bellings	Bellengreville	Bellinger, *Hants.*
Basings	Bazenville	Basing, *Hants.*
Bobbings	Baubigny	Bobbing, *Kent.*
Callings	Caligny	Callington, *Cornwall.*
Ceafings	Chavigny	Chalvington, *Sussex.*
		Chevington, *Suffolk.*
Cofings	Cavigny	Covington, *Huntingdon.*
Ceardings	Cartigny	Cardington, *Beds.*, *Salop.*
		Cardingham, *Cornwall.*
Græfings	Gravigny	Grayingham, *Linc.*
Hardings	Hardinvast	Hardenhuish, *Wilts.*
Ifings	Juvigny	Jevington, *Sussex.*
Essings	Isigny	Issington, *Hants.*
Mærings	Marigny	Marrington, *Salop.*
Potings	Potigny	Podington, *Dorset.*
Seafings	Savigny	Sevington, *Kent.*
Sulings	Soulangy	Sullington, *Sussex.*
Dhyrings	Thorigny[2]	Torrington, *Devon.*

Local names are of great value when we attempt to estimate the amount and the distribution of the Teutonic element in the population of France. Any historical notices which might aid us are very vague, and the philological analysis of the modern French vocabulary [3] would give a most inadequate

[1] La Roquette, *Noms en Normandie*, p. 53; Charnock, *Local Etym.* p. 53. *Cat* is perhaps a corruption of Goth or Geat, or it may be the proper name Geit.
[2] The Gothic *igg* becomes *ing* in the Teutonic, and *ign* in the Romance languages. Grimm, *Gesch. Deut. Spr.* p. 775.
[3] Not more than five hundred words were introduced into the French language by the German conquerors. Diez, *Gram. d. Rom. Spr.* vol. i. p. 52. Most of them are names of weapons and military terms, such as *gonfanon, massacre* from *metzger*, a butcher, *bivouac* from *beiwacht*, and *guerre*, from *werra*, war. *Ib.* p. 55; Max Müller, *Lectures*, 2nd series, p. 263; Perticari; and Milman, *Hist. Latin Christianity*, vol. vi. p. 332. The other words are chiefly the names of articles of dress, of beasts of the chase, and terms belonging to the feudal system. Diez, *Gram.* p. 56; Lewis, *Romance Languages*, p. 270. To these must be added the points of the compass, *nord, sud, est, ouest.* The

notion of the actual numbers of the Frank and Burgundian colonists. In fact, the local names enable us to prove that certain parts of modern France are as thoroughly Teutonic in blood as any portion of our own island.

The Germanization of France commenced with settlements of subsidized colonists, *læti*,[1] who were introduced by the Roman rulers to defend the frontier. According to the Notitia there were Batavian *læti* at Arras. The Emperor Julian transported thousands of the Chattuarii, Chamavi, and Frisii, to the neighbourhood of Amiens, Beauvais, and Langres.[2] The system was continued at a later period. Charlemagne transported into France a vast multitude of Saxons—multitudinem Saxonorum cum mulieribus et infantibus.[3] After another Saxon conquest he transplanted every third man—tertium hominem—of the vanquished people.[4] Many of the German names in France may be due to these forced emigrations,[5] but by far the greater number are, no doubt, records of the settlements of the Frank and Burgundian conquerors. The area and intensity of this German colonization may conveniently be traced by means of the patronymic village-names, of which there are more than 1,100 in France.[6]

About 250, or nearly one-fourth, of these clan-names are also to be found in England—the proportional number of identifications being far smaller than in the case of the Litus Saxonicum in Picardy.

fact that in these cases the Teutonic terms should have displaced their Romance equivalents is a striking indication of the more mobile habits of the German tribes as contrasted with the stationary life of the Celto-Latin inhabitants. Lewis, *Romance Lang.* p. 267. The radical meaning of the word *west* is perhaps the vast [?] the vastitudo, or great unknown region lying before the conquerors as they advanced from the east. See Pictet, *Orig. Indo-Europ.* part i. p. 112 ; Müller, *Marken des Vaterl.* p. 209. The Romance words introduced into the Teutonic languages are chiefly ecclesiastical, a fact which, connected with the nature of the terms conversely introduced into the Romance languages, suggests curious speculations as to the reciprocal influence of the rude conquerors and their more civilized subjects. See Diez. *Gram. d. Rom. Spr.* vol. i. p. 209. German was spoken in France more or less for some 400 years after the Teutonic conquest. So late as the year 812 A.D. the Council of Tours ordained that every bishop should be able to preach both in the Romance and Teutonic languages. Diez, *Gram. d. Rom. Spr.* vol. i. p. 48 ; Milman, *Hist. Latin Christianity*, vol. vi. p. 341.

1 Probably a Latinization of the German word ¥eute, people. The *lathes* of Kent are probably a vestige of the *lætic* organization.

2 Latham, *Channel Islands*, p. 343 ; *Nationalities of Europe*, vol. ii. p. 294.

3 *Annal. Laureshamenses*, apud Pertz., *Mon. Germ.* vol. i. p. 38 ; Warnkönig, *Flandrische Staatsgeschichte*, vol. i. p. 92.

4 *Annal. Laur. Minores*, apud Pertz, vol. i. pp. 119, 120.

5 Guilmot, quoted by Warnkönig, *Flandrische Staatsgesch.* vol. i. p. 92, believes all the Flemish patronymics to be due to this cause.

6 See Appendix C [p. 355].

Thus we have the

Families of the	In France at	In England at
Æbings . . .	Aubinges, *Burgundy* (3), Franche-Comté, *Poitou* (2)	Abington, *Camb.*
Æcings . . .	Acquing, *Isle of France* . .	Oakington, *Camb.*
Ælings . .	Alligny, *Burgundy*. . . . Allinges, *Burgundy* . . .	Allington, *Dev., Hants.,* Kent.
Antings. . .	Antigny, *Burgundy, Poitou* (2)	Antingham, *Norf.*
Arrings . .	Arrigny, *Champagne* . . .	Arrington, *Camb.*
Bælings. . .	Balagny, *Isle of France* . .	Ballingdon, *Essex.*
Basings . . .	Bazegny, *Champagne* . . . Bazainville, *Isle of France* .	Basing, *Hants.*
Beadings . .	Bettigny, *Champagne* . . .	Beddingham, *Sussex.*
Bellings. . .	Belligneux, *Burgundy* . . . Belligni, *Anjou*	Bellinger, *Hants.*
Bessings . .	Bissines, *Limousin* . . .	Bessingham, *Norf.*
Billings . . .	Billanges, *Limousin* . . .	Billing, *Northumb.*
Bings . . .	Binges, *Burgundy*	Bing, *Suff.*
Bobbings . .	Bibigny, *Isle of France* . . Beaubigny, *Burgundy* . . .	Bobbing, *Kent.*
Bollings. . .	Boligneux, *Burgundy* . . . Bolligney, *Fr. Comté* . . .	Bollington, *Essex.*
Bondings . .	Bontigny, *Lorraine* . . .	Bondington, *Somers.*
Brantings . .	Brantigny, *Champagne* . .	Brantingham, *Yorks.*

The map will give an approximate idea of the distribution of these names.

They cluster most thickly in the old province of Lorraine, where, especially in the departments of the Meurthe and the Moselle, almost every village name bears witness to the extensive colonization effected by the Frankish conquerors. The Isle of France, especially the department of the Aisne, the Upper Valley of the Loire above Orleans, and the provinces of Franche-Comté and Burgundy, present numerous names of the patronymic class.

It is difficult to account for these resemblances on the ordinary theory that England was colonized exclusively by the Saxon and Angles, and France by the Franks and Burgundians. A large number of Frank adventurers must have joined in the descents which the Saxons made on the English coast : [1] and many Saxons must have found a place in the ranks of the Frankish armies which conquered North-eastern

---

[1] Dr. Latham thinks that Kent was largely colonized by Franks. *English Language,* vol. i. p. 178. Ammianus Marcellinus places Alemanni in Britain. Lappenberg believes that the Saxons were accompanied by large numbers of Franks, Frisians, and Lombards. The Welshman Llywarc Hen uses Frank as an equivalent for Saxon.

France. The chroniclers, when mentioning the earlier invasions and piratical attacks, attribute them to Franks and
Saxons,[1] or to Saxons and Lombards in conjunction. The

GERMAN PATRONYMIC VILLAGE NAMES IN FRANCE.

The towns indicated by initials are Amiens, Caen, Rouen, Paris, Rheims,
Treves, Chalons, Troyes, Dijon, Strasbourg, and Maçon. The shaded
district (Alsace) is full of names of the pure German type, few of which,
however, are patronymic.

tribes between the Rhine and the Elbe—Franks, Saxons,
Angles, Sueves, Lombards, and Burgundians—were probably
united by a much closer connexion—ethnological, geographical
and political—than historians have hitherto been willing
to admit. At all events, the speech of all these invading
tribes must have been mutually intelligible.[2] Indeed, there
seems to be strong reason for believing that the names of

[1] Eutropius, Julian, and Ammianus Marcellinus associate the Franks and Saxons
in this manner.
[2] Diez, *Gram. d. Rom. Spr.* vol. i. p. 46 ; Marsh, *History of Eng. Lang.* p. 55 ; Poste,
British Researches, p. 74 ; Donaldson, *English Ethnog.* p. 61.

Frank, Saxon, or Lombard are not true ethnic names, but that they were only the designations of temporary confederations for military purposes,[1] an hypothesis which would be almost reduced to a demonstration if we could succeed in establishing that plausible etymology of these names which makes them *descriptive* terms relating to the equipment of the invading hosts—whether armed with javelin (*franca*), sword (*seax*), or partisan (*lang-barta*).[2] This hypothesis, which I was first inclined to reject somewhat cavalierly, has commended itself more and more to my judgment during the progress of a laborious comparison of the village names of France, Germany, Italy, and England.

Little need be said about the German names in Northern Italy. Paulus Diaconus and Gregory of Tours assert that the conquest was effected by Saxons and Lombards. We find the names of the early Lombard kings are of a pure Anglo-Saxon type. Thus Audouin and Alboin are, no doubt, the same names as Edwin and Elfwine.[3] My friend, Mr. G. P. Marsh, the United States Minister at Turin, has kindly pointed out to me several clusters of Saxon patronymics in Northern Italy. One of these is to be found on the Southern side of the Po, opposite the mouth of the Dora Baltea, where we have the villages of VARENGO, ODALENGO, TONENGO, GONENGO, and SCALENGHE. Near Biella there is another cluster of these names—VALDENGO, ARBENGO, BOLENGO, and TERNENGO. Near Milan we find MARENGO and MORENGO; and near Brescia—BOVENGO and PISOGNE.[4] In the villages of RONCEGNO and TORCEGNO, in the Valle Sugana, German is still spoken.[5]

I have not succeeded in discovering any undoubtedly Teutonic names in Spain, with the notable exception of BURGOS.[6] Such, however, doubtless exist within the confines of the kingdom of the Swabian conquerors, which comprised Galicia, the Asturias, and part of Portugal.[7]

---

[1] See Zeuss, *Die Deutschen*, pp. 326, 380–384 ; Sheppard, *Fall of Rome*, p. 130.

[2] See p. 59, *supra*. [3] Latham, *Nationalities of Europe*, vol. ii. p. 246.

[4] Compare the English village-names of Warrington, Athelney (p. 99), Donnington, Connington, Skillington, Waldingfield, Erpingham, Bolingbroke, Thurning, Marrington, Bovington, Bessingham, Rockingham, and Torkington.

[5] Latham, *Nationalities of Europe*, vol. ii. p. 283 ; Schmeller, *Ueber die sogenannten Cimbern*, p. 561. The Lombard German was commonly spoken in Northern Italy, till the year 800 A.D. Diez, *Gram. d. Rom. Spr.* vol. i. p. 48.

[6] And, possibly, Collunga and Meville, both within the limits of the Swabian kingdom.

[7] See Grimm, *Gesch. d. Deut. Spr.* p. 501 ; Keferstein, *Ansichten*, vol. ii. p. 313 ; Zeuss, *Die Deutschen*, p. 456.

It has been generally assumed that the original home of the Saxons is to be sought in the modern kingdom of Hanover, between the mouths of the Elbe and the Weser. I have made a careful search in this region for names identical or analogous with those which are found in Saxon England. In Westphalia a small group of patronymics was discovered.[1] But on the whole the investigation was remarkably barren of results, the names, for the most part, proving to be of an altogether dissimilar type.[2] The search was continued over Mecklenburg, Holstein,[3] Friesland, and the greater part of Germany. A few sporadic names were found, but always surrounded and outnumbered by names possessing no distinctive Anglo-Saxon character. There is, however, in a most unlikely corner of the Continent, a well-defined district, rather larger than Devonshire, where the names, though slightly disguised in form, are as characteristically Saxon as those found in the Boulogne Colony. This district is confined chiefly to the Valley of the Neckar, but just crosses the watershed between the Neckar and the Danube. It occupies the Northern half of the modern kingdom of Würtemburg, and includes a small portion of Bavaria in the neighbourhood of Donau-werth. It also stretches into the State of Baden, between Heidelberg and Bruchsal. It does not extend to the left bank of the Rhine, or to the right bank of the Lower Neckar. In Würtemberg, however, it occupies both banks of the Neckar. The railway from Bruchsal to Ulm, with its serpentine windings and fearful gradients, carries the tourist through the centre of this district, which has attractions for the artist and the angler, as well as for the ethnologist.[4]

This district comprehends the Southern portion of what was known in mediaeval times as FRANKEN, or Franconia, and

[1] See Appendix B.
[2] Names in *wick* and *wich*, so common in England, are found on the Continent only in the Netherlands, Friesland, and old Saxony. Lappenberg, *Anglo-Saxon Kings*, vol. i. p. 86. The *horsts* which abound in Kent and Sussex, are found also on the Weser in Westphalia.
[3] Some curious coincidences between the local names in Kent and in Jutland have been pointed out by Maack, in the *Germania*, vol. iv. pp. 396–398.
[4] There are many points of analogy between this part of Germany and England. It is the hop garden and brewery of the Continent. It was in the midst of this district that I met with the only case of downright English beery drunkenness that it has been my lot to encounter during many rambles on the Continent. The people are the only Protestants in South Germany, and they are distinguished by the English love of field sports. It may be curious to note that the battles of Blenheim and Dettingen were fought on the borders of this Saxon district, and that of Agincourt on the borders of the Boulogne colony.

the northern part of SWABIA, or Schwabenland.[1] Etymologically and historically, Franconia is the land of the Franks, and Schwabenland is the land of the Suevi, just as England is the land of the Angles. Tacitus locates the Suevi near the Angles ; and Ptolemy even speaks of the Suevi as one division of the Angles.[2]

The ancient charters of this district, extending from the eighth to the twelfth centuries, have been admirably edited, and published by the Government of Würtemberg.[3] The local names which occur in these charters are, to a surprising extent, *identical* with those in the Anglo-Saxon charters, published by the English Historical Society.[4] Twenty-four very remarkable correspondences are given by Professor Leo,[5] and it would be easy largely to increase the list.

But confining ourselves to the names which have survived to modern times, I find in the maps of the admirable government survey of Würtemberg no less than 344 patronymics, of which 266, or 80 per cent. occur also in England ; [6] and the number of identifications might, doubtless, be largely increased by a more careful comparison. The evidence is overwhelming. It proves that the villages of Würtemberg and the villages of England were originally settled by men bearing the *same family names.* One or two instances of these correspondences may here be given, and others will be found in the appendix.[7] Thus the Æslingas are mentioned in a Kentish charter,[8] we have Eslingaforda in the Exon Domesday, and ISLINGTON in Norfolk and Middlesex. In Artois we find ISLINGHEM and ESLINGHEN ; and in Würtemburg there are several villages named ESSLINGEN, EISLINGEN, and AISLINGEN. Again, the Besingas, who are mentioned in an Anglo-Saxon charter, appear at BESSINGHAM in Norfolk,

---

[1] On the close connexion of the Franks and Suevi, see Zeuss, *Die Deutschen,* pp. 328, 338.

[2] τῶν δὲ ἐντὸς καὶ μεσογείων ἐθνῶν μέγιστα μέν ἐστι τό τε τῶν Σουήβων τῶν Ἀγγει, λῶν. See Zeuss, *Die Deutschen,* p. 153. It is a very significant fact that in mediaeval times the district south of Heidelberg was called the ANGLA-DEGAU.

[3] *Wirtembergisches Urkundenbuch, herausgegeben von dem Königlichen Staatsarchiv in Stuttgart.* Edid. Kausler ; two vols. 4to. 1849 and 1858. A large number of ancient Swabian names are also to be found in the *Codex Laureshamensis,* in Dümges, *Regesta Badensia,* and in Trehere, *Origines Palatinæ.* See also Förstemann, *Alt-deutsches Namenbuch,* vol. ii. *passim.*

[4] *Codex Diplomaticus Ævi Saxonici,* opera Joh. M. Kemble ; five vols, 8vo.

[5] *Anglo-Saxon Names,* pp. 116-119.

[6] The proportion is the same as in the Boulogne colony.

[7] Appendix B.

[8] *Cod. Dipl.* no. 111.

at BEZINGHAM in Artois, and at BISSENGEN in Würtemberg. The Birlingas appear in a Worcestershire charter, we have BIRLING in Kent, BIRLINGHAM in Worcestershire, BARLINGHEM and BERLINGHEN in Artois, and BIERLINGEN in Würtemberg —a place which has been identified with the Birlingen of an ancient charter. So we have BOCKING in Essex, BOUQUINGHEM in Artois, and BÖCHINGEN in Würtemberg.

It will be observed that these Swabian names terminate almost universally in *ing-en*. The suffix *en* is usually the sign of the dative plural. Thus Birlingen would mean ' At the Birlings ', that is, ' at the place where the family of Birl lives '.[1] It should, however, be noted that a name like Birlingen may be a corruption of the Berling*hen*, which we find in Artois.[2] The *hen* in this case is, undoubtedly, a corruption of *hem*, for we find that, close to the coast, the village-names end in *hem*, a suffix which passes into *hen* as we approach the Belgian frontier. The *hem* of Artois is undoubtedly only a phonetic modification of the English *hăm* ; and it is, therefore, a question whether the *-ing-en* of Würtemberg is not the same as the *-ing-ham* of England, since we can trace it through the intermediate stages of *inghen* and *inghem*.[3]

What interpretation shall we put upon these facts ? Shall we conclude that the cradle of the Saxon race is to be sought in the Valley of the Neckar, or were Swabia and England both colonies from a common motherland ? In the case of a fluviatile migration the descent of the river would be far more easy, and therefore far more probable, than the ascent against a rapid current like that of the Rhine.[4] But this

[1] So Bad*en* is a dative plural answering to Thermis or Aquis. Holste*in*, Swed*en*, Hess*en*, and Preuss*en* are also dative plurals. Pott, *Personen-Namen*, p. 169 ; Förstemann, *Alt-Deutschcs Namenbuch*, vol. ii. p. 835 ; *Ortsnamen*, pp. 194, 195 ; Grimm, *Deut. Gram.* vol. ii. p. 349 ; Meyer, *Ortsnamen des Kantons Zürich*, p. 139 ; Bender, *Deutschen Ortsnamen*, p. 103 ; Vilmar, *Ortsnamen*, pp. 264, 265 ; and p. 50, *supra*.

[2] That the Suevi were associated with the Saxons in the formation of the Flemish settlement is proved by the names of some fifteen villages in Flanders which contain their name, e.g. Suevezele, Sueveghem, etc. Warnkönig, *Flandrische Staatsgeschichte*, vol. i. p. 91.

[3] In Switzerland *heim* often becomes *en*, e.g. Altheim is now Alten, Dachsheim is now Dachsen, Sickingen was anciently Sickingheim. Pott, *Personennamen*, p. 169 ; Meyer *Ortsnamen*, p. 125. In Hesse we find Sielen, anciently Siliheim, and Heskem, anciently Heistinche*i*m. Vilmar, *Ortsnamen*, p. 271 ; Förstemann, *Ortsnamen*, pp. 98, 231. Some of the names, instead of the suffix *ing-en*, terminate in *ig-heim*. This is clearly the Anglo-Saxon *hăm*, a home, while *hăm*, an inclosure, would be represented by *en*. The distinction which has been lost in England has been preserved in Swabia. Since *heim* is a long syllable, the penultimate is shortened for phonetic reasons by the omission of a letter, and *ingheim* becomes *igheim*, or *enheim*, as in the cases of Bönigheim, Besigheim, Bietigheim, Billigheim and Dackenheim.

[4] Along the whole course of the Rhine, from the Neckar to the sea, a distance of more than 250 miles, we find scattered, here and there, isolated names undoubtedly akin

argument is of small force, when weighed against the con-
currence of ancient tradition, which places the Saxons on the
coast of the German ocean. Ptolemy speaks of the ' islands
of the Saxons ' ; and the geographer of Ravenna says, ' con-
finalis Daniæ est patria quæ nominatur Saxonia.' Orosius
speaks of the Saxons, ' gentem Oceani in litoribus et paludibus
inviis sitam '.[1]

These and other early notices render it difficult to avoid
the conclusion that the ' old Saxons ' were seated somewhere
between the mouths of the Elbe and of the Rhine, in juxtaposition with the Suevi, the Franks, the Lombards, and the
Angles. As we have already seen, it was here that, for thirty-
two years, they withstood the power of Charlemagne, who
avenged their obstinate resistance by the massacre of thousands of their warriors in cold blood, and dispersed a third
of the nation into distant provinces.[2] This extermination
of the Saxons on the Weser, coupled with the subsequent
influx of a Sclavonic population, as evinced by the local names,
may serve to account for the absence of characteristic Saxon
names in that region, while the Swabians and Angles of
Würtemberg may possibly have formed one of the transported colonies of Charlemagne ; if, indeed, the Swabian
colony was not a settlement brought about at the same time
and by the same causes that produced the descents upon the
English coast.[3]

to those which we have been considering. There is no cluster of them to be discovered
anywhere, nothing but single names, such as Bingen, Wellingen, Rellinghaus, and
Eppinghofen, which seem to have been waifs by the roadside, dropped by the passing
host of pilgrims.

[1] On the original seat of the old Saxons see Lappenberg, *Anglo-Saxon Kings*, vol.
i. p. 87; Zeuss, *Die Deutschen*, pp. 380–394. The modern kingdom of Saxony was
Sclavonic to a late date, as is shown by the local names. It is out of the question to
locate the ' old Saxons ' in this region.

[2] Eginhard, in his life of Charlemagne, sec. vii. and again in his Annals, A.D. 804,
says that Charlemagne transplanted 10,000 men of the Saxons, with their wives and
children, into Germany and Gaul. All these were from the Duchy of Bremen. The
names of Sachsenhausen, near Frankfort, and Katzellenbogen in the gorge of the Rhine,
may be records of some of these settlements. See p. 101, *supra*; Pertz, *Mon. Ger.*
vol. ii. p. 447; vol. i. p. 191; Palgrave, *English Commonwealth*, vol. i. p. 40.

[3] Both Zeuss and Latham think that the Suevi left the shores of the Weser for those
of the Danube and the Neckar in the third century. The Saxons moved southwards
in the sixth century. See Zeuss, *Die Deutschen*, p. 316; Turner, *Anglo-Saxons*,
vol. i. p. 208.

CHAPTER VIII

THE NORTHMEN

Incursions of the Northmen—Norse test words : ' by ', ' thorpe ', ' toft ' ' ville ', ' garth ', ' ford ', ' wick '—Vestiges of the Danes near the Thames —Essex, Suffolk, Norfolk, and Lincolnshire—The Danelagh—Norwegians in Sutherland, the Orkneys, Shetlands, Hebrides, and Isle of Man—Cumberland and Westmoreland—The Wirall—Colony in Pembrokeshire—Devonshire and the South Coast—Northmen in Ireland— Intensity of the Scandinavian element in different parts of England— Northmen in France—Names in Normandy—Norse Names in Spain, Sicily, and the Hellespont—Local vestiges of the Anglo-Norman conquest—Anglo-Norman nobles in Scotland.

FOR three centuries the Northmen were the terror of Western Europe. They sailed up the Elbe, the Scheldt, the Rhine, the Moselle, and the Neckar.[1] They ravaged the valleys of the Somme, the Seine, the Marne, the Yonne, the Loire, and the Garonne. They besieged Paris, Amiens, Orleans, Tours, Troyes, Chalons, Poictiers, Bordeaux, and Toulouse.[2] They plundered the coasts of Italy, and encountered the Arabs at Seville and Barcelona.[3] Over the entrance to the arsenal at Venice may still be seen one of the sculptured lions which once adorned the Piræus at Athens. The marble is deeply scored with Norse runes, which, by the aid of photography, have been deciphered by Professor Rafn of Copenhagen, and which prove to be a record of the capture of the Piræus by Harold Hardráda, the Norwegian king who fell at Stamford Bridge.[4] The Northmen established themselves as conquerors or colonists over the half of England, in the isles and western coasts of Scotland, in Greenland, in Iceland, in the Isle of Man, and in the north of France—they founded kingdoms in Naples, Sicily, France, England, and Ireland—

[1] Strinnholm, *Wikingzüge*, p. 81.
[2] Ib. pp. 34, 35, 98, 144 ; Crichton, *Scandinavia*, vol. i. p. 165.
[3] Gayangos, *Moham. Dynasties*, vol. ii. pp. 116, 431, 435 ; Strinnholm, *Wikingzüge*, p. 36 ; Depping, *Expéditions*, vol. i. pp. 110, 134.
[4] Laing, *Heimskringla*, vol. iii. pp. 3, 4 ; Dasent, *Burnt Njal*, vol. i. p. 10 ; vol. ii, p. 499 ; St. John, *Four Conquests*, vol. ii. p. 248.

while a Norse dynasty ruled Russia for seven hundred years,[1] and for centuries the Varangian guard upheld the tottering throne of the Byzantine emperors.

The historic annals of these conquests are scanty and obscure. But the Norse names which are still found scattered over the north-west of Europe supply a means of ascertaining many facts which history has left unrecorded. By the aid of the names on our modern maps we are able to define the precise area which was ravaged by the Scandinavians, and we can, in many instances, detect the nature of the descent, whether for purposes of plunder, trade, or colonization. Sometimes, indeed, we can even recover the very names of the Viking chiefs and of their followers, and ascertain from whence they sailed, whether from the low-lying coasts of Denmark, or from the rock-bound fjords of Norway.

Before we proceed to attempt the solution of any of these curious problems, it will be necessary to exhibit the tools with which the historical lock is to be picked. We must analyse and classify the characteristic names which the Northmen have left upon the map.

The most valuable and important of these test-words is *byr* or *by*. This word originally meant a dwelling, or a single farm, and hence it afterwards came to denote a village.[2] In Iceland, at the present day, the ordinary name given to a farmstead is *boer*,[3] and in Scotland a cow-stall is still called a *byre*. We find this word as a suffix in the village-names of Denmark, and of all countries colonized[4] by the Danes. In Normandy we find it in the form *bue* or *boeuf*, and in England it is usually contracted into *by*.[5] In the Danish district of England—between Watling Street and the River Tees—the suffix *by* frequently takes the place of the Anglo-Saxon *-ham*

---

[1] Of the fifty Russian ambassadors to Constantinople in the year 945, as many as forty-seven bear Norse names, such as Rulov (Rolf), Phrelaf (Frideleif), Grim, Karl, Ulf, Asbrand, and Sven. Strinnholm, *Wikingzüge*, p. 296.

[2] A *by-law* is the local law enacted by the township. Compare the Burlaw, or Birlaw, of Scotland. [But see *N.E.D. s.v.*]. Palgrave, *Eng'ish Commonwealth*, vol. i. p. 80. On the suffix *by*, see Donaldson, *English Ethnog*, p. 54 ; Worsaae, *Danes and Norwegians*, pp. 67, 159 ; Latham, *English Language*, vol. i. p. 431 ; Ansted and Latham, *Channel Islands*, p. 333 ; Ferguson, *Northmen*, p. 42.

[3] *Peaks and Passes*, Second Series, vol. i. p. 47.

[4] It denotes Danish *colonization*. In places visited only for purposes of trade or plunder no dwellings would be required. [See G. S. Streatfeild, *Lincolns. and the Danes*, 19.]

[5] The Devonshire suffix *bere* or *bear* comes still nearer to the Icelandic form. See p. 125, *infra*. The Normand *boeuf* seems to be represented in the English *booth*, and the Scotch *bothie*. Le Prevost, *Recherches*, p. 40 ; Ferguson, *Northmen*, p. 46.

or -*ton*. In this region there are numerous names like GRIMS-
BY,[1] WHITBY, DERBY,[2] RUGBY, KIRBY, NETHERBY, SELBY,
or ASHBY. In Lincolnshire alone there are one hundred
names ending in *by*. To the north of Watling Street there
are some six hundred instances of its occurrence—to the
south of it, scarcely one. There are scores and scores of
names ending in *by* in Jutland and Sleswic, and not half-a-
dozen throughout the whole of Germany.[3] The suffix is
common both to the Norwegian and Danish districts of England, though it is more frequent in the latter.

Another useful test-word is *thorpe, throp*, or *trop*,[4] which
we find in ALTHORPE, COPMANSTHORPE, and WILSTROP, near
York. It means an aggregation of men or houses—a village.
This suffix is very useful in enabling us to discriminate between
the settlements of the Danes and those of the Norwegians,
being confined almost exclusively to the former. It is very
common in Denmark and East Anglia, it is very rare in Norway, it does not occur in Lancashire, only once in Cumberland, and very seldom in Westmoreland.

The word *toft*, which in Normandy takes the form *tot*, is
also distinctly Danish and East Anglian. It is very scarce
in Norway and Westmoreland, and is unknown in Cumberland. It signifies a homestead or inclosure, and, like *by* and
thorpe, it is an indication of permanent colonization.

Thwaite, on the other hand, is the distinctive Norwegian
suffix. The meaning is nearly the same as the Saxon *field*,
a forest clearing. It is very common in Norway, it occurs
forty-three times in Cumberland, and not once in Lincolnshire,
while *thorpe*, the chief Danish test-word, which occurs sixty-three
times in Lincolnshire, is found only once in Cumberland.

In Normandy the greater proportion of Norse names end

---

[1] At the port of Elsinore, previous to the recent abolition of the Sound dues, the
vessels of Grimsby could claim certain privileges and exemptions conferred by the Danish
founder of the town. Palgrave, *Eng. Commonwealth*, vol. i. p. 50 ; *Normandy and England*, vol. iii. p. 349.

[2] In a few cases we have documentary evidence of a change of name consequent upon
the Danish conquest. Thus we know that the Norse name of Deoraby or DERBY took
the place of the former Saxon name of Northweorthig, or Norworth as it would now be
written. So the Saxon Streoneshalch became the Norse WHITBY.

[3] Even these are chiefly found on the Eyder and north of the Elbe—a Danish district.

[4] It corresponds to the German *dorf*, a village, seen in the names ALTORF, DUSSELDORF,
etc. Cf. Arnold, *Hist. Rome*. vol. i. p. 526. In Westphalia and Münster the form *trup*
or *drup* is very common, as HOLTRUP, ALDRUP, SANDRUP, BARNSTRUP, WESTRUP. Mass-
man, in Dorow's *Denkmäler*, vol. i. pp. 187–192. The etymological affinities of *thorpe*
are discussed by Diefenbach, *Vergleichendes Wörterbuch*, vol. ii. p. 698 ; Leo, *A.-S.
Names*, pp. 43–50; Förstemann, *Namenbuch*, vol. ii. p. 1391.

in *ville*, as TANCARVILLE or HACONVILLE. This has always, I believe, been referred to the Romance word *villa*, but a careful study of the regions in which it occurs has convinced me that it must be the Teutonic *weiler*, an abode,[1] a single house, which is so common in the Khinegau and in many parts of Germany.[2] Toward the edge of the Norman occupancy it takes the form *villiers*,[3] as in the name HARDIVILLIERS. In England it is found in the form *well* or *will*, as at KETTLE-WELL, and BRADWELL.

The Norse *garth*, an inclosure, which corresponds to the Anglo-Saxon *yard*, has already been discussed.[4]

The work *beck*,[5] a brook, is more frequent in the Norwegian than in the Danish region, and this also is the case with the suffixes *-haugh, -with, -tarn,* and *-dale*.[6] The word *force*, which is the ordinary name for a waterfall in the lake district, is exclusively Norwegian, and corresponds to the Icelandic and Norwegian *foss*.[7] The word *fell* is also derived from Norway, where it takes the form *fjeld* (pronounced *fi-ell*). It is the usual name for a hill in the north-west of England.[8]

We now come to the words which do not necessarily imply any permanent colonization by the Northmen. The suffix *ford* occurs both in Anglo-Saxon and in Norse names, but with characteristic difference of meaning. In either case *ford* is a derivative of *faran* or *fara*, to go.[9] The *fords* of the Anglo-Saxon husbandmen, which are scattered so abund-

---

[1] Old High German *wilari* or *wilre*. Now High German *weiler*. Förstemann, *Alt-deutsches Namenbuch*, vol. ii. pp. 1527–1533; Bender, *Ortsnamen*, p. 131.

[2] In Canton Zürich it occurs more than seventy times, as in BREITWIL. Meyer, *Ortsnamen des Kantons Zürich*, p. 75.

[3] This form alone may suffice to show how inadequate the Romance *villa* is as a source of these names.

[4] See p. 85, *supra*. MICKLEGARTH or 'Greatgarth' was the Norse name of Constantinople.

[5] In Mercia we find the form *batch*, as in Woodbatch, Comberbatch, and Sandbach.

[6] The Anglo-Saxon form is *dell*, as in ARUNDEL. The Norse form *dale* is seen in KENDAL, ANNANDALE, and LONSDALE. The German equivalent is *thal*. When *dal* is a prefix it is usually a corruption of the Celtic *dol*, a field, as in the cases of DALKEITH and DALRYMPLE.

[7] e.g. the waterfall of SKOGAROSS in Iceland.

[8] The Anglo-Saxon *field* or *feld* is from the same root as the Norse *fell*. A *fell* is a place where the ground is on the fall; *a field* or *feld* is where the trees have been felled. [? Probably 'open ground' akin to Lat. *pala-m*, Curtius, i, 337.] In old writers wood and feld are continually contrasted. Just like the American term 'a clearing', the word *field* bore witness to the great extent of unfelled timber which still remained. With the progress of cultivation the word has lost its primitive force. The word *fold* is from the same source [?]. See p. 86, *supra*; Trench, *Study of Words*, p. 200; Sparschuh, *Berichtigungen*, p. 17.

[9] A cabman's or waterman's *fare* is the person who goes with him. *Fare*-well is an imperative—journey well. The field-*fare* is so called from its characteristic habit of moving across the fields. See Diefenbach, *Vergl. Wört.* vol. i. pp. 364–366; Sparschuh, *Berichtigungen*, p. 65.

antly over the south of England, are passages across rivers for men or cattle ; the *fords* of the Scandinavian sea-rovers are passages for ships [1] up arms of the sea, as in the case of the fjords of Norway and Iceland,[2] and the firths of Scotland. These Norse fords are found on the coasts which were frequented for purposes of trade or plunder. We have instances in WEXFORD, CARLINGFORD, WATERFORD, and STRANGFORD in Ireland, in MILFORD and HAVERFORD in Wales, in ORFORD and CHILLSFORD in Suffolk, and perhaps in SEAFORD [3] in Sussex, and DEPTFORD, the ' deep reach ' on the Thames.

Wick is also found in both Anglo-Saxon and Norse names, but here also there is a difference in the application, analogous to that which we have just considered. The primary meaning in either case seems to have been a station.[4]   With the Anglo-Saxons it was a station or abode on land—hence a house or a village : with the Northmen it was a station for ships [5]— hence a small creek or bay. The sea-rovers derived their name of *vik-ings*,[6] or ' creekers,' from the *wics* or creeks in which they anchored. The inland wicks, therefore, are mostly Saxon, while the Norse wicks fringe our coasts,[7] and usually indicate the stations of pirates, rather than those of colonists. Thus we have WICK and SANDWICH, in Kent ; WYKE, near Portland ; BERWICK, in Sussex and Northumberland ; and WICKLOW, in Ireland, all of which occur in places

[1] While many of our agricultural terms, as basket, crook, kiln, fleam, barrow, ashlar, gavelock, rasher, and mattock, are of Celtic origin, seafaring words, such as cockswain, boatswain, and skipper, are mostly Norse. Garnett, *Essays*, p. 31. Cf. Diez, *Gram. d. Rom. Spr*, vol. i. p. 56.

[2] e.g. FAXA FIORD, HAFNAFIORD, and HVALFIORD in Iceland.

[3] Still pronounced Seafoord.

[4] See Marsh, *Lectures on the Origin and Hist. of the English Language*, p. 132. The root runs through all the Aryan languages. We have the Sanskrit *vêça*, the Zend *vîç*, the Greek οἶκος, a house, and the Latin *vicus*, the Mæso-Gothic *veihs*, the Polish *wies*, the Irish *fich*, the Cymric *gwic*, all meaning an abode or village. Diefenbach, *Vergleichendes Wörterbuch*, vol. i. p. 138 ; Pictet, *Orig. Indo-Europ.* vol. ii. p. 238 ; Vilmar, *Ortsnamen*, p. 270 ; Crichton, *Scandinavia*, vol. i. p. 37 ; Sparschuh, *Berichtigungen*, p. 95 ; Förstemann, *Namenbuch*, vol. ii. p. 1509.

[5] [A.-Sax. *wîc*, a village, and Lat. *vik*, a creek, are really distinct words.] There is, however, an Anglo-Saxon verb *wîcian*, to run a ship on shore, to take up a station.

[6] Afterwards the work viking came to be used for any robber. Thus in a Norse Biblical paraphrase Goliath is termed a viking. Dasent, *Burnt Njal*, vol. ii. p. 353.

[7] The whole of the Essex coast is lined with names ending in *wick*. About thirty of the farmhouses in the salt marshes bear this name. We have the Wick (three times), Eastwick (twice), Westwick (twice). Northwick (twice), as well as Jewick, Raywick, Frowick, Langwick, and Lastwick. These names may be derived either from the Anglo-Saxon, or from the Norse, *wic*. More probably, however, they should be referred to an entirely different source, namely the Anglo-Saxon *vîc.*, a marsh, a word which is related to the German *weich*, soft, and the modern English word *weak*. Diefenbach, *Vergleichendes Wörterbuch*, vol. i. p. 139 ; Leo, *Rectitudines Sing. Pers.* p. 53. The numerous places in South Tyrol called Vigo seem to derive their names from the Latin *vicus*. Gilbert and Churchill, *Dolomite Mountains*, p. 74.

where there are no inland names denoting Norse colonization. The names of NORTHWICH, MIDDLEWICH, NANTWICH, DROIT-WICH, NETHERWICH, SHIRLEYWICH, WICKHAM, and perhaps of WARWICK, although inland places, are derived indirectly from the Norse *wic*, a bay, and not from the Anglo-Saxon *wic*, a village. All these places are noted for the production of salt, which was formerly obtained by the evaporation of sea-water in shallow wiches or bays, as the word baysalt testifies. Hence a place for making salt came to be called a wych-house, and Nantwich, Droitwich, and other places where rock-salt was found, took their names from the wych-houses built for its preparation.[1]

Another word which denotes the occasional presence of the sea-rovers is *ness* or *naze*, which means a nose, or promontory of land. Thus we have CAITHNESS, WRABNESS, CAPE GRINEZ, near Calais, and the NAZE in Norway and in Essex.

We may also detect the visits of the Northmen by the word *scar*, a face of rock or cliff—from *skera*, to *shear*, or cut asunder.[2] Instances are to be found in the names of SCAR-BOROUGH, the SKERRIES, and SKERRYVORE. A *holm* means an island, almost always an island in a lake or river.[3] STOCK-HOLM stands on such an island. We have also FLATHOLM in the Severn, and LINGHOLME on Windermere. An island in the sea is denoted by the suffix *œ*, *a*, *ay*, or *ey*,[4] as in the case of the FAROE ISLANDS ; MAGEROE, in Norway ; STAFFA, IONA, and CUMBRAY, on the western coast of Scotland ; and LAMBAY on the Irish coast.

Furnished with these test-words we may endeavour to trace the various settlements of the Danes and of the Norwegians.

To begin with our own island. As will be seen by a reference to the coloured map, the Danes of Jutland appear to

---

[1] See Knapp, *English Roots and Ramifications*, p. 18. Domesday Book mentions salt works at Wick, Upewic, Helperic, Midelwic, and Norwiche, all in Worcestershire. From the same authority we learn that at Droitwich certain *dues* of salt were payable. Ellis, *Introduction to Domesday*, pp. xl. and xli. [See Duignan, *Worcestershire Place Names*, 54.]

[2] Cf. the Gaelic and Erse *sgeir*, a cliff, and the Anglo-Saxon *sciran*, to divide. Hence the *shire*, a division of land, the *shore* which divides land from sea, a *skewer*, the plough-*share* and the *shears*, instruments for dividing, and a *share*, a divided part. To *score* is to make notches on a stick, and the numeral a *score* denotes the number of notches such a stick would contain. A *scar* is the mark where the flesh has been divided. [No. It was properly a burn, from Greek.] A *shard* is a bit of broken pottery *Sharp* and *sharp* denote that something has been cut off.]

[3] [Sometimes low ground partly submerged.]

[4] The suffix *ey* is Anglo-Saxon as well as Norse.

have frequented the south-eastern portion of the island for
purposes of trade or plunder rather than of colonization,
This we gather from the fact that the Norse names in this
district are found chiefly in the immediate vicinity of the
coast, and designate either safe anchorages, or dangerous
headlands. We find hardly one solitary instance of the occur-
ence of the suffixes *by, toft, thorpe,* or *thwaite,* which would
indicate permanent residence.

London was repeatedly besieged by the Danes. With the
hope of capturing the rich and unrifled prize, their fleets lay
below the city for many months together.[1] Their stations
were at DEPTFORD, ' the deep fiord ' ; at GREENWICH [2], the
' green reach ' : and at WOOLWICH, the ' hill reach ',[3] so
called apparently from its being overhung by the conspicuous
landmark of Shooter's Hill. The spits and headlands, which
mark the navigation along the Thames and the adjacent
coasts, almost all bear characteristic Norse names—such as
the FORENESS, the WHITENESS, SHELLNESS, SHEERNESS, SHOE-
BURYNESS, FOULNESS, WRABNESS, ORFORDNESS, and the NAZE,
near Harwich. On the Essex coast we find DANESEY FLATS,
LANGENHOE, and ALRESFORD.[4] DENGEY Hundred, in the
south-east of Essex, is spelt Daneing in a charter of
Edward the Confessor.[5] PRETTLEWELL and HAWKSWELL,
in the same neighbourhood, may probably contain the
suffix *-ville,* which is so common in Normandy ; and
THOBY, near Ingatestone,[6] SCAR House, and LEE BECK, indicate
the presence of Danish settlers. In the extreme north-eastern
corner of the county we find a little compact Danish colony
—planted on a spot well guarded by marshes and the sea.
Here we discover the Danish names of HARWICH, HOLMES
Island, KIRBY, THORPE-le-Soken, and East THORPE. At
WALTON ON THE NAZE there seems to have been a walled
inclosure, to defend the intruders from the assaults of their
hostile Saxon neighbours. In the south-eastern corner of

---

[1] *Saxon Chronicle,* A.D. 1013, 1014, 1016.
[2] There is a GRENIVIK in Iceland, which is mentioned in the *Landnamabok,* p. 255.
[3] This etymology is confirmed by the fact that Woolwich is written Hulviz in
Domesday.
[4] Stansgate Wick, Wigborough, and Battleswick may be either Saxon or Norse. See
p. 113, *supra.*
[5] Gough's *Camden,* vol. ii. p. 132.
[6] Not far from hence Cnut gained a great victory over Eadmund Ironside, which may
have led to the settlement of some of the conquerors in the neighbourhood. See Chapter
XII.

Suffolk we have another WALTON, probably a second fortified outpost of the Danish kingdom.[1]

In Suffolk there are a few scattered Danish names, chiefly near the coast—such as IPSWICH, DUNWICH,[2] WALDERSWICK, ORFORD, CHILLESFORD, THORPE, BARNBY, and LOWESTOFT.

The name of NORWICH is probably Norse. The city is situated on what was formerly an arm of the sea, and it was visited by Danish fleets.[3] In the extreme south-eastern corner of Norfolk there is a dense Danish settlement—occupying the Hundreds of East and West FLEGG,[4] a space some eight miles by seven, well protected on every side by the sea, and the estuaries of the Bure and the Yare. In this small district eleven names out of twelve are unmistakably Norse, compounded mostly of some common Danish personal name, and the suffix *by*. We find the villages of STOKESBY, BILLOCKBY, FILBY, HEMSBY, ORMSBY, SCROTEBY, ROLLESBY, MALTBY, HERRINGBY and CLIPPESBY. The parish of REPPS reminds us of the Icelandic districts called *Hreppar*,[5] and St. Olave's Bridge preserves the name of the royal saint of Scandinavia. In the remaining part of Norfolk there are scattered names of a distinctively Danish character, though they by no means preponderate.[6] Here, however, we are met by an element of uncertainty, since the dialectic peculiarities of the Danes from Jutland merge into those of the East Anglians[7] who

[1] In England we find some forty places called Walton. With one or two exceptions these occur in the neighbourhood of some isolated Danish or Norwegian colony. There are places bearing the name in the neighbourhood of Harwich, Ipswich, Fenny Stratford, Lynn, Wisbeach, Liverpool, and Haverford West, all regions inhabited by an intrusive population, to whom the security afforded by a *walled town* would be a matter of prime necessity.

[2] Beda writes the name Dunmoc. It would seem, therefore, that the last syllable of the modern name is due to Danish influence.

[3] *Saxon Chronicle*, A.D. 1004 ; Turner, *Anglo-Saxons*, vol. ii. p. 317 ; Palgrave, *Normandy and England*, vol. iii. p. 398.

[4] From the Norse word *flegg*, or Danish *vlak*, flat. Compare the names of FLECKNEY, in Leicestershire, and FLEKKESFJORD and FLECKEROE, on the Norwegian coast.

[5] See p. 135, *infra*.

[6] In the list of Suffolk surnames given in Donaldson's *English Ethnography*, pp. 62–65, there are several which occur in the *Landnamabok* of Iceland. The sons of Njal were Skarphethin, Helgi, and Grimmr ; these three names are common in Norfolk in the form Sharpin, Heely, and Gryme. Dasent, *Burnt Njal*, vol. i. p. 79 ; Borrow, *Wild Wales*, vol. i. p. 352, note.

[7] In the Rev. R. Garnett's *Essay on the Language and Dialects of the British Isles* (*Essays*, pp. 139, 140, 143) an attempt is made to distinguish the Anglian districts by means of the hard forms, Carlton, Fiskerton, Skipton, Skelbrooke, Skephouse, etc., which take the place of the Charltons or Chorltons, Fishertons, Shelbrookes, and Sheephouses, which are found to the south of the Thames and the west of the Teme. But it may be doubted how far these forms are Anglian and how far Scandinavian. Mr. R. Garnett's Anglian districts are : 1. *East Anglian*—Norfolk and Suffolk. 2. *Middle Anglian*—Lincoln, Notts, and Derbyshire. 3. *North Anglian*—West Riding. 4. *Northumbrian*—Durham, Northumberland, and the North and East Ridings. All these

migrated from the contiguous districts of Holstein and Sleswic ; and it is often difficult to discriminate between the names derived from either source.

When, however, we cross the Wash and come to Lincolnshire, we find overwhelming evidence of an almost exclusive Danish occupancy.[1] About one-fourth of the village names in Lincolnshire present the characteristic Danish suffix *by*, while the total number of Danish names in this county amounts to about three hundred—more than are found in all the rest of Southumbrian England.

The fens which border the Witham, the Welland, and the Nen effectually guarded the southern frontier of the Danish settlers ; and this natural boundary they do not seem to have crossed in any considerable numbers. A line drawn from east to west, about eleven miles to the north of Boston, will mark the southern limit of the purely Danish, as distinguished from the Anglian settlement.[2] North of this line is a district about nine miles by twelve, between Tattershall, New Bolingbroke, Horncastle, and Spilsby, which would appear to have been more exclusively Danish than any other in the kingdom,[3] In this small space there are some forty unmistakable Danish village-names ; such as KIRBY, MOORBY, ENDERBY, WILKSBY, CLAXBY, MININGSBY, HAGNABY, DANDERBY, SCRIVELSBY, HAREBY, LUSBY, REVESBY, RAITHBY, SOMMERSBY, SALMONBY, FULLETBY, ASHBY, ASGARDBY, HEMINGBY, TOFT, and others, all denoting the fixed residence of a Danish population.

From Lincolnshire the Danes spread inland over the contiguous counties. The Danelagh, or Danish district, by agreement between Alfred and Guthrum, renewed by Eadmund and Anlaf in 941, was divided from the Saxon kingdom by a line passing along the Thames, the Lea, and the Ouse, and then following the course of Watling Street, the Roman road which runs in a straight line from London to Chester.[4] North of this

---

so-called Anglian districts are also, it will be seen, decisively Scandinavian. In fact, the Saxon peculiarities pass into those of the Anglians, the Anglian into those of the Danes, and these again into those of the Norwegians. The Danish inroads were the continuation, under another name, of the *earlier* Anglo-Saxon expeditions. See Palgrave, *Eng. Comm.* vol. i. p. 568.

1 [See Rev. G. S. Streatfeild's excellent book *Lincolnshire and the Danes*, 1884.]

2 See the coloured map.

3 A list of surnames compiled from the parish registers of this district, and compared with the names in the *Landnamabok* of Iceland, would probably prove of great ethnological interest and value.

4 Roger de Hoveden, p. 423 ; St. John, *Four Conquests*, vol. i. p. 354 ; Robertson, *Scotland under her Early Kings*, vol. i. p. 273 ; Turner, *Anglo-Saxons*, vol i. p. 378 ; Worsaae, *Danes and Norwegians*, p. 21.

line we find in the local names abundant evidence of Danish occupancy, while to the south of it hardly a single name is to be found denoting any permanent colonization. The coloured map will show the manner in which the Danish local names radiate from the Wash. In Leicestershire, Rutland, Northamptonshire, and Yorkshire, the Danish names pieponderate over those of the Anglo-Saxon type ; while Cambridgeshire, Huntingdonshire, Bedfordshire, and the adjacent counties, protected by the fens, present scarcely a single Danish name.[1]

We have, however, the Danish village-names of HEYTHROP, and COCKTHORPE in Oxfordshire. DACORUM Hundred, in Herts, is called Danais in Domesday : it contains the hamlets of ELSTROP, AYSTROPE, CAUSEWELL, HAMWELL, and a place called DANEFURLONG ; and on the borders of the hundred, close to the dividing line of Watling Street, are KETTLEWELL,[2] CHISWILL, and DANESEND.[3] It will be seen also how the Danish names cluster round each of the Danish fortresses of Leicester, Derby, Stamford, Nottingham, Lincoln, and York.[4]

As we leave Yorkshire and approach Durham and Northumberland the Norse names rapidly diminish in frequency, and north of the Tweed they almost entirely disappear. The few that we find are usually only stations on the coast, as ALNWICK, and BERWICK. The names of a few bays and headlands[5] prove that the Northmen weie familiar with the navigation of the coast, while the absence of any Norse names of villages or farms proves that the soil, for some reason, was left in the undisturbed possession of the Saxons or the Celts. In Fife we find *by* once or twice, and *thorpe* appears once in the form of *threap*.[6] The map proves conclusively that the district between the Tees and the Forth is one of the most purely Saxon portions of the island, thus remarkably corroborating the historical fact that in the eleventh century even the Lothians were reckoned as a part of England.[7]

---

[1] Toft, in Cambridgeshire, is almost the only instance.
[2] An unmistakably Norse name. In the *Landnamabok* Ketell occurs repeatedly as a personal name.
[3] Gough's *Camden*, vol. ii. p. 67.
[4] On the Danish burghs, see Worsaae, *Danes and Norwegians*, p. 31 ; Kemble, *Saxons n England*, vol. ii. p. 320.
[5] e.g. Alnwick, Berwick, the Firths of Forth, Tay, and Moray, Blackness, Borrowstowness, Fifeness, Buttonness, Burleness.
[6] See Chalmers, *Caledonia*, vol. i. p. 487.
[7] See Palgrave, *Normandy and England*, vol. iv. p. 346.

But as we approach the north-eastern extremity of Scotland a new phenomenon presents itself. We find a large number of Norse names ; they are, however, no longer Danish as heretofore, but exclusively Norwegian. We find, in fact, that the local nomenclature bears decisive witness to the historical fact that, down to a comparatively late period,[1] the Shetlands, the Orkneys, the Hebrides, and the Isle of Man, were not dependencies of the Crown of Scotland, but jarldoms attached to the kingdom of Norway.

It may seem strange to us that the extreme north-western corner of Great Britain should be called SUTHERLAND.[2] No inhabitants of Scotland could have bestowed so inappropriate a name. And, accordingly, we find that the Gaelic peasantry call the county Catuibh.[3] The name of Sutherland was evidently given by a people living still further to the north. Sutherland, in short, was the mainland to the *south* of the Orkney jarldom.[4] Here, as well as in Caithness, we find numerous Norwegian names, such as BRORA, THURSO, WICK, SKEROAR, Loch SKERROW, and SANDWICK bay. The barren uplands were left to the Gael ; while in the more fertile straths and glens we find the Norse suffixes *-dale*, *-seter*, and *-ster*. Names like LOCH LAXFORD [5] or STRATH HELMSDALE, in which a Celtic synonym is prefixed to the Norse word, seem to point to the recovery by the Celts of that preponderance of which, for a time, they had been deprived.

In the Shetlands every local name, without exception, is Norwegian. The names of the farms end, as in Norway, in *-seter* or *-ster*, and the hills are called *-how*, *-hoy*, and *-holl*. The names of the small bays have the Norwegian suffix *-voe*, as WESTVOE, AITHSVOE, LAXVOE, and HAMNAVOE.[6] We find also BURRAFIORD, SAXAFORD, LERWICK, and SANDWICK. In the whole of the Orkneys there are only two, or perhaps three, Celtic names.[7] The names of the islands of which the group

---

[1] A.D. 1266.   [2] See p. 54, *supra*.

[3] This word, and the first syllable of Caithness, are probably vestiges of an Ugrian occupation, which preceded the arrival of the Celts. In the Lapp language *ketje* means an end or extremity. See Robertson, *Early Kings*, vol. i. p. 33 ; Worsaae, *Danes*, p. 253.

[4] [Compare *Sodor*, *infra*, 120.]   [5] i.e. Salmon fjord.

[6] Worsaae, *Danes*, p. 230.

[7] One of these is the name of the group. In the word ORKNEY the terminal syllable *ey* is the Norse for island. The *n* which precedes is, I imagine, a vestige of the Gaelic *innis* or *inch*, an island. *Orc* is probably from the Gaelic *orc*, a whale. [Rather the porpoise=Lat. *porcus*.] Diefenbach, *Celtica*, vol. i. p. 41. Milton speaks of ' the haunt of seals and orcs '. Dr. Guest and Chalmers think that the root is the Cymric word *orch*, which means a border or limit. Guest, *On Gentile Names*, in *Phil. Proc.* vol. i. p. 9.

is composed present the Norwegian suffix, *a*, island. We have SANDA (sand island), STRONSA (stream island), and WESTRA (west island) ; and often, as in the case of RONALDSA and EGILSA, we find the name of the first Norwegian chief who found here a safe island home.[1]

It was the practice of the Vikings to retire during the winter months to one of the small islands off the coast, and to issue forth again on the return of summer to recommence their piracies.[2] The names of the innumerable islets of the Hebrides bear curious testimony to the prevalence of this practice. The small islands, with few exceptions, bear Norse appellations, while the local names on the mainland are almost wholly Celtic.[3]

The name of LEWIS is the Norwegian *ljod-hus*,[4] the wharf or landing-place ; and in this island we find bays called SAND-WICK and NORWICK. UIG was anciently Wig, [5] and HARRIS is a corruption of Harige.[6] BROADFORD bay, in Skye, is a name identical with BREIDA FIORD in Iceland, and there are also the capes of TROTTERNISH and VATTERNISH (water-ness). The first portion of this name contains the characteristic Norse word *vatn*, which appears in the names of no less than ten of the Hebridean lakes—as, for example, in those of Lochs LANGAVAT and STEEPAVAT.[7]

The Norsemen called the Hebrides the SUDREYJAR, or Southern Islands. The two sees of the Sudreyjar and of the Isle of Man were united in the eleventh century, and made dependent on the Archbishop of Trondhjem, in Norway, by whom, till the year 1334, the Episcopi Sudorenses were always consecrated. The Anglican Bishop of SODOR and Man still retains his titular supremacy over those ' southern isles ' which

---

[1] The Faroe Islands are wholly Norwegian. We have the islands of SANDOE, MEGGANAES, HESTOE, VAAGOE, NAALSOE, and the chief town is THORSHAVN.

[2] Skene, *History of the Highlanders*, vol. i. p. 91.

[3] There are three islands called Bernera, two called Scalpa, two called Pabbay. We have also the islands of Skarpa, Tarransay, Gillisay, Barra, Sundera, Watersay, Mingalay, Sanderay, Plottay, Uidhay, Eriskay, Fiaray, Wiay, Grimsay, Rona, Calvay, Lingay, and Hellesay. Nearer to the coast we find Rona, Fradda, Raasay, Soa (twice), Longa, Sanday, Canna, Ulva, Gommeray,Staffa (cf. Stafafell, in Iceland), Iona, Colonsay, Oronsay, Kerrera, Skarba, Jura, Islay, Gigha, Cara, Cumbray, Ailsa, and many others.

[4] Ansted and Latham, *Channel Islands*,p. 333 ; Innes, *Orig. Par.* Possibly, however, the root is *lod*, a bundle of fishing lines.

[5] Innes, *Orig. Par.* vol. ii. p. 385.

[6] *Ib.* p. 376.

[7] In Iceland there are lakes called Langer-vatn, Apa-vatn, Grœna-vatn, Fiski-vatn, Torfa-vatn, Sand-vatn, etc. On Norse names in the Scottish Isles, see Worsaae, *Danes*, pp. 218–276 ; Barry, *Hist. of Orkneys*, p. 232.

have so long been under the pastoral care of a presbyterian Church.[1]

In the south of Scotland the only Scandinavian settlement on the mainland was in Dumfriesshire. Here we find more than a dozen names with the suffix *by*, and others ending in *garth*, *beck*, and *thwaite*. In the neighbouring counties of Kirkcudbright and Wigton there are also a few outlying names of the same class.

The Isle of Man, which at one time formed a portion of the kingdom of Norway, must have contained a considerable Norwegian population, as appears from the Norse names of the villages, such as COLBY, GREENABY, DALBY, BALEBY, KIRBY, SULBY, and JURBY. On the coast we find the bays of PERWICK, FLESWICK, GREENWICK, SANDWICK, ALDRICH, SODER-ICK, GARWICK, and DRESWICK, the capes of LANGNESS and LITTLENESS, and the islands of EYE, HOLM, the CALF, and RONALDSAY; while SNEEFELL (snow hill), the highest mountain in the island, bears a pure Norwegian name.[2] The distribution of these Norse names is very noteworthy. It will be seen by a reference to the coloured map that they are confined mainly to the south of the island, a circumstance for which I was at a loss to account, till I discovered the historical fact that when Goddard of Iceland conquered Man he divided the fertile southern portion among his followers, while he left the natives in possession of the northern and more mountainous region, where, consequently, Celtic names still prevail.[3]

In the same way that the Danish names in England are seen to radiate from the Wash, so the Norwegian immigration seems to have proceeded from Morcambe Bay and that part of the coast which lies opposite to the Isle of Man. Cumberland, Westmoreland, Lancashire, and Dumfriesshire contain a very considerable number of Scandinavian names, but comparatively few of a distinctively Danish cast. The lake district seems to have been almost exclusively peopled by Celts and Norwegians. The Norwegian suffixes, *-gill*, *-garth*, *-haugh*, *-thwaite*, *-force*, and *-fell*, are abundant; while the Danish forms, *-thorpe* and *-toft*, are almost unknown; and the Anglo-

---

[1] [See *Orkneyingar Saga*, ed. Anderson, p. cxii; M. Walcott, *Ancient Church of Scotland*, p. 166].

[2] See p. 4, *supra*; and Worsaae, *Danes*, p. 279.

[3] Train, *Isle of Man*, vol. i. p. 78.

Saxon test-words, -*ham*, -*ford*, -*worth*, and -*ton*, are comparatively rare.[1]

Of the other test-words we find *ey* in WALNEY and FOULNEY,[2]
and *holm* in LINGHOLM and SILVERHOLM on Windermere, and
in RAMPSHOLME on Ulleswater. *Ness* occurs in the names of
BOWNESS, SHINBURNESS, SCARNESS, and FURNESS :—*wick* in
KESWICK on Derwentwater, and in BLOWICK on Ulleswater.
The Norwegian word *stackr*, a columnar rock, was appropriately
applied to the mountains which bear the names of STAKE,
the STICKS, PIKE O' STICKLE, and the HAY STACKS (the high
rocks).

More than 150 different personal names of the Icelandic
type are preserved in the local topography of the lake district.
According to the last census [3] there are now only sixty-three
surnames in Iceland, of which the commonest are Kettle,
Halle, Ormur, and Gils. In Cumberland and Westmoreland
these are preserved in the local names, KETTLEWELL, HALL-
THWAITE, ORMATHWAITE, and GELLSTONE. By far the most
common Christian names in Iceland are Olafur (borne by 992
persons), Einer (by 878), and Bjarni (by 869). These are
found in ULVERSTON, ENNERDALE, and BARNEYHOUSE. We
find the name of Hrani (now Rennie) in RANSDALE, RAINS-
BARROW, and WRENSIDE ; Loki in LOCKTHWAITE, LOCKHOLM,
LOCKERBY, and LOCKERBARROW ; Buthar in BUTTERMERE,
BUTTERHILL, and BUTTERGILL ; Geit [4] in GATESWATER,
GATESGARTH, and GATESGILL ; and Skögul in SKEGGLES WATER.[5]

The Norse *haugr*, a sepulchral mound, is often found in
the names of mountains crowned by conspicuous tumuli.
The name of the old Viking who lies buried here is often preserved in the first portion of such local names. Thus, SILVER
HOW, BULL HOW, SCALE HOW, and BUTTERLIP HOW, are, probably, the burial-places of the forgotten heroes, Sölvar, Böll,
Skall, and Buthar Lipr.[6]

In Cheshire, with one remarkable local exception, we find
no vestiges of Norse colonists. But the spit of land called

---

[1] See pp. 84–87, *supra*.
[2] The suffix *a*, which denotes a river as well as an island, appears in the river names
of the Greta, Liza, Wiza, Rotha, Bretha, Rathay, Calda, as well as in the Ea, and the
Eamont. See Ferguson, *Northmen*, p. 113.
[3] Symington, *Iceland*, p. 182.
[4] Ferguson, *Northmen in Cumberland*, pp. 105, 130.
[5] Ferguson, *Northmen*, pp. 128–135. See the *Landnamabok*, passim.
[6] Ferguson, *Northmen in Cumberland*, p. 55.

the Wirral, between the Dee and the Mersey, seems to have
allured them by its excellent harbours, and the protection
afforded by its almost insular character.[1] Here, in fact,
we find geographical conditions similar to those which gave
rise to the two isolated Norse colonies at the mouths of the
Stour and the Yare,[2] and the result is no less remarkable.
In this space of about twelve miles by six there is scarcely a
single Anglo-Saxon name, while we find the Norse villages of
RABY, PENSBY, IRBY, FRANKBY, KIRBY, WHITBY, and GREASBY.
We find also the Norse names of SHOTWICK, HOLME, DALPOOL
HOWSIDE, BARNSTON, THORNTON, THURSTANSTON, BIRKENHEAD,
and the BACK Brook ; and in the centre of the district is the
village of THINGWALL, a name which indicates the position of
the meeting place of the Thing, the assembly in which the
little colony of Northmen exercised their accustomed privileges
of local self-government.[3]

The Vikings cruised around the coasts of North Wales,
but we find no trace of settlements. The names of the ORME'S [4]
HEAD, the NORTH STACK, the SOUTH STACK, FENWICK ROCK,
the SKERRIES, and PRIESTHOLME, show their familiar acquaintance with the dangerous points on this rockbound coast ;
while PORT DYN NORWIG, the ' Port of the Norway Man ', near
Bangor, may probably indicate a haven which they frequented.

There is a curious exception to the broad assertion that has
been made [5] as to the non-existence of Norse names to the
south of Watling Street. The sea-rovers, with infallible
instinct, seem to have detected the best harbour in the
kingdom, and to have found shelter for their vessels in the
fjords of the Pembrokeshire coast—the deep land-bound
channels of MILFORD, HAVERFORD, [6] WHITEFORD, [7] and
SKERRYFORD, and the neighbouring creeks of WATHWICK,
LITTLE WICK, OXWICH, HELWICK, GELLYSWICK, MOUSSELWICK,
WICK HAVEN, and MUGGLESWICK BAY. The dangerous rocks

---

[1] We read of a large body of Scandinavian invaders who took refuge here. Turner,
Anglo-Saxons, vol. i. p. 397.

[2] See pp. 116, *supra*.

[3] See Chapter XII.

[4] From the Norse *ormr*, a serpent. The Wurmshead in South Wales presents the
Saxonized form of the same word. In Stanfield's admirable picture of this rock we
seem to see the sea serpent raising its head and the half of its huge length above the
waves.

[5] See p. 118, *supra*.

[6] Havenfjord. So there is a Hafnafjord in Iceland.

[7] Whiteford Sands show that the estuary of the Burry must have received from the
Norsemen the appropriate name of *Hvit-fjora*.

and islands which fringe this coast likewise bear Norwegian names ; such are the STACK Rocks, STACKPOLE Head, the STACK, PENYHOLT STACK, ST. BRIDE'S STACK, STACK Island STOKHOLM Island, SKERRYBACK, SKERPOINT, the NAZE, STRUMBLE Head, the WORM'S Head, NASH (Naze) Point, and DUNGENESS (Dangerness). Most of the names on the mainland are Celtic, but the neighbouring islands bear the Norse names of CALDY (Cold Island), BARRY (Bare Island), SULLY (Ploughed Island), LUNDY (Grove Island), SKOKHOLM (Wooded Island), DENNEY (Danes' Island), RAMSEY, SKOMER, BURRY HOLMES, GATEHOLM, GRASSHOLM, FLATHOLM [1] and STEEPHOLM.

No less than twenty-four of the headlands on the Pembroke-shire coast are occupied by camps, which we may regard as the first beginning of a Scandinavian occupation of the soil. Round the shores of Milford Haven a little colony of perma-nent settlers was established in the villages of FREYSTROP (Freysthorpe), STUDDA, VOGAR, ANGLE, TENBY (Daneby), DERBY, HASGUARD, FISHGUARD, DALE, LAMBETH, and WHITSAND. Of the Vikings who founded this Welsh colony, Harold, Bakki, Hamill, Grim, Hiarn, Lambi, Thorni, Thor, Gorm, Brodor, Sölvar, Hogni, and Buthar have left us their names at HAROLD-STON, BUCKSTON, AMBLESTON, CREAMSTON, HEARSTON, LAMB-STON, THORNSTON, THURSTAN, GOMᴲRESTON,[2] BROTHER HILL, SILVER HILL, HONEY HILL, and BUTTER HILL, several of which may be the burial-places of those whose names they bear.[3]

There is, occasionally, in Pembrokeshire, a difficulty in dis-tinguishing between the Norse names and those which are due to the colony of Flemings which was established in this dis-trict during the reign of Henry I. ' Flandrenses, tempore Regis Henrici pimi . . . ad occidentalem Walliæ partem, apud Haverford, sunt translati '.[4] These colonists came from a portion of Flanders which was submerged by an irruption of the sea in the year 1110. LEWESTON, RICKESTON, ROBESTON. ROGESTON, JOHNSTON, WALTERSTON, HERBRANDSTON, THOMAS-TON, WILLIAMSTON, JAMESTON, and JEFFREYSTON belong to a class of names which we find nowhere else in the kingdom—

---

[1] A large body of Danes took refuge in Flatholm in the year 918. St. John, *Four Conquests*, vol. i. p. 322.

[2] The last syllable in these names would seem not to be the Anglo-Saxon *ton*, but was probably derived from the memorial *stone* erected over the grave of some departed hero.

[3] See Ferguson, *Northmen*, pp. 10, 66, 68.

[4] Higden's *Chronicle*, apud Gale, *Scriptores*, vol. iii. p. 210.

names given, not by Saxon or Danish pagans, but by Christian-
ized settlers, men bearing the names, not of Thurstan, Gorm,
or Grim, but of Lewes, Richard, Robert, Walter, and others
common in the twelfth century.[1] The names of the village
of FLEMINGSTON, and of the VIA FLANDRICA, which runs along
the crest of the Precelly mountains, afford ethnological evidence still more conclusive, and TUCKING Mill (Clothmaking
Mill) shows the nature of the industry which was imported.

This Pembrokeshire settlement was, probably, at first, little
more than a nest of pirates, who sallied forth to plunder the
opposite coast of the Channel, and to prey upon any passing
merchant craft.   That the Somersetshire coast was not unknown to them we see from the Norse names of WICK Rock at
one entrance of Bridgewater Bay, and HOW Rock at the other.
The sands which lie in the estuary of the Yeo are called Langford grounds—an indication that this ' long fiord ' was known
to the Northmen by the appropriate name of LANGFORD.

The chief port of Scilly bears the name of GRIMSBY, and ST.
AGNES, the name of the most southern island, is a corruption
of the old Norse name Hagenes.   On the mainland of Cornwall only one station of the Northmen can be discovered, but
the position is admirably adapted for refitting ships, and
obtaining necessary supplies.   Near the Lizard Point a deep
inlet bears the name of HELFORD, and the village at its head is
called GWEEK, evidently a corruption of Wick.[2]

In Devonshire there are two or three clusters of Norse
names.   These present the characteristic suffix *by* in a form
nearly approaching to the old Norse form *byr*, which is preserved in the *boer* of the Icelandic farms.[3]   In North Devon
we find ROCKBEER and BEAR, both in the neighbourhood of the
fjord of BIDEFORD.   On the left bank of the estuary of the Exe,[4]
in South Devon, we have another cluster of such names, comprising the villages of AYLESBERE, ROCKBERE, LARKBEER, and
HOUNDBERE.   We find also BYESTOCK and THORP, EXWICK

---

[1] See Cliffe, *South Wales*, p. 257 ; Lappenberg, *Anglo-Norman Kings*, p. 345 ; Giraldus
Cambrensis, *Itin.*, lib. i. cap. 11 ; and the notes of H. Lluyd, Camden, and Sir R. C.
Hoare upon the passage.
[2] See the review of the 1st edition of *Words and Places* in the *Times* of March 26,
1864.
[3] e.g. Ossaboer, in Iceland.   In Essex and Suffolk we find Buers and Bures.   See
p. 157, *supra*.
[4] On the numerous Danish incursions into Devonshire see Strinnholm, *Wikingzüge*,
p. 57 ; Turner, *Anglo-Saxons*, vol. i. pp. 542, 591, 601 ; vol. ii. pp. 306, 312, 317.   In
877 the Danes were in possession of Exeter.   St. John, *Four Conquests*, vol. i. p. 266,

and COWICK, the NESS at Teignmouth, the SKERRIES close by, and a place called NORMANS (i.e. Northman's) CROSS. Here a portion of the Roman road to Exeter takes the Danish name STRAIGHTGATE. The Northmen penetrated up the estuary of the Tamar as well as up that of the Exe. In the Saxon Chronicle (A.D. 997) we read of a descent of the Danes at Lidford ; and in this neighbourhood we find LANGABEER, BEARDON, BEER ALSTON, BEARON, BEER FERRERS, DINGWELL, and THURSHELTON, as well as BURN and BEARA (byr water), both on the banks of brooks. At the mouth of the Otter, again,[1] we find the villages of BEER, BEREWOOD, and BOVY [2] IN BEER. Near Poole Harbour [3] we have East HOLME, BERE Regis, and SWANWICK. There was another Swanwick on Southampton Water, which has been corrupted to SWANAGE. In the Saxon Chronicle (A.D. 877) we read of the defeat of a Danish fleet at Swanawic on the south coast ; and it has been conjectured, with some probability, that a chief bearing the common Danish name of Sweyn may have been in command, from whom we derive the name of ' Sweyn's Bay '.[4] SWAN-THORPE, IBTHROP, and EDMUNDSTHROP, all in Hampshire, exhibit the suffix which is so characteristic of Danish settle-ments. At HOLMSDALE, in Surrey, we find an isolated Danish name. At this spot the crews of 350 ships, who had marched inland, were cut off by Ethelwulf, in the year 852,[5] and it is probable that the survivors may have settled in the neighbour-hood. Further to the north we find THORPE, near Chertsey. There seem to be traces of the Danes at BERWICK and SEAFORD near Beachy Head, and at HOLMSTONE [6] and WICK in Romney Marsh, as well as at the point of DUNGENESS or ' Danger Cape '. Finally, we find them on the Kentish coast at SAND-WICH, the sandy bay—a name which occurs also in Iceland, in Norway, in the Orkneys, in the Hebrides, and in the Shet-lands. Sandwich in Kent was one of the favourite stations

---

[1] The Danes landed at Seaton in 937. See *Saxon Chronicle*.
[2] This approximates to the Norman form *Coeuf*. See pp. 110, 131.
[3] We frequently read of Danish descents in Dorset. See Turner, *Anglo-Saxons*, vol. ii. pp. 306, 312 ; Strinnholm, *Wikingzüge*, p. 55 ; St. John, *Four Conquests*, vol. i. p. 443.
[4] See Gough's *Camden*, vol. i. p. 329. Sweyn was a common Danish name. There are three SWANTONS in Norfolk. At SWANESCOMB, near Greenhithe, there are several barrows ; and here, it has been thought, Sweyn, king of Denmark, landed.
[5] St. John, *Four Conquests*, vol. i. p. 227. Cf. Turner, *Anglo-Saxons*, vol. i. p. 590.
[6] Here a battle was fought between Danes and Saxons. The Danes had a fortress in Romney Marsh. Turner, *Anglo-Saxons*, vol. i. p. 387.

for the Danish fleets ; they were there in the years 851 and 1014, as we learn from the Saxon Chronicle.

The Northmen would appear to have established themselves in Ireland rather for purposes of trade than of colonization. Their ships sailed up the great fjords of WATERFORD, WEXFORD,[1] STRANGFORD, and CARLINGFORD, and anchored in the bays of LIMERICK and WICKLOW. In Kerry we find the name of SMERWICK, or ' butter bay ', then apparently, as now, a trading station for the produce of the surrounding district. The name of COPLAND Island, near Belfast, shows that here was a trading station of the Norse merchants, who trafficked in English slaves [2] and other merchandise. As we approach Dublin the numerous Norse names along the coast—LAMBAY Island, DALKEY Island, Ireland's EYE, the SKERRIES, the Hill of HOWTH, and LEIXLIP, the ' salmon leap ', on the Liffey—prepare us to learn that the Scandinavians in Dublin were governed by their own laws till the thirteenth century, and that, as in London, they had their own separate quarter of the city, guarded by walls and gates—OXMANTOWN, that is, Ostmantown, the town of the men from the East.[3]

The general geographical acquaintance which the Northmen had with the whole of Ireland is shown by the fact that three out of the four Irish provinces, namely, LEINSTER, MUNSTER, and ULSTER, present the Norse suffix *ster*, a place, which is so common in local names in the Shetlands and in Norway.[4]

In order to estimate with some exactitude the proportionate amount of the Scandinavian element in the different parts of England, the following table has been carefully compiled. It gives the proportion of Norse names to the acreage of the several counties—the proportion in Kent being taken as the unit of computation. The names in those counties which are printed in italics exhibit a Norwegian rather than a Danish character.

Intensity of the Scandinavian element of population, as indicated by village names :—

1 To the south of Wexford is the Barony of FORTH (fjord).
2 See Goldwin Smith, *Irish History and Irish Character*, p. 48.
3 Worsaae, *Danes and Norwegians*, pp. 323, 349. The Ostmen possessed the four cities of Dublin, Waterford, Limerick, and Cork. There were Ostman kings of Limerick, Dublin, and Waterford. Lappenberg, *Anglo-Norman Kings*, p. 64 ; Strinnholm, *Wiking-züge*, p. 57.
4 See p. 119, *supra*.

Kent .		.	.	.	.	1	Lancashire .		.	.	. 28
Glamorgan	.	.	.	.	1	Durham .		.	.	. 30
Hants	.	.	.	.	4	West Riding		.	.	. 60
Essex	.	.	.	.	5	Nottingham.		.	.	. 62
Warwick.		.	.	.	5	Norfolk .		.	.	. 76
Bucks	.	.	.	.	6	Northampton		.	.	. 83
Cheshire .		.	.	.	8	Rutland .		.	.	. 83
Devon	.	.	.	.	9	North Riding		.	.	. 111
Suffolk	.	.	.	.	10	*Cumberland* .		.	.	. 124
Bedford .		.	.	.	13	*Westmoreland*		.	.	. 125
Pembroke		.	.	.	15	East Riding		.	.	. 126
Northumberland		.	.	15	Lincolnshire		.	.	. 165
Derbyshire .		.	.	.	16	Leicestershire		.	.	. 169 [1]

The actual number of names is—in Lincolnshire, about 300 ; in Leicestershire, Westmoreland, Cumberland, and each of the Ridings about 100 ; in Norfolk, Northampton, Notts, and Lancashire, about 50 ; in Durham and Northumberland, about 20 ; in Suffolk, Derby, Cheshire, Rutland, and Pembroke, about a dozen ; in Bucks, Bedford, and Warwick, not more than half that number.

From the character of the Norse names upon the map of the British Isles, we may class the districts affected by Scandinavian influence under three general divisions :—

I. Places visited only for trade or booty. These fringe the coast, and are the names of bays, capes, or islands. The surrounding villages have Saxon or Celtic names. To this class belong, mostly, the names along the estuaries of the Thames and Severn, and along the coasts of Kent, Sussex, Essex, North Wales, Ireland, and Eastern Scotland.

II. Isolated settlements amid a hostile population. These are found in places which are nearly surrounded by water, and which are furnished with good harbours. In this class we must include the settlements near Harwich, Yarmouth, Birkenhead, and Milford.

---

[1] In several particulars this table will be found to differ from that given by Mr. Worsaae, *Danes and Norwegians*, p. 71.

1. I have excluded suffixes common to the Anglo-Saxon and the Norse languages.

2. I have excluded names on the coast not denoting colonization.

3. I have calculated the proportion of names to the acreage of each county, instead of giving the absolute number of names.

The latter mode of computation is deceptive. An example will make this plain. From Mr Worsaae's table it appears that the Scandinavian names in Lincolnshire, a very large county, are three times as numerous as those in Leicestershire, a much smaller one, whereas, in reality, the Norse element is actually less *intense* in Lincolnshire than it is in Leicestershire. In fact, portions of Lincolnshire are almost destitute of Norse names : for example, the Fens, which in their nomenclature are neither Saxon nor Danish, but English, having been reclaimed at a period when the distinction between Dane and Saxon had died away. See the coloured map.

III. The Danelagh or Danish kingdom, where the Norse element of the population was predominant. Yet even here the names are clustered, rather than uniformly distributed. Such clusters of names are to be found near Stamford, Sleaford, Horncastle, Market Rasen, Melton Mowbray, Leicester, Ashby-de-la-Zouch, Newark, Lincoln, Grimsby, York, and Bridlington.

The Scandinavians who settled in France have left few memorials of their speech in our French dictionaries—few permanent conquests have had so slight an influence on the language of the conquered nation. The conquerors married native women, and their sons seem only to have learned the language spoken by their mothers ; so that, except in the neighbourhood of Bayeux, where the Norman speech was grafted on the nearly-related and firmly-established language of the Saxon shore, the sons of the soil at no time spoke a Scandinavian dialect.[1] But the map of Normandy supplies abundant traces of the Scandinavian conquest. The accompanying sketch-map shows the distribution of these names, and, as has been already observed, it proves how carefully the Scandinavians avoided all encroachment on the district already occupied by Saxon colonists.

We find the names of the original Scandinavian settlers are thickly scattered over the land. We have seen that in England the former abodes of the Northmen—Grim, Biörn, Harold, Thor, Guddar, and Haco [2]—go by the names of Grimsby, Burnthwaite, Harroby, Thoresby, Guttersby, and Hacconby ; so in Normandy these same personal appellations occur in the village-names, and we find GRIMONVILLE, BORNEVILLE, HEROU-VILLE, TOURVILLE, GODARVILLE, HACONVILLE, and HACQUE-VILLE.[3]

[1] A few Norse words still survive in the dialect of Normandy. Thus we have—

In Normandy.	In Iceland.	
davre.	dagverdr.	*breakfast.*
fikke.	ficki.	*pocket.*
grande.	granni.	*neighbour.*
gild.	gildr.	*clever.*
feig.	feigr.	*dying* [' *fey* '].
kaud.	kot.	*cottage.*

These are not the terms used either in French or Danish. The French expressions would be déjeuner, poche, voisin, habile, moribond, and cabane ; and the modern Danish would be frokost, lomme, nabo, flink, dödsens, and hytte. See Etienne Borring, *Sur la Limite Méridionale de la Monarchie Da noise,* p. 4. In modern French there are a few nautical terms of Danish origin. See Diez, *Rom. Gram.* vol. i. p. 51. Cf. Max Müller, *Lectures,* 2nd series, p. 264.

[2] All these names are found in the *Landnamabok* of Iceland.

[3] See Depping, vol. ii. p. 339 ; Palgrave, vol. i. p. 702 ; Ferguson, p. 128 ; Worsaae,

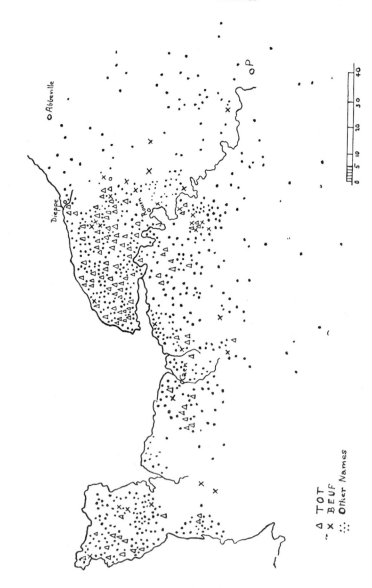

The Norse *gardr*, an inclosure, or yard, occurs in Normandy at FISIGARD, AUPPEGARD, and EPEGARD—names which we may compare with Fishguard in Pembrokeshire, Applegarth in Yorkshire, and Æblegaard in Denmark. *Toft*, which also means an inclosure, takes the form *tot* in Normandy, as in YVETOT, Ivo's toft ; PLUMETOT, flower toft ; LILLETOT, little toft ; ROUTOT, Rödtot, or red toft ; CRIQUETOT, crooked toft ; BERQUETOT, birch toft ; HAUTOT, high toft ; LANGETOT, long toft. We have also Prétot, Tournetot, Bouquetot, Grastot, Appetot, Garnetot, Ansetot, Turretot, Hebertot, Cristot, Brestot, Franquetot, Raffetot, Houdetot, and others, about one hundred in all. Toft being a Danish [1] rather than a Norwegian suffix, would incline us to suppose, from its frequent occurrence, that the conquerors of Normandy were Danes rather than Norwegians ; and the total absence of *thwaite*, the Norwegian test-word, tends to strengthen this supposition.

The suffix *by*, so common in Danish England, generally takes, in Normandy, the form *bœuf*, *buf*, or *bue*, as in the cases of CRIQUEBUF (Crogby, or crooked-by), MARBŒUF (Markby), QUITTEBEUF (Whitby, or Whiteby), DAUBEUF (Dale-by), CARQUEBUF (Kirkby), QUILLEBEUF (Kil-by [2]), ELBŒUF, PAINBEUF, and LINDEBEUF. The form *buf*, or *bœuf*, seems very remote from the old Norse *boer* ; but a few names ending in *bue*, such as LONGBUE and TOURNEBUE,[3] and still more the village of BURES, exhibit the transitional forms through which the names in *buf* may probably have passed. HAMBYE and COLOMBY are the only instances of the English form which I can find.

The village of LE TORP gives us the word *thorpe*, which, however, more usually appears in the corrupted form of *torbe*, *tourp*, or *tourbe*, as in the case of CLITOURPS.[4]

The name of the castle-crowned rock of FALAISE reminds us of the *fells* of Cumberland.[5]

The name of the river DIEPPE, which was afterwards [6] given

---

p. 69 ; Gerville ; Petersen. This suffix *ville* has been usually supposed to be the Romance word *villa*. It is far more probable, however, that it is the Teutonic *weiler*, a single house. See. p. 115, *supra*.

[1] Moreover, in Denmark we often find combinations identical with some of those just enumerated. Such are Blumtofte, Rodtofte, Langetofte, and Grastofte. See Le Prevost, *Recherches*, pp. 41, 64.

[2] Norse *kellda*, German, *quelle*, a *well* or river-source. La Roquette, *Recherches*, p. 46 ; Ferguson, *Northmen*, p. 119.

[3] Cf. Taarnby, in Denmark.

[4] See Leo, *Anglo-Saxon Names*, pp. 43–50. Cf. the German *felsen*.

[5] Petersen, p. 49.   [6] In the tenth century.

to the town which was built beside it, is identical with that
of the Diupa, or 'deep water' in Iceland; and it may be
compared with 'The Deeps' near Boston.[1]

From the Norse *beckr* (Danish *bæc*), a brook, we have
CAUDEBEC, the 'cold brook', the same name as that of the
Cawdbeck in the Lake District, and the Kaldbakr in Iceland.
The name of the BRIQUEBEC, the 'birch-fringed brook', is the
same as that of the Birkbeck in Westmoreland. The HOUL-
BEC, the 'brook in the hollow', corresponds to the Holbeck
in Lincolnshire, and the Holbeck in Denmark. The name of
BOLBEC we may compare with Bolbek in Denmark; and the
name of FOULBEC, or 'muddy brook', is identical with that
of the Fulbeck in Lincolnshire.

The Danish *ö*, an island, is seen in Eu, Cantaleu, Jersey,
Guernsey, and Alderney.

The suffix -*fleur*, which we find in HONFLEUR and other
names, is derived from the Norse, *fliot*,[2] a small river or channel, which we have in Purfleet, Northfleet, and many other
English names. The phonetic resemblance between *fleur* and
fleet may seem slight, but the identification is placed beyond
a doubt by the fact that HARFLEUR was anciently written
Herosfluet; while Roger de Hovenden calls BARFLEUR by
the name of Barbeflet, and Odericus Vitalis calls it Barbeflot.
VITTEFLEUR is the 'white river', and FIQUEFLEUR seems to
be a corruption of Wickfleet, 'the river in the bay'.[3]

Holme, a river island, appears in the names of TURHULME,
NIHOU,[4] and LE HOULME, near Rouen. Cape de la HOGUE,
Cape HOC, and Cape le HODE, may be compared with the Cape
near Dublin, called the Hill of Howth. This is the old Norse
haugr, a sepulchral mound, the same word which appears in
the *haughs* of Northumberland. LES DALLES, OUDALES, CRO-
DALE, CROIXDAL, DANESTAL, DEPEDAL, DIEPPEDAL, DARNETAL,
and BRUQUEDALLE, remind us of the dales of Westmoreland
and the North Riding.

ESCOVES[5] seems to be the Icelandic *skogr*, and corresponds

---

[1] Palgrave, *Normandy and England*, vol. ii. p. 111; La Roquette, p. 55.
[2] Danish *flod*, English *flood*. See Petersen, *Recherches*, p. 38; Depping, *Expéditions*,
vol. ii. p. 341.
[3] HAVRE may be either from the Norse *höfn*, a haven, or from the Celtic *aber*, a river's
mouth. See Adelung, *Mithridates*, vol. ii. p. 41; Diefenbach, *Celtica*, i. p. 23.
[4] Granted to one Niel, or Njal, A.D. 920. Gerville, *Noms*, p. 229; La Roquette,
p. 48.
[5] Peterson, p. 50.

to the English *shaw*, a wood, or *shady* place. *Bosc*, a wood, or *bushy* place, is a very common suffix in Normandy, as in the names VERBOSC, BRICQUEBOSQ, and BANDRIBOSC. *Holt*, a wood, occurs in the name TERHOULDE, or Theroude.[1] The Calf of Man is repeated in LE CAUF.[2]

Beyond the district of Norse colonization we have a few scattered names of bays and capes, indicating occasional visits of the Vikings. Such are Cape GRINEZ, or Greyness, near Calais; WYK in Belgium; QUANTOVIC; VIGO Bay in the North of Spain,[3] and possibly VICO in the bay of Naples. The BERLINGAS, a group of rocky islets forty miles north-west of Lisbon, would appear, from the name, to have been a station of the Northmen.[4] HASTINGUES, a river-island near Bayonne, probably takes its name from the renowned Viking Hasting, who was long the terror of France, Spain, and Italy,[5] and the Ile de BIERE in the Loire was no doubt so called from the huts which the Danes erected upon it for the accommodation of their prisoners.[6]

SCARANOS, on the southern coast of Sicily,[7] is an almost solitary memorial of the visits of the Vikings to the Mediterranean.[8] With this name we may compare those of Scarnose on the coast of Banff, Scarness in Cumberland, and Sheerness on the Thames. The SKERKI rocks, also on the Sicilian coast, may not improbably have received from the Northmen the name of the Skerries, or Scar Isles, which was so frequently given to similar dangerous needles of sea-washed rock.

The most easterly Norse name is KIBOTUS (Chevetot), near Helenopolis, on the Hellespont. Here was the station of the Væringer, or Varangian guard of the Byzantine Emperors, who were afterwards reinforced by the Ingloi, or Saxon refugees, who fled from the Norman conquerors.[9]

---

1 Peterson, p. 50; Depping, vol. ii. p. 344.
2 On the Norse names in Normandy, see Depping, *Expéditions Maritimes des Normands*, vol. ii. pp. 339–342; Lappenberg, *England under the Anglo-Norman Kings*, pp. 97–100; Borring, *Sur la Limite Méridionale de la Monarchie Danoise*: and the essays of Palgrave; Petersen; La Roquette; Le Prevost; Gerville; and Latham.
3 A Danish fleet was destroyed at Compostella. Strinnholm, *Wikingzüge*, vol. i. pp. 144, 145; Depping, vol. i. p. 110.
4 This patronymic is found on the Baltic coast, in Friesland, and in England, see p. 107, *supra*.
5 Crichton, *Scandinavia*, vol. i. p. 166; Strinnholm, *Wikingzüge*, vol. i. p. 26: Depping, *Expéditions des Normands*, vol. i. pp. 122, 132.
6 See Strinnholm, *Wikingzüge*, vol. i. p. 34.
7 On the exploits of the Northmen in Sicily, see the Saga of Harold Hardráda, in Laing's *Heimskringla*, vol. iii, p. 7.
8 Talbot, *English Etymologies*, p. 376.
9 See Lappenberg, *Anglo-Norman Kings*, p. 114. We find the name of these Warings'

The Norman conquest of England has left few traces on the map. There was in no sense any colonization, as in the case of the previous Saxon and Danish invasions; nor was there even such a general transference of landed property as took place in Normandy, and which is there so fully attested by the local names. The companions of the Conqueror were but a few thousands in number, and they were widely dispersed over the soil. A few Norman-French names, however, may be still pointed to as memorials of the conquest.[1] Of these RICHMOND [2] in Yorkshire, and MONTGOMERY [3] on the Welsh border, are the most conspicuous. At MALPAS was a castle built by the first Norman Earl of Chester to guard the 'bad pass' into the valley of the Dee.[4] MONTFORD, or Montesfort, in Shropshire, and MOLD in Flintshire, anciently Monthault [5] (Mons Altus) were also frontier fortresses; MONTACUTE Hill, in Somerset, has Mortaine's Norman castle on its summit, and a Norman abbey at its foot. The commanding situation of BELVOIR castle justifies its Norman name. At BEAUMONT [6] near Oxford, was a palace of the Norman kings; and at PLESHY (*plaisir*) in Essex, the seat of the High Constables of England, the ruins of the Norman keep are still visible.[7] BEAUCHAMP-OTTON, near Castle Hedingham, bears the name of Ottone, the skilful goldsmith who fashioned the tomb of the Conqueror at Caen.[8] We find the Norman abbeys of RIEVAUX and JORVEAUX in Yorkshire, BEAULIEU in Hampshire, DELAPRE in Northamptonshire, and the Augustinian Priory of GRACEDIEU in Leicestershire. The Norman family of St. Clare, or Clarence, has bestowed its name upon an English town, an Irish county, a royal dukedom, and a Cambridge college.[9] We have the names of Norman barons at

or Varangians, at VARENGEFJORD in Norway, VARENGEVILLE in Normandy, WIERINGER-WAARD on the coast of Holland, and at many places in England. See p. 91, *supra*. On the etymology of the name see Strinnholm, *Wikingzüge*, vol. i. pp. 301, 312.

[1] The only Anglo-Norman suffixes seem to be *clere, manor*, and *court*, as in HIGHCLERE, BEAUMANOIR, and HAMPTON COURT. We have also a few names like CHESTER-LE-STREET, BOLTON-LE-MOOR, and LAUGHTON-EN-LE-MORTHEN.

[2] Thierry, *Conquest*, p. 90. Henry IV transferred to his Surrey palace the name of his Yorkshire earldom.

[3] The same story is told in another language by the Welsh name of Montgomery—Tre-faldwyn, or Baldwin's Town. See Borrow, *Wild Wales*, vol. iii. p. 97.

[4] Ormerod, *Hist. of Chester*, vol. ii. p. 328 ; Charnock, *Local Etymol.* p. 173.

[5] *Cambro-Briton*, vol. i. p. 136.

[6] Gough's Camden, vol. ii. p. 21.

[7] Gough's Camden, vol. ii. pp. 121, 133.

[8] Palgrave, *Normandy and England*, vol. iv. p. 2.

[9] See Donaldson, *English Ethnography*, p. 60 ; Yonge, *Christian Names*, vol. i. p.

STOKE-MANDEVILLE,   CARLTON-COLVILE,   MINSHALL-VERNON, ASHBY-DE-LA-ZOUCH,   NEWPORT-PAGNELL,   BURY-POMMEROYE, ASTON-CANTELOUPE,   STOKE-PIROU,   ACTON-TURVILLE,   and NEVILLEHOLT. The names of HURST MONCEAUX, HURST PIERPOINT, and HURST COURTRAY all occur in the county of Sussex, where the Conqueror landed, and where the actual transfer of estates seems to have taken place to a greater extent than in other counties. Sussex is the only English county which is divided into rapes, as well as into hundreds or wapentakes. While the hundred seems to indicate the peaceful settlements of Saxon families, and the wapentake the defensive military organization of the Danish intruders, the *rape*, as it would appear, is a memorial of the violent transference of landed property by the Conqueror—the lands being plotted out for division by the *hrepp*, or rope,[1] just as they had been by Rolf in Normandy. Illam terram (Normandy) suis fidelibus funiculo divisit.[2]

There are some curious memorials of that influx of Anglo-Norman nobles into Scotland which took place during the reigns of David I and Malcolm Canmore. In ancient records the name of Maxwell is written in the Norman form of Maccusville. The name of Robert de Montealt has been corrupted into Mowatt and MOFFAT ; and the families of Sinclair, Fraser, Baliol, Bruce, Campbell, Colville, Somerville, Grant (le Grand), and Fleming, are all, as their names bear witness, of continental ancestry.[3] Richard Waleys—that is, Richard the Foreigner —was the ancestor of the great Wallace, and has left his name at RICHARDTUN in Ayrshire. The ancestor of the Maule family has left his name at Maleville, or MELVILLE, in Lothian. SETON takes its name from a Norman adventurer called Say. TANKERTON, in Clydesdale, was the fief of Tancard, or Tancred, a Fleming who came to Scotland in the reign of Malcolm IV.

385. The Clarenceaux King-at-Arms had jurisdiction over the Surroys, or men south of the Trent, and the Norroys' king over those to the north of that river.
1 [These words are not connected, notwithstanding the parallelism of Heb. *chebel* (1) a cord, measuring line,](2) a measured portion, an allotment, Ps. xvi. 6, Vulg. *funis*.]
2 Dudo, *De Moribus Norm. Ducum*, apud Duchesne, *Hist. Norm. Script*. p. 85. The districts of Iceland are called Hreppar. The hyde, the Saxon unit of land, seems to have been a portion measured off with a *thong*, as the rape, was with a *rope* [?]. See Palgrave, *Normandy and England*, vol. i. p. 692 ; vol. iii. p. 395 ; Robertson, *Early Kings*, vol. ii. p. 213.
3 See Buchanan, *Scottish Surnames*, pp. 42, 43 ; Palgrave, *Normandy and England*, vol. iii. Appendix, and vol. iv. p. 298 ; Dugdale, Chalmers, and the Charters. Skene, *History of the Highlanders*, vol. ii. p. 280, etc., attempts to disprove the supposed Norman origin of the Campbells and other Scottish families. He admits, however, the case of the Grants ; vol. ii. p. 255.

And a few village names like INGLISTON, NORMANTON, and FLEMINGTON, afford additional evidence of the extensive immigration of foreign adventurers which was encouraged by the Scottish kings.

CHAPTER IX [1]

THE CELTS

Prevalence of Celtic Names in Europe—Antiquity of River-names—The roots Avon, Dur, Stour, Esk, Rhe, and Don—Myth of the Danaides—Hybrid composition, and reduplication of synonyms—Adjectival river-names : the Yare, Alne, Ban, Douglas, Leven, Tame, Aire, Cam, and Clyde—Celtic mountain-names : cefn, pen, cenn, dun—Names of Rocks—Valleys—Lakes—Dwellings—Cymric and Gadhelic test-words—Celts in Galatia—Celts in Germany, France, and Spain—Euskarian Names—Gradual retrocession of Celts in England—Amount of the Celtic element—Division of Scotland between the Picts and Gaels—Inver and Aber—Ethnology of the Isle of Man.

EUROPE has been peopled by successive immigrations from the East. Five great waves of population have rolled in, each in its turn urging the flood which had preceded it further and further toward the West. The mighty Celtic inundation is the first which we can distinctly trace in its progress across Europe, forced onward by the succeeding deluges of the Romance, Teutonic, and Sclavonic peoples, till at length it was driven forward into the far western extremities of Europe.

The Celts were divided into two great branches, which followed one another on their passage across Europe. Both branches spoke languages of the same stock, but distinguished by dialectic differences as great or greater than those which divide Greek from Latin, or English from German. There are living tongues belonging to each of these branches. The first, or Gadhelic branch, is now represented by the Erse of Ireland, the Gaelic of the Scotch Highlands, and the Manx of the Isle of Man ; the second, or Cymric, by the Welsh of Wales, and the Brezonec or Armorican of Brittany, which is still spoken by a million and a half of Frenchmen.[2]

---

[1] [Many of the origins suggested in this chapter must be received with reserve, as mere conjectures.]

[2] Diefenbach, *Celtica*, ii. pt. ii. p. 162 ; Meyer, in Bunsen's *Philos of Univ. History*, vol. i. p. 145.

Although both of these branches of the Celtic speech now survive only in the extreme corners of western Europe, yet, by the evidence of local names, it may be shown that they prevailed at one time over a great part of the continent of Europe, before the Teutonic and Romance nations had expelled or absorbed the once dominant Celts.   In the geographical nomenclature of Germany, Switzerland, Italy, France, Spain, and England, we find a Celtic substratum underlying the superficial deposit of Teutonic and Romance names.   These Celtic roots form the chief available evidence on which we can rely when investigating the immigrations of the Celtic peoples.

We shall now proceed to adduce a few fragments of the vast mass of evidence which has been collected by numerous industrious explorers, and which seems to justify them in their belief as to the wide extension of the Celtic race at some unknown prehistoric period.[1]

One class of local names is of special value in investigations relating to primaeval history.   The river-names, more particularly the names of important rivers, are everywhere the memorials of the very earliest races.[2]   These river-names survive where all other names have changed—they seem to possess an almost indestructible vitality.   Towns may be destroyed, the sites of human habitation may be removed, but the ancient river-names are handed down from race to race ;   even the names of the eternal hills are less permanent than those of rivers.   Over the greater part of Europe—in Germany,[3] France, Italy, Spain—we find villages which bear Teutonic or Romance names, standing on the banks of streams which still retain their ancient Celtic appellations. Throughout the whole of England there is hardly a single river-name which is not Celtic.   By a reference to the map prefixed to this volume it will be seen that those districts of our island which are dotted thickly with Anglo-Saxon and Scandinavian village-names, are traversed everywhere by red lines, which represent the rivers whose names are now almost

---

[1] [See Prof. J. Rhys, *Celtic Britain*, 1882.]
[2] See Förstemann, in Kuhn's *Zestschrift für Vergl. Spr.* vol. ix. p. 284; Monkhouse *Etymologies*, p. 64; Müller, *Marken d. Vaterl.* p. 124 ;   Schott, *Deut. Col.* p. 218.
[3] Almost every river-name in Germany is Celtic.   Leo, *Vorlesungen*, vol. i. p. 198 ; Zeuss, *Gram. Celt.* vol. ii. p. 760.

the sole evidence that survives of a once universal Celtic occupation of the land.

The Celtic words which appear in the names of rivers may be divided into two classes. The first may be called the substantival class, and the second the adjectival.

The first class consists of ancient words which mean simply water or river. At a time when no great inter-communication existed, and when books and maps were unknown, geographical knowledge must have been very slender. Hence whole tribes were acquainted with only one considerable river, and it sufficed, therefore, to call it ' The Water ', or ' The River '. Such terms were not at first regarded as *proper* names ; in many cases they only became proper names on the advent of a conquering race. To take an example—the word *afon*. This is the usual Welsh term for a river. On a map of Wales we find at Bettws-y-Coed the ' Afon Llugwy ', or, as it is usually called by English tourists, the ' River Llugwy '. So also at Dolwyddelen we find the Afon Lledr, or River Lledr, and the Afon Dulas and the Afon Dyfi at Machynlleth. In England, however, the word *avon* is no longer a *common* name as it is in Wales, but has become a *proper* name. We have a River AVON which flows by Warwick and Stratford, another River AVON flows past Bath and Bristol, and elsewhere there are other rivers of the same name, which will presently be enumerated. The same process which has converted the word *afon* from a common name into a proper name has also taken place with other words of the same class. There is, in fact, hardly a single Celtic word meaning stream, current, brook, channel, water, or flood, which does not enter largely into the river-names of Europe.

The second class of river-names comprises those which may be called adjectival. The Celtic words meaning rough, gentle, smooth, white, black, yellow, crooked, broad, swift, muddy, clear, and the like, are found in the names of a large proportion of European rivers. For example, the Celtic word *garw*, rough, is found in the names of the GARRY, the YARE, the YARROW, and the GARONNE.

We may now proceed to enumerate some of the more important names which belong to either class.

I. AVON. This, as we have seen, is a Celtic word meaning ' a river '. It is written *aon* in the Manx language, and *abhainn* (pronounced *avain*) in Gaelic. We find also the ancient forms *amhain* [1] and *auwon*. This word has become a proper name in the case of numerous rivers in England, Scotland, France, and Italy. The Stratford AVON flows through Warwickshire and Worcestershire. The Bristol AVON divides the counties of Gloucester and Somerset. The Little AVON, also in Gloucestershire, runs near Berkeley Castle. One Hampshire AVON flows past Salisbury to Christchurch, another enters the sea at Lymington. We also have rivers called AVON or EVAN in the counties of Devon, Monmouth, Glamorgan, Lanark, Stirling, Banff, Kincardine, Dumfries, and Ross. We find the IVE in Cumberland, the ANNE in Clare, and an INN in Fife and in the Tyrol. The AUNE in Devon keeps close to the pronunciation of the Celtic word. The AUNEY, in the same county, is the Celtic diminutive ' Little Avon ', which we find also in the EWENNY in Glamorgan, the EVENENY in Forfar, the INNEY in Cornwall, and the ANEY in Meath. The AWE in Argyll, and the EHEN in Cumberland, are probably corrupted forms of the word Avon.

We find it in composition in the AVEN-GORM in Sligo, the AVEN-BANNA in Wexford, the BAN-ON in Pembrokeshire, the AVEN-BUI in Cork, the AVEN-MORE in Mayo and Sligo, and the ANTON in Hampshire, as well, possibly, as in the case of the D-OVE,[2] the T-OWY, the T-AFF, the T-AVY, the T-AW, and the D-EE, anciently the Deva.[3]

A very large number of French river-names [4] contain the root *afon*. In Brittany we find the AFF, and two streams called AVEN. There are two streams called AVON in the river system of the Loire, and two in that of the Seine. The names of the chief French rivers often contain a fragment—sometimes only a single letter—of this root, which may, however, be identified by a comparison of the ancient with the modern name. Thus, the Matrona is now the Marne, the

---

[1] Cognate to the Latin *amnis*. Ultimately *afon* is to be referred to the Sanskrit root *ap*, water, which we see in the names of the Punj-*ab*, or land of the ' five rivers '; the Do-*ab*, the district between the ' two rivers ', Ganges and Jumna; as well as in the river-names of the Z-*ab*, and of the Dan-*ub*-ius, or Dan-*ub*-e.

[2] Compare the name of the Dovebridge over the Avon.

[3] This initial *d* or *t* may be a fragment of an ancient preposition, as will be shown below, p. 149, *infra*. These names are more probably to be referred to the Welsh *dof*, gentle; or *dyfi*, smooth.

[4] There are some remarks on the Celtic river-names of France in a paper by Kennedy, in *Philological Trans.* for 1855, p. 166; Betham, *Gael*, pp. 194–196; Astruc, *Hist. de Languedoc*, p. 424; Thierry, *Hist. Gaul.* vol. ii. p. 2; Ferguson, *River Names*, passim; Pott, *Etymolog. Forsch.* vol. ii. pp. 103, 528; Salverte, *Essai sur les Noms*, vol. ii. p. 289.

Axona is the Aisne, the Sequana is the Seine, the Antura is the Eure, the Iscauna is the Yonne, the Saucona is the
Saone, the Meduana is the Mayenne, the Duranius is the
Dordogne, the Garumna is the Garonne. The names of an
immense number of the smaller French streams end in on, onne,
or one, which is probably a corruption of the root afon. In
the department of the Vosges, for instance, we find the Madon,
the Durbion, the Angronne, and the Vologne. In the department of the Alpes-basses we have the Verdon, the Jabron, the
Auon, the Calavon, and the Bléone. In the department of the
Ain there are the Loudon, the Sevron, the Solman, and the Ain.
Elsewhere we have the Avenne, the Vilaine, the Vienne, the
Arnon, the Ausonne, the Odon, the Iton, the Seran, the Aveyron,
the Roscodon, the Maronne, the Jourdanne, the Douron, and
scores of similar names.

The same termination occurs frequently in the names of
German streams, as for example, in the case of the Lahn, anciently the Lohana, the Isen, anciently the Isana, the Mörn,
anciently the Merina, and the Argen, anciently the Argana,[1]
the Drave and the Save preserve the latter instead of the former
portion of the ancient word.

In Portugal we find the AVIA, and in Spain the ABONO or
AVONO. The GUADI-ANA is the Anas of Strabo, with the
Arabic prefix Wad.

In Italy we may enumerate the Aventia, now L Avenza,
the Savo, now the Savone, the Ufens, now the Aufente, the
Vomanus, now the Vomano, as well as the Amasenus, the
Fibrenus, and the Avens.[2]

The names of Oundle (Avondale), Wandle, Wandsworth,
Wanstead, Wansford,[3] Verona, and Avignon, anciently Aven-
ion, the town on the afon or stream of the Rhodanus, or Rhone,[4]
have all been thought to contain the same root.

II. DUR. Another word, diffused nearly as widely as
afon, is the Welsh dwr, water.[5]   Prichard gives a list of forty-

---

[1] Vilmar, Ortsnamen, p. 254.
[2] Williams, in Edinburgh Transactions, vol. xiii. p. 521 ; Essays, p. 70.
[3] [These two, like Wansdike, are more probably called after Woden, as indeed suggested, infra, 229.]
[4] Salverte, Essai sur les Noms, vol. ii. p. 289.
[5] Brezonec and Cornish dour ; Gaelic and Irish dur, and dobhar, pronounced doar ;
cf. the Greek ὕδωρ. On this root see Diefenbach, Celtica, i. p. 155 ; Adelung, Mithridates, vol. ii. p. 57 ; Davies, Celtic Researches, p. 207 ; Duncker, Orig. Germ. p. 55 ;
Charnock, Local Etym. p. 93 ; Ferguson, River Names, pp. 37, 69 ; Radlof, Neue Untersuchungen, p. 317 ; De Belloguet, Ethnogénie, vol. i. p. 218.

four ancient names containing this root in Italy, Germany,
Gaul, and Britain. We find the DOUR in Fife, Aberdeen, and
Kent, the DORE in Hereford, the DUIR in Lanark, the THUR
in Norfolk, the DORO in Queen's County and Dublin, the
DURRA in Cornwall, the DAIRAN in Carnarvonshire, the DURAR-
WATER and the DEARGAN in Argyle, the DOVER or Durbeck
in Nottinghamshire, the Glasdur, or grey water in Elgin, the
Rother, or red water (Rhuddwr), in Sussex, the Calder,[1]
or winding water, in Lancashire (twice), Yorkshire, Cumberland, Lanark (three times), Edinburgh, Nairn, Inverness,
and Renfrew, the Adder in Wilts, and two of the same name
in Berwick, the Adur in Sussex, the Adar in Mayo, the Noder in
Wiltshire, the Cheddar in Somerset, the cascade of Lodore,
the lakes of Windermere and Derwent-water. The name
Derwent is probably from dwr-gwyn, the clear water.[2] There
is a river Derwent in Yorkshire, another in Derbyshire, a
third in Cumberland, and a fourth in Durham. The Darwen
in Lancashire, the Derwen in Denbighshire, the Darent in
Kent, and the Dart in Devon, are contractions of the same
name,[3] as well, possibly, as the TRENT.

DORCHESTER was the city of the Dur-otriges, or dwellers
by the water, and a second ancient city of Dorchester, in
Oxfordshire, stands upon the banks of the Thames.

In France[4] we have the Duranius, now the Dordogne,
the Antura, now the Eure, and the Aturus, now the Adour.
The Alpine Durance, anciently the Druentia, reminds us
of our English Derwents. We find the THURR in Alsace and
again in Switzerland, the Durbion in the Vosges, the Durdan
in Normandy, the Dourdon and the Dourbie in the department of the Aveyron, as well as the Douron in Brittany.

In the North-Western, or Celtic part of Spain, there are
the Durius, now the DOURO, the Duerna, the Duraton, the
Torio, the Tera, the Turones, and the Tormes.

In Italy are the TORRE, the two Durias, or DORAS in

---

[1] Perhaps, however, from the Norse kalldr, cold.

[2] Whitaker, Hist. Whalley, p. 8; Charnock, Local Etym. p. 85; Williams, Edin.
Trans. vol. xiii. p. 522; Essays, p. 72; Poste, Brit. Researches, p. 143. Ferguson prefers
Baxter's etymology, from the Welsh derwyn, to wind, River Names, p. 141. I believe,
however, that none of the Derwents are very tortuous, though they are all very clear.

[3] That the Darent was anciently the Derwent is shown by the name of DERVENTIO,
the Roman station on the Darent. The further contraction into the form Dart is exhibited in the name of Dartford, the modern town on the same river. See Baxter, Glossarium, p. 103.

[4] Pott, Etym. Forsch. vol. ii. p. 104; Philolog. Proc. vol. i. p. 107; King, Italian
Valleys, p. 75.

Piedmont, and the TURIA, a tributary of the Tiber. In the slightly changed form of *ter* we find the root *dur* in the names of the *Tru*entum, now the *Tr*onto, the *Tra*ens, now the *Tri*onto,[1] as well as the *Tr*ebia, the *Ter*ias, the *Ter*mus, the Dnies*ter*, and the Is*ter*.[2]

In Germany we find the *Oder*, the *Dr*ave, the *Dur*bach the *Dür*renback in Würtemberg, the *Dür*nbach in Austria, the *Dür*renbronne near Eppingen,[3] and the city of Marco*dur*um, now *Dur*en.[4]

STOUR is a very common river-name. There are important rivers of this name in Kent, Suffolk, Dorset, Warwickshire, and Worcestershire ; we have the STÖR in Holstein, the Stura, in Latium, is now the STORE, and STURA is a very common river-name in Northern Italy. The etymology of this name Stour is by no means certain. In Welsh, words are augmented and intensified in meaning by means of the prefix *ys*.[5] Thus we have—

Llwc,	a lake ;	*Ylswc,*	a slough.
Ber,	a bar ;	*Yspar,*	a spear.
Llac,	lax ;	*Yslac,*	slack.
Crecian,	to creak ;	*Ysgrec,*	a shriek.
Crafu,	to scratch ;	*Ysgrafu,*	to scrape.
Pin,	a point ;	*Yspin,*	a spine.
Mwg,	vapour (muggy) ;	*Ysmwg,*	smoke.
Mal,	light, fickle ;	*Ysmal,*	small.
Pig,	a peak, or point ;	*Yspig,*	a spike.
Brig,	a shoot ;	*Ysbrig,*	a sprig.

Stour, therefore, may be only the intensive of *dur*. On the other hand, it is possible that by a common process of

---

[1] Compare the name of the English *Tr*ent, anciently the *Tr*eonta.

[2] Rawlinson, *Herodotus*, vol. iii. p. 202. See, however, p. 144, *infra*.

[3] Mone, *Celtische Forschungen*, p. 68.

[4] In ancient Gaul we find many names of towns in which this root indicates that their sites were on the banks of rivers. We may specify, among others, Erno*dur*um, Salo*dur*um, Icto*dur*um, Divo*dur*um, Brevio*dur*um, Gano*dur*um, Velato*dur*um, Antisso*dur*um, Octo*dur*um, Brivo*dur*um Marco*dur*um, *Dur*onum, *Dur*ocatalaunum, and Veto*dur*um. In the valley of the Danube we find Gabano*dur*um, Brago*dur*um Ebo*dur*um, Ecto*dur*um, Boio*dur*um ; and in Britain, *Dur*overnum, *Dur*obrivæ, *Dur*olevum, *Dur*olitum, *Dur*ocornovium, *Dur*ocobrivium, and *Dur*olipsus. Prichard, *Researches*, vol. iii. pp. 114–119. So ZURICH, in Switzerland, is a corruption of *Tur*icum, SOLOTHURN of Salo*dur*um, and WINTERTHUR of Vito*dur*um. Förstemann, *Altdeutsches Namenbuch*, vol. ii. p. 446 ; Keferstein, *Kelt. Alt.* vol. ii. p. 375.

[5] Some forty instances of this augmentation may be found in Garnett's *Essays*, p. 174 ; Cf. Diefenbach, *Celtica*, i. pp. 90–96 ; Charnock, *Local Etym.* pp. 258, 26(; Mayhew, *German Life and Manners*, vol. i. p. 557 ; Zeuss, *Gram(Celtica*, vol. i. p. 142. On the name Stour, see Ferguson, *River Names*, p. 58 ; and Bo(idard, *Num. Iber.* p. 127, who thinks it is the Euskarian *ast-ur*, rock water,

reduplication of synonyms, which will presently be discussed, the word Stour may be formed from a prevalent root—*is*, water ; and *dwr*, water. There is also a further complication, arising from a Teutonic river-root *st-r*, which has been discussed by Förstemann, a great authority.[1] He finds this root in the names of more than one hundred German streams, such as the Elster, Alster, Lastrau, Wilster, Ulster, Gelster, Innerste, Agistra, Halsterbach, Streu, Suestra, Stroo, Ströbeck, Laster, Nister, and others.

III. Esk. The Gaelic and Erse word for water is *uisge*.[2] This is represented in Welsh by *wysg*, a current, and by *gwy* or *wy*, water. This root, subject to various phonetic mutations, is found in the names of a vast number of rivers.[3] There is an Esk in Donegal, in Devon, in Yorkshire, in Cumberland, in Dumfries, two in Forfarshire, and two in Edinburghshire. We have an Esky in Sligo, an Esker in King's County and in Brecknock, an Eskle in Herefordshire, and an Isle in Somerset. *E*sthwaite Water, and *E*asedale, in the Lake District, contain the same root, as well as the Ewes in Northumberland and Dumfries, the Ise near Wellingborough, the *I*sbourne, a tributary of the Stratford Avon, the *E*aseburn in Yorkshire, the *A*shbourne in Sussex, and the Ash in Hertfordshire and Wiltshire. In Bedfordshire and in Hertfordshire we have the Iz ; the *I*schalis was the ancient name of the Ivel, and the T*i*sa of the Tees.[4] The Isis contains the root in a reduplicated form, and the Tam*esis*, or Thames, is the ' broad Isis'. In Wales we have the river which the Welsh call the wysg, and the English call the usk. This Celtic word was Romanized into Isca, while another Isca in Devonshire, now the Exe, has given its name to *Ex*eter, *Ex*moor, and *Ex*mouth. There is also an Ex in Hampshire and in Middlesex. The Somersetshire axe flows by *A*xbridge, and the Devonshire axe gives its name to *A*xminster, and *A*xmouth. The ancient name of the Chelm must have also been the Axe, for Chelmsford was formerly Trajectus ad Axam, and Thaxted has been supposed to be a corruption

---

[1] In Kuhn's *Zeitschrift für Vergleichende Sprachforschung*, vol. ix. pp. 276–289.
[2] Whisky is a corruption of *Uisge-boy*, yellow water. [Rather of *uisge-beatha* (usquebaugh) ' water of life ', like *eau-de-vie*.]
[3] Diefenbach, *Celtica*, ii. part i. p. 327; Donaldson, *English Ethnography*, p. 39 ; Radlof, *Neue Untersuchungen*, p. 286. The word has been thought to have some Norse affinities. See Dietrich, in Haupt's *Zeitschrift*, vol. v. p. 228.
[4] More probably from the Gadhelic *taise*, moisture.

of The Ax Stead.[1] The town of *Ux*bridge stands on the River Colne, a later Roman appellation, which apparently superseded the Celtic name Ux. The OCK joins the Thames near Oxford, the OKE is in Devon, and the Ban*oc*burn near Stirling, has given its name to a famous battle-field. The few Gadhelic names in England are found chiefly towards the Eastern part of the island ; here consequently we find three rivers called the OUSE [2], as well as the OUSEL, the OUSEBURN, the USE in Buckinghamshire, UGG Mere, and OS-EY Island. *Oseney* [3] Abbey is on an island near Oxford. The WISK and the *Wash*burn in Yorkshire, the *Guash* in Rutland, the *Wiss*ey in Norfolk, and the local names of *Wish*ford, *Wi*sley, *Wish*anger, *Wis*borough, *Wisk*in (water-island) in the Fens, formerly an island ; *Wi*stow and *As*beach, in the fens of Huntingdonshire, *Wis*beach, and the WASH, seem to be derived from the Welsh *wysg* rather than from the Gaelic *uisge*.[4]

In Spain there are the ESCA and the *Es*la, the latter of which we may compare with the two *Is*las in Scotland, the *Is*le in Somerset, and the *Is*le in Brittany, where also we find the *Is*ac, the *Oust*, the Cou*es*non, and the Cou*es*an ; and in other districts of France are the ESQUE, the ASSE, the OSE, the *Is*olé, the *Is*ère, the *Ous*che, the *Ais*ne, the *Aus*onne, and the Ach*as*e.[5]

There are several French rivers called the AÈS or AÈSE. The *Is*ara, or *Es*ia, has become the OISE, the *Ax*ona is now the *Ais*ne, the *Is*cauna is the Yonne, the Liger*is* is the Loire, and the *Ux*antis insula is the island of *Oues*sant or *Us*hant. The name of the town of Orange, near Avignon, is a corruption of Ar*ais*ion.[6]

The *Is*ella is now the *Y*ssel, the Scald*is* is the Scheldt, the Vahal*is* is the Waal. In central Europe we have the Alb*is* now the Elbe, the Tan*ais* now the Don, the Borysthenes now the Dan*asper* or Dn*ie*per, the Tyr*as* now the Dan*aster* or Dni*es*ter, the Tib*is*cus now the The*is*, the *Is*ter now the

[1] Baxter, *Glossarium*, p. 31.

[2] The Huntingdonshire peasant to this day calls the Ouse the Usey, thus preserving the ancient Gaelic form. Monkhouse, *Etymologies*, p. 64.

[3] The *n* is probably a relic of the Celtic *innis*, island, as in the case of Orkney. See page 119, *supra*.

[4] [Rather from A. Sax. *wascan*, to steep in water, so ' flooded ground ', a pool, Fr. *gâschis*.]

[5] [The account of river names given in this and the following paragraphs is largely conjectural.]

[6] Salverte, *Essai sur les Noms*, vol. ii. p. 289.

Danube, to which may, perhaps, be added the Hyphan*is*, the Hyphas*is*, the Phas*is*, the Tiber*is*, the Ter*is*, the *I*saurus, the *I*saphis, and the *I*sœus [?].

Among German streams we find the ISE, the AXE, the *I*sen, the *I*sar, the *Ei*sach, the *E*schaz, the *S*ave, the *A*hse, the *Ei*sbach, the *Ei*senbach, the *Ei*schbach, the *E*sbach, the *E*selbach ; and a very large number of small streams bear the names of *E*tchbach, *A*schbach, *E*schelbach, and *E*schel-bronn or *E*schelbrunn. We find, also, the *E*sseborn, the *E*sterbach, the *A*gsbach, and the Et*sch*.[1]

The word Etsch is a German corruption of the ancient name At*esis* or Ath*esis*, which the Italians have softened into the Ad*ige*. In Italy we find the Bed*esis*, the *I*s now the *I*ssa, the *Æ*sis now the Fium*esino* (Flumen Æsinum), the *Æ*sar*us* now the *I*sro, the Nat*iso* now the Nat*isone*, the Gal*æ*sus now the Gal*eso*, the Ver*esis* now L'*o*sa, the *O*sa, which still retains its name unchanged, the *Au*sar now the Serchio, the Apr*usa* now the *Au*sa, and the Pad*usa* a branch of the Po.[2] The name of ISTRIA—half land, half water—is derived from the Celtic roots, *is*, water, and *ter*, terra ; and Tri*este*, its chief town, exhibits a Celtic prefix *tre*, a dwelling, which will presently be discussed.[3]

From the closely related Welsh word *gwy* or *wy* (water), we may derive the names of the WYE in Wales and in Derbyshire, and of the WEY in Hampshire, in Dorset, and in Surrey. The Llug*wy* (clear water), the Myn*wy* (small water), the Gar*way* (rough water), the Dowrd*dwy* (noisy water), the El*wy* (gliding water), the Con*way* (chief water), the So*wy*, the Ed*wy*. the On*wy*, the Ol*way*, the Vry*wy*, are all in Wales ; the Med*way* is in Kent, and the Sol*way* on the Scottish border. There is an *I*vel (*Gui*vel) in Somersetshire and in Bedfordshire. The Solent was anciently called Y*r wyth*, the channel, and the Isle of Wight was Y*nys yr wyth*, the Isle of the Channel, from which the present name may possibly be derived.[4] We find the *Vieh*bach, *Wip*pach, and many similar names in Germany.[5] In France the *Gy*, the *Gui*save, and the *Gui*l, in the department

---

1 See Donaldson, *Varronianus*, pp. 45–48 ; Mone, *Celtische Forschungen*, pp. 12, 13, 14, 18 ; Ferguson, *River Names*, pp. 31–33.
2 Arch. Williams, in *Edinb. Trans.* vol. iii. p. 519 ; *Essays*, p. 69.
3 Pott, *Etymol. Forsch.* vol. ii. p. 233 ; Mone, *Celt. Forsch.* p. 224.
4 Walters, in *Philological Proceedings*, vol. i. p. 65. See, however, p. 51, *supra*.
5 Mone, *Celtische Forsch.* pp. 35, 36.

of the Hautes Alpes, and the *Gui*ers, in the department of the Ain, seem to contain the same root.[1]

IV. RHE. The root *Rhe* or *Rhin* is connected with the Gaelic *rea*, rapid ; with the Welsh *rhe*, swift ; *rhedu*, to run ; *rhin*, that which runs :[2] and also with the Greek ῥέω, the Sanskrit *ri*, and the English words *run* and *rain*.[3]

Hence we have the RYE in Kildare, Yorkshire, and Ayrshire, the REA in Salop, Warwick, Herts, and Worcestershire, the REY in Wilts, the RAY in Oxfordshire and Lancashire, the RHEE in Cambridgeshire, the RHEA in Staffordshire, the WREY in Devon, the ROY in Inverness, the ROE [4] in Derry, the RUE in Montgomery, the ERYN in Sussex, the *Ro*den in Salop and Essex, and the *Ri*bble in Lancashire. We also find this root in the names of the RHINE (Rhenus), the RHIN, the REGEN, the REGA and the *Rha*danau, in Germany, the *Rei*naç̧h and the *Reu*ss in Switzerland, the *Re*gge in Holland, the *Rh*one in France, the *Ri*ga in Spain, the RHA or Volga in Russia, the *Eri*danus, now the Po, and the *Rhe*nus, now the *Re*no, in Italy.

V. DON. Whether the root *Don*, or *Dan*, is connected with the Celtic *afon*, or whether it is an unrelated Celtic or Scythian gloss, is a point which has not been decided. It appears, however, that in the language of the Ossetes— a tribe in the Caucasus, which preserves a very primitive form of the Aryan speech—the word *don* means water or river.[5] If this be the true meaning of the word it enables us to assign an esoteric explanation to certain primaeval myths.[6]

---

[1] The Welsh names of many aquatic animals contain the root *gwy*, water, e.g. *hwyad*, a duck ; *gwydd*, a goose ; *guillemot*, etc. Morris, in *Gentleman's Magazine* for October, 1789, p. 904. *Guit* is the Provençal term for a duck. Courson, *Peup. Bret.* vol. i. p.32.

[2] *Rhyn* is a promontory, a point of land which *runs* out to sea [?]. Penrhyn near Bangor, Rynd in Perth, Rhind in Clackmannan, Rindow Point near Wigton, the Rins of Galloway, Penryn in Cornwall, Rien in Clare, Rinmore in Devon, Argyle, and Aberdeen, and several Rins in Kerry, are all projecting tongues of land.

[3] So the *raindeer* is the running deer [?]. Cf. Diefenbach, *Celtica*, i. p. 56 ; *Orig. Europ.* p. 408 ; Pictet, *Orig. Indo-Eur.* vol. i. p. 136 ; Zeuss, *Grammatica Celtica*, vol. i. p. 13 ; Astruc, *Languedoc*, p. 448 : Betham, *Gael*, p. 212. [Compare O. Eng. *rin*, a streamlet or *runnel*. *Rain* is not connected.]

[4] [Rather ' the red ' river, Ir *ruadh*.]

[5] Arndt, *Europ. Spr.* pp. 117, 174, 241 ; Cf. Hartshorne, *Salopia Antiqua*, p. 261 ; Wheeler, *Geography of Herodotus*, p. 145. There is a Gadhelic word *tain*, water. Armstrong says *don* is an obsolete Gaelic word for water, and that it is still retained in the Armorican. Compare the Sclavonic *tonu*, a river-deep. Schafarik, *Slawische Alterth.* vol. i. p. 498. Ultimately, we may probably refer *don* to the conjectural Sanskrit word *udan*, water—which contains the root *und* [read *ud*], to wet. Hence the Latin *unda*. The Sanskrit *udra*, water, comes from the same root *und* [*ud*], and is probably the source of the Celtic *dwr*. Pictet, *Orig. Indo-Eur.* vol. i. p. 141.

[6] Karl v. Müller, *Mythologie* pp. 185, 312 ; Pott, *Mytho-Etymologica*, in Kuhn's *Zeitschrift für Vergleich. Sprachforsch.* vol vii. pp. 109-111 ; Gladstone, *Homer.* p. 366 ; Kelly, *Curiosities*, pp. 142, 212 ; Creuzer, *Symbolik*, vol. iii. p. 480 ; Preller, *Griechische Mythologie*, pp. 33-38.

Thus Hesiod informs us that *Dan*aus, the grandson of Poseidon and Libya (λίβα, moisture), relieved Argos from drought: Αργος ἄνυδρον ἐὸν Δαναὸςποίησεν ἔνυδρον. Again, we are told that the fifty Danaides, having slain their husbands, the fifty sons of Ægyptus, on the wedding night, were condemned to carry water in broken urns to fill a bottomless vessel. This myth receives a beautiful interpretation as an esoteric exposition of a natural phenomenon, if we interpret the ancient gloss *dan*, as meaning water. We then see that the *Dan*aides, daughters of *Dan*, are the waters of the inundation, which overwhelm the fifty provinces of Egypt in their fatal embrace, and for a penalty have to bear water up the mountain sides in their broken urns of cloud, condemned ceaselessly to endeavour to fill the valley, a bottomless gulf through which the river carries forth the outpourings of the clouds into the sea.

But whatever may be the signification of this root, we find it in a large number of the most ancient and important river-names.

On the Continent we have the *Dan*ube,[1] the *Dan*astris, the *Dan*aster, or *Dn*iester, the *Dan*apris, *Dan*asper, or *Dn*ieper, the DON, anciently the *Tan*ais, and the *Don*etz, a tributary of the Don, in Russia, the Rha*dan*au, in Prussia, the Rho*dan*us or Rho*ne*, the A*don*is, the Are*don* in the Caucasus, the Ti*don*e, and the *Tan*aro, affluents of the Eri*dan*us or Po, the Dur*dan* in Normandy, the *Don* in Brittany, and the Ma*don*, the Ver*don*, the Lou*don*, the O*don*, and the Rosco*don* in other parts of France.

In the British Isles this word is found in the names of the DON in Yorkshire, Aberdeen, and Antrim, the Ban*don* in Londonderry, the DEAN in Nottinghamshire and Forfar, the DANE in Cheshire, the DUN in Lincolnshire and Ayrshire, the TONE in Somerset, and probably in the E*den* in Yorkshire, Cumberland, Kent, Fife, and Roxburgh, the DAVON in Cheshire and Glamorgan, the DEVON in Leicestershire, Perth, Fife, and Clackmannan, and possibly the TYNE in Northumberland and Haddington, the TEIGN in DEVON, the TIAN in the Island of Jura, the TEANE in Stafford, the TEYN in Derbyshire, and the TYNET in Banff.[2]

---

[1] Zeuss, *Gram. Celt.* vol. ii. p. 994, thinks the root is the Erse *dana*, strong. He is followed by Förstemann, *Alt-deut. Namenbuch*, vol. ii. p. 409; De Belloguet, *Eth.* p. 104; and Glück, *Kelt. Namen*, p. 92.

[2] Some of these names may be from the Celtic *tian*, running water, or, perhaps, from

It thus appears that the names of almost all the larger rivers of Europe, as well as those of a very great number of the smaller streams, contain one or other of the five chief Celtic words for water or river, viz.—

1. Avon, *or* aon.
2. Dwr, *or* ter.
3. Uisge, *or* wysk, wye, is, es, oise, usk, nesk, ex, ax.
4. Rhe, *or* rhin.
5. Don, *or* dan.

It will, doubtless, have been remarked that several rivers figure more than once in the foregoing lists; we find, in short, that two or even three of these nearly synonymous roots enter into the composition of their names.

Thus it seems probable that the name of the

Dan-as-ter, or } Dn-ies-ter }	contains roots (5) (3) (2)		Hypan-is.	.	.	.	. (1) (3)
Rha-dan-au .	. . . (4) (5) (1)		Tan-ais	.	.	.	. (5) (3)
Is-ter .	. . . . (3) (2)		Eri-dan-us	.	.	.	. (4) (5) (3?)
Rho-dan-us	. . . (4) (5) (3 ?)		Ex-ter	.	.	.	. (3) (2)
Dan-ub-ius	. . . (5) (1) (3 ?)		Tyr-as	.	.	.	. (2) (3)
Dur-dan .	. . . (2) (5)		Ax-ona	.	.	.	. (3) (1)
Dur-an-ius	. . . (2) (1) (3 ?)		S-avone .	.	.	.	. (3) (1)
Rhe-n-us .	. . . (4) (1) (3 ?)		Aus-onne	.	.	.	. (3) (1)
Isc-aun-a .	. . . (3) (1)		Is-en .	.	.	.	. (3) (1)
Dan-as-per	. . (5) (3)		Dour-on .	.	.	.	. (2) (1)
Ter-ab-ia .	. . . (2) (1)		S-tour	.	.	.	. (3 ?) (2)
			An-ton	.	.	.	. (1) (5)

Some of these cases may be open to criticism, but the instances are too numerous to be altogether fortuitous. The formation of these names appears to be in accordance with a law,[1] which, if it can be established, will enable us to throw light on the process of slow accretion by which many of the most ancient river-names have been formed.

The theory supposes that, when the same territory has

Ta-aon, the still river—see page 153, *infra*. The names of the Davon and the Tone show how *dwr-avon*, by crasis, might possibly become D'avon, *d-aon*, or *don*. In many river-names we find a *d* or a *t* prefixed, which has been thought to be due to the Celtic preposition *di*, *do*, or *du*, which means at. The Tees, the Taff, the Tavon, are perhaps instances of this usage, which we see exemplified in the indisputable cases of Zermat, Andermat, Amsteg, Stanko (ἐς τὰν Κῶ), Utrecht (ad trajectum), Armorica, Arles, etc. See pp. 61, 162; and Whitaker, *Hist. Manchester*, vol. i. p. 220; *Hist. Whalley*, p. 9; Zeuss, *Gram. Celt.* vol. ii. pp. 566, 595, 597, 626; Baxter, *Glossarium*, p. 8; Charnock, *Local Etym.* p. 269.

[1] The existence of this law, *hybrida compositio,* as it was termed by Baxter, who discovered it, has been strenuously upheld. See, however, Donaldson, *Varronianus*, pp. 46, 47; *New Cratylus*, p. 14; Rawlinson, *Herodotus*, vol. iii. p. 188; Mone, *Celt. Forsch.* p. 5; Davies, in *Phil. Trans.* for 1857, p. 91; Poste, *Brit. Researches*, p. 144.

been subject to the successive occupancy of nations speaking different languages, or different dialects of the same language, the earliest settlers called the river, on whose banks they dwelt, by a word signifying in their own language ' The Water', or ' The River '. As language changed through conquest, or in the lapse of ages, this word was taken for a proper name, and another word for ' River ' or ' Water ' was superadded. This process of superimposition may have been repeated again and again by successive tribes of immigrants, and thus ultimately may have been formed the strange aggregations of synonymous syllables which we find in so many river-names. The operation of this law we may detect with certainty in the case of names unaffected, as are most of the names which have been cited, by the phonetic changes of many centuries. It will be well, therefore, to illustrate this process in the case of some familiar and more modern names, where it must, beyond possibility of doubt, have taken place.

In the case of the DUR-BECK in Nottinghamshire, and the DUR-BACH in Germany, the first syllable is the Celtic *dwr*, water. The Teutonic colonists, who in either case dispossessed the Celts, inquired the name of the stream, and being told it was DWR, *the* water, they naturally took this to be a *proper* name instead of a *common* name, and suffixed the German word *beck* or *bach*, a stream. In the names of the ESK-WATER and the DOUR-WATER in Yorkshire, we have a manifest English addition to the Celtic roots *esk* and *dwr*.

The IS-BOURNE, the EASE-BURN, the ASH-BOURNE, the WASH-BURN, and the OUSE-BURN, present the Anglian *burne*, added to various common modifications of the Celtic *uisge*.

In the name of WAN-S-BECK-WATER we first find *wan*, which is a slightly corrupted form of the Welsh *afon*. The *s* is, perhaps, a vestige of the Gadhelic *uisge*. As in the case of the Durbeck, the Teutonic *beck* was added by the Anglian colonists, and the English word *water* was suffixed when the meaning of Wansbeck had become obscure, and Wansbeckwater, or Riverwaterriverwater, is the curious agglomeration which has resulted.[1]

The mountain at the head of the Yarrow is called MOUNT-BENJERLAW. The original Celtic name was *Ben Yair*, or ' Yarrow Head '. The Angles added their own word *hlaw*, a

[1] Donaldson, *Varronianus* ; *New Cratylus*, p. 14.

hill; and the *mount* is an Anglo-Norman addition of still later date.[1]

In the name of BRINDON HILL, in Somersetshire, we have first the Cymric *bryn*, a hill. To this was added *dun*, a Saxonized Celtic word, nearly synonymous with *bryn*; and the English word *hill* was added when neither *bryn* nor *dun* were any longer significant words.

PEN-DLE-HILL, in Lancashire, is similarly compounded of three synonymous words—the Cymric *pen*, the Norse *holl*, and the English *hill*.[2] In PEN-TLOW HILL, in Essex, we have the Celtic *pen*, the Anglo-Saxon *hlaw*, and the English *hill*. SHAR-PEN-HOE-KNOLL, in Bedfordshire, contains four nearly synonymous elements. The names of PIN-HOW in Lancashire, PEN-HILL in Somersetshire and Dumfriesshire, PEN-D-HILL in Surrey, and PEN-LAW in Dumfriesshire, are analogous compounds.

MON-GIBELLO, the local name of Etna, is compounded of the Arabic *gebel*, a mountain, to which the Italian *monte* has been prefixed.

Trajan's bridge, over the Tagus, is called the LA PUENTE DE ALCANTARA. Here we have the same process. *Al Cantara* means ' The Bridge ' in Arabic, and *La Puente* means precisely the same thing in Spanish.

In the case of the city of NAG-POOR we have *nagara*, a city, and *pura*, a city.

The VAL DE NANT, in Neufchâtel, presents us with the Celtic *nant* and the French *val*, both identical in meaning. HERT-FORD gives us the Celtic *rhyd*, a synonym of the Saxon *ford*.[3] In HOLM-IN ISLAND there are three synonyms. We find, first, the Norse *holm*; secondly, the Celtic *innis*; and, lastly, the English *island*. INCH ISLAND is an analogous name. In the case of the Isle of Sheppey, Canvey Island, Osey Island, and Ramsey Island, we have the Anglo-Saxon *ea*, which is identical in meaning with the English *island*.

In like manner, we might analyse the names of the Hill of Howth, the Tuskar Rock, Smerwick Harbour, Sandwich Bay, Cape Griznez, Start Point, the Aland Islands, Hampton, Hamptonwick, Bourn Brook in Surrey, the Bach Brook in

---

[1] Garnett, *Essays*, p. 70.
[2] Davies, in *Philolog. Trans.* p 218; Whitaker, *Hist. of Whalley*, pp. 7, 8.
[3] Baxter, *Glossarium*, p. 69. [The ancient form of the name *Heorot-ford* shows that it is merely the ' hart's ford '.]

Cheshire, the Oehbach[1] in Hesse, Knock-knows, Dal-field, *Kinn*aird *Head*, the King-horn River, Hoe Hill in Lincoln, Mal-don (Celtic *maol* or *moel*, a round hill) Maserfield (Welsh *maes*, a field), Romn-ey Marsh (Gaelic *ruimne*, a marsh), Alt Hill (Welsh *allt*, a cliff),[2] and many others.

In short, it would be easy to multiply, almost without end, unexceptional instances of this process of aggregations of synonyms ; but the cases cited may probably suffice to make it highly probable that the same process has prevailed among the Celtic and Scythian tribes of central Europe, and that this law of hybrid composition, as it is called, may, without extravagance, be adduced in explanation of such names as the Rha-dan-au, or the Dn-ies-ter, and with the highest probability in cases like the Ax-ona or the Dur-dan.

It now remains briefly to consider the second or adjectival class of river-roots.

Two have been already mentioned. From the Welsh *garw*, rough,[3] we obtain the names of the GARA in Sligo and Hereford, the GARRY in Perth and Inverness, the YARE in Normandy, in Norfolk, in the Isle of Wight, and in Devon, the GARWAY in Carmarthen, the GARNERE in Clare, the GARNAR in Hereford, the YARRO in Lancashire, the YARROW and the YAIR in Selkirk,[4] the GARVE and the GARELOCH in Ross, the GARONNE, the GERS, and the GIRON in France, and the GUER in Brittany.

From the Gaelic *all*, white, we obtain *al-aon*, ' white afon '. The Romans have Latinized this word into Alauna.[5] In Lancashire the Alauna of the Romans is now the LUNE.[6] There is another LUNE in Yorkshire. We find a River ALLEN in Leitrim, another in Denbigh, another in Northumberland, and a fourth in Dorset. There is an ALLAN in Perthshire, and two in Roxburghshire. The ALAN in Cornwall, the ALLWEN in Merioneth, the ELWIN in Lanark, the ELLEN in Cumberland, the ILEN in Cork, and the ALN or AULN, which we find in

---

[1] Old High German, *aha*, water. See Vilmar, *Ortsnamen*, p. 258.
[2] Davies, in *Philolog. Trans.* for 1857, p. 91.
[3] Gaelic and Irish, *garbh*. [Joyce, *Irish Names of Places*, ii. 444.]
[4] Compare the name of the monastery of Jarrow, where Beda lived.
[5] See Diefenbach, *Celtica*, ii. part i. p. 310.
[6] *Lan*caster, anciently Ad Alaunam, is the *castra* on the Lune. The name of *Alces*ter, which stands on the *Aln*, the Warwickshire Alauna, is written Ellencaster by Matthew Paris. See Baxter, *Glossarium*, p. 10.

Northumberland, Cumberland, Hampshire, Warwick, Roxburgh, and Berwickshire, are all modifications of the same name, as well as the AULNE and the ELLÉE in Brittany. The name of the ELBE is probably connected with the same root [if not rather from Teutonic *elf, elv*, 'river '].

To the Gaelic and Erse *ban*, white, we may refer the BEN in Mayo, the BANN in Wexford, the BANE in Lincoln, the BAIN in Hertford, the AVEN-BANNA in Wexford, the *Ban*on (Ban Afon) in Pembroke, the BANA in Down, the *Ban*don in Cork and Londonderry, the *Ban*ney in Yorkshire, the *Ban*ac in Aberdeen, the *Ban*oc-burn in Stirling, the BAUNE in Hesse, and the *Ban*itz in Bohemia.

The word *dhu*, black, appears in five rivers in Wales, three in Scotland, and one in Dorset, which are called *Du*las. There are also two in Scotland and one in Lancashire called the *Dou*glas,[1] and we have the *Dou*las in Radnor, and the *Dow*les in Shropshire.

From *llevn*, smooth, or from *linn*, a deep still pool,[2] we obtain the names of Loch LEVEN and three rivers called LEVEN in Scotland, beside others of the same name in Gloucestershire, Yorkshire, Cornwall, Cumberland, and Lancashire. To one of these words we may also refer the names of Loch LYON in Perth, the River LYON in Inverness, the LOIN in Banff, the LEANE in Kerry, the LINE in Cumberland, Northumberland, Nottingham, Peebles, and Fife, the LANE in Galloway, the LAIN in Cornwall, and perhaps one or more of the four LUNES which are found in Yorkshire, Durham, and Lancashire.[3] Deep pools, or lynns, have given names to LINCOLN, King's LYNN, DUBLIN, GLASLIN, LINLITHGOW, LINTON, KILLIN, and ROSLIN.[4]

The word *tam*, spreading, quiet, still, which seems to be related to the Welsh *taw* and the Gaelic *tav*, appears in the names of the *Tam*esis or THAMES, the TAME in Cornwall, Cheshire, Lancashire, Stafford, and Bucks, the TAMAR in Devon, the TEMA in Selkirk, the TEME in Worcester, and

---

1 The Diggles, also in Lancashire, is a corruption of the same name. Whitaker, *Hist. Whalley*, p. 9.
2 [Or better Gaelic *leamhan*, an elm, J. B. Johnston, *Place Names of Scotland*, 200.]
3 We know that the Lune is, in one case, a contracted form of Alauna, the white river. See p. 152, *supra*.
4 Zeuss derives the name of the Lacus Lemanus from this root. *Gram. Celt.* vol. i. p. 100; De Belloguet, *Ethnogénie*, vol. i. p. 249.

perhaps [1] in those of the TAW in Devon and Glamorgan, the TA Loch in Wexford, the TAY (anciently the Tavus) in Perth and Waterford, the TAVY in Devon, and the TAVE in Wales. Pliny tells us, Scythæ vocant Mæotim Temarundam,—the 'Broad Water'.[2]

The widely-diffused root *ar* causes much perplexity. The ARAR, as Cæsar says, flows 'incredibili lenitate'; while, as Coleridge tells us, the ARVE and the ARVEIRON 'rave ceaselessly'. We find, however, on the one hand, a Welsh word *araf*, gentle, and an obsolete Gaelic word *ar*, slow, and on the other we have a Celtic word *arw*, violent, and a Sanskrit root *arb*, to ravage or destroy. From one or other of these roots, according to the character of the river, we may derive the names of the ARW in Monmouth, the ARE and the AIRE in Yorkshire, the AYR in Cardigan and Ayrshire, the ARRE in Cornwall, the ARRO in Hereford and Sligo, the *Ar*ay in Argyle, the *Ar*a-glin and the *Ar*a-gadeen in Cork, the ERVE, the ARVE, the OURCQ, the ARC, the *Ar*riège, and the *Ar*veiron, in France, the *Ar*ga and three rivers called *Ar*va in Spain, in Italy the *Ar*no and E*ra*, in Switzerland the AAR and the *Ar*bach, in Germany the OHRE, AHR, Isa*r*, Au*r*ach, O*rr*e, E*r*l, E*r*la, A*r*l, O*r*la, A*r*gen, and several mountain streams called the ARE; besides the well known ancient names of the O*ar*us, the *Ar*axes, the AR-AR-AR, the Napa*r*is, the *Ar*as, and the Jaxa*r*tes.[3]

The word *cam*,[4] crooked, we find in the CAM in Gloucester and Cambridgeshire [?], the CAMIL in Cornwall, the CAMLAD in Shropshire, the CAMBECK in Cumberland, the CAMLIN in Longford, and the CAMON in Tyrone. MORCAMBE BAY is the crooked-sea bay, and CAMDEN is the crooked vale. We have also the rivers KAMP and CHAM in Germany, and the KAM in Switzerland.

---

[1] See p. 148, *supra*.

[2] Donaldson, *Varron*. p. 51. We find a Sanskrit word *támara*, water. The ultimate root seems to be *tam*, languescere. Pictet, *Orig. Indo-Europ*. p. 142.

[3] See Latham, *Germania*, p. 13; Rawlinson, *Herodotus*, vol. iii. p. 202; Mone, *Celt, Forsch*. p. 204; Prichard, *Researches*, vol. iii. p. 132; Glück, *Kelt. Namen*, p. 58; Radlof, *Neue Untersuchungen*, p. 285; De Belloguet, *Ethnogénie*, vol. i. p. 116; Förstemann *Ortsnamen*, p. 32.

[4] Diefenbach, *Celtica*, i. p. 110. This word was adopted into English, though it is now obsolete So Sicinius Velutus says of the crooked reasoning of Menenius Agrippa, 'This is clean kam'; to which Brutus replies, 'Merely awry'. *Coriolanus*, Act iii. scene i. The root appears in the phrase, arms in kembo, or a-kimbo [?]. To *cam*, in the Manchester dialect, is to cross or contradict a person, or to bend anything awry. Kennett, *Parochial Antiquities*, Glossary, s. v. Camera; Whitaker, *Hist. Manchester*, vol. ii. p. 274; Davies, in *Philolog. Proc*. vol. vi. p. 129; Halliwell, *Archaic Glossary*, s. v.; Glück, *Kelt. Namen*, p. 34. [But see Prof. Skeat, *Notes and Queries*, 8th. s. viii. 265.]

To the Gaelic *clith*, strong, we may refer the CLYDE [1] and the CLUDAN in Scotland, the CLWYD, the CLOYD, and the CLYDACH, in Wales, the GLYDE and several other streams in Ireland, and, perhaps, the CLITUMNUS in Italy. [2]

There are many other clusters of river-names which invite investigation, but of which a mere enumeration must suffice. [3] Such are the groups of names of which the NEATH, the SOAR, the MAY, the DEE, the TEES, the CHER, the KEN, the FROME, the COLNE, the IRKE, the LID, the LEA, the MEUSE, the GLEN, and the SWALE, may be taken as types. It is indeed a curious fact, that a unique river-name is hardly to be found. Any given name may immediately be associated with some dozen or half-dozen names nearly identical in form and meaning, collected from all parts of Europe. This might suffice to show the great value of these river-names in ethnological investigations. Reaching back to a period anterior to all history, they enable us to prove the wide diffusion of the Celtic race, and to trace that race in its progress across Europe.

For antiquity and immutability, the names of mountains and hills come next in value to the names of rivers. [4] The names of these conspicuous landmarks have been transmitted from race to race very much in the same way, and from the same causes, as the names of rivers.

The modern Welsh names for the head and the back are *pen* and *cefn*. We find these words in a large number of mountain-names. The Welsh *cefn*, [5] (pronounced keven) a back, or ridge, is very common in local names in Wales, as in the case of CEFN COED or CEFN BRYN. In England it is found in the CHEVIN, a ridge in Wharfdale ; in CHEVIN Hill near

---

[1] [Clyde (anciently *Cloithe*) is probably ' the grey water ', akin to Welsh *llwyd*, grey (whence the name Lloyd). *Scottish Rev.* xxii., 91.]

> ' They had him to the *wan* water,
> For a' men call it Clyde '.—*Old Scotch Ballad*]

[2] Williams, *Essays*, p. 71, prefers the Welsh *clyd*, warm.

[3] On river-roots see Ferguson, *River Names of Europe* ; Baxter, *Glossarium* ; Chalmers *Caledonia*, vol. i. ; Förstemann, *Altdeutsches Namenbuch*, vol. ii. ; *Deutschen Ortsnamen*, pp. 31–37 ; Whitaker, *History of Manchester*, vol. i. p. 220 ; *History of Whalley*, pp. 8, 9. Betham *Gael.* pp. 205–215 ; Vilmar, *Ortsnamen*, p. 254 ; *Church of England Quarterly*, No. 73, p. 153 ; Schott, *Deutsch. Col.* pp. 210, 225 ; Pictet, *Orig. Indo-Eur.* part i. pp. 119, 134–145: and the works of Pott, Arndt, Glück, Diefenbach, De Belloguet, Williams, Davies, Latham, Rawlinson, Donaldson, etc.

[4] ' Helvellyn and Skiddaw rise as sepulchral monuments of a race that has passed away '.—Palgrave, *English Commonwealth*, vol. i. p. 451.

[5] See Diefenbach, *Celtica*, i. p. 104 ; Glück, *Kelt. Namen*, p. 51 ; Boudard, *Numat. Ibér.* p. 121 ; Morris, in *Gentleman's Mag.* for 1789, p. 905.

Derby; in KEYNTON, a name which occurs in Shropshire, Dorset, and Wilts; in CHEVENING, on the great ridge of North Kent; in CHEVINGTON in Suffolk and Northumberland; also in CHEVY Chase, and the CHEVIOT Hills; [1] in the Gebenna Mons, now LES CEVENNES, in France; and in Cape CHIEN, in Brittany.

The Welsh *pen*,[2] a head, and by metonymy, the usual name for a mountain, is widely diffused throughout Europe. The south-easterly extension of the Cymric race is witnessed by the names of the PENN-INE chain of the Alps, the A-PENN-INES, a place called PENNE, anciently Pinna, in the high Apennines, and Mount PINDUS, in Greece. The ancient name of PENIL UCUS, near Villeneuve, is evidently a Latinized form of *Pen-y-llwch*, the head of the lake.[3] We find PENHERF and the headland of PENMARCH in Brittany, and there is a hill near Marseilles which is called LA PENNE. In our own island, hills bearing this name are very numerous. We have PENARD, PENHILL, and PEN in Somerset, Upper and Lower PENN in Staffordshire, and PANN Castle near Bridgenorth. The highest hill in Buckinghamshire is called PEN. One of the most conspicuous summits in Yorkshire is called PENNI-GANT. INKPEN stands on a high hill in Berkshire. We have PENDLETON and PENKETH in Lancashire, PENSHURST in Sussex; in Cumberland we find PENRITH, the head of the ford; and in Herefordshire, PENCOID, the head of the wood. In Cornwall and Wales the root *pen* is of perpetual occurrence, as in the cases of PENRHYN and PENDENNIS (*Pen Dinas*) in Cornwall, and PENMAENMAWR, PEMBROKE,[4] and PENRHOS, in Wales.

In Argyleshire and the northern parts of Scotland the Cymric *pen* is ordinarily replaced by *ben* or *cenn*, the Gaelic forms of the same word.

---

[1] [More likely from Gaelic *c(h)iabach*, ' bushy ',—J. B. Johnston, *Place Names of Scotland*, 72.]

[2] From the root *pen*, originally a head or point, come probably [?], pinnacle, penny (?), pin, spine, and the name of the pine-tree. It is curious that the Cymric *pyr*, a fir, bears the same relation to the name of the Pyrenees that *pina* does to those of the Apennines and Pennine Alps. Compare the Pyern mountains in Upper Austria, and the Ferner in Tyrol. In the case of many of the Pyrenean giants the topmost pyramid of each is called its ' penne '. *Peña* is the name for a rock in Spanish, and in Italian *penna* is a mountain summit. Diez, *Etym. Wörterb.* p. 258. Cf. *Quarterly Review*, vol. cxvi. p. 12. On the root *pen*, see Diefenbach, *Celtica*, i. p. 170; *Orig. Eur.* p. 397; Keferstein, *Kelt. Alt.* vol. ii. p. 186; Adelung, *Mithridates*, vol. ii. p. 67; Forbes, *Tour of Mont Blanc* p. 210; Zeuss, *Gram. Celt.* vol. i. p. 77; Wedgwood, in *Philolog. Proceed.* vol. iv. p. 259; Davies, *ibid.* vol. vi. p. 129; De Belloguet, *Ethnogénie*, vol. i. p. 73.

[3] Robertson, *Early Kings*, vol. ii. p. 229.

[4] *Pen-bro*, the head of the land.

This distinctive usage of *pen* and *ben* in local names enables us to detect the ancient line of demarcation between the Cymric and Gadhelic branches of the Celtic race. We find the Cymric form of the word in the Gram-*pian*-s, the PENTLAND Hills, the PENNAGAUL Hills and PENPONT in Dumfries, the PEN of Eskdalemuir, PEN CRAIG in Haddington, PENWALLY in Ayrshire, and PENDRICH in Perth. On the other hand the Gaelic *ben*, which is conspicuously absent from England,[1] Wales, and south-eastern Scotland, is used to designate almost all the higher summits of the north and west, as, for instance, BENNEVIS, BENLEDI, BENMORE, BENWYVIS, BENLOMOND, BENCRUACHAN, and many more, too numerous to specify.

The Gadhelic *cenn*, a head, is another form of the same word. It is found in KENMORE,[2] CANTIRE, KINNAIRD, and KINROSS, in Scotland, KINSALE and KENMARE in Ireland, in the English county of KENT [?], KENNE in Somerset, KENNEDON in Devonshire, KENTON in Middlesex, KENCOT in Oxfordshire, and KENCOMB in Dorset.

The position of ancient Celtic strongholds is frequently indicated by the root *dun*, a hill fortress, a word which is closely related to the modern Welsh word *dinas*.[3] The features of such a natural stronghold are well exhibited at SION in Switzerland, where a bold isolated crag rises in the midst of an alluvial plain. Like so many other positions of the kind, this place bears a Celtic name. The German form SITTEN is nearer than the French SION to the ancient name Se*dun*am, which is the Latinized form of the original Celtic appellation. In a neighbouring canton the ancient Edre*dun*um has become YVERDUN, a place which, as well as THUN (pronounced *Toon*), must have been among the fortress-cities of the Celts of Switzerland. In Germany, Campo*dun*um is now KEMP-TEN, and Taro*dun*um, in the modern form of DOR-N-STADT, preserves only a single

[1] Ben Rhydding, in Yorkshire, is a name of very recent concoction.
[2] Kenmore, the ' great summit ', from the Gaelic *mor*, or the Welsh *mawr*, great. This name is found also in Switzerland. There is a mountain called the KAMOR in Appenzell, and another called the KAMMERSTOCK between Uri and Glarus. Mont CENIS was anciently Mons Cinisius. GENEVA is probably *cenn afon*, the head of the river. See Mone, *Celtische Forschungen*, p. 27. [More likely from Celtic *genava*, a mouth or opening.]
[3] Glück, *Kelt. Namen*, p. 139 ; Diefenbach, *Celtica*, i. p. 157 ; *Orig. Eur.* pp. 325–328 ; Adelung, *Mithridates*, vol. ii. p. 57 ; Holtzmann, *Kelten und Germanen*, p. 100 ; Menage, *Origines*, pp. 264–267 ; Förstemann, *Altdeutsches Namenbuch*, vol. ii. p. 442 ; *Cambro-Briton*, vol. iii. p. 43. From the Celtic the root has penetrated into Italian and Spanish as *duna*, into English as *down*, and into French as *dune*. The *Dhuns* of the Himalayas, as Kjarda Dhun, Dehra Dhun, etc., seem to be related words. Diez, *Etym. Wörterb.* p. 129 ; Lassen, *Indische Alterth*, vol. i. pp. xlv. 48.

letter of the Celtic *dun*. The same is the case with Carro-
*dun*um (carraighdun, the rock fort), now KHAR-N-BURG on
the Danube ; while I*dun*um, on the same river, is now I-DIN-O.
THUN-DORF and DUN-ESTADT also witness the eastern extension of the Celtic people.[1] In Italy we find nine ancient
names into which this Celtic root enters, as Vin*din*um, A*tin*a,
and Re*tin*a.[2] But in France, more especially, these Celtic
hill-forts abounded. Augusto*dun*um is now AU-TUN, and
Julio*dun*um is LOU-DUN near Poictiers. Lug*dun*um, on the
Rhone, is now LYONS ; Lug*dun*um or Lugo*din*um, in Holland,
is now LEYDEN ; and Lugi*dun*um, in Silesia, is now GLOGAU.
The rock of LAÔN, the stronghold of the later Merovingian
kings, is a contraction of Lau*dun*um.[3] Novio*dun*um, the
' new fort ', is a common name : one is now NOYON, another
NEVERS, another NYON, another JUBLEINS. Melo*dun*um
(*mealldun*,[4] the hill fort), now MELUN, Vero*dun*um, now VER-
DUN, and Uxello*dun*um in Guienne, were also Celtic strongholds.

In England there seem to have been fewer Celtic fortresses
than in France. Lon*dun*um or Lon*din*ium, the fortified hill
on which St. Paul's Cathedral now stands, is now LON-DON.
LEX-DON, near Colchester, seems to have been Legionis dunum ;[5]
and Camulo*dun*um is probably MAL-DON, in Essex.[6]   Sorbio-
*dun*um, now Old SARUM ; Branno*dun*um, now Brancaster ;
Mori*dun*um,   now   CARMAR-THEN ;   Rigio*dun*um,   perhaps
Ribblechester ; Mori*dun*um, probably Seaton ; and Tao*dun*um,
now DUN-DEE, were all British forts which were occupied by
the Romans.   The same root *dun* is found also in DUNSTABLE,
DUNMOW, and DUNDRY Hill in Somerset. In Scotland we
have DUMBLANE, DUMFRIES, DUNKELD, the ' fort of the
Celts ', and DUMBARTON, the ' fort of the Britons '.   In Ireland we find DUNDRUM, DUNDALK, DUNGANNON, DUNGARVON,
DUNLEARY, DUNLAVIN, and scores of other names, which exhibit
this word.   It was adopted by the Saxons from the Celts,

---

[1] See Mone. *Celtische Forschungen,* p. 68.   The ancient name of Belgrade was SEGODU-
NUM, *Seigha-dun,* equivalent to Hapsburg, or Hawks'-hill. Leo, *Vorlesungen,* vol. i.
p. 195.
[2] Williams, *Edinburgh Proceedings,* vol. xiii. p. 532 ; *Essays,* p. 80. Cor*tona* is evidently *Caer-dun.*
[3] Palgrave, *England and Normandy,* vol. ii. p. 7 ; Kennedy, in *Philolog. Trans.* for
1855, p. 170 ; Salverte, *Essai sur les Noms,* vol. ii. pp. 265, 266. See p. 227, *infra.*
[4] Glück, *Kelt. Nam.* p. 139.
[5] Baxter, *Glossarium,* p. 174.
[6] Horsley, *Brit. Rom.* p. 31 ; Gough's Camden, vol. ii. pp. 122, 135.

and, in accordance with the genius of their language, it is used as a suffix instead of as a prefix, as is usually the case in genuine Celtic names. We have instances in the names of HUNTINGDON, FARRINGDON, and CLARENDON.

The Celtic languages can place the substantive first and the adjective last, while in the Teutonic idiom this is unallowable. The same is the case with substantives which have the force of adjectives. Thus the Celtic Strathclyde and Abertay corresponds to the Teutonic forms Clydesdale and Taymouth. This usage often enables us to discriminate between Celtic and Saxon roots which are nearly identical in sound. Thus, Balbeg and Strathbeg must be from the Celtic *beg*, little ; but Bigholm and Bighouse are from the Teutonic *big*, great.[1] Dalry, Dalgain, Dalkeith, Daleaglis, Dolberry in Somerset, and Toulouse must be from the Celtic *dol*, a plain ; while Rydal, Kendal, Mardale, and Oundle, are from the Teutonic *dale*, a valley.[2]

The Welsh word *bryn*, a brow [3] or ridge, is found in BRANDON, in Suffolk, which is the Anglicized form of *Dinas Bran*, a common local name in Wales. A ridge in Essex is called BRANDON. BREANDOWN is the name of a high ridge near Weston-super-Mare. BRENDON Hill forms part of the great ridge of Exmoor. BIRNWOOD Forest, in Buckinghamshire, occupies the summit of a ridge which is elevated some 300 feet above the adjacent country. BRAINTREE in Essex, and BRINTON and BRANCASTER in Norfolk (anciently Brannodunum), contain the same root, which is found in numerous Swiss and German names, such as BRANNBERG, BRANDENBURG, BRENDENKOPF, and the BRENNER in the Tyrol.[4]

PENRHOS, a name which occurs in Wales and Cornwall, contains a root—*rhos*, a moor [5]—which is liable to be confused with the Gaelic *ros*, which signifies a prominent rock or headland. ROSS in Hereford and in Northumberland, ROSNEATH by Loch Long, and ROSDUY on Loch Lomond, are all on pro-

---

1 [There is no Teutonic word *big*, great ; perhaps Gaelic *beag*, little, or Norse *bygg* barley.]
2 See Zeuss, *Grammatica Celtica*, vol. ii. pp. 824, 825, 862 ; Chalmers, *Caledonia*, vol. i. p. 492 ; Robertson, *Early Kings*, vol. ii. p. 244.
3 Cf. the Sanskrit *bhrû*, eyebrow. The English word *brow*, the Scotch *brae*, and the old German *brâwa*, all seem to be connected with this root. See Diefenbach, *Celtica*, i. p. 178 ; *Vergl. Wörterb.* vol. i. pp. 316–318.
4 Mone, *Celtische Forschungen*, pp. 15, 16.
5 The *rush* is the characteristic moorland plant. The Latin *rus* is a cognate word [?], and indicates the undrained moorland condition of the country.

jecting points of land. Every Rigi tourist will remember the projecting precipice of the ROSSBERG, in Canton Schwytz, whose partial fall overwhelmed the village of Goldau. There are six other mountains of the same name in Germany.[1] To the same source we may probably refer the names [2] of Monte ROSA, Piz ROSATSCH, ROSEG, and ROSENLAUI in Switzerland, and ROSTRENAN in Brittany. In our own islands we find this root in the names of WROXETER, ROSLIN, KINROSS, CARDROSS, MONTROSE, MELROSE, ROXBURGH, ARDROSSAN, and ROSCOMMON.

Craig, a rock, so common in Welsh names, is found in CRICK in Derbyshire and Northampton, and CRICKLADE in Wilts. In Ireland this word takes the form *carraig* as in the case of CARRICKFERGUS. The root is probably to be found in the name of the three ranges called respectively the GRAIAN,[3] the CARNIC, and the KARAVANKEN Alps. The prefix *Kar* is very common near Botzen.[4] In Savoy it takes the form *crau*. This form also appears in the name of a rocky district between Arles and Marseilles, which is called LA CRAU.[5]

Tor, a projecting rock, is found in the names of Mount TAURUS, TORBAY, and the TORS of Devonshire and Derbyshire.[6] The higher summits of the TYROL are called Die *Taur*ren. [Tyrol is said to be from Tyr, a mountain fortress—Grohman.]

The word *ard*, high, great, which forms the first portion of the name [?] of the legendary King Arthur, [7] occurs in some 200 Irish names,[8] as ARDAGH, ARDGLASS, and ARDFERT. In Scotland we have ARDROSSAN, ARMEANAGH, ARDNAMURCHAR, and ARDS. The name of ARRAN, the lofty island, has been appropriately bestowed on islands off the coast of Scotland and Ireland, and it attaches also to a mountain in Wales. The LIZARD Point is the high cape.[9] In combination with the

---

[1] Mone, *Celtische Forschungen*, p. 127.
[2] Some of these may be the 'red ' mountains. The red hue of Monte Rosso, a southern outlier of the Bernina, is very markedly contrasted with the neighbouring ' black peak ' of Monte Nero.
[3] Petronius tells us that this name means a rock. See Diefenbach, *Celtica*, i. p. 104 ; Adelung, *Mithridates*, vol. ii. p. 54 ; Keferstein, *Kelt. Alt.* vol. ii. p. 186 ; Radlof, *Neue Untersuchungen*, p. 312 ; De Belloguet, *Ethnogénie*, vol. i. p. 249.
[4] Gilbert and Churchill, *Dolomite Mountains*, p. 84.
[5] According to Pliny, the Scythian name of Caucasus was Grau-casis.
[6] We find YES TOR, FUR TOR, HEY TOR, MIS TOR, HESSARY TOR, BRENT TOR, HARE. TOR, and LYNX TOR, in Devon ; and ROW TOR, MAM TOR, ADYN TOR, CHEE TOR, and OWLAR TOR, in Derbyshire. HENTOE, in Lancashire, is a corruption of Hen Tor. See Diefenbach, *Celtica*, ii. pt. i. pp. 337, 340. [Akin to Lat. *turris*, a tower.]
[7] Yonge, *Christian Names*, vol. ii. p. 125.
[8] Sullivan, *Dictionary of Derivations*, p. 282.
[9] Baxter, *Glossarium*, p. 186.

word *den*, a wooded valley, it gives us the name of the Forest of ARDEN in Warwickshire and in Yorkshire, and that of the ARDENNES, the great forest on the borders of France and Belgium. AUVERNE is probably *ar fearann*, the 'high country'.[1]

The word *cwm*[2] is very frequently used in Wales, where it denotes a cup-shaped depression in the hills. This word, in the Saxonized form *comle*,[3] often occurs in English local names, especially in those counties where the Celtic element is strong. In Devonshire we have ILFRACOMBE, YARCOMBE, and COMBE MARTIN ; and the combes among the Mendip hills are very numerous. The Celtic county of Cumberland has been supposed to take its name from the *combes* with which it abounds.[4] Anderson, a Cumberland poet, says of his native county :—

> There's *Cum*whitton, *Cum*whinton, *Cum*ranton,
> *Cum*rangan, *Cum*rew, and *Cum*catch,
> And mony mair *Cums* i' the County,
> But nin wi' *Cum*divock can match."[5]

High WYCOMBE in Buckinghamshire, COMBE in Oxfordshire, APPLEDURCOMB, GATCOMB, and COMPTON Bay, in the Isle of Wright, FACOMB and COMBE in Hampshire, and COMPTON,[6] GOMSHALL, and COMBE, in Surrey, are instances of its occurrence in districts where the Celtic element is more faint than in the west : and abroad we find the root in the name of the Puy de BELLECOMBE in Cântal, and not improbably even in the name of COMO.

The Welsh *llwch*, a lake, morass, or hollow, corresponds to the Scotch *loch* and the Irish *lough*. This word constitutes the first syllable of the common ancient name Lugdunum, which has been modernized into LYONS and LEYDEN. We can trace the first portion of the Romanized Celtic name Lugu-ballium in the mediaeval Caerluel which superseded it, and which, with little change, still survives in the modern form

---

[1] Thierry, *Hist. Gaul.* vol. i. pp. xxxvi. 5 ; Keferstein, *Kelt. Alt.* vol. ii. p. 295.

[2] A *comb*, a measure for corn, and the *comb* of bees, are both from this root, which is found in several local dialects in the Celtic parts of France, Spain, and Italy, as, for example, the Piedmontese *comba*. Diez, *Etym. Wört.* p. 107 ; Diefenbach, *Celtica*, i. p. 112 ; Glück, *Kelt. Namen*, p. 28 ; Kemble, *Cod. Dipl.* vol. iii. p. xvi.

[3] Professor Leo, however, maintains the Anglo-Saxon *combe* was not adopted from the Celtic *cwm*. *Anglo-Saxon Names*, p. 83.

[4] See, however, p. 51, *supra*.

[5] Sullivan, *Dictionary of Derivations*, p. 286.

[6] There are twenty three parishes of this name in England.

CARLISLE. The lake which fills a remarkable bowl-shaped crater in the Eifel district of Germany is called LAACH. We find the same root in Lukotekia, Lukotokia, or Lutetia, the ancient name of Paris.[1]

The Cymric prefix *tre*, a place or dwelling,[2] is a useful test-word, since it does not occur in names derived from the Gaelic or Erse languages.[3] It occurs ninety-six times in the village-names of Cornwall,[4] more than twenty times in those of Wales ; and is curiously distributed over the border counties. We find it five times in Herefordshire, three times in Devon, Gloucester, and Somerset, twice in Shropshire, and once in Worcester, Yorkshire, Lancashire, Cumberland, and North-umberland.[5] It is frequent in Brittany, it occurs some thirty times in other parts of France, and twice or thrice in the Celtic part of Spain.[6] TRÊVES, anciently Augusta *Tre*-virorum, TROYES, anciently Civitas Tricassium, and TRICASTIN, near Orange, exhibit this widely-diffused Cymric root. The tribe of the Duro*trig*es, the dwellers by the water, have given a portion of their name to DORSET, and the A*tre*bates bestowed theirs upon ARRAS and ARTOIS. In Italy we find the name Treba, now TREVI, Trebula, now TREGLIA, TRESSO, TREVISO, TREBBIA, and TRIESTE, besides TRIENT in the Italian Tyrol, and other similar names in the most Celtic part of Italy, near the head of the Adriatic.

[1] Old Paris was confined on the island which divides the Seine into two branches. The name seems to be from *llwch*, and *toki*, to cut. Prichard, *Researches*, vol. iii. p. 132. From the related Welsh word *llaith*, moist, we have the name of ARLES, anciently Arelate, the town ' on the marsh '. See p. 61, *supra* ; Glück, *Kelt. Namen*, pp. 30, 114, 115 ; Pott, *Etym. Forsch.* vol. ii. pp. 42, 536 ; Astruc, *Hist. Languedoc*, p. 424 ; Menage, *Origines*, p. 57 ; Davies, *Celtic Researches*, pp. 221, 500 ; Radlof, *Neue Untersuchungen*, p. 290 ; De Belloguet, *Ethnogénie*, vol. i. p. 115.

[2] The Tref or Hamlet was the primary division of a British sept.

[3] It is related to the Irish *treabh*, a clan, and, more distantly, to the Latin *tribus*. Mone, *Celtische Forsch*, p. 204 ; Leo, *Vorlesungen*, vol. i. p. 149 ; Diefenbach, *Celtica*, i. pp. 146, 147 ; Williams, *Essays*, p. 85 ; Gerville, *Noms*, p. 225 ; Latham, *Germania*, p. 98 ; Pictet, *Orig. Indo-Europ*. vol. ii. p. 291 ; Glück, *Kelt. Namen*, pp. 39, 40.

[4] More than a thousand times, if we include hamlets and single homesteads. Hence it enters into a vast number of Cornish territorial surnames. There is an old adage which says :—

> ' By Tre, Pol, and Pen,
>   You may know the Cornish men.'

[5] We have, for example, such names as—Trefonen, Tre-evan, Tretire, Trevill, and Trewen, in Herefordshire ; Trebroader, in Shropshire ; Treborough in Somerset ; Treton in Yorkshire ; Trebroun in Berwickshire ; Trehorn in Cunningham, in Ayrshire ; Tretown in Fifeshire ; Tregallon in Kirkcudbright ; Treuchan in Perthshire. Such names as Uchiltre in Ayrshire, Wigtonshire, and Linlithgow ; Wavertree in Lancashire ; Braintree in Essex ; Oswestry in Shropshire ; and Coventry in Warwickshire, may, or may not, contain this root. The substantive in Celtic names is usually, but not invariably, the prefix. See p. 159, *supra*.

[6] e.g. TREVENTO, CONTREBIA.

Bod, a house, is very common in Cornwall,[1] and appears also in Wales. *Ty* means a cottage, and is universally prevalent in Wales, though it enters into few important names. In Cornwall it takes also the forms *Chy* and *Ky*,[2] and in Brittany it appears as *Qui* and *Cae*.[3]

Llan, an inclosure, and hence, in later times, the sacred inclosure, or church, is also a useful Cymric test-word. It occurs ninety-seven times in the village-names of Wales, thirteen times in those of Cornwall, in Shropshire and in Herefordshire seven times, in Gloucestershire four times, and in Devon twice. It is also found in the Cymric part of Scotland,[4] and is very common in Brittany.[5]

The original meaning of *lan* was probably not an inclosure, but a level plain,[6] such as the LANDES, the vast sandy flats near Bayonne, or the LLANOS, the sea-like plains of South America. In a mountainous country like Wales such level spots would be the first to be inclosed, and it is easy to perceive the process by which the transition of meaning might be effected. The root, in its primary meaning, appears in the name of MILAN, which stands in the midst of the finest plain in Europe. The Latin name Medio*lan*um, probably embodies, or perhaps partly translates, the ancient enchorial word. [7]

The Celtic word, *man*, a district, is probably to be sought in MAINE, MANS, MANTES, and MAYENNE in France, in MANTUA in Italy, in LA MANCHA and MANXES in Spain, in England in MANSFIELD, in Mancunium, now MANCHESTER, in Manduessedum, now MANCESTER, as well as in MONA, the MENAI Straits, the Isle of MAN,[8] and several Cornish names.[9]

Nant, a valley, is a common root in the Cymric districts

---

1 e.g. BODMIN, the stone house.
2 e.g. CHYNOWETH, the new house, KYNANCE, the house in the valley. Pryce, *Arch. Cornu-Brit.* sub voc.
3 e.g. QUIBERON.
4 e.g. LANARK and LANRICK.
5 e.g. LANGEAC, LANNION, LANDERNEAU, LANDIVIZIAN, LANOE.
6 Cf. Talbot, *Eng. Ety.* p. 55 ; Pryce, *Arch. Cornu-Brit.* s. v. Our words *lawn* and *and* come from the same ultimate root. [Lat. *pla(c)nus*.] Compare however the Persian *lán*, a yard. Pictet, *Orig. Indo-Europ.* vol. ii. p. 19.
7 Niebuhr, *Lectures on Geography and Ethnology*, vol. ii. p. 235. Leo, *Vorlesungen*, vol. i. p. 194, makes Milan *meiden llan*, the great temple. Adelung, *Mithridates*, vol. ii. p. 64, thinks the first syllable is *medu*, a low place. See Salverte, *Essai sur les Noms*, vol. ii. p. 279 ; De Belloguet, *Ethnogénie*, vol. i. p. 222.
8 [Probably from Manannan, God of the Sea, A. W. Moore, *Manx Names* ; J. Rhys, *Celtic Heathendom*, 663-4.]
9 See *Philolog. Proceed.* p. 118. Mona and the Isle of Man are perhaps from the Welsh *mon*, separate. Cf. the Greek μόνος. *Cambro-Briton*, vol. iii. p. 170 ; *Notes and Queries*, 2d series, vol. ii. p. 20.

of our island, as in NANT-FRANGON, the beavers' valley, in Carnarvonshire; or NANTGLYN in Denbighshire. NAN BIELD is the name of a steep pass in Westmoreland, and NANTWICH stands in a Cheshire valley. In Cornwall we find NANS, NAN-CEMELLIN, the valley of the mill, PENNANT, the head of the valley, and TRENANCE, the town in the valley. It is also found in NANTUA in Burgundy, NANCY in Lorraine, NANTES in Brittany, and the VAL DE NANT in Neufchâtel. All Chamounix tourists will remember NANT BOURANT, NANT D'ARPENAZ, NANT DE TACONAY, NANT DE GRIA, NANT DANT, NANGY, and the other *nants* or valleys of Savoy, which were once, as this word proves, possessed by the same people who now inhabit the valleys of North Wales.[1]

The ancient kingdom of GWENT comprised the counties of Monmouth and Glamorgan, and Monmouth still locally goes by this name. A Newport newspaper is called the Star of Gwent. The word denotes an open champaign country, and the uncouth Celtic word was Latinized by the Romans into Venta. Venta Silurum is now CAER-WENT in Monmouthshire, Venta Belgarum is now WIN-CHESTER, and Bennaventa is now DAVENT-RY. The *Veneti* were the people who inhabited the open plain of Brittany, and they have left their name in the district of LA VENDÉE and the town of VANNES. The vast plain at the mouth of the Po, where Celtic names abound, has from the earliest times been called VENETIA,[2] a name which may probably be referred to the same root, as well perhaps as Beneventum, now BENEVENTO, and Treventum, now TRIVENTO.[3]

Most of the Celtic roots which we have hitherto considered are distinctively Cymric rather than Gaelic or Erse. Such are *cefn, bryn, cwm, llan, tre, nant,* and *gwent. Dun* and *llwch* are common to both branches of the Celts, while the Gaelic

[1] Smith, *Dict. of Gr. and Rom. Geogr.* sub voc. Nantuates; Diefenbach, *Celtica,* i. p. 82; Court de Gebelin, *Monde Prim.* p. xxiv; Thierry, *Hist. Gaul.* vol. ii. p. 34; Adelung, *Mithridates,* vol. ii. p. 64; De Belloguet, *Ethnogénie,* vol. i. p. 211. The singular way in which this root *nant* is confined to Wales and the region of the High Alps, has suggested the doubt whether it be an original Cymric gloss, or not rather one adopted from an earlier Liguro-Iberian wave of population. See Robertson, *Scotland under her Early Kings,* vol. ii. p. 223.

[2] Vannes and Venetia may possibly be from *venna,* a fisherman. See however p. 56, *supra.* Mommsen thinks the Veneti of the Adriatic were not Celts, but Illyrians. *Hist. Rome,* vol. ii. p. 76.

[3] See Guest on Early Settlements in South Britain, in *Proceedings of Arch. Instit.* for 1849, p. 33; Guest in *Philolog. Pr.* vol. i. p. 10; Archdeacon Williams, *Ed. Trans.* p. 535; *Essays,* p. 82; *Cambro-Briton,* vol. i. pp. 17, 168; Diefenbach, *Celtica,* ii. pt. i. p. 343; Mone, *Gesch. Heidenth.* vol. ii. p. 424.

ben, cenn, and *carraig* are closely related to the Cymric *pen* and *craig.*

The next root to be considered is decisively Gadhelic, and is, therefore, very useful as a test-word in discriminating between the districts peopled by the two great branches of the Celtic stock.

The word *magh,*[1] a plain or field, is found in more than a hundred Irish names, such as MAGH-ERA, MAY-NOOTH, AR-MAGH. On the Continent it is found in many ancient and modern names.[2] In Germany we find *Mage*toburgum, now MAG-DEBURG ; *Mogo*ntiacum, now MAI-NTZ, and other names ;[3] and in north-eastern France this root was equally common.[4]

The chief Cymric roots are found scattered over Spain, Northern Italy, Switzerland, and Southern Germany ; but the root *magh,* the Gadhelic test-word, seems to be confined almost entirely to the district of the lower Rhine and its tributaries. In Switzerland it does not appear,[5] and in Italy it occurs only in the district peopled by the intrusive Boii.[6] In southern and western France it hardly occurs at all, and it is found only once or twice in Britain.[7] We may therefore conclude that while the Cymry came from the region of the Alps, the Gadhelic branch of the Celts must have migrated from the valleys of the Rhine and the Moselle. It seems to have been from this district that the earliest historic movement of the Celts took place. Three Celtic

---

[1] Sanskrit, *mahi,* terra. The Welsh form is *maes,* as in Maes Garmon, Mesham, Maesbury, Maserfield, Masbrook, Woodmas. The MAES or MEUSE is the river of meadows. The English *math,* and to *mow,* and the Latin *meto* are cognate words [?]. Se Diefenbach, *Celtica,* i. p. 77 ; Mone, *Celtische Forschungen,* p. 228 ; Sullivan, *Dict. of Derivations,* p. 291 ; Astruc, *Hist. Languedoc,* p. 437 ; Pictet, *Orig. Indo-Europ.* vol. ii. p. 101 ; Glück, *Kelt. Namen,* pp. 123–125 ; Zeuss, *Grammatica Celtica,* vol. i. p. 5.

[2] The suffix *magus* occurs forty-seven times in Prichard's lists. *Researches,* vol. iii.

[3] e.g. Marco*magus,* now Marmagen, Novio*magus* (Newfield), now Nimegen, Rigo-*magus* (Kingsfield), now Rheinmagen, Borbeto*magus,* now Worms, and Durno*magus,* a place near Cologne.

[4] We have it in Roto*magus,* now Rouen, Noio*magus,* now Nemours, Novio*magus* Lexoviorum, now Lisieux, Cæsaro*magus,* now Argenton, Catori*magus,* now Chorges, and Sermanico*magus,* now Chermez.

[5] The Swiss form *mat,* a meadow, which appears in ZERMAT and ANDERMAT, is found only in the Cymric, and not in the Gaelic portions of Great Britain. e.g. MATHERN in Monmouth and in Hereford.

[6] We have Rigo*magus* near Turin, Bodinco*magus* on the Po, and Cameliom*agus* near Placentia.

[7] We have *Magi*ntum, now Dunstable. Close to the town is an ancient earthwork, called the Maiden Bower, or the Maidning Bourne, which seems to be a corruption of the Celto-Saxon name Mageburg. See Gough's Camden, vol. ii. pp. 49, 55. The original name of Cæsaro*magus* was probably Dunomagus, as is indicated by the modern name DUNMOW. Sito*magus* is, perhaps, Thetford. The position of these places is a strong corroboration of the opinion held by many Celtic scholars, that East Anglia was Gaelic rather than Cymric. See various Papers by the Rev. J. Davies, in the *Transaction of the Philological Society* ; and Davies, *Celtic Researches,* p. 203.

tribes burst through the Alps ; they pillaged Rome, and, after returning to Illyria for a while, they broke in upon Greece, and plundered the treasures at Delphi.[1] They settled for a time in Thrace, where we have local traces of a still earlier abode of a Celtic people, and then crossing the Bosphorus, they took possession of the central parts of Asia Minor, to which they gave the name of Galatia, the land of the Gael, and where they long retained their Celtic speech,[2] and the ethnical peculiarities of their Celtic blood.[3] Here, curiously enough, we again encounter this root *mag*, which is found so abundantly in the district from which they emigrated. In the Galatian district we find the names of *Mag*ydus, *Mag*abula, *Mag*aba, *Myg*dale, *Mag*nesia (twice), and the *Myg*dones. In Thessaly, where these Celts settled for a time, we also find two of these names, *Mag*nesia, and the district of *Myg*donia, which lay on the banks of the Axius, a Celtic river-name.[4] *Mag*aba is on the Halys, which is a Celtic word, meaning salt river. In Lycia, according to Strabo, there was an enormous rocky summit, steeply scarped on every side, called Κράγος.[5]

The accumulative evidence furnished by these Celtic names has been exhibited in a very imperfect manner, but enough has probably been adduced to lead irresistibly to the conclusion that large portions of Italy, Spain, France, Switzerland,

[1] See Contzen, *Wanderungen der Kelten*, pp. 97–262 ; Conybeare and Howson, *Life of St. Paul*, vol. i. p. 284 ; Zeuss, *Die Deutschen*, pp. 180–184 ; Rawlinson, *Herodotus*, vol. iii. p. 190 ; Arnold, *History of Rome*, vol. i. p. 522 ; Niebuhr, *History of Rome*, vol. ii. p. 524 ; Latham, *Germania*, pp. 83, 98 ; Prichard, *Eastern Origin of Celt. Nat.* pp. 104–110 ; Lindsay, *Progression*, p. 62 ; Duncker, *Orig. Germ.* pp. 36–39 ; Keferstein, *Kelt. Alt.* vol. ii. p. 348 ; Radlof, *Neue Untersuchungen*, pp. 430–435.

[2] Galatas . . . propriam linguam eandem pene habere quam Treviros. Jerome, *Commentary on the Epistle to the Galatians*, Prœmium.

[3] We see, from many indications in St. Paul's Epistle, that the ‘ foolish Galatians ’, who were so easily ‘ bewitched ’, were like the rest of the Gaelic race—fickle, enthusiastic, fond of glory and display, and at the same time lively, witty, eloquent, and full of good sense and good feeling. The Galatians, like all other Celtic peoples, made admirable soldiers, and overthrew the invincible phalanx of Macedonia. We recognize in them the same military qualities which have made the charge of the Highland clans and of the Irish regiments so terrible, and which have rendered so famous the brilliant Celtic mercenaries of France and Carthage.

[4] These Thessalian names, occurring as they do in Homer and Herodotus, must be attributed to the earlier Celtic occupancy of this region.

[5] Diefenbach, *Celtica*, i. p. 104. There are many other Celtic names in Galatia and the neighbouring parts of Bithynia and Magnesia ; such as the Rivers Æsius, Æsyros, and Æson, which apparently contain the root *es*, water. See p. 144, *supra*. Abr-os-tola seems to contain the root *aber* as well. See p. 245, *infra*. Vindia, Cinna, and Brianiæ call to mind the roots *gwent*, *cenn*, and *bryn*. See pp. 164, 157, 159, *supra*. Armorium reminds us of Armorica. Olenus, in Galatia, reminds us of Olenæum in Britain, and Olin in Gaul. Agannia reminds us of Agennum in Gaul. An Episcopus Taviensis came from Galatia to attend the Nicene Council. We have also the apparently Celtic names Acitorizacum, Ambrenna, Eccobriga, Landrosia, Roslogiacum, and the River Siberis. Diefenbach, *Celtica*, ii. pt. i. pp. 256, 313, etc. ; Thierry, *Histoire des Gaulois* vol. i. pp. 145, *seq.* ; De Belloguet, *Ethnogénie*, vol. i. p. 249.

and Germany, were at some period inhabited by the race which now retains its speech and its nationality only in a few of the western corners of Europe—Ireland, the Scotch Highlands, the Isle of Man, Wales, and Brittany.

The following may be offered as a brief summary of the results disclosed by the evidence of these Celtic names.

There is no ground for any probable conjectures as to the time and place at which the division of the Celts into their two great branches may be supposed to have taken place.

In central Europe we find traces of both Cymry and Gael.

The most numerous people of primaeval Germany were of the Gadhelic branch. They were not only the most numerous, but they were also the earliest to arrive. This is indicated by the fact that throughout Germany we find no Cymric, Sclavonic, or Teutonic names which have undergone phonetic changes in accordance with the genius of the Erse or Gaelic languages. Hence it may be inferred that the Gaels, on their arrival, found Germany unoccupied, and that their immigration was therefore of a peaceful character.

Next came the Cymry. They came as conquerors, and in numbers they were fewer than the Gaels whom they found in possession. This we gather from the fact that there are comparatively few pure Cymric names in Germany, but a large number of Gadhelic names which have been Cymricized. From the topographical distribution of these names we infer that the Gaels arrived from the east, and the Cymry from the south.[1]

The large number of Cymric names in northern Italy,[2] and the fact that several of the passes of the Alps [3] bear Cymric

[1] See Meyer, in Bunsen's *Phil. of Univ. Hist.* vol. i. p. 148 ; and Mone, *Celtische Forschungen*. In the lists given by Keferstein (vol. ii. pp. 1–101) there are about 2,400 German words which bear more or less resemblance to their Celtic synonyms. The resemblance, in many cases, is only what is due to the common Aryan source ; but, from other instances, we may fairly infer the existence, for a time, of a Celtic remnant among the Teutonic conquerors. On Celtic names in Germany see Leo, *Vorlesungen*, vol. i. p. 194, *seq.* ; Mahn, *Namen Berlin und Köln*, p. 7 ; Keferstein, *Kelt. Alt.* vol. ii ; Mone, *Celtische Forschungen*, passim ; Müller, *Marken d. Vaterl.* pp. 117–128 ; Duncker, *Origines Germ.* pp 44–70.

[2] We find the roots *llan, gwent, afon, is, stour, dwr, tre, ter.* See pp. 163, 164, etc. ; Williams, in vol. xiii. of *Trans. of Royal Society of Edin.* passim ; Latham, note to Prichard's *Eastern Origin*, pp. 121–133. A large number of words are common to the Celtic and Latin languages—lists will be found in Keferstein, *Kelt. Alterth.* vol. ii. pp. 102–172 ; Newman, *Regal Rome*, pp. 17–25 ; Donaldson, *English Ethnography*, p. 37 ; and see Diez, *Etym. Wörterbuch*, passim. Compare, for instance, the words *sagitta* and *saighead*, *lorica* and *luireach, telum* and *tailm.*

[3] Celtic names are very numerous in the Alps. See Meyer, *Ortsnamen* ; Schott, *Deut. Pied. Col.* pp. 216, 225 ; Keferstein, *Kelt. Alt.* vol. ii. p. 375 ; Latham, in Prichard's *Eastern Origin*, p. 84, *seq.* ; Zeuss, *Deutschen*, pp. 228–238.

names, seem also to indicate the quarter whence the Cymric invasion proceeded.

Lastly came the Germans from the north—they were conquerors, and fewer in number than either the Cymry or the Gael. They have Germanized many Gadhelic names which had previously been Cymricized.[1]

The names of northern and central France are still more decisively Celtic than those of Germany.[2]   In Brittany the Armorican, a language closely allied to the Welsh, is still spoken, and the local names, with few exceptions, are derived from Cymric roots, and are in a much purer and more easily recognizable form than in other parts.   But we find that the same names which occur in Brittany are also scattered over the rest of France, though more sparingly, and in more corrupted forms.   Brandes[3] has compiled a list of more than three hundred Breton names, which also occur in other parts of France.[4]   In the north-east of France we find a few Gaelic and Erse[5] roots, which are altogether absent from the local nomenclature of the west, a fact which suggests that the Gaels of Germany may have crossed this part of France on their way to the British Isles.

But in south-western France—the region between the Garonne and the Pyrenees—the Celtic names, which are so universally diffused over the other portions of the kingdom, are most conspicuously absent.   The names which we find

[1] See Mone, *Celtische Forschungen*, p. 172.

[2] Though the Celtic tongue was spoken in France down to the sixth century, very few Celtic words have found their place in the French language.   A good many, however, linger in the provincial dialects.   A list will be found in Courson, *Histoire des Peuples Bretons*, vol. i. pp. 31–41.   But without the evidence of local names we should have no conception of the real amount of the Celtic element in France.   See Milman, *Hist. Lat. Christianity*, vol. vi. p. 340 ; Diez, *Gram. Rom. Spr.* vol. i. p. 80 ; Adelung, *Mithridates*, vol. ii. p. 35.   On Celtic names in France, see Diefenbach, *Celtica* ; Gück, *Keltischen Namen* ; De Belloguet, *Ethnogénie Gaulois* ; Kennedy, in *Philolog. Trans.* for 1855, ¹p. 166 ; and two silly books—Astruc, *Hist. Nat. de Languedoc*, pp. 422–457, and Court de Gebelin, *Monde Primitif*, vol. v. pp. xx–xxv.

[3] *Das Ethnographische Verhältniss der Kelten und Germanen*, pp. 257–261.   Courson, *Histoire des Peuples Bretons*, vol. i. pp. 42–45, gives a similar list.   Cf. Souvestre, *Les Derniers Britons*, vol. ii. p. 164, on the two races inhabiting respectively the mountains and the plains.

[4] Thus we have *avon* four times, *bryn* nine times, *tre* thirty times, as well as *llan, is, ar, dwr, garw,* etc.   The theory has been advanced that the Bretons of Brittany were a colony from Cornwall or Devon.   No doubt there was a great amount of intercourse.   The Cornwall and Devon of France afforded refuge to the emigrants expelled by the Saxons from the Cornwall and Devon of England ; but the local names of France prove conclusively that the Bretons were once more widely spread.   See Palgrave, *Eng. Com.* vol. i. p. 382 ; Turner, *Anglo-Saxons*, vol. ii. p. 213.

[5] The *Glossa Malperga*, recently disinterred by Leo, contains the laws of a Belgian tribe, written in a language nearly akin to Irish.

in this district are not even Indo-European,[1] but belong to quite another family of human speech—the Turanian, which includes the languages which are now spoken by the Turks, the Magyars, the Finns and Lapps of Northern Europe, and their distant congeners, the Basques, who inhabit the western portion of the Pyrenees. These Spanish mountaineers, who now number three-quarters of a million, seem to be the sole unabsorbed remnant of the powerful nation which once occupied the greater portion of Spain, the half of France, the whole of Sardinia and Corsica, and large portions of Italy. Whether these Iberians, or Euskarians as they are called, were the earliest inhabitants of Spain, or whether they were preceded by Celtic tribes, is still a disputed question among ethnologists. It is doubtful whether they crossed into Spain by the Straits of Gibraltar, or whether they crept along the coast of the Mediterranean from Liguria, and penetrated by the north-eastern defiles of the Pyrenees.[2] The whole subject of the ancient ethnology of Spain has been discussed in an admirable and exhaustive manner by Baron Wilhelm von Humboldt, in his work entitled ' Prüfung der Untersuchungen über die alter Bewohner Hispaniens '.[3] The materials of this investigation consist chiefly of the ancient names which are found in Pliny, Ptolemy, Strabo, and the Itineraries. These names he endeavours to trace to Celtic or Euskarian roots, and compares them with the Basque names now found in the Asturias. One of the most prevalent words is *asta*, a rock, which we have in ASTURIA, ASTORGA, ASTA, ASTEGUIETA, ASTIGARRAGA, ASTOBIZA, ASTULEZ, and many other names. The root *ura*, water, occurs in ASTURIA,[4] ILURIA, URIA, VERURIUM, URBIACA, and URBINA. *Iturria*, a fountain, is found in the names ITURISSA, TURAS, TURIASO, TURDETANI, and TURIGA. The

---

[1] Pott, Art. *Indo-Germ. Sprach-Stamm*, in Ersch und Gruber, p. 250 ; Arndt, *Europ. Spr.* pp. 19–23 ; Brace, *Races of Old World*, p. 252.

[2] The absence of Iberic names from Eastern Europe and Asia seem to make it probable that the Iberians crossed from Africa, and spread over Spain, and thence to France, the Italian coast land, and the Mediterranean Islands. The Celts seem to have been the conquering, and the Iberians the conquered people. Pott, *Indo-Germ Spr.* p. 25. See, however, Niebuhr, *Hist. Rome*, vol. ii. p. 520. There appear to be a few Euskarian names in Thrace. Humboldt, *Prüfung*, pp. 118–120.

[3] On Iberic names see also Zeuss, *Die Deutschen und die Nachbarstämme*, pp. 160–164 ; Prichard, *Researches into the Physical History of Mankind*, vol. iii. p. 20–48 ; Diefenbach, *Celtica*, ii. pp. 1–52 ; Robertson, *Scotland under her Early Kings*, vol. ii. p. 221 ; Adelung, *Mithridates*, vol. ii. pp. 12–30. The work by S. F. W. Hoffmann, *Die Iberer im Westen und Osten*, I have not been able to procure.

[4] On the name Asturia see Humboldt, *Prüfung*, pp. 23, 30 ; Diefenbach, *Celtica*, ii. part i. p. 312, and i. p. 27.

characteristic Euskarian terminations are *uris, pa, etani, etania,*[1] *gis, ilia,* and *ula.* The characteristic initial syllables are *al, ar, as, bae, bi, bar, ber, cal, ner, sal, si, tai,* and *tu.* These roots are found chiefly in eastern and northern Spain, in the valley of the Tagus, and on the southern coast, while in Galicia, in the valleys of the Minho [2] and the Guadiana, and in southern Portugal, the names are purely Celtic,[3] and there seems to have been no infusion of an Euskarian element. Various fortresses in the Iberic district bear Celtic names, while in the mountainous district of central Spain a fusion of the two races would seem to have taken place, probably by a Celtic conquest of Iberic territory, and the Celtiberians, as they are called, separated the pure Celts from the pure Iberians.

In Aquitania proper [4] there is hardly a single Celtic name —all are Iberic or Romance. In Italy Iberic names are not uncommon,[5] and it has been thought that some faint traces of a Turanian, if not of an Iberic population are perceptible in the names of north-western Africa, of Sicily, and even of the extreme west of Ireland.[6]

In the British Isles, the Gaelic, the Erse, the Manx, and the Welsh, are still living languages. Just as in Silesia and Bohemia the Sclavonic is now gradually receding before the German language, so in the British Isles a similar process has been going on for more than fourteen centuries. We have documentary evidence of this process. The ancient documents relating to the parishes north of the Forth, exhibit a gradually increasing proportion of Teutonic names. In the Taxatio of the twelfth century, only 2½ per cent. are Teutonic ; in the Chartularies, from the twelfth to the fourteenth century, the proportion rises to 4 per cent., and in the tax rolls of 1554 to nearly 25 per cent.[7] In the south of the island a similar retrocession of the Celtic speech may be traced. Thus in the

---

[1] See p. 41, *supra.*
[2] The Mynnow or Mynwy, on which Monmouth stands, is the same name.
[3] Dr. Latham has noticed the significant fact that the Celtic roots *mag* and *dun*, which occur so abundantly in other districts peopled by the Celts, are not found in Spain. This may indicate that the Spanish Celts were separated from their kinsfolk at an early period.
[4] On Euskarian names in France see Humboldt, *Prüfung,* pp. 91–95.
[5] We find URIA in Apulia, ASTURA near Antium, ASTA in Liguria, as well as LIGURIA, BASTA, BITURGIA, and others which are compounded with the Euskarian roots, *asta,* a rock, *ura,* water, and *ilia* or *ulia* a city. Humboldt, *Prüfung,* pp. 111–118.
[6] Professor Keyser, of Christiania, has endeavoured to prove a wide extension of Iberic tribes over the extreme Western shores of Europe. See Prichard, *Report on Ethnology to Brit. Assoc. in* 1847, p. 246 ; Meyer, *ib.* ; Wilson, *Prehist. Annals,* p. 11 ; Robertson, *Early Kings,* vol. i. p. 33.   [7] Chalmers, *Caledonia,* vol. i. pp. 484, 485.

will of Alfred, Dorset, Somerset, Wilts, and Devon, are enumerated as ' Wealhcynne ', a phrase which proves that these
counties were then thoroughly Celtic in blood and language,
although politically they belonged to the Anglo-Saxon commonwealth.[1]   Dr. Guest has shown that the valleys of the
Frome and the Bristol Avon formed an intrusive Welsh wedge,
protruding into the Saxon district.[2]   Athelstan found Britons
and Saxons in joint occupation of the city of Exeter.   He expelled the former, and drove them beyond the Tamar, and
fixed the Wye as the boundary of the Northern Cymry.
Harold, son of Godwin, ordered that every Celt found east of
Offa's Dyke should have his right hand struck off.[3]   But
even so late as the time of Henry II Herefordshire was not
entirely Anglicized, and it was only in the reign of Henry
VIII that Monmouthshire was first numbered among the
English counties.   In remote parts of Devon the ancient Cymric speech feebly lingered on till the reign of Elizabeth, while
in Cornwall it was the general medium of intercourse in the
time of Henry VIII.   In the time of Queen Anne it was confined to five or six villages in the western portion of the
county, and it has only become extinct within the lifetime
of living men (A.D. 1777),[4] while the Celtic race has survived
the extinction of their language with little intermixture of
Teutonic blood.   In the west of Glamorgan, in Flint, Denbigh,
and part of Montgomery, the English language has almost
entirely displaced the Welsh, and in the other border counties
it is rapidly encroaching.   In fact, we may now see in actual
operation the same gradual process which has taken place
throughout the rest of Britain.   In Wales, the change of
language, now in progress, is accompanied by very little
infusion of Saxon blood.   The same must also have been the
case at an earlier period.   In Mercia and Wessex, at all events,
we must believe that the bulk of the people is of Celtic blood.
The Saxon keels cannot have transported any very numerous
population, and, no doubt, the ceorls, or churls, long continued
to be the nearly pure-blooded descendants of the aboriginal
Celts of Britain.[5]

[1] Palgrave, *English Commonwealth*, vol. i. p. 410.
[2] *Archæolog. Journal*, vol. xvi.   [3] Lappenberg, *Anglo-Saxon Kings*, vol. i. p. 231.
[4] Gough's Camden, vol. i. p. 15 ; Halliwell, *Cornwall*, pp. 167–174.   Many Cornish
words still survive, as *quilquin*, a frog.
[5] Palgrave, *English Common.* vol. i. p. 26 ; Davies, in *Philolog. Trans.* for 1857, p. 75 ;
Diefenbach, *Celtica*, ii. part ii. p. 140.

These theoretical conclusions are thoroughly borne out by the evidence of the local names. Throughout the whole island almost every river-name is Celtic, most of the shire-names contain Celtic roots,[1] and a fair sprinkling of names of hills, valleys, and fortresses, bears witness that the Celt was the aboriginal possessor of the soil ; while in the border counties of Salop, Hereford, Gloucester, Dorset, Somerset, and Devon, and in the mountain fastnesses of Derbyshire and Cumberland, not only are the names of the great natural features of the country derived from the Celtic speech, but we find occasional village-names, with the prefixes *lan* and *tre*, interspersed among the Saxon patronymics. A large number of the chief ancient centres of population, such as LONDON, WINCHESTER, GLOUCESTER, EXETER, LINCOLN, YORK, MANCHESTER, LANCASTER, and CARLISLE bear Celtic names, while the Teutonic town names usually indicate by their suffixes that they originated in isolated family settlements in the uncleared forest,[2] or arose from the necessities of traffic in the neighbourhood of some frequented ford.[3] These facts taken together, prove that the Saxon immigrants, for the most part, left the Celts in possession of the towns, and subdued, each for himself, a portion of the unappropriated waste. It is obvious, therefore, that a very considerable Celtic element of population must, for a long time, have subsisted, side by side with the Teutonic invaders, without much mutual interference. In time the Celts acquired the language of the more energetic race, and the two peoples at last ceased to be distinguishable. Just in the same way, during the last two centuries, Anglo-Saxon colonists have been establishing themselves among the aborigines of North America, of the Cape, and of New Zealand, and the natives have not been at once exterminated, but are being slowly absorbed and assimilated by the superior vigour of the incoming race.

To exhibit the comparative amount of the Celtic, the Saxon, and the Danish elements of population in various portions of the island, an analysis has been made of the names of villages,

---

[1] Cambridge, Cornwall, Cumberland, Devon, Dorset, Durham, Gloucester, Hertford Huntingdon, Kent, Lancaster, Lincoln, Monmouth, Northumberland, Oxford, Worcester and York, together with all the Welsh and Scotch shires, except Anglesea, Montgomery Haddington, Kircudbright, Stirling, Sutherland, and Wigton.
[2] e.g. Buckingham, Reading, Derby, etc.
    e.g. Stafford, Bedford, Chelmsford, etc.

hamlets, hills, woods, valleys, etc.[1] in the counties of Suffolk, Surrey, Devon, Cornwall, and Monmouth.

Percentage of Names from the	Suffolk.	Surrey.	Devon.	Cornwall.	Monmouth.	Isle of Man.	Ireland.
Celtic . . .	2	8	32	80	76	59	80
Anglo-Saxon .	90	91	65	20	24	20	19
Norse . . .	8	1	3	0	0	21	1

By far the greater number of Celtic names in England are of the Cymric type. Yet, as we have already seen,[2] there is a thin stream of Gadhelic names which extends across the island from the Thames to the Mersey, as if to indicate the route by which the Gaels passed across to Ireland, impelled, probably, by the succeeding hosts of Cymric invaders.

The Cymry held the lowlands of Scotland as far as the Perthshire hills.[3] The names in the valleys of the Clyde and the Forth are Cymric, not Gaelic. At a later period the Scots,[4] an Irish sept, crossed over into Argyle, and gradually extended their dominion over the whole of the north-west of Scotland, encroaching here and there on the Cymry who held the lowlands, and who were probably the people who go by the name of Picts. In the ninth century the monarchy of the Picts was absorbed by the Scots. The Picts, however, still maintained a distinct ethnical existence, for we find them fighting in the battle of the Standard against Stephen. In the next century they disappear mysteriously from history.[5]

To establish the point, that the Picts, or the nation, whatever was its name, that held central Scotland, was Cymric, not Gaelic, we may refer to the distinction already mentioned [6] between *ben* and *pen*. *Ben* is confined to the west and north ;

---

[1] River names are excluded from the computation.
[2] e.g. Dun*mow*, Ouse, etc. See pp. 145, 165, *supra*.
[3] On the limits of the Cymry and Gael in Scotland, see Garnett, 'On the relation of the Picts and Gael', in *Philolog. Proceed.* vol. i. and *Essays*, pp. 196–204 ; Chalmers, *Caledonia*, vol. i.; Robertson, *Scotland under her Early Kings*, vol. ii. pp. 360–381 ; Skene, *Hist. of the Highlanders*, vol. i. pp. 67–87 ; Donaldson, *English Ethnography*, pp. 36, 37 ; Diefenbach, *Celtica*, ii. pt. ii. pp. 176, *seq.*
[4] In ancient records Scotia means Ireland. North Britain was called Nova Scotia. In the twelfth century the Clyde and Forth were the Southern boundary of what was then called Scotland. Palgrave, *English Commonwealth*, vol. i. p. 420 ; vol. iv. p. 308.
[5] Palgrave, *English Commonwealth*, vol. i. p. 418.
[6] See p. 157, *supra*.

pen to the east and south.   *Inver* and *aber* are also useful test-words in discriminating between the two branches of the Celts. The difference between the two words is dialectic only ; the etymology and the meaning are the same—a confluence of waters, either of two rivers, or of a river with the sea.   *Aber* occurs repeatedly in Brittany,[1] and is found in about fifty Welsh names, such as ABERDARE, ABERGAVENNY, ABERGELE, ABERYSTWITH, and BARMOUTH, a corruption of Abermaw.   In England we find *Aber*ford in Yorkshire, and *Ber*wick in Northumberland and Sussex ; and it has been thought that the name of the HUMBER is a corruption of the same root.   *Inver*, the Erse and Gaelic form, is common in Ireland, where *aber* is unknown.   Thus we find places called INVER, in Antrim, Donegal, and Mayo, and INVERMORE, in Galway and in Mayo. In Scotland, the *invers* and *abers* are distributed in a curious and instructive manner.   If we draw a line across the map from a point a little south of Inverary, to one a little north of Aberdeen, we shall find that (with very few exceptions) the *invers* lie to the north-west of the line,[2] and the *abers* to the southeast of it.[3]   This line nearly coincides with the present southern limit of the Gaelic tongue, and probably also with the ancient division between the Picts and the Scots.   Hence, we may conclude that the Picts, a people belonging to the Cymric branch of the Celtic stock, and whose language has now ceased to be anywhere vernacular, occupied the central and eastern districts of Scotland, as far north as the Grampians ; while the Gadhelic Scots have retained their language, and have given their name to the whole country.   The local names prove, moreover, that in Scotland the Cymry did not encroach on the Gael, but the Gael on the Cymry.   The intrusive names are *invers*, which invaded the land of the *abers*.   Thus on the shore of the Frith of Forth we find a few *invers* among the *abers*.[4]   The process of change is shown by an old charter, in which King David grants the monks of May, ' Inverin qui fuit Aberin '.   So Abernethy became Invernethy, although the old

---

[1] e.g. ABERVRACK, AVRANCHES, etc.
[2] Inverary, Inverness, Inveraven, Inverury, Inveroran, Inverlochy, Invercannich, Inverfankaig, Invercaslie, Inverallen, Inverkeithnie, Inveramsay, Inverbroom, Invereshie, Invergarry, Invernahavon.
[3] Arbroath or Aberbrothwick, Abercorn, Aberdeen, Aberdour, Abernethy, Abertay, Aberledy, Abergeldie, Abernyte, Aberfeldie, Aberfoyle.
[4] e.g. Inveresk, near Edinburgh, Inverkeithing in Fife, Inverbervie in Kincardine.

name is now restored.[1]   The Welsh word *uchel*, high, may also be adduced to prove the Cymric affinities of the Picts. This word does not exist in either the Erse or the Gaelic languages, and yet it appears in the name of the OCHIL Hills, in Perthshire. In Ayrshire, and again in Linlithgow, we find places called OCHIL-TREE ; and three is an UCHEL-TRE in Galloway. The suffix in this case is undoubtedly the characteristic Cymric word *tre*, a dwelling.[2] Again, the Erse *bally*,[3] a town, occurs in 2,000 names in Ireland ; and, on the other hand, is entirely absent from Wales and Brittany. In Scotland this most characteristic test-word is found frequently in the *inver* district while it never appears among the *abers*. The evidence of these names makes it impossible to deny that the Celts of the Scottish lowlands must have belonged to the Cymric branch of the Celtic stock.

The ethnology of the Isle of Man may be very completely illustrated by means of local names. The map of the island contains about 400 names, of which about 20 per cent. are English, 21 per cent. are Norwegian, and 59 per cent. are Celtic. These Celtic names are all of the most characteristic Erse type. It would appear that not a single colonist from Wales ever reached the island, which, from the mountains of Carnarvon, is seen like a faint blue cloud upon the water. There are ninety-six names beginning with *Balla*, and the names of more than a dozen of the highest mountains have the prefix *Slieu*, answering to the Irish *Slievh* or *Sliabh*. The Isle of Man has the *Curragh*, the *Loughs*, and the *Allens* of Ireland faithfully reproduced. It is curious to observe that the names which denote places of Christian worship [4] are all Norwegian ; they are an indication of the late date at which Heathenism must have prevailed.[5]

---

[1] See Kemble, *Saxons in England*, vol. ii. pp. 4, 5 ; Chalmers, *Caledonia*, vol. i. p. 480 ; Latham, *Ethnology of Brit, Is.* pp. 80, 81.   Skene, *History of the Highlanders*, vol. i. p. 74, and Diefenbach, *Celtica*, i. p. 23, think that too much ethnological importance has been attributed to the distinction between *inver* and *aber*.

[2] See p. 162, *supra*.

[3] The root of *bally* is found in the words *wall, vallum, bailey*, etc.   [Ir. *baile* (1) a place, (2) a town or townland, see Joyce, *Irish Names of Places*, i. 335.]

[4] In the Channel Islands the names of *all* the towns and villages are derived from the names of saints, indicating that before the introduction of Christianity these islands were inhabited only by a sparse population of fishermen and shepherds. Cf. Latham, *Channel Is.* p. 311.

[5] An account of the heathen superstitions and legends, which still linger in the Island, will be found in Train, *Isle of Man*, vol. ii. pp. 114-184. [And A. N. Moore, *Folklore of the Isle of Man*].

CHAPTER X

THE HISTORIC VALUE OF LOCAL NAMES

Contrast between Roman and Saxon civilization, as shown by Local Names —Roman roads—' Gates '—Bridges and fords—Celtic bridges—Deficiency of inns—Cold Harbour—Saxon dykes—Roman walls—Saxon forts—' Bury '—Ancient camps—Chester, caster, and caer—Stations of the Roman Legions—Frontier districts—Castile—The Mark—Pfyn, Devizes—Ethnic shire-names of England—Intrusive colonization.

THERE is a striking contrast between the characteristics of Saxon and Roman names. The Saxon civilization was domestic, the genius of Rome was imperial ; the Saxons colonized, the Romans conquered. Hence, the traces of Roman rule which remain upon the map are surprisingly few in number. Throughout the whole island, we scarcely find a single place of human habitation denoted by a name which is purely Roman.[1] The names of our English villages, with few exceptions, are Scandinavian or Teutonic ; while the appellations of the chief centres of population and of the great natural landmarks— the rivers and the mountains—are the legacy of a still earlier race.

The character of Roman names is very different. Rome, with her eagle eye, could cast a comprehensive glance over a province or an empire, and could plan and execute the vast physical enterprises necessary for its subjugation, for its material progress, or for its defence. The Romans were essentially a constructive race. We still gaze with wonder on the massive fragments of their aqueducts, their bridges, their amphitheatres, their fortresses, and their walls ; we still find their altars, their inscriptions, and their coins. The whole island is intersected by a network of Roman roads, admirably planned, and executed with a constructive skill which is able to excite the admiration even of modern engineers. These are the true monuments of Roman greatness.

[1] Exceptions are SPEEN, anciently Spinæ, PONTEFRACT, CAERLEON, PORCHESTER, and CHESTER.

The Saxons were not road-makers. Vast works undertaken with a comprehensive imperial purpose were beyond the range of Saxon civilization. The Saxons even borrowed their name for a road from the Latin language. The Roman *strata*, or paved roads, became the Saxon *streets*. This word street often enables us to recognize the lines of Roman road which, straight as an arrow-course, connect the chief strategic positions in the island.

Thus, from the fortified port of Lymne an almost disused road runs across the Kentish Hills to Canterbury, bearing the name of STONE STREET. From the fortified port of Richborough the road which is called WATLING [1] STREET went to Canterbury and London, and thence, by STONY STRATFORD (the paved Street-ford), to Chester, the 'castra' of the northern army. RYKNIELD STREET led from Tynemouth, through York, Derby, and Birmingham, to St. David's. ICKNIELD STREET led from Norwich to Dorchester and Exeter. The ERMIN [2] STREET joined London and Lincoln. The Roman road by which sick men journeyed from London to bathe in the hot springs at Bath, went, in Saxon times, by the appropriate name of AKEMAN STREET. The Westmoreland mountain called HIGH STREET, derives its name from the Roman road which crosses it at a height of 2,700 feet. [3]

Even where the Roman roads have become obliterated by the plough, we may often trace their direction by means of the names of towns, which proclaim the position they occupied on the great lines of communication. Such are the names of ARDWICK LE STREET in Yorkshire, CHESTER LE STREET in Durham, STRETTON, STRATTON, STREATHAM, STREATLEY, and several places called STRETFORD or STRATFORD, all of which inform us that they were situated on some line of Roman road. [4] Roman roads which do not bear the name of *street* are often called *Portways*. There are nine Portways in different parts of the kingdom. [5] The FOSSWAY [6] also was a Roman road, running from Cornwall to Lincoln.

---

[1] Probably from *vadla*, a mendicant pilgrim. [A.-Sax. *Wætlinga Stræte*, ' the way of the Wætlingas ' or sons of Wætla, whom Rydberg identifies with the mythical hero Wate or Vate (*Teut. Mythology*, 667) ; W. H. Duignan, *Staffordshire Place Names*, 162–168.]

[2] Probably from *earm*, a pauper. [*Erminge-strete*, or *Irming-stræt*, where *Irmin*= mighty, as in *Irmin-sul*, De la Saussaye, *Rel. of the Teutons*, 125 ; Grimm, *Teut. Myth.* 356.] See Lappenberg, *Anglo-Saxon Kings*, vol. i. p. 51 ; Poste, *Britannic Researches*, p. 94 ; Horsley, *Brit. Rom.* p. 388. [3] Ferguson, *Northmen in Cumberland*, p. 49. Wright, *Wanderings*, p. 326.

[4] Hartshorne, *Salopia Antiqua*, p. 238 ;

[5] Hartshorne, *Salopia Antiqua*, p. 272.

[6] *Foss* is a Saxon synonym for a dyke. The source seems to be the Latin *fossa*.

In the Scandinavian districts of the island the word *gate* [1] is commonly used to express a road or street, as in the case of HARROWGATE. In York, Leeds, Lincoln, and other northern towns, the older streets usually bear this suffix. In Leeds we find BRIGGATE or Bridge Street, and KIRKGATE or Church Street. In York this suffix was borne by no less than twenty of the streets, as in the case of MICKLEGATE, WALMGATE, JUBBER-GATE, FEASEGATE, GODRAMGATE, CASTLEGATE, SKELMERGATE, PETERSGATE, MARYGATE, FISHERGATE, and STONEGATE. We find MILLGATE STREET and ST. MARYSGATE in Manchester, and COWGATE and CANONGATE in Edinburgh.

In the South the word *gate* usually takes the sense of the passage through a town wall, as in the case of NEWGATE, BISHOPSGATE, and the other gates of London. In the name of HIGHGATE, however, we have the sense of a road.

The passes through lines of hill or cliff are frequently denoted by this root. Thus REIGATE is a contraction of Ridgegate, the passage through the ridge of the North Downs. GATTON, in the same neighbourhood, is the town at the passage. CATER-HAM and GODSTONE may possibly be referred to the same root, as well as GATCOMBE in the Isle of Wight. RAMSGATE, MAR-GATE, WESTGATE, KINGSGATE, and SANDGATE, are the passages to the shore through the line of Kentish cliffs. In Romney Marsh *gut* takes the place of *gate*, as in the case of JERVIS GUT, CLOBESDEN GUT, and DENGE MARSH GUT.

The difficulties of travelling must formerly have interposed great obstacles in the way of commercial intercourse. Local names afford various intimations that the art of bridge-building, in which the Romans had excelled,[2] was not retained

---

1 The Danish word *gata* means a street or road. The Anglo-Saxon *geat* means a gate. The distinction is analogous to that which exists in the case of the word ford. See p. 160, *supra*. The one is a passage *along*, the other a passage *through*. The root is seen in the German verb *gehen*, and the English *go*. Compare the Sanskrit *gati*, and the Zend *gâtu*, which both mean a road. From the same primary meaning of a passage, we obtain *gut*, the intestinal passage, and the nautical term *gat*, a passage through a narrow channel, as the CATTEGAT [?]. A *gate* is the passage into a field. A man's *gait* is the way he goes; his *gaiters* are his goers [!]. Other*gates* is the Sussex provincialism for otherways. See Warton, *Seaboard and the Down*, vol. ii. p. 28. The *ghats*, or *ghauts*, of India are the passages to the riverside, and the passes through the western line of hills. See Pictet, *Orig. Indo-Europ.* pt. ii. p. 292 ; Worsaae, *Danes and Norwegians*, p. 40 ; Ferguson, *Northmen*, p. 49 ; Leo, *Anglo-Saxon Names*, p. 63 ; Diefenbach, *Vergleich. Wörterbuch*, vol. ii. p. 394 ; *Philolog. Proc.* vol. i. p. 40 · and several letters in the *Guardian*, December, 1861.
2 The importance attached by the Romans to the art of bridge-building is indicated by the fact that the chief ecclesiastical functionary bore the name of the bridge-builder —*Pontifex*. See Donaldson, *Varronianus*, p. 270. [Ihering, *Evolution of the Aryan*, 351–6 ; Mommsen, *Hist. of Rom.* vol. i.]

by the Anglo-Saxons. Thus the station on the Tyne, which in Roman times had been called Pons Ælii,[1] received from the Anglians the name GATESHEAD, or, as we may translate it, ' road's end ' ; an indication, it would seem, of the destruction of the bridge. At the spot where the Roman road crosses the Aire, the name of PONTEFRACT (Ad Pontem Fractum) reminds us that the broken Roman bridge must have remained unrepaired during a period long enough for the naturalization of the new name, and the name of STRATFORD LE BOW contains internal evidence that the dangerous narrow Saxon ford over the Lea was not replaced by a ' bow ', or ' arched bridge ' till after the time of the Norman conquest.[2]

But nothing shows more conclusively the unbridged state of the streams than the fact that where the great lines of Roman road are intersected by rivers, we so frequently find important towns bearing the Saxon suffix -*ford*.[3] At OXFORD, HEREFORD, BEDFORD, STRATFORD ON AVON, STAFFORD, WALLINGFORD, GUILFORD, and CHELMSFORD, considerable streams had to be forded. In the kingdom of Essex, within twenty miles of London, we find the names ILFORD, ROMFORD, STAPLEFORD, PASSINGFORD, STANFORD, WOODFORD, CHINGFORD, STORTFORD, OLD FORD, and STRATFORD. We find the same state of things in Kent. The Medway had to be forded at AYLESFORD, the Darent at DARTFORD and at OTFORD, and the Stour at ASHFORD.

The great deficiency of bridges is still more forcibly impressed upon us when we remember that while the names of so many large towns present the suffix *ford*, there are only a very few which terminate in *bridge*. We have TUNBRIDGE, WEYBRIDGE, UXBRIDGE, STOCKBRIDGE, CAMBRIDGE,[4] and a few more, all of which stand on small and easily-bridged streams. But in all these cases the English form of suffix seems to show the

---

[1] The piles on which the Roman bridge rested were discovered in 1771. Bruce, *Roman Wall*, p. 130. There seems to have been another bridge built by Ælius on the continuation of the Roman road northward. Six miles from Newcastle we find the village-name of PONTELAND, apparently from Ad Pontem Ælianum. Baxter, *Gloss.* p. 196. There was a Roman bridge at PAUNTON, Ad Pontem. Baxter, *Glossarium*, p. 7.

[2] The bridge was built by Matilda, Queen of Henry I.

[3] Hartshorne, *Salopia Antiqua*, pp. 262–265.

[4] Cambor*itum*, the ancient name of Cambridge [?], gives us the Celtic root *rhyd*, a ford, which we find also in *Rhede*cina, the British name of Oxford, and in *Hert*-ford (Rhyd-ford) [?], where, probably, we have two synonymous elements. The Celtic *rhod*, a roadstead, and *rhyd*, or *red*, a ford, bear much the same relation to each other as the Norse *fjord* and the Saxon *ford*. See p. 112, *supra* ; Glück, *Keltischen Namen*, p. 25 ; Adelung, *Mithridates*, vol. iii. p. 68 ; Diefenbach, *Celtica*, i. p. 58.

comparatively modern date of the erection, and names which take a Saxon form, such as BRIXTON, or BRISTOL, anciently Bricgstow, are extremely rare.

It should be noticed that *pont*, the Welsh word for a bridge, is derived from the Latin, probably through the monks, who were the great bridge-builders. Nevertheless it has been thought that the art of bridge-building was known at a very early period to the Celtic nations, and was subsequently lost. In the most purely Celtic parts of Spain and France, a very large number of the names of riverain cities terminate in *briga* and *briva*, which, in the opinion of many Celtic scholars, must have meant a bridge.[1] They think it is an ancient Aryan word, older than the epoch of the separation of the Teutonic and Celtic stems, and which disappeared from the Celtic speech at the time when the art of bridge-building was lost.[2]

The hardships incident to travelling must have been much increased by the fewness of houses of entertainment along the roads. Where no religious house existed to receive the way-farer, he would usually be compelled to content himself with the shelter of bare walls. The ruins of deserted Roman villas were no doubt often used by travellers who carried their own bedding and provisions, as is done by the frequenters of the khans and dak houses of the East. Such places seem commonly to have borne the name of COLD HARBOUR.[3] In the neighbourhood of ancient lines of road we find no less than

[1] Thus the ancient name of Brivisara has been replaced by the modern equivalent, Pontoise.

[2] In Spain we have Turobriga, Mirobriga, Mertobriga, Segobriga, Lacobriga, Arcobriga, Juliobriga, and others, thirty-five in all. In Celtic Gaul there are Eburobriga, Limno-briga, Amagenbriga, and Brigiosum ; and Brivate and Durocobrivis in Britain. An allied form is *bria*, which we find in Mesembria, Selymbria, and Poltyobria, in the Celtic colonies on the Euxine. Brescia was in the Celtic part of Italy. The names of Bregentz, Braganza, Briançon, and perhaps of the Brigantes, contain the same root. For lists of these names see Diefenbach, *Celtica*, ii. pt. i. p. 317 ; Prichard, *Researches*, vol. iii. pp. 30, 120. The word *brigand* may not improbably be derived from the name of the Brigantes, who served as mediaeval mercenaries. See Dufresne, vol. i. pp. 775–778 ; Diefenbach, *Orig. Eur.* p. 271 ; *Celtica*, i. p. 17 ; Diez, *Etym. Wörterb.* s. voc. ; Rawlinson, *Herodotus*, vol. iii. p. 220 ; Prichard, *Eastern Origin of Celtic Nat.* p. 120 ; Humboldt, *Prüfung*, pp. 82–86, 144 ; Salverte, *Essai sur les Noms*, vol. ii. p. 258 ; Radlof, *Neue Untersuchungen.* pp. 304, 305 ; Zeuss, *Grammatica Celtica*, vol. i. p. 101 ; vol. ii. pp. 758, 772 ; Hume, *Geogr. Terms*, p. 10 ; *Cambro-Briton*, vol. iii. p. 285 ; De Belloguet, *Ethno-génie*, vol. i. pp. 214–217 ; Baxter, *Gloss.* p. 50. Glück, as usual, laments the sad ignor-ance displayed by all preceding writers, except himself and Zeuss, and asserts that the root is the same as that of the German *berg*, the Irish *brig*, and the Cymric *bre*, a hill. *Kelt Namen*, pp. 126, 130. On the whole I am inclined to believe that the words *briga* and *briva* are unconnected, *briga* meaning a hill, and *briva* a bridge.

[3] Compare [Icel. *kald hereberga*, Ger. *Kaltern herberg*, a bare caravanserai—R. F. Burton, *Ultima Thule*, i, 72] the German *Herberg*, shelter, and the French *auberge*. See *Notes and Queries*, second series, vol. vi. pp. 143, 317.

seventy places bearing this name,[1] and about a dozen more bearing the analogous name of CALDICOT, or ' cold cot '.[2]

The only great works constructed by the Anglo-Saxons were the vast earthen ramparts which served as the boundaries between hostile kingdoms. For miles and miles the dyke and ditch[3] of the WANSDYKE—the ancient boundary of Wessex —still stretches across the bleak downs of Somerset and Wilts, Beginning near Portishead, on the Bristol Channel, it runs by Malmesbury and Cirencester, to Bampton in Oxfordshire ; it then crosses the Thames, and reappears at a place called KINSEY. This name is a corruption of King's Way, and shows that the dyke must have been used as a road as well as for purposes of defence.[4] OFFA'S DYKE, which stretched from Chester to the Wye, guarded the frontiers of Mercia against the Welsh.[5] GRIM'S DYKE near Salisbury, OLD DITCH near Amesbury, and BOKERLY DITCH, mark the position of the Welsh and Saxon frontier at an earlier period.[6] The ditch called the PICTS' WORK, reaching from Galashiels to Peel Fell, seems to have been at one time the northern boundary of the kingdom of Northumbria. A vast work, variously called the RECKEN DYKE, the DEVIL'S DYKE, ST. EDMUND'S DYKE, and CNUT'S DYKE, served as the defence of the kingdom of East Anglia against Mercia ; unless, indeed, we suppose, as is not improbable, that it was constructed at a time when the Mercian kingdom was still British, and the East-Englian settlement was the sole possession of the Teutons in the island.[7]

But these Saxon defences were at the best mere earthworks, and are not to be compared, in a constructive point of view,

[1] There are three on Akeman Street, four on Ermin Street, two on Icknield Street, two on Watling Street, two on the Portways, and one on the Fossway. Hartshorne, *Salopia Antiqua*, pp. 253–258.

[2] Hartshorne, *Salopia Antiqua*, p. 249.

[3] The Anglo-Saxon *dic* is derived from the root which supplies us with the verb to dig, and is used to mean both the mound and the excavation. In modern English we call one the dyke and the other the ditch. Probably the masculine and feminine of the Anglo-Saxon *dic* supplied the original germ of the distinctive use. Kemble, *Cod. Dip.* vol. iii. p. xxii. ; Leo, *Anglo-Saxon Names*, p. 78. The common village name of DITTON (dyketon) may sometimes guide us as to the position of these dykes. Fen Ditton and Wood Ditton in Cambridgeshire, stand respectively on the Fleam Dyke and the Devil's Dyke.

[4] Leo, *Anglo-Saxon Names*, p. xiv.

[5] Lappenberg, *Anglo-Saxon Kings*, vol. i. p. 231 ; Hartshorne, *Salopia Antiqua*, pp. 181–193.

[6] Guest, in *Proceedings of Archæol. Instit. for* 1849, p. 28.

[7] Lappenberg, *Anglo-Saxon Kings*, vol. i. p. 242. The Mercian kingdom was founded 140 years after that of Kent, and the East-Anglian settlement was, no doubt, much earlier than that in Kent. Thrupp, *Anglo-Saxon Home*, p. 7.

with the two Roman walls which stretched across the island from sea to sea. The Wall of Hadrian, or of Severus, as it is called, ran from Newcastle to Carlisle, and is still in wonderful preservation. But even if the massive masonry and huge earthen rampart of this wall had perished, it would be easy to trace its direction by means of the continuous series of memorial names which are furnished by the villages and farmhouses along its course. It began at WALLSEND, now famous as the place where the best Newcastle coals are shipped. We then come in succession to places called Ben*well*, *Wal*bottle, Heddon-on-the-*Wall*, *Wel*ton, *Wall*houses, *Wall*, *Wal*wick Chesters, *Wall*shiels, *Wall*town, Thirl*wall*, Birdos*wald*, *Wall*bours, *Wal*ton, Old*wall*, *Wall*knoll, *Wall*mill, and *Wall*by, with *Wall*end, *Wall*foot, and *Wall*head at the western end. The wall was, moreover, protected by fortified posts at regular intervals. The sites of these fortresses go by the names of BLAKE (Black) CHESTERS, RUTCHESTER, HALTON CHESTERS, CARROWBURGH, CHESTERHOLM, GREAT CHESTERS, BURGH, and DRUMBURGH.[1]

The northern wall, or Wall of Antoninus, extended from the Forth to the Clyde, and goes by the name of GRIME'S DYKE.[2] DUMBARTON, DUMBUCK Hill, and DUNGLAS were probably fortified stations along its course.

Fortified camps, whether of British, Roman, Saxon, or Danish construction, are very commonly marked by the suffix *bury*. To enumerate any considerable portion of these names would far exceed our limits ; but merely to show how this suffix may guide the antiquarian in his researches, it may suffice to exhibit the results obtained from a single county. In Wiltshire alone there are, or were in Camden's time, military earthworks in existence at places called Chisbury, Boadbury, Abury, Yanesbury, Ambresbury, Selbury, Sidbury, Badbury, Wanborough, Burywood, Barbury, Oldbury, Rybury, Westbury, Battlesbury, Avesbury, Heytesbury, Scratchbury, Waldsbury, Bilbury, Winklebury, Chiselbury, Clerebury, Whichbury, Frippsbury, and Ogbury or Okebury. At Malmesbury, Salisbury, Heytesbury, Ramesbury, Titsbury, and Marlborough, the sites of British or Saxon earthworks seem to have been used for the erection of Norman castles.

---

[1] Bruce, *The Roman Wall*, passim.
[2] There is also a Grimesditch in Cheshire, and there are four other earthworks bearing the same name, slightly altered. Chalmers, *Caledonia*, vol. i. p. 119.

A competent etymological investigation of the first syllable in these names might probably yield results not destitute of value.

The Roman stations throughout the island may very frequently be recognized by the fact that their modern names contain a modification of the Latin word *castra*.[1] These modifications are very curious, as exhibiting the dialectic tendencies in different portions of the island.[2] Throughout the kingdoms of Essex, Sussex, Wessex, and other purely Saxon districts, the form *chester* is universal. Here we have the names of Colchester, Godmanchester, Grantchester, Chesterford, Irchester, Rochester, Winchester, Ilchester, Chichester, Silchester, Porchester, and two Dorchesters. But as we pass from the Saxon to the Anglian kingdoms, we find *chester* replaced by *caster*. The distinctive usage of these two forms is very noticeable, and is of great ethnological value. In one place the line of demarcation is so sharply defined that it can be traced within two hundred yards. Northamptonshire, which is decisively Danish, is divided by the Nen from Huntingdonshire, which is purely Saxon. On the Saxon side of the river we find the village of CHESTERTON, confronted on the other side by the town of CASTOR, the two names recording, in two different dialects, the fact that the bridge was guarded by the Roman station of Durobrivæ.[3] Throughout the Anglian and Danish districts we find this form *caster*, as in Tadcaster, Brancaster, Ancaster, Doncaster, Lancaster, Casterton, Alcaster, Caster, and Caistor. As we pass from East Anglia to Mercia, which, though mainly Anglian, was subject to a certain amount of Saxon influence, we find *cester*, which is intermediate in form between the Anglian *caster* and the Saxon *chester*. The *e* is retained, but the *h* is omitted ; and there is a strong tendency to further elision, as in the case of Leicester,

---

[1] One syllable of names containing *chester, caster,* or *caer,* is almost always Celtic, and seems to have been a Latinization of the enchorial name. In *Win*chester the first syllable is the Latin *venta,* a word which was constructed from the Celtic *gwent,* a plain. *Bin*chester contains a portion of the Latinized name Binovium. In *Dor*chester and *Exe*ter we have the Celtic words *dwr* and *uisge,* water ; in *Man*chester we have *man,* a district. See pp. 141, 143, 144, *supra*.

[2] See Robertson, *Early Kings,* vol. ii. p. 240 ; Latham, *Opuscula,* p. 152 ; Wright, *Wanderings,* p. 208 ; Hartshorne, *Salopia Antiqua,* pp. 158, 199.

[3] See a paper by Latham *On the Traces of a Bilingual Town in England,* read before the British Association in 1853 ; Latham, *Opuscula,* p. 152 ; *English Language,* vol. i. p. 434 ; Ansted and Latham, *Channel Is.* p. 335 ; Smith, *Dictionary of Geogr.* s. v. Durobrivæ ; Gough's Camden, vol. ii. p. 286. Durobrivæ means water-bridge. See p. 180, *supra*.

pronounced Le'ster ; Bicester, pronounced Bi'ster ; Worcester, pronounced Wor'ster ; Gloucester, pronounced Glos'ter, and Cirencester, pronounced S'isester or Si's'ter. The same tendency is seen in the cases of Alcester, Mancester, and Towcester. It is still more noteworthy that beyond the Tees, where the Danish and Mercian influence ceases, and where almost all the local names resume the pure Saxon type,[1] we find that the southern form *chester* reappears ; and we have the names Lanchester, Binchester, Chester-le-Street, Ebchester, Ribchester, Rowchester, Fichester, Chesterknows, Chesterlee, Chesterholm, Rutchester, and a few others on the Wall.

Towards the Welsh frontier the *c* or *ch* becomes an *x*, and the tendency to elision is very strong. We have Uttoxeter, pronounced Ux'ter ; Wroxeter, and Exeter, which in Camden's time was written Excester.

These names on the Welsh frontier exhibit a gradual approximation to the form which we find in the parts where the Celtic speech survived. Here the *t* also disappears, and we find the prefix *caer* in the names of Caerleon, Caergai, Caergwyle, Caersws, Caerwent, Caerphilly, Caerwis, and the still more abbreviated forms of Carstairs, Carluke, and Carriden in Scotland, Carhayes in Cornwall, Carmarthen, Cardigan, Cardiff, and Carnarvon in Wales, Carhallock, Carlisle, and Carvoran [2] in England, Carlow [3] and Cardross in Ireland. With these forms we may compare Caerphili and Caerven in Brittany, Cherbourg in the Celtic peninsula of Cornuaille, and Carsoli, Carosio, Carmiano, Carovigno, and Cortona, in the Celtic part of Italy.[4]

The Latin word *colonia* is found in the names of LINCOLN

---

[1] See p. 117, *supra*.

[2] Great Chesters, on the Wall, is an exact reproduction of the Celtic name Carvoran, from which it is only three miles distant. As in the case of Chesterton and Castor, we have here an indication of the close geographical proximity in which different races must have lived. See Wright, *Essays*, vol. i. p. 103.

[3] [Carlow, formerly *Caherlough, Catherlogh*, is from Irish *Cether-loch*, ' Four lakes ', Joyce, *Irish Names of Places*, i. 433.]

[4] Chester and caster are, undoubtedly, from the Latin *castra*. Compare the Anglo-Saxon word *ceaster*. Kemble, *Codex Diplom*. vol. iii. p. xx. But there is considerable doubt whether *caer* is a modification of *castra*, or an independent Celtic root. We have the British and Cornish *caer*, the Amorican *ker*, and the Irish *cathair* and *ca'ir*, a fortress, and the Welsh *cae*, an inclosure, and *cor*, a close. See Owen's *Welsh Dictionary* ; Diefenbach, *Celtica*, i. p. 107 ; Davies in *Philolog. Trans. for* 1857, p. 43 ; Williams, *Essays*, pp. 79, 80 ; Wright, *Essays*, vol. i. p. 103 ; Mone, *Celt. Forsch*. p. 200 ; De Belloguet, *Ethnog*. vol. i. p. 210 ; Guest in *Philolog. Proceed*. vol. v. p. 187 ; *Cambro-Briton*, vol. ii. p. 409. Compare the Hebrew and Phœnician word *Kartha*, which is seen in the names of *Kir*jath, *Ker*ioth, *Kir*, and *Cart*hage, and is identical in meaning with the Celtic *caer*. Wilton, *Negeb*, p. 103. If there is no affiliation, this is a very remarkable coincidence of sound and meaning.

and COLOGNE,[1] and perhaps also in those of COLCHESTER and the two rivers called the COLNE, one of which rises near the site of the *colonia* of Verulamium, and the other flows past Colchester. In the immediate vicinity of Colchester a legion was stationed for the protection of the colony. The precise spot which was occupied by the camp of this legion is indicated by the remains of extensive Roman earthworks at LEXDON, a name which is a corruption of *Legionis Dunum*.[2]   The Second Legion—Legio Augusta—was stationed on the river Usk, or Isca, at a place called, in the Roman time, Isca Legionis. The process by which the modern name of CAERLEON has been evolved, is indicated in the work which bears the name of Nennius : ' bellum gestum est in urbe Leogis, quæ Brittanice Cair Lion dicitur '.[3]   Another legion we find at LEICESTER (Legionis castra).

The station of the seventh legion was in Spain, at LEON (Legio), that of the Claudian legion at KLOTEN in Switzerland.[4] Megiddo in Palestine, where another legion was quartered, now goes by the name of LEDJÛN, or LEJJUN.[5] (Legio, or Castra Legionis.)

The numerous ' peels ' along the border are an evidence of the insecurity arising from border warfare in times when every man's house was, in a literal sense, his castle also.[6]

The hill where the border clan of the Maxwells used to assemble previous to their dreaded forays bears the appropriate name of the WARDLAW (guard hill). A reference to this trysting place is contained in the war-cry of the clan, ' I bid you bide Wardlaw '.

A similar state of society is indicated by the name of CASTILE, as well as by the castle which appears on the armorial bearings of that kingdom. The name and the device date from the times of continuous border warfare, when the central portion of the peninsula was, mile by mile, being wrested from the Moors, and secured by an ever advancing line of frontier castles.[7]

[1] See Mahn, *Ueber die Namen Berlin und Köhn*, p. 2.   Compare the name of KULÔNIA in Palestine.   Robinson, *Later Researches*, p. 158.
[2] Baxter, *Glossarium*, p. 64 ; Gough's Camden, vol. ·ii. p. 138.
[3] Nennius, c. 56.   [4] Meyer, *Ortsnamen*, p. 70.
[5] Robinson, *Biblical Researches*, vol. iii. pp. 177–180 ; *Later Researches*, p. 118 ; Stanley, *Jewish Church*, p. 322.
[6] Peel is from the Celtic *pill*, a castle.   Davies in *Philolog. Proc.* vol. vi. p. 131.   [Geo. Nelson, *On the word Peel*, 1894 ; Lat. *pila*.]
[7] The same fact is expressed by the Arabic name for Castile—*Ardhu-l-kila*, the land

At a later period, when the unbelievers had been finally expelled from Northern and Central Spain, the debateable ground was the province which now goes by the name of MURCIA. This word means the district of the 'march' or *marg*in, the de*marc*ation between two alien races. To make a *mark* is to draw a boundary. Letters of *marque* are letters which contain a licence to harass the enemy beyond the frontier. A Margrave, Mark-graf, Earl of March, or Marquess was the warden of the Marches, who held his fief by the tenure of defending the frontier against all aggression, and this important office gave him rank next to the Duke or Dux, the leader of the forces of the shire. The root is found in all the Indo-Germanic languages, and is probably to be referred to the Sanskrit *maryâ*, a boundary, which is a derivative of the verb *smri*, to remember.[1] We may compare the Latin *margo*, and the Persian *marg*, a frontier. The uncleared forest served as the boundary of the *gau* of the Teutonic settlers. Hence the Scandinavian *mörk*, a forest, and the English word *murky*,[?] which originally denoted the gloom of the primaeval forest. The chase took place in the forest which bounded the inhabited district, hence the Sanskrit *mrga*, chase hunting. A huntsman being nearly synonymous with a horseman, we have the Celtic *marc*,[2] a horse, which has found its way into the English verb, to *march*, and the French word *maréchal*, a groom or farrier [?]. The Earl *Marshal* was originally the 'grand farrier', or 'master of the horse'—a great officer of state, like the grand falconer.[3]

The Scotch and the Welsh marches for many centuries, occupy an important place in English history as the border-lands between England, and her ancient enemies in Scotland and Wales. The Anglo-Saxon kingdom of MERCIA was the frontier province between the East Angles and the Welsh. On the

---

of castles. Gayangos, *Dynasties*, vol. i. p. 316 ; Prescott, *Ferdinand and Isabella*, vol. i. p. 28.

[1] [Rather Sanskrit *márga*, a trace, from the root *mrij. mar*. See Skeat, *Etym. Dict. s.v.*]

[2] Gaelic and Erse, *marc* ; Welsh, Cornish, and Brezonec, *mar'ch*. Compare the Anglo-Saxon *mear*, a horse, whence the English *mare*. According to Ammianus Marcellinus, the war-cry of the Sarmatians was—Marha, Marha, ' to horse, to horse '. Diefenbach, *Orig. Europ.* p. 90.

[3] On the word *mark* see Diefenbach, *Celtica*, i. p. 67 ; *Origines Europ.* p. 429. ; *Vergleichendes Wörterbuch*, vol. ii. pp. 50–53 ; Leo, *Vorlesungen*, vol. i. p. 144 ; Zeuss, *Die Deutschen*, p. 114 ; Diez, *Etymolog. Wörterbuch*, pp. 217, 682 ; Pictet, *Orig. Indo-Europ.* part ii. p. 408 ; Müller, *Marken des Vaterlandes*, pp. 216, 217 ; Verstegan, *Restitution*, pp. 171, 172 ; Kemble, *Codex Diplom.* vol. iii. p. xi ; Blackstone, *Commentaries*, book i. c. 7, § 4 ; Garnett, *Essays*, p 16 ; Pott, *Etymologische Forschungen*, vol. ii. p. 116.

frontier line we find MARBROOK and MARCHOMLEY in Shropshire, MARBURY in Cheshire, and MARKLEY in Herefordshire.[1] On the frontier between the Celts of Cornwall and the Saxons of Devon, stands the village of MARHAM. We have seen that the valleys of the Frome and Avon remained Celtic long after the surrounding country had been occupied by the Saxons. Some three or four miles to the south-west of Bath stands the village of MERKBURY, the 'fortress of the march' or boundary of the Welsh district. The names of the adjoining villages of ENGLISHCOMBE[2] and ENGLISH BATCH seem to mark outlying portions of the English territory.[3] The town of MARCH in Cambridgeshire is close to the sharply defined frontier line of the Scandinavian kingdom,[4] and on the frontier of the little outlying Danish colony in Essex we find a place called COMARQUES.

Throughout Europe we find this word march or mark entering into the names of outlying or frontier provinces. The MARCOMANNI of Tacitus were the marchmen of the Sclavonic frontier of Germany.[5] The names of the provinces of ALTMARK, MITTELMARK, UKERMARK,[6] and NEUMARK, which collectively constitute the MARK of Brandenburg, show the successive encroachments of the Germans on the Poles ; Altmark, or the ' Old Mark ', being the farthest to the west, while Neumark, the ' New Mark ', is the farthest to the east. DENMARK was the Danish frontier. FINMARK, and four provinces called LAPPMARK, show the five successive stages by which the Scandinavian invaders encroached upon the territory of the Fins and Lapps. MORAVIA takes its name from the March, or Mor-ava, a bordering river.[7] STEYERMARK, or Styria, as we Anglicize the word, formed the south-eastern frontier between the Germans, and the Hungarians and Croats. Here

---

1 There are fifteen English parishes called Marston, i.e. Markstone or boundary stone one of which gives a name to the well-known battlefield of Marston Moor.

2 The name of Englishcombe is found in Domesday.

3 Guest, in *Archæolog. Journal*, vol. xvi. pp. 111, 112.

4 See p. 117, *supra*.

5 Latham, *Germania*, prolegomena, pp. liii.–lvi. ; Latham in *Philolog. Proceedings*, vol. iv. p. 190. Grimm thinks that the Marcomanni were the men of the forest, rather than the men of the frontier. *Gesch. d. Deut. Spr.* p. 503.

6 The name of the Ukermark contains two synonymous elements—Ukraine being a Sclavonic word, meaning a frontier. The UKRAINE on the Dnieper was the southern frontier of the ancient kingdom of Poland. See Latham, *Nationalities of Europe*, vol. i. pp. 5 and 376; vol. ii. p. 358.

7 Grimm, *Gesch. d. Deut. Spr.* p. 505. The suffix *ava* is the Old High German *aha*, a river.

we find the border town of MARCHBURG. The boundary of the Saxon colony in Westphalia is shown by the district called MARCH, and there is a place called MARBACH on the frontier of the Swabian settlement in Würtemberg. On the frontiers of the Saxon colony in Picardy we find the Rivers MARBECQ and NORBECQUE, a dike called the MARDICK, and the village of MARCK. In the Vosges, on the frontier of the Alemannic population of Alsace, we find the town of LA MARCHE. One of the old provinces of France, called MARCHE, was the frontier between the Franks and the Euskarians of Aquitaine. The March of Ancona, and the other Roman Marches which have been recently annexed to the kingdom of Italy, together with the Marquisate of Tuscany, formed the southern boundaries of the Carlovingian empire. The Marquisate of Flanders [1] was erected at a later period as a barrier against the Danes In fact, all the original Marquisates, those of Milan, Verona, Carniola, Istria, Moravia, Cambe, Provence, Susa, Montserrat, and many others, will be found to have been marks or frontier territories.

Two names survive which mark boundaries of the Roman empire. The name of the Fiume Della FINE, near Leghorn, is a corruption of the ancient name, Ad Fines. This river, about the year 250 B.C., formed the extreme northern limit of the Latin confederacy.[2] The Canton Valais in Switzerland is curiously divided between a German and a French-speaking population. The Romans left the upper end of the valley to the barbarous mountaineers, and their descendants now speak German. The lower part, which was included within the Roman rule, is now French in language. The line of linguistic demarcation is sharply drawn in the neighbourhood of Leuk. Here we find a village which is called PFYN, a name which marks the *fines*, the confines both of the Roman rule, and of the language of the conquerors.

A somewhat similar name is found in England. DEVIZES is a barbarous Anglicization of the Low Latin *Divisæ*, which denoted the point where the road from London to Bath passed into the Celtic district.[3] Even so late as the time of Clarendon, the name had hardly become a proper name, being called

---

[1] On the frontier of the Marquisate of Flanders are two towns called MARCHIENNES
[2] Mommsen, *Hist. Rome*, vol. i. p. 441.
[3] Guest, in *Archæolog. Journal*. vol. xvi. p. 116.

The Devizes, in the same way that Bath was called The Bath in the time of Addison.[1]

The former state of our island, divided between hostile peoples—Saxon, Celt, and Dane—is indicated not only by such names as Mercia and March, but by those of several of our English counties.[2] CUMBERLAND is the land of the Cymry. CORNWALL, or Corn-wales, is the kingdom of the Welsh of the Horn. DEVON is the land of the Damnonii, a Celtic tribe ; KENT that of the Cantii ; WORCESTERSHIRE that of the Huicii. SUSSEX, ESSEX, WESSEX, and MIDDLESEX, were the kingdoms of the southern, eastern, western, and central Saxons. In Robert of Gloucester, the name of SURREY appears in the form of Sothe-reye, or the south realm.[3] NORFOLK and SUFFOLK were the northern and southern divisions of the East-Anglian folk. The position on the map of what we call NORTHUMBERLAND—the land north of the Humber— proves that it was by aggression from the south that the Northumbrian kingdom, which once stretched northward from the Humber, was reduced to the restricted limits of the modern county. HEREFORD, the ' ford of the army ', was an important strategic point in the Marches of Wales, being one of the few places where an Anglo-Saxon army could cross the Severn to harry the Welsh borders.

These county names may serve to remind us of the discordant fragments that have at length been welded into a national unity, while numerous village-names, such as SAXBY, FLEMINGSBY, FRANKBY,[4] FRISBY,[5] SCOTTHORPE, NORMANDBY, FINSTHWAITE,[6] and DANBY, prove from how wide an area those bands of adventurers were collected who made their swords the title-deeds to portions of our English soil.

At the close of the period of Roman occupation, the Barbarian auxiliaries must have formed a not inconsiderable element in the population of Britain. From the ' Notitia

---

[1] See *Saturday Review*, August 22, 1863.

[2] See Grimm, *Gesch. d. Deut. Spr.* p. 658.

[3] On the forms in which this name appears, see Guest, *On Gentile Names*, in *Philolog. Proceedings*, vol. i. p. 111.

[4] We have Frankby in Cheshire, four Franktons in Salop, and one in Warwick, Frankley in Worcester, and Frankham in Dorset.

[5] We find a Friesthorpe in Lincolnshire, two Frisbys in Leicestershire, Frieston in Lincolnshire and Sussex, and two in Suffolk, Frystone in Yorkshire, Friesden in Bucks, and Frisdon in Wilts.

[6] We have Finsthwaite in Lancashire, Fineston in Lincolnshire, Finsham, in Norfolk, Finstock in Oxon. [A.S. *Súthrig, Suthri-gēa* (*A.Sax. Chron.* an. '836) *i.e.* southern-district—Skeat, *Notes and Queries*, 10th s. xi. 171.]

Imperii ', and from inscriptions, we learn that there were legions recruited from Moors, Indians,[1] Cilicians, Dacians, Thracians,[2] Dalmatians,[3] Sarmatians, Tungrians, Batavians, and from sundry tribes of Gaul, Spain, and Germany, which were located in various parts of Britain.[4]   Local names preserve a few traces of these military colonies.   The names of QUAT and QUATFORD,[5] near Bridgenorth, in Salop, have, been thought to bear witness to a settlement of Quadi ; and TONG,[6] in Yorkshire, of the Tungrians.   The ancient name of HUNNUM on the Wall, and the modern one of HUNSTANTON, in Norfolk, may possibly be due to the Huns.   There is only one name of this class, however, which can be referred to with any confidence.   We are informed by Zosimus that large bodies of Vandal auxiliaries were settled in Britain by the Emperor Probus, and Gervase of Tilbury informs us that Vandalsburg in Cambridgeshire was a fortification raised by them.   Vandalsburg is undoubtedly to be identified with the huge earthwork called WANDLESBURY, which occupies the summit of the Gogmagog Hills.   WENDLEBURY, near Bicester, in Oxfordshire ; WINDLESHAM, near Woking, in Surrey ; WINDLEDEN and WENDEL Hill, in Yorkshire ; and WINDLE, in Lancashire, may, some of them, be Vandal settlements.[7]

Henry of Huntingdon informs us that the Picts, during one of their incursions, advanced as far as Stamford, where they suffered a bloody repulse.   The remnant of this invading host may with some probability be traced at PITCHLEY in Northamptonshire, a place which, in Domesday, is called Picts-lei and Pihtes-lea, the *laga* or settlement of the Picts or Pehtas.[8]

Beyond the confines of England we find numerous names which denote intrusive colonization, or the settlement of the remains of defeated armies.   One of the most curious of these

[1] At Cirencester.
[2] In Yorkshire, Shropshire, at Cirencester, and on the Wall.
[3] In Norfolk, Lincolnshire, and on the Wall.
[4] See Wright, ' On the Ethnology of South Britain at the extinction of the Roman Government ', *Essays*, vol. i. pp. 70, 71 ; Poste, *Britannic Researches*, pp. 99, 100 ; Latham, *Ethnol. Brit. Is.* pp. 99–101 ; *Edinb. Review*, vol. xciv. p. 187 ; Horsley, *Brit. Rom.* pp. 88–97, 102 ; Bruce, *Roman Wall*, p. 60.
[5] More probably from the Celtic *coed*, a wood.
[6] More probably Norse.
[7] See Kennett, *Parochial Antiquities*, vol. i. p. 18 ; Palgrave, *English Commonwealth*, vol. i. p. 355 ; Gough's Camden, vol. i. p. cxxxix. and vol. ii. p. 213.
[8] See Poste, *Brit. Researches,* p. 47.   The pronunciation of this name, Peitchley, strongly favours the etymology suggested in the text.   Compare also the phrases Sexena-laga, the seat or district of the Saxons, and Danelagh, that of the Danes.

is SCYTHOPOLIS, a strong natural rock-fortress in Eastern Palestine, the name of which is probably a record of the Scythian invasion in the reign of Josiah, which is recorded by Herodotus.[1]

The names of SERVIANIKA and CRAVATTA show that Servians and Croats penetrated into the Morea. In Westphalia we find the adjacent villages of FRANKENFELD and SASSENBERG,[2] and in Hesse Cassel FRANKENBERG and SASSENBERG stand face to face.[3] In the Rhineland, FRANKFURT and FRANKENTHAL[4] are settlements of the Franks, just as KATZELLENBOGEN[5] and SACHSENHAUSEN are of the Saxons. FLAMANDVILLE and SASSETOT in Normandy, and SUEVEGHEM in Flanders, are among the numerous names of the kind which might easily be collected.[6] The WESTMANN ISLES, opposite Hjörleif's Head on the coast of Iceland were the refuge of some *westmen*, or Irish slaves, who slew their master, Hjörleif, and then fled for their lives.[7] We must, I fear, give up the curious tradition which derives the name of Canton SCHWYTZ from a Swedish colony which settled there at some remote period.[8]

1 Herodotus, i. c. 105 ; Zephaniah ii. 5, 6 ; see Stanley, *Jewish Church*, p. 338 ; *Sinai and Pal.* p. 340 ; Bergmann, *Les Gètes*, p. 26 ; Robinson, *Biblical Researches*, vol. iii. p. 175 ; *Later Researches*, p. 330 ; Brace, *Races of the Old World*, pp. 60, 61. It is possible that there may be truth in the tradition which asserts that the Frank Mountain, in the same neighbourhood, was a refuge of the Crusaders. See Stanley, *Sinai and Pal.* p. 163 ; Robinson, *Bibl. Researches*, vol. ii. p. 171.
2 Massmann, in Dorow's *Denkmäler*, vol. i. p. 199.
3 Vilmar, *Ortsnamen*, p. 243.
4 The ancient forms of these two names show that they are derived from the nationality of the inhabitants, and not, as is usually supposed, from the possession of certain franchises. Zeuss, *Herkunft der Baiern*, p. 38.
5 See, however, Dixon, *Surnames*, p. 4.
6 Many instances have been collected by Zeuss and Förstemann. See *Die Deutschen*, pp. 608, 635, etc.; *Die Deutschen Ortsnamen*, p. 170.
7 Baring-Gould, *Iceland*, p. 2.
8 The Haslithalers affirm that they are Swedes. Hassle is a common local name in Sweden. See Geijer, *De Colonia Svecorum in Helvetiam deducta*, quoted extensively by Strinnholm, *Wikingzüge*, pp. 190–199.

CHAPTER XI

THE STREET NAMES OF LONDON

*The walls of Old London—Gradual extension of the town—Absorption of
surrounding villages—The Brooks ; the Holborn, the Tyburn, and
the Westbourne—Wells, conduits, ferries—Monastic establishments
of London—Localities of certain trades—Sports and pastimes—
Sites of residences of historic families preserved in the names of streets
—The Palaces of the Strand—Elizabethan London—Streets dating
from the Restoration.*

THE history of many cities has been deciphered from inscriptions, and so the history of Old London may, much of it, be
deciphered from the inscriptions which we find written up
at the corners of its streets. These familiar names, which
catch the eye as we pace the pavement, perpetually remind
us of the London of bygone centuries, and recall the stages
by which the long unlovely avenues of street have replaced
the elms and hedgerows and have spread over miles of pleasant
fields till scores of outlying villages have been absorbed into
a ' boundless contiguity ' of brick and mortar.

By the aid of the street names of London let us then endeavour to reconstruct the history of London, and, in the first
place, let us take these names as our guide-book in making
the circuit of the old City Walls. The ancient wall started
from the Norman fortress on TOWER HILL, and ran to ALDGATE
—the ' Old Gate '. Between ALDGATE and BISHOPSGATE the
wall was protected by an open ditch, two hundred feet broad,[1]
whose name, HOUNDSDITCH, sufficiently indicates the unsavoury
nature of its contents. CAMOMILE STREET and WORMWOOD
STREET remind us of the desolate strip of waste ground which
lay immediately within the wall, and of the hardy herbs which
covered it, or strove to force their rootlets between the stones
of the grey rampart. In continuation of the street called
Houndsditch, we find a street called LONDON WALL. Here

[1] Pennant, *London*, p. 234.

no ditch seems to have been needed, for the names of FINS-
BURY, MOORFIELDS, MOOR LANE, and MOORGATE STREET, hand
down the memory of the great Fen or Moor—an ' arrant fen ',
as Pennant quaintly calls it—which protected the northern
side of London.

On this moor, just outside the wall, was the ARTILLERY
GROUND,[1] where the bowmen were wont to assemble to display their skill.

Where the fen terminated the wall needed more protection,
and here accordingly we find the site of the BARBICAN,[2] one
of the gateway towers, which seems to have guarded ALDERS-
GATE, the chief entrance from the north. Considerable
remains of the wall are still visible in CASTLE STREET, as well
as in the churchyard of St. Giles', CRIPPLEGATE.[3] Passing
by NEWGATE we come to the OLD BAILEY, a name which is
derived from the *ballium* or *vallum*, an open space between
the advanced gate of the city and the line of the outer wall.[4]

The wall now turned southward, and ran along the crest
of LUDGATE HILL, its western face being protected by the FLEET,
a small stream which flowed through the ditch of the city
wall, which was here called the FLEET DITCH. The river
Fleet also gave its name to the street which crossed it at right
angles, and entered the city by Fleetgate, Floodgate, or LUD-
GATE.[5]

[1] Hard by we find ARTILLERY STREET, where the Bowyers and Fletchers fabricated
longbows and cloth yard shafts. The word *artillery*, in old English, denotes bows and
arrows, and it retained this meaning till the seventeenth century, for we find the word
used in this sense in 1 Sam. xx. where our version reads, ' And Jonathan gave his
artillery unto his lad, and said unto him, Go, carry them to the city'.
[2] The whole tribe of modern Londonologists have followed Stow in deriving the word
barbican from the Saxon *burgh kenning*, or ' town watching ' tower. A barbican was,
strictly, a projecting turret over a gateway. The true etymology of the word is undoubtedly that given by Camden (vol. ii. p. 85), from the Persian *bála khaneh*, an upper
chamber [more probably *barbār kāhnah*, ' house on 'the wall ', *N.E.D.*], whence also
we derive the word balcony [?]. We find this form in the case of BALCON LANE, which
was parallel to, and just outside, the town wall of Colchester. See Wedgwood, *Eng.
Etym.* vol. i. p. 97 ; and Wedgwood in *Phil. Proc.* vol. iii. p. 156.
[3] The wall gives its name to the parish of Allhallows-in-the-Wall, as well as to that
of Cripplegate.
[4] In a similar position with respect to the city wall, we find the Old Bayle at York
the church of St. Peter in the Bailey at Oxford, and Bailey Hill at Sheffield and Radnor
A *bailiff* was originally the Bayle-reeve, or officer in charge of the Ballium ; just as the
sheriff is the shire-reeve. A *bail* is etymologically a palisade. Thus the *bails* at cricket
were originally the stumps, the present restricted meaning of the word being of later
origin. See Knapp, *English Roots*, pp. 79–81 ; Timbs, *Curiosities of London*, p. 556 ;
Wedgwood, *Dict. of Eng. Etym.* vol. i. p. 96 ; Hartshorne, *Salopia Antiqua*, p. 241 ; Diez,
Etym. Wörterbuch, p. 37 ; Whitaker, *Hist. of Manchester*, vol. ii. p. 244.
[5] The words *flood*, *fleet*, and *float*, come from the Anglo-Saxon verb *fleotan*, to float
or swim. A *fleet* is either that which is afloat, or a place where vessels can float—that
is, a channel, or where water fleets or runs. Hence the names EBBFLEET, NORTHFLEET

At the angle formed by the wall and the Thames stood a Norman fortress erected at the same time with the Tower of London.[1] A wharf which occupies the site, as well as one of the city wards, still retain the name of CASTLE BAYNARD, although every vestige of the fortress has long disappeared. DOWGATE [2] and BILLINGSGATE were two of the passages through that part of the wall which protected the city from assailants coming from the riverside.[3]

The small space within the walls of Old London was almost exactly of the same shape and the same area as Hyde Park. In fact, as the last syllable of its name indicates, LONDON was originally a *dun* or Celtic hill-fortress, formed by Tower Hill, Cornhill, and Ludgate Hill, and effectually protected by the Thames on the south, the Fleet on the west, the great fen of Moorfields and Finsbury on the north, and by the Hounds-ditch and the Tower on the east.[4]

For a long period London was confined within the limit of its walls. In the reign of Edward I. CHARING was a country village lying midway between the two cities of London and Westminster, and ST. MARTIN'S-IN-THE-FIELDS long continued to be the village church. Along the STRAND of the river hardly a house had been built in the time of Edward III., and no continuous street existed till the reign of Elizabeth. Even then, to the north of this straggling line of houses, the open country extended from LINCOLN'S INN FIELDS to the village church of ST. GILES' IN THE FIELDS. James I. ordered the justices to commit to prison any person presuming to build in this open space.[5] LONG ACRE, formerly a field called 'The Elms', or 'The Seven Acres',[6] was not built upon till the reign of Charles 1. And scarcely a century ago a man with a telescope used to station himself in LEICESTER FIELDS—now Leicester Square—and offer to the passers-by, at the charge of one half penny, a peep at the heads of the

---

SOUTHFLEET, PURFLEET, and PORTFLEET. The word *vley*, which the boers of the Cape use for the smaller rivers, is the same word fleet (Dutch, *vliet*,) in a somewhat disguised form. Kemble, *Cod. Dip.* vol. iii. p. xxv. See p. 132, *supra*.

[1] See Thierry, *Norman Conquest*, p. 76; Cunningham, *Handbook for London*, p. 65.
[2] Possibly the Dourgate or water-gate. Gough's Camden, vol. ii. p. 80.
[3] Pauli, *Pictures of Old England*, p. 416.
[4] The natural advantages of the site have been well brought out by Dean Stanley in his admirable lecture on *The Study of Modern History*, pp. 352-355. [Sir H. Maxwell suggests *Lon-dún*, ' the marsh fort '—*Scottish Landnames*, 3.]
[5] Smith, *Antiquarian Ramble*, vol. i. p. 302; Mackay, *History of London* p. 272.
[6] Timbs, *Curiosities of London*, p. 473.

Scotch rebels which garnished the spikes on Temple Bar [1].

If, two or three centuries ago, what now forms the heart of London was unbuilt upon, it was at a still more recent period that Kensington, Brompton, Paddington, Dalston, Stoke Newington, and Islington, remained detached country villages, though they are now districts incorporated with the wilderness of streets. There was a coach which took three hours to run, or rather to flounder, from the village of Paddington to London ; and Lord Hervey, in country retirement at Kensington, laments that the impassable roads should cause his entire isolation from his friends in London.

The names SPITALFIELDS, BETHNAL GREEN, FIELD LANE, CLERKENWELL GREEN, PADDINGTON GREEN, VINE STREET, MOORFIELDS, SMITHFIELD, East and West, COLDBATH FIELDS, ST. GEORGE'S FIELDS, SPA FIELDS, ROSEMARY LANE, COPENHAGEN FIELDS, and KINGSLAND, indicate the rural character of the districts that separated the outlying villages from the neighbouring city. In these fields the citizens could take pleasant country walks with their wives, while their children clambered over Goodman's STYLE, in GOODMAN'S FIELDS, or, on rare occasions, went nutting on Nutting or NOTTING HILL. There were windmills in WINDMILL STREET, at the top of the Haymarket, and in WINDMILL STREET, Finsbury ; there was a water-mill in MILFORD LANE, Strand ; while the hounds of the Lord Mayor's pack were kenneled at DOG-HOUSE BAR, in the City Road.

In TOTHILL FIELDS there was a bear garden, and in the fields by the side of the brook which has given its name to Brook Street, an annual fair was held on the site of Curzon Street and Hertford Street—a rural fête whose memory is preserved in the name of the fashionable region of MAYFAIR.

The names of the present streets will enable us to trace the courses of the brooks which ran through these country fields. The little stream called the HOLBORN, rising near Holborn Bars, gave its name to the street down which it flowed,[2]

---

1 Smith, *Antiquarian Ramble*, vol. i. p. 117.

2 The ' Old Bourne ', or burn, is the etymology of ' The Holborn ', which is universally given—thoughtlessly copied, according to the usual custom, by one writer from another. That a village or town should be called Oldham, Aldborough, or Newton is intelligible, but how a name like Oldbourne should have arisen is difficult to explain. The introduction of the *h* is another difficulty in the way of this etymology. It seems far more in accordance with etymological laws to refer the name to the Anglo-Saxon *hole*, a hollow, or ravine ; the Holborn will therefore be ' the Burn in the hollow ' like the Holbeck

and after turning the mill at TURNBULL or Turnmill Street, it joined the FLEET river at Holborn Bridge. From this point to the Thames the Fleet was navigable, at all events by barges, as is attested by the names of SEACOAL LANE and NEWCASTLE LANE.

Finsbury and Moorfields were drained by the WALBROOK, which passed through the wall in its course to the Thames. Two or three centuries ago this stream was vaulted over, and WALBROOK STREET was built upon the ground thus gained. At BUDGE ROW [1]—a corruption of Bridge Row—there was a bridge over the brook. The LANGBOURNE, another of the city streams, has given its name to one of the London wards ; and SHERBOURNE LANE, near London Bridge, marks the course of the Sherbourne. Further to the west, the positions of two small rivulets which crossed the Strand are denoted by IVYBRIDGE LANE and STRAND-BRIDGE LANE.

The TYBURN, a much larger stream, after passing by the church of St. Mary le bourne, or MARYLEBONE, and crossing the great western road near Stratford Place, passed across BROOK STREET, and down ENGINE STREET, to the depression of Piccadilly. The hollow in the Green Park is, in fact, the valley of the Tyburn, and the ornamental water in front of Buckingham Palace was the marsh in which it stagnated before its junction with the Thames.

To the west of the Holborn and the Tyburn we find the WESTBOURNE, with its affluent the KILBURN. [2] Where this stream crossed the great western road, it spread out into a shallow BAY-WATER,[3] where cattle might drink at the way-side. On the formation of Hyde Park a dam was constructed across the valley of the Westbourne, so as to head up the water, thus forming the SERPENTINE RIVER, which leaves the park at Albert Gate, and crosses the Kensington Road at KNIGHTSBRIDGE.

It would appear that the water supply of Old London, when not derived from the Thames, the Holborn, or the Tyburn,

---

in Lincolnshire, and the Holbec in Normandy. The Charters in the *Codex Diplomaticus* supply apposite instances of the usage of the Anglo-Saxon word *hole*. See Leo, *Anglo-Saxon Names*, p. 80.

[1] [Named from the dealers in *budge* fur who lived there, as Stow mentions in his *Survey*, 1598.]

[2] Either the Cold-burn, or, more probably, the Well-burn. See p. 132, *supra*.

[3] A different etymology of Bayswater is, however, proposed in *Notes and Queries*, first series, vol. i. No. 11, p. 162.

was obtained from numerous wells—CLERKENWELL or the priest's well, BRIDEWELL or St. Bridget's well, HOLYWELL, [1] SADLER'S WELLS, BAGNIGGE WELLS, and others—and in later times from the conduits or fountains which gave a name to LAMB'S CONDUIT STREET, and CONDUIT STREET, Regent Street. The use of the SHOREDITCH, the Walbrook, the Sherbourne, the Langbourne, and the Fleet, was, we will hope, discontinued at a comparatively early period.

REDRIFF, which is a corruption of Rotherhithe, St. Mary SOMERSET, a corruption of Summer's Hithe, STEPNEY,[2] anciently Stebenhithe, QUEENHITHE, and LAMBETH, or Loamhithe, mark some of the chief ' hithes ' or landing-places on the banks of the Thames.[3]

Close to London Bridge we find the church of St. Mary OVERY, or St. Mary of the Ferry.[4] This name, if we may believe the old traditions, recalls the time when the Thames was unbridged, and when the proceeds of the ferry formed the valuable endowment of the conventual church, just as HORSEFERRY ROAD is a reminiscence of the ferry which Westminster Bridge has superseded.

The Thames was formerly by no means confined to its present bed, but both above and below the city spread out into broad marshes, where the varying channels of the river inclosed numerous islands.[5] LAMBETH MARSH, and perhaps MARSHAM STREET, may remind us of the former. Some of the islands are commemorated by such names as CHELSEA, which is a corruption of *chesel-ey*, or shingle isle ; BATTERSEA, which is St. Peter's-ey ; as well as BERMONDSEY, PUTNEY, and the ISLE OF DOGS.[6]

The monastic establishments were chiefly situated in the fields

---

[1] I am not aware that any etymology of the name of WYCH STREET has been proposed. Like Wynch Street in Bristol, it may be probably derived from the wynch of the public well of Holywell.

[2] The name was anciently written Stebenhethe, which would mean either the ' timber wharf ', or perhaps ' Stephen's wharf '. Cunningham, *Handbook for London*, p. 780.

[3] The names of Erith and Greenhithe, lower down the river, contain the same root.

[4] This etymology, as well as the myths of the miserly ferryman and his fair daughter, are open to grave suspicion. St. Mary Overy is probably St. Mary Ofer-ea, or St. Mary by the water-side. The Anglo-Saxon *ofer* is the same as the modern German *ufer*, a shore.

[5] See Chambers, *Ancient Sea Margins*, p. 14. Thorney Island, on which Westminster Abbey was built, seems to have been completely surrounded by the river. The ornamental water in St. James's Park occupies a part of the bed of the northern branch of the Thames. During the excavation of St. Katharine's Docks old ships were dug out, showing that here also the Thames must have shifted its channel. Lyell, *Antiquity of Man*, p. 129.

[6] Perhaps a corruption of the Isle of Digues, or dikes. [Impossible.]

around the city, their sacred character rendering unnecessary the protection of the walls. Convent, or COVENT GARDEN,[1] was the garden of the monks of WESTMINSTER ABBEY. The name of the Chartreuse, or Carthusian convent, has been corrupted into the CHARTERHOUSE. At CANONBURY, Islington, was an affiliated establishment of the canons of St. Bartholomew's Priory, now St. Bartholomew's Hospital. SPITAL SQUARE occupies the site of the churchyard belonging to the church of the priory and hospital of St. Mary, which stood beyond the walls in SPITAL FIELDS. In AUSTIN FRIARS, Broad Street, stood the convent of the Augustines ; that of the Minoresses, or Nuns of St Clare, was in the MINORIES, just outside the eastern wall ; and in CRUTCHED FRIARS, Tower Hill, was that of the Crutched Friars, distinguished by the cross upon their dress.[2] ST. KATHARINE'S DOCKS occupy the site of the abbey of St. Catherine. The Knights of the Temple of Jerusalem occupied what is now the TEMPLE ; the round church, built on the model of the church of the Holy Sepulchre, being the only part of the ancient building still remaining. At ST. JOHN'S GATE, Clerkenwell, we find a vestige of the other great military order, the Hospitallers, the Knights of the Hospital of St. John, of Jerusalem, Rhodes, and Malta.

To several of the convents belonged sanctuaries, or precinct possessing the valuable privilege of freedom from arrest. The BROAD SANCTUARY belonged to the abbot and monks of Westminster. The monastic establishment of the SAVOY enjoyed similar privileges. The *Times* is now printed within the precincts of the convent of the BLACK FRIARS,[3] or Dominicans,[4] who together with the WHITEFRIARS, or Carmelites, and the GREY FRIARS,[5] or Franciscans, possessed the privileges

---

[1] So Orchard Street, Bristol, was the garden of a monastery, and Culver Street was the columbarium. Lucas, *Secularia*, p. 98.

[2] A *crutch* is the old English word for a cross. A cripple's *crutch* has a cross piece of wood at the top. *Crouchmass* was the festival on the 14th of September, in honour of the Holy Cross. To *crouch* is to bend the body into the form of a cross. *Crochet* work is performed with a crooked needle. A person who has a *crotchet* has a crook in the mind. A *crotchet* in music is a crooked note. A shepherd's crook is crooked at the top.

[3] GLOSTER COURT, Blackfriars, is a corruption of Cloister Court. See Whewell, in *Philological Proceedings*, vol. v. p. 140.

[4] The Augustines, the Dominicans, the Franciscans, and the Carmelites, were the four mendicant orders, whose sphere of labour lay among the crowded population of great cities. The Benedictines and Cistercians had their establishments, for the most part, in country districts, where they discharged the duties of great feudal landowners. See Pauli, *Pictures of Old England*, pp. 53–64.

[5] The monastery of the Greyfriars is now Christ's Hospital. The cloisters and the buttery are the only parts of the old edifice now remaining. The Greyfriars were sometimes called the Minorites, but the name of the Minories is derived, as has been said above, from the Minoress nuns, and not from the Minorite friars.

of sanctuary, the abuse of which has conferred an unenviable notoriety upon the districts to which these immunities were attached.[1]

Special districts in the city, or in the suburbs, were assigned to aliens, or appropriated by those who carried on certain trades. TOOLEY STREET, a corruption of St. Olaf's Street,[2] and ST. CLEMENT DANES [3] mark respectively the colony and the burying-place of the Danes in the southern and western suburbs. The Jews were admitted within the walls, and resided in the two districts which still retain the names of JEWIN STREET and the OLD JEWRY. The LOMBARD pawn-brokers and money dealers established themselves in the street which bears their name, between the two chief centres of trade, the positions of which are denoted by the names of CHEAPSIDE and EASTCHEAP.[4] The corn-market on CORNHILL adjoined the grass-market in Grasschurch or GRACECHURCH STREET, and the hay-market in FENCHURCH STREET.[5] The wool-market was held round the churchyard of ST. MARY WOOLCHURCH. The grocers were established in SOPERS' LANE ; [6] the buckler-makers in BUCKLERSBURY ; [7] and LOTHBURY, a corruption of Lattenbury, was inhabited by the workmen in brass and copper. The names of the POULTRY, the VINTRY, FISH STREET, BREAD STREET, MILK STREET, LEADEN-HALL,[8] LEATHER LANE, SILVER STREET, SHIREMONGERS' [9] or Sermon LANE, and SMITHFIELD, indicate the localities appropriated to other trades.

The streets in the neighbourhood of ST. PAUL'S were occu-pied by those who ministered to the temporal and spiritual necessities of the frequenters of the church. DEAN'S COURT, DOCTORS' COMMONS, and GODLIMAN STREET, still form an oasis of ecclesiastical repose amid the noise and whirr of the city. At the great entrance of the cathedral the scene must have resembled that which we see at the doors of continental

---

1 Pauli, *Pictures of Old England*, pp. 425–427.
2 St. Olaf was the great saint of Scandinavia.
3 See Worsaae, *Danes and Norwegians*, p. 16 ; Stanley, *Study of Modern History*, p. 361 ; Stow, *Survey*, bk. iv. p. 113 ; Timbs, *Curiosities of London*, p. 123.
4 From the Anglo-Saxon *ceap*, sale.
5 The name of Fenchurch is probably from *fœnum* or *foin*, hay. [?] The western HAY-MARKET dates from a much later period.
6 Now Queen Street, Cheapside.
7 Stow, however, gives another derivation for this name. *Survey*, Book iii. p. 27.
8 A corruption of Leather Hall.
9 A Sheremonier was a man who cut bullion into shape ready for coining. The MINT, in Bermondsey, was the issuing place at a later date.

churches, which are often blocked up by stalls for the sale of rosaries, crucifixes, and breviaries. We read in Stow's Survey : 'This street is now called PATERNOSTER ROW, because of the stationers or text-writers that dwelled there, who wrote and sold all sorts of books then in use, namely A B C or Absies, with the Paternoster, Ave, Creed, Graces, etc. There dwelled also Turners of Beads, and they were called Paternoster-makers. . . . At the end of Paternoster Row is AVE MARY LANE, so called upon the like occasion of text-writers and bead-makers then dwelling there. And at the end of that lane is likewise CREED LANE, late so called. . . . and AMEN CORNER is added thereunto betwixt the south end of Warwick Lane, and the north end of Ave Mary Lane '.[1]

Of the recreations of old London but few memorials are preserved in names. It is difficult to realize the fact that tournaments were held on London Bridge, or in the middle of Cheapside. The name of QUEEN STREET, Cheapside, seems to have arisen from an ancient stone balcony which had been erected at the corner of the street in order to enable the queens of England to enjoy the spectacle of the tourneys which on special occasions were held in this great thoroughfare.[2]

Drury Lane Theatre was built on the site of a cockpit called the Phœnix, the memory of which is perpetuated, not only in the ' Rejected Addresses ', but by the names of PHOENIX ALLEY, leading to Long Acre, and of COCKPIT ALLEY in Great Wyld Street.

The names of many of our streets preserve the remembrance of the sites of the town houses of great historical families. These were originally within the walls.[3] ADDLE STREET, near the Guildhall, is believed by Stow to owe its name to the royal residence of Athelstane, which once stood upon the site. In the time of Henry VI. the Percys, Earls of Northumberland, had their town house near Fenchurch Street, on the

---

[1] Stow, *Survey of the Cities of London and Westminster*, vol. i. p. 174. Contiguous to the Cathedral at Geneva are streets called Des Toutes Ames, Des Limbes, Du Paradis, and D'Enfer. Salverte, *Essai*, vol. ii. p. 336.

[2] The permanent stone balcony was erected in 1329, in consequence of the fall of one of the temporary wooden structures previously used. The name of the street was bestowed in 1667, when it was rebuilt after the Great Fire. See Mackay, *History of London*, p. 97 ; Cunningham, *Handbook*, p. 185.

[3] Richard III. resided in Castle Baynard, and Duke Humphrey of Gloucester, and Prince Rupert, in the Barbican. OLD PALACE YARD reminds us of the ancient palace of the kings of England, the site of which is now occupied by the Houses of Parliament.

spot which still goes by the name of NORTHUMBERLAND ALLEY. The De la Poles, Dukes of Suffolk, lived in SUFFOLK LANE, Cannon Street ; DUCK'S FOOT LANE, close by, is probably a corruption of Duke's Foot Lane ; the Manners family resided in RUTLAND PLACE, Blackfriars ; the Earls of Devonshire in DEVONSHIRE SQUARE, Bishopsgate ; and the Earls of Bridge-water in BRIDGEWATER SQUARE, Barbican. LONDON HOUSE YARD, in St. Paul's Churchyard, marks the site of the palace attached to the See of London.

The greater security which existed under the Tudor princes is shown by the fact, that the protection of the walls was gradually found to be unnecessary, and mansions began to cover the ground between London and Westminster, where hitherto churchmen only had found it safe to reside.

The Bishops of Bangor, Chichester, Durham, and Ely lived, respectively, in BANGOR COURT, Shoe Lane ; CHICHESTER RENTS, Chancery Lane ; DURHAM STREET, Temple Bar ; and Ely Place, Holborn. SAFFRON HILL, near ELY Place, has obtained its name from the saffron which grew abundantly in the gardens of Ely House. Between the river Fleet and Temple Bar, we find SALISBURY SQUARE, which occupies the site of the courtyard of the old Salisbury House, be-longing to the see of Sarum ; while DORSET STREET and DORSET COURT, Fleet Street, mark the position of the residence of the Sackvilles, Earls of Dorset. In Clerkenwell we find a NORTHAMPTON SQUARE, which was formerly the garden of the Earls of Northampton ; and in AYLESBURY STREET and COBHAM ROW, both in the same fashionable locality, were the houses of the Earls of Aylesbury, and of the celebrated Sir John Oldcastle, Lord Cobham. The Wriothesleys, Earls of South-ampton, lived in SOUTHAMPTON BUILDINGS, Chancery Lane, and Christopher Hatton, Elizabeth's chancellor, had his house in HATTON GARDEN.

But the neighbourhood of the Strand [1] was the favourite residence of the great nobles, probably because the execrable condition of the roads rendered necessary the use of the Thames as the chief highway. At the beginning of the seven-teenth century the Strand must have presented the appear-ance of a continuous line of palaces, with gardens sloping down to the brink of the then silvery Thames. ESSEX STREET,

[1] See Cunningham, *Handbook for London*, pp. 783, 784.

DEVEREUX COURT, and ESSEX COURT, point out the spot where Elizabeth's favourite plotted and rebelled. The great space which is now occupied by SURREY STREET, HOWARD STREET, NORFOLK STREET, and ARUNDEL STREET, is a proof of the wide extent of the demesne attached to Arundel House, the residence of ' all the Howards '. The present SOMERSET HOUSE stands on the site of the palace built by the Protector Somerset, which afterwards became the residence of Henrietta Maria, queen of Charles I. Those nests of poverty and crime called CLAREHOUSE COURT, CLARE MARKET, and NEWCASTLE STREET, replace the mansion and gardens of Clare House, the residence of the Earls of Clare, afterwards Dukes of Newcastle. Near CRAVEN BUILDINGS, Drury Lane, stood the house of Lord Craven, a soldier of the Thirty Years' War, celebrated as the hero of Creutznach, and the champion of the Winter Queen. CLIFFORD'S INN and GRAY'S INN were the mansions of the Barons Clifford and Gray de Wilton. Peter de Savoy, uncle of Eleanor of Provence, the queen of Henry III., built for himself a palace at the SAVOY, which was afterwards converted into a conventual establishment. Facing each other, on opposite sides of the Strand, stood the mansions of the two sons of the great Sir William Cecil, Lord Burleigh. The elder son, created Earl of Exeter, occupied his father's house, which has now made way for BURLEIGH STREET, EXETER HALL, and EXETER STREET ; while the younger son, Sir Robert Cecil, Earl of Salisbury, built Salisbury House on the site where CECIL STREET and SALISBURY STREET are now standing.[1]

In close proximity to the houses of the Cecils was, as we have seen, the ' convent garden ', belonging to the abbot and monks of Westminster. After the dissolution of the monasteries this property came into the hands of the Russell family, and here the Earls of Bedford built a mansion, which, about a century and a half ago, gave place to SOUTHAMPTON STREET, RUSSELL STREET, TAVISTOCK STREET, and BEDFORD STREET. The Russells then removed to Bloomsbury, where BEDFORD SQUARE, SOUTHAMPTON STREET, RUSSELL SQUARE, TAVISTOCK SQUARE, and CHENIES STREET, preserve the memory of

---

[1] The Adelphi [i.e. ' Brothers ' in Greek] with the five streets—Robert Street, John Street, George Street, James Street, and Adam Street, was built in 1760, by four brothers of the name of Adam.

the great house they occupied. SYDNEY ALLEY, and LEICESTER SQUARE, remind us of another historic name—that of Robert Sydney, Earl of Leicester, whose house stood on what is now called LEICESTER PLACE. GEORGE STREET, VILLIERS STREET, DUKE STREET, OR ALLEY,[1] and BUCKINGHAM STREET, preserve every syllable of the name and titles of ' Steenie ',the fortunate and unfortunate favourite of James I. and ' baby Charles '. Of all the palaces which once lined the Strand, Northumberland House is the only one which still remains.

If the Strand is full of memories of the statesmen and favourites of Elizabeth, PICCADILLY [2] brings us to the time of the Restoration. ALBEMARLE STREET and CLARGES Street,[3] ARLINGTON Street and BENNET Street,[4] The CLARENDON, CORK Street,[5] COVENTRY Street,[6] DOVER Street, JERMYN Street and ST. ALBAN'S Place,[7] SACKVILLE Street and DORSET Place,[8] CLEVELAND Row,[9] KING Street, CHARLES Street, St. JAMES' Street, DUKE Street, YORK Street, and The ALBANY,[10] are in convenient proximity to PALL MALL, and the MALL in St. James's Park, where the courtiers from whom these streets derived their names played at *Paille Maille* while the merry monarch fed his ducks.

There are a few scattered names to remind us of persons and events memorable in later times. HARLEY Street, OXFORD Street, HENRIETTA Street, CAVENDISH Square, and HOLLES Street, take their names from Harley, Earl of Oxford, and his wife Lady Henrietta Cavendish Holles. HANS Place and SLOANE Street bear the names of Sir Hans Sloane, who invested his fees in the purchase of the manor of Chelsea, and in the formation of a collection of natural curiosities as celebrated as Harley's collection of MSS. or the marbles of the Earl of Arundel. PIMLICO takes its name from a celebrated character of a very different order—one Ben Pimlico, who

---

[1] Now improved away.   See Stanley, *Lecture on the Study of Modern History*, p. 362.
[2] So called from Piccadilla Hall, a shop for the sale of piccadillas, the fashionable peaked or turn-over collars.
[3] Monk, Duke of Albemarle, and Nan Clarges, Duchess of Albemarle.
[4] Henry Bennet, Earl of Arlington.
[5] Boyle, Earl of Cork.
[6] Lord Keeper Coventry.
[7] Henry Jermyn, Earl of St. Albans, one of the heroes of Grammont's Memoirs.
[8] Edward Sackville, Earl of Dorset.
[9] The ' beautiful fury,' Barbara Villiers, Duchess of Cleveland, mistress of Charles II.
[10] Charles II., and James, Duke of York and Albany.

kept a suburban tavern, first at Hoxton, but afterwards transferred to the neighbourhood of Chelsea.[1]

The dates at which other streets were built can, in many cases, be determined by the names they bear. If the SAVOY reminds of the queen of Henry III., PORTUGAL Street, Lincoln's Inn, carries us to the time of the marriage of Charles II. QUEEN ANNE Street, MARLBOROUGH Street, HANOVER, Square, Great GEORGE Street, REGENT Street, KING WILLIAM Street, and VICTORIA Street, afford dates, more or less definite, of certain metropolitan extensions or improvements ; while BLENHEIM Street, QUEBEC Street, VIGO Street, WATERLOO BRIDGE, and TRAFALGAR Square, are instances of that system of nomenclature which has been so extensively carried out in Paris.

---

[1] The MALAKOFF, in like manner, was called from a tavern kept by Alexander Ivano-vitch Malakoff, a ropemaker discharged for drunkenness from the arsenal at Sebastopol. Strange origin for a ducal title. See Charnock, *Local Etymology*, pp. 172, 210.

CHAPTER XII

HISTORIC SITES

Places of popular assembly—Runnimede—Moot-hill—Detmold—The Scandinavian ' things ' or parliaments—The Thingvellir of Iceland—The Thing walls and Dingwells of Great Britain—Tynwald Hill in the Isle of Man—Battle-fields: Lichfield, Battle, Slaughter—Conflicts with the Danes—Eponymic Names—Myths of Early English History—Carisbrooke—Hengist and Horsa—Cissa—Ælle—Cerdic—Offa—Maes Garmon—British Chieftains—Valetta—Alexander—Names of the Roman Emperors—Modern Names of this Class.

IN the preceding chapter it has been shown how the history of a great city tends to perpetuate itself in its street-names. It would be easy, did space permit, to apply the same method of investigation to other cities, such as Paris,[1] Rome, or Athens. We might show, from the evidence of names, how Paris was originally confined to the little island in the Seine upon which the cathedral of Nôtre Dame now stands ; and how the LOUVRE was at first a hunting-seat; and the TUILERIES a tile-yard (French *tuile*, a tile). The names of the Palatine, the Vatican, and the Janiculum, of the Forum, and the Latin Gate at Rome, or of the Ceramicus, the Acropolis, and the Pnyx at Athens, would prove similarly suggestive. [2]

But the instance of London may suffice as an example of the value of local names in city history, and in this chapter we will rather pursue another department of the subject and collect the names of various scattered HISTORIC SITES—names which conserve the remembrance of historic personages, which denote the localities of great battles, or of places otherwise memorable in the history of the human race.

[1] This has been imperfectly attempted for Paris in a work by M. Ferdinand Heuzey, entitled, *Curiosités de la Cité de Paris, Histoire Etymologique de ses Rues*, etc. Paris, 1864.
[2] There are monographs of greater or less value on the street-names of the cities of Brunswick, Heiligenstadt, Hildesheim, Köln, Nuremberg, and Amsterdam. A curious list of German street-names will be found in Förstemann, *Deut. Ortsnamen*, pp. 167–169.

The places where popular self-government has at any time been exercised, are frequently indicated by local names.

RUNNIMEDE, the ' meadow of the runes ', was the ancient Anglo-Saxon field of council ; [1] and, on the spot thus consecrated to national liberty, the privileges of the great feudatories of England were afterwards secured by the Magna Charta.

In Scotland the ancient place of assembly was the MOTE HILL at Scone, near the ancient capital of Scotland.[2] In the midst of the town of Hawick there is a singular conical mound called the MOAT HILL. We may notice also the names of the MOOT HILL at the eastern end of Lyne Bridge, and the MOTE OF THE MARK in Galloway. On the confines of the Lake District, there are hills called MOUTAY and CAERMOTE ; and there is a MOOT-HILL at Naseby, all of which have probably served as the meeting-places of assemblies.[3]

The Stannary Court of the Duchy of Cornwall is an assembly which represents, in continuous succession, the local courts of the ancient Britons. The court was formerly held in the open air, on the summit of CROKERN TOR,[4] where the traveller may still see concentric tiers of seats hewn out of the rock. The name of Crokern Tor seems to point to a deliberative assembly,[5] and WISTMAN'S WOOD, in the immediate neighbourhood, suggests the wisdom traditionally imputed to the grave and reverend seniors who took part in the debates. [?]

In Germany there are several places called Ditmold. We find the names DETMOLD, DIETMALE, RODENDITMOL, and KIRCHDITMOLD. These were all places of popular assembly, as the names imply. The first portion of the name is *diet*, people, which we have in the name of Deutschland.[6] The suffix is *mal*, a place of assembly, or a court of justice.[7]

---

[1] Matthew of Westminster, A.D. 1215.

[2] This, perhaps the most interesting historical memorial in Scotland, has been recently removed, to improve the view from the drawing-room window ! Palgrave, *Normandy and England*, vol. iv. p. 336.

[3] Ferguson, *Northmen in Cumberland*, p. 33 ; Pennant, *Scotland*, vol. iii. p. 115.

[4] See Gough's Camden, vol. i. pp. 43, 49 ; Murray, *Handbook of Devon*, p. 95.

[5] We have the Welsh word *gragan*, to speak loud, whence [?] comes the English verb to *croak*, to make a loud noise like a frog or raven. The *creak*ing of a door and the name of the corn*crake* are from the same root. Compare the Sanskrit *kruç*, to call out, the Greek κρώζω, and the Latin *crocire*. See Diefenbach, *Vergleichendes Wörterb.* vol. ii. 591 ; *Celtica*, Glossary, No. 184 ; Whitaker, *History of Manchester*, vol. ii. p. 313.

[6] See p. 42, *supra*.

[7] Piderit, *Ortsnamen*, pp. 309, 310 ; Förstemann, *Die Deutschen Ortsnamen*, p. 95 ; Diefenbach, *Vergleich. Wörterb.* vol. ii. pp. 59, 706.

But the most noticeable traditions of ancient liberties are associated with the places where the *Things*,[1] the judicial and legislative assemblies of the Scandinavian nations, were wont to meet. These institutions, of which we find traces in all the regions colonized by the Northmen, were derived from the parent country, Norway, where there was an *Althing*, or general assembly, and four district *Things* for the several provinces.[2] The Norwegian parliament still goes by the name of the *Stor-thing*, or great council. The *Thing* usually met on some island, hill, or promontory, where its deliberations could be carried on secure from lawless disturbance.

The Swedish parliament used to assemble on a mound near Upsala, which still bears the name of TINGSHOGEN (*Thinghough*).[3]

One of the chief attractions for Icelandic tourists is a vast sunken lava-plain which bears the name of the THINGVELLIR [4] or 'council plains'. In the midst of this plain there is an isolated area, some two hundred feet long and fifty broad, which is guarded on every side by deep rifts,[5] produced by the cooling of the lava. Across these rifts the sole access is by one narrow bridge of rock. This spot, so well guarded by nature, is called the ALTHING, and was the assembly-place of the 'general council' of the whole island. A mound, in the midst of the Althing, bears the name of the LÖGBERG,[6] the sacred 'hill of laws', from whose summit, for nine hundred years, all the enactments of the Althing had to be promulgated before they could receive the force of laws.[7]

---

1 The word *thing* is derived from the Old Norse *tinga*, to speak, and is allied to the English word *to think*. See Ihre, *Glossarium Suiogothicum*, vol. ii. p. 901 ; Haldorsen, *Islandske Lexicon*, vol. ii. p. 407. The bodyguard of the Danish kings was called *thingamanna lith*, its chief duty being to escort the monarch at these assemblies.

2 Laing, *Heimskringla*, vol. i. pp. 103, 114–119.

3 Ibid, vol. i. pp. 89, 117.

4 Often wrongly called the Thingvalla. This, however, is the genitive case. The word *völlr* means a plain or field. The root is the Norse *völr*, a stick or post (Mæso-Gothie *valus*: cf the English *goal*, a winning-*post*). The *völlr* takes its name from the nature of the inclosing fence, like *ton*, *ham*, *garth*, etc. See pp. 85–87, and the notes on the words *bally* and *bail*, pp. 175, 193, *supra* ; also Diefenbach, *Vergleich. Wörterb.* vol. i. p. 179.

5 A tradition which still lingers on the spot avers that during the battle which ensued upon the hearing of the suit for the burning of Njal's house, Flosi, the leader of the burners, took a wild and desperate leap across one of these chasms. Dasent, *Burnt Njal*, vol. i. p. cxxviii.

6 The upper chamber of the Norwegian parliament is called the *Lag*. Crichton, *Scandinavia*, vol. i. p. 158.

7 The Thingvellir have been described sixteen times by recent travellers. Perhaps the most graphic accounts are those given by Dasent, *Burnt Njal*, vol. i. pp. cxxv.– cxxxix. ; *Norsemen in Iceland*, p. 207 ; Dufferin. *Letters from High Latitudes*, pp. 84– 95 ; and Baring-Gould, *Iceland*, pp. 67–71. The Icelandic parliament, with full legisla-

Each of the twelve districts into which Iceland is divided had also its *Thing*, where the peasant-nobles carried into effect their privileges of local self-government. THINGANES, THINGSKALER, ARNESTHING, THINGORE, and THINGMULI, were, as the names denote, places at which some of these subordinate assemblies were accustomed to be held.

The Northmen introduced their *Things* into England. The very name survives among us as a household word. A ' meeting ', according to Dr. Dasent, is the *mot thing*, or assembly of freeholders, and at the ' HUSTINGS ', or *house things*, the duly qualified householders still assemble to delegate their legislative powers to their representatives in parliament.[1]

In the Danelagh, as well as in most of the detached Scandinavian colonies, we find local names which prove the former existence of these *Things*.

In the Shetland Islands, SANDSTHING, AITHSTHING, DELTING, NESTING, and LUNZIESTING, were the places of assembly for the local *Things* of the several islands,[2] while TINGWALL seems to have been the spot where the *Althing*, or general assembly, was held. In a fresh-water lake, in the parish of Tingwall, there is an island still called the SAWTING. On it are four great stones, the seats for the officers of the court, and the access is by stepping stones laid in the shallow waters of the lake.[3] In the Shetlands, the old Norwegian laws are even now administered at open courts of justice, which still go by the ancient name of *Lawtings*.

In the Ross-shire colony we find the names of DINGWALL and TAIN,[4] while TINWALD Hill, near Dumfries, was the assembly place of the colonists who settled on the northern shore of the Solway.[5] Not far from the centre of the Cheshire colony in the Wirall, we find the village of THINGWALL.[6] Near Wrabness, within the limits of the little colony in the northeast of Essex, we find a place whose name, DENGEWELL,

tive and judicial powers, continued to meet at the Thingvellir till the year 1800. The legislative powers have now ceased ; the judicial functions were restored in 1845, since which time the meeting-place has been at Reykjavik.

[1] Dasent, *Burnt Njal*, vol. i. p. li. ; Worsaae, *Danes*, p. 19.

[2] These were usually held in the centre of circles of upright stones, perhaps the erection of an earlier race. See Wilson, *Pre-historic Annals*, p. 113 ; Poste, *Brit. Researches*, p. 256 ; Worsaae, *Danes*, p. 232.

[3] Martin, *Description of the Western Isles*, p. 383 ; quoted by Train, *Isle of Man*, vol. i. p. 299.

[4] Worsaae, *Danes and Norwegians*, p. 260.

[5] Ib. p. 204 ; Crichton, *Scandinavia*, vol. i. p. 158 ; See p. 123, *supra*.

[6] Worsaae, *Danes*, p. 70.

probably marks the spot where the local jurisdiction was exercised. The three neighbouring Danish parishes of Thorp le Soken, Walton le Soken, and Kirby le Soken, possessed the privilege of holding a *soke,* or local court, independent of the jurisdiction of the hundred—a vestige, probably, of their ancient Scandinavian franchises.

In the absence of all documentary evidence, I was inclined to believe that the apparently Danish names in Devonshire [1] must be explained from Saxon sources ; I felt that I should hardly be justified in placing a Scandinavian colony in that county, so far removed from their compatriots in the Danelagh. But all cause for hesitation was removed by the accidental discovery of an isolated farmhouse bearing the name of DINGWELL. It stands on a plateau, steeply scarped on three sides, and about a mile from the village of THUR-SHEL-TON, a name every syllable of which is of the Icelandic type, denoting the *tun* or enclosure round the *skaaler,* or wooden booths, which were usually erected at some little distance from the *Thingvellir* for the convenience of persons attending the meeting. The *Thing* was inaugurated by sacrifices and religious ceremonies, which enables us to understand why the name of the deity Thor should appear in the first syllable of this name Thurshelton.[2] These two names, Thurshelton and Dingwell, surrounded as they are by names of the Norse type, seem to prove conclusively [3] that the Northmen must have settled in this remote corner of the island in sufficient numbers to establish their usual organized self-government.

In the Danelagh we meet with several places bearing names of the same class, which may, with greater or less certainty, be regarded as meeting places of local *Things.* In Northamptonshire we have, near Kettering, a place called FINEDON, which was anciently written Thingdon, and there is a place called DINGLEY near Market Harborough. Not far from Stamford we find TINWELL in the county of Rutland, and TINGEWICK, in the north of Buckinghamshire. In Yorkshire,

---

[1] See pp. 125, 126, *supra.*

[2] Near Tingwall, in Shetland, we find SCALLOWAY, or Booth Bay. Worsaae, *Danes,* p. 232. Mr. Ferguson thinks Porting*scale,* near Keswick, is an analogous name. *Northmen,* p. 31.

[3] This conclusion, it is fair to add, has been ably controverted by Mr. King, in *Notes and Queries,* Nov. 5th, 1864. He would derive the name of Thurshelton from a neighbouring stream called the Thistle Brook, and is of opinion that all the apparently Norse names in Devonshire may be explained from Saxon sources. *Valeat quantum.*

there are TINSLEY near Rotherham, and THWING near Bridlington. In Durham, on the extreme northern border of the Danelagh, we find DINSDALE,[1] a place which is almost entirely surrounded by one of the bends of the Tees, and is thus well protected from hostile intrusion, as is the case with so many of these sites. I cannot discover the place where the Lincolnshire *Thing* assembled, unless indeed it be at THIMBLEBY or LEGBOURN.

In the Scandinavian district of Cumberland and Westmoreland, the word *Thing* does not appear in any local name ; but the Vale of LEGBERTHWAITE, no doubt, contained the *lögberg*, or ' hill of laws ', from which the local enactments were promulgated.[2]

By far the most interesting of these ancient Westminsters is TYNWALD HILL in the Isle of Man. Less than a century ago the Isle of Man preserved a sort of *quasi* independence of the British crown, and it was only in the year 1764 that the Duke of Athol parted with the last of the royal rights, which had descended to him from the ancient Norwegian kings. But though the representative of the Norwegian jarls has divested himself of his regal prerogatives, the descendants of the vikings still retain a shadow of their ancient legislative powers. The old Norse *Thing* has survived continuously in the Isle of Man to the present day, though in Iceland, in Norway, and in Denmark, its functions have been intermitted, or have long ceased. The three estates still assemble every year, and no laws are valid in the island unless they have first been duly proclaimed from the summit of TYNWALD HILL.[3] This is an ancient mound some eighteen feet in height, and constructed with four concentric circular stages, whose diamters are, respectively, 80, 27, 15, and 7 feet.[4]

The ancient place of the coronation of the kings of England was KINGSTON in Surrey, where, in the centre of the town, is still to be seen the stone on which the Saxon monarchs sat while the ceremony was performed.[5] TRONDHJEM, or DRON-

---

[1] Tindale in Northumberland is probably the Tyne dale.
[2] Ferguson, *Northmen in Cumberland*, p. 32.
[3] Palgrave, *English Commonwealth*, vol. i. p. 122 ; Worsaae, *Danes*, p. 295 ; Crichton, *Scandinavia*, vol. i. p. 158. A full account of the powers of the estates, and of the ceremonies observed when they are convened, will be found in Train, *Isle of Man*, vol. ii pp. 189–201.
[4] Train, *Isle of Man*, vol. i. pp. 271–273 ; Poste, *Brit. Res.* p. 256.
[5] [Compare $\beta\alpha\sigma\iota\text{-}\lambda\epsilon\acute{\nu}\text{-}\varsigma$, king, according to Curtius (i. 452) the ' Stone-treader.']

THEIM, was in like manner the 'throne home', or coronation seat of the kings of Norway,[1] and KÖNIGSBERG,[2] in the extreme east of Prussia, shows the way in which that agglomerated kingdom has extended itself westward from the ancient central seat of the grand master of the Teutonic Knights.[3] KINGSGATE, in the Isle of Thanet, marks the spot where Charles II. landed after his exile ; and QUEENBOROUGH, in the Isle of Sheppey, is a proof of the development of the English navy in the time of Edward III. The manor of Hull, or KINGSTON-UPON-HULL, was purchased by Edward I. ; and Coningsby, Coneysby, Conington, Cunningham, Kingthorpe, Kinsby, King's Lynn, Lyme Regis, and many similar names, denote the residences, or manors, of Saxon, Danish, and English monarchs.

Local names often conserve the memory of famous battles, or sometimes they tell us of forgotten contests of which no other memorial remains.

Probably the greatest reverse ever suffered by the Roman arms was the defeat which Hannibal inflicted on Flaminius at Thrasymene. The brook which flows through this scene of slaughter is still called the SANGUINETTO, and the name of the neighbouring village of OSSAIA shows that the plain must have long been whitened by the bones of the fallen Romans.[4]

The Teutonic division of the Cimbric horde which invaded Italy, was annihilated by Marius in the year 102 B.C., and the slaughter is said to have reached the immense number of 100,000 men. The battlefield afterwards bore the name of the Campi Putridi, a name which is preserved by the Provençal village of POURRIÈRES. The Temple of Victory built by the conqueror is now the parish church of St. VICTOIRE.[5]

Of the great battles which have changed the course of the world's history, few are more important than the defeat of the Huns by the Emperor Otho in the tenth century. This

---

1 It is possible, however, that the root may be the same as that of Thrandia. Crichton, *Scandinavia*, vol. i. p. 32.

2 Mone, *Celtische Forschungen*, p. 265, makes Argos the equivalent of Königsberg ! *arg*, a prince ; *ais*, a fortress ! !

3 There are ten Königsbergs in Germany. See Buttmann, *Ortsnamen*, p. 38 ; Förstemann, *Ortsnamen*, p. 299.

4 Dennis, *Etruria*, vol. ii. p. 457 ; Duke of Buckingham, *Private Diary*, vol. iii. pp. 658–666.

5 Sheppard, *Fall of Rome*, p. 164.

battle, regarded as to the magnitude of its results, can only be compared with the overthrow of the Saracens by Charles Martel. The one rescued Christianity, the other saved civilization. The Magyar host, like that of the Saracens, was all but exterminated, and the name of the LEICHFELD, or 'Field of Corpses', near Augsburg, informs us of the precise locality of the fearful slaughter.[1]

Our two English LICHFIELDS,[2] one in Staffordshire[3] and the other in Hampshire, where are seven barrows,[4] as well as LECKHAMPSTEAD in Buckinghamshire, are probably memorials of battles of which history has preserved no certain record. The chroniclers tell us that in the year 1173, an army of 10,000 Flemings under Robert, Earl of Leicester, was almost totally annihilated at LACKFORD, near Bury St. Edmund's by Richard Lucy, Chief Justice of England. LECKFORD in Hampshire may also not improbably indicate the site of a bloody battle which was gained by Cymen over the Britons in this immediate neighbourhood.

The final overthrow of the Britons by Athelstan in the year 936 occurred at a place called BOLLEIT, in Cornwall. This name means in Cornish the 'House of Blood'.

The name of BATTLEFIELD,[5] about three miles from Shrewsbury, is a memorial of the decisive contest which Shakespeare has so vividly brought before us; and an additional memorial of the fiery Welsh chieftain is found in an ancient tumulus near Corwen, which bears the name of Dinas Mont Owain Glyndwr, and from the summit of which he is said to have been in the habit of gazing down the valley of Dee.

Close to Bannocburn is the inclosure of BLOODY FOLD, where the Earl of Gloucester fell, and the name of GILLIES HILL commemorates the station of the camp followers who created the fatal panic.

Of the destruction of the Spanish Armada, we have a geo-

---

[1] Palgrave, *Normandy and England*, vol. ii. pp. 658–666.

[2] The German word *leich*, a corpse, is preserved in the *lychgate* of our churchyards, where the corpse awaits the approach of the priest; and in the *lykewake*, or funeral feast, which is celebrated in some parts of Scotland. See Drake, *Shakspeare and his Times*, vol. i. p. 234. [Cf. Lichmere, *infra* 220.]

[3] The city arms are a field surcharged with dead bodies. Tradition refers the name to the martyrdoms of a thousand Christian converts. See Fuller, *Church History*, vol. i. p. 34. [Mr. Duignan holds Lichfield to be the ' field of the leche ' or morass, *Staffordshire Placenames*, 94.]

[4] Gough's Camden, vol. i. p. 205.

[5] The collegiate church of Battlefield was founded by Henry IV. in commemoration of the victory. Pennant, *Wales*, vol. ii. p. 411.

graphical reminiscence in the name of PORT-NA-SPANIEN in Ireland, where one of the galleons of the Invincible Armada was dashed to pieces.[1]

There is a place called BATTLE FLATS north of Bosworth, though perhaps hardly near enough to be confidently referred to as the scene of the struggle. CROWN HILL, a small eminence on the plain, is pointed out as the spot where Stanley placed Richard's crown on the head of Henry VII.

The flying cavaliers, after the defeat at Naseby, were overtaken and cut to pieces at a place now called SLAUGHTER-FORD, where the road to Harborough crosses the Welland ; [2] and a part of the route by which Monmouth's army marched to the night attack at Sedgemoor, still goes by the name of WAR LANE.[3]

The names of the town of BATTLE in Sussex, and of BATTLE FLATS near Stamford Bridge, have already been mentioned as instances in point.[4] SENLAC (*Sangue Lac*), the Norman name of the battle-field of Hastings, still survives as a local name in the neighbourhood of the town of Battle. STANDARD HILL close by, is said to be the place where the Conqueror raised his standard previous to the commencement of the engagement, and MONTJOIE, one of the four wards of the town, com-memorates the spot to which he rode in triumph at the conclu-sion of the fight.[5]

About six miles south of Poictiers there is a place called MAUPERTUIS, a name supposed to commemorate the exact site of the battle-field which proved so disastrous to the chivalry of France. Frederick the Great's victory over the Austrians at Hohenfriedberg, has given the name of SIEGESBERG, or ' Victory Hill ', to an eminence which stands within the confines of the battlefield.[6]

The terror which was inspired by the inroads of the Danes, and the joy with which their discomfiture was hailed, is evidenced by numerous local names, which are often associated with traditionary battle-legends which still linger among the

1 Goldwin Smith, *Irish History and Irish Character*, p. 85.
2 James, *Northamptonshire*, p. 50.
3 Macaulay, *History of England*, vol. i. p. 608.
4 See p. 5, *supra*.
5 Hartshorne, *Salopia Antiqua*, p. 241 ; Palgrave, *Normandy and England*, vol. iii. p. 406.
6 Carlyle, *Frederick the Great*, vol. iv. p. 137.

surrounding villagers. Such a tradition is connected with a camp in Hampshire called Ambrose Hole, hard by which runs a rivulet called DANESTREAM.[1] At SLAUGHTERFORD in Wiltshire,[2] and at BLEDLOE[3] (*bloody hlaw*) in Buckinghamshire, there are traditions that great slaughters of the Danes took place.

In the Saxon Chronicle (A.D. 1016) we have an account of the great victory gained by Cnut over Eadmund Ironside, which led to the division of the kingdom between the two monarchs. The Chronicle places the battle at Assandun in Essex. Near Billericay there is a place now called Assingdon, and in the neighbourhood we find twenty barrows, and the names of CANEWDON and BATTLEBRIDGE.[1]

On CAMPHILL near Rochdale, the Danes are said to have encamped on the eve of the battle that was fought in the neighbourhood ; and KILLDANES, the name of the valley below Camphill, tells us the story of that bloody day.[5]

Near Stow-on-the-Wold in Gloucestershire is a Danish earthwork called Bury Camp, and the adjacent villages bear the names of SLAUGHTER and LEACH.[6] In a field called KNAP DANE in the parish of Nettlecombe, a vast quantity of bones was found, supposed to be those of the Danes who landed at Watchet in the year 918.[7]

At DANEBURY near Chelmsford, and at DANES-BANKS in the parish of Chartham in Kent[8] the outlines of camps are still to be traced. GRAVENHILL is also the legendary scene of a battle with the Danes. It is surrounded with entrenchments, and is covered with mounds, which are probably the graves of the fallen warriors.[9] At DANES GRAVES on the Yorkshire wolds numerous small tumili are still visible.[10] The name of DANESFORD, in Shropshire, is supposed to be a memorial of the Danes who wintered at the neighbouring town of Quatford in the year 896.[11] DANTSEY or 'Danes Island' in Wiltshire, was formerly the property of the

---

[1] Gough's Camden, vol. i. p. 187.
[2] Ibid, vol. i. p. 141.   [3] Ibid. vol. ii. p. 41.
[4] Gough's Camden, vol. ii. p. 131.
[5] Davies, in *Philological Transactions*, for 1855, p. 261.
[6] Ibid, vol. i. p. 407.   [7] Ibid, vol. i. p. 90.
[8] Ibid, vol. i. p. 354.
[9] Kennett, *Parochial Antiquities*, vol. i. p. 50.
[10] Worsaae, *Danes and Norwegians*, p. 40.
[11] Hartshorne, *Salopia Antiqua*, p. 260.

family of the Easterlings ,[1] a name usually given to the Vikings from the East.

WARE in Hertfordshire seems to have been the place at which Alfred constructed his *weir* across the river Lea, in order to cut off the retreat of the Danish fleet.[2]

On Brent Knoll near Athelney in Somersetshire, is a camp which tradition ascribes to Alfred, and at the foot of the hill, half a mile from its summit, stands the village of BATTLEBURY.[3] There is also a camp near Salisbury which goes by the name of BATTLESBURY, and there is a place called BATTLEWIC near Colchester.

By the side of the Dee in Scotland there is an ancient earthwork called NORMAN (Northmen's) DIKES, in the front of which there is a piece of land which bears the name of BLOODY STRIPE.[4] Near Burnham in Norfolk there is a camp surrounded by tumuli, the road leading to which goes by the name of BLOODGATE.[5] At Chelsham in Surrey there is a Roman camp crowning the summit of a knoll called BOTLE or BATLE HILL.[6] Two Roman camps in Forfarshire go by the names of BATTLE DIKES and WAR DIKES.[7] There is a camp near Caterham called WAR COPPICE; and the name of CATERHAM itself may perhaps be referred to the Celtic word *cath*, battle. CADBURY, a name which occurs in Somersetshire and in Devon, means the 'Battle entrenchment'. CATERTHUN, a remarkable Celtic fortress which overlooks Strathmore, is no doubt 'Battle Hill'. The numerous Cat Stanes in Scotland are supposed to be memorials of battles. Such are the CATT STANE in Kirkliston parish, and the CAIG STONE near Edinburgh.[8] From the Anglo-Saxon *camp*, battle, we have a few names like CAMPTON and KEMPSTON in Bedfordshire.[9]

In the case of several of these battle-fields we find tradi-

---

1 Gough's Camden, vol. i. p. 130.
2 St. John, *Four Conquests*, vol. i. pp. 298, 299 ; Turner, *Anglo-Saxons*, vol. i. p. 398 ; Gough's Camden, vol. ii. p. 68.
3 Gough's Camden, vol. i. p. 103.
4 Chalmers, *Caledonia*, vol. i. p. 125.
5 Gough's Camden, vol. ii. p. 197.
6 Ibid, vol. i. p. 256.
7 Chalmers, *Caledonia*, vol. i. pp. 148, 176.
8 The name of the Caturiges, 'the battle kings', and the personal names of Catullus, Cadwallon, Cadwallader, St. Chad, and Katleen, contain this word. See Zeuss, *Grammatica Celtica*, vol. i. p. 6 ; Yonge, *Christian Names*, vol. ii. p. 93 ; Wilson, *Pre-historic Annals of Scotland*, pp. 95. 412 ; Monkhouse, *Etymologies*, p. 58.
9 Monkhouse, *Etymologies*, pp. 6, 20.

tions which assign a local habitation to the names of British chieftains or Anglo-Saxon kings. It is possible that in some of these instances minute fragments of historic truth have been conserved, but it is needless to say that the greatest caution must be exercised as to the conclusions which we allow ourselves to draw. The traditions are generally vague and obscure, and the personages whose names are associated with these sites have often only a mythical, or, to speak technically, an *eponymic* existence. This convenient phrase is used to convey the suggestion that a personal name has been evolved by popular speculation to account for some geographical term, the true meaning of which has not been understood.

A full discussion of this subject would form a curious and important chapter in what we may call the history of History.

Most nations have supposed themselves to be descended from some mythical or eponymic ancestor. The Lydians, the Phœnicians, the Pelasgians, the Dorians, the Æolians, the Hellenes, the Sicilians, and the Italians, have respectively traced themselves to mythical personages whom they called Lydus, Phœnix, Pelasgus, Dorus, Æolus, Hellen, Siculus, and Italus. Rome was said to have been built by Romulus ; Nineveh by Ninus ; Memphis by Menes. When we come down to a later time we are encountered by the still more extravagant absurdities which fill the pages of Geoffrey of Monmouth, Layamon, Wace, Matthew Paris, and Matthew of Westminster, by whom the origin of all the nations and cities of Europe is traced to heroes of the Trojan war. We are gravely told that France takes its name from Francus, a son of Hector, and Britain from Brute, Prydain, or Pryd, a son of Æneas ; that Lisbon (Olisopo) was built by Ulysses ; and Paris by the well-known son of Priam. Tours was the burial-place of a Trojan named Turonus, and Troyes was, of course, a colony from Troy. Nuremberg was built by Nero, and Prussia takes its name from one Prussus, a brother of Augustus. But these are modest pretensions when compared with that of the Scots, who claimed to be descended from Scota, a daughter of Pharaoh, while the Saracens are assigned to Sarah the wife of Abraham.[1]

[1] See a series of papers by Pott, in Kuhn's *Zeitschrift für Vergleich. Sprachforschung*, entitled ' Mytho-Etymologie ' ; Grimm, *Geschichte d. Deut. Spr.* pp. 776, 784 ; Buckle, *History of Civilization*, vol. i. pp. 284–286, 295 ; Wright, on ' Geoffrey of Monmouth ', *Essays*, vol. i. p. 216 ; Lewis, *Credibility of Early Roman History*, vol. i. p. 278 ; Welsford,

These wild absurdities are mostly the creation of authors of a late date, and seldom conceal any esoteric truths. The case is often different with the earliest legends. Thus we are told that Pedias was the wife of Cranaus, one of the mythical kings of Attica. Under this disguise we recognize a statement of the fact that Attica is formed by the union of the mountain district (κραναός, rocky), and the plain (πεδιάς, level).[1]

But the extravagances of Geoffrey of Monmouth, or the more recondite myths of Grecian history, concern us less nearly than the eponymic names which fill the earlier pages of Beda and the Saxon Chronicle. These narratives are still regarded as historical by the great mass of half-educated Englishmen,[2] who seem to have hardly a conception that, in the ordinary school histories of England, the chapter ' On the arrival of the Saxons ' relates the deeds of personages who, in all probability, have only an eponymic existence.

To take a few instances. The name of PORTSMOUTH undoubtedly dates from the time when the commodious harbour was used as a *portus* by the Romans. But when we read in the Saxon Chronicle that Portsmouth derives its name from a Saxon chieftain of the name of Port, who landed there, we conclude at once that the name of Port is eponymic, that no such personage ever existed except in the imagination of some early historical speculator. Again, CARISBROOKE, in the Isle of Wight, was anciently written *Wiht-gara-byrig*. Respecting the etymology of this name there can be little doubt.[3] *Wiht* is a corruption of Vectis, the Roman name of the island. The inhabitants of the island would be called *Wiht-ware*, and the chief town of the island would be called *Wiht-gara-byrig*, ' the burgh of the men of Wight ', just as Canterbury, or Cant-wara-byrig, is ' the burgh of the men of Kent '. But when the Saxon Chronicle asserts that Wiht-gara-byrig was the burgh of a Saxon chief named Wihtgar, who was buried there, we can entertain no doubt that the

English Language, pp. 6–16 ; Movers, *Die Phönizier*, part ii. vol. ii. p. 297 ; Verstegan, *Restitution*, p. 102 ; Davies, *Celtic Researches*, pp. 167, 169 ; Buttmann, *Mythologus*, vol. i. p. 219 ; vol. ii. pp. 172–193.

[1] See a paper by J. K[enrick], in the *Philological Museum*, vol. ii. p. 359 ; Pott, ' Mytho-Etymologie ', in Kuhn's *Zeitschrift*, vol. ix. p. 403.

[2] A well-known M.P. has lately, before a London audience, gravely reproduced the still more extravagant absurdities of Layamon and Geoffrey as veritable English history.

[3] See p. 50, *supra*.

name of Wihtgar, like that of Port, is eponymic.[1]   But we should undoubtedly be wrong were we to extend our scepticism to some other cases.   For instance, we read in a later and more historical portion of the Saxon Chronicle, and in the Latin version which bears the name of Florence, that King Harthacnut drank himself to death at a feast which Osgod Clapha, one of the great nobles of Wessex, gave in his house at Lambeth to celebrate the marriage of his daughter Gytha with Tovi the Proud.   In this case there is a very high probability that the London suburb of CLAPHAM takes its name from the *ham* of the Saxon thane.

Or to take another case of a somewhat different character. Near Christchurch, in Hampshire, there is a place called TYRRELL'S FORD, around which a tradition used to linger that here Tyrrell passed on the day of the death of Rufus.[2] There is nothing intrinsically improbable about this tradition, and Tyrrell is certainly not an eponymus.   We may even go so far as to lend an ear to the assertion that Jack Cade was killed at CAT STREET, near Heathfield in Sussex—especially when we find that the name was anciently written Cade Street.[3]

Bearing in mind, then, the necessity of great caution as to the eponymic character of many of the heroes who figure in Beda and the Saxon Chronicle, we may proceed to enumerate a few of the more conspicuous of the localized traditions of the Saxon conquest.

Whether the names of Hengist and Horsa are wholly eponymic, or whether there remains a substratum of historic fact, after all due concessions have been made to the demands of modern criticism, is a question respecting which scholars are not agreed.   But we find their names in many places. Thus at HENGISTBURY HEAD on the Hampshire coast, there is a large funeral barrow protected by an entrenchment; and a tumulus of flints at HORSTED, in Sussex, is said to mark the sepulchre of Horsa.[4]   There is also a mound near the castle wall of Conisbrough which bears the name of Hengist. Camden asserts that it was his tomb; and we learn from

---

[1] See Latham, *English Language*, vol. i. pp. 37–40.
[2] Aubrey, quoted in Gough's Camden, vol. i. p. 187.
[3] Ibid, vol. i. p. 295.
[4] Lappenberg, *Anglo-Saxon Kings*, vol. i. p. 72 ; Gough's Camden, vol. i. pp. 311, 336.

Polydore Virgil that in the sixteenth century a local tradition still survived respecting a great battle which had been fought upon the spot.[1] Henry of Huntingdon informs us that Hengist and Horsa fought a battle with the Picts and Scots at Stamford, in Lincolnshire. A local tradition affirms that the Saxons came from Kent by sea, and landed near Peterborough, after sailing up the Nene. This tradition is supported by the fact, that at about two miles from Peterborough there is an ancient entrenchment which goes by the name of HORSEY HILL.[2] There is a camp near Chesterford in Essex, called HINGESTON barrows.[3] We have also the names of HINKSEY near Oxford, anciently *Hengestesige* ; HENSTRIDGE in Somerset, anciently *Hengestesricg* ; [4] HINXWORTH in Hertfordshire, anciently *Haingesteworde* ; and HENGESTON, anciently *Hengestesdun*, in Cornwall. There are many other names of the same class. The numerous Horsleys and Hinkleys,[5] are probably only forest leys or pastures for horse or steed (*hengst*). Other names, such as two Horsteads in Sussex, and one in Norfolk, Horsham in Sussex and in Norfolk, Horsey in Norfolk, and Horsell in Sussex, certainly seem specially to connect some person, or persons, bearing the name of Horsa with the two English counties of Sussex and Norfolk.[6]

According to the Saxon Chronicle the kingdom of the South Saxons was founded by Ælle and his three sons, Cymen, Wlencing, and Cissa. If these names are not altogether eponymic, as is probably the case, the account in the Chronicle receives very remarkable confirmation from local names. The landing is said to have taken place at KEYNOR in Selsea, anciently *Cymenesora* [7] or Cymen's shore, where we may suppose the eldest son was left to guard the ships while the father and the brothers advanced into the interior.[8] We find the name of Ælle at ELSTEAD in Sussex and ELSTEAD in

---

[1] Haigh, *Conquest of Britain*, p. 257. This is an uncritical work, but contains a large store of carefully collected, and sometimes valuable facts.

[2] Ibid, p. 209.   [3] Gough's Camden, vol. ii. p. 141.

[4] *Codex Dipl.* No. 1002. [Elton, *Origins of Eng. Hist.*, 381.]

[5] Horsley in Surrey and Derby, Horseley in Gloucester and Stafford, and three in Northumberland ; Hursley in Hants (Horsanleah, *Cod. Dipl.* No. 180), and Hinkley in Leicester.

[6] We have also Hinxton in Cambridgeshire, Hensting in Hants, Hincksford in Stafford, Hinxhill in Kent, Hinckford in Essex, Hinchcliff in Yorkshire, as well as Horsey Isle in Essex, Horsall in Surrey, Horsdun in Hants, and many other similar names. See Haigh, *Conquest of Britain*, p. 151.

[7] See Dugdale, *Monast. Ang.* vol. vi. p. 1163 ; *Cod. Dipl.* No. 992.

[8] CUMNOR in Berks was anciently *Cumenora*. *Cod. Dipl.* No. 214 ; Dugdale, *Monast. Ang.* vol. i. p. 527.

Surrey.[1] The name of LANCING near Shoreham is certainly very remarkably coincident with that of Wlencing. The name of Cissa may be sought at CISSBURY, a rude camp on a lofty hill near Worthing,[2] as well as at another camp in Wiltshire called CHISBURY; also at CISSANHAM [3] in Hampshire, and at CHICHESTER, anciently *Cissan-ceaster*, the ' fortress of Cissa ', who, according to the Chronicle, succeeded in taking the old Roman city, and made it the capital of his kingdom of the South Saxons.[4]

The kingdom of Wessex was founded, we are told, by Cerdic, through whom Queen Victoria claims to be lineally descended from Woden ! The name of Cerdic we find at CHARFORD, anciently *Cerdices-ford*, where was fought the decisive battle which gave the Saxons the supremacy as far west as the Hampshire Avon.[5] The name of LICHMERE, the moor of corpses, not far from Charford, seems to mark the precise locality of the struggle, and is of a more historic character than many of the rest.[6] The nephew of Cerdic was the eponymic Wihtgar of Carisbrooke Castle, whose claims to an historical existence have already been discussed.

In SEWARDSTONE near Waltham Abbey we have, perhaps, the name of Seward, king of the East Saxons; and Offa, another king of the same people, had a palace and a tomb at OFFLEY near Hitchin.[7] Another Offa, king of the Mercians, had a palace at OFFENHAM in Worcestershire, and in 773 he is said to have gained a victory over Eadmund, king of Kent, at OTFORD on the Darent. The name of Wuffa, king of the East Angles, may perhaps be found at UFFORD in Suffolk. RENDLESHAM, in the same county, was in the seventh century the residence of Redwald, another king of the East Angles. Among other Anglian traditions we are told that king Atla of Norfolk was the founder of ATTLEBURY,[8] and that the name

1 There was another Ælle, founder of the Anglian kingdom of Northumbria. To him we may perhaps refer Ellakirk, Ellaby, Ellard, Ellerbeck, Ellerburn, and other Yorkshire names. Ellescroft is said to be the burial place of the Ælle who was killed in a battle with Regner Lodbrook. Worsaae, *Danes*, p. 33.

2 Gough's Camden, vol. i. p. 270.   3 *Codex Diplom.* No. 658.

4 Lappenberg, *Anglo-Saxon Kings*, vol. i. pp. 104–106; *Saxon Chronicle*, A.D. 490. There are the remains of a Saxon camp at Chichester.

5 *Saxon Chronicle*, A.D. 519; Lappenberg, *Anglo-Saxon Kings*, vol. i. p. 109. The locality of Cerdices-oora, where the Chronicle (A.D. 514) asserts that Cerdic landed, has not been satisfactorily identified. Perhaps it may be Charmouth in Dorset. See Haigh, *Conquest of Britain*, p. 312; Turner, *Anglo-Saxons*, vol. i. p. 271.

6 Gough's Camden, vol. i. p. 178. [Compare, *supra*, 212.]

7 Knapp, *English Roots*, pp. 11, 12; Gough's Camden, vol. ii. p. 66.

8 Lappenberg, *Anglo-Saxon Kings*, vol. i. p. 116.

of Bebbe, the queen of Ida of Northumbria, is to be found in *Bebban-burk*, now BAMBOROUGH, near Berwick-upon-Tweed.[1] Oswald, a Christian prince of Mercia, gave his name to OSWESTRY. The strong natural fortress of EDINBURGH bears the name of Edwin, king of Northumbria, who extended his kingdom to the shores of the Forth.[2]

Ammianus Marcellinus, a more trustworthy authority than the earlier portion of the Saxon Chronicle, says, that Valentinan sent over to Britain one Fraomarius, the king of the Bucinobantes, an Alemannic tribe near Mayence. These names are perhaps preserved at BRAMERTON and four BUCKENHAMS, all in Norfolk.[3]

Attempts have been made to identify the spots selected for an abode by other less distinguished settlers. The results are of course highly conjectural, to say the least, but they are perhaps sufficiently curious to justify the insertion of a few specimens in a note.[4]

The British traditions conserved in local names are often more trustworthy than those of the Saxon period. There is a high probability that MAES GARMON near Mold was the scene of the famous Alleluia victory, which was obtained by St. Garmon over the Picts. The good bishop placed the members of his church militant in ambush, and when the invaders were fairly entangled in the intricacies of the valley, a loud shout of Alleluia from the Welsh created a panic which enabled them to gain an easy but decisive victory.[5]

---

[1] Ibid, p. 119; *Saxon Chronicle*, A.D. 547.
[2] Dixon, *Fasti Ebor.* vol. i. p. 44.   [3] Haigh, *Conquest*, p. 163.
[4] Thus we have—

Personal name.	Ancient local name.	Modern local name.
Heremod	Harmodestone (*Domesday*)	Harmstone, *Lincoln.*
	Hermodesthorpe (*Domesday*)	Harmthorpe, *Lincoln.*
	Hermodesworde (*Domesday*)	Harmondsworth, *Mid.*
Heorogar	Herigerby (*Domesday*)	Harrowby, *Lincoln.*
Halga	Helgiby (*Domesday*)	Hellaby, *Yorks.*
	Helgefelt (*Domesday*)	Hellifield, *Yorks.*
	Halgeforde (*Cod. Dip.* No. 483)	Halliford, *Mid.*
	Halganstok (*Cod. Dip.* No. 701)	Halstock, *Dorset.*
Wærmund	Wærmundes hlæw (*Cod. Dip.* No. 1368)	Warmlow, *Worces.*
	Wærmundesham (*Cod. Dip.* No. 18)	Mundham, *Sussex.*
Scylf	Scylftun (*Cod. Dip.* No. 775)	Shilton, *Oxford.*
Bedca	Bedan ford (*Saxon Chronicle*)	Bedford.
Childeric	Hildericesham (*Domesday*)	Hildersham, *York.*

At Navistock, in *Essex*, and Navesby, in *Northamptonshire*, we seem to have a name like that of Hnæf, which we find in the Traveller's Tale. At Ripley, in *Yorkshire*, we have a founder Hryp, and there are also local names which have been supposed to refer to the semi-historic personages who were called Alr, Beonæt, Beowa, Brada, Cynfar, Fear, Hlyd, Hræfn, Hungar, Nægel, Pendere, Sumær, etc.—See Haigh, *Conquest*, pp. 150-160.
[5] Beda, *Hist. Ecc.* book i. cap. 20; Haigh, *Conquest*, p. 238; St. John, *Four Conquests of England*, vol. i. p. 56; Rees, *Welsh Saints*, pp. 121, 122.

The CARADOC, the most picturesque of the Shropshire hills, is crowned by an earthwork bearing the name of Caer Caradoc, and here, as tradition affirms, was the stronghold of Caractacus. [1]

A camp near Verulamium, called OISTER HILLS, has been supposed to bear the name of the Roman general Ostorius,[2] and we have a CÆSAR'S CAMP near Farnham, and a VESPASIAN'S CAMP in Wiltshire.

CHILHAM in Kent was anciently called *Jul*ham, and is supposed to be the site of the battle fought by Julius Cæsar, in which Laberius was slain. This supposition is curiously corroborated by a tradition which calls a large tumulus in the neighbourhood by the name of JULABER'S GRAVE.[3]

According to the Chronicles, it fell to the lot of Catigern, a Kentish chieftain, to oppose the earliest invasion of the Saxons. We are told that he fought a battle with the forces of Hengist and Horsa, in the neighbourhood of Aylesford. On the summit of the downs which overlook the battle-field there is a Celtic tomb, constructed of vast vertical and horizontal slabs of sandstone. This, the most remarkable megalithic erection in the south-eastern portion of the kingdom goes by the name of KITS COTY HOUSE, and may not improbably bear the name of the British prince.[4]

We also read that the body of Ambrosius, the successor of Vortigern, was buried, according to his dying request, at AMBRESBURY on Salisbury Plain.[5]

In the year 945 the British population of Cumbria, under a chief who bore the name of Donald, made a final and unsuccessful attempt to shake off the Saxon yoke. A cairn at the summit of the desolate pass which leads from Keswick to Ambleside is called DUNMAIL-RAISE, and in all probability it marks the precise scene of the struggle with Eadmund, as well as the burial-place of the British leader.[6]

---

1 The real name of Caractacus was probably [Caratac=] Cradock, which is still a common surname in the West of England.
2 Gough's Camden, vol. ii. pp. 63, 73 ; Hartshorne, *Salopia Antiqua*, p. 153.
3 Gough's Camden, vol. i. pp. 313, 353.
4 Lappenberg, *Anglo-Saxon Kings*, vol. i. p. 73 ; Gough's Camden, vol. i. pp. 311, 336.
5 Haigh, *Conquest of Britain*, p. 264. There is a large camp in Epping Forest called Ambresbury Banks.
6 Palgrave, *English Commonwealth*, vol. i. p. 442 ; Ferguson, *Northmen in Cumberland*, pp. 15, 57.

In Strathearn there is a barrow which goes by the name of CARN-CHAINICHIN, that is, the Cairn of Kenneth. This name no doubt preserves the memory of the burial-place of Kenneth IV. of Scotland, who in the year 1003 was slain by Malcolm II. in a battle which was undoubtedly fought in the near neighbourhood of the cairn .[1]

An entrenchment on Barra Hill in Aberdeenshire bears the name of CUMMIN'S CAMP, and thus preserves the memory of the defeat of Comyn, Earl of Buchan, by Robert Bruce ; [2] while DALRY, the ' king's field ', is the spot where John of Lorn defeated Bruce, and from whence he tracked him with blood-hounds, as is so inimitably told in the ' Tales of a Grandfather.[3]

The names of GIBRALTAR and TARIFA have already been noticed.[4] VALETTA, the port and chief town of Malta, preserves the name of John Parisot de la Vallette, the heroic Grand Master of the Knights of St. John. Together with the suburb of VITTORIOSA it was founded in the year 1566, at the close of the memorable siege in which some 500 knights, assisted by 9,000 men at arms, successfully withstood for four months the assaults of an army of 30,000 Turks, until at last there survived only 600 of the Christians, utterly worn out by the toils and perils of the siege.[5]

The rulers of the ancient world seem to have anxiously desired to stamp their names upon cities of their own creation. Of the fifteen cities upon which Alexander the Great bestowed his name, only six retain it, and only two still possess any geographical importance. The name of Alexandria in Egypt has been corrupted into the Arabic form of ISCANDERIEH, and Alexandria in Bokhara is now SAMERCAND. The city of Alexandria which was built near the battle-field of Issus, though now a miserable village, has given a name to the Bay of SCANDEROON or ISKENDEROON. ALEXANDRETTA and CANDAHAR still maintain an obscure existence.[6]

---

1 Chalmers, *Caledonia*, vol. i. p. 397.
2 Ibid. vol. i. p. 90.
3 Skene, *History of the Highlanders*, vol. ii. p. 109.
4 See p. 73, *supra*.
5 Porter, *Knights of Malta*, vol. ii. pp. 70–166. One of the gates of Valetta is called the Port des Bombes, from its bearing the marks of the cannonade which took place when the French were attacked by the English and Maltese.
6 ALESSANDRIA, an important fortress in Piedmont, takes its name from a Roman Pope. Several places in Russia and Siberia are called ALEXANDROV and ALEXANDRIA, from the Russian Emperor. See Yonge, *Christian Names*, vol. i. p. 200.

Antiochus and Seleucus, and the princes of their dynasties, followed the example of their great captain, but while the once important name of SELEUCIA [1] has vanished from the map, Antioch,[2] now ANTAKIEH, still ranks among the cities of the East.

Philippi, now FELIBEDJIK, built by the father of Alexander, would be now forgotten were it not for the epistle addressed by St. Paul to its inhabitants ; and the mention of PHILADEL-PHIA in the Apocalypse still causes us to bear in mind that it was built by Attalus Philadelphus, king of Pergamus.

The names of the Roman Emperors are scattered over Europe, and some of them are found under very curious phonetic disguises. Who would expect, for instance, to find the name of Cæsar in JERSEY, a name which nevertheless is probably a corruption of Cæsarea ? [3] In the East the phonetic changes have been less ; the Cæsareas in Palestine and Cilicia are now called KAISARIYEH ; and KESRI, on the Dardanelles, is probably a corruption of the same name. The city of Cæsarea Jol, built by Juba in honour of Augustus, is now ZERSHELL in Algeria.[4] Two of the most curious of these transmutations are Cæsarea Augusta into ZARAGOSSA, and Pax Augusta into BADAJOZ. Augusta Emerita has been clipped down into MERIDA. Augustodunum is now AUTUN, and Augusta is AOSTA and AUGIA. We find the same Imperial name preserved in AUGSBURG, AUGST in Canton Bâle and Canton Zurich,[5] AOUST in the department of the Drôme, AUCH near Toulouse, and the AUST passage over the Severn.

The names of Julius and Julia we have in LOUDON (Julio-dunum), BEJA in Portugal (Pax Julia), TRUXILLO in Spain (Turris Julia, or Castra Julia), JÜLICH or JULIERS (Juliacum), the valley of ZSIL (Julia) in Hungary, pronounced *Jil*, ZUGLIO (Julium), ITUCCI (Victus Julius), and LILLEBONNE (Julia bona) ; while FRIULI, FORLI, and FREJUS are all corruptions of Forum Julii. ORLEANS, VALENCIENNES, GRENOBLE, and

[1] There were seven cities called Seleucia. The only one that retains the name is Seleucia in Cilicia, now Selefkieh.

[2] There were ten cities called Antiochia.

[3] The names of GUERNSEY and CHERBOURG are possibly to be traced to a similar origin, as well as Jerbourg in Guernsey ; though it is more probable that the first is Norse, and that the root of the two latter is the Celtic word *Caer*. Latham, *Channel Isles*, pp. 429, 452 ; *Notes and Queries*, second series, vol. vi. p. 163.

[4] Smith, *Dictionary of Greek and Roman Geography*, s. v. Jol ; *Quarterly Review*, xcix. p. 341.

[5] Meyer doubts this. See *Ortsnamen des K. Zurich*, p. 76.

ADRIANOPLE, bear the names of the Emperors Aurelian, Valentinian, Gratian, and Hadrian, by whom they were respectively founded or rebuilt. Forum Aurelii is now FIORA, Aurelia is ORLEANS,[1] Claudii Forum is KLAGENFURT, and PAMPELUNA and LODI (Laus Pompeii) bear the name of Pompey. TIBERIAS, in Palestine, was built by the younger Herod (Antipas) in honour of his imperial friend and master. Constantius Chlorus gave his name to CONSTANCE or CONSTANTZ on the Boden See, and to COUTANCES (Constantia) in Normandy, where Roman antiquities are still occasionally found. The surrounding district, now called the CÔTANTIN, exhibits very curiously a parallel but independent corruption of the name Constantinum. KUSTENDJE is the Turkish corruption of Constantiana. CONSTANTINEH is the strongest place in Algeria. Constantine, the son of Constantius, had a palace a few miles from Trêves, at a place now called CONZ, a name which, after a long eclipse, is again becoming audible among men, in the novel character of a great railway junction. I could not but think, as I once whiled away a tedious hour in the waiting-room at Conz, of the waiting-rooms on the same spot once thronged by the nobles of Western Europe, worshipping the rising sun, who was afterwards to imprint his name on CONSTANTINOPLE, the new capital of the Roman world.

Of the modern cities which are thus inscribed with the dates of their foundation, ST. PETERSBURG and VICTORIA, the capitals of two distant empires, occur at once to the memory. EKATERINENBURG was founded by the great Empress Catherine. CHRISTIANA, CHRISTIANSTAD, and CHRISTIANSAND, are memorials of the subjection of Norway and Sweden to the crown of Denmark in the seventeenth century, during the reign of Christian IV of Denmark. The little kinglets of Germany, otherwise unknown to fame, have not been slow in endeavouring to rescue their obscure names from oblivion by a geographical immortality of this kind. As we fly past upon the railway the names of CARLSRUHE, FRIEDRICHSHAFEN, LUDWIGSHAFEN, LUDWIGSBURG, or WILHELMSBAD may, perhaps, induce the traveller to endeavour to learn from his open Murray the deeds of the monarchs who have thus eagerly striven after fame.

The form of the modern name suggests that the place must have ordinarily been called Aureliana, rather than Aurelia.

W.P.   Q

A far more inconvenient practice prevails in the United States, where the names of popular Presidents have been bestowed so liberally on towns and counties as to occasion no little confusion. There are no less than 169 places, which bear the name of Washington, 86 that of Jefferson, 132 that of Jackson, while Munroe and Harrison have respectively to be contented with 71 and 62 places named in their honour.[1]

[1] See *Notes and Queries*, second series, vol. i. p. 508.

CHAPTER XIII

SACRED SITES

*Local Vestiges of Saxon Heathendom—Tiw, Frea, Woden, Thor, Balder—
Celtic Deities—Teutonic Demigods—Wayland Smith—Old Scratch
—Old Nick—The Nightmare—Sacred groves and temples—Vestiges
of Sclavonic Heathendom—The Classic Pantheon—Conversion of
the Northern Nations—Paulinus at Goodmanham—' Llan ' and ' Kil '
—The Hermits of the Hebrides—The Local Saints of Wales—Places
of Pilgrimage—The Monastic Houses.*

DAY after day, as the weeks run round, we have obtruded
upon our notice the names of the deities who were worshipped
by our pagan forefathers. This heathenism is indeed so
deeply ingrained into our speech, that we are accustomed
daily, without a thought, to pronounce the sacred names of
Tiw, Woden, Thunor, Frea, and Sætere.[1] These names are
so familiar to us, that we are apt to forget how little is really
known of the mythology of those heathen times. We have,
it is true, Beowulf and the Traveller's Song, the verse Edda,
and other parallel Norse and Teutonic legends, but the Anglo-
Saxon literature dates only from the Christian period, and
proceeds mostly from the pens of Churchmen, who naturally
preferred to recount thaumaturgic histories of Christian saints,
and willingly allowed the pagan legends to die away out of
the memories of men. So small, in fact, are the materials
at our disposal for an account of the Anglo-Saxon Pantheon,
that the very name of Sætere is conjectural—it is not found in
any literary document till long after the extinction of the Anglo-
Saxon paganism—and it would almost appear that the name,
the attributes, and the cult of this deity have been constructed
in comparatively recent times, in order to illustrate the assumed etymology of the word Saturday.[2] Our knowledge of

[1] On the names of the days of the week, see Mone, *Gesch. Heidenthums*, vol. ii. p. 110;
Turner, *Anglo-Saxons*, vol. ii. p. 217 ; Trench, *Study of Words*, p. 93 ; Müller, *Alt-deut.
Relig.* pp. 86–88 ; Mannhardt, *Götterwelt*, vol. i. p. 262.
[2] That the worship of Sætere was very local, appears also from the fact that Saturday,

Anglo-Saxon mythology being thus scanty, it will bear to be supplemented by the information which may be derived from local names.

We may, in the first place, arrive at some vague estimate of the relative mythological importance of the various Anglo-Saxon deities by means of a comparison of the number of places which severally bear their names, and which were probably dedicated to their worship. Judging by this standard, we conclude that Tiw,[1] Frea, and Sætere, had but a small hold on the religious affections of the people, for TEWESLEY in Surrey, Great TEW and TEW DUNSE in Oxfordshire, TEWIN in Hertfordshire, DEWERSTONE [2] in Devon, FRATHORPE and FRIDAYTHORPE [3] in Yorkshire, FRAISTHORPE in Holderness, FREASLEY [4] in Warwickshire, three FRIDAYSTREETS in Surrey, and one in Suffolk, SATTERLEIGH in Devon, and SATTER-THWAITE in Lancashire, seem to be the only places which bear their names.

But of the prevalence of the worship of Woden and Thunor, we have widespread evidence. WEDNESBURY in Stafford-shire, WISBOROW Hill in Essex, WANBOROUGH in Surrey, WAN-BOROUGH in Wilts, two WARNBOROUGHS in Hampshire, WOOD-NESBOROUGH in Kent [5] and Wilts, and WEMBURY in Devon, are all corruptions of the Anglo-Saxon word *Wodnesbeorh*, a

as a name for the last day of the week, is found only in the Frisian, Anglo-Saxon, and other Low-German languages. *Laugardagr*, the Norse equivalent for Saturday, the Swedish *Lôrdag*, and the Danish and Norwegian *Lôversdag*, mean the washing-day, or laving-day ; if, indeed, they do not refer to the Scandinavian deity Loki. See Grimm, *Deutsche Mythologie*, pp. 115, 226 ; Kemble, *Saxons*, vol. i. p. 372 ; Yonge, *Christian Names*, vol. i. p. 439 ; Donaldson, *English Ethnography*, p. 67.

[1] This word was used as the name of the Deity by all the Aryan nations. The San-skrit *déva*, the Greek θεός, the Latin *deus*, the Lithuanian *déwas*, the Erse *dia*, and the Welsh *dew* are all identical in meaning. The etymology of the word seems to point to the corruption of a pure monotheistic faith. The Sanskrit word *dyâus* means the expanse of blue sky, the heaven. This sense is retained in the Latin word *dies*, and in the phrase *sub Jove*, in the open air. (Horace, *Odes*, lib. I. i. 25.) Jupiter, Diupiter, or Diespiter. is the 'heavenly father'. See Pictet, *Orig. Indo-Eur.* part ii. pp. 653, 663, 664 ; Bunsen, *Philos. of Universal History*, vol. i. p. 78 ; *Edinburgh Review*, vol. xciv. pp. 334–338 ; Mannhardt, *Götterwelt*, vol. i. pp. 57, 69 ; Buttmann, *Mythologus*, vol. ii. p. 74 ; Müller, *Alt-deut. Relig.* pp. 223, 225 ; Kelly, *Curiosities*, p. 29 ; Max Müller, *Lectures*, second series, p. 425.

[2] In Saxe Weimar we have Tisdorf and Zeisberg ; in Hesse, Diensberg and Zierenberg ; in Bavaria, Zierberg ; in Zeeland, Tisvelae ; in Jutland, Tystathe and Tüslunde ; in Swe-den, Tistad, Tisby, Tisjo, and Tyved. Grimm, *Deutsche Mythol.* p. 180 ; Müller, *Alt-deut. Religion*, p. 87 ; Vilmar, *Ortsnamen*, p. 244 ; Knobel, *Völkertafel*, p. 41 ; Mann-hardt, *Götterwelt*, vol. i. p. 262.

[3] An elaborate account of Frekkenhorst, a chief German seat of the worship of Frigge, or Frea, is given by Massmann, in Dorow's *Denkmäler*, pp. 199–203. We have also Frekeleve near Magdeburg, Freyenwald on the Oder, and Freyenburg in Belgium. Müller, *Alt-deut. Rel.* p. 121 ; Salverte, *Essai sur les Noms*, vol. ii. p. 238.

[4] Fraisthorpe and Freasley are more probably *Frisian* settlements.

[5] Close to Woodnesborough is a tumulus called Winsborough.

name which indicates the existence of a mound or other similar erection dedicated to Woden.[1] WANSTROW in Somerset was formerly *Wodnestreow,* and WANSDIKE in Wiltshire was *Wodnesdic.* WODEN HILL on Bagshot Heath, WONSTON in Hampshire, WAMBROOK in Dorset, WEDNESHOUGH in Lancashire, WAMPOOL in Cumberland, WANSFORD in Northamptonshire, and another place of the same name in the East Riding, WANSTEAD in Essex, WAMDEN in Bucks, WADLEY in Berks, two WANSLEYS and WEDNESFIELD in Staffordshire, WENDON in Essex and in Somerset, WEDESLEY in Derbyshire, WEDNESHAM in Cheshire, WANTHWAITE in Cumberland, and WONERSH in Surrey, with other more doubtful names of the same class, enable us to form some estimate of how wide was the diffusion of Woden's worship.[2]

The Scandinavian Thor was worshipped by the Anglo-Saxons under the name of Thunor, a name identical with the English *thunder* and the German equivalent $\mathfrak{Donner}$.[3] We find traces of the worship of the Saxon god in the names of THUNDERSFIELD in Surrey, two places called THUNDERSLEIGH in Essex, and one in Hants, as well as THUNDRIDGE in Herts, and THUNDERHILL in Surrey.[4] To the name of Thor we may assign THURSLEY in Surrey, THURSLEIGH in Bedfordshire,[5] KIRBY THORE in Westmoreland, THURSCROSS in Yorkshire, THURSTON in Suffolk, THURSTABLE and THUR-

---

[1] Kemble, *Saxons,* vol. i. p. 344 ; Haigh, *Conquest of Britain,* p. 141 ; Morris, *Local Names,* p. 8 ; Guest, in *Archæolog. Journal,* vol. xvi. p. 107.

[2] In Germany we have Godesberg, near Bonn, anciently Wodenesberg ; Gudensberg, in Hesse, anciently Wuodenesberg, as well as another Gudensberg, and a Gudenberg ; also Godensholt, anciently Wodensholt, in Oldenburg ; Woensdrecht, near Antwerp, and Vaudemont, in Lorraine, anciently Wodani Mons.   In Denmark we find Odensberg ; Onsberg, anciently Othensberg ; Onsjö, anciently Othänsharet ; Onsala, anciently Othänsäle ; Onsley, anciently Othänslef ; Odinsey, on the island of Funen ; and in Norway, Onso, anciently Odinsey.   Grimm, *Deut. Myth.* pp. 133, 140, 144 ; Vilmar, *Ortsnamen,* p. 244 ; Bender, *Deutschen Ortsnamen,* pp. 107, 108 ; Mone, *Gesch. Heidenthums,* vol. i. p. 269 ; vol. ii. p. 154.   On the occurrence of the names of Woden and Thunor in the Saxon Charters, see Kemble, *Codex Dip.* vol. iii. p. xiii.

[3] The identity of Thunor and Indra has been proved by Mannhardt, by a laborious comparison of the Teutonic and Indian myths. *Germ. Mythen,* pp. 1–242.   The names also of Indra and Donnor, different as they may seem, are, no doubt, ultimately identical. We have seen (p. 147, *supra*) that *udra* and *udan* are related Sanskrit words, meaning water.   The first gives us the name of Indra, the second that of Donnor or Thunor, both of whom are the storm and rain gods ; both were born out of the water, both fill the rivers, and pour the milk of the cloud-cows of heaven upon the earth.   See Mannhardt, *Germ. Myth.* pp. 3, 38, 50, 143, 147, 213, 216 ; Mannhardt, *Götterwelt,* vol. i. p. 61 ; Max Müller, *Lectures,* second series, p. 430.

[4] The little scholars who enjoy catching a great scholar tripping, may amuse themselves with Mr. Kemble's attempt to find an allusion to the Thunderer's Hammer, in the Hammer ponds in Surrey ; the fact being, that the name originated from some iron works now disused.

[5] There is a remarkable tumulus in the middle of the village called Bury Hill.

LOW in Essex, THURSFIELD in Staffordshire, THURSFORD in Norfolk, TURSDALE in Durham, THURSHELTON in Devon, THURSBY in Cumberland, THURSO in Caithness, TORNESS in Shetland, and THORIGNY in Normandy, all of which, as we have seen, are in regions settled more or less by Scandinavian colonists.[1]   In some of these cases it is probable that the name may have been derived from some Viking who bore the name of Thor.[2]   The Anglo-Saxon names, however, are not liable to this ambiguity, since it does not appear that any Anglo-Saxon—more timid, or more reverent than the North-man—ever dared to assume the name of the dreaded Thunor.

Names like BALDERBY or BALDERTON, may probably be derived from the personal name Balder, rather than from that of the deity.   Pol, another form of the name of the god Balder, is probably to be found in such names as POLBROOK, POLSTEAD, POLSDEN and POLSDON, as well perhaps as in BELL HILL, and HILL BELL.   The last two names, however, are, more probably, vestiges of a still earlier *cultus*—Celtic, or possibly Semitic.[3]   It has been thought that there must have been some original connexion, etymologic or mythologic, between the Syrian Baal, the Celtic Bel or Belen, the Sclavonic Biel-bog, and the Teutonic Pol.[4]   To the Celtic deity we may probably assign the local names of BELAN, near Trefeglwys in Montgomeryshire, BELAN near Newtown, two BELAN BANKS in Shropshire, and the BAAL HILLS in Yorkshire, besides three mountains called BELCH in the Vosges and the Black Forest.[5] BALERIUM, the ancient name of the Land's End, may possibly be due to the Phœnicians.   BEL TOR in Devon may be either Teutonic, Celtic, or Semitic.   Several of the Devon-

---

[1] On the continent we find Thuneresberg, in Westphalia, where stands a sacred oak, under which, to this day, an annual festival is held ; Donnersberg, near Worms, anciently Thoneresberg ; Donnerkaute and Donnersgraben in Hesse ; Donnersreut in Franconia ; Donnerbühel in Berne ; Donnersted in Brunswick ; Donershauk in Thuringia ; Thorsborg in Gothland ; Donnerschwee, anciently Donerswe (*ve*, holy), in Oldenburg ; Donnersbach in Styria ; Torslunde (*lundr*, a sacred grove), and Thorsbro in Denmark ; and Thôrsbiörg, Thôrshöfn, and others, in Norway. Grimm, *Deutsche Mythol.* pp. 64, 155, 169 ; Grimm, *Namen Donners* ; Vilmar, *Ortsnamen*, p. 244 ; Mannhardt, *Germanische Mythen*, p. 235.
[2] In the case of several villages called Thursby this is the more probable supposition.
[3] Grimm, *Deutsche Mythol.* pp. 208, 580 ; Leo, *Vorlesungen*, vol. i. p. 205 ; Thierry, *Hist. Gaulois*, vol. ii. pp. 77, 78 ; Müller, *Alt-deutsche Religion*, pp. 253, 256 ; Ferguson, *Northmen*, pp. 95, 98 ; Mone, *Geschichte Heidenthums*, vol. ii. p. 345 ; Barth, *Druiden*, p. 69.   The Beltane fires are still kept up in the Isle of Man, and in Yorkshire. Train, *Isle of Man*, vol. i. p. 328.
[4] [These suggestions are, to the last degree, improbable.]
[5] Mone, *Geschichte Heidenthums*, vol. ii. p. 337 ; Barth, *Druiden*, p. 86.   Cf. Piderit, *Ortsnamen*, p. 300.

shire Tors seem also to bear names derived from a primaeval mythology. MIS TOR and HAM TOR have been supposed to bear Semitic names derived from Misor, the moon,[1] and Ham or Ammon. The name of HESSARY TOR can with greater confidence be referred to the Celtic deity Esus or Hesus,[2] mentioned by Lucan—

> Teutates, horrensque feris altaribus Hesus,
> Et Taranis Scythicæ non·mitior ara Dianæ.[3]

The Celtic deity Taith referred to in these lines under the name of Teutates, must not be confounded with the Teutonic Tiw, though the names are probably not unconnected. Places called TOT HILL, TOOT HILL, or TOOTER HILL, are very numerous, and may possibly have been seats of Celtic worship.[4]

The word Easter, as we learn from Beda, is derived from the name of Eostre,[5] or Ostâra, the Anglo-Saxon goddess of Spring, to whom the month of April was sacred. As in other instances the Catholic clergy seem to have given the heathen festival a Christian import, and to have placed 'Our Lady' on the throne previously occupied by the virgin goddess of the spring.[6] She seems to have bestowed her name on two parishes in Essex which are called GOOD EASTER,[7] and HIGH EASTER; we find also the more doubtful names of EASTER-FORD in the same county, EASTERLEAKE in Nottinghamshire, and EASTERMEAR in Hampshire.

The name of Hel, the mistress of the gloomy underworld, seems to be confined to Yorkshire; it may possibly be pre-served in the names of HELLIFIELD, HELLATHYRNE, HELWITH, two HEALEYS, HEALIGH, and HELAGH, all in Yorkshire.[8] HELWELL in Devonshire is probably only the covered well,

---

[1] [These suggestions are not worthy of serious consideration.]
[2] Cf. the Sanskrit *Asura*, the supreme, self-existent Spirit, a name probably derived from a root *as* = esse. A statue inscribed with the name of Esus was exhumed at Paris. Pictet, *Orig. Indo-Eur.* part ii. p. 655; Barth, *Druiden*, p. 71; Prichard, *Researches*, vol. iii. p. 185; Thierry, *Hist. Gaulois*, vol. ii. p. 78.
[3] *Pharsalia*, book i. l. 445.
[4] See Davies, in *Philolog. Trans.* for 1855, p. 219; Barth, *Druiden*, p. 64; Thierry, *Hist. Gaulois*, vol. ii. p. 78; Prichard, *Researches*, vol. iii. p. 185.
[5] Cf. the Sanskrit *ushas* = Aurora, from a root *ush*, to burn or glow. Hence the Greek ἠώς, the Latin *auster*, the south, and the English *east*. Grimm, *Deut. Mythol.* p. 266; Neus, in *Zeitschrift für Deut. Myth.* vol. iii. pp. 356–368; Pictet, *Orig. Indo-Eur.* part ii. pp. 672–674; Leo, *Rectitudines*, p. 206.
[6] Mayhew, *German Life*, vol. ii. pp. 332, 377.
[7] In Domesday this name appears in the form ESTRA. GOOD EASTER is probably the *god* Eostre.
[8] We have Helgraben, Helwald, Helleberg, and other similar names in Germany. Panzer, *Deut. Myth.* p. 275.

the word hell originally meaning only the 'covered' place. Thus a wound *heals* when it becomes covered with skin.[1] The *heel* is that part of the foot which is covered by the leg [!],[1] *helmet* covers the head. The *hull* is the covered part of the ship.[1] To *hele* potatoes is to clamp or tump them. In Kent to *heal* a child is to cover it up in its cradle, and to *heal* a house is to put on the roof or covering. A *hellier* is a slater.

Of the mythic heroes of Scandinavian legend, the name of Weland, the Northern Vulcan, who fabricates the arms of the heroes of the early Sagas, is preserved at a place in Berkshire called WAYLANDSMITH. Here, appropriately placed at the foot of that sacred HILL OF THE WHITE HORSE, which from immemorial times has borne the colossal symbol of Saxon conquest, there still stands the structure which our ancestors called Weland's forge,[2] a huge megalithic monument, consisting of two chambers constructed of upright stones and roofed with large slabs. Here the hero-smith was supposed to fabricate shoes for the sacred horse. Though bearing a Saxon name, and connected with a Saxon legend, it is doubtless only a Celtic grave.[3]

The name of Eigil, the hero-archer, is probably to be sought at AYLESBURY, formerly *Æglesbyrig*, as well perhaps as at AYLESFORD, AYSWORTH, and AYLSTONE.[4] ASGARDBY and AYSGARTH, however, probably refer to Asgard, the home of the gods.

Curious legends often linger round the numerous places called the Devil's Dyke, the Devil's Punchbowl, and the like,[5] and results, not without value, might doubtless be obtained by a comparative analysis of the names of the various celebrated witch mountains.[6]

---

[1] [These words are not connected with one another or with A. Sax. *helan*, to cover.]

[2] In the charters the place is called *Welandes Smidde*, Wayland's Forge. *Codex Diplom*, No. 1172.

[3] Grimm, *Deutsche Mythol.* p. 350 ; Wilson, *Pre-hist. Annals of Scotland*, p. 210 ; Scott, *Kenilworth*, chap. xiii. and note ; Singer, *Wayland Smith*, p. xxxv. ; Wright, in *Journal of Archæolog. Association*, vol. xvi. pp. 50–58 ; Kemble, *Saxons in England*, vol. i. pp. 419–421 ; Grimm, *Heldensage*, pp. 41, 322, 323 ; Gough's Camden, vol. i. p. 221.

[4] Grimm, *Deutsche Mythol.* p. 349 ; Kemble, *Saxons*, vol. i. p. 422.

[5] We find Teufelstein near Dürkheim, Teufelsberg in Bavaria, and Teufelsmauer in Austria. See Panzer, *Deut. Myth.* pp. 46, 100, 204 ; Piderit, *Ortsnamen*, p. 301. There are also many places called Drachenfels, Drachenbogen, Drachenkammer, etc. Panzer, *Deut. Myth.* p. 293 ; Grimm, *Heldensage*, p. 316.

[6] The chief of these are the Blocksberg, or Brocken, in the Hartz ; several Blocksbergs in Mecklenburg ; the Huiberg near Halberstadt ; the Horselberg in Thuringia ; the Bechelsberg in Hesse ; the Köterberg and the Weckingstein in Westphalia ; the Kandel the Heuberg, and the Staffelstein in the Black Forest ; the Bischenberg and the Büchel

A dark and rugged rock in the Lake District bears the name of SCRATCH MEAL SCAR. Here we may perhaps detect the names of two personages who figure in the Norse mythology, Skratti, a demon, and Mella, a weird giantess.[1] There is also a SCRATTA WOOD on the borders of Derbyshire. The demon Skratti still survives in the superstitions of Northern Europe. The Skratt of Sweden, with a wild horse-laugh, is believed to mock travellers who are lost upon the waste, and sundry haunted rocks on the coast of Norway still go by the name of 'SKRATTASKAR'.[2] In the north of England the name of Skratti continues to be heard in the mouths of the peasantry, and the memory of 'Old Scratch', as he is familiarly called, may probably be yet destined to survive through many future Christian centuries, in company with 'Old Nick', who is none other than Nikr,[3] the dangerous water-demon of Scandinavian legend. This dreaded monster, as the Norwegian peasant will gravely assure you, demands every year a human victim, and carries off children who stray too near his abode beneath the waters. In Iceland also, Nykr, the water-horse, is still believed to inhabit some of the lonely tarns scattered over the savage region of desolation which occupies the central portion of the island.

Many similar traces of the old mythology are to be found in that well-stored antiquarian museum, the English language. In the phrase 'Deuce take it', the deity Tiw still continues to be invoked.[4] The Bogie, with whose name nurses are wont to frighten children, is probably Bogu, the Sclavonic

berg in Alsace; the Blåkulla (Black Mountain) in Sweden; and the Blaakolle in Norway, See Thorpe, *Northern Mythology*, vol. i. p. 243; Grimm, *Deut. Myth.* p. 1004. Hanenkamm and Hanenbuck in Bavaria were places of heathen worship. Mone, *Gesch. Heid.* vol. ii. p. 218. Heidenberg is the name of a hill near Zurich, down which on winter nights a headless horseman is seen to ride. Meyer, *Ortsnamen*, p. 165.

[1] Grimm, *Deutsche Mythologie*, p. 493; Ferguson, *Northmen*, p. 99; *Edinburgh Review*, vol. cxi. p. 386. Mella, when tired of the company of Skratti, had a separate abode on MELL FELL; unless, indeed, this name be Celtic rather than Scandinavian, and allied to the word *mull*, a headland, which we have in the Mull of Cantyre and other names. Or the name of Mell Fell may be from the Icelandic *melr*, a sandy hill. There is a Mœlifell in Iceland.

[2] Grimm, *Deut. Myth.* p. 447; Thorpe, *Northern Mythology*, vol. ii. p. 95; vol. i. p. 250. The name of Skratti is found also in the Sarmatian legends. In Bohemian *Screti* means a demon. See Latham, *English Language*, vol. i. p. 360.

[3] Norwegian *nök*, Swedish *neck*, German *nix*, plural *nixen*, English *nixies*, and old *Nick*. The name of the River Neckar probably comes from the same root. Thorpe, *Northern Mythology*, vol. i. p. 246; vol. ii. p. 20; Grimm, *Deut. Myth.* p. 456; Kemble, Preface to *Translation of Beówulf*, p. xvii.; Kemble, *Saxons*, vol. i. pp. 389-392; Laing, *Heimskringla*, vol. i. p. 92; Baring-Gould, *Iceland*, p. 149.

[4] Compare Augustine, *De Civitate Dei*, book xv. cap. 23, 'quosdam dæmones quos dusios Galli nuncupant'.

name of the Deity,[1] and the name of Puck has been referred to the same source.[2]   The nursery legend of ' Jack and Jill ' is found in the younger Edda, where the story of Hjuki (the flow) and Bil (the ebb), the two children of the Moon, is seen to be merely an exoteric version of the flowing and ebbing of the tides.[3]   The morning gossamer is the *gott-cymar*, the veil or trail left by the deity who has passed over the meadows in the night.[4]   The word *brag* has an etymological connexion with the name of Bragi,[5] the Norse god of song and mirth, while the faithful devotees of Bragi fall after awhile under the power of Mara,[6] a savage demon, who tortures men with visions, and crushes them even to death, and who still survives, though with mitigated powers, as the Nightmare of modern days.[7]

There is another class of names of sacred sites, those, namely, which are not associated with the names of particular deities.

The name of REDRUTH in Cornwall is written in old deeds. Dre-druith, the town of the Druids.[8]   From the Celtic *nemet*, a sacred grove, we may deduce the name of NYMET ROWLAND in Devonshire, and of NISMES, anciently Nemausus, in Provence, as well as many ancient Gaulish names, such as Nemetacum or Nemetocenna (Arras), Vernemetum, and Tascinemetum.[9]   LUND and LUNDGARTH, both in Holderness, are probably from the Norse *lundr*, a sacred grove.[10]   The name of HOFF,

---

[1] Sanskrit *bhaga*, god, the sun. Pictet, *Orig. Indo-Europ.* part ii. p. 654 ; *Edinburgh Review*, vol. xciv. p. 332. See, however, Davies, in *Philolog. Proceed.* vol. vi. p. 136 ; *Notes and Queries*, second series, vol. xi. p. 97.
[2] De Belloguet, *Ethnog.* vol. i. p. 222.
[3] Grimm, *Deut. Myth.* p. 679 ; Müller, *Alt-deut. Relig.* p. 161 ; Baring-Gould, *Iceland*, p. 189.
[4] [This suggestion has no basis, being purely imaginary.]
[5] Diefenbach, *Vergleich. Wörterb.* vol. i. p. 266 ; Grimm, *Deut. Myth.* p. 215 ; Baring-Gould, *Iceland*, p. 161 ; *Notes and Queries*, second series, vol. v. p. 32.
[6] Thrupp, *Anglo-Saxon Home*, p. 263 ; Grimm, *Deut. Myth.* p. 215 ; Kelly, *Curiosities*, p. 240 ; Laing, *Heimskringla*, vol. i. p. 92.
[7] On the subject of the Teutonic and Scandinavian mythology, as illustrated by local names, the reader may consult Jacob Grimm, *Deutsche Mythologie*, passim ; Buttmann, *Die Deutschen Ortsnamen*, pp. 162–169 ; Kemble, *Anglo-Saxons*, vol. i. p. 243–422 ; Ferguson, *Northmen in Cumberland*, pp. 28, 95 ; Bender, *Die Deutschen Ortsnamen*, pp. 107, 108 ; Leo, *Anglo-Saxon Names*, p. 5 ; Panzer, *Deutsche Mythologie* ; Förstemann, *Ortsnamen*, p. 172 ; Worsaae, *Danes and Norwegians*, p. 69.   A list of mythologic names in the Tyrol is given in a paper by Zingerle, in the *Germania*, vol. v. p. 108.
[8] Pryce, *Arch. Cornu-Brit.* s. v.
[9] Sanskrit *nam*, to worship, Greek νέμω, Irish *nemhta*, holy, Latin *nemus*, a grove, Gaulish *nemetum*, a temple, Brezonec *nemet*, a sacred grove. Pictet, *Orig. Indo-Europ.* part ii. p. 691 ; Zeuss, *Gram. Celt.* vol. i. p. 186 ; Astruc, *Languedoc*, p. 439 ; Davies, in *Philolog. Trans.* for 1857, p. 91 ; Glück, *Kelt. Namen*, p. 75 ; Adelung, *Mithridates*, vol. ii. p. 65 ; Maury, *Hist. des Forêts*, p. 160.
[10] LUNDEY Island in the Bristol channel, and LUNDHOLME near Lancaster may be from this source, but more probably from the Norse *lundi*, a puffin.   There is an islet called LUNDEY on the Icelandic coast.   Baring-Gould, *Iceland*, p. 244.

near Appleby, seems to be from the Anglo-Saxon and old Norse *hof*, a temple.[1] The vast inclosure of SILBURY is probably the holy hill.[2] The names of WYDALE, WIGTHORP, and WEIGHTON, as well as WEIHBOGEN in the Tyrol, WYBORG and WISBY, all of them holy places, probably come from the Norse *vé*, a sacred place.[3]

HELIGOLAND—which means 'holy island land'—has been with great probability identified [4] with the insula oceani, which is described by Tacitus as the seat of the secret rites of the Angli and other adjacent continental tribes. Of the numerous places bearing the name of HOLYWELL, HOLY ISLAND, and HOLY HILL,[5] many were probably the sites of an ancient pagan cultus, to which, in accordance with Gregory's well weighed instructions, a Christian import was given by Augustine and his brother missionaries.[6] The churches of St. Martin and St. Pancras, at Canterbury, as well as Westminster Abbey and St. Paul's Cathedral, were built on the sites of heathen temples, and are instances of this practice of enlisting, in favour of the new faith, the local religious attachments of the people.[7]

It would demand more space than the interest of the subject would warrant, to trace the local vestiges of the worship of the Sclavonian deities. They have left their names scattered far and wide over Eastern and Central Europe—a testi-

[1] There are two places called HOF in Iceland.
[2] *Selig*, holy. See Poste, *Brit. Res.* p. 263. So Jerusalem is called by the Arabs EL KUDS, the holy. Compare also the name of BETHEL, the 'house of God', with the Beit-allah of Mecca, and the Bætulia of early Phœnician worship. Behistun is the abode of the gods, from the Sanskrit *Bhaga*. See *Edin. Rev.* vol. xciv. p. 333 ; Stanley, *Jewish Church*, p. 59.
[3] We have the Gothic *veihs*, holy, and *veihan*, to consecrate ; the old High German *vih*, a sacred grove, or temple, the German *weihnacht*, Christmas, and the Anglo-Saxon *wiccian*, fascinare, whence the English word *witch*. Pictet, *Orig. Indo-Europ.* part ii. p. 643 ; Grimm, *Deutsche Mythol.* p. 581 ; Yonge, *Christian Names*, vol. ii. p. 238 ; Diefenbach, *Vergleich. Wörterbuch*, vol. i. pp. 137, 138 ; Mone, *Geschichte Heidenthums*, vol. i. p. 269 ; Thaler, in the *Zeitschrift für Deut. Myth.* vol. i. p. 286 ; Adelung, *Mithridates*, pp. 144, 169.
[4] See Latham, *Germania*, pp. 145, 146 ; *Eth. of Brit. Is.* p. 155 ; Grimm, *Deutsche Myth.* p. 211 ; Crichton, *Scandinavia*, vol. i. p. 75 ; and a paper by Maack, in the *Germania*, vol. iv.
[5] Holy Hill is the highest point of ground in Kent. Cf. the numerous Heiligenbrunns and Heilbrunns in Germany, to the waters of many of which a supernatural efficacy was supposed to attach. The original meaning of *holy* is healing [hale]. See Grimm, *Deutsche Myth.* p. 553 ; Pictet, *Orig. Indo-Europ.* vol. ii. p. 647.
[6] Gregory, ' diu cogitans ', came to the conclusion that ' fana idolorum destrui minime debeant ', but that the idols should be destroyed, and the temples, well sprinkled with holy water, should be supplied with relics, so that the gens Anglorum ' ad loca quæ consuevit familarius concurrat '. Beda, *Hist. Ecc.* lib. i. c. 30 ; Gregorii Magni *Epistol.* lib. xi. ep. lxxvi. ; Thorpe, *Northern Mythology*, vol. i. p. 268.
[7] See Rees, *Welsh Saints*, p. xii. ; Dixon and Raine, *Fasti Eboracenses*, p. 3 ; Stanley, *Memorials of Canterbury*, p. 21 ; Pauli, *Pictures of Old England*, p. 12.

mony to the long duration and great difficulty of the process by which the Sclavonic nations were converted to Christianity. Thus the name of Radegast, a god of light, is found at two places called RADEGAST in Mecklenburg Schwerin, one of the same name in Anhalt Dessau, and another in Oschatz; as well as at RADEGOSZ in Posen, RADIHOSCHT in Bohemia, the village of RODGES near Fulda in Hesse, anciently written *villa Radegastes*, and many villages bearing the names of RADIBOR, RADEBURG, RADENSDORF, and the like.[1] We also find traces of the worship of Swjatowit,[2] a deity with attributes similar to those of Radegast, of Juthrbog [3] the god of spring, of Ciza [4] the goddess of fertility, of Mita [5] a malevolent cynoform [6] deity, of Marsana [7] the Sclavonic Ceres, and of Perun,[8] a deity who corresponds to the Scandinavian Thor.

The subject of names derived from the eastern and classic mythologies is too extensive for discussion in this place. It would require a chapter, or even a volume to itself. There are many such places in India, Syria is full of them, they abound in Italy and Greece. Thus CALCUTTA and CALICUT are the Kali-Ghauts, the steps, or landing-places by the river-side, where the great festival of Kali was celebrated. BAALBEC was the chief seat of the worship of Baal, the ruins of whose temple, with its substructure of colossal stones, is still one of the wonders of the world.[9] Panium, now BANIAS, was a sanctuary of Pan.[10] The shores of the Mediterranean were covered with places bearing the names of the deities of Greece and Rome. More than a dozen might be enumerated taking their names from Neptune or Poseidon, of which PAESTUM, the ancient Posidonia, is the only one that still

[1] Buttmann, *Deutschen Ortsnamen*, pp. 164, *seq.*; Vilmar, *Ortsnamen*, p. 26.
[2] At Zwettnitz in Bohemia, Schautewitz in Pomerania, and Zwitto in Brandenburg. Buttmann, *Ortsnamen*, p. 162; Maclear, *Hist. of Christian Missions*, p. 33.
[3] Hence Jüterbogk, a large town near Berlin. Buttmann, *Ortsnamen*, p. 168.
[4] Hence Zeitz, near Leipsig. Buttmann, *Ortsnamen*, p. 168.
[5] Hence Mitau in Courland.
[6] [Meant for ' caniform '.]
[7] Hence Marzahn near Berlin, Marzahna near Wittenberg, and Marzana in Illyria. Buttmann, *Ortsnamen*, p. 169.
[8] Grimm, *Deut. Myth.* p. 156.
[9] In the Old Testament we find many traces of the Canaanitish worship still lingering in Palestine. For a long time, probably, the devotions of the people were attracted by the old idolatrous sanctuaries, such as Baal Gad, Baal Hermon, Baal Tamar, Baal Hazor, Baal Judah, Baal Meon, Baal Perazim, and Baal Shalisha. In the genealogies of families we find evidence of the same lingering superstitions. Thus in the family of Saul we find persons bearing the names of Baal, Eshbaal, and Meribaal. Stanley, *Jewish Church*, p. 291.
[10] Robinson, *Biblical Researches*, vol. iii. p. 348.

retains both its name and any human interest.   Hercules
seems to have been deemed the most powerful protector of
colonies, for from him we find that some thirty or forty places
were named HERACLEIA, HERACLEOPOLIS, or HERCULANEUM.[1]
Twenty, under the protection of Apollo, were called APOLLONIS
or APOLLONIA, and fifteen bore the name of Pallas Athene, all
of which, except Athens,[2] have sunk into obscurity.

It is pleasant to leave these dry bones of a dead paganism,
and turn to the names which speak to us of the first propaga-
tion of Christianity in our native land.   One of the most
striking scenes in the whole history of missionary enterprise
was enacted in the East Riding of Yorkshire, at GOODMAN-
HAM, or GODMUNDINGAHAM,[3] a mile from WEIGHTON [4] where,
as the name implies, stood a large heathen temple.   Beda
tells that the Bishop Paulinus presented himself on this
spot before Edwin King of the Northumbrians, and urged
eloquently the claims of the new faith.   Coifi, the pagan high-
priest, to the surprise of all, proclaimed aloud that the old
religion had neither power nor utility.   'If', said he, 'the
gods were of any worth they would heap their favour upon
me, who have ever served them with such zeal'.   The demoli-
tion of the temple was decreed, but with a lingering belief
in the ancient faith, all shrank from incurring the possible
hostility of the old deities, by taking part in its destruction.
'As an example to all', said Coifi, 'I am myself ready to
destroy that which I have worshipped in my folly'.   Arming
himself with spear and sword, he mounted on a horse, and
having profaned the temple by casting his lance against it,
it was set on fire and consumed.[5]

GODNEY near Glastonbury, GODMANCHESTER in Huntingdonshire, GODMANSTONE in Dorset, GODLEY in Cheshire, GOD-
STOW near Oxford, GODSHILL in the Isle of Wight, and GOD-
STONE in Surrey, were probably, like Godmundham, pagan
sites consecrated to Christian worship.

[1] MONTERCHI, in Umbria, is Mons Herculis.
[2] In this case the name of the city is probably the source from which the cognomen
of the goddess was derived.
[3] The home of the *mund*, or protection of the gods, or from the Norse *godi*, a priest ;
hofs godi, a temple priest.   Grimm, *Deut. Myth.* p. 78.
[4] The 'sacred inclosure', see pp. 120, 332, *supra*. The ruins of the temple are to
be seen near Goodmanham Church.
[5] Beda, *Hist. Ecc.* lib. ii. c. 13.   Cf. Lappenberg, *Anglo-Sax. Kings*, vol. i. p. 153 ;
St. John, *Four Conquests*, vol. i. p. 110 ; Turner, *Anglo-Saxons*, vol. i. pp. 356–360 ;
Dixon and Raine, *Fasti Eboracenses*, vol. i. pp 40, 41 ; Maclear, *History of Missions*,
p. 114.]

The prefix *llan* which, as we have seen,[1] occurs so frequently in Cornwall, Wales, and the border counties, often enables us to detect the spots which were the first to be dedicated to purposes of Christian worship.

The Cymric *llan* is replaced in Scotland and Ireland by the analogous Gadhelic word *kil*. Originally this denoted only a hermit's ' cell ', though it was afterwards used to mean the ' church ', of which the hermit's cell was so often the germ.

The numerous village-names which have this prefix *kil* possess a peculiar interest. They often point out to us the earliest local centres from which proceeded the evangelization of the half-savage Celts ; they direct us to the hallowed spots where the first hermit missionaries established each his lonely cell, and thence spread around him the blessings of Christianity and of civilization.

In Ireland alone there are no less than 1,400 local names which contain this root, and there are very many in Scotland also.[2] In Wales and the neighbouring counties, a few names occur with the prefix *kil* instead of *llan*. These names may probably be regarded as local memorials of those Irish missionaries, who about the fifth century resorted in considerable numbers to the shores of Wales.[3]

It seems to have been by means of these Irish hermits that the fierce Scandinavians who settled in the islands off the Scottish coast were brought to submit to the gentle influences of Christianity. The Norse name for these anchorite fathers was *Papar*. Three islets among the Hebrides,[4] two in the Orkneys,[5] two in the Shetlands,[6] and others among the Faroes and off the coast of Iceland, bear the names of PABBA, or PAPA, the ' Father's isle '. In the Mainland of Orkney, and again in South Ronaldshay, we find places called PAPLAY,[7] the ' hermit's abode ', and at ENHALLOW, and at one of the PAPAS in the Orkneys, the ancient cells are still preserved.[8]

---

[1] See p. 163, *supra*.

[2] e.g. Kilmore, Kilkenny, Killin, Icolmkill.

[3] We find Kilcwm, Kilsant, and Kilycon in Carmarthen ; Kilgarran and Kilred in Pembrokeshire ; Kilkenin, Kiluellon, and Kilwy in Cardigan ; Kilowen in Flint ; Kilgwri in Cheshire ; Kilmersdon and Kilstock in Somerset ; Kildare and Killow in Yorkshire ; and Kilpisham in Rutland.

[4] Pabba off Skye, Pabba off Harris, and Pabba off Barra.

[5] Papa Westray and Papa Stronsay.   [6] Papa Stour and Papa Little.

[7] There is a Papil in Unst, and a Pappadill in Rum.

[8] Wilson, *Pre-historic Annals*, p. 486 ; Dasent, *Burnt Njal*, vol. i. p. viii. ; Worsaae, *Danes*, p. 231.

In that part of England which was settled by the Danes, the missionary efforts seem to have been more of a parochial character. We find the prefix *kirk*, a church, in the names of no less than sixty-eight places in the Danelagh, while in the Saxon portion of England we find it scarcely once.[1] KIRBY means church-village, and the Kirbys which are dotted over East Anglia and Northumbria speak to us of the time when the possession of a church by a village community was the exception, and not, as is now happily the case, the rule. These names point to a state of things somewhat similar to that now prevailing in Australia or Canada, where often but a single church and a single clergyman are to be found in a district fifty miles in circumference.[2] Thus we may regard these Kirbys, distributed throughout the Danelagh, as the sites of the mother churches, to which the surrounding parishes, whose names contain no such prefix, would bear a filial relationship.

Joined with the prefixes *kil* and *llan* we find not unfrequently the name of the apostle of each wild valley or rocky islet—the first Christian missionary who ventured into the mountain fastnesses to tame their savage denizens. From the village-names of Wales, Scotland, and Ireland, it would be almost possible to compile a Hagiology of these sainted men, who have been canonized by local tradition, though their names are seldom to be found in the pages of the Bollandists.

In a few of these cases, where the same name is repeated again and again, we can only infer the fact of the dedication of the church to some saint of widely extended fame. Thus the repute of St. Bridget has given rise to no less than eighteen Kilbrides in Scotland alone. At ICOLMKILL, or Iona,[3] as well as at INCHCOLM, COLONSAY, and KIRKCOLM, we find the name of St. Columba, the great apostle of the Picts, who is said to have founded an hundred monasteries in Ireland and Scotland. So the name of St. Ciarran, the apostle of the Scoto-Irish, and the founder of a monastic rule, is found at KILKIARAN in Islay, as well as at KILKERRAN in Ayrshire

---

[1] It is found over the whole track of the Norsemen from Kirkwall in the Orkneys, to Dunkerque in Flanders, and Querqueville in Normandy.

[2] See Dixon and Raine, *Fasti Eboracenses*, vol. i. p. 27.

[3] Iona, the chief monastery and seminary of North Britain, and the burial-place of innumerable kings and saints, was originally bestowed on St. Columba by one of the Pictish kings. Lappenberg, *Anglo-Saxon Kings*, vol. i. p. 132 ; Maclear, *History Christian Missions*, pp. 84-90.

and in Connemara. But a very large number of these saint-names are locally unique, and the parishes which bear such names are almost always the most ancient, their ecclesiastical position being that of the mother parishes, affiliated to which are the churches dedicated to saints in the Romish calendar.[1] Hence these village-names may fairly be adduced as evidence in any attempt to localize the scene of the labours of these primitive missionaries.[2]

Our space would fail were we to attempt such a commemoration in this place ; it may suffice to indicate the names of a few of the local saints who are associated with some of the more familiar localities. Thus the watering place of LLAN-DUDNO takes its name from St. Tudno, a holy hermit who took up his abode among the rocks of the Orme's head. LLAN-BERIS, now the headquarters of Welsh tourists, commemorates the labours of St. Peris, an apostolically-minded cardinal.[3] In the case of BEDDGELERT, the legend of the hound Gelert, which Spencer has so gracefully inshrined in verse, must give place to the claims of St. Celert, a Welsh saint of the fifth century, to whom the church of LLANGELLER is consecrated. LLANGOLLEN is so called from St. Collen, a man more fortunate, or unfortunate, than the majority of his brethren, in that a Welsh legend of his life has come down to us, recounting the deeds of valour which he performed when a soldier in the Roman armies ; how he became Abbot of Glastonbury, and finally retired to spend the remainder of his days in a cave scooped out in that rugged wall of cliff which bounds the lovely valley on which the saint has bestowed his name.[4]

The name of MERTHYR TYDFIL commemorates the spot where the heathen Saxons and Picts put to death the martyr Tydfyl, daughter of the eponymic King Brychan, who is asserted by Welsh legend to have given his name to the county of Brecknock.[5]

St. David or St. Dewi was a Welsh prince, whose preaching is compared to that of St. John the Baptist. He lived on

---

[1] Rees, *Welsh Saints*, pp. 57, 59.
[2] Great use has been made of local names in the *Lives of the Cambro-British Saints*, by the Rev. W. J. Rees, and in the *Essay on the Welsh Saints*, by Professor Rice Rees, who enumerates 479 local saints.
[3] Rees, *Welsh Saints*, p. 302.
[4] See Borrow, *Wild Wales*, vol. i. p. 57 ; Rees, *Welsh Saints*, p. 302.
[5] Borrow, *Wild Wales*, vol. iii. p. 411 ; Haigh, *Conquest of Britain*, p. 251 ; Rees, *Cambro-British Saints*, pp. 602–608 ; Rees, *Welsh Saints*, p. 151.

herbs, and clothed himself in the skins of beasts. LLANDDEWI BREFI marks the spot where, at a synod assembled for the purpose, he refuted Pelagius. He was buried at his see of TY DDEWI, ' the house of David ', a place which the Saxons call St. Davids.[1] The names of St. Asaph,[2] the apostle of North Wales, and of St. Maughold or Macull, the apostle of the Isle of Man, are to be found on the maps of the countries where they laboured. A few more of these names are appended in a note.[3]

At KIRKCUDBRIGHT and elsewhere, we find the name of St. Cuthbert, a shepherd-boy who became abbot of Melrose, and the Thaumaturgus of Britain. St. Beya, an Irish virgin, lived an ascetic life at ST. BEES, where her shrine was long a great place of pilgrimage. We find the name of St. Jia, another female saint, at ST. IVES in Cornwall. There is another place called ST. IVES, which takes its name, we are told, from St. Ivon,[4] a Persian bishop ; but how his body reached Huntingdonshire, where it was miraculously discovered by a ploughman in the year 1001, tradition sayeth not. The neighbour-

---

[1] Alban Butler, *Lives of the Saints*, March 1 ; Lappenberg, *Anglo-Saxon Kings*, vol. i. p. 133 ; Rees, *Cambro-British Saints*, pp. 402–448 ; Rees, *Welsh Saints*, pp. 43–56, 191–201.

[2] Rees, *Welsh Saints*, p. 265.

[3] The names of .... are attributed to

LLANGATTOCK, Brecknock, and Monmouth . . . . CADOXTON, Glamorgan	St. Cadoc, a martyr.
LLANBADERN, Radnor, and Cardigan .	St. Padern, an Armorican bishop who came to Wales.
LLANGYBI, near Caerleon . . . . . CAERGYBI, at Holyhead	St. Cybi.
LLANILLTYD, Glamorgan . . . . . ILLSTON, Glamorgan	St. Illtyd, an Armorican.
CRANTOCK, Cardigan	St. Carannog.
LLANGADOG, Carmarthenshire . . .	St. Gadoga, a British saint of the fifth century, who died in Brittany.
LLANIDLOES	St. Idloes.
ARDFINNAN, in Tipperary . . . . INISFALLAN, in Kerry	St. Finian the leper, a royal saint.
KILBAR, in the Isle of BARRA . . .	St. Bar.
ST. KENELM'S WELL	St. Kenelm, a Mercian prince, murdered in a wood by his aunt at the age of seven.
KILLALOE	St. Lua. [St. Dalua—Joyce.j
PERRANZABULOE, or St. Perran in Sabulo, Cornwall, a church buried in the drifting sand	St. Piran, a bishop consecrated by St. Patrick for a mission to Cornwall.
PADSTOW, i.e. Petrocstow, in Cornwall	St. Petroc, one of St. Patrick's missionary bishops.
PENZANCE, i.e. Saint's Headland . .	St. Anthony [rather St. John].

The legends of St. Cadoc, St. Padern, St. Cybi, St. Illtyd, and St. Carannog will be found at length in Rees, *Cambro-British Saints*, pp. 309, 306, 465, 495, 502 ; and those of the others, in Alban Butler, *Lives of the Saints*, and Rees, *Welsh Saints*.

[4] Cf. Gough's Camden, vol. ii. p. 248. There is a third St. Ivo, the popular saint

ing town of ST. NEOTS bears the name of St. Neot, who was a relative of King Alfred.[1]

ST. MALO takes its name from St. Maclou, as the chronicles call him. He appears to have been one of those wandering evangelists [2] of whom Ireland and Scotland sent forth so many in the sixth century, and we may perhaps conjecture that his real name was McLeod, and that his cousin St. Magloire was really a McClure.[3] A more historical personage is St. Gall (the Gael), the most celebrated of the successors of St. Columba :—he occupied high station in France, and founded in the uncleared forest the Scotch abbey of ST. GALLEN, from which one of the Swiss cantons takes its name.[4] Another Swiss canton, that of GLARUS, belonged to a church founded by St. Fridolin, an Irish missionary, and dedicated to St. Hilarius, a saint whose name has been corrupted into Glarus.[5] ST. GOAR built a hut beneath the dangerous Lurlei rock, at the spot which bears his name, and devoted himself to the succour of shipwrecked mariners.[6] St. Brioc fled from the Saxon invaders of Britain, and founded a monastery at ST. BRIEUX in Brittany.[7] The town of ST. OMER was the see of St. Audomar, a Suabian favourite of Dagobert, and ST. CLOUD was the scene of the retirement of St. Hlodowald, one of the saints whose royal birth facilitated their admission to the honours of the calendar.[8]

Legends more or less marvellous often attach to names of this class.

The history of St. Brynach, who gave his name to LLANFRY-NACH, is, to say the least, somewhat remarkable ! We are

of Brittany. He was an honest lawyer, and hence he is represented as a black swan in certain mediæval verses in his honour :—

> ' Sanctus Ivo erat Brito
> Advocatus, sed non latro
> Res miranda populo '.
> Jephson, *Tour in Brittany*, p. 81.

[1] Turner, *Saxons*, vol. i. pp. 549–553.
[2] A catalogue of some of these Irish saints will be found in Alban Butler, *Lives of the Saints*, vol. xii. pp. 415–432.
[3] For an account of St. Magloire see Ansted, *Channel Islands*, p. 324 ; Rees, *Welsh Saints*, p. 256.
[4] Maclear, *History of Missions*, pp. 146–152 ; Lappenberg, *Anglo-Saxon Kings*, vol. i. p. 183.
[5] Lappenberg, *Anglo-Saxon Kings*, vol. i. p. 183.
[6] Maclear, *History of Christian Missions*, p. 132.
[7] Jephson, *Tour in Brittany*, p. 31.
[8] SANTAREM, SANTIAGO, and SANTANDER, in the Peninsula, take their names respectively from St. Irene, a holy virgin, St. James, and St. Andrew ; ARCHANGEL, in Russia, from St. Michael ; MARSABA, on the Dead Sea, from the celebrated St. Saba, hermit and abbot,

gravely told how, for lack of a boat, he sailed from Rome to Milford Haven mounted on a piece of rock, and how among other proofs of supernatural power he freed Fishguard from the unclean spirits, who by their howlings had rendered the place uninhabitable.[1]

Sometimes we have legends of a totally different class, as in the case of ST. HELIERS in Jersey. Here, we are told, was the retreat of St. Helerius,[2] who mortified the flesh by standing on sharp stones with spikes pointed against his shoulders, and others against his breast, in order to prevent him from falling backwards or forwards in his weariness.[3]

A far more picturesque legend is that which accounts for the name of the castle of ST. ANGELO at Rome. We are told that, in the time of Gregory the Great, while a great plague was desolating Rome, the Pontiff, walking in procession at the head of his monks, and chaunting a solemn litany for the deliverance of the city, saw, or thought he saw, St. Michael, the destroying angel, standing upon the very summit of the vast mausoleum of Hadrian, in the act of sheathing his avenging sword. The plague ceased, and thenceforward, in memory of the miracle, the tower bore the name of the castle of the angel, whose effigy, poised upon its summit in eternal bronze, is pointed out as a perpetual evidence of the truth of the legend.[4]

Where the reputed burial-places of celebrated saints have become great places of pilgrimage, the name of the saint has often superseded the original appellation. Thus the reputed tomb of Lazarus has changed the local name of Bethany to EL LAZARIETH; and Hebron, the place of interment of Abraham, who was called the friend of God, is now called by the Arabs EL KHALIL, or 'the friend'.[5] ST. EDMUND'S BURY in Suffolk was the scene of the martyrdom of St. Edmund, king of the East Angles. He was taken prisoner by Ingvar the Viking, and having been bound to a tree, he was scourged, and made a target for the arrows of the Danes, and was

1 Rees, *Cambro-British Saints*, pp. 289–298; Rees, *Welsh Saints*, p. 156.
2 Not to be confounded with St. Hilarius, Bishop of Poitiers, or with Hilarius, Bishop of Arles, to whom Waterland has assigned the authorship of the Athanasian Creed.
3 Latham, *Channel Islands*, pp. 320–323.
4 Dean Milman has ruthlessly pronounced this picturesque legend to be inconsistent with Gregory's own letters. *History of Latin Christ*, vol. i. p. 409.
5 Stanley, *Jewish Church*, p. 488.

finally beheaded.[1]   ST. OSYTH in Essex is said to bear the
name of a queen of the East Angles who was beheaded by the
Danes.[2]   ST. ALBANS claims to be the scene of the sufferings
of the protomartyr of Britain, and the still more marvellous
legend of Dionysius the Areopagite finds a local habitation
at ST. DENIS, the burial-place of the kings of France. The
name of SANTIAGO DE COMPOSTELLA in Spain has been curiously
formed out of the Latin phrase Sancto Jacobo Apostolo.[3]

Of the great monastic edifices of later ages, most of which
are now demolished wholly or in part, or devoted to other
purposes, we find traces in the names of AXMINSTER, LEOMIN-
STER, KIDDERMINSTER, WESTMINSTER, WARMINSTER, BED-
MINSTER, BEAMINSTER, STURMINSTER, UPMINSTER, and others.
Minster is the Anglo-Saxon form of the Low Latin Mona-
sterium. From the same word come the names of several
places called MONSTIERS, MOUSTIERS, or MOUTIER in France and
Switzerland, and various MONASTIRS in Greece and Thessaly.
The bay of ABER BENIGUET in Brittany, takes its name from the
lighthouse which the Benedictine monks maintained to warn
vessels from the dangerous rocks upon the coast.[4]   MÜNCHEN,
or Munich as we call it, takes its name from the warehouse in
which the monks (German mönche) stored the produce of their
valuable salt-mines at Reichenhall and Salzburg. ABBEVILLE
was the township belonging to the Abbot of St. Valeri, seized
and fortified by Hugh Capet.[5]   Numerous names, such as
NUNTHORPE and NUNEATON, STAPLEFORD ABBOTS and ABBOTS
LANGLEY, BISHOPSLEY and BISHOPS STORTFORD, MONKTON
and MONKLANDS, PRESTON and PRESTWICH, PRIORS HARDWICK,
BUCKLAND MONACHORUM, KINGSBURY EPISCOPI, and TOLLER
FRATRUM record the sites of the long-secularized possessions
of nuns, abbots, priors, bishops, friars, monks, and priests.[6]
The word Temple often appears as a prefix or suffix in village
names, and marks the possession of the Templars : such are
CRESSING TEMPLE and TEMPLE ROYDON in Essex, TEMPLE

---

[1] Matthew of Westminster, Roger Wendover, and John of Brompton, apud Lappenberg, Anglo-Saxon Kings, vol. ii. p. 39 ; St. John, Four Conquests, vol. i. p. 253 ; Sharon
Turner, Saxons, vol. i. pp. 521–525.

[2] Gough's Camden, vol. ii. pp. 124, 138. The name seems to be eponymic. Osyth
means ' water channel ', and would correctly characterize the natural features of the
spot.

[3] Yonge, Christian Names, vol. i. p. 54.

[4] Ibid. vol. i. p. 382.

[5] Palgrave, Normandy and England, vol. iii. p. 56.

[6] Sion House, near Kew, was a nunnery. Gough's Camden, vol. ii. p. 88.

CHELSING, and TEMPLE DINSLEY in Herts. TERREGLES in Dumfries is a corruption of *Terra Ecclesiæ*, a phrase which is usually translated into the form of KIRKLANDS, or corrupted into ECCLES. The name of AIX-LA-CHAPELLE [1] reminds us of the magnificent shrine erected over the tomb of Charlemagne, and CAPEL CURIG of the chapel of a humble British saint.

[1] Mr. Burgon, in his amusing letters from Rome, has recently pointed out an undoubted etymology for this word *chapel*, which has so long puzzled etymologists. It seems to have been the name given to the arched sepulchres excavated in the walls of the catacombs of Rome, which afterwards became places where prayer was wont to be made. The Low Latin *capella* is the hood or covering of the altar. Hence our words *cape* and *cap*. See Wedgewood, *Dictionary of English Etymol.* vol. i. p. 322. The inscription in the catacombs which gave Mr. Burgon the clue is *literatim* as follows : ' EGO SECUNDA FECI CAPELLA BÖNE MEMORIE FILIEM MEEM SECUNDINEM QE RECESSIT IN FIDEM CUM FRATREM SUM LAURENTIUM IN PACE RECESERUND '. *Letters from Rome*, p. 206. Any of our *young* schoolboy readers may correct the grammar, and then translate the inscription for their sisters' benefit.

CHAPTER XIV

PHYSICAL CHANGES ATTESTED BY LOCAL NAMES

The nature of geological changes—The valley of the Thames once a lagoon filled with islets—Thanet once an island—Reclamation of Romney Marsh—Newhaven—Somersetshire—The Traeth Mawr—The Carse of Gowrie—Loch Maree—The Fens of Cambridgeshire—The Isle of Axholme—Silting up of the lake of Geneva—Increase of the Delta of the Po—Volcanoes—Destruction of ancient Forests—Icelandic Forests—The Weald of Kent—Increase of population—Populousness of Saxon England—The nature of Saxon husbandry—English vineyards—Extinct animals : the wolf, badger, auroch, and beaver—Ancient Salt Works—Lighthouses—Changes in the relative commercial importance of towns.

Vast geological operations are still in progress on this globe ; continents are slowly subsiding at the rate of a few inches in a century ; while new lands are uprising out of the waters, and extensive deltas are in process of formation by alluvial deposition. But these changes, vast as is their aggregate amount, are so gradual that generations pass away without having made note of any sensible mutations. Local names, however, form an enduring chronicle, and often enable us to detect the progress of these physical changes, and occasionally even to assign a precise date to the period of their operation.

Thus it is not difficult to prove that the present aspect of the lower valley of the Thames is very different from what it must have been a thousand years ago. Instead of being confined within regular banks the river must have spread its sluggish waters over a broad lagoon, which was dotted with marshy islands. This is indicated by the fact that the Anglo-Saxon word *ea* or *ey*, an island, enters into the composition of the names of many places by the river-side which are now joined to the mainland by rich pastures. BERMONDSEY, PUTNEY, CHERTSEY, MOULSEY,[1] IFFLEY, OSNEY, WHITNEY,

---

[1] The island at the confluence of the Mole and the Thames.

and ETON or Eaton, were all islands in the lagoon. The Abbey Church of Westminster was built for security on THORNEY Island, and the eastern portion of the water in St. James' Park is a part of that arm of the Thames which encircled the sanctuary of the monks, and the palace of the Anglo-Saxon kings. The name CHELSEA is a contraction of *chesel-ea*, or ' shingle island ', and in its natural features the place must have once resembled the eyots which are found in the Thames near Hampton. In Leland's time there was a shingle bank at the mouth of the Axe in Devon called the Chisille. The long ridge of shingle which joins the Isle of Portland to the mainland is also called the Chesil bank ; and the name of the *Isle* of Portland proves that the foundation of this ridge took place in modern times, subsequent to the period when Anglo-Saxon gave place to modern English.

The *Isle* of Thanet was formerly as much an island as the Isle of Sheppey is at the present time. Ships bound up the Thames used ordinarily to avoid the perils of the North Foreland by sailing through the channel between the island and the mainland, entering by Sandwich and passing out by Reculver, near Herne Bay. SANDWICH, or ' sandy bay ', was then one of the chief ports of debarkation ; but the sands have filled up the wick or bay, the ancient port is now a mile and a half distant from high-water mark ; and the ruins of Rutupiæ, now Richborough, the port where the Roman fleets used to be laid up, are now surrounded by fine pastures. EBBFLEET, which is now half a mile from the shore, was a port in the twelfth century,[1] and its name indicates the former existence of a ' tidal channel ' at the spot.[2] This navigable channel, which passed between the Isle of Thanet and the mainland, has been silted up by the deposits brought down by the River Stour. STOURMOUTH—the name, be it noted, is English, not Anglo-Saxon—is now four miles from the sea, and marks the former embouchure of this river. CHISELET, close by, was once a shingle islet, and the name of FORDWICK,[3] five miles farther inland, proves that in the time of the Danes

---

1 Stanley, *Memorials of Canterbury*, p. 13.
2 The Celtic name of DURLOCK, more than a mile from the sea, means ' water lake ', and indicates the process by which the estuary was converted into meadow.
3 Fordwick means in Danish the bay on the arm of the sea. (See p. 113, *supra*.) Fordwick was anciently the port of Canterbury, and a corporate town. Gough's Camden, vol. i. p. 356. Norwich in the thirteenth and fourteenth centuries was ' on the banks of an arm of the sea '. Lyell, *Principles of Geology*, p. 307.

the estuary must have extended nearly as far as Canterbury.[1]

ROMNEY Marsh,[2] which is now a fertile tract containing 50,000 acres of the best pasturage in England, must, in Saxon times, have resembled the shore near Lymington—a worthless muddy flat, overflowed at every tide. OLD ROMNEY, NEW ROMNEY, and SCOTNEY, were low islands which afforded sites for the earliest fisher-villages. The name of WINCHELSEA, or *gwent-chesel-ey,* enlightens us as to the process by which these islands were formed—namely, by the heaping up of shingle banks at the seaward edge of the muddy flats.[3] The recent origin of this tract of land, and the gradual progress of its reclamation, are moreover curiously illustrated by the fact that over the greater portion of the marsh the local names present a marked contrast to the ancient names which so abound in Kent. They are purely English, such as IVYCHURCH, FAIRFIELD, BROOKLAND, and NEWCHURCH. In a few of the more elevated spots the names are Saxon or Celtic, as WINCHELSEA or ROMNEY, while it is only when we come to the inland margin of the marsh that we meet with a fringe of ancient names like LYMNE or APPLEDORE,[4] which show the existence of continuous habitable land in the times of the Romans or the Celts.[5]

LYMNE, the ancient Portus Lemanus, is the καινὸς λιμὴν of Ptolemy, and was one of the three great fortified harbours which protected the communications of the Romans with the Continent. The ruins of the Roman port are now nearly two miles from the sea. The names of WEST HYTHE, which is more than a mile from the shore, and of HYTHE, which is only half a mile, chronicle the silting up of the backwater which formed the ancient port, and the successive seaward

---

[1] Beyond Canterbury is Olantigh, anciently Olantige, whose name shows that in Saxon times it must have been an *ige*, or island.

[2] From the Gaelic word *ruimne,* a marsh. The name of RAMSEY, in the Fens, is derived from the same source.

[3] Dungeness, at the southern extremity of Romney Marsh, is a long spit of shingle, derived from the disintegration of the cliffs at Beachy Head, and has for the last two centuries been advancing seaward at the rate of nearly twenty feet per annum. Lyell, *Principles,* p. 316.

[4] From the Celtic *dwr,* water. Appledore was once a maritime town. See Gough's Camden, vol. i. p. 368.

[5] The same is the case in the Fens. The portions reclaimed at an early period show English names surrounded by a border of Danish names on the north, and of Saxon names on the south. The same is the case with the Delta of the Rhone. Places lying to the north of the old Roman road between Nismes and Beziers have Celtic names, while all those to the south of the road have names of Romance derivation. Astruc, *Hist. Languedoc,* pp. 374, 375 ; Lyell, *Principles,* p. 258.

advances of the shingle since the time when the Saxon word
hithe was superseded by its English equivalent ' haven '.[1]

The name of NEWHAVEN commemorates a geological event
of an opposite character. LEWES was anciently a port,[2]
and HAMSEY was a marshy island in the estuary of the River
Ouse, which then entered the sea at SEAFORD,[3] but a great
storm in the year 1570 permanently changed its course, and
the port of Newhaven has arisen at the new outlet of the
river.[4]

PEVENSEY and SELSEY are now no longer islands, the channels which divided them from the mainland having been
silted up. The name of SELSEY (seal's island) reminds us of
the remote period when seals lay basking on the Sussex coast.[5]

The central part of Somersetshire presents many names which
show great physical changes.[6] In Celtic times STICKLINCH,
MOORLINCH and CHARLINCH were islands, as was the case in the
Saxon period with MUCHELNEY, RODNEY, GODNEY, ATHELNEY,
HENLEY, BRADNEY, HORSEY, HACKNEY, OTHERY, MIDDLENEY,
THORNEY, CHEDZOY, WESTONZOYLAND, MIDDLEZOY, and WEST-
HOLME, while the pasture-land called MEARE must once have
been the bed of an inland lake.

The whole district of the TRAETH MAWR or ' Great Sand '
in North Wales was an estuary at no very remote period.
The action of the sea may be distinctly traced along the rocks
near Tremadoc.[7] Almost every rocky knoll on the wide flat
pasture land bears the name of *ynys*, or island,[8] and must
once have been surrounded by every tide, as is still the case
with Ynys-gifftan and Ynys-gyngar. YNYS FAWR and YNYS
FACH, the ' Great Island ' and the ' Little Island ' are now
two miles from the sea.[9] From YNYS HIR, now some way
inland, Madoc is said to have sailed in quest of unknown
lands. Ywern, two miles from the sea, was once a seaport
as is proved by the parish register of Penmorpha.[10]

---

[1] Wright, *Wanderings of an Antiquary*, p. 123. [2] See p. 120, *supra*.
[3] Probably from the Danish *fjord*.
[4] The name of NEWPORT in South Wales reminds us in like manner of the decay of
the Roman port at Caerleon, and the erection of another a little nearer to the sea ; and
NEWPORT in the Isle of Wight has taken the place of an older harbour near Carisbrooke
[5] See Gough's Camden, vol. i. p. 268.
[6] See Macaulay, *History of England*, vol. i. p. 604.
[7] The site of this town was reclaimed from the sea in 1813 by means of an embankment
made by Mr. Maddock.
[8] e.g. YNYS-GWELY, YNYS-CEILIOG, YNYS-CALCH, YNYS-TYWYN.
[9] YNYS GWERTHERYN, south of Harlech, is a mile inland.
[10] Davis, on the Geology of Tremadoc, in *Quarterly Journal of the Geological Society*,
for May, 1846, vol. ii. pp. 70–75 ; Chambers, *Ancient Sea Margins*, p. 20.

The tract of land near Dartmouth called NEW GROUND was only reclaimed from the river a century ago,[1] ROODEY, which now forms the racecourse at Chester, was formerly an island surrounded by the river Dee, like the INCHES, or islands of Perth. The Carse of Gowrie is the bed of an ancient arm of the sea, which having been nearly filled up by the alluvium of the Tay and the Earn, has, in common with the whole of central Scotland, .undergone an elevation of twenty to thirty feet since the Roman period. INCHTURE, INCHMARTIN, INCHMICHAEL, INCHYRA, and MEGGINCH were, as the names witness, islands in this frith.[2]   In the plain a little below Dunkeld, a hillock containing 156 acres goes by the name of INCHTUTHILL, ' the island of the flooded stream ', showing that the Tay must once have surrounded it.[3]

This secular elevation of Scotland may also be traced by means of the raised beaches on the western coast. Here also we meet with a remarkable etymological confirmation of the results arrived at on independent grounds by geological investigators.   ' Loch Ewe, in Ross-shire, one of our salt sea locks,' says Hugh Miller, ' receives the waters of Loch Maree —a noble freshwater lake, about eighteen miles in length, so little raised above the sea level that ere the last upheaval of the land it must have formed merely the upper reaches of Loch Ewe. The name Loch Maree—Mary's Loch [4]—is evidently mediæval. And, curiously enough, about a mile beyond its upper end, just where Loch Ewe would have terminated ere the land last arose, an ancient form has borne, from time immemorial, the name of KINLOCH EWE—the head of Loch Ewe '. [5]

START ISLAND, in the Orkneys, has in comparatively recent times been separated from the Island of Sanda. The word start means a tail, as in the case of Start-point, in Devon, and the redstart or red-tailed bird. Thus the name of this island proves that it was once only a long promontory projecting from the island of Sanda.[6]

[1] Murray, *Handbook to Devonshire and Cornwall*, p. 58.
[2] Chambers, *Ancient Sea Margins*, p. 19 ; Geikie, ' On the Date of the Last Elevation of Central Scotland ', in *Quarterly Journal of Geological Society*, vol. xviii. p. 227.   An anchor has been dug up at Megginch, and at the farm of Inchmichael a boat-hook was found at a depth of eight feet below the soil, and twenty feet above the present high watermark.
[3] Chambers, *Ancient Sea Margins*, p. 44.
[4] Or, perhaps, from the Celt c *mor*, the sea.
[5] Hugh Miller, *Lectures on Geology*, p. 23.   [6] Lyell, *Principles*, p. 302.

The Fens of Cambridgeshire and Huntingdonshire constitute a vast alluvial flat of more than a thousand square miles in extent, and must formerly have been a shallow bay six times as large as the Wash, which has been silted up by the deposits of the Nen, the Welland, and the Ouse.

The local names in this district show, as might have been expected, great alterations in the distribution of land and water. HOLBEACH is now six miles from the coast, and WISBEACH, the beach of the Wash or Ouse, is seven miles inland.[1] The ancient sea-wall, now at a considerable distance from the shore, has given rise to the local names of WALSOKEN, WALTON, and WALPOLE.

The tide does not now come within two miles of TYDD, and almost all the present villages in the Fen country were originally islands, as is shown by their names. Thus Tilney, Gedney, Stickney, Ramsey, Thorney, Stuntney, Southery, Norney, Quaney, Helgae, Higney, Spinney, Whittlesey, Yaxley, Ely, Holme, Oxney, Eye, Coveny, Monea, Swathesey, Sawtrey, Raveley, Rowoy, and Wiskin,[2] are no longer, as they once were, detached islands in the watery waste ; the great island seas of Ramsey Mere and Whittlesey Mere are now drained, and the flocks of Wildfowl have given place to flocks of sheep.

The Isle of AXHOLME or AXELHOLME, in Lincolnshire, is now joined to the main land by a wide tract of rich cornland. The name shows that it has been an island during the time of the Celts, Saxons, Danes, and English. The first syllable *Ax* is the Celtic word for the water by which it was surrounded. The Anglo-Saxons added their word for island to the Celtic name, and called it Axey. A neighbouring village still goes by the name of HAXEY. The Danes added *holm,* the Danish word for island, to the Saxon name, and modern English influences have corrupted Axeyholme into Axelholme, and contracted it into Axholme, and have finally prefixed the English word *Isle.* The internal evidence afforded by the name is supplemented by historical facts. In the time of Henry II. the island was attacked and taken by the Lincolnshire men in boats, and so late as the time of James I it was surrounded

---

[1] We have also LANDBEACH, WATERBEACH, ASBEACH, OVER (Anglo-Saxon *ufer,* a shore), and ERITH (*ora,* shore, and *hithe,* haven), which are all places on the edge of the present Fen district.

[2] Both syllables of this name are Celtic. It is evidently the ' water island '. See p. 145, *supra.*

by broad waters, across which the islanders sailed once a week to attend the market at Doncaster.[1]

We can trace similar changes on the Continent.   The city of LISLE is built on *L'isle*, once an island.   MONTREUIL SUR MER, formerly Monasteriolum super Mare, was built in the year 900, on the banks of an estuary which has been silted up, and the town is now separated from the sea by many miles of alluvial soil.[2]   A Danish fleet once sailed up to *Ba*vent, which is now ten miles from the sea.   WISSAN is now four miles from the sea. The name is a corruption of the Norse Wissant or Witsand, and refers to the ' White sand ' which has choked up the harbour from which, in all probability, Cæsar first sailed for Britain.[3]   ST. PIERRE-SUR-LE-DIGUE, near Bruges, is six miles from the present seawall, and the town of DAMME, which once possessed an harbour and considerable maritime trade, is now an inland   agricultural   town.[4]   NOTRE DAME DES PORTS, at the mouth of the Rhone, was an harbour in the year 898, but is now three miles from the sea.[5]   OSTIA, as the name implies, and as we are expressly told, was founded at the mouth of the Tiber, but the alluvial matter from the Apennines brought down by the yellow river has now advanced the coast line three miles beyond Ostia [similarly GENEVA, Curtius].[6]

There are but few islands in the world whose names do not contain some root denoting their insular character.   A remarkable exception to this rule is to be found in the names of the islands which lie off the mouth of the Scheldt, and at the entrance of the Zuyder Zee.   Does not the circumstance bear a striking testimony to the historical fact that it is only within comparatively recent times that the delta of the Scheldt has been broken up, and the Zuyder Zee formed by incursions of the ocean ?

PORT VALAIS, the Portus Valesiæ of the Romans, occupies the site of the ancient harbour at the upper end of the Lake of Geneva.   The alluvium of the Rhone has advanced the land nearly two miles in less than two thousand years, being at the rate of between four and five feet per annum.   VILLENEUVE, the new town, has taken the place of the old port.

[1] Smiles, *Lives of the Engineers*, vol. i. p. 37.
[2] Palgrave, *England and Normandy*, vol. ii. p. 57.
[3] Ibid. vol. ii. p. 200.
[4] Burn, *Tour in Belgium*, p. 14.
[5] Lyell, *Principles*, p. 259.
[6] Bunbury, in Smith's *Dict. of Geogr.* s. v. Ostia.

The southern face of the Alps is bare and precipitous, and from meteorological causes, which are well understood, the district is peculiarly liable to sudden and violent falls of rain. The rivers of Lombardy are, in consequence, charged with an exceptional amount of alluvial matter. The whole plain of the Po is rapidly rising, so much so that at Modena the ruins of the Roman city are found forty feet beneath the surface of the ground. Hence at the embouchures of the Po and the Adige, we might anticipate rapid changes in the coast line ; and this we find to be the case. We find a range of ancient dunes and sea beaches stretching from Brandolo to Mesola. Ravenna, now four miles inland, stood on the coast two thousand years ago. One of the suburbs of Ravenna is called CLASSE, a corruption of Classis,[1] the ancient name of the port, which was capable of giving shelter to 250 ships of war. Classe is now separated from the sea by a dense forest of stone-pines two miles in breadth. The Adriatic takes its name from the town of ADRIA, which was its chief port, B.C. 200. ATRI, the modern town upon the site, is now nearly twenty miles from the coast.

The present delta of the Po, containing 2,800 square miles, was probably at no very distant date a shallow lagoon, resembling that which is crossed by the railway viaduct between Mestre and Venice. The delta commences at the town of OSTEGLIA, now eighty-six miles from the sea. The name of Osteglia would indicate that here formerly was the embouchure of the Po. ESTE is nearly thirty miles inland, and the name seems also to be a corruption of the word *ostia*. The Po has, moreover, frequently changed its channel, and two of these deserted river-beds are known by the names of the PO MORTO, the PO VECCHIO.[2]

The name of VESUVIUS is probably Oscan, and proves, as Benfey thinks, that this volcano must have been in eruption some 2,400 years ago, before the Greeks arrived in Italy.[3] A similar conclusion may be deduced from the fact that the name of ETNA means a ' furnace ' in the Phœnician language.[4] On the Bay of Baiæ we find MONTE NUOVO, the ' new moun-

---

[1] Niebuhr, *Lectures on Ethnol. and Geogr.* vol. ii. p. 240 ; Lyell, *Principles*, p. 256 ; Marsh, *Man and Nature*, p. 256.
[2] Lyell, *Principles*, p. 255 ; Beardmore, *Hydrology*, pp. 164–180.
[3] Benfey, in Höfer's *Zeitschrift*, vol. ii. p. 118. Cf. the Sanskrit *vasu*, fire.
[4] See p. 66, *supra*. The name of SODOM means burning, thereby indicating, as Dr. Stanley has suggested, the volcanic character of the region in which the catastrophe took place. *Sinai and Pal.* p. 289.

tain ', which, at the time of the eruption in the year 1538, was thrown up to a height of 440 feet in less than a week.[1]

Near Primiero, in the Italian Tyrol, is a lake, three miles long, called LAGO NUOVO. This was formed a few years ago by a landslip which choked up the entrance to one of the narrow mountain valleys.[2]

The physical condition and the climate of the northern hemisphere have been largely affected by the destruction of the forests which once clothed the greater part of Europe.[3] The notices of ancient writers are seldom sufficiently definite or copious to enable us to discover the extent of the old woodland. Occasionally we have tangible evidence such as is supplied by the bog oak of Ireland, or the buried trees of Lincolnshire. But ancient names here stand us in good stead, and enable us, at certain definite periods, to discover with considerable precision, the extent of primaeval forests now partly or entirely destroyed.

The local names of Iceland show in a very curious manner the way in which the rigour of the climate and the scarcity of fuel have caused the total destruction of the few forests of dwarf trees which existed at the time when the island was first discovered. At the present time, a solitary tree, about thirty feet in height, is the sole representative of the former Icelandic forests ; and the stunted bushes growing on the heaths are so eagerly sought for fuel that, as a recent traveller has observed, the loss of a toothpick is likely to prove an irreparable misfortune. The chief resource of the inhabitants is the drift-wood cast upon the coast by the gulf stream, or the costly substitute of Norwegian timber. But at the time of the first settlement of the island there must have been considerable tracts of woodland. In the *Landnamabok* we find no less than thirty-one local names containing the suffix *holt*, a wood, and ten containing the word *skogr*, a shaw. Most of these names still remain, though every vestige of a wood has disappeared. Thus there are several places still called HOLT ; and we also find HOLTFORD, SKALHOLT, REYKHOLT (where Snorro Sturleson was murdered), SKOGARFOSS, Cape SKAGI, SKOGCOTTR, and BLASKOGIHEIDI or Blue-wood-Heath.

---

[1] Lyell, *Principles of Geology*, pp. 366–372.
[2] Gilbert and Churchill, *Dolomite Mountains*, p. 451.
[3] See Marsh, *Man and Nature*, pp. 128–329.

The name of HOLSTEIN, or Hol-satia, means the Forest settlement, and it probably indicates, as Dr. Latham has observed,[1] that the now barren Segeberger Heath was once a vast forest which supplied a portion of the Angles with the materials for the fleets with which they invaded the shores of England.

In southern Europe names like BROGLIO, BROLO, and BREUIL attest the former existence of forests in districts now entirely bare. The name of the island of MADEIRA bears witness to the vast forests which clothed the mountains of the island, and which were wantonly destroyed by fire soon after the discovery by the Portuguese.[2]

The bare heaths to the south-west of London seem to have been at one time partially clothed with forest. This is indicated by the root *holt* (German $\mathfrak{Hol}$), which we find in the names of BAGSHOT, BADSHOT, EWSHOT, LODSHOT, BRAMSHOT, ALDERSHOT, and ALDERSHOLT.

The vast tract in Kent and Sussex which is now called the WEALD,[3] is the remains of a Saxon forest called the *Andredesleah*, which, with a breadth of 30 miles, stretched for 120 miles along the northern frontier of the kingdom of the South Saxons. In the district of the Weald almost every local name, for miles and miles, terminates in *hurst*, *ley*, *den*, or *field*. The *hursts*[4] and *charts*[5] were the denser portions of the forest ; the *leys* were the open forest glades where the cattle love to lie ;[6] the *dens*[7] were the deep wooded valleys, and the *fields* were[8] little patches of 'felled' [?] or cleared lands in the midst of the surrounding forest. From PETERSFIELD and MIDHURST, by BILLINGHURST, CUCKFIELD, WADHURST, and LAMBERHURST,

---

[1] *English Language*, vol. i. p. 123.
[2] Marsh, *Man and Nature*, p. 129. So also local names attest the former existence of the forests which covered the now bare slopes of the High Alps of Dauphiny. *Ib.* p. 24.
[3] Cf. the German *wald*, wood. WELL Street is the name of the Roman road which ran through the wooded district. Maury, *Hist. des Forêts*, p. 129.
[4] e.g. Penshurst, Lyndhurst, and Chiselhurst.
[5] As in Seal Chart and Chart Sutton in Kent. The word *chart* is identical with the *hart* (wood, or forest), which we find in such German names as the HARTZ Mountains, the HERCYNIAN Forest, HUNHART, LYNDHART, etc. *H* and *ch* are interchangeable, as in the case of the Chatti, who have given their name to Hesse. There seems to have been a German word *harud* or *charud*, from which *hart* and *chart* are derived. We find it in the names of the 'forest tribes', the Harudes and the Cherusci. Cf. Latham, *English Language*, vol. i. p. 57 ; Maury, *Hist. des Forêts*, p. 187.
[6] The root of the word *leah* or *lea*, is the verb 'to lie'. Kemble, *Codex Dipl.* vol. iii. p. xxxiii. [A mistake ; see Skeat s. p. *Lea*.]
[7] *Den* is probably a Celtic word adopted by the Saxon. The ARDENNES is the 'great forest' on the frontiers of Belgium and France. On the word *den*, see Leo, *Rectitudines*, p. 91 ; Kemble, *Saxons*, vol. i. p. 481 ; Maury, *Hist. des. Forêts*, p. 167.
[8] e.g. Cuckfield, Lindfield, Uckfield. On *field* see note on p. 112, *supra*.

as far as HAWKSHURST and TENTERDEN, these forest names
stretch in an uninterrupted string.[1]   The *dens* were the swine
pastures ; and down to the seventeenth century the ' Court
of Dens ', as it was called, was held at Aldington to determine disputes arising out of the rights of forest pasture.[2]
Another line of names ending in *den* testifies to the existence of
the forest tract in Hertfordshire, Bedfordshire, and Huntingdonshire, which formed the western boundary of the East
Saxon and East Anglian kingdoms.   HENLEY IN ARDEN, and
HAMPTON IN ARDEN, are vestiges of the great Warwickshire
forest of ARDEN, which stretched from the forest of Dean to
Sherwood Forest.

The BLACK FOREST in Argyle is now almost entirely desti-
tute of trees, and the same is the case with the COTSWOLD
Hills in Gloucestershire.   This name contains two synony-
mous elements.[3]   The second syllable is the Anglo-Saxon
WEALD, a weed, which we find in the now treeless WOLDS of
Yorkshire ; and the first portion is the Celtic *coed*, a wood, which
we find in CHAT MOSS, CATLOW, COITMORE, GOODGRAVE, and
CADBEESTON.[4]

The name of DERBY, the ' village of wild beasts ',[5] shows us

[1] An analysis of the forest names in the Weald gives the following results :—

	hurst	den	ley	holt, hot	field	Total.
Central Kent	33	42	22	1	19	117
Northern Sussex	40	16	21	4	28	109
Southern Surrey	1	0	8	11	2	22
Eastern Hants	26	1	15	3	6	51
Total	100	59	66	19	55	299

[2] The surnames Hayward and Howard are corruptions of Hogwarden, an officer
elected annually to see that the swine in the common forest pastures or *dens* were duly
provided with rings, and were prevented from straying.   The Howard family first comes
into notice in the Weald, where their name would lead us to expect to find them.   So the
family name of Woodward is *vudu veard*, the wood warden, whose duties were analogous
to those of the howard.   There are many evidences of the importance attached to swine
in Anglo-Saxon times.   *Flitch* is etymologically the same word as *fleisch* or *flesh*, [rather
as *flake—Skeat*,] showing that the flesh of swine was pre-eminently ' the flesh ' to which
our ancestors were accustomed.   Sir Walter Scott, in the well-known forest dialogue
in Ivanhoe, has pointed out the fact that while veal, beef, mutton, and venison are
Norman terms, bacon is Saxon.   [*Bacon* though ultimately of Teutonic origin came to
us from the old Freach.   See *N.E.D.*] Cf. Mrs. Grote, *Collected Papers*, p. 165 ; Kemble,
Anglo-Saxons, vol. i. pp. 481–486 ; Leo, *Rectitudines*, p. 129 ; Marsh, *Lectures on English
Language*, p. 248.
[3] See pp. 150–152, *supra*.
[4] Whitaker, *History of Whalley*, p. 9 ; Verstegan, *Restitution*, p. 262.
[5] The German word *thier* still means any wild animal ; but in England the extermina-

the state of things on the arrival of the Danes. The Midland Derby lay between the forests of Arden and Sherwood. The hundred of Derby, which occupies the southern portion of Lancashire, and includes the populous towns of Liverpool and Wigan, was one vast forest, with the solitary village of Derby standing in the midst, till at length the villages of Ormskirk and Preston grew up around the church built by Ormr, and the priest's house.[1]

Indeed, Lancashire, which is now such a busy hive of workers, was one of the most desolate and thinly peopled parts of England before coal had been discovered underlying her barren moorlands and thick forests. An analysis of the local names will enable us to make a rough comparison of the area anciently under cultivation with that which was unreclaimed. Throughout Lancashire we find very few names ending in *borough, by,* or *thorpe,* and hence we conclude that the number of villages and towns was small. There is a fair sprinkling of names in *ham, worth,* and *cote,* suffixes which would denote detached homesteads; while the very large number of names which are compounded with the words *shaw, holt, ley, hill,* and *mere,* prove that the greater portion of the county consisted only of woodland or wild moor.[2]

In order to arrive at somewhat definite results an analysis has been made of the local names in the counties of Surrey and Suffolk. Of the total number of names in Surrey 36 per cent. have terminations like *wood, holt, hurst, ley, den,* or *moor,* and 12 per cent. end in *don, combe, ridge, hill,* etc., while 40 per cent. *exhibit* such suffixes as *ham, worth, cote, ton, sted,* or *borough,* whence we gather that the proportion of uninhabited to inhabited places was 48 to 40. In Suffolk, on the other hand, the population seems to have been much more dense, for 65 per cent. of the names denote habitations, 18 per cent. denote wood and moorland, and 7 per cent. denote hills.[3]

tion of the wolf, the wild ox, and the badger, has left the 'deer' as the solitary representative of the German *thier.*

[1] See Whitaker, *History of Manchester,* vol. ii. p. 403.
[2] Davies, in *Philolog. Trans.* for 1855, p. 262.
[3] We may tabulate these results as follows :—

Names in	ham.	ton.	ing.	thorpe.	borough or bury.	field.	ley.	wood.	hurst.
Suffolk . .	84	88	17	5	12	31	27	1	0
Surrey . .	36	30	10	1	10	9	40	14	15

It would thus appear that the ratio of the density of the population in Suffolk to that in Surrey was approximately as 13 to 8, whereas at the present time the population of Suffolk is 215 to the square mile, and that of Surrey 842, or in the ratio of 13 to 48.

The names which we have been considering indicate the former existence of ancient forests that have been cleared. In Hampshire we are presented with the converse phenomenon ; we meet with names which establish a fact which has been doubted by some historical inquirers, that extensive populated districts were afforested to form what now constitutes the New Forest.   The very name of the NEW FOREST has its historical value—and within its present reduced area, the sites of some of the villages that were destroyed are attested by names like TROUGHAM, FRITHAM, WOOTON, HINTON, BOCHAMPTON, TACHBURY, WINSTED, CHURCH WALK, and CHURCH MOOR, while the villages names of Greteham, Adelingham, Wolnetune, and Bermintone survive only in the Domesday record.[1]

The hundred is supposed to have been originally the settlement of one hundred free families of Saxon colonists, just as the canton was a similar Celtic division.[2]   In rural districts the population must have increased at least tenfold— often in a much larger proportion—since the period of the formation of the present hundreds.   Many single agricultural parishes contain a hundred families removed above the labouring class, and we may probably conclude that the population is equal to that of one of the Saxon hundreds.

The manner in which the island was gradually peopled, and the distribution and relative density of the Saxon population, are curiously indicated by the varying sizes of the hundreds. In Kent, Sussex, and Dorset, which were among the earliest settlements, the small dimensions of the hundreds prove that the Saxon population was very dense, whereas, when we approach the borders of Wales and Cumberland, where the Saxon tenure was one rather of conquest than of colonization, and where a few free families probably held in check a con-

---

[1] Ellis, *Introduction to Domesday*, p. xxxiv.   A colony of the dispossessed villagers was established at Carlisle by Rufus.   Of this I can find no trace in local names.   See Palgrave, *Eng. Common.* vol. i. p. 449.
[2] From the Welsh *cant*, a hundred.   See Diefenbach, *Celtica*, i. pp. 113–115 ; Hallam, *Middle Ages*, vol. ii. p. 391.   [But the word really comes from the Teutonic *Kant*, through Old Fr. *canton*, a nook or corner ; see *N.E.D.*]

siderable subject population, we find that the hundreds include a much larger area.

Thus the average number of square miles in each hundred is,

In Sussex	. . . . .	23	
Kent	. . . . .	24	
Dorset	. . . .	30	
Wiltshire	. . . .	44	
Northamptonshire	. .	52	
Surrey	. . . . .	58	

In Herts	. . . .	79
Gloucestershire	. .	97
Nottinghamshire	.	105
Derbyshire	. . .	162
Warwickshire	. .	179
Lancashire	. . .	302

We arrive at somewhat similar conclusions from the proportions of the slaves to the rest of the population, as returned in Domesday. In the east of England we find no slaves returned, the Celtic population having become entirely assimilated. In Kent and Sussex the slaves constitute 10 per cent. of the population ; in Cornwall and Devon, 20 per cent. ; and in Gloucestershire, 33 per cent.

The knowledge which we possess of several thousand names which have been preserved in Anglo-Saxon charters, enables us to ascertain, in many cases, the original forms of names which have now become more or less corrupted. From the study of these names Professor Leo, of Halle,[1] has arrived at the conclusion that agriculture was in a more advanced state among the Anglo-Saxons than on the Continent. A three-course system of husbandry was adopted ; wheat and flax are the crops which seem to have been the most cultivated. We meet with indications of the existence of extensive estates, on which stood large houses, occasionally of stone, but more frequently of wood, for the residence of the proprietor, surrounded by the *tun* or inclosure for cattle, and the *bartun* or inclosure for the gathered crops. Round the homestead were inclosed fields, with barns, mills, and weirs. There were detached outlying sheepfolds and sheepcotes, with residences for the serfs, and special pasturages were allotted to swine and goats. The estates were separated from one another by a *mark*, or broad boundary of woodland. There were open forest-pastures fed by swine, which must have presented an appearance resembling that of the open parts of the New Forest at the present day. In these woodlands the prevalent vegetation consisted of the thorn,

[1] Leo, *Anglo-Saxon Names*, p. 72. See also *Codex Diplomaticus Ævi Saxonici*, passim ; St. John, *Four Conquests of England*, vol. ii. p. 191 ; Ellis, *Introduction to Domesday Book*, pp. xxx,–xliv.

hazel, oak, ash, elm, lime, and fern.   The maple, beech, birch, aspen, and willow grew less abundantly.   There were planta-tions of osiers, and the names of the rush and sedge occur so frequently as to indicate a very defective state of drainage.

One fact, however, which we gather from these ancient names indicates a marked peculiarity in the aspect of Anglo-Saxon England.   In no single instance throughout the charters do we meet with a name implying the existence of any kind of pine or fir, a circumstance which curiously corroborates the assertion of Cæsar, that there was no fir found in Britain.[1] The names of fruit-trees are also very unfrequent, with the exception of that of the apple-tree, and even this appears very rarely in conjunction with Anglo-Saxon roots, being found chiefly in Celtic [2] names, such as APPLEDORE,[3] APPLEDURCOMBE, and AVALON ; or in Norse names, such as APPLEBY, APPLE-GARTH, and APPLETHWAITE.

At the period of the Conquest, vineyards do not seem to have been uncommon in the south of England.   In Domesday Book vineyards are mentioned in the counties of Hertford, Middlesex, Norfolk, Suffolk, Kent, Hampshire, Dorset, and Wilts.   At the present day a part of the town of Abingdon is called the VINEYARD, and there is also a field so called near Beaulieu Abbey in Hampshire, and another near Tewksbury.   The same name is borne by lands which were formerly attached to monastic foundations in the counties of Worcester, Hereford, Somerset, Cambridge, and Essex.   The very early existence of vine culture in England is indicated by the name of WINNAL in Hampshire, which is derived from the Celtic *gwinllan*, a vineyard.[4]

Local names occasionally preserve evidence of the former existence of animals now extinct.   The names of the wolf and the bear were so commonly used as personal appellations by the Danes and Saxons, that we are unable to pronounce with certainty as to the significance of names like WOLFERLOW in Herefordshire, or BARNWOOD in Gloucestershire.   WOL-VESEY, a small island at Winchester, was, however, the place

---

[1] See, however, Whitaker, *History of Manchester*, vol. i. p. 309.
[2] The root *apple* or *apul* runs through the whole of the Celtic, Scandinavian, Teutonic and Sclavonic languages. See Diefenbach, *Vergleich. Wörterb*, vol. i. p. 88.
[3] Appledore in Romney Marsh was a favourite station of the Vikings. See *Saxon Chronicle*. Hasting the Dane built a castle there.
[4] Redding, *Wines*, pp. 33, 34 ; Gough's Camden, vol. i. p. 189 ; Lappenberg, *Anglo-Saxon Kings*, vol. ii. p. 360 ; *Edinburgh Review*, vol. cxi. p. 392.

where the Welsh tribute of wolves' heads was annually paid.[1] The badger or broc gave its name to BAGSHOT, BROX-BOURNE, [BROCKLEY, BROCKENHURST] and BROGDEN ; the wild boar (eofer) was found at EVERSHAW, EVERSHOT, EVERTON, and EVERSLEY ; [2] and the crane at CRANFIELD and CRAN-BOURN.

The huge aurochs, which once roamed over the forests of Germany, is mentioned in the Niebelungen Lied by the name of the Wisent ; [3] and in Hesse we find a place called WIESEN-FELD, the ' aurochs' field ', and another called WIESENSTIEGE, the ' aurochs' stair '.[4] We find traces of the elk at ELBACH and ELLWANGEN ; and of the Schelch, a gigantic elk, now everywhere extinct, at SCHÖLLNACH.[5]

The fox is unknown in the Isle of Man, and not even a tradition survives of its former presence. A place called CRONK-SHYNNAGH, which means ' Fox hough ', is, however, sufficient to prove that this animal was once a denizen of the island.[6]

The vestiges of the Beaver are very numerous. BEVERLEY in Yorkshire is the ' beaver's haunt ', and we find a BEVERSTONE in Gloucestershire, and a BEVERCOATES in Nottinghamshire. The valley which stretches northwards from the Glyders, scored with glacial striæ and dotted over with moraines, bears the name of NANT FRANGON, or ' the beaver's dale ' ; and across this valley stretches SARN YR AFRANGE, or ' the beaver's dam '.[7] The magnificent pool, well known both to the artist and to the angler, which lies just below the junction of the Lledr and the Conway, is called LLYN YR AFRANGE, ' the beaver's pool '.[8] In Germany we have the names of BIBERS-BURG,[9] BIVERBIKE (the beaver's beck),[10] and the BEBRA (anciently Piparaha, or beaver's river).[11] From the Sclavonic bobr, a beaver, we have the River BOBER in Silesia, as well as BOBERN, BOBEROW, BOBERSBURG, BOBERWITZ and BOBRAU.[12]

1 Yonge, Christian Names, vol. ii. p. 269.
2 Leo, Anglo-Saxon Names, p. 12 ; Morris, Local Names, p. 10 ; Monkhouse, Etymologies, p. 40.
3 [The same word as bison.]
4 Piderit, Ortsnamen, p. 296 ; Förstemann, Ortsnamen, p. 145.
5 Förstemann, Ortsnamen, p. 145 ; Marsh, Man and Nature, p. 85.
6 Train, Isle of Man, vol. i. p. 20. [Irish sionnach, a fox.]
7 Pennant, Wales, vol. ii. p. 299.
8 Ibid. vol. ii. p. 134.
9 Pictet, Orig. Indo-Europ, vol. i. p. 444.
10 Vilmar, Ortsnamen, p. 258.
11 Piderit, Ortsnamen, p. 297 ; Vilmar, Ortsnamen, p. 256.
12 Buttmann, Ortsnamen, p. 124 ; Jacobi, Ortsnamen um Potsdam, p. 34.

BIÈVRE on the Aisne has been identified with the BIBRAX of Cæsar, and BIBRACTE, now Autun, was the chief city of the Ædui. The tribe of the BIBROCI no doubt called themselves 'the Beavers', in the same way that North American tribes take their names from the snakes, the foxes, or the crows.[1]

In the Saxon charters we find many allusions to quarries, but there is a remarkable absence of names denoting iron-works or mines, such names, for instance, as the GOLDBERG, EISENBERG, KUPFERHÜTTE, and ERZGEBERGE, which we find in Germany. In the Forest of Dean, however, we find on the map CINDER-FORD and CINDERHILL, names derived from vast heaps of scoriæ, from which the iron had been so imperfectly extracted by the Roman miners, that these mounds form a valuable consideration in the purchase of the ground on which they lie.[2] The charters contain numerous indications of the localities where salt was procured or manufactured.[3] Domesday Book enumerates no less than 385 salt-works in the single county of Sussex. The *wics* in the Essex marshes were probably once salt-works, and we have already traced the singular way in which the *wych* or bay-houses on the coast came to give a name to the inland salt-works of DROITWICH and NANTWICH.[4] But the evidence of names enables us to prove that many existing salt-works were worked before the advent of the Teutonic race. This we can do by means of the Celtic word *hal*, salt, which we find in the name of PWLLHELLI, the 'salt pools', in Carnarvonshire. At HALING, on the Hampshire coast, salt-works still exist, which apparently date from Celtic times ; and we find a place called HALTON in Cheshire, and HALSAL,[5] and HALLATON in Lancashire. In the salt-producing districts of Germany several towns whose names contain the Celtic root *hal* stand on rivers which contain the Teutonic synonym *sal*.[6] Thus HALLE, in Prussian

---

[1] Zeuss, *Grammatica Celtica*, vol. i. p. 44 ; vol. ii. p. 761 ; Glück, *Kelt. Namen*, p. 43 ; Förstemann, *Ortsnamen*, p. 145. The word beaver is common to most of the Aryan languages. Latin *fiber* (= beber), Cornish *befer*, Gaelic *beabhor*, Gaulish *biber*, German *befer*. The Welsh names are *afrange*, and *llost lydan*, ' the broad-tailed '. On the former existence of the beaver in Scotland, see Wilson, *Pre-historic Annals*, p. 193.

[2] Nicholls, *Forest of Dean*, p. 216.

[3] Ellis, *Introduction to Domesday*, p. xl. ; Lappenberg, *Anglo-Saxon Kings*, vol. i. p. 363.

[4] See p. 114, *supra*.

[5] [This name, with some of the others, is probably from the Norse *hall(r)*, slope, hill (H. Harrison, *Place Names of the Liverpool District*, 48).]

[6] An ingenious attempt to account for this distinction will be found in Leo, *Vorlesungen*, vol. i. p. 196.

Saxony, stands on the river SAALA (salt river) ; REICHEN-HALL,
in Bavaria, is also on a river SALE ; [1] HALLEIN, in SALZBURG,
stands on the SALZA. We find towns called HALL near the
salt mines of the Tyrol, of Upper Austria, and of Swabia ;
there is a HALLE in Ravensberg, a HALLSTADT in the Salzkam-
mergut, and HALEN and HAL in Brabant.[2]

The institution of lighthouses dates from very early times,
as names bear witness. The names of the PHAROS, at Dover
and Alexandria, and the GIBEL EL FARO, near Malaga, take
us back beyond the Christian era. In Sicily, the cape by the
side of Charybdis, and opposite Scylla, was called CAPE PELORUS
(Cape Terrible). It has now become CAPO DI FARO—the
erection of the lighthouse having caused the Cape to lose
at once its terrors, and its name of terror.[3] CAPE COLONNA,
in Greece, takes its name from the conspicuous white columns
of the ruined Doric temple which served as a landmark
to the Genoese and Venetian seamen ; [4] and CAPE CORUNNA,
in Spain, is so called from the columna or tower which
served the purpose of a Pharos. The name of FLAMBOROUGH
HEAD speaks of the rude fires of coal or wood that used to
' flame ' by night on that dangerous headland.[5] At the
extremity of the peninsula of FURNESS [6] (Fireness) is a small
island, on which stands a ruined building, called the PILE
OF FOUDRY—that is, the ' peel ' or tower of the ' fire isle '.[7]
Furness and Foudry are Norse names, and are an indication
of the antiquity of the lighthouse which guided the Northmen
in their voyages from the Isle of Man to Lancaster.[8] The
numerous BEACON HILLS throughout the island call to mind
the rude though efficient means by which, before the days
of the Electric Telegraph, the tidings of great events could

[1] There were six German rivers anciently called SALA. Förstemann, *Alt-deut. Namenbuch*, vol. ii. p. 1209. We find the river HALYS (salt water) in Galatia, and the river
HALYCUS in Sicily.

[2] On names containing the root *hal*, see Leo, *Rectitudines*, p. 203 ; and an article
by the same writer in Haupt's *Zeitschrift*, vol. v. p. 511 ; Grimm, *Deut. Mythol.* p. 1000 ;
Garnett, *Essays*, p. 150 ; Bender, *Deutschen Ortsnamen*, p. 113 ; Mahn, *Namen Berlin*,
p. 6.

[3] Duff, in *Oxford Essays*, for 1857, p. 93 ; Duke of Buckingham, *Diary*, vol. i.
p. 226.

[4] Bremer, *Greece*, vol. i. p. 313.

[5] This name may, however, mean the ' camp of refuge '. Anglo-Saxon *fleam*, a
fugitive. The extremity of the headland has been converted into a stronghold by an
ancient dyke still called Danes' Dyke.

[6] Ferguson, *Northmen*, p. 109.

[7] It is possible, however, the Furness may be only the ' fore ness ', and Foudry the
' isle of fowls '.

[8] There is also a FURNESS on the Belgian coast.

be communicated from one end of the island to the other. There are those now alive who can remember looking out, the last thing every night, towards the Beacon Hill to know if the dreaded landing of Bonaparte had taken place.

Though the commerce of the Anglo-Saxons was not extensive, yet our local names indicate considerable changes in the relative commercial importance of various towns. The natural advantages of the site of London have enabled it to maintain, at all times, its ancient pre-eminence—for its Celtic name implies that, even in pre-historic times, it was, as it is still, the ' city of ships '.[1]

From the Anglo-Saxon *ceapian*, to buy, *cypan*, to sell, and *ceap*,[2] price, or sale, we derive many names which indicate early seats of commercial activity. A *chipping* was the old English term for a market-place ; thus Wicliffe translates Luke vii. 32, ' They ben like children sitting in cheping and spekinge togidre '. Hence we see that CHIPPING NORTON, CHIPPING CAMDEN, CHIPPING SODBURY, CHIPPING ONGAR, CHIPPING BARNET, CHEPING HILL on the south side of the church at Witham, CHEPSTOW, and CHIPPINGHAM, are ancient market-towns — once of much greater *relative* commercial importance than they are at present. CHEAPSIDE and EAST-CHEAP were the old market-places of London. In Norse names the form *cope* takes the place of the Anglo-Saxon *ceap*. COPENHAGEN[3] is equivalent to Chipping Haven. In like manner we infer from the name of the COPELAND Islands near Belfast, that here were the storehouses of the goods brought by Norwegian traders. COPMANSTHORPE, near York, would be equivalent to the German Kaufmansdorf,

---

[1] [Welsh *llong*, Ir. *long*, a ship, from Lat. (*navis*) *longa* (W. Stokes, *Ir. Glosses*, 80).]
[2] To this root we may trace many idiomatic English words. A *chapman* is an itinerant seller : *chap* was originally an abbreviated form of chapman. *Cheap*, an abbreviation of good cheap, answers to the French *bon marché* ; while good cheap still survives in the phrase *dog cheap* [?], where the letters *d* and *g* have been interchanged according to a well-known phonetic law. The original sense of the root is that of bargaining—the ancient method of making a purchase—which is preserved in the word to *chaffer*. To *chop* horses is to sell them. A horse *couper* is one who deals in horses. To *chop* and change is to sell and barter. To *swop* and to *swab* are probably phonetic variations of to chop (?). Thus we say the wind chops, i.e. changes. The ultimate root is the Sanskrit *kupa*, the beam of a balance. Compare the old Sclavonic *kupiti*, to buy, the Gothic *kaupon*, the Latin *caupo*, and the Greek κάπηλος. Wedgwood, *Eng. Etym.* vol. i. p. 327 ; Pictet, *Orig. Indo-Europ.* part ii. pp. 416, 417.
[3] Anciently Kiobmans havn. The Norse word *köping*, is pronounced chaping. Hence we derive the names of JÖNKÖPING, LIDCÖPING, NYKÖPING, NORRKÖPING. See Thompson, *Travels in Sweden*, p. 42, quoted in Crichton, *Scandinavia*, vol. i. p. 226. KIEL and KIELERFIORD take their names from the Danish *keol*, a ship. Morris, *Local Names*, p. 29. The name of the HANSE towns seems to be from *hansel*, a contract, or *hanse*, a company or association. Wedgwood, in *Philolog. Trans*, for 1860–61, p. 37.

the merchants' village ; and the form of the word shows us that here the Danish traders resided, just as those of Saxon blood dwelt together at CHAPMANSLADE. The word *staple* also enables us to detect some of the local centres of Anglo-Saxon trade. This word has undergone some changes in meaning. It now denotes the established merchandize of a place ;—thus we should say lace is the staple of Nottingham. But the term was formerly applied to the place rather than to the merchandize, and our forefathers would have said Nottingham is the staple of lace.[1] In local names—as DUNSTABLE, BARNSTAPLE, and ETAPLES in France—this word staple denotes a place where merchants were wont to store their goods.[2]

When the English word market takes the place of the Anglo-Saxon *chipping*, or *staple*, as in the case of STOW-MARKET, MARKET BOSWORTH, or WICKHAM MARKET, we may fairly conclude that the commercial importance of the town in question dates from a more recent period.

[1] See Trench, *Glossary*, p. 205.
[2] It may be noted that the name of AMPURIAS in Spain retains, nearly unchanged, the name of the Hellenic settlement of *Emporiæ*.

CHAPTER XV

CHANGES AND ERRORS

Vitality of Local Names—Recurrence to ancient Names—Changes: in Names often simply phonetic—Lincoln—Sarum—Whitehall—Phonetic corruptions among savage tribes—Interchange of suffixes of analogous sound—Tendency to contraction—Laws of Phonetic change—Examples—Influence of popular etymological speculation on the form of Names—Tendency to make Names significant—Examples—Transformations of French Names—Invention of new Saints from Local Names—Transformed names often give rise to legends—Bozra—Thongcastle—The Dun Cow—Antwerp—The Mouse Tower—The Amazons of the Baltic—Pilatus—The Picts—The Tatars—Poland—Mussulman—Negro pont—Corruptions of Street Names—America—The Gypsies.

PROFESSOR MAX MÜLLER, in his deservedly popular lectures, has well illustrated the process of phonetic decay by which the words of a nation's speech are clipped and worn down by constant currency, until, like ancient coins, the legend which they bore at first has become effaced. Many words, whose paternity is nevertheless indisputable, do not retain a single letter, sometimes not even a single vocable, of the ancestral form, and exhibit still less resemblance to collateral descendants from the parent stock. Who would imagine, for instance, that the French word *larme* is the same as the English *tear* ; that the French *jour* is a lineal descendant of the Latin *dies*,[1] or that *dies*, and the two syllables of Tuesday are all descended from the same original Aryan root ?

In the case of local names the raw materials of language do not lend themselves with the same facility as other words to the processes of decomposition and reconstruction, and many names have for thousands of years remained unchanged, and even linger round the now deserted sites of the places to which they refer. The names of five of the oldest cities

---

[1] *Dies—diurnum tempus—giorno—jour. Aujourd'hui* contains the root *dies* twice, the *hui* being a corruption of *hodie*=hoc die. Max Müller, *Lectures*, p. 48 ; Lewis, *Romance Languages*, pp. 213, 220.

of the world—DAMASCUS, HEBRON, GAZA, SIDON, and HAMMATH —are still pronounced by the inhabitants in exactly the same manner as was the case thirty, or perhaps forty, centuries ago, defying oftentimes the persistent attempts of rulers to substitute some other name. During the three hundred years of the Greek rule, an attempt was made by the conquerors to change the name of HAMATH to Epiphania, but the ancient appellation lingered on the lips of the surrounding tribes, and has now resumed its sway, while the Greek name has been utterly forgotten. The name of Accho, which we find in the Old Testament, was superseded for some time by the Greek name of Ptolemais. This is now forgotten, and the place goes by the name of AKKA.[1] The Greeks attempted to impose their name of Nicopolis on the town of Emmaus, but in vain ; for the modern name, 'AMWÂS, still asserts the vitality of the ancient designation.[2] We read, in the Book of Chronicles, that Solomon built TADMOR in the wilderness. The Romans attempted to impose on it the name of Adrianopolis, but this appellation has utterly perished, and the Bedouin still give the ancient name of Tadmor [3] to the desolate forest of erect and prostrate columns, which marks the site of the city of the palms. TENEDOS and ARGOS still bear the names which they bore in the time of Homer. Most of the islands of the Grecian archipelago, and many of the neighbouring cities, retain their ancient names with little variation,[4] and several of the Etruscan cities are called by the same names which they bore at the first dawn of Italian civilization.[5]

But we need not go to the East for instances of the persistency with which names adhere to the soil. The name of LONDON is now, in all probability, pronounced exactly as it was at the time when Cæsar landed on the coast of Kent. The Romans attempted to change the name, but in vain. It mattered little what the city on the Thames was called in

[1] Stanley, *Sinai and Palestine*, p. 381 ; Robinson, *Later Researches*, p. 92.
[2] Robinson, *Later Researches*, p. 146.
[3] PALMYRA is an Italian translation of the enchorial name of Tadmor, and is known only in the West. See Beaufort, *Egyptian Sepulchres and Syrian Shrines*, vol. i. pp. 34, 302.
[4] Delos is now DILI, Paros is PARO, Scyros is SKYRO, Naxos is NAXIA, Patmos is PATIMO, Samos is SAMO, Thasos is THASO, Sardis is SART, Sparta is SPARTI, Arbela is ARBIL, Tyre or Tzur is SÛR, Nazareth is NAZIRAH, |Joppa is YAFA, Gaza is GHUZZEH.
[5] The names of SATURNIA and POPULONIA are unaltered. Cortona is now CORTONO, Volaterræ is VOLATERRA, Sena is SIENNA, Pisæ is PISA, and Perusia is PERUGIA.

the edicts of prefects and proconsuls. The old Celtic name continued in common usage, and has been transmitted in turn to Saxons, Normans, and Englishmen. It is curious to listen to Ammianus Marcellinus speaking of the name of London as a thing of the past—an old name which had gone quite out of use, and given place to the grand Roman name ' Augusta '.[1]

In like manner the ancient Indian name of HAITI has replaced the appellation of ST. DOMINGO, which the Spanish conquerors attempted to impose upon the island. But though so many names remain substantially unchanged in spite of efforts to supplant them, yet, as the successive waves of population have flowed on, many influences have been set at work which have sometimes produced material modifications, and it often requires the utmost care, and no inconsiderable research, to detect the original form and signification of very familiar names, and to extract the information which they are able to afford.

These modifying influences are of two kinds. The first is simply phonetic. A conquering nation finds it difficult to pronounce certain vocables which enter into the names used by the conquered people, and changes consequently arise which bring the ancient names into harmony with the phonetic laws of the language spoken by the conquerors. Many illustrations of this process may be found in Domesday. The ' inquisitors ' seem to have been slow to catch the pronunciation of the Saxon names, and were, moreover, ignorant of their etymologies, and we meet consequently with many ludicrous transformations. The name of LINCOLN, for example, which is a hybrid of Celtic and Latin, appears in the Ravenna Geographer in the form Lindum Colonia, and in Beda as Lindocolina. The enchorial name must have been very nearly what it is now. This, however, the Norman conquerors were unable to pronounce, and changed the name into Nincol or Nicole.[2] The name of SHREWSBURY is an English corruption of the Anglo-Saxon *Scrobbes-byrig* or Shrubborough. The Normans, however, corrupted Scrobbes-

---

[1] Ab Augustâ profectus, quam veteres adpellavêre Lundinium. *Amm. Marc.* lib. xxviii. cap. 3, § 1. Lundinium, vetus oppidum, quod Augustam posteritas adpellavit. Ibid. lib. xxvii. cap. 8, § 7.

[2] Dugdale, *Monast. Anglic.* vol. ii. p. 645, apud Thierry, *Norman Conquest*, p. 84.

bury into Sloppesburie, whence the modern name of SALOP is derived. So also the Roman Sorbiodunum was contracted into the English SARUM, and then, as in the case of Salop, the Normans changed the *r* into an *l*, and have thus given us the form SALISBURY.

In the Arabic chronicles of Spain we meet with many curious transformations of familiar names, such, for instance, as that of the Visigoths into the Bishtolkat.[1]

Mr. Motley, in his United Netherlands, has given an amusing instance from the archives of Simancas. A dispatch of the ambassador Mendoja stated that Queen Elizabeth was residing at the palace of St. James'. Philip II., according to his custom, has scrawled on the margin of this dispatch, ' There is a park between it and the palace which is called Huytal, but why it is called Huytal I am sure I don't know '. WHITEHALL seems to have presented an insurmountable etymological difficulty to the ' spider ' of the Escurial.

Among unlettered nations phonetic changes of this kind are especially likely to arise. The word YANKEE is probably an Indian corruption of either *Anglois* or *English*.[2] The Chinese call an Englishman *Yingkwoh*,[3] the Bengalee calls him *Inrej*, and corrupts the words champagne and coachman into the forms *simkin* and *gurrawaun*.[4] At Fort Vancouver, the medium of intercourse a few years ago was a curious Lingua Franca, composed of Canadian-French, English, Iroquois, Cree, Hawaian, and Chinese. The word for rum was *lum*, for money *tula*, a corruption of dollar, and an Englishman went by the name of a *Kintshosh*, a corruption of King George.[5] The Kaffirs of Natal call Harry *Hali*, and Mary *Mali*. The Egbas have turned Thompson into *Tamahana*, and Philip into *Piripi*.[6] The Maoris make sad havoc of biblical names ; they have transformed Lot to *Rota*, and

---

[1] Gayangos, *Dynasties*, vol. i. p. 324. So the Indian names Misachibee and Tlaltelolco have been corrupted into MISSISSIPPI and GUADALUPE. Russell, Diary *North and South*, vol. i. p. 381 ; Yonge, *Christian Names*, vol. i. p. 81.
[2] Drake, *Book of the Indians*, book i. p. 23. [Prof. Skeat thinks that *yanky* meant active, spry, from Dialect Eng. *yank*, to jerk.—*Etym. Dict.*, p. 834 ; *Notes on Etymology*, p. 324.]
[3] Fleming, *Travels on Horseback*, p. 116.
[4] Hotten, *Slang Dictionary*, pp. 148, 231.
[5] Wilson, *Pre-historic Man*, vol. ii. p. 431. An American is called *Boston*, and the ordinary salutation is *Clakhohahyah*, which is explained by the fact that the Indians, frequently hearing a trader named Clark, long resident in the Fort, addressed by his companions in the village, ' Clark, how are you ? ' imagined that this sentence was the correct English form of salutation.
[6] Burton, *Mission to Gelele*, vol. i. p. 32.

Philemon to *Pirimona*.[1]   Sailors are especially given to such innovations. Jos-house, for instance, the name applied to the Buddhist temples in China, has been formed by English sailors out of the Portuguese word *dios*, god.[2]

Anglo-Saxon suffixes of nearly similar sound sometimes come to be interchanged. This has very frequently taken place in the case of *stone* and *ton*. Thus Brigges-stan has been transmuted into BRIXTON, and Brihtelmes-stan into Brighthelmstone, Brighthampton, and BRIGHTON. The change from don to *ton* is also common. Seccan-dun is now SECKINGTON,[3] and Beamdun is BAMPTON.[4]   The suffix *hithe*, a haven, is changed into *ey*, an island, in the case of STEPNEY, formerly Stebenhithe, and into *head*, in the case of Maidenhead, formerly Maydenhithe. In CARISBROOK, which was anciently Wihtgara-byrig, we have a change from *burgh* to *brook*.[5]   The suffix in the name DURHAM is properly not the Saxon *ham*, but the Norse *holm*, and Dunelm—the signature of the bishop—reminds us also that the Celtic prefix is *Dun*, a hill fort, and not *Dur*, water.[6]

Many of these changes seem to be simply phonetic, among which we may reckon Gravesham into GRAVESEND, Edgeworth into EDGEWARE, Ebbsham into EPSOM, Swanwick into SWANAGE, and Badecanwylla or Bathwell into BAKEWELL. The great tendency is to contraction ; as Horne Tooke puts it, ' letters, like soldiers being very apt to desert and drop off in a long march.'[7] Thus we find Botolph's ton contracted into BO'STON, Agmondesham into AMERSHAM, and Eurewic into YORK. In London St. Olaf's Street has been changed into TOOLEY Street, and in Dublin into TULLOCH Street.[8] St. Mary's Hall, Oxford, has been transformed into Skimmery Hall, and this has been abbreviated into the disrespectful appellation SKIM. St. Bridget is turned into St. Bride, St. Benedict into St. Bennet, St. Etheldreda into St. Awdrey, St. Egidius into St. Giles.[9]

---

[1] Yonge, *Christian Names*, vol. i. p. 10.
[2] The sailors' transformations of H.M.S. *Bellerophon* into the *Billy Ruffian*, of the *Andromache* into the *Andrew Mackay*, of the *Æolus* into the *Alehouse*, of the *Courageux* into the *Currant Juice*, and of the steamer *Hirondelle* into the *Iron Devil*, belong to another class of changes, which we shall presently consider. See p. 274, *infra*.
[3] *Sax. Chron.* A.D. 755.
[4] *Sax. Chron.* A.D. 614.   [5] See p. 217, *supra*.
[6] Durham is written Dunholm in the *Saxon Chronicle*, A.D. 1072.
[7] Tooke, *Diversions of Purley*, part i. ch. vi. p. 94.
[8] Now pulled down. It was standing in the sixteenth century.
[9] Territorial surnames show still more startling changes. St. Denys has been corrupted into Sydney, St. Maur into Seymour, St. Paul into Semple, Sevenoaks into Snooks, and St. John and St. Leger are pronounced Sinjun and Sillinger.

This tendency to contraction is often to be detected in the pronunciation of names of which the more lengthened form is retained in writing. Thus CIRENCESTER is pronounced Cisester; GLOUCESTER, Gloster; WORCESTER, Worster; BARFREESTONE, Barston; and TROTTERSCLIFFE, Trosley.[1] In America, on the other hand, owing to the universal prevalence of reading, the tendency is to pronounce words exactly as they are spelt, and WORCESTER is pronounced Wor-ces-ter, and ILLINOIS is called Illinoys.[2]

In endeavouring to recover the original forms of names, it becomes important to discover the phonetic tendencies which prevailed among different nations. This is not the place to exhibit or discuss the laws of phonetic change which have been detected; [3] all that can here be attempted is to illustrate them by a few characteristic instances.

[1] In Switzerland *inghofen* is generally contracted into *ikon*, as Benninghofen into Bennikon. Meyer, *Ortsnamen*, pp. 127–136.
[2] In Samuel Rogers' youth every one said Lunnon; we have now returned to Lundun.
[3] ' Grimm's law ', as it is called, enables us to identify cognate words in the Teutonic and Romance languages. It is—

In Greek and generally in Sanskrit and Latin, the letters .	*p*	*b*	*ph (f, φ)*	*t*	*d*	*th (θ]*	*k (c)*	*g*	*kh (χ)*
Correspond in Gothic to	*ph (f)*	*p*	*b*	*th*	*t*	*d*	*kh(h,g)*	*k*	*g*
And in Old High German to	*b (v,f)*	*ph (f)*	*p*	*d*	*th (z)*	*t*	*g (h)*	*kh*	*k*

The changes from the Latin to the modern Romance languages are more simple. The chief correspondences are—

Latin	*p*	*b*	*f*	*v*	*c*	*q*	*g*	*j*
Romance Languages .	*b, v*	*v, f*	*h*	*b*	*g, ch, k, z, s*	*c, p*	*y, i, j*	*g, d, y*

Latin	*t*	*d*	*s*	*m*	*n*	*l*	*r*
Romance Languages .	*d, z*	*z, j, l, s, c*	*k, z, x*	*n*	*l, r*	*r, n, lh*	*l,d*

See Bopp, *Vergleich. Gramm.*; Grimm, *Geschichte der Deut. Sprache*, vol. i. pp. 294–434; Schleicher, *Die Sprachen Europas*; Bunsen, *Brit. Assoc. Reports* for 1847, p. 262; *Edinb. Rev.* vol. xciv. pp. 318, 319; Prichard, *Eastern Origin*, pp. 179–200; Mone, *Celt. Forsch-*

The tendency among the German nations is to develop the sibilants and gutturals; among the Romance nations to suppress these and develop the mutes and liquids. Thus in the name of the river Atesis or Atygis, how harsh is the German name—the ETSCH; how soft and harmonious the Italian development of the same word—the ADIGE. Again we may compare the German LUTTICH with the French LIÉGE, or we may contrast the German change of Confluentes into COBLENTZ with the soft effect produced even in cases when the Italians have introduced sibilants, as in the change of Florentia into FIRENZE, or Placentia into PIACENZA.

But the best illustration of these phonetic tendencies will be to enumerate a few cases where the same root has been variously modified by different nations. Let us take the Latin word *forum*. The Forum Julii, in Southern France has become FRÉJUS; and, in Northern Italy, the same name has been changed to FRIULI. In the Emilia we find FORLI (Forum Livii), FOSSOMBRONE (Forum Sempronii), FERRARA (Forum Allieni), and FORNOVO (Forum Novum). In Central Italy we have FORCASSI (Forum Cassii), FIORA (Forum Aurelii), FORFIAMMA (Forum Flaminii), and FORLIMPOPOLI (Forum Popilii).

With these compare the German name KLAGENFURT (Claudii forum), the Dutch VOORBOURG (Forum Hadriani), the French FEURS (Forum Segusianorum), and the Sardinian FORDONG-IANUS (Forum Trajani).

Or let us take the changes effected in the Greek word πόλις, a city. Neapolis, in Italy, has become NAPLES, in the Morea it has become NAUPLIA. Neapolis, near Carthage, is now NABEL, and Neapolis, in Syria, is NÁBULUS or NÁBLÚS.[1] TRIPOLI is little changed; Amphipolis is now EMBOLI, Callipolis is GALLIPOLI, Antipolis is ANTIBES, Gratianopolis is GRENOBLE. STAMBOUL, or ISTAMBOUL, the modern name of Byzantium, is not, as might be imagined, a corruption of Constantinopolis, but of ἐς τὰν πόλιν,[2] a phrase analogous to that which we use when we speak of a journey to London,

ungen; Donaldson, *Varronianus*; *New Cratylus*, pp. 144–190; Max Müller, *Lecture*, second series, pp. 198–222; Pott, *Etymol. Forschungen*; Diez, *Rom. Gram.* vol. i. pp. 175–253; Lewis, *Romance Languages*; Milman, *Hist. Latin Christianity*, vol. vi. p. 343.
[1] Robinson, *Biblical Researches*, vol. iii. pp. 96, 119.
[2] Stanley, *Sinai and Palestine*, p. 246; Leo, *Vorlesungen*, vol. i. p. 196.

as going ' to town '. In like manner STANKO, the modern name of the Island of Cos, is a corruption of ἐς τὰν Κῶ.[1]

We find the word Trajectus in ATRECHT or ARRAS (Atrebatum Trajectus), MAESTRECHT (Mosæ Trajectus), and UTRECHT (Ultra Trajectum).[2]

The Romanized Celtic suffix *iacum* is changed into *ay* in France and *ach* in Germany, while in Brittany and Cornwall the original form is ordinarily retained.[3] Thus Cortoriacum is now COURTRAY, Camaracum is CAMBRAY, Bagacum is BAVAY, and Tournacum is TOURNAY. Antunacum is now ANDERNACH, Olimacum is LYMBACH, Vallacum is WILNPACH, and Magontiacum is MAINTZ.

The manner in which personal names have entered into the names of places has been referred to in a previous chapter.[4] A few instances may be here again enumerated as affording admirable illustrations of diverse phonetic tendencies. Thus the name of Augustus is found in the Spanish ZARAGOSSA (Cæsarea Augusta), and BADAJOZ (Pax Augusta) ; in the Italian AOSTA (Augusta) ; in the French AOUST (Augusta), AUCH (Augusta), and AUTUN (Augustodunum) ; in the German AUGSBURG (Augusta), and AUGST (Augusta) ; and the English AUST passage (Trajectus Augusti). We find the word Julius or Julia in LILLEBONNE (Julia Bona), LOUDON (Juliodunum), in BEJA in Portugal (Pax Julia), in JÜLICH or JULIERS (Julicacum), in ZUGLIO (Julium), and in FRIULI and FRÉJUS (Forum Julii) ; and the name of Constantius or Constantinus is found in CONZ, COUTANCES, CÔTANTIN, CONSTANZ, and CONSTANTINOPLE. Some additional changes, valuable as illustrating phonetic laws, are added in a note.[5]

The changes that have hitherto been discussed may be

---

[1] The same process of the incorporation of preposition and articles may be seen in ZERMAT, ANDERMAT. Many German names beginning with M are due to *am* or *im* prefixed to Celtic names. Thus Oersberg has become changed to MARSBERG, Eppenthal to MEPPENTHAL, Achenthal to MACHENTHAL. So with MOSBACH, MEICHES, and many others. Mone, *Celt. Forsch.* pp. 157, 180. THAXTED is probably The Axstead, THISTLEWORTH is The Istle-worth, ATFORD and OTFORD are At the ford, and ABRIDGE is At the bridge. Also in Spain the Arabic article *Al* is often incorporated into the name. See p. 75, *supra.* LUXOR, one of the four villages which stand on the site of ancient Thebes, is a contraction of El Eksor, the palaces. Fairholt, *Up the Nile*, p. 266.
[2] The word *trajectus* may have sometimes been confounded with the Celtic *traeth*, sands. See Diefenbach, *Origines Europææ*, p. 429 ; De Belloguet, *Ethnog.* p. 139 ; Ludlow, in *Philolog. Trans.* for 1857, p. 15.
[3] *E.g.* Plabenec, Bourbriac, Loudeac, and Gourarec in Brittany, and Bradock, Boconnoc, Isnioc, Ladock, Phillack, Polbathick, and Polostoc in Cornwall.
[4] See pp. 224, 225, *supra.*
[5] Eburovices and Évreux, Vesontio and Besançon, Vinovium and Binchester, Bononia

W.P. T

considered as natural phonetic changes—changes bringing combinations of letters from one language into harmony with the laws of another.

We have now to consider a class of corruptions which have arisen from a totally different cause. Men have ever felt a natural desire to assign a plausible meaning to names — to make them, in fact, no longer sounds, but words. How few children, conning the atlas, do not connect some fanciful speculations with such names as the CALF OF MAN, or IRELAND'S EYE ; they suppose that JUTLAND is the land which ' juts out ', instead of the land of the Jutes ; [1] they suppose that Cape HORN has received its name, not, as is the fact, from the birth-place of its discoverer,[2] but because it is the extreme southern horn of the American continent, and names like the ORANGE River, or the RED Sea are, unhesitatingly, supposed to denote the colour of the waters, instead of being, the first a reminiscence of the extension of the Dutch empire under the house of Orange, and the second a translation [3] of the Sea of Edom.[4]

This instinctive causativeness of the human mind, this perpetual endeavour to find a reason or a plausible explanation for everything, has corrupted many of the words which we have in daily use,[5] and a large allowance for this source of

and Boulogne, Chatti and Hesse, Aquitania and Guienne, Olisippo and Lisbon, Agrigentum and Girgenti, Aletium and Lecci, Aquæ and Aix. In French names a final n or s is often added, as in the case of Dibio and Dijon, Matesco and Maçon, Brigantio and Briançon, Massilia and Marseilles, Londinium and Londres.

[1] Trench, *Study of Words*, p. 86.

[2] See p. 51, *supra*.

[3] [Some maintain that the name comes from the ' redskins ' (*Phœnices*) who lived on its borders (Ebers ; Bochart, *Phaleg*. ii. 22) ; others from the Erythræi, red men, a Greek rendering of Phæni=Pæni, the men of Pun-t (Delitzsch, *New Comm. on Genesis*, 2, 318. See also F. Paley, *Ovid's Fasti*, p. 214). Otherwise, Brinton, *Myths of the New World*, 83 ; Byron, *Don Juan*, ii. 141.] So the YELLOW SEA and PALMYRA are trans-lated names. Magna, the Roman station, is now Car-voran, from the Celtic *vawr*, great.

[4] Similar misconceptions are BLACKHEATH (bleak heath) ; the Isle of Wight, see p. 217 ; Trinidad, p. 12 ; Gateshead, p. 179, *supra*. FLORIDA is not the flowery land, but the land discovered on Easter Day, Pascua florida, p. 10. The FINSTER-AAR-HORN is not, as guidebooks tell us, the peak of the Black Eagle, but the peak which gives rise to the Glacier of the black Aar.

[5] We may enumerate the well-known instances of buffetier corrupted into beefeater [?], lustrino into lute-string, asparagus into sparrow-grass, coat-cards into court-cards, shuttlecork into shuttlecock [?], mahlerstock into maulstick, écrevisse into crayfish, dormeuse into dormouse [?], dent de lion into dandy lion, quelques choses into kickshaws contre danse into country dance [?], ver de gris into verdigrease, weissager into wiseacre and hausenblase or sturgeon's bladder into isinglass. A groom used to call Othello and Desdemona—two horses under his charge—by the names of Old Fellow and Thursday Morning. The natives called Miss Rogers (authoress of ' Domestic Life in Palestine " by the name of narâjus, ' the lily ', as the nearest approximation to her name which they were able to pronounce. Ibrahim Pacha, during his visit to England, was known to the mob as Abraham Parker. See Whewell, in *Philolog. Proceedings*, vol. v. p. 138 ; Wedgwood, in *Philolog. Trans.* for 1855, pp. 66–71 ; Wilton, *Negeb*, pp. 140, 218 ; Farrar, *Origin of Language*, pp. 57, 58 ; Mayhew, *German Life and Manners*, vol. ii. p. 404

error must be made when we are investigating the original forms of ancient names. No cause has been more fruitful in producing corruptions than popular attempts to explain from the vernacular, and to bring into harmony with a supposed etymology, names whose real explanation is to be sought in some language known only to the learned.[1] Names, significant in the vernacular, are constructed out of the ruins of the ancient unintelligible names, just as we find the modern villages of Mesopotamia built of bricks stamped with the cuneiform legend of Nebuchadnezzar.[2]

Teutonic nations, for instance, inhabiting a country covered with ancient Celtic names, have unconsciously endeavoured to twist those names into a form in which they would be susceptible of explanations from Teutonic sources. The instances are innumerable. The Celtic words *alt maen* mean high rock. In the Lake District this name has been transformed into the OLD MAN of Coniston.[3] In the Orkneys a conspicuous pyramid of rock, 1,500 feet in height, is called the OLD MAN of Hoy; and two rocks on the Cornish coast go by the name of the OLD MAN and his MAN. The DEAD MAN, another Cornish headland, is an Anglicization of the Celtic *dod maen*. BROWN WILLY, a Cornish ridge, some 1,370 ft. in height, is a corruption of *Bryn Huel*, the tin-mine ridge.[4] Abermaw, the mouth of the Maw, is commonly called BARMOUTH;[5] Kinedar has been changed into KING EDWARD; Dun-y-coed, a 'wooded hill' in Devonshire, is now called the DUNAGOAT; and EASTBOURNE was, no doubt, the eas-bourne,[6] or water-brook; the *t* having crept in from a desire to make the Celtic prefix significant in English.[7]

Similar transformations of Celtic and Sclavonic names are to be found on the Continent.[8] In Switzerland the

Dixon, *Surnames*, p. v.; Trench, *English Past and Present*, pp. 243–253; *Study of Words*, p. 87. [See on the whole subject A. S. Palmer, *Folk Etymology*, 1883, and *The Folk on their Word-lore*, 1904.]

[1] Erroneous etymologies are unfortunately by no means confined to the unlearned. Witness Baxter's derivation of KIRCUDBRIGHT (i.e. Church of St. Cuthbert). It is, he says, *forsan*, Caer gui aber rit, i.e. Arx trajectus fluminei Æstuarei!! *Glossarium*, p. 40.

[2] See *Edinburgh Review*, vol. xciv. p. 331.

[3] Davies, in *Philolog. Trans.* for 1855, p. 219.

[4] Welli, or wheal, which occurs so often in the mining share list, is a corruption of the word *huel*, a tin mine.

[5] Baxter, *Glossarium*, p. 69.

[6] A reduplicated name. See p. 150, *supra*. [Probably for *egesa-(bourne)*, suggested by *Egesa-uude* (Charter, A.D. 683), and *Eas-writh, South-ease*, all in Sussex.—W. D. Birch.]

[7] Gough's *Camden*, vol. i. p. 296.

[3] See a paper by Förstemann in Kuhn's *Zeitschrift*, vol. i. p. 10, *seq.* The numerous instances given by Mone, in his *Celtische Forschungen*, must be received with caution.

Celtic Vitodurum has been Germanized into WINTERTHUR [1];
Noviomagus is now NIMWEGEN; Alcmana is ALTMÜHL [2];
and the FREUDENBACH, or joyful brook, is, probably, a corruption of the Celtic *ffrydan*, a stream.[3]   The Sclavonic Potsdupimi has become POTSDAM, Melraz is MÜLLROSE, and Dub-
rawice DUMMERWITZ.[4]

Anglo-Saxon and Norse names have not escaped similar
metamorphoses. The name of MAIDENHEAD has given rise
to the myth that here was buried the head of one of the eleven
thousand virgins of Cologne,[5] but Mayden hithe, the ancient
form of the name, shows that it was the wharf midway between Marlow and Windsor.   So MAIDSTONE and MAGDE-
BURG are not the towns of maids, but the town on the Medway,
and the town on the plain,[6] HUNGERFORD, on the border
between the Saxons and the Angles, was anciently Ingleford,
or the ford of the Angles.[7]

FITFUL HEAD, in Shetland, familiar to all readers of the
Waverley Novels as the abode of Norna in 'The Pirate,' has
received its present not inappropriate name, by reason of a
misconception of the original Scandinavian name *Hvit-fell*,
the white hill;[8] CAPE WRATH, beaten, it is true, by wrathful
storms, was originally Cape *Hvarf*, a Norse name, indicating a
point where the land trends in a new direction;[9] and the
Norse *Vedrafiordr*, the firth of Rams (wethers), is now WATER-
FORD in Ireland.[10]

In the Lake District we also find some curious transformations of Norse Names. SILLY WREAY is the happy nook,

---

[1] Förstemann, *Alt-deut. Namenbuch*, vol. ii. p. 446.

[2] Förstemann, *Ortsnamen*, p. 313.

[3] Förstemann, *Ortsnamen*, p. 314.   On the Germanization of Sclavonic names see
a paper by Bronisch in the *Neues Lausitzisches Magazin*, vol. xvii. pp. 57–73.

[4] Mone, *Celt. Forsch.* p. 7.   Mone thinks the OELBACH, or oily brook, is from the Irish
oil, a stone, and that the TEUFELSTEIN, or Devil's Stone, is from the Celtic *dubhail*, the
black rock. Ibid. p. 175.

[5] The Cologne myth of the eleven thousand virgins seems to have arisen from the
name of St. Undecemilla, a virgin martyr.   The insertion of a single letter in the calendar
has changed this name into the form, ' Undecem millia Virg. Mart '.   The bones of
the eleven thousand, which are reverently shown to the pious pilgrim, have been pronounced by Professor Owen to comprise the remains of all the quadrupeds indigenous
to the district.

[6] See p. 165, *supra*. For the legends respecting the *Mons Puellarum*, as Magdeburg
was called, see Panzer, *Deut. Myth.* pp. 122, 272, 370.

[7] Inglefield, in the immediate neighbourhood, has retained the ancient form. See
Gough's Camden, vol. i. p. 215.

[8] Symington, *Faroë and Iceland*, p. 8.

[9] Laing, *Heimskringla*, vol. i. p. 144.

[10] [The first part of the name is probably Icel. *vadh.*, a wading place, Dan. *vad*, Lincolns. *wath*, a ford.]

CUNNING GARTH is the King's Yard, CANDY SLACK is the bowl-shaped hollow.[1]

As might have been expected, French and Norman names in England have been peculiarly liable to suffer from these causes. *Château Vert*, in Oxfordshire, has been converted into SHOTOVER Hill ; *Beau chef* into BEACHY Head ; and *Burgh Walter*, the castle of Walter of Douay, who came over with the Conqueror, now appears in the form of BRIDGEWATER. *Beau lieu* in Monmouthshire, *Grand pont*, the great bridge over the Fal in Cornwall, and *Bon gué*, or the good ford, in Suffolk, have been Saxonized into BEWLEY Woods, GRAMPOUND,[2] and BUNGAY. Leighton *Beau-désert* has been changed into LEIGHTON BUZZARD ; and the brazen eagle which forms the lectern in the parish church is gravely exhibited by the sexton to passing strangers as the original buzzard from which the town may be supposed to derive its name.[3]

In Canada, where an English speaking population is encroaching on the old French settlers, the same process of verbal translation is going on. ' Les Chéneaux ', or channels, on the River Ottawa, are now the SNOWS. So ' Les Chats ' and ' Les Joachims ' on the same river are respectively becoming the SHAWS and the SWASHINGS, while a mountain near the head of the bay of Fundy, called the ' Chapeau Dieu ', from the cap of cloud which often overhangs it, is now known as the SHEPODY Mountain. The River Quah-Tah-Wah-Am-Quah-Duavic in New Brunswick, probably the most breakjaw compound in the Gazetteer, has had its name justifiably abbreviated into the Petamkediac, which has been further transformed by the lumberers and hunters into the TOM KEDGWICK.[4]

Anse des Cousins, the Bay of Mosquitoes, has been turned by English sailors into NANCY COUSINS Bay ; they have changed Livorno into LEG-HORN ; and the nautical mind has canonized a new saint, unknown even to the Bollandists, by the change of Setubal into ST. UBES. So Hagenes, the Norse name of one of the Scilly Isles, has become ST. AGNES.[5] Sor-

---

1 Cf. Mealy Sike, Heedless Gill, etc. Ferguson, *Northmen*, p. 126.
2 Gough's Camden, vol. i. p. 20.
3 The French colony of Beauregard, in Brandenburg, has been Germanized into BURENGAREN or Bauerngarten (peasants' garden). Förstemann, in Kuhn's *Zeitschrift*, vol. i. p. 21.
4 Hon. Arthur Gordon, in *Vacation Tourists* for 1862–3, p. 484 ; *Quarterly Review*, vol. cxvi. p. 27.   5 Times, *March 26th*, 1864.

acte, the mountain whose snowy summit is sung by Horace,[1] has been added to the list of saints by the Italian peasantry, and receives their prayers under the name of ST. ORESTE.[2] The name and legend of ST. GOAR, who is said to have dwelt in a cavern on the Rhine, where the river furiously eddies round the Lurlei rock, is supposed by certain sceptics to have originated in a corruption of the German word *gewirr*, a whirl-pool.[3] In this instance it is not improbable that the hagiologists may be right and the philologists wrong. The name of a well-known saint is sometimes substituted for one less familiar. Thus St. Aldhelm's Head, in Dorset, has become ST. ALBAN'S HEAD.[4] Occasionally the name of the saint apparently disappears, submerged beneath some obtrusively tempting etymology, as in the case of St. Maidulf's borough, which has become MARLBOROUGH.

The Hebrew name JERUSALEM was reproduced under the form *Hierosolyma*, the holy city of Solomon, owing to a mis-taken derivation from the Greek ἱερός.[5] A mountain on the eastern coast of Africa, opposite Aden, received the Arabic name of GEBEL FIEL [*Fil*] (elephant mountain), from the re-markable resemblance of the outline to the back of the elephant. From the resemblance of the sound the name was corrupted in the Periplus into Mons Felix.[6]

Many instances may be cited of the manner in which legends are prone to gather round these altered names. The citadel of Carthage was called BOZRA, a Phœnician word meaning an acropolis. The Greeks connected this with βύρσα, an ox-hide, and then, in harmony with the popular notions of Tyrian acuteness, an explanatory legend was con-cocted, which told how the traders, who had received permis-sion to possess as much land as an ox-hide would cover, cut the skin into narrow strips, with which they encompassed the spot on which the Carthaginian fortress was erected.[7] [See Appendix, Note E.]

---

[1] Vides, ut alta stet nive candidum Soracte.
[2] Duke of Buckingham, *Private Diary*, vol. iii. p. 171 ; Whewell, in *Philolog. Proceedings*, vol. v. p. 141.   [3] Mayhew, *German Life and Manners*, vol. ii. pp. 370, 398.
[4] Farrar, *Origin of Language*, p. 59. The process of the creation of new saints is illus-trated by the case of the eleven thousand virgins (see p. 276, *supra*), as well as by that of St. Veronica, whose name arose from a transposition of the letters of the mongrel phrase *vera icon*. See Whewell, in *Philolog. Proceed.* vol. v. p. 141 ; Yonge, *Christian Names*, vol. i. p. 424.
[5] Trench, *English Past and Present*, p. 237 ; Farrar, *Origin of Lang.* p. 59.
[6] Buckingham, *Autobiography*, vol. ii. p. 395.
[7] Bochart, vol. iii. p. 470 ; Trench, *English Past and Present*, p. 238.

We find the same legend repeated in the traditions of other countries. The name of THONG castle, near Sittingbourne, is derived from the Norse word *tunga*, a tongue of land, which we find in the Kyle of Tongue in Sutherlandshire. This name has given rise to the tradition, that Dido's device was here repeated by Hengist and Horsa. The same story is told of Ivar, son of Regnar Lodbrok, in order to account for the name of THONG CASTOR, near Grimsby.[1]

The legend of the victory gained by Guy of Warwick, the Anglian champion, over the dun cow, most probably originated in a misunderstood tradition of his conquest of the *Dena gau*, or Danish settlement in the neighbourhood of Warwick.[2]

The name of ANTWERP denotes, no doubt, the town which sprang up ' at the wharf '. But the word Antwerpen approximates closely in sound to the Flemish *handt werpen*, hand throwing. Hence arose the legend of the giant who cut off the hands of those who passed his castle without paying him black mail, and threw them into the Scheldt.[3]

The legend of the wicked Bishop Hatto is well known. It has been reproduced by Southey in a popular ballad, and it is annually retailed and discussed on the decks of the Rhine steamers. At a time of dearth he forestalled the corn from the poor, but was overtaken by a righteous Nemesis—having been devoured by the swarming rats, who scaled the walls of his fortress in the Rhine. The origin of this legend may be traced to a corruption of the name of the *maut-thurm*, or custom-house, into the MÄUSE-THURM, or Mouse-tower.[4]

The story of Roland the crusader, and his hapless love for the daughter of the Lord of Drachenfels, is perhaps a still greater favourite with the fairer portion of the Rhine tourists. It is sad to have to reject the pathetic tale, but a stern criticism derives the name of ROLANDSECK from the rolling waves of the swift current at the bend of the river, which caused the place to be called the *rollendes-ecke* by the passing boatmen.[5]

---

[1] The legend is found also among the Thuringians and the Russians. Grimm, *Deut. Rechtsalt.* p. 90, apud Pictet, *Orig. Indo-Europ.* part ii. p. 51 ; Latham, *Channel Isles,* p. 338 ; Gough's Camden, vol. ii. p. 338 ; Verstegan, *Restitution,* p. 133 ; Skinner, *Etymol.* s. v.

[2] Donaldson, *English Ethnography,* p. 54.

[3] Motley, *Dutch Republic,* vol. i. p. 711 ; Salverte, *Essai sur les Noms,* vol. ii. p. 294 ; Charnock, *Local Etymology,* p. 14. The giant was killed by Brabo, the eponymus of Brabant.

[4] Förstemann, in Kuhn's *Zeitschrift für Vergleich. Sprachforschung,* vol. i. p. 6.

[5] Mayhew, *German Life and Manners,* vol. ii. p. 405.

Near Grenoble is a celebrated tower, which now bears the name of LA TOUR SANS VENIN, the tower without poison. The peasantry firmly believe that no poisonous animal can exist in its neighbourhood. The superstition has arisen from a corruption of the original saint-name of San Verena into *sans venin*.[1] The superstitions which avouch that birds fall dead in attempting to fly across the DEAD SEA and the LAKE AVERNUS (ἄορνος) have originated in similar etymological fancies.

In the Swedish language a woman is called *quinna*, or *quinn*, a word nearly allied to the obsolescent English word *quean*,[2] as well as to the appellation of the highest lady in the land. The Finns also call themselves Qvœns, a Euskarian word, which is no way related to the Teutonic root. The misunderstood assertions of travellers as to this nation of Qvœns gave rise to the legend respecting a tribe of Northern Amazons ruled over by a woman. This myth must have come into existence even so early as the time of Tacitus, and we find it repeated by the geographer of Ravenna, by King Alfred, and by Adam of Bremen.[3] The last-named writer confuses all our notions of ethnological propriety by the assertion that there are Turks to be found in Finland. He has evidently been misled by the fact that Turku was the ancient enchorial synonym for the city of Abo.[4]

PILATUS, the mountain which overhangs Lucerne, takes its name from the cap of cloud which frequently collects round this western outlier of the mountains of Uri. The name has originated the poetic myth of the banished Pilate, who, torn by remorse, is said to have haunted the rugged peak, and at last to have drowned himself in the lonely tarn near the summit of the mountain.[5]

Drepanum, now TRAPANI, in Sicily, was so called from the sickle-shaped curve of the sea-shore—δρέπανον, a sickle. A Greek legend, preserved by Pausanias, affirms that the name is a record of the fact that it was here Kronos threw away

[1] Max Müller, *Lectures*, 2d series, p. 368.
[2] Gay speaks of ' the dread of every scolding quean '.
[3] ' Circa hæc litora Baltici maris ferunt esse Amazonus, quod nunc terra feminarum dicitur ', etc. Adam of Bremen, *De situ Daniæ*, p. 15. See also Zeuss, *Die Deutschen*, p. 687 ; Prichard, *Researches*, vol. iii. p. 273 ; Latham, *Nationalities of Europe*, vol. i. p. 164 ; Latham, *Germania*, p. 174 ; Buckle, *Hist. of Civilization*, vol. i. p. 275.
[4] *De situ Daniæ*, p. 11 ; Cooley, *Hist. of Maritime and Inland Discovery*, vol. i. p. 211 ; Buckle, *Hist. of Civiliz.* vol. i. p. 275.
[5] Salverte, *Essai sur les Noms*, vol. ii. p. 291 ; Murray, *Handbook for Switzerland*, p. 39.

the *sickle* with which he had killed Uranos.[1]   And various myths have clustered round the river LYCUS, as if it had been the Wolf river (λύκος, a wolf) instead of the White river (λευκός, white), as is no doubt the case.[2]

The names of countries and nations have often suffered in this way.   The Celtic named *Pehta*, or *Peicta*, ' the fighters ', has been Latinized into PICTI, the painted savages of the Scottish Lowlands.[3]   In the case of the Berbers, a people in Northern Africa, the *e* in the enchorial name seems to have been changed into an *a*, from a desire to establish a connexion with the Greek word βάρβαροι, and the name of BARBARY still remains on our maps to remind us of the error.[4]

A similar instance of the change of a single letter in accordance with a fancied etymology occurs in the case of the TATAR hordes, which, in the thirteenth century, burst forth from the Asiatic steppes.   This terrible invasion was thought to be a fulfilment of the prediction of the opening of the bottomless pit, spoken of in the ninth chapter of the Revelation, and in order to bring the name into relation with Tartarus the word *Tatar* was written, and still continues to be written, in the form *Tartar*.[5]

Our English name of POLAND is likewise founded on a misconception.   The country consists of vast plains, and from the Sclavonic *polie*, a plain, is derived the German plural form *Polen* or *Pohlen*, the men of the plains.   In the old English writers we meet with the name Polayn, which is an admissible Anglicization of the German word.   But the more recent change of Polayn into Poland is due to the desire of substituting an intelligible word for an unintelligible sound.   The correct formation, following the analogous case of Switzerland, would be Polenland.

[1] Movers, *Phönizier*, pt. ii. vol. ii. p. 312 ; Welsford, *English Language*, p. 194.

[2] So around the name of the Lycian Apollo, the light-giver, have collected mythologic legends of the wolf-destroyer. Müller, *Dorians*, vol. i. p. 315.

[3] See p. 57, *supra* ; Trench, *Study of Words*, p. 86.

[4] See p. 42, *supra* ; Barth, *Travels*, vol. i. p. 224 ; Movers, *Die Phönizier*, pt. ii. vol. ii. pp. 390, 391 ; cf. Gibbon, *Decline and Fall*, vol. vi. p. 427, chap. li. The name of the Berbers is found in an ancient Egyptian inscription. Kenrick, *Ancient Egypt*, vol. ii. p. 248. In the time of Herodotus the word βάρβαροι was applied to all nations who spoke languages unintelligible to the Greeks. Afterwards it was restricted to all tribes beyond the pale of the Roman empire, and is now confined to certain tribes of northern Africa.

[5] Plebs Sathanæ detestanda Tartarorum . . . exeuntes ad instar dæmonum solutorum à tartaro, ut bene Tartari, quasi tartarei nuncupentur. Matt. Paris, *Hist. Major*, p. 546, A.D. 1240. See p. 42, *supra* ; Prichard, *Researches*, vol. iv. p. 278 ; Wedgwood, in *Philolog. Trans.* for 1855, p. 72 ; *Edinburgh Rev.* vol. xciv. p. 308 ; Trench, *English past and Present*, p. 239 ; Buckle, *Hist. of Civilization*, vol. i. p. 288.

So the Arabic MOSLEMIN, already a plural form, has been corrupted into Mussulman, which is taken for a singular, and from which have been formed those anomalous double plurals—Mussulmen and Mussulmans.[1]

NEGROPONT, the modern name of the island of Eubœa, is a corruption due, probably, to Genoese and Venetian mariners. The channel dividing the island from the mainland was anciently called Euripus, in allusion to the swiftness of the current; and at one time the land on either side projected so far as nearly to bridge the space between the two shores. The town built at this spot received the name of the channel, and was called Evripo, or Egripo, a name which has been converted by Italian sailors into Negripo, or NEGROPONT, the black bridge '; and, finally, the name of the town was extended to the whole island.[2]

Some of the most curious transformations which have been effected by popular attempts at etymologizing are those which have taken place in the names of the streets of London.

Sheremoniers Lane was so called from being the dwelling-place of the artizans whose business it was to shear or cut bullion into shape, so as to be ready for the die. The name, as its origin became forgotten, passed into Sheremongers Lane, and after a while, from the vicinity of St. Paul's Cathedral, and an analogy with Amen Corner, Ave Maria Lane, and Paternoster Row, it became SERMON Lane.[3] After the loss of Calais and its dependencies, the artizans of Hames and Guynes, two small towns in the vicinity of Calais, took refuge in England. A locality in the east of London was assigned for their residence, and this naturally acquired the name of the old home from which they had been expelled, and was called Hames et Guynes. The vicinity of the place of execution on Tower Hill probably suggested the change of the name to HANGMAN'S GAINS.[4] Among many similar changes we may enumerate that of the Convent of the Chartreuse into the

---

[1] See Förstemann, in Kuhn's *Zeitschrift*, vol. i. p. 17.

[2] Talbot, *English Etymologies*, p. 53 ; Salverte, *Essai sur les Noms*, vol. ii. p. 301 ; Bremer, *Greece*, vol. ii. p. 89. So also the name of the MOREA seems to have arisen from a transposition of the letters of Romea, the ancient name. The usual explanation is that the name Morea is due to the resemblance of the peninsula in shape of a mulberry leaf. This is too abstract an idea, and it argues a knowledge of geographical contour which would hardly be possessed by the mediæval sailors among whom the name arose. See Salverte, *Essai sur les Noms*, vol. ii. p. 305.

[3] Cunningham, *Handbook of London*, p. 734.

[4] Stow, *Survey*, book v. p. 2.9 ; Cunningham, *Handbook*, p. 369.

chartered school now called the CHARTER HOUSE. Guthurun Lane, which takes its name from some old Danish burgher, has become GUTTER Lane, the change having been, doubtless, suggested by the defective condition of the drainage. Grass-church Street, where the old grass market was held, became —first, Gracious Street, and then GRACECHURCH Street. Knightengild Lane has become NIGHTINGALE Lane, Mart Lane is now changed to MARK Lane, Desmond Place to DEAD-MAN'S Place, Snore Hill to SNOW Hill, Candlewick Street to CANNON Street, Strype's Court to TRIPE Court, Leather Hall to LEADENHALL, Cloister Court, Blackfriars, to GLOSTER Court, Lomesbury to BLOOMSBURY, St. Olave's Street to TOOLEY Street,[1] St. Osyth's Lane to SISE Lane, St. Peter's-ey to BATTERSEA, and Stebenhithe to STEPNEY.[2]

In New York there is a square called GRAMMERCY SQUARE, a name popularly supposed to be of French origin. But the true etymology is indicated in one of the old Dutch maps, in which we find that the site is occupied by a pond called *De Kromme Zee*, the crooked lake.

In addition to the corruptions already considered, there are misnomers which are due to mistakes or misconceptions on the part of those by whom the names were originally be-stowed. Prominent among these is one which has been already referred to, and which has bestowed the name of Amerigo Vespucci upon the continent which Columbus had discovered. The names of the WEST INDIES, and of the RED INDIANS of North America, are due to the sanguine supposition of Colum-bus that his daring enterprise had in truth been rewarded by the discovery of a new passage to the shores of India. The name of CANADA is due to a mistake of another kind. Canada is the enchorial word for 'a village'. When the French ex-plorers first sailed up the St. Lawrence, it would seem that,

---

[1] Compare the name of TIBBS Row, in Cambridge, a corruption of St. Ebbe's Row.
[2] The curious transformations in the signs of inns have often been commented upon. For instance, we have the change of the Belle Sauvage to the Bell and Savage; the Pige washael, or the Virgin's greeting, to the Pig and Whistle; the Boulogne Mouth, *i.e*. the mouth of Boulogne harbour, the scene of a naval victory, to the Bull and Mouth; the Bacchanals to the Bag o' Nails; the vintner's sign of the Swan with two Nicks to the Swan with two Necks; and the Three Gowts (sluices) in Lincoln, to the Three Goats. Mr. Wedgwood, however, in a paper in the *Transactions of the Philological Society* for 1855, pp. 62–72, is inclined to hold as apocryphal some of the cases usually cited. Cf. Whewell, in *Phil. Proc.* vol. v. p. 140; Timbs, *Curiosities of London*, pp. 397–402; Taylor, *Antiquitates Curiosæ*, p. 60; Cunningham, *Handbook*. Cf. also the change of the name of the lust-garten, or tea-garden, called *Philomeles lust*, nightingales' delight, into *Viellmann's lust*, many men's delight. Förstemann, in Kuhn's *Zeitschrift*, vol. i. p. 21.

pointing to the land, they asked its name, while the natives thought they inquired the name given to the collected wigwams on the shore, and replied Canada.[1]

A notable instance of a name arising from an erroneous ethnological guess occurs in the case of the GIPSIES. Their complexion, their language, and many of their customs, prove them to be a Turanian tribe which has wandered from the hill-country of India. Dr. Wilson, an Indian missionary, found some gipsies in Palestine with whom he could converse in one of the dialects of Western India. When they appeared in Europe in the beginning of the fifteenth century, their dark complexion and their unknown language seem to have suggested the erroneous ethnological guess that they were Egyptians, a word which has been corrupted into Gipsies. Their own name for themselves, ROMANI, indicates their temporary sojourn in the ' Roman ' colony of Wallachia.[2]   A belief that they came immediately from Eastern Europe is also implied by the French name BOHÉMIENS, unless, indeed, as has been suggested, the name Bohemian be derived from an old French word *boem*, a Saracen.[3]   The Danes and Swedes regard them as Tatars, the Dutch call them HEIDEN or Heathen, the Spaniards call them GITANOS, (Gentiles,[4]) and the Germans and Italians call them ZIGANAAR, ZIGEUNER, or ZINGARI, that is, the wanderers.[5]

[1] [See E. J. Payne, *Hist. of the New World*, vol. i. p. 139; vol. ii. pp. 237, 368.] *Notes and Queries*, vol. ii. p. 428 ; Cooley, *History of Maritime and Inland Discovery*, vol. ii. p. 140 ; Charnock, *Local Etymol.*, p. 58 ; Drake, *Book of the Indians*, book i. p. 23. The etymology from the Indian words *kan*, mouth, and *ada*, a country, has also been suggested. The etymology from the Portuguese *ca nada*, ' Here is nothing ', has been gravely proposed ! This Portuguese exclamation is supposed to express the disappointment of the French discoverers at the desolate aspect of the country. [For similar mistakes see R. H. Codrington, *The Melanesians*, p. 4.]

[2] See p. 42, *supra*, note.

[3] In Germany they are popularly regarded as Saracens. Pott, *Zigeuner*, vol. i. p. 30.

[4] Or, perhaps, a corruption of the name Egyptians. Pott, *Zigeuner*, vol. i. p. 31.

[5] See Buyers, *Northern India*, pp. 151–153 ; Gardner, *Brazil*, p. 147 ; *Frontier Lands of the Christian and the Turk*, vol. i. p. 385 ; Trench, *Study of Words*, p. 86 ; Pott, *Die Zigeuner in Europa und Asien*, vol. i. p. 58 ; Prichard, *Researches*, vol. iv. p. 616. [Bulgarian *Atsiganinu*, said to be from Low Greek *a-thinganoi* (' touch-nots ') an heretical sect in Asia Minor—Miklosich.]

CHAPTER XVI

WORDS DERIVED FROM PLACES [1]

Growth of Words out of names—Process of Transformation—Examples; cherry, peach, chestnut, walnut, quince, damson, Guernsey lily, currant, shallot, coffee, cocoa, and rhubarb—Tobacco—Names of wines and liqueurs—Gin, negus, and grog—Names of animals : turkey, ermine, sable—Breeds of horses—Fish—Names of Minerals : loadstone, magnet, agate, jet, nitre, ammonia—Textile fabrics—Manufactures of the Arabs : muslin, damask, gauze, fustian—Manufactures of the Flemings : cambric, diaper, duck, ticking, frieze—Republics of Northern Italy—Cravats —Worsted—Names of vehicles—The coach—Names of weapons— Inventions called from the name of the inventor—Pasquinade, punch, harlequin, charlatan, vaudeville—Mythical derivations—Names of coins—Moral significance attached to words derived from Ethnic Names — Examples ; Gothic, bigot, cretin, frank, romance, gasconade, lumber, ogre, fiend, slave—Names of servile Races—Tariff—Cannibal—Assassin —Spruce—Words derived from the practice of Pilgrimage : saunter, roam, canter, fiacre, tawdry, flash—History of the word palace.

ALL local names were once words. This has been the text of the preceding chapters ; we have hitherto been endeavouring to make these words—long dumb—once more to speak out their meaning, and declare the lessons which they have to teach. We now come to the converse proposition. Many words were once local names. We find these words in all stages of the process of metamorphosis—some unchanged— —some so altered as to be scarcely recognisable. In fact, it is only by watching the process of transmutation in actual progress in the linguistic laboratory of Nature that we are able to trace the identity of some of the products, so strangely are they altered.

Let us take a few familiar instances. So short a time has elapsed since the introduction of French beans or Brussels' sprouts, that the names have undergone no phonetic changes —the information which they convey needs no interpreter. We may now proceed to an analogous case where the first stage in the transformation of names into words has already com-

1 [Some of the derivations advanced in this chapter have since been disproved.]

menced.   We have almost ceased to speak of Swede turnips, Ribstone pippins [1] or Savoy cabbages, but the adjectives Swede, Ribstone, and Savoy have already become substantives, and the farmer talks of his SWEDES and the gardener of his RIBSTONES and his SAVOYS.   In these instances the words themselves have as yet remained uncorrupted ; but in the case of the cherries called MAYDUKES a further process of transformation has taken place.   The word Mayduke is a corruption or Anglicization of the name Medoc, a town in the Gironde, from which these cherries were introduced.[2]   But the word CHERRY is itself a local name, still more disguised, since it has passed through the alembic of two or three languages instead of one. The English word Cherry, the German Κirſche, and the French Cerise,[3] all come to us from the Greek, through the Latin, and inform us that this fruit was first introduced from Cerasus,[4] a town on the Black Sea.

We shall find it instructive thus to examine the names of a few of our common plants and animals, with the double object of tracing historically the process by which words become disguised, and of showing the aid which etymology is able to render to the naturalist.

To begin with the PEACH.   This word, like Cherry, has had an adventurous life, and has retained still less resemblance to its original form, the initial *p* alone remaining to remind us of the native country of the peach.   The English word is derived immediately from the old French *pesche*.   The *s*, which has been dropped in the English form, gives us a clue to the origin of the word ; and when we find that the Italian name is *pesca* or *persica*, the Spanish *persigo*, and the Latin *persicum*, we discover that the peach is a Persian fruit.[5] The Nectarine comes also from the same region, but tells us its story in a different way.   The name is itself a Persian word, meaning ' the best ' kind of peach ; and the Latin name of Apricots,[6] *mala armeniaca*, refers them to a neighbouring district.

The CHESTNUT is often improperly spelt chesnut, as if it were

[1] First grown in the Garden of Ribstone Hall in the West Riding.
[2] Sankey, *Portfeuille*, p. 52.
[3] Compare the Armenian *geras*, and the Persian *carásiyha*.
[4] Now, probably, Kheresoun. See, however, Pictet, *Orig. Indo-Europ.* part i. p. 244.
[5] Talbot, *English Etymologies*, p. 475 ; Diez, *Etym. Wörterb.* p. 259. Compare the Dutch name *persikboom*.
[6] Abricot is an Arabic word. For its curious history see Engelmann, *Glossaire*, p. 13.

the cheese-like nut. But the mute *t*, which could never have crept into the word, whatever may be the danger of its ultimate disappearance, is valuable as an indication of the true etymology, as well as of the country in which the tree was indigenous. The French *Châtaigne* or *Chastaigne*, and still more plainly the Italian Castagna, and the Dutch *Kastanie*, point us to Castanæa, in Thessaly, as its native place.[1]

The London urchins, whose horticultural studies have been confined to Covent Garden, probably suppose that the WALNUT is a species of Wallfruit. In German, however, the word takes the form 𝔚𝔞𝔩𝔰𝔠𝔥𝔢 𝔑𝔲𝔟, which would indicate that it is either the foreign nut, or the nut from Wälschland or Italy.[2] Though the former is, perhaps, the more probable etymology, yet we must remember that the walnut is pre-eminently the tree of Northern Italy, as will be acknowledged by all who have rested beneath the spreading shade of the gigantic walnut-trees of the Piedmontese valleys, or who have crossed the wide plains of Lombardy, where the country for miles and miles is one vast walnut orchard, with the vines swinging in graceful festoons from tree to tree.

The word QUINCE preserves only a single letter of its orginal form. The English word is a corruption of the French *coing*,[3] which we may trace through the Italian *cotogna* to the Latin *cotonium* or *cydonium malum*, the apple of Cydon, a town in Crete.

The cherry, the peach, the quince, and the chestnut are very ancient denizens of Western Europe. Not so the DAMSON, which was only imported a few centuries ago. If we write the word according to the older and more correct fashion—damascene—we are able at once to trace its identity with the *Prunum Damascenum*, or plum from Damascus.[4] The DAMASK ROSE came from the same city in the reign of Henry VII., and

1 See, however, Pictet, *Orig. Indo-Europ.* part i. p. 249.
2 See p. 45, *supra* ; Talbot, *English Etymol.* p. 307 ; Max Müller, Lectures, 2nd series, p. 367. Compare the Anglo-Saxon *wealh-hnut*, and the Old Norse *val-hnot.*
3 See the ' Romaunt of the Rose ' :—

> ' And many homely trees there were
> That peaches, *coines*, and apples bere ;
> Medlers, plummes, peeres, chesteines,
> Cherise, of which many one faine is '.

This passage also exhibits chestnut and cherry in a transitional stage of adoption from the French.
4 The greengage was introduced by one Gage, belonging to an old Suffolk family of that name. Borrow, *Wild Wales*, vol. ii. p. 99.

we learn how rapidly the culture of the beautiful flower must have extended from the fact, that in less than a century Shakespeare talks of the damask cheek of a rosy maiden, showing that the name had already become an English word.[1]

The science of etymological botany has its pitfalls, which must be avoided. The GUELDER ROSE, for instance, is not, as might be supposed, the rose from Guelderland, but the elder rose, as is shown by the natural affinities of the plant, as well as by the ancient spelling of the name [2] [?]   An attempt to give a geographical significance to the name has probably led to the modification of the spelling. The same cause has undoubtedly been at work in corrupting the name of the *girasole*—the Italian turnsole or sunflower—into the JERUSALEM ARTICHOKE, out of which some ingenious cook has concocted palestine soup ! [3]

The name of the GUERNSEY LILY contains a somewhat curious history. The flower is a native of Japan, where it was discovered by Kæmpfer, the Dutch botanist and traveller. The ship which contained the specimens of the new plant was wrecked on the coast of Guernsey, and some of the bulbs having been washed ashore, they germinated and spread in the sandy soil. Thence they were sent over to England, in the middle of the seventeenth century, by Mr. Hatton, a botanist, and son of the Governor of Guernsey.[4]

The small dried grapes called CURRANTS were, in the last century, called ' corinths ', or Corinth grapes, Corinth being the chief port from which they were shipped. The currants of our gardens seem to have received their name from their superficial resemblance to the currants of commerce.

The SHALLOT, a species of onion, comes to us from Ascalon, as will appear if we trace the name through the French form *échalotte*, and the Spanish *escalona*, to the Latin *Ascalonia*.[5] SPINAGE is, perhaps, *olus Hispanicum*, and the Arabs call it *Hispanach*, the Spanish plant.[6]   COFFEE has been traced to the mountains of Caffa, south of Abyssinia, where the plant grows wild ; and MOCHA,[7] where it was first cultivated, still

---

[1] See Whewell, in *Philolog. Proceed.* vol. v. p. 136.
[2] Talbot, *English Etymologies*, p. 88.
[3] Max Müller, *Lectures*, second series, p. 368.
[4] Beckmann, *History of Inventions*, vol. i. p. 516 ; Ansted, *Channel Islands*, p. 499.
[5] Diez, *Etymolog. Wörterb.* p. 305 ; Ménage, *Origines*, pp. 278, 786.
[6] Or, perhaps, the name is derived from the spines on the seed. See Beckmann, *Hist. of Inventions*, vol. ii. p. 340 ; *Notes and Queries*, vol. xii. p. 253.
[7] Hartwig, *Tropical World*, p. 189.

gives a name to the choicest growth. In like manner BOHEA, CONGOU, HYSON and SOUCHONG are geographical terms on a map of China. JALAP comes from Xalapa, or Jalapa, a province of Mexico. Another Mexican province, Choco, has given us the names of CHOCOLATE and CACAO. The coco or cocoa nut, however, has no botanical [1] or etymological connexion with cacao. The Portuguese term for a bugbear is *coco*, and the word seems to have been applied to the palm nut on account of the appearance of a mask or face which is produced by the three holes at the extremity of the shell. [2] CAYENNE, CHILIS, SEVILLE and CHINA oranges, PERUVIAN bark, and BRAZIL nuts are examples of names that have remained undisguised by etymological changes. The BRAZIL WOOD of commerce does not, however, as might have been thought, derive its name from the country ; but, on the contrary, that vast empire was so called from the discovery on its shores of a dye wood, [3] which produced the Brazil colour, or colour of glowing coals. [4] The slopes of Sinai were formerly overgrown with the SENEH, or wild acacia-tree, a shaggy thornbush ; and it is more probable that the plant takes its name from the mountain than the mountain from the plant. [5] SQUILLS are possibly from Squillace, and CARRAWAYS, Pliny tells us, are from Caria. RHUBARB is a corruption of *Rha barbarum*, or *Rha barbaricum* (German *Rhabarber*, Italian *Rabarbaro*), the root from the savage banks of the River Rha, or Volga. [6] DRAGONWORT is a curiously corrupted name, It comes from Tarragona in Spain. The word TAMARIND is from the Arabic *tamarhendi*, which means the Indian date. [7] INDIGO

---

1 The cacao, or cocoa nibs, which produce the beverage, are beans borne in the pods of a shrub, (*Theobroma cacao*,) which has no resemblance or affinity to the palm-tree, (*Cocos nucifera*,) which produces the coco nut, or to the coca or coco (*Erythroxylon coca*,) a herb whose leaves are chewed by the Peruvians, as a powerful stimulant-narcotic. The distinctive spelling of these three productions, cacao, cocoa, and coca should be carefully observed. See Burton, *Abeokuta*, vol. i. p. 47.

2 Marsh, *Lectures on English Language*, p. 143.

3 The *Cæsalpinia crista*, which grows profusely in the forests of Brazil. Hartwig, *Tropical World*, p. 240.

4 The word *brazil* is found in our literature as early as the reign of Edward I. Talbot, *English Etymologies*, p. 451 ; Hinchliff, *South American Sketches*, p. 232. French *braise*, Portuguese *braza*, live coals. Hence the English *braser*, sometimes improperly written brasier, a vessel for containing live coals.

5 Stanley, *Jewish Church*, p. 108 ; *Sinai and Palestine*, p. 18. Cf. Greek μύρρα= σμύρνα, myrrh.

6 Huic Rha vicinus est amnis, in cujus superciliis quædam vegetabilis ejusdem nominis gignitur radix, proficiens ad usus multiplices medelarum. *Ammianus Marcellinus*, lib. xxii. cap. 8, § 28. See Müller, *Ugrische Volkstamm*, vol. ii. p. 87. [Old It. *rabbarbaro*, the drug Reubarbe. Florio].

7 Diez, *Etym. Wörterbuch*, p. 340 ; Freytag, vol. i. p. 424, b.

W.P.   U

is *indicum*, the Indian dye ; and GAMBOGE is from Cambodia. *Jenjibre*, the Spanish form of the word GINGER, looks as if the root had been imported from Zanzibar, while the Arabic form *Zenjebel* seems to point to the mountains of Zend, or Persia. Sugar CANDY seems to be from Candia ; and this view is supported by the fact that *kand* is the Turkish word for sugar of every kind.[1]   The CYPRESS tree comes from the island of Cyprus, and the SPRUCE fir is the Prussian fir.

   ' There is an herbe ', says an old voyager, ' which is sowed apart by itselfe, and is called by the inhabitants *Vppowoc* ; in the West Indies it hath diuers names according to the seuerall places and countreys where it groweth and is used ; the Spanyards generally call it TOBACCO. The leaues thereof being dried and brought into pouder, they use to take the fume or smoake thereof, by sucking it through pipes made of clay, into their stomacke and head. . . . This *Vppowoc* is of so precious estimation amongst them (the Indians), that they think their gods are maruellously delighted therewith : whereupon sometime they make hallowed fires, and cast some of the pouder therein for a sacrifice '.[2]   The general estimation in which the growth of Tobago [3] was held has caused the name of this island to become the general designation of the ' herbe '. Laodicea, the mother of Seleucus Nicator, gave her name to a city on the Syrian coast, and the ' herbe ' shipped from this port goes by the name of LATAKIA tobacco—a name which exhibits a curious geographical juxtaposition. Another choice growth is called YORK RIVER, a name familiar to the readers of telegrams from the seat of war, and derived from the Duke of York, afterwards James II.   CUBAS, HAVANNAHS, VEVAYS, and MANILLAS are also among the ' diuers names ' derived from ' the seuerall places and countreys where thei herbe groweth '.

   The names of wines are, with few exceptions,[4] derived from

   [1] In Moslem countries an inordinate quantity of sugar is consumed. A very large number of the Arabic words now existing in the Spanish and Portuguese languages denote preparations of sugar. See Engelmann, *Glossaire*, passim.
   [2] See Hariot, ' Brief and true report of the new found land of Virginia ', apud Hackluyt, *Voyages*, vol. iii. p. 271.
   [3] There is also a province of Yucatan called Tabaco. Adelung thinks that the word tobacco is not derived from either of these local names, but *vice versâ :* the word may, perhaps, be derived from the Haitean *tambaku*, a pipe, or, as some have thought, the word may have been adopted from an Indian name of the plant. Against this it may be urged that the Indian word for tobacco is *úppówoc*. Wilson, *Pre-historic Man*, vol. i. p. 383 ; Drake, *Book of the Indians*, book iv. p. 6.
   [4] Such as TENT, which is derived from the Spanish *tinto*, in allusion to its rich

geographical sources. The CHIAN and the SAMIAN came from islands of the Grecian archipelago. The FALERNIAN, of which Horace was so fond, was the produce of a volcanic hill-side near Naples. Falernian has already been driven from the cellar to the schoolroom, and the vine disease threatens to do the same with CANARY and MADEIRA. CAPE comes from South Africa. Three of the old provinces of France give their names to CHAMPAGNE, BURGUNDY, and ROUSILLON. There is a vine-yard near Rheims called SILLERY, CHABLIS is a town in northern Burgundy not far from Auxerre, and SAUTERNE is a village near Bordeaux. MEDOC is the name of the vast sandy plain which lies between the Gironde and the ocean. The town of MAN-ZANARES and the VAL DE PENAS, or valley of rocks, are both in the province of La Mancha. ASTI is a town near Marengo. TOKAY is situated in the north-east of Hungary.

Many of the wines of commerce, as BORDEAUX and LISBON, receive their English names from the port of shipment rather than from the place of growth. So PORT is the wine exported from Oporto, and the wines of Sicily are shipped from MARSALA, an Arabic name meaning ' the Port of God ', and reminding us, as we drink it, of the almost forgotten story of the Mahometan conquests in Southern Europe. MALMSEY is a contraction of MALVASIA, having been originally shipped from Napoli di Malvasia, a port in the Morea.

MALAGA and XERES are also places of export rather than of production. The Spanish *x* being pronounced like the *ch* in German, the word sherris, on English lips, is a very fair approximation to the name of the town of Xeres, which, since Shakespeare's time, has been the grand emporium of the Spanish wine trade. The sack or sherris sack, upon whose excellent ' twofold operation ' Falstaff so feelingly dilates,[1] is Xeres sec, or dry sherry as we should call it. The term sack was applied to all the dry wines of Canary, Xeres, and Malaga; thus we read of Canary sack, Malaga sack, Xeres sack.[2]

It would be curious to trace the progress of the perversion whereby the wines which in the fifteenth century used to be correctly designated ' wines of Rhin ' have come to be called

colour. The name of CLARET is derived from its clearness. No Frenchman, however, speaks of, or drinks, *clairet*. This is the mixture manufactured solely for the English market. [1] *Henry IV*, second part, act iv. scene 2.
[2] See Hackluyt, apud Redding, *Wines*, p. 211 ; Drake, *Shakespeare and his Times*, vol. i. p. 130 ; Ducange, s. v. saccatum ; Ford, *Gatherings from Spain*, p. 150.

HOCKS. Hocheim, from which the name is derived, lies on the Mayn and not on the Rhine, and neither the excellence nor the abundance of the Hocheim vintage seems to afford adequate reason for the fact that the name has become a generic term for the whole of the Rhine wines. It may probably be due to special commercial interests connecting some London firm with Hocheim, for in no European language except English do these wines go by the name of hocks. It might seem that JOHANNISBERG, with its white Schloss, STEINBERG, NIERSTEIN, GEISENHEIM, RUDESHEIM, ASSMANNHAUS, or some other of the venerable towns or smiling villages which delight the eye of the traveller, as he passes the romantic ruins and steep vineyards which fringe the broad rolling stream, might have asserted a better claim to bestow their names upon the delicate vintage of the Rhine, than an obscure village, which stands upon another river, and which is by no means unsurpassed in the excellence or abundance of its growth.

The volcanic slopes of all the river-banks in this district offer a congenial soil and site for the growth of the vine. LAUBENHEIM on the Nahe, LAHNSTEIN on the Lahn, and ZELTINGEN and PIESPORT on the MOSELLE, compete with the more celebrated villages on the Rhine and the Mayn. The Germans have a saw which compares the qualities of their chief growths :

> Rhein-wein, fein wein ;
> Neckar-wein, lecker wein ;
> Franken wein, tanken wein ;
> Mosel-wein, unnosel wein.

HUNGARY WATER is said to have been first distilled by Elizabeth, Queen of Hungary.[1] CHARTREUSE is prepared from a recipe in the possession of the monks of the celebrated monastery ruled over by St. Bernard. CURAÇAO [2] came originally from the island of that name in the Carribean Sea. COGNAC is a town in the department of the Charente. HOLLANDS and SCHIEDAM, as their names import, came to us from the Dutch. Since GIN is a contraction of Geneva, it might be supposed that geneva was originally distilled in the city of that name. The word geneva is, however, only an Anglicized

---

[1] Beckmann, *History of Inventions*, vol. i. p. 316.
[2] Often wrongly spelt Curaçoa. Cf. the analogous names Macao, Bilbao, Callao, etc.

form of the Dutch *jenever*,[1] the juniper, from the berries of which plant the peculiar flavour is derived. WHISKEY is a corruption of the Celtic word *uisge*, water, a root which, as we have seen,[2] appears in the names of the Wisk, Esk, Usk, Exe, Thames, and other Celtic rivers. USQUEBAUGH is the ' yellow water ', from the Erse *boy*, yellow [No, see p. 144]. GLENLIVAT is the name of a highland valley in Banffshire, famous for its stills. SPRUCE BEER is either Prussian beer, or beer tinctured with the sap of the spruce or Prussian fir. Colonel NEGUS has been immortalized by the beverage which he first concocted. The etymology of GROG is curious. Admiral Vernon, a sailor of the old school, used to wear a grogram coat,[3] and hence the seamen bestowed upon him the nickname of ' Old Grog ', which was afterwards transferred to the mixture of rum and water which he was the first to introduce into the navy.[4]

The names of animals, like those of plants, are able to supply us, in many cases, with information as to the countries from which they have been introduced, as well as with examples of the curious phonetic changes which the names of those countries have undergone.

The naturalization of the COCHIN CHINA fowl has been too recent to permit any of these changes to take place. The same is the case with DORKINGS and SPANISH FOWLS. The GUINEA FOWL came from the Guinea coast,[5] and the CANARY was brought from the Canary Isles in the middle of the sixteenth century.[6] BANTAMS came from the Dutch settlement of Bantam in Java. The PHEASANT is of much older introduction. The name is derived from the Latin *avis phasiana*—the Phasian bird—whence we conclude, with Pliny, that the bird was originally brought from the banks of the river Phasis, in Colchis. The EIDER duck takes its name from the river Eider in Holstein, whence, however, the bird has long disappeared. The TURKEY was so named by a mistake. It is an American fowl, but was

---

[1] Gin being originally a Dutch drink, the name is undoubtedly derived from the Dutch *jenever*, rather than from the French equivalent *genièvre*, as is usually alleged.

[2] See pp. 144-145, *supra*.

[3] The word Grogram is an Anglicization of the French *gros-grain*, coarse textured.

[4] Taylor, *Antiquitates Curiosæ*, p. 58 ; *Notes and Queries*, first series, vol. i. pp. 58, 168 ; Sullivan, *Dict. of Derivations*, p. 110.

[5] The GUINEA-pig is a native of Brazil, but it may probably have been originally brought to this country by some ship engaged in the Guinea trade.

[6] Hence CANARY seed and the CANARY colour.

popularly supposed to have come from the Levant. The German name, *Kalekuter*, would imply that it came from Calicut, and the French *Dinde*, a contraction of *poulet d' Inde*, appears to endorse the same error.

ERMINE is the fur of the animal of the same name ; Chaucer calls it the Armine.[1] By a parallel phonetic change, Ville Hardouin calls the Arminians the Hermines. Hence we may with great probability assign the animal to Armenia, and its scientific name, *Mus Ponticus*, points to the same region.

The SABLE, like the Ermine, bears the corrupted name of a large country. The English form affords no clue to the etymology, but we find that the word in Italian takes the form *Zibellino*, which appears to be a corruption of Sibelino or Siberino—the fur from Siberia. The POLECAT is from Poland. SHAMOY leather is often erroneously spelt chamois, as if it were prepared from the hide of the Alpine antelope. But, like RUSSIA or MOROCCO, the word shamoy has a geographical origin, and means the leather from Samland, a district on the Baltic.

Many of the breeds of domestic cattle are of such recent origin, that the names have as yet suffered no corruption. Thus the names of LEICESTERS, and SOUTHDOWNS, DEVONS and HEREFORDS, as well as of ANGOLAS, CASHMERES, SHETLANDS and NEWFOUNDLANDS, are still in the second stage of word formation.[2] In the third stage we may place the SPANIEL, which is either the Spanish dog, or the dog from Hispaniola. The GREYHOUND is the Grecian dog (*canis graius*). PUSS is an endearing corruption of Pers, the Persian cat.[3] The meaning of the word BARB [4] is slowly changing ; it was at first used strictly of a horse brought from Barbary, just as an ARAB was a horse from Arabia. Of kindred blood to Barbs aud Arabs is the Spanish horse called a JENNET, a name which may not improbably be derived from Jaen, the capital of one of the Moorish kingdoms in the Peninsula. Nor have we yet acknowledged all the obligations of our horse-breeders to the Arabian blood. One of the galleons of the Armada, which had succeeded in weathering Cape Wrath and the storm-beaten Hebrides,

[1] We find also the forms Harmelinus and Arminiæ pellis, and the Italian name is Armellino. Diez, *Etymol. Wörterbuch*, p. 26.
[2] See p. 286, *supra ;* and compare the names CHEDDER, CHESHIRE, STILTON, PARMESAN, etc.
[3] Hume, *Geographical Terms*, p. 9. [An imitative word everywhere.]
[4] German, *barbar :* Old French, *barbare*.

was lost on the coast of Galloway, and tradition avers that a Spanish stallion, rescued from the wreck, became the ancestor of the strong and serviceable breed of GALLOWAYS. A curious instance of change of application in a name occurs in the case of the strong Normand horses which were imported from Rouen. They were called rouens or ROANS—a word which has now come to denote the colour of the horse rather than the breed.

Collectors of insects often give topic names to rare or local species, such as the Camberwell beauty, the Kentish glory, the Bath white ; and there are scores of similar names which might be added to the list. The venomous spider called the TARANTULA takes its name from Taranto in Southern Italy. The Cantharides of the druggist's shop often go by the name SPANISH FLIES. Mosquitoes, however, do not take their name from the Musquito coast, the word being the diminutive of the Spanish word *mosca*, a fly.[1]

The CARP is in Latin *cupra* or *cyprinus*, the fish from Cyprus. SARDINES are caught off the coast of Sardinia, but we should be wrong in supposing that the SARDINE stone or the SARDONYX came to us from that island, for the true origin of these names is to be sought at Sardis in Asia Minor. The loadstone and the magnet are both local names. The LOADSTONE is a corrupted [2] translation of *Lydius lapis*, the stone of Lydia [?]. In the same region we must seek for the source of the name MAGNET, which is derived from Magnesia, a Lydian city. From Magnesia we also obtain the names of MANGANESE, or *manganesis*, MAGNESIA, and MAGNESIAN LIMESTONE. COPPER is *cuprum* or *æs cyprium*, the brass of Cyprus.[3] The neighbouring island of Crete gave its name to the *creta*, a sort of pipeclay which the Romans used for seals, the knot with which the packet was tied being enveloped in a ball of clay, and the seal impressed upon it. From the Latin *creta* the English adjective CRETACEOUS has been formed, and from the same root we get our CRAYONS through the medium of the French *craie*. TRIPOLI powder is composed of the flinty skeletons of diatomaciæ,

---

1 The word musket (Italian, *moschetto*) is from the same root. Diez, *Etym. Wörterb.* p. 232.

2 The notion of a leading or guiding-stone seems to have influenced the present form of the word. Cf. the loadstar, or leading-star. [Both from *lode*, a way.]

3 The Sanskrit name is nearly identical, which would indicate that copper first reached India from the West. See Pictet, *Orig. Indo-Europ.* part i. p. 173.

of which large beds exist near Tripoli. The TURKEY STONE on which we whet our razors is derived from the same region, and possibly from the same quarries as the *cos*, to which the Romans gave the name of the island from which they were accustomed to procure it.[1] The TURQUOISE is a sort of misnomer. It came from Nishapore in Persia, but being imported by the Turkey merchants, was supposed to be a Turkish stone. CHALCEDONY came from Chalcedon, and ALABASTER from Alabastrum in Egypt, as we are told by Pliny, who also informs us that the TOPAZ came from Topazos, an island in the Red Sea. AGATES were first found in the bed of the Achates, a Sicilian river.[2] In like manner the Gagates, a river of Lycia, gave its name to the black stone which the French call *gagate, jayet*, or *jaet*, a word which we have abbreviated into JET. The crystal called SPA came originally from the Belgian watering-place whose name has been transferred to so many mineral springs, and the word CHALYBEATE is itself indirectly derived from the name of the Chalubes, a tribe which inhabited the iron-producing district of Armenia, SEIDLITZ in Bohemia has given its name to the well-known effervescing draughts, and genuine SELTZER water comes from Nieder Selters, near Maintz. On Epsom Common may still be discovered the forsaken, but once fashionable well, from whose waters EPSOM SALTS were first procured. GYPSUM, when written in its ancient form *egipsum*, tells us that it came from Egypt. PLASTER of PARIS was procured in great abundance from the catacombs of Paris, and UMBER and SIENNA, as the names import, are earths from Northern Italy. SYENITE is the granite of Syene in Upper Egypt.[3] PARIAN marble is from the isle of Paros, and CAEN and BATH stone have suffered no corruption. Two of the newly discovered metals take their names respectively from YTTRIUM in Sweden and STRONTIAN in Argyleshire. NATRON and NITRE are found in the Egyptian province of Nitria, where natron lakes still exist, though it is fairly open to dispute whether the salt gave its name to the province, or, as Jerome asserts, the province

---

[1] Or the island may have derived its name from the stone. In favour of this view it may be urged that the Sanskrit *ço* means to sharpen. Cf. the Latin *acuo*. [Or, more probably, the two words are quite unconnected.]

[2] Bochart, vol. iii. p. 549.

[3] There are many terms of local origin used by geologists, such as Devonian, Silurian, Wealden, Cambrian, etc.

performed the like office for the salt. AMMONIA abounds likewise in the soil of the Libyan desert, and in the writings of Synesius, bishop of Pentapolis, we have an account of the preparation of the *sal ammoniacus* by the priests of Jupiter Ammon and its transmission to Egypt in baskets made of the leaves of palms.

A large number, we might almost say the greater number, of the fabrics which we wear, are called by names derived from the places at which they were originally made. Political and social revolutions, aided by the invention of the spinning jenny, of the power-loom, and of the steam-engine, have, it is true, transferred the great seats of manufacture from India, from the Levant, from Holland, from Northern Italy, and from East Anglia, to the neighbourhood of our English coal-fields, but the fabrics retain the ancient names which still testify of the places which saw the earliest developments of industrial energy. Our CASHMERE SHAWLS [1] are now made at Paisley ; our JAPANNED ware comes from Birmingham, our CHINA from Staffordshire, our NANKEEN from Manchester, and we even export our CALICO to Calicut, the very place from whence, three hundred years ago, it used to come. [2]

Names of this class resolve themselves, for the most part, into three divisions, which indicate in a characteristic manner the three chief centres of mediaeval industry.

The ingenuity and inventive skill of the Arabs gave the first impulse to the industrial progress of the West. Thus SARCENET (low Latin, *saracenicum*) was a silken fabric obtained from the Saracens. Mouseline, the French form of the word MUSLIN, clearly refers us to Moussul, [3] in the neighbourhood of the eastern capital of the Caliphs. In Bagdad, the street inhabited by the manufacturers of silken stuffs was called Atab, and the fabrics woven by them were called Atabi. [4] From a corruption of this word we probably derive the words TAFFETY and TABBY. [5] The rich figured silk called DAMASK, [6] and the famous DAMASCUS swords were produced at the central seat

---

[1] The word SHAWL is itself the name of a valley and district in Affghanistan.
[2] The French for calico is *calicot*. The fact that the *t* is dropped in English indicates that we got the word through the French. Hackluyt calls it ' Calicut cloth '.
[3] Diez, *Etymol. Wörterbuch*, p. 236 ; Pihan, *Glossaire*, p. 210.
[4] Gayangos, *Dynasties*, vol. i. pp. 358, 51 ; Yonge, *Christian Names*, vol. i. p. 122.
[5] A tabby cat has the wavy markings of watered silk.
[6] Scarlet, it may be noted, is an Arabic word.

of the Moslem dominion,[1] and the TOLEDO blades remind us
that the Arab conquerors carried their metallurgic skill with
them to the West. From another Moslem kingdom came
CIPRESSE, the black 'cobweb lawn' behind which Olivia, in
'Twelfth Night', 'hides her heart', and which the pedlar
Autolycus, in the 'Winter's Tale', carries in his pack.

GAUZE was made at Gaza, as is indicated by *gaze*, the French,
and *gasa* the Spanish form of the name ; [2] and in the same way
we are guided by the Italian *baldacchino* in assigning BAUDEKIN,
which we read of in old authors, to Baldacca or New Bagdad,
one of the suburbs of Cairo. Baudekin originally meant a rich
silken tissue embroidered with figures of birds, trees, and flowers,
in gold and silver thread, but the word was subsequently used
for any rich canopy, especially that over the altar, and pre-
eminently the canopy in St. Peter's under which stands the
throne of the Pope.[3] Previous to the tenth century an important suburb of Cairo was Fostat,[4] where flourished the manufacture of FUSTIAN ; *fostagno*, the Italian name of the fabric,
indicates this more clearly than the English disguise.[5]

MOHAIR, or MOIRE, is a fabric[6] of the Moors or Arabs of Spain ;
and the same skilful race, after the Spanish conquest, manufactured JEAN at Jaen ; and at Cordova, cordovan or CORD-
WAIN,[7] a kind of leather prized by the *cordonniers* or CORD-
WAINERS of the middle ages as highly as MOROCCO is by the
leather-workers of the present day. Truly the most elaborate
history of the civilization[8] of the Arabs would fail to give us

---

[1] Diez, *Etymol. Wörterbuch*, p. 121.

[2] Pihan, *Glossaire*, p. 132 ; Diez, *Etymol. Wörterb.* p. 641.

[3] Fairholt, *Up the Nile*, p. 59. Wedgwood (*English Etym.* p. 126) copies Diez, *Etym.
Wörterb.* p. 39, in assigning this manufacture to Bagdad on the Tigris. The ecclesiastical
vestment called a DALMATIC was invented in Dalmatia.

[4] Gibbon, chap. li. vol. vi. p. 403.

[5] Diez, *Etymol. Wörterb.* p. 157. Dimity is not, as has been asserted, the fabric from
Damietta, but that woven with two threads ($\delta i \varsigma$ and $\mu i \tau o \varsigma$) just as twill and drill are
respectively made with two and three threads, as the names imply.

[6] In Almeria there were at least 4,000 looms. Gayangos, *Dynasties*, vol. i. p. 51.
MERINO is woven from the wool of the Merino sheep, a name which Southey has ingeniously
derived from the emirs, or shepherd princes of Spain. The name of MOREEN may be
due to the same source, though it is more probably derived from the dark colour.

[7] Diez, *Etymol. Wörterb.* p. 111 ; Ménage, *Origines*, pp. 229, 696.

[8] To the Arabs we also owe much of the early science of the West, as is shown by
the words *chemistry, alchemy, alembic, borax, elixir, alkaii, alcohol, azul, lapis lazuli,
algebra, almanac, azimuth, zenith*, and *nadir*, which are all of Arabic origin. How feeble,
too, would be our powers of calculation without the ARABIC NUMERALS, and the Arabic
system of decimal notation. It is also a very suggestive fact that almost every Spanish
word connected with irrigation—some dozen in all—is of Arabic origin. e.g. *alberca*,
a tank ; *azequia*, a canal ; *azena*, a water-wheel ; *aljibe*, a well. Gayangos, *Dynasties*,
p. 487. Many nautical terms used in Spain are also Arabic. e.g. *saetia*, a boat ; the
small three-masted vessel called a *xabeque ; almadia*, a raft ; *arsenal ;* and *almirante*,

any such vivid sense of their industry and ingenuity as is conveyed by the curious fact, that the seats of their empire, whether in Europe, in Africa, or in Asia, have stamped their names indelibly on so many of the fabrics in our daily use.

As the energies of the Moslem races decayed, the Flemings took their place as the chief manufacturing people.[1]   When Leeds and Manchester were country villages, and Liverpool a hamlet, Flanders was supplying all Europe with textile fabrics. The evidence of this fact is interwoven into the texture of our English speech. We have seen that many silken and cotton fabrics come from the Arabs ; the Flemings excelled in the manufactures of flax and wool. From Cambrai we have CAMBRIC, as is clear from the French form *cambray*, or *toile de Cambray*. DIAPER, formerly written *d'ipre* or *d'Ypres*, was made at Ypres, one of the chief seats of the cloth manufacture, as we learn from Chaucer, who says of his wife of Bath :—

> Of cloth making she hadde swiche an haunt,
> She passed hem of Ipres and of Gaunt.

Another colony of clothworkers was settled on the River Toucques in Normandy. From the name of this river a whole family of words has been derived.[2]   In German the general name for cloth is Tuch, and in old English *tuck*. We read in Hackluyt a description of ' the great Turke himselfe ', who had ' upon his head a goodly white tucke, containing in length by estimation fifteene yards, which was of silke and linnen wouen together, resembling something of Calicut cloth '.[3] White trousers are made of DUCK, our beds are covered with TICKING, and our children wear TUCKERS at their meals. A TUCKER was originally a narrow band of linen cloth worn by ladies round the throat. Hence any narrow strip of cloth fastened on the dress was called a TUCK or TUCKER, and when this mode of ornamentation was imitated by a fold in the fabric, the fold or plait itself received the same name. A weaver used to be called a tucker, and Tucker is still a common surname among us. In Somerset and in Cornwall there

an admiral, which is a corruption of *emir-al-bahr*, commander at sea. Gayangos, *Dynasties*, vol. ii. appendix, p. xxxvi. ; Engelmann, *Glossaire*, p. 53.

[1] The Flemish manufactures arose in the twelfth century. See Hallam, *Middle Ages*, vol. iii. p. 375.

[2] See Knapp, *English Roots*, p. 46.

[3] Anthony Ienkinson, ' The manner of the entring of Soliman the great Turke, with his armie into Aleppo in Syria ', apud Hackluyt, *Voyages*, vol. ii. p. 113.

are villages called Tucking Mill, and Tucker Street in Bristol [1] was that occupied by the weavers.[2]

From the Walloons we have GALLOON,[3] that is, Walloon lace, as well as the finer fabrics which take their names from VALENCIENNES and MECHLIN. GINGHAM was originally made at Guingamp in French Flanders.[4] From the same region came LISLE thread, the rich tapestry called ARRAS, and BRUSSELS CARPETS. In the marshes of Holland the fabrics were of a less costly type than among the wealthy Flemings. From this region we obtain the names of DELF ware, brown HOLLAND, and homely FRIEZE,[5] or cloth of Friesland.

Passing from the ingenious Arabs and the industrious Netherlanders, we find among the luxurious republics of Northern Italy a third series of names, as characteristic and as suggestive as those we have already considered. The fiddles of CREMONA, the PISTOLS of Pistoja [6] in Tuscany, the bonnets of LEGHORN, the PADS and PADDING of Padua, the rich fabric called PADUASOY, and the scent called BERGAMOT, are fair specimens of the wares which would be articles of foremost necessity to the fine gentleman and fair ladies who figure in the pages of Boccace ; and it is easy to understand that ITALIAN IRONS might be suitably introduced by those MILLINERS and MANTUAMAKERS[7] who derive their names from two cities where their services were so abundantly appreciated.[8] On the other hand, ITALICS and ROMAN type still bear witness in every printing office that the newly discovered art was no-

---

1 Lucas, *Secularia*, p. 101.

2 I have left this paragraph as it stood in the first edition, though I am now far from certain as to the correctness of the etymology suggested. The very early use of the word *tuck* suggests some independent Teutonic root.

3 The GALLEON was probably a Walloon vessel, one of the great Antwerp merchantmen.

4 Hume, *Geographical Terms*, p. 7.

5 Compare, however, the Welsh *ffris*, the nap of cloth. To FRIZZLE, in French *friser*, is to curl the hair in the Frisian fashion. See, however, Grimm, *Gesch. Deut. Spr.* p. 669 ; Diez, *Etym. Wörterb.* p. 155. The architectural term FRIEZE is probably derived from Phrygia, certainly not from Friesland. The ATTICS of our houses may be traced to the Attic order of architecture, which displayed an upper tier of columns.

6 The name of pistoyers was originally given to certain small daggers, and was afterwards transferred to the small concealed firearms. H. Stephanus, apud Diez, *Etym. Wörterbuch*, p. 267 ; Menage, *Origines*, p. 527. To this last we may add the *pavois*, or shield of Pavia. Diez, *Etym. Wörterbuch*, p. 256.

7 Whewell, in *Phil. Proc.* vol. v. p. 136, thinks this is an erroneous derivation. He prefers *manteau*. The best bells for hawks were called MILANS, because imported from Milan. See Drake, *Shakspeare and his Times*, vol. i. p. 268.

8 The tureen is not from Turin, but is a *terrine*, or earthen vessel. Whewell, in *Philolog. Proc.* vol. v. p. 136. We have also POLONIES or [Bologna sausages, and SAVELOYS from Savoy. Cf. Perigord pies, Bath buns, Banbury cakes, etc. The MAGENTA colour derives its name from a Lombard village, but the name commemorates the date, and not the locality of the discovery.

where more eagerly welcomed, or carried to a higher perfection than in the country in which the revival of learning first began.

From the rest of Europe we may glean a few scattered names of the same class—though they mostly denote peculiarities of local costume rather than established seats of manufacture. Thus, we have the word CRAVATS from the nation of the Cravates, or Croats as they are now called.[1] There was a French regiment of light horse called ' le royal Cravate ', because it was attired in the Croat fashion, and the word cravat was introduced in 1636, when the neck-ties worn by these troops became the mode. GALLIGASKINS were the large open hose worn by the Gallo-vascones, or Gascons of Southern France. GALLÔCHES, or galloshoes,[2] are the wooden sabots worn by the French peasants, and the name has been transferred to the overshoes of caoutchouc which have been recently introduced. The French city from which we first obtained SHALLOON is indicated by Chaucer in the ' Reves Tale '. The Miller of Trumpington, we read,

> Made a bedde
> With shetes and chalons fair yspredde.

JERSEYS and GUERNSEYS remind us how the mothers and wives of the fishermen in the Channel islands used to toil with their knitting-needles while their sons and husbands were labouring at sea. TWEEDS were made at Hawick, Galashiels, Selkirk, and other towns on the Scottish border. The name was first suggested by the misreading of an invoice, and the appropriateness of this substitution of Tweeds for Twills gave rapid currency to the new name. WORSTED [3] takes its name from Worstead, a village not far from Norwich, and informs us that the origin of our English textile manufactures dates from the settlement, in the time of Henry I, of a colony of Flemings, who made Norwich one of the chief manufacturing towns of England. The importance of the East Anglian

---

[1] Whewell, in *Phil. Proc.* vol. v. p. 136 ; Zeuss, *Die Deutschen*, p. 608.

[2] The etymology here suggested is doubtful. The word is very ancient, for the Roman *caliga*, from which Caligula derived his name, and the Lancashire *clog*, are from the same root. Compare the Old Spanish *gallochas*, Erse *galoig*, Brezone *galochou*. Spenser speaks of ' My galage grown fast to my heel '. Diefenbach, *Celtica*, i. p. 133 ; Diez, *Etymol. Wörterbuch*, p. 162 ; Whitaker, *History of Manchester*, vol. ii. p. 258 ; Ménage, *Origines*, p. 338.

[3] Blomefield, *Hist. of Norfolk*, vol. v. p. 1455 ; Gough's Camden, vol. ii. p. 190 ; Hallam, *Middle Ages*, vol. iii. p. 378.

woollen trade [1] is also shown by the fact that two contiguous
Suffolk villages, Lindsey, and Kersey with its adjacent *mere*,
have given their names to LINDSEY WOLSEY and KERSEYMERE.
BAIZE is said [2] to be from Baiæ near Naples, though this appears
to be only an ingenious etymological guess.   It is said also that
DRUGGET, or droget, was first made at Drogheda in Ireland, and
that BONNETS came from the Irish village of that name.[!] From
the name of Hibernia is derived the French word *berne*, a
blanket,[3] and hence, perhaps, we have obtained the semi-
naturalized word BERNOUSE.[4]   Llanelly, I believe, was a
great place for the Welsh flannel manufacture, though whether
the word FLANNEL is derived from the name Llanelly is
doubtful.[5]   The etymology at all events seems quite as
probable as that which Diez proposes, from *velamen*.[6]   The
word SILK may be traced to the *sericæ vestes*, the garments of
the Seres or Chinese, who, ever since the time of Pliny, have
been the chief producers of this material.

It must suffice briefly to enumerate a few inventions whose
names betray a local origin.

The towns of Sedan in France, and Bath in England, have
given us SEDANS and BATH CHAIRS.   From Kottsee, a town in
Hungary, comes the Hungarian word KOTCZY, and the German 𝔎𝔲𝔱𝔰𝔠𝔥𝔢,[7] of which the English word COACH [8] is a corruption.[9]

The first BERLINE was constructed for an ambassadorial
journey from Berlin to Paris.   The LANDAU is said to derive
its name from the town of Landau in the Palatinate.[10]   It

---

[1] See *Good Words*, March, 1864 ; Hume, *Geographical Terms*, p. 6.
[2] Hume, *Geographical Terms*, p. 7.
[3] Italian and Spanish *bernia*.   Diefenbach, *Celtica*, i. p. 201 ; Diez, *Etym. Wörterbuch*, p. 51.
[4] The general use of this word in the East suggests a doubt whether it may not be of Semitic origin. [Devic says from Arab. *bûrnûs*].
[5] *Notes and Queries*, second series, vol. ix. p. 177.
[6] Diez, *Etymol. Wörterbuch*, p. 147. [From Welsh *gwlanen* woollen].
[7] John Cuspinianus, physician to Maximilian I, says that the Hungarians rode in carriages, called in their native tongue *kottschi*.   *Ungriches Mag.* vol. i. p. 20, vol. ii. p. 460.   See two most exhaustive treatises on this word, by M. Cornides, in the *Ungriches Magazin*, vol. i. pp. 15–21 ; vol. ii. pp. 412–465.   See also Beckmann, *Hist. of Inventions*, vol. i. p. 77.
[8] Coaches were introduced into England from Hangary, by the Earl of Arundel, in 1580.   *Ung. Mag.* vol. ii. p. 424 ; Smith, *Antiquarian Ramble*, vol. i. p. 367.
[9] The *Kutsche* was a carriage in which the traveller might sleep, as appears from a passage of Avila, quoted by Diez, p. 105.   Charles V he says, ' se puso á dormir en un carro cubierto, al qual en Hungria llaman coche, el nombre y la invencion es de aquella tierra '.   Hence it has been [proposed to connect the English word COUCH, and the French verb COUCHER with the same root, but the influence is probably only of a reflex nature, the ultimate source of these two words being to be sought in the Latin *collocare*.
[10] Whewell, in *Philolog. Proc.* vol. v. p. 136 ; Hume, *Geogr. Terms*, p. 17.   It seems

has been supposed that Hackney coaches were first used at the London suburb of Hackney ; [1] the true etymology, however, seems to be the French word *hacquenée*, an ambling nag, of which the English *hack* is an abbreviation.[2]

CHEVAUX DE FRISE, the wooden horses of Friesland, are due to Dutch ingenuity. They were first drawn up at the siege of Groningen, in 1658, to oppose the Spanish cavalry. A nearly contemporaneous invention is that of the BAYONET, which was first used at the storming of Bayonne in 1665.[3] The BURGONET, probably, takes its name from Burgundy, and the CARABINE from Calabria, as is indicated by the obsolete Italian form of the word—*calabrino*. The word CALIBRE, though apparently cognate, is really from an Arabic source.[4] The POLE-AXE was the national weapon of the Poles. The LOCHABER axe has disappeared along with Highland warfare, and that other national weapon, the SHILLELAH,[5] will, we may hope, soon be confined also to the museums of the antiquary. Improved weapons, according to the modern rule of nomenclature, are named after the inventor, as in the case of Congreve rockets, Minié and Whitworth rifles, and Armstrong, Dahlgren, and Parrot guns. An exception, however, exists in the case of long Enfields and short Enfields, which are made in the Government factory at Enfield, just as the obsolete ordnance called CARRONADES were cast at the celebrated Carron Foundry on the Clyde.

The word PARCHMENT is derived from the Latin *charta pergamena*, or *pergamentum*, which was used for the multiplication of manuscripts for the great library at Pergamus. From the Campagna of Rome we have the Italian *campana* a bell,[6] and the naturalized English word CAMPANILE,

---

probable, however, that it may have been named after Marshal Landau, like the STANHOPE, TILBURY, and BROUGHAM. There is a coachmaker, in Longacre, called Rumball, and a writer in *Notes and Queries* (second series, vol. ix. p. 177) suggests that the RUMBLE was invented by him.

[1] Taylor, *Antiquitates Curiosæ*, p. 115.
[2] In the seventeenth century we have mention of the *coche à haquenée*. See Diez, *Etym. Wörterbuch*, p. 192 ; Diefenbach, *Vergleich. Wörterbuch*, vol. i. p. 30 ; Ménage, *Origines*, p. 375.
[3] Diez, *Etym. Wörterbuch*, p. 561. Grenades have no connexion with the famous siege of Granada, but are so called from their resemblance to the granate or pomegranate. The tallest and strongest men in the regiment, who were chosen to throw them, were called *grenadiers*.
[4] Englemann, *Glossaire*, p. 76.
[5] The oak saplings which grow in a certain wood in the parish of Shillelah, County Wicklow, are believed to be of a peculiarly tough and knotty quality.
[6] See Ducange, s. v. ; Diez, *Etym. Wörterb.* p. 84.

a bell tower. The first ARTESIAN well was sunk through the
chalk basin of the province of ARTOIS. VARNISH [1] is said to
be from the city of Berenice on the Red Sea. The BOUGIE,
that constant source of altercation at Continental hotels,
takes its name from Bougiah, a town in Algeria which exports
large quantities of beeswax. [2]   Venetian blinds, prussic acid
and prussian blue, Dresden, Sev es, Worcester, Chelsea, and
other names of the class present no etymological difficulties.
MAJOLICA is Majorca ware, and Mr. Marsh thinks that the
glass vessel called a DEMIJOHN may take its name from Dam-
aghan, a town in Khorassan formerly famous for its glass
works. [3]

Many names of this description are personal rather than
local. Thus the DOILEY is supposed to have been introduced
by a tradesman in the Strand, [4] one Doyley, whose name
may still be seen cut in the stone over the office of the *Field*
newspaper ; and the etymology of the word MACKINTOSH is
not likely to be forgotten while the shop at Charing Cross
continues to bear the name of the inventor. In like manner
JACKET, in French *jaque*, was so called from Jaque of
Beauvais, [5] and GOBELIN tapestry from the brothers Gobelin,
dyers at Paris, whose house, called the Hotel des Gobelins,
was bought by Louis XV for the manufacture of the celebrated fabric. [6]   The invention of SPENCERS and SANDWICHES
by two noblemen of the last century is commemorated in a
contemporaneous epigram, which may perhaps bear tran-
scription :—

> Two noble earls, whom, if I quote,
>   Some folks might call me sinner,
> The one invented half a coat,
>   The other, half a dinner.
> The plan was good, as some will say,
>   And fitted to console one,
> Because, in this poor starving day,
>   Few can afford a whole one. [7]

---

[1] Cf. the Italian *vernice*, and the Spanish *berniz*.

[2] Diez, *Etym. Wört.* p. 76 ; Ménage, *Origines*, p. 130 ; Pihan, *Glossaire*, p. 63.

[3] Marsh, *Lect. on Eng. Language*, p. 145 ; English edition, p. 101. The *dame Jeanne*,
however, seems to have been a bottle made near Arras. See *Philolog. Trans.* vol. i.
p. 62–72.

[4] *Notes and Queries*, second series, vol. ii. p. 476.

[5] Diez, *Etym. Wörterb.* p. 172 ; compare Yonge, *Christian Names*, vol. i. p. 110 ;
Ménage, *Origines*, p. 353.

[6] See *Notes and Queries*, November 10, 1860 ; Beckmann, *Hist. of Inventions*, vol.
i. p. 403.

[7] Booth, *Epigrams*, p. 83. The invention of Lord Sandwich is said to have enabled

The invention of Earl Spencer may be classed with the
WELLINGTONS and BLÜCHERS which came into fashion
at the close of the European war ; and that of the Earl of
Sandwich with Maintenon cutlets. It has been suggested [1]
that we owe the BRAWN on our breakfast tables to a German
cook named Braun who lived in Queen Street. The word,
however, is doubtless of much greater antiquity, the true etymology being to be sought in the old French *braion*, a roll of
flesh.

From two Greek philosophers we derive the terms PLAT-
ONIC love, and EPICURE. The GUILLOTINE takes its name
from Dr. Guillotin, who introduced it. [2] The DERRICK, a
machine for raising sunken ships, by means of ropes attached
to a sort of gallows, perpetuates the memory of a hangman
of the Elizabethan period. [3] TRAM roads and MACADAMIZATION
we owe to Outram [?] and Macadam. A strict disciplinarian
in the army of Louis XIV has given us the word MARTINET,
and from a French architect we obtain the MANSARDE roof. [4]
Mr. PINCHBECK was one of the cheap goldsmiths of the last
century, and has left numerous disciples in our own. [5] An
ingenious astronomical toy bears the name of the Earl of
ORRERY. [6] Galvani, Volta, Daguerre, and Talbot have stamped
their names upon two of the greatest discoveries of modern
times. The value of MESMERISM is more open to question. [7]
The name of SILHOUETTE was bestowed in the time of Louis
XV on the meagre shadow portraits which were then in
vogue, and it contains a sarcastic allusion to the niggardly
finance of M. de Silhouette, an unpopular minister of the
French monarch. [8]

Paschino was a cobbler at Rome ; he was a noted char-

---

him to remain at the gaming-table for 24 consecutive hours, without having to retire
for a regular meal. Taylor, *Antiq. Curiosæ*, p. 17.

[1] *Notes and Queries*, second series, vol. ii. pp. 196, 235.

[2] Dr. Guillotin only introduced the bill in the Convention ; a Dr. Louis was the real
inventor of the machine, which was at first called the Louisette. See *Times*, June 11,
1864.

[3] Hotten, *Slang. Dict.* p. 119.

[4] Whewell, in *Philolog. Proc.* vol. v. p. 136.

[5] Hotten, *Slang Dict.* p. 201.

[6] The Orrery was invented by a Mr. Rowley, who gave it the name of his patron.

[7] This method of nomenclature has naturally prevailed among religious sects. We
have ARIANS, ARMINIANS, CALVINISTS, WESLEYANS, SIMEONITES and PUSEYITES.

[8] Sismondi, *Hist. de Français*, vol. xxix. pp. 94, 95, apud Diez, *Etym. Wörterb.*
p. 725. So Mr. Joseph Hume's unpopular fourpenny pieces were called JOEYS by the cab-
men ; and Sir Robert Peel's substitute for the London watchmen are still called BOBBYS
and PEELERS. Hotten, *Slang. Dict.* pp. 163, 198.

W.P. X

acter, and a man of a very marked physiognomy. The statue of an ancient gladiator having been exhumed, and erected in front of the Orsini palace, the Roman wits detected resemblance to the notorious cobbler, and gave the statue his name. It afterwards became the practice to post lampoons on the pedestal of the statue, whence effusions of this nature have come to be called PASQUINADES.[1] Pamphylla, a Greek lady, who compiled a history of the world in thirty-five little books, has given her name to the PAMPHLET.[2][?] The name of PUNCH, or to give him unabbreviated Italian title, Pulcinello, has been derived from the name of the person who is said to have first performed the world-known drama, one Puccio d'Aniello, a witty peasant of Acerza in the Roman Campagna.[3] It has also been supposed, with some reason, that Punch and Judy and the dog Toby are relics of an ancient mystery play, the actors in which were Pontius Pilate, Judas, and Tobias' dog.[?] For the word HARLEQUIN, in Italian *Arlechino*, a local origin has, however, been suggested ; the name being, perhaps, derived from the Arle-camps, or Champ d'Arles, where the performance was first exhibited.[4] The word CHARLATAN we may trace through the Italian forms *ciarlatano* and *cerretano* to the city of Cerreto.[5] VAUDEVILLE is from Vau-de-Ville in Normandy, where the entertainment was introduced by Olivier Basselin, at the end of the fourteenth century.[6]

Many analogous derivations which we find in classical authors are obviously fanciful or mythical. Thus we read that the art of grinding was discovered at Alesiæ (ἀλέσαι, to grind), by Myles (μύλη, a millstone).[7] In like manner we are told that the tinder-box was invented by Pyrodes, and the spindle by Closter ; and that the oar was first used at two Bœotian towns—Copæ (handle), and Platææ (blade).[8] This, it need not be said, is as absurd as if a modern Pliny were to assure us that needles were first manufactured by a Mr. Steel at the

[1] Yonge, *Christian Names*, vol. i. p. 437.
[2] *Athenæum*, November 11, 1863, p. 715.
[3] Diez, *Etymolog. Wörterbuch*, p. 425.
[4] Diez, *Etymol. Wörterb.* p. 26. See, however, Max Müller, in *Reports of Brit. Assoc.* for 1847, p. 322. [A. S. Palmer. *Quarterly Rev.* No. 392, pp. 462–482].
[5] Diez, *Etymol. Wörterb.* p. 100 ; Ménage, *Origines*, p. 202.
[6] Du Bois, p. 13, apud Diez, *Etymol. Wörterb.* p. 742.
[7] Kenrick, *Primæval History*, p. 82 ; Pott, in Kuhn's *Zeitschrift für Vergleich. Spr.* vol. ix. p. 181.
[8] Kenrick, *Phœnicia*, p. 217.

Names of Coins 307

western extremity of the Isle of Wight, or that the game of draughts was originally played in Ayrshire.

The etymology of the names of coins is often curious. The GUINEA was first coined in 1663 from gold brought from the Guinea coast. It was struck as a twenty-shilling piece, but from the fineness of the metal the new coins were so highly prized that they commanded an agio of a shilling. The BYZANT a large gold coin of the value of £15 sterling, was struck at Byzantium. The DOLLAR was originally the same as the German THALER, which took its name from the silverworks in the Thal or valley of Joachim in Bohemia. Its currency throughout the New World bears witness to the extension of the Spanish-Austrian empire in the reign of Charles V. The FLORIN was struck at Florence, and bore the Florentine device of the lily-flower,[1] which has been reproduced on the new English coins of the same name. The MARK was a Venetian coin, stamped with the winged lion of St. Mark, and since Venice was the banker to half the world, it became the ordinary money of account.[2] CUFIC coins, silver pieces with Arabic characters, were coined at Cufa. The JANE which is mentioned by Chaucer and Spenser was a small coin of Genoa (Janua). The FRANC is the *nummus francicus*—the coin of the Franks or French, and the Dutch GUILDER may possibly take its name from Gelderland.[3]

MONEY and MINT remind us that the coinage of the Romans was struck at the temple of Juno Moneta, the goddess of counsel (*moneo*). The word STERLING is a contraction of *esterling*—the pound or penny sterling being a certain weight of bullion according to the standard of the Esterlings or eastern merchants from the Hanse towns on the Baltic.[4] The convenience of the local standard of Troyes has given us TROY

[1] Ménage, *Origines*, p. 793 ; *Notes and Queries*, second series, vol. v. p. 258.
[2] Yonge, *Christian Names*, vol. i. p. 291.
[3] A DUCAT is the coin issued by a duke, just as a SOVEREIGN is that issued by a king. A TESTER bore the image of the king's head (*teste*, or *tête*, and the PENNY is, possibly, in like manner, the diminutive of the Celtic *pen*, a head. The modern Welsh word *ceiniog*, a penny, is analogously from *cenn*, a head. A SHILLING or skilling bore the device of a shield or schild, and a SCUDO had a scutum. An EAGLE, an ANGEL, and a KREUTZER bear respectively the American eagle, an angel, and a cross. English GROATS, like the German GROSCHEN, were the *great* coins, having been four times the size of the penny. Twenty shillings used to weigh a POUND (*pondus*). So the Italian *lira* and French *livre* were of the weight of a *libra*. A FARTHING is the fourthing, or fourth part of a penny, just as the square furlong is the fourthling of an acre, and as the Ridings of Yorkshire were the thirdings or third parts of the county.
[4] Robertson, *Scotland under her Early Kings*, vol. ii. p. 350 ; Ménage, *Origines*, pp. 616–618 ; Hume, *Geogr. Terms*, p. 19 ; Skinner, *Etymologicon*, s. v.

weight ; and the STEELYARD is not, as is commonly supposed, a balance made with a steel arm, but is the machine for weighing which was used in the Steelyard, the London factory of the Hanse towns.[1] That the name originated in England is proved by the fact that it is confined to this country ; the French equivalent being *Romaine*, and the German *ruthe*.

Not the least interesting, and by far the most instructive, of the words that have been derived from geographical names are those which have been furnished by the names of nations, and which will mostly be found to have a sort of moral significance, ethnical terms having become ethical.

Thus, when we remember how the Vandals and the Goths, two rude northern hordes, swept across Europe, blotting out for a time the results of centuries of Roman civilization, and destroying for ever many of the fairest creations of the Grecian chisel, we are able to understand how it has come about that the wanton or ignorant destruction of works of art should go by the name of VANDALISM, and also how the first clumsy efforts of the Goths to imitate, or adapt to their own purposes the Roman edifices, should be called GOTHIC.[2] It is interesting to note the stages by which this word has ascended from being a word of utter contempt to one of highest honour. Yet we may, at the same time, regret that the same word— Gothic—should have been misapplied to designate that most perfect system of Christian architecture which the northern nations, after centuries of honest and painsful labour, succeeded in working out slowly for themselves, and in the elaboration of which the nations of pure Gothic blood took comparatively little share.

The fierce and intolerant Arianism of the Visigothic conquerors of Spain [3] has given us another word. The word Visigoth has become BIGOT, and thus on the imperishable tablets of language the Catholics have handed down to perpetual infamy the name and nation of their persecutors.[4]

---

[1] See Pauli, *Pictures of Old England*, pp. 176–203.
[2] Cf. Grimm, *Gesch. d. Deut. Spr.* p. 475 ; Milman, *Hist. of Latin Christianity*, vol. vi. p. 405.
[3] See Brace, *Races of Old World*, p. 283.
[4] The doubtful point in this etymology seems to be set at rest by a passage in the romance of Gerard of Roussillon, in which Bigot is used as an ethnic name :—

> ' Bigot, e Provenzal, e Rouergues,
> E Bascle, e Gasco, e Bordales '.

See Michel, *Hist. des Races Maudites*, vol. i. p. 539. This seems, therefore, to be a more

From the name of the same nation—the Goths of Spain—are derived, curiously enough, two names, one implying extreme honour, the other extreme contempt. The Spanish noble, who boasts that the *sangre azul* of the Goths runs in his veins with no admixture, calls himself an HIDALGO, that is, a son of the Goth, as his proudest title.[1] Of Gothic blood scarcely less pure than that of the Spanish Hidalgos, are the CAGOTS of Southern France, a race of outcast pariahs, who in every village live apart, executing every vile or disgraceful kind of toil, and with whom the poorest peasant refuses to associate. These Cagots are the descendants of those Spanish Goths, who, on the invasion of the Moors, fled to Aquitaine, where they were protected by Charles Martel. But the reproach of Arianism clung to them, and religious bigotry branded them with the name of câ Gots,[2] or 'Gothic Dogs', a name which still clings to them, and keeps them apart from their fellow-men. In the Pyrenees these Arian refugees were anciently called *Christaas*, and in French *Chrétiens*, or Christians, probably to distinguish them from Jewish or Moorish fugitives. Confinement to narrow valleys, and their enforced intermarriages, often resulted in the idiotcy of the children, and the name of the outcasts of the Pyrenees has been transferred to the poor idiotic wretches, who, under the name CRETINS, are painfully familiar to Swiss tourists.[3] The word *goître* is not, as has been thought, derived from the name of these Gothic refugees, but is a corruption of the Latin *guttur*, which we find in Juvenal:—'Quis tumidum guttur miratur in Alpibus'.[4]

probable etymology than any of those which are ordinarily given. The explanation of Ménage, *Origines*, p. 116, from *Bi got*, the Norman oath, is out of the question. That proposed by Wachter, and supported by Trench, *Study of Words*, p. 80 ; and by Wedgwood, *Philological Trans.* for 1855, p. 113–116, from the *beguins*, or Franciscans, involves serious phonetic difficulties. That from *bigotte*, a moustache, is almost a ὕστερον πρότερον, for *bigotte*, a moustache is itself probably from Visigoth. Compare the Spanish phrase *hombre de bigote*, a man of fixed purpose, and the French *un vieux moustache*. Cf. Ford, *Gatherings from Spain*, p. 256. Bigot appears as a personal name in the case of Hugh Bigod, Earl of Norfolk.

1 The old etymology *hijo d' algo*, son of something, has been universally given up in favour of *hi d' al Go*, son of the Goth. See a paper ' On Oc and Oyl ', by J. E. Biester, in the *Berlin Transactions* for 1812–13, translated by Bishop Thirlwall for the *Philological Museum*, vol. ii. p. 337.

2 From the Provençal *câ*, canis, or the Béarnais *caas*, and *Got*, Goth. This etymology, first proposed by De Marca, and stamped with the approval of Scaliger, is now generally adopted. Compare the French *cagoterie*, bigotry. See Michel, *Histoire des Races Maudites*, vol. i. pp. 284, 294, 355 ; and a paper by the same author in vol. i. of *Le Moyen Age et la Renaissance* ; Ménage, *Origines*, pp. 165–171 ; Diez, *Etymol. Wörterbuch*, p. 584.

3 See Michel, *Histoire des Races Maudites*, vol. i. pp. 59, 162, 180, etc.

4 Juvenal, Sat. xiii. l. 162

The MARRONS of Auvergne are a race of pariahs, descended from the Mauriens or Moorish conquerors of the Maurienne. Hence the French word *marrane*, a renegade or traitor, and the Spanish adjective *marrano*, accursed, and the substantive *marrano*, a hog.[1]

Again, when we remember how the soldierlike fidelity, and the self-reliant courage [2] of the Franks enabled them with ease to subjugate the civilized but effeminate inhabitants of northern Gaul, we can understand how the name of a rude German tribe has come to denote the FRANK, bold, open, manly character of a soldier and a freeman, and the word FRANCHISE to denote the possession of the full civil rights of the conquering race.[3]

In the south-east of Gaul the Roman element of the population had ever been more considerable than elsewhere, and in this region the influence of the northern conquerors was comparatively transient. Hence the *langue d'oc*, or language of Provence, the Roman Provincia, was called the Romance, retaining as it did a much greater resemblance to the language of the Romans than the *langue d'oyl*, the tongue of that part of Gaul which had been conquered and settled by the Franks. Here, in the region of the Languedoc, civilization was first re-established ; here was the first home of chivalry ; here the troubadour learned to beguile the leisure of knights and ladies with wild tales of adventure and enchantment—ROMANCES, ROMANTIC narratives—so called because sung in the Romance tongue of the Roman province.[4]

In the south-west of Gaul, on the other hand, the Celtic or Celtiberic element of the original population was little influenced either by Roman colonization, or by Frankish or Gothic conquest. The Gascons afforded an exhibition of the peculiar characteristics of the Celtic stock—they were susceptible, enthusiastic, fickle, vain, and ostentatious.[5]   The random and

---

[1] See p. 79, *supra* ; Michel, *Histoire des Races Maudites*, vol. ii. pp. 45, 96 ; Ménage, *Origines*, p. 451.

[2] So the haughty character of the Norman conquerors, well illustrated by the story of Rollo's homaging, explains how the French *norois* (normand) came to mean proud. Diez., *Gram. der Rom. Spr.* vol. i. p. 47.

[3] I agree with Leo, *Vorlesungen*, vol. i. p. 255, that the arguments of Jacob Grimm, *Geschichte d. Deut. Sprach.* p. 512, on the name of the Franks exhibit virtually a ὕστερον πρότερον. Cf. Diez, *Etym. Wörterbuch*, p. 153 ; Diefenbach, *Vergleich. Wörterbuch*, vol. i. p. 403 ; Diez., *Gram. der Rom. Spr.* vol. i. p. 47.

[4] Diez, *Etym. Wörterbuch*, p. 295 ; Ménage, *Origines*, pp. 565-572 ; Sheppard, *Fall of Rome*, p. 133.

[5] See p. 167, *supra*.

boastful way of talking in which these Gascons were prone to indulge, has, from them, received the name GASCONADE.[1]

The Langobardes, or Lombards, who settled in Northern Italy, appear to have been distinguished by national characteristics very different from those of Frank, Gascon, Goth, Visigoth, or Vandal. They seem to have been actuated by the spirit of commercial rather than of chivalrous adventure ; and at an early period we find them competing with the Jews as the capitalists and pawnbrokers [2] of the middle ages. As we have already seen,[3] Lombard Street—still the street of bankers —marks the site of the Lombard colony in London ; [4] and the Lombards have left their name not only in our streets but in our language, as a curious witness to the national characteristics which distinguished them from the other tribes which overran the Roman Empire. A lumber-room is the Lombard room,[5] the room where the Lombard pawnbrokers stored their unredeemed pledges. Hence, after a time, furniture stowed away in an unused chamber came to be called LUMBER ; and since such furniture is often heavy, clumsy, and out of date, we call a clumsy man a lumbering fellow ; and our American cousins have given heavy timber the name of lumber, and call the man who fells it a LUMBERER—a curious instance of the complicated process of word manufacture—by which the name of a barbarous German tribe has been transferred to American backwoodsmen.

When the Bulgarians and Huns, under Attila, overran the

---

1 The Spaniards call the Basque language, the *Bascongada*. RODOMONTADE, a word of somewhat similar meaning, is derived from Rodomonte, a braggart who figures in Ariosto's poem of Orlando Furioso. The immortal romance of Cervantes has given us the word QUIXOTIC. HECTORING comes from ' Sir Hector ' of Troy. GIBBERISH comes from Geber, an obscure eastern writer on alchemy, and FUDGE, perhaps, from a certain inventive Captain Fudge, who flourished in the reign of Charles II. BURLESQUE, in Italian *burlesco* or *Berniesco*, is derived from Francesco Bernia, who invented this species of composition. ALEXANDRINES and LEONINES probably from a French poet, Alexandre Pâris, and the monk Leo, of Marseilles. We speak of the SPENSERIAN stanza, and a CICERONIAN style. The summary proceedings of Judge LYNCH have given our American cousins a verb, of which they stood in need. The words BOGUS (Borghese), and BLENKERISM hand down to fame the names of two other transatlantic worthies, while BURKING is the peculiar glory of this island. See Bowditch, *Suffolk Surnames*, pp. 256-258.

2 The Sicilian word *lumbardu*, an innkeeper, shows that the Lombards also exercised this calling. Diez, *Etym. Wörterbuch*, p. 676. There is an old French adjective, *lombart*, usurious. Thom. de Cant. Ed. Bekker, p. 41 ; apud Diez, *Etym. Wörterbuch*, p. 676.

3 See p. 199, *supra*.

4 The Caorsini, *i.e.* the men of Cahors (Dept. Lot), were in mediæval times the rivals of the Lombards in the money-markets of Europe. Their name, however, has not been perpetuated to the same extent as that of the Lombards, having left only the Provençal word *chaorcin*, a usurer. Hallam, *Middle Ages*, vol. iii. p. 405 ; Ducange, s. v.

5 French *lombard*, a pawnshop. See the passages cited by Trench, *Glossary*, p. 127.

Roman Empire, the terror which they inspired was due not
only to their savage ferocity, but in part to the hideousness
of the Kalmuck physiognomy, with its high cheek bones, and
grinning boar-tushed visage. Their name became the synonym
for an inhuman monster. Hence the German Hüne, a giant,[1]
the French *Bulgar*, or *Bougre*,[2] the Russian *Obri*, and the
English OGRE.[3]

When the Asi approached Scandinavia they found the
shores peopled by wandering Finns, whom tradition represents as malignant imps and deformed demons, lurking among
rocks and in the forest gloom. Hence, it has been thought
[quite wrongly] have arisen the words FIEND and FIENDISH,
and the German Feind, an enemy.[4]

The relations of the Sclavonic races of Eastern Europe to
their western neighbours is also indicated by a curious piece
of historical etymology. The martial superiority of the
Teutonic races enabled them, as we have seen, gradually to
advance their frontier toward the east, and in so doing, to keep
their slave markets supplied with captives taken from the
Sclavonic tribes.[5] Hence, in all the languages of Western
Europe, the once glorious name of SCLAVE has come to express
the most degraded condition of man.[6] What centuries of
violence and warfare does the history of this word disclose !
and the contempt and hatred of race which the use of the word
implies, is strongly shown by the fact that even so late as the
last century no person of Sclavonic blood was admissible
into any German guild of artisans or merchants.[7]

We have, however, an earlier and an analogous case of

---

[1] The Norse word for a giant is JOTUNN, *i.e.* Jute or Goth. Schafarik, *Slaw. Alt.*
vol. i. pp. 50, 52.

[2] The Bulgarians were given to manichæism, hence the French word *bougerie*, heresy.
Cf. Ducange, s. v. Bulgarus ; Diez, *Etym. Wörterbuch*, p. 576 ; Ménage, *Origines*, p. 131.'

[3] The Ogres or Ugrians, to which stock the Bulgarians and Magyars belong, were the
tribes north of the Ural. The ethnic name of the *Ugrians* seems to have become *Ogres*,
from a fancied connexion with Orcus, analogous to that of the Tatars with Tartarus, which
has been already referred to (p. 396, *supra*). Compare Prichard, *Researches*, vol. iii.
pp. 273, 324 ; Grimm, *Deut. Myth.* p. 454 ; Diez, *Etym. Wörterbuch*, p. 244 ; Wilson,
Pre-historic Man, vol. ii. p. 302.

[4] Palgrave, *English Commonwealth*, vol. i. p. 103.

[5] See p. 37, *supra*.

[6] The word *sclave*, in the sense of *servus*, appears first in Lombardy, in the ninth century.
The earliest known occurrence of the word in Germany is in the year 996 :—' Ecclesiæ
servos vel sclavos '. Schafarik, *Slaw. Alterth.* vol. ii. p. 27 ; *Monumenta boica*, 28, 1,
p. 267, quoted by Mone, *Celtische Forschungen*, p. 251.

[7] See Schafarik, *Slaw. Alterth.* vol. ii. p. 42 ; Arndt, *Europ. Sprach.* p. 291 ; Donaldson,
New Cratylus, p. 385 ; *Varronianus*, p. 66 ; Gibbon, chap. lv. vol. vii. p. 76 ; Palgrave,
Normandy and England, vol. i. p. 379 ; Sheppard, *Fall of Rome*, p. 143 ; Zeuss, *Die
Deutschen*, p. 646 ; Pictet, *Orig. Indo-Eur.* part ii. p. 204.

word-formation, which has not attracted the same attention as the word slave. That Sclavonic people which was in the closest geographical proximity to Italy called themselves Serbs or Servians,[1] and it seems probable that the Latin word *servus*, and our own derivative SERF, originated from causes similar to those which have given us the word slave. The probability of this being the true etymology of *servus* is much increased by the numerous parallel cases of ethnic terms being perverted to be the designation of servile races. The manner in which the words Davus, Geta, and Syrus are applied to slaves in the Græco-Latin comedies, exhibits in a half completed state the same linguistic process which has given us the words slave and serf, and at the same time indicates that the Grecian slave markets must have been largely supplied by Dacians, Goths, and Syrians.[2] Aristophanes uses the word σκύθαινα in the sense of a female house-servant.[3] The word δοῦλος is probably [?] derived from the Δόλοπες, a subject race of Thessaly ; and the HELOTS were the aboriginal inhabitants of the Peloponnesus, who were reduced to slavery at the time of the Dorian conquest. The rich treasure-house of language has preserved a curious memorial of the fact that the Saxon conquest of England was accompanied by a reduction to servitude of the indigenous race. Till within the last three centuries the word VILLAIN retained the meaning of a peasant.[4] In Domesday the *villani* are the prædial serfs. The root of the word is, not improbably, the Anglo-Saxon *wealh*, a foreigner, or Welshman,[5] an etymology which, if correct, proves that servitude must have been the ordinary condition of the Celts under Saxon rule.[6]

We have a somewhat analogous case in British India. Porters and palanquin-bearers go by the name of COOLIES, a name which has been extended to include the Indian labourers

[1] The root *s-rb* denotes 'kinsmanship'. The modern usage of the word servility is an illustration of the habits engendered by a state of slavery.

[2] Pott, in Kuhn's *Zeitschrift*, vol. ix. p. 216. We have also the less frequent slave-names Λάκων, in Theocritus (v. 5), Μεσσηνίων, in Plautus, and Θετταλοικέτης, in Athenæus (vi. 264).

[3] So St. Paul uses Σκύθης as an equivalent of barbarian. *Colossians*, chap. iii. v. 11.

[4] The change to the present meaning of the word is analogous to that which has transformed the significations of *boor* (*bauer*, or peasant), *knave* (boy), and *imp* (child).

[5] See pp. 45–47, *supra*. Schafarik, *Slaw. Alterth.* vol. i. p. 50. The word *vile* may be from the same root, *wealh*. Ibid. vol. i. p. 377. Much may doubtless be said in favour of the old derivation of these words from the Latin *villa* and *vilis*. But at all events we may believe that the obvious Teutonic analogy exercised a reflex influence on the usage of the words.

[6] Cf. the name of the Teilfali of Poitou.

who have replaced the negro slaves in the sugar plantations of Tropical America. The word Coolie is a corruption of the name of a Turanian hill-tribe, the Coles or Kôlas, who occupy the lowest place in the Indian labour-market.[1]

The word κάρ is used in Greek to denote a mercenary soldier, the Carians having habitually hired themselves out to fight the battles of their neighbours. In like manner the Shawi, a tribe of desert nomads, were enlisted by the French after their Algerian conquest, and the name has been corrupted into ZOUAVE, while the ranks are filled by the gamins of the streets of Paris.[2] The word Sikh may possibly be destined to undergo a similar change of meaning.

The luxurious sensuality which prevailed at Sybaris has attached a disgraceful signification to the word SYBARITE, and the moral corruption which poisoned the mercantile and pleasure-loving city of Corinth caused the word κορινθιάζεσθαι to become a synonym for ἑταιρεῖν,[3] just as the more healthy pleasures of the Sicelian peasant made the word σικελίζειν equivalent to ὀρχεῖσθαι.[4]   The dry upland sheep pastures of the Peloponnesus, and the rich corn-flats of Thebes have given us the two adjectives ARCADIAN and BŒOTIAN. An heroic man we call a TROJAN, a morose man a TURK, a benevolent man a good SAMARITAN, and 'catching a TARTAR' is a process more familiar than agreeable. The terse, pregnant way in which the Spartans expressed themselves still causes us to talk of LACONIC speech,[5] the pithy wit of the Athenians has left us the phrase ATTIC salt, and the bitter laughter of the Sardinians is commemorated in the expression, 'a SARDONIC smile'.

From Thrax, a Thracian, the Romans, by the change of a single letter, derived the word threx, a gladiator, a fact which indicates the region from which the arena was supplied with hardy mountain combatants. The usage of the words Κρής, Παφλάγων, and Μύσος would prove equally suggestive.[6]

---

[1] Brace, *Races of the Old World*, p. 103.
[2] Ibid. p. 172.
[3] See Becker, *Charicles*, p. 246.
[4] Müller, *Dorians*, vol. ii. p. 339.
[5] The Italian word *ladino*, easy, shows that Latin was the easiest language for an Italian to acquire. Compare the German *deutlich*, plain, and our own phrase, ' It is Greek to me '.
[6] See Donaldson, *Varronianus*, p. 449 ; Müller, *Dorians*, vol. ii. p. 300 ; Schafarik, *Slaw. Alterth.* vol. i. p. 52.

The word BRIGAND, as we have seen,[1] is not improbably derived from the name of the Brigantes, or perhaps from Briga, a border town near Nice. The word *brigant* first appears in the sense of a light-armed soldier, and then it takes the meaning of a robber. Next we find *brigante*, a pirate ; and the pirate's ship is called a BRIGANTINE, of which the word BRIG is a contraction.[2]

' Jeddart justice ', which denotes the practice of hanging the criminal first and trying him afterwards, is a reminiscence of the wild border life of which the town of Jedburgh was the centre.

From Tarifa [*supra*, 73] the Moorish cruisers sallied forth to plunder the vessels passing through the Straits of Gibraltar, but discovering the impolicy of killing the goose that laid the golden egg, they seem to have levied their black mail on a fixed scale of payment, which, from the name of the place where it was exacted, came to be called a TARIFF.[3]

The word CANNIBAL is probably a corruption of the name of the Caribs or Caribals, a savage West Indian people, among whom the practice of cannibalism was supposed to prevail.[4] The horrible custom of scalping fallen enemies was usual among the Scythian tribes, and Herodotus gives us a picture of the string of bloody trophies hanging to the warrior's rein. Hence arose the word ἀποσκυθίζειν, to scalp, which we find in Euripides. The word ASSASSIN probably comes from the name of a tribe of Syrian fanatics who, like the Thugs of India, considered assassination in the light of a religious duty.[5]

During the last century false political rumours were often propagated from Hamburg, then the chief port of communication with Germany. ' A piece of Hamburg news ' seems to have become a proverbial expression for a *canard* [?], and it is easy to see how this phrase has been pared down into the

---

[1] See p. 180, *supra*.

[2] See Diez, *Etymolog. Wörterbuch*, p. 69 ; Ménage, Origines, p. 149.

[3] See, however, Freytag, s. v. ; Diez, *Etymol. Wörterbuch*, p. 342 ; and Pihan, *Glossaire*, p. 271, who prefer a derivation from the Arabic ' *tarif*, a declaration. [So Devic—Skeat.] The word *to sally* is no doubt from *salire*, though there is a temptation to deduce it from Sallee, another chief station of the Moorish pirates. *Corsair* is certainly not from Corsica ; though, possibly, *riff*, *raff* may be derived from the Riff pirates. [From F. *rif et raf*, *rifle et rafle*.]

[4] Trench, *Study of Words*, p. 137.

[5] Diefenbach (*Celtica*, i. p. 24) derives the name from the Kurdish word *asen* or *hassin*, iron. The name of the tribe, perhaps, [certainly] comes from the *hashish*, an intoxicating preparation of hemp with which the members of the sect worked themselves up to the requisite degree of recklessness. Ménage, *Origines*, p. 64 ; Pihan, *Glossaire*, pp. 43, 147 ; De Sacy, in *Memoires de l'Institute* for 1818, apud Diez, *Etym. Wörterbuch*, p. 29.

modern slang term HUMBUG.[1] The expressive American term
BUNCUM is due to the member for the county of Buncombe, in
North Carolina. In the State Legislature he made a speech,
full of highflown irrelevant nonsense, and when called to
order he explained that he was not speaking to the House,
he was talking to Buncombe. Castle BLARNEY is, of course,
in Ireland, and the famous stone can still be seen and kissed
by those who desire to test its virtues. By a good-natured
allusion to another peculiarity of our Irish fellow-countrymen, we term a certain characteristic confusion of ideas an
Hibernianism.

A SPRUCE person was originally a person dressed in the
Prussian fashion. Thus Hall, the chronicler, describes the
appearance of Sir Edward Haward and Sir Thomas Parre ' in
doblettes of crimosin veluet, voyded lowe on the backe, and
before to the cannell bone, lased on the breastes with chaynes
of siluer, and ouer that shorte clokes of crimosyn satyne,
and on their heades hattes after dauncers fashion, with fea-
sauntes fethers in theim : They were appareyled after the
fashion of Prusia or Spruce '.[2] [So *Spruce fir*, Prussian fir.]

Though the pilgrims of the eighth and succeeding centuries
were often only ' commercial travellers ', and still more frequently ' vacation tourists ',[3] and although the visitation of
foreign shrines did much to dispel national prejudices and to
unite nations, yet we may be glad, on moral as well as on religious grounds, that the practice of pilgrimages, which formed
so noticeable a feature in the life of the Middle Ages, has now
ceased, at least among ourselves ; for in the word SAUNTERER
we have a proof that, in popular estimation, idle and vaga-
bond habits were acquired by those who made the pilgrimage
to the *Sainte Terre*, or Holy Land.[4] A ROAMER was one
who had visited the tombs of the two Apostles at Rome, and
this word conveys also in its present usage an intimation of

[1] See *Outlines of Humbug*, a brochure ascribed to the late Archbishop Whately. The
word has also been derived from an alchemist named Homberg, who professed to have
discovered the Philosopher's stone. Hotten, *Slang Dictionary*, p. 157. The analogous
slang word BOSH has, I imagine, been imported from the Cape, the metaphor having
been taken from the rubbishing and worthless ' *!ush* ', which is burned regularly every
autumn. See, however, Hotten, *Slang. Dict.* p. 81. [Turkish, *bosh*, worthless, an imported
word.]

[2] Hall, *Chronicle*, p. 513.

[3] See Thrupp, *Anglo-Saxon Home*, p. 241.

[4] [Really an ' ex-adventurer '—Skeat.] The Palestine pilgrims were also called *palmers*,
from the palm branches which they brought home with them from the Holy Sepulchre.

unsettled habits similar to that which is contained in the word saunterer. The Italian word *romeo* implies no moral censure, but means simply a pilgrim ; and hence we may perhaps infer, that where the distance to be traversed was small, the evil effects of the pilgrimage were not so manifest.

From the Canterbury pilgrimages to the shrine of St. Thomas comes the word CANTER,[1] which is an abbreviation of the phrase ' a Canterbury gallop '[2]—the easy ambling pace of the pilgrims as they rode along the grassy lane which follows the foot of the North Downs of Kent for many miles, and which still retains its title of the Pilgrims' Road.

St. Fiacre (Fiachra) was an Irish saint of great renown, who established himself as a hermit at Meaux, some five-and-twenty miles from Paris. His tomb became a great place of pilgrimage, which was performed even by royal personages, such as Anne of Austria. The miracle-working shrine being frequented by many infirm persons who were unable to perform the pilgrimage on foot, carriages were kept for their convenience at an inn in the suburbs of Paris, which had the sign of St. Fiacre ; and now, long after the pilgrimages have ceased, the hired carriages of Paris retain the name of FIACRES.[3]

St. Etheldreda, or, as she was commonly called, St. Awdrey, was the patron saint of the Isle of Ely. She is said to have died of a swelling in the throat, which she considered as a judgment on her for her youthful fondness for necklaces. Hence, at the fair held at the time of the annual pilgrimage, it was the custom for the pilgrims to purchase, as mementoes of their journey,[4] chains of lace or silk, which were called ' St. Awdrey's chains'. These being of a cheap and flimsy structure, the name of St. Awdrey, corrupted into TAWDRY,

---

[1] The word canter is not found in any continental language, as it would be, if it were derived, as has been supposed, from *cantherius*, a gelding. See Wedgwood, *Eng. Etym.* vol. i. p. 295 ; Stanley, *Memorials of Canterbury*, p. 196.

[2] It is possible [?] that the word *gallop* may be in like manner connected with Galoppe in Flanders. Diefenbach derives it from *wallen*, to wander. From the Cheviot hills we have the slang verb to CHEVY, a reminiscence of Chevy Chase.

[3] See Ménage, *Origines*, p. 315 ; Alban Butler, *Lives of the Saints* ; Yonge, *Christian Names*, vol. ii. p. 97. [His tomb at Clonmacnois with the inscription ' Or Do Fiachraich', ' Pray for Fiachra ', is still shown (died Aug. 30, ab. 670.)—G. Petrie, *Christian Inscriptions*, vol. i. p. 46.]

[4] So keys were brought away by the romeos who had visited the tomb of St. Peter, palm-branches by the palmers from the Holy Land, and scallop-shells from the sea-shore near Compostella. St. James' day is still commemorated by London urchins by oyster-shell grottos, for the construction of which the contributions of passers-by are solicited. On the various signs of pilgrimage see the description of a pilgrim in Piers Ploughman, lines 3541-3552 :—

has come to be the designation of cheap lace and showy finery.[1]

In a wild district of Derbyshire, between Macclesfield and Buxton there is a village called Flash, surrounded by uninclosed land. The squatters on these commons, with their wild gipsy habits, travelled about the neighbourhood from fair to fair, using a slang dialect of their own. They were called the Flash men, and their dialect Flash talk ; and it is not difficult to see the stages by which the word FLASH has reached its present signification.[2]   A SLANG is a narrow strip of waste land by the roadside, such as those which are chosen by gipsies for their encampments. To be ' out on the slang ', in the lingo used by thieves and gipsies, means to travel about the country as a hawker,[3] encamping by night on the roadside *slangs*. A travelling show is also called a *slang*. It is easy to see how the term was transferred to the language spoken by hawkers and itinerant showmen.[4]   The phrase, ' using BILLINGSGATE ', which has spread from England to America, reminds us that the language of London fishwives is not so choice as their fish ; and ' a BABEL of sounds,' refers to the confusion of tongues at the Tower of Babylon or Babel.

A few remaining terms, derived from places, may be here collected.

The winding river MEANDER has given us a verb ; and the name of the RUBICON has now almost passed into our vocabulary. From the Moriscoes of Spain we have the words MORRIS boards, and MORRIS dances.[5]

> ' A bolle and a bagge
> He bar by his syde,
> And hundred of ampulles
> On his hat seten,
> Signes of Synay,
> And shelles of Galice,
> And many a crouche on his cloke,
> And keyes of Rome,
> And the vernycle bi-fore ;
> For men sholde knowne,
> And se bi hise signes,
> Whom he sought hadde '.

[1] See *Notes and Queries*, second series, vol. xi. pp. 226, 300 ; Taylor, *Antiquitates Curiosæ*, p. 65 ; Stanley, *Memorials of Canterbury*, p. 221.   [A.S. Palmer, *Word-Collector's Cabinet*, 13–15.]

[2] Smiles, *Lives of the Engineers*, vol. ii. p. 307.   [More than doubtful.]

[3] Hotten, *Slang Dictionary*, p. 234.   [? Probably language *slung* at one.]

[4] A writer in *Notes and Queries*, second series, vol. xi. p. 471, and vol. iii. p. 445, derives *slang* from the name of the Dutch General Slangenberg, who commanded a part of the English forces, and whose unintelligible objurgations seem to have puzzled the troops under his command. [!]

[5] Skinner, *Etymologicon*, s. v. ; Drake, *Shakspeare and his Times*, vol. i. pp. 157, 158.

Political parties have sometimes assumed names derived from local sources. The leaders of the GIRONDISTS were the deputies from the department of the Gironde. The JACOBINS took their name from the convent of St. James, in which the meetings of the revolutionary club were held. A TEMPLAR now studies law in the former residence of the crusading Knights of the Temple of Jerusalem. The Court of Arches was originally held in the arches of *Bow* Church—St. Mary de Arcubus—the crypt of which was used by Wren to support the present superstructure. When we talk of finding ourselves in a perfect BEDLAM we do not always remember that the rapacity and the vandalism of the English Reformers were redeemed by some good deeds—one of which was the assignment of the Convent of St. Mary of Bethlehem for the reception of lunatics, who used previously to be chained to a post, if indeed they were not left utterly uncared for. The hospital of St. Lazarus, at Naples, has, in a somewhat similar way, given a name to those who would be its most fitting occupants—the Neapolitan LAZZARONI.

The porch of a cathedral is called the GALILEE, probably because to the crusaders and pilgrims advancing from the North, Galilee formed the frontier or entrance to the Holy Land [1] [inhabited by semi-pagans or outsiders].

On the Mons Palatinus—a name the etymology of which carries us back to the time when sheep were bleating on the slope [2]—was the residence of the Roman emperors, which, from its site, was called the Palati(n)um, or Palatium. Hence the word PALACE has come to be applied to all royal or imperial residences. The Count Palatine was, in theory, the official who had the superintendence of the household of the Carolingian emperors. As the foremost of the twelve peers of France, the Count Palatine took a prominent place in mediæval romance, and a PALADIN is the impersonification of chivalrous devotion. His feudal fief was the Palatinate—the rich Rhine valley above Frankfort. The counties Palatine of Chester, Durham, and Lancaster, are so called on account of the delegated royalty—the *jura regalia*—formerly exercised by the

[1] Stanley, *Sinai and Palestine*, p. 356.
[2] So the CERAMICUS, or ' Potter's field ', at Athens, was converted into the most beautiful quarter of the city, containing the academy, lyceum, etc. The name of the TUILERIES denotes that the site was once a ' Tile yard' ; and that of the ESCURIAL shows that the palace was built upon a ' heap of refuse [*scoria*] from an exhausted mine '. See p. 205, *supra*.

Earls of Chester, the Bishops of Durham, and the Dukes
of Lancaster.[1]   It is one of the curiosities of language that a
petty little hill-slope in Italy should have thus transferred
its name to a hero of romance, to a German state, to three
English counties, to a glass house at Sydenham, and to all
the royal residences in Europe.[2]

[1] Pembroke and Hexham, also march or border towns, had palatine rights. Lappenberg *Anglo-Saxon Kings*, vol. ii. p. 62.
[2] See Yonge, *Christian Names*, vol. ii. p. 353 ; Ménage, *Origines*, p. 506 ; Max Müller, *Lectures*, second series, p. 251.

CHAPTER XVII

ONOMATOLOGY ;

OR, THE PRINCIPLES OF NAME-GIVING

Dangers which beset the Etymologist—Rules of Investigation—Names in the United States—List of some of the chief components of Local Names.

THE study of local names can, as yet, hardly claim the dignity of a science. With the exception of Ernst Förstemann, those who have written on the subject have too often been contented to compile collections of 'things not generally known', without attempting either to systematize the facts which they have brought together, or to deduce any general principles which might serve to guide the student in his researches.

There are few subjects, perhaps, in which such numerous dangers beset the inquirer. The patent blunders, and the absurdly fanciful explanations of etymologists have become a byeword. It may be well, therefore, to clear the way for a scientific treatment of the subject by an examination of some of these sources of error, and by the suggestion of a few obvious rules which should be constantly kept in view by those who attempt the investigation of the meaning of ancient names.

The fundamental principle to be borne in mind is an axiom which alone makes the study of local names possible, and which has been tacitly assumed in the title of this volume, and throughout the preceding chapters. This axiom asserts that local names are in no case arbitrary sounds. They are always ancient WORDS, or fragments of ancient words—each of them, in short, constituting the earliest chapter in the local history of the PLACES to which they severally refer.

Assuming, therefore, as axiomatic, the significancy of local names, it need hardly be said that in endeavouring to detect the meaning of a geographical name, the first requisite is to discover the language from which the name has been derived. The choice will mostly lie within narrow limits—geographical and historical considerations generally confining our choice to the three or four languages which may have been vernacular in the region to which the name belongs. No interpretation of a name can be admitted, however seemingly appropriate, until we have first satisfied ourselves of the historical possibility, not to say probability, of the proposed etymology. For example, LAMBETH, as we have seen, is a Saxon name meaning the loam-hithe, or muddy landing-place. We must not, as a *Saturday Reviewer* has amusingly observed, plume ourselves on the discovery that *lama* is a Mongolian term for a chief priest, and *beth* a Semitic word for a house, and thus interpret the name of the place where the primate lives as the ' house of the chief priest '.[1]

In the next place the earliest documentary form of the name must be ascertained. In the case of an English name Kemble's collection of Anglo-Saxon Charters,[2] Domesday Book, and Dugdale, must be diligently searched. For Scottish names Innes' *Origines Parochiales Scotiæ* will generally supply the necessary information. For names in France, the *Dictionnaire des toutes les Communes de la France*, by Girault de Saint Fargeau, may often be consulted with advantage. But if the name to be investigated occurs in Germany, all trouble will be saved by a reference to Förstemann's systematic list of mediæval German names—the *Altdeutsches Namenbuch* —a work which only a German could have conceived or executed, and which, even in Germany, must be considered a marvellous monument of erudite labour.

If no early form of the name can be discovered, we must, guided by the analogy of similar names, endeavour to ascertain it by conjecture, bearing carefully in mind those well-known laws of phonetic change to which reference has already been made.[3]

This having been done, it remains to interpret the name

---

[1] Etymologies quite as absurd have been seriously propounded. Thus Jacobin, his *Bedeutung der böhmischen Dorfnamen*, derives from the Sclavonic the names of Jerusalem, Jericho, Africa, the Tigris [see Appendix p. 369.] and the Euphrates. His absurdities are, if possible, surpassed by George Dyer, who, in his *Vulgar Errors Ancient and Modern*, derives from Welsh roots all Scriptural names—Adam, and Eve, Shem, Ham, and Japhet, the Nile, the four rivers of Paradise, etc.; and he naively says of those who refuse to accept his absurdities, ' Our mistakes . . . afford melancholy instances of want of judgment, . . . and they prove that our opinions may not rest so much on rational grounds, as on weak imaginations, which in such cases as herein cited produce ridiculous and chimerical allusions or ludicrous and delusive explanations '.—p. LXXXV.
[2] *Codex Diplomaticus Ævi Saxonici.*
[3] See p. 271, *supra.*

which has been thus recovered or reconstructed. To do this with success requires a knowledge of the ancient grammatical structure and the laws of composition which prevailed in the language in which the name is significant [1]—the relative position, for instance, of adjective and substantive,[2] and the usage of prepositions and formative particles.

Great aid will be derived from the analogy of other names in the same neighbourhood. A sort of epidemic seems to have prevailed in the nomenclature of certain districts. There is hardly a single English county, or French province, or German principality, which does not possess its characteristic clusters of names—all constructed on the same type.[3] The key that will unlock one of these names will probably also unlock the rest of those in the same group.

Having thus arrived at a probable interpretation of the name in question, we must proceed to test the result. If the name be topographic or descriptive, we must ascertain if it conforms to the physical features of the spot ; if, on the other hand, the name be historic in its character, we must satisfy ourselves as to the historic possibility of its bestowal.

This scientific investigation of names is not, indeed, always possible. In the case of the Old World, the simple-minded children of semi-barbarous times have unconsciously conformed to the natural laws which regulate the bestowal of names. The names of the Old World may be systematized —they describe graphically the physical features of the country, or the circumstances of the early settlers.

But in the New World, settled, not by savages but by civilized men, a large proportion of the names are thoroughly barbarous in character. We find the map of the United States thickly bespattered with an incongruous medley of names— for the most part utterly inappropriate, and fulfilling very insufficiently the chief purposes which names are intended to fulfil. In every State of the Union we find repeated, again and again, such unmeaning names as Thebes, Cairo, Memphis,

---

[1] For Celtic names, the *Grammatica Celtica*, of Zeuss, will be found indispensable, and for Teutonic names, Grimm's *Deutsche Grammatik*.

[2] See p. 159, *supra*.

[3] The local names invented by our popular novelists frequently set all etymologica propriety at defiance. We have all sorts of impossible compounds, we have *thorpes*, *holms*, and *thwaites* in Wessex, Cornish names in Wales, and Kentish forms in the Midland counties. Mrs. Howitt's novel of *The Cost of Caergwyn* forms a praiseworthy exception to the general rule.

Troy, Rome, Athens, Utica, Big Bethel, and the like. What a poverty of the inventive faculty is evinced by these endless repetitions, not to speak of the intolerable impertinence displayed by those who thus ruthlessly wrench the grand historic names from the map of the Old World, and apply them, by the score, without the least shadow of congruity, to collections of log huts in some Western forest. The incongruity between the names and the appearance of some of these places is amusing. Thus Corinth 'consists of a wooden grog-shop and three log shanties ; the Acropolis is represented by a grocery store. . . . All that can be seen of the city of Troy . . . is a timber house, three log huts, a saw mill, and twenty negroes '.[1]

The more ancient names in the States are for the most part far less objectionable. Indian names, such as Niagara, Massachusetts, Missouri, or Arkansas, though not always euphonious, are otherwise unexceptionable. And the same may be said of most of the names given by the trappers and pioneers of the Far West, names such as Blue Ridge, North Fork, Pine Bluff, Red River, Hickory Flats, Big Bone Lick, Otter Creek, and the town of Bad Axe. Henpeck City and Louse Village, both in California, are, to say the least, very expressive, and the town of Why Not, in Mississippi, seems to have been the invention of some squatter of doubtful mind.[2] Such names as Louisiana, Columbia, Pittsburg, Charleston, New York, Albany, Baltimore, Washington, Raleigh, Franklin, or Jefferson, have an historical significance and appropriateness which incline us to excuse the confusion arising from the frequency with which some of them have been bestowed.[3] Much also may be said in favour of names like Boston, Plymouth, and Portsmouth, whereby the colonists have striven to reproduce in a land of exile, the very names of the beloved spots which they had left. Smithtown and Murfreesboro' may perhaps pass muster, though Brownsville[4] and Indianopolis have a somewhat hybrid appearance. Flos, Tiny, and the other townships which a late Canadian Governor named after his wife's lapdogs, are at all events distinctive names, though perhaps

[1] Russell, *Diary North and South*, vol. ii. pp. 45, 46.
[2] See Bowditch, *Suffolk Surnames*, p. 259.
[3] See p. 226, *supra*.
[4] Brownwill or Brownell would more correctly denote the abode of Brown : see p. 115, *supra*. The *villes* and *cities* which we find so profusely in the States show the land-speculating and grandiose character of the nation, just as the *hams*, *tons*, and *worths* of England are a proof of Anglo-Saxon seclusiveness. See p. 87, 91, *supra*.

showing a want of respect to the inhabitants.[1]   But the
scores of Dresdens, Troys, and Carthages, are utterly indefen-
sible ;   they betray quite as much poverty of invention as
Twenty-fourth Street, Fifth Avenue, or No. 10 Island, while
they do not possess the practical advantages of the numerical
system of nomenclature, and must be a source of unending
perplexity in the post-office, the booking-office, and the schoolroom.   The geographical etymologist regards a large portion
of the names in the United States with feelings which are akin
to those experienced by the ecclesiologist who, having traced
with delight the national developments of the pointed architecture of western Europe, beholds the incongruous restora-
tions—so called—for which the last century is to blame, or
the Pagan temples, the Egyptian tombs, and Chinese pagodas
with which architectural plagiarists have deformed our cities.
Such plagiarisms and incongruities are as distasteful as the
analogous barbarisms with which the map of the United States
is so woefully disfigured.   The further perpetration of such
æsthetic monstrosities as those to which reference has been
made is now happily impossible.   Our architects have taken
up the idea of Gothic art, and developed, from its principles,
new and original creations, instead of reproducing, *usque ad
nauseam,* servile copies or dislocated fragments of ancient
buildings.   Would that the same regeneration could be effected
in the practice of name-giving.   If the true principles of
Anglo-Saxon nomenclature were understood, our Anglo-
American and Australian cousins might construct an endless
series of fresh names, which might be at once harmonious,
distinctive, characteristic, and in entire consonance with the
genius of the language.[2]

When we attempt a scientific analysis and classification of
local names, we find that by far the greater number contain
two component elements.   One of these, which in Celtic names
is generally the prefix, and in Teutonic names the suffix, is
some general term meaning island, river, mountain, dwelling,

---

[1] *Quarterly Review*, vol. cxvi. p. 3.
[2] Many of the Swabian patronymics which have not been reproduced in England
would furnish scores of new names of a thoroughly characteristic Anglo-Saxon type, if
combined with appropriate suffixes, such as ham, ton, hurst, ley, worth, by, den, don,
combe, sted, borough, thorpe, cote, stoke, set, thwaite, and holt.   Thus Senningham,
Wickington, Erkington, Frelington, Moringham, Hermingham, Lennington, Teppington,
Ersingham, Steslingham, Mensington, Relvington, Plenningham, Aldington, Delkington,
Weighingham, Ensington, Melvington, are characteristic Anglo-Saxon names, which
nevertheless do not appear in the list of English villages.

or inclosure, as the case may be. Thus we have the Celtic prefixes, Aber, Inver, Ath, Bally, Dun, Kil, Llan, Ben, Glen, Strath, Loch, Innis, Inch ; and the Teutonic suffixes, borough, by, bourn, den, don, ton, ham, thorpe, cote, hurst, hill, ley, shiels, set, stow, sted, wick, worth, fell, law, dale, gay, holm, ey, stone, and beck.

This element in names is called the 'Grundwort' by Förstemann.[1] We have already, in the case of river names, called it the *substantival* element. The other component serves to distinguish the island, river, or village, from other neighbouring islands, streams, or villages.[2] This portion of the name, which we have called *adjectival*, has been denominated the " Bestimmungswort " by Förstemann.[3] It is frequently a personal name [4]—thus GRIMSBY is Grim's dwelling, ULLSTHORPE is Ulf's village, BALMAGHIE is the town of the Maghiesr CLAPHAM is the home of Clapha, KENSINGTON the homestead of the Kensings. In a large, number of cases, instead of a personal name we have a descriptive adjective denoting the relative magnitude, the relative position or antiquity, the excellence, or, sometimes, the inferiority of the place, the colour or nature of the soil, or its characteristic productions.[5] A full enumeration, not to say a discussion, of these roots would occupy a volume—a few of the more important are enumerated below.

---

[1] Förstemann, *Die Deutschen Ortsnamen*, pp. 26–107.

[2] There are only about 500 German *Grundwörter*, which, variously combined with the *Bestimmungswörter*, constitute the 500,000 names which are found upon the map of Germany. Förstemann, *Ortsnamen*, p. 108.

[3] Förstemann, *Ibid.*, pp. 109–174 ; Bender, *Deutschen Ortsnamen*, pp. 97, 98.

[4] While local names are frequently derived from personal names, the converse has been the case in a still greater number of instances. See Pott, *Personennamen*, p. 330, and passim ; Dixon, *Surnames*, passim.

[5] On German roots of this class, such as *breit, platt, alt, neu, weiss, schwart*, etc., see Förstemann, *Die Deutschen Ortsnamen*, and Bender, *Die Deutschen Ortsnamen*, pp. 97, 98.

LIST OF SOME OF THE
CHIEF ADJECTIVAL COMPONENTS OF
LOCAL NAMES

I. WORDS DENOTING RELATIVE MAGNITUDE

From the Celtic word *mor* or *mawr*, great, we have the names of Benmore, and Penmaen-Mawr, the great mountains, Kilmore, the great church, and Glenmore, the great glen. Much Wenlock, Macclesfield, Maxstoke in Warwickshire, Great Missenden, Grampound, and Granville, contain Teutonic and Romance roots of the same import. Similarly MISSISSIPPI is an Indian term of precisely the same meaning as the neighbouring Spanish name Rio Grande, which, as well as the Arabic GUADALQUIVER (*keber*, great,, and the Sarmatian word WOLGA, signifies ' the great river '.[1] [Algonquin] *mici-sipi*, 'great river '.[2]]

From the Celtic *beg* or *bach*, little, we have Bally begg and Inis beg, Glydwr Fach, Pont Neath Vechan, and Cwm Bychan. We find several Teutonic Littleboroughs, Littleburys, Littletons and Clintons. MAJORCA and MINORCA are the greater and lesser isles. BOCA CHICA is the great mouth. We find the prefix *broad*, in Braddon, Bradley, Bradshaw, Bradford, and Ehrenbreitstein, and some of the Stratfords and Strettons are probably from the root ' strait ', and not ' street '.

II. RELATIVE POSITION

The points of the compass afford an obvious means of distinguishing between the places of the same name. Thus we have Norfolk and Suffolk, Wessex, Essex, and Sussex, Northampton and Southampton, Surrey, Westmoreland, Northumberland, and Sutherland ; Norton (57) and Sutton (77), Norbury (7) and Sudbury (7), Easton (14) and Weston (36), Eastbury (21) and Westbury (10), Easthorpe and Westhorpe, Norleigh, Sudley and Westley.[3] The Erse *iar*, the west, appears in the name of ORMUNDE or West Munster, as well, possibly, as in those of IRELAND and ARGYLE.[4] [But see p. 61 note.]

The ZUYDER ZEE is the southern sea ; DEKKAN means the south in Sanskrit ; and ALGARBE is an Arabic name meaning the west.[5] The OSTROGOTHS and VISIGOTHS were the eastern and western divisions of the Goths, as distinguished from the Massagetæ, or the great Goths, the chief

---

[1] Müller, *Ugrische Volkstamm*, vol. ii. p. 105.
[2] [E. J. Payne, *Hist. of the New World*, i, 58.]
[3] See Leo, *Anglo-Saxon Names*, p. 10 ; Vilmar, *Ortsnamen*, p. 239 ; Förstemann, *Ortsnamen*, p. 133.
[4] See Betham, *Gael*, p. 81.
[5] See pp. 54, 76, *supra*.

body of the nation.[1] AUSTRIA (Oestreich) is the eastern empire, WEST-
PHALIA the western plain, and the WESER (anciently Wisaraha) is the
western river.[2] From the close resemblance of the sounds it is sometimes difficult to distinguish between roots meaning the east and those
meaning the west. Thus OSTEND in Belgium is at the west (*ouest*) end of
the great canal ; and OSTEND in Essex is the east end of the land. In
Chinese, *pih* and *nan* mean respectively north and south. Hence we
have PIH-KING and NAN-KING, the northern and southern courts ; PIH-
LING and NAN-LING, the northern and southern mountains ; NAN-HAI,
the southern sea,[3] and the kingdom of AN-NAM, or the 'peace of the
south '.[4]

PERÆA is the country 'beyond' the Jordan. ANTILIBANUS is the
range 'opposite' Lebanon. TRANSYLVANIA is the country beyond the
forest-clad range of mountains which bounds Hungary to the south-
east. Hinton (14) is a common name for a village behind a hill, as in the
case of Cherry Hinton, near Cambridge. [Probably Hind-town—Skeat,
Camb. Place Names, p. 7.]

From the German prepositions, *an*, *in*, and *zu*, we have the names
of Amsteg, Andermat, Imgrund, Zermatt, Zerbruggen, and Zermägern.
From the Anglo-Saxon *æt*, at, we have Atford, Adstock, Otford, and
Abridge.[5] From the Celtic preposition *ar*, upon, we obtain ARMORICA,
the land ' upon the sea ', and ARLES (*ar-laeth*), the town ' upon the marsh '.[6]
In the names of POMERANIA, and of PRUSSIA, we have the Sclavonic preposition *po*, by. With Netherby, Dibden, Dibdale, Deeping (the low
meadow), Holgate and Holloway, we may contrast High Wycombe, High
Ercal, Upton (42), Higham, Highgate, and Highstreet.

III. RELATIVE AGE

There are numerous English villages which go by the names of Althorp
Alton, Elston, Elton, Eltham, Elbottle, Alcester, Aldbury, Abury, Albury,
Aldborough, Aldburgh, and Oldbury [many of these do not contain ' old '
as an element ; *e.g.* Alton (Hants) stands for Aewel-tun, ' town of the
water-spring '], and on the Continent we find Altorf, Starwitz,[7] Torres
Vedras, Civita Vecchia near Rome, and Citta Vecchia in Malta.

On the other hand, there are in England alone more than 120 villages
called Newton, besides Newport (12), Newnham (11), Newland (11),
Newark, Newbiggen (17), Newbold (11), Newbottle, Newstead, Newbury,
Newby, Newcastle [8] (10), Newhall and Newburgh, which we may compare
with Continental names like Villeneuve, Villanova, Neusiedel, Neustadt,
Novgorod, Neville, Neufchâtel, Nova Zembla, Naples,—Newfoundland,
and Nâblus.

---

[1] Bosworth, *Origin*, p. 114 ; Pictet, *Orig. Indo-Europ.* part i. p. 83 ; Förstemann,
Ortsnamen, p. 212.
[2] Förstemann, *Ortsnamen*, p. 134.
[3] Charnock, *Local Etymology*, pp. 159, 204 ; Gibson, *Etym. Geogr.* p. 147.
[4] *Quarterly Review*, vol. cxvi. p. 284.
[5] Ingram, *Saxon Chron.* p. 425.
[6] See pp. 61, 162, *supra*.   [7] From the Sclavonic *stary*, old.
[8] The New Castle built by the Normans on the Tyne is now 800 years old, yet still
keeps its name ; and Nâblus (Neapolis) in Palestine is twice that age, having been founded
by Vespasian after the destruction of Samaria. New College is one of the oldest colleges
in Oxford, having been founded in 1386, and New Palace Yard, Westminster, is a memorial of the palace built by Ruf s

IV. NUMERALS

In ancient Anglo-Saxon and German names, the numerals which most commonly occur are four and seven, numbers which were supposed to have a mystical meaning. Such are Sevenoaks, Klostersieben and Siebenbürgen. Nine-elms dates from a later period. We have a mountain group called the Twelve Pins, in Ireland, and Fünfkirchen and Zweibrücken in Germany. Neunkirchen, however, is only a corruption of Neuenkirchen, or New Church.[1] The modern names of the ancient Roman stations in the Upper Rhine valley, near Wallenstadt, are curiously derived from the Roman numerals. We find, at regular intervals, as we proceed up the valley, the villages of Seguns, Tertzen, Quarten, Quinten and Sewes.[2]

The three cities of Oea, Sabrata, and Leptis in Africa, went collectively by the name of TRIPOLIS.[3] TRIPOLI in Syria was a joint colony from the three cities of Tyre, Sidon, and Aradus.[4] On the lake Ontario there is the Bay of the Thousand Isles. TERCEIRA, one of the Azores, is the third Island. The LACCADIVES are the ten thousand islands, and the MALDIVES are the thousand isles. The PUNJAB is the land of the five rivers, and the DOAB[5] is the country between the 'two rivers', the Ganges and the Jumna. PLYNLIMMON is a corruption of Pum-lumon, the five hills ; and MIZRAIM, the Biblical name of Egypt, describes either the 'two' banks of the Nile, or the 'two' districts of Upper and Lower Egypt.[6]

V. NATURAL PRODUCTIONS

A far larger number of names are derived from natural production. Mineral springs are often denoted by some corruption of the Latin word Aquæ. Thus we have Aix in Savoy, and Aix near Marseilles ; Aix la Chapelle, or Aachen, in Rhenish Prussia ; Acqui in Piedmont ; and Dax, or Dacqs, in Gascony. The misunderstood name Aquæ Solis, or Aq uæ, probably suggested to the Anglo-Saxons the name of Ake mannes ceaster,[7] the invalid's city, which was changed at a later period to Bath, from a root which also supplies names to Bakewell, anciently Badecanwylla, in Derbyshire, and to the numerous Badens on the Continent. THERMOPYLÆ took its name from the hot springs in the defile ; TIERRA DEL FUEGO from its volcanic fires ; and REIKJAVIK, or 'reek bay ', was the Norse settlement in the neighbourhood of the GEYSERS,[8] or 'boilers '. HECLA was so called

---

[1] Bender, *Ortsnamen*, p. 98. On names of this class see Förstemann, *Ortsnamen*, p. 125.

[2] Tschudi, *Hauptschlüssel*, p. 290 ; Holtzmann, *Kelten und Germ.* p. 137.

[3] Bochart, vol. iii. 479.

[4] See p. 5, *supra*.

[5] The *ab* here is the Sanskrit and Persian word for water, which comes to us from the Persian through the Arabic, and which we have in the word jula*p* (*gul*, rose ; and *ab*, water), as well as in shrub and syrop (schara*b*) [No ; from Arab. *sharib*, to drink.] Diez, *Etymol. Wörterb.* pp. 175, 319 ; cf. Latham, *Eng. Lang.* vol. i. p. 355 ; Pihan, *Glossaire*, p. 169 ; Engelmann, *Glossaire*, p. 83.

[6] The word survives in Misr, the enchorial name of Cairo. Stanley, *Jewish Church*, p. 76 ; p. 57, *supra*.

[7] The road from London to Bath long went by the name of Akeman Street, which survives in the name of a hollow still called Jacuman's Bottom. Gough's Camden, vol. i. p. 119.

[8] The words *geyser, yeast, geist, gust,* and *ghost*, [?] are from the same root, which signifies something boiling, bubbling up, or overflowing. Cf. the cognation of ἄνεμος and *animus*. Pictet, *Origines*, pt. ii. p. 540 ; Gladstone, *Homer*, p. 303.

from the ' cloak' of smoke hanging over the mountain. VESUVIUS is an Oscan name, meaning the emitter of smoke and sparks.[1] The basaltic columns of STAFFA are well described by its name, ' the isle of steps ', a Norse name which we have repeated in the case of the basaltic rocks of STAPPEN in Iceland. [Rather Norse *staf-ey*, ' isle of staves ', i.e. columnar rocks.]

MISSOURI is the muddy river, and the name may be compared with those of the FOULBECK and the LAMBOURN ; while the names of ACCHO or ACRE, and of SCINDE, describe the sandy nature of the country.[2] SAND-WICH is the sandy bay : we have many analogous names, such as Sandhurst, Sandon, Sandford, Sandbach, and Peschkow, which last is derived from *pesk*, the Sclavonic word for sand.[3] ALUM BAY, in the Isle of Wight, is a modern name of the same class.

The RIO DE LA PLATA, or river of plate, took its name from a few gold and silver ornaments which Sebastian Cabot found in the possession of the natives, and which he hoped were indications of an El Dorado, or golden land, in the interior. The GOLD COAST and the IVORY COAST were names appropriately bestowed by early traders. The name of the ANDES is derived from the Peruvian word *anta*, which means copper.

Many names are derived from animals. We find that of the Ox in Oxley, and perhaps in Oxford ; and that of the Cow in Cowley ; *wol*, the Sclavonic name for an ox, appears in the names of Wollau (14), Wollin (6), and many other places.[4] We find Swine at Swindon, Swinford, and Swingfield :—Kine at Kinton :—Neat Cattle at Nutford, and Netley ; [5] and Sheep at Shipton and Shipley. The names of the FAROE Islands, and of FAIRFIELD, a mountain in Westmoreland, are probably from the Norse *faar*, sheep.

Deer, or perhaps wild animals generally (German, *Thier* ; Anglo-Saxon, *deor*) are found at Deerhurst and Dyrham in Gloucestershire, Dereham in Norfolk, Dereworth in Northamptonshire, and Derby, anciently Deoraby. SCHWERIN, which serves as a name for a German principality and three other places in Germany, is the exact Sclavonic equivalent of Derby.

Other wild animals whose names often occur are :—

The Stag at Hertford and Heurtley : the Fox or Tod at Foxley, Foxhill, Foxhough, Todburn, and Todfield : the Wild Boar at Evershot and Eversley : the Seal at Selsey : the Otter at Otterbourn in Hants : the Beaver at Beverley and Nant Frangon : [6] the Badger, or Broc, at Bagshot, at Broxbourne, and at Brokenborough in Wilts, anciently Broken-eber-egge, or Badger-boar-corner.[7]

The Crane is found at Cranbourne, and the Eagle at Earnley in Sussex, and Arley in Warwickshire, both of which are written Earneleáh in the Saxon charters.

Ely was once famous for the excellence of its eels. In the Isle of Ely rents used to be paid in eels.

---

[1] Benfey, in Höfer's *Zeitschrift*. vol. ii. pp. 115, 116 ; Humboldt, *Cosmos*, vol. i. p. 449. See p. 253, *supra*.
[2] See Stanley, *Sinai and Pal.*, p. 264.
[3] Buttmann, *Ortsnamen*, p. 103.
[4] Buttman, *Ibid*. p. 122.
[5] Morris, *Local Etymology*, p. 10.
[6] See p. 261, *supra*. [Beverley, Bevorlac, is from the British *Pedwarllech*, ' Four Stones '.]   [7] See p. 261, *supra*.

The Norse word for a salmon is *lax*. Hence we have Laxvoe, or ' salmon bay ' in Shetland, Loch Laxford in Sutherland, the Laxay, or ' salmon river ', in the Hebrides, and also in Cantire, and the river Laxey in the Isle of Man, and five rivers called Laxa, in Iceland. We have Laxweir on the Shannon, Leixlip, or salmon-leap, on the Liffey, and Abbey Leix, in Queen's County.

ZEBOIM is the ravine of hyænas and AJALON the valley of stags. BERNE takes its name from the bears with which it formerly abounded. ARLBERG in the Tyrol is the Adlers berg, or eagle's mountain : and HAPSBURG, the *stammschloss* of the Austrian dynasty, is hawk castle.[1]

SWAN RIVER was so called from the number of black swans seen there by Vlaming, the first discoverer.[2] The AZORES when discovered were found to abound in hawks ; the CANARIES in wild dogs ; the CAMAROONS[3] in shrimps ; the GALAPAGOS Islands in turtles ; and the Bay of PANAMA in mud fish. There are five islands called TORTUGA, either from the turtles found on the coast, or possibly from the turtle-like shape.[4] The island of MARGARITA received its name from the pearls which Columbus obtained from the inhabitants.

The island of BARBADOES is said to have derived its name from the long beard-like streamers of moss hanging from the branches of the trees ;[5] the island of BARBUDA from the long beards of the natives ; and the LADRONES from their thievish propensities. The PATAGONIANS were so called by Magalhaens from their clumsy shoes. The name of VENEZUELA, or little Venice, is due to the Indian villages which were found built on piles in the late Maracaybo.[6]

Names derived from those of plants are found in great abundance.[7] We have, for example—

The Oak—Acton, Auckland, Okely, Oakley, Sevenoaks.[8] From the Erse *doire*, an oak, we deduce the names of Derry and Kildare.

Elm—Nine Elms, Elmdon, Elmstead, Elmswell.

Ash—Ashton, Ashley.

Beech—Buckland, Buckhurst.

Birch—Berkeley, Bircholt, Birbeck.

Lime—Lyndfield, Lyndhurst.

Thorn—Thorney. Names derived from the thorn are very frequent in the Saxon charters.

Hazel—Hasilmere.

Alder—Allerton, Aldershot, Allerdale, Olney, Ellerton.

Apple—Avallon, or Apple Island,[9] Appleby, Appleton.

Cherry—Cherry Hinton.

---

[1] On German names from animals, see Förstemann, *Ortsnamen*, pp. 143–147 ; Butt-mann, *Ortsnamen*, p. 18. On Sclavonic Names, see Buttmann, *Ortsnamen*, p. 120. On Norse Names, see Ferguson, *Northmen*, p. 124.

[2] Charnock, *Local Etymol*. p. 261.

[3] Portuguese, *camaroēs*, shrimps. Burton, *Abeokuta*, vol. i. p. 18 ; vol. ii. p. 48.

[4] Thornbury, *Monarchs of the Main*, vol. i. p. 28.

[5] Burton, *Abeokuta*, vol. ii. p. 78.

[6] Cooley, *Hist. of Discovery*, vol. ii. p. 49 ; Thornbury, *Monarchs*, vol. i. p. 205.

[7] On German names from plants, see Buttmann, *Ortsnamen*, p. 9 ; Bender, *Ortsnamen*, p. 114 ; Förstemann, *Ortsnamen*, pp. 60, 140. For Norse names, see Ferguson, *Northmen*, p. 124.

[8] Ingram, *Sax. Chron*. p. 425.

[9] Mone, *Geschichte, Heidenthums*, vol. ii. p. 456.

Broom—Bromley, Brompton.

Fern—Farnham, Farnborough.

Rushes—Rusholme.

Sedge—Sedgemoor, Sedgeley.

Reeds—Rodney, Retford.

Shrubs—Shrewsbury and Shawbury. The names of Brescia and Brussels have been referred to a root connected with the low Latin *bruscia*, thicket, or brushwood.[1]

The chief Sclavonic roots [2] of this class are :—

dub, the oak. There are 200 places called Dubrau.

brasa, the birch, occurs in the names of 40 places. *E.g.* Braslaf.

lipa, the lime, occurs in the names of 600 places. *E.g.* Leipsig, the 'linden town'.

topol, the poplar. *E.g.* Toplitz.

The Mount of Olives and the Spice Islands are familiar instances of this mode of nomenclature. Saffron Walden took its name from the saffron, the cultivation of which was introduced in the reign of Edward III. and which still to some extent continues.[3] GULISTAN is the place of roses.[4] The name of SCIO comes from *scino*, mastic. TADMOR, or PALMYRA, is the city of palms. PHŒNICIA is perhaps the land of palms.[5] EN RIMMON is the Fountain of the Pomegranate. CANA, which stands close to the lake, is the reedy.[6] BETH TAPUAH is the apple orchard,[7] and ANAB means the grape. JAVA is the isle of nutmegs [8] (*jayah*), and PULOPENANG means, in Malay, the island of the areca nut. BRAZIL, as we have seen,[9] was named from the red dye-wood, which was the first article of export. MADEIRA, when discovered by the Portuguese in 1418, was found uninhabited and covered with dense forests. It received its name from the Portuguese word *madera*, timber [Lat. *materies*]. The RIO MADEIRA, an affluent of the Amazons, still flows through the immense forests from which it took its name.

VI. NAMES IMPLYING EXCELLENCE OR THE REVERSE

Names implying the excellence of the locality are far more common than those implying the reverse. Thus FORMOSA, FUNEN, and JOPPA, in Portuguese, Danish, and Hebrew, mean fine, or beautiful. VALPARAISO is Paradise Valley, and GENNESARETH is nearly identical in meaning.[10] The name of BUENOS AYRES describes the delicious climate of Southern Brazil. The PACIFIC Ocean seems calm to those who have just weathered the tempests of Cape Hoorn. BUNGAY is probably from the French [11]

---

[1] See Diefenbach, *Celtica*, i. p. 217. Brussels may, however, be from the Flemish *breecksal*, a swamp.

[2] See Buttmann, *Ortsnamen*, pp. 88–94.

[3] Loudon, *Encyclopædia of Plants*, p. 38 ; Gough's Camden, vol. ii. p. 125.

[4] Pihan, *Glossaire*, p. 146.

[5] See page 67, *supra*.

[6] Stanley, *Sinai and Pal.* p. 260.

[7] Wilton, *Negeb*, p. 232.

[8] Talbot, *English Etymologies*, p. 451. [Rather, of *yava*, grain.]

[9] See p. 289, *supra*.

[10] Stanley, *Sinai and Pal.* p. 374.

[11] The Norman castle of Hugh Bigot accounts for the French name. See Gough's Camden, vol. ii. p. 157.

bon gué, fair ford. PALERMO, a corruption of Panormus, is the haven sheltered from every wind. The Genoese gave BALACLAVA its name of the beautiful quay, *bella chiava*.[1] The name of BOMBAY is from the Portuguese *bona bahia*, the good bay, and well describes the harbour, one of the largest, safest, and most beautiful in the world.[2] [Compare Bayonne from the Basque *bai ona*, *ibai ona*, ' the good bay '—L. L. Bonaparte.]

CAIRO is the Anglicized form of the Arabic El Kahirah, the ' victorious ',[3] and the name may be compared with that of VITTORIOSA, a suburb of Valetta which was built at the conclusion of the great siege. The Romans often gave their colonies names of good omen,[4] as Pax, Liberalitas, Fidentia, Placentia (now PIACENZA), Valentia (now VALANCE, VALENTZ, and VALENTIA), Pollentia (now POLENZA), Potentia (now S. MARIA POTENZA), Florentia (now FIRENZE or FLORENCE), Vicentia (now VICENZA), Faventia (now FAENZA), and the queenly city Basilia (now BASEL or BÂLE).

Names of bad omen[5] are rare. From the Anglo-Saxon *hean*, poor, [rather, ' high '], we have Henlow, Hendon, and Henley.[6] PERNAMBUCO means the mouth of hell [*parana*, the river] and BAB-EL-MANDEB the gate of the devil.[7] MALPAS is the bad frontier pass.[8] DUNGENESS and Cape PELORUS express the terrors of the sailor. Caltrop, Colton, Caldecote, and Cold Harbour, are all cold places, and the name of Mount Algidus may be paralleled by that of Coleridge. A volcano broke out on the ' most beautiful ' island of CALLISTE, which caused the name to be changed to THERA, ' the beast '. At the time of a subsequent eruption the island was placed under the protection of the Empress St. Irene, whose name it still bears in the form of SANTORIN.[9]

VII. CONFIGURATION

A few names, chiefly those of islands, bays, and mountains, are derived from the configuration of the land. Thus ANGUILLA is the eel-shaped island. Drepanum, now TRAPANI, is from a Greek word, meaning a sickle. ZANCLE, the original name of Messina, is said to be derived from a Siculian root of the same significance. SICILY perhaps comes from a root allied to *sica*, a sickle, and the name seems to have been first applied to the curved shore near Messina, and then extended to the whole island. ANCONA, which preserves its original name unchanged, is built at the place where Monte Conero juts out into the sea and then recedes, forming a sort of bent ' elbow ' (ἀγκών).[10]

The name of GOMPHI, near Pindus, expresses the ' wedge-shaped ' formation of the rocks,[11] and may be compared with that of the NEEDLES in

[1] Charnock, *Local Etymology*, p. 24.
[2] See Buckingham, *Autobiography*, vol. ii. p. 338.
[3] The real name of Cairo is Misr ; El Kahirah or Cairo is only a title of honour applied to the city, just as Genoa is called ' La Superba ', Verona, ' La Degna ', Mantua, ' La Gloriosa ', Vicenza, ' L'antica ', and Padua, ' La Forte '. Fairholt, *Up the Nile*, p. 42.
[4] See Niebuhr, *Lectures on Ethnology and Geogr.* vol. ii. p. 291.
[5] On names of ill omen, see Grimm, *Gesch. d. deut. Spr.* p. 780.
[6] Monkhouse, *Etymologies*, p. 48. [Henlow, anciently Haneslau, is probably ' Hann's Low ' or ' mound '—Skeat, *Bedford Place Names*, 40.]
[7] Pihan, *Glossaire*, p. 49. [Rather, ' of tears '.]
[8] See p. 159, *supra*.
[9] Bremer, *Greece*, vol. i. p. 329.
[10] Trollope, *Lenten Journey in Umbria*, pp. 281, 290.
[11] Müller, *Dorians*, vol. i. p. 27.

the Isle of Wight. At METEORA the convents are poised ' aloft in the air ' on the summits of rocky columns.[1] The name Trapezus, now TREBIZOND, on the Black Sea, is identical in meaning with that of TABLE MOUNTAIN at the Cape. The ORGAN Mountains in Brazil derive their name from the fantastic forms of the spires of rock, resembling the pipes of an organ.[2] PHIALA, in Palestine, is the ' bowl'.[3] RHEGIUM is the ' rent' between Sicily and Italy. TEMPE is the ' cut ' ($\tau\epsilon\mu\nu\omega$) in the rocks through which the Peneus flows,[4] and DETROIT the ' narrows ', between Lake Erie and Lake St. Clair.

VIII. COLOUR

The adjectival element in names is frequently derived from colour.[5] Names of this class are often admirably descriptive. How well, for instance, the Northmen described a conspicuous chalk cliff, past which they steered to Normandy, by the name of Cape GRISNEZ, or the grey nose. Cape BLANCNEZ, close by, is the white nose. Cape VERDE is fringed with green palms.

The local name for the Indus is the Nilab, the blue river ; and the name of the Blue Nile is, perhaps, an unconscious reduplication.[6] The XANTHUS is the yellow river. The RIO COLORADO takes its name from its deep red colour ; RATBY, RUGBY, and RUTLAND, from their red soil. RATCLIFFE, Bristol, is the red cliff. The Red Sea,[7] the Black Sea, the Yellow Sea, and the White Sea, are translated names.

The city of Hatria or ADRIA, from which the Adriatic took its name, is the black town, so called, perhaps, because built on a deposit of black mud.[8] The KEDRON is the black valley.[9] From the Celtic *dhu*, black, we have the names of DUBLIN, the black pool or linn, and the DOUGLAS, or black water, in Lancashire, Scotland, and the Isle of Man.[10] The RIO NEGRO and the River MELAS are also the black rivers. The River LYCUS is, as we have seen, the white river, and not the wolf river.[11] The HVITA, a common Norse river-name, is the white water. Names like Blackheath, Blackmore, Blakeley, or Blackdown, are very ambiguous, as they may be either from the English *black*, or from the Norse *blakka*, which means white.[12] From the Sclavonic *bel*, white, we have BELGRADE and BOLGRAD, the ' white castles',[13] and scores of names in eastern Germany, such as

---

[1] See Curzon's *Monasteries of Levant* ; Müller, *Dorians*, vol. i. p. 26.
[2] Hinchcliff, *South American Sketches*, p. 275. [Cf. Staffa, p. 329.]
[3] Robinson, *Later Researches*, p. 400.
[4] Müller, *Dorians*, vol. i. p. 21.
[5] Buttmann, *Deutschen Ortsnamen*, pp. 6, 7.
[6] Pott (*Indo-Germ. Spr.* p. 29) thinks the name of the Nile is only an accidental coincidence with the Sanskrit *nila*, blue, whence, through the old French *neel*, we obtain the verb, to anneal. Cf. *neelah*, the Indian name of indigo. See Wilkinson, *Ancient Egypt*, vol. ii. p. 57.
[7] Probably a translation of Sea of Edom. Renan, *Lang. Semit.* p. 39 ; Knobel, *Völkertafel*, p. 135. [But see *supra*, p. 274.]
[8] Mommsen, *Inhabitants of Italy*, p. 46.
[9] Stanley, *Sinai and Pal.* p. 172.
[10] See Diefenbach, *Celtica*, i. p. 139.
[11] See p. 281, *supra*.
[12] Cf. the English verb, to *bleach* or make white, the German *bleich*, pale, and the French *blanc*. Some of these names may be from the Celtic *blaighe*, a hill. See Hartshorne, *Salopia Antiqua*, p. 243.
[13] Cf. the Turkish Ak-kerman, white castle.

Biela, Bielawa, Beelow, Bilau, and Bülow.[1] From the Wendish *zarny*, black, we have Sarnow, Sarne, and many other names : from *seleny*, green, come Zielonka, Zelenetz, etc. ; and so on through the whole range of the spectrum.[2]

The names of mountains are naturally derived in many cases from their prevailing hue. Thus we have the NILGHERRIES, or the ' blue hills ' of India, the BLUE RIDGE of Virginia, and the BLUE MOUNTAINS of New South Wales and Jamaica. From the Gadhelic *gorm*, blue, we have BENGORM in Mayo, and the CAIRNGORM group in the Highlands.[3] Roger Williams tells us that the name MASSACHUSETTS is an Indian word, meaning the blue hills.[4] The hills of VERMONT are clothed to the summit with green forests, while the SIERRA MORENA of Spain is the ' sombre range ',[5] and the SIERRA VERMEJA is the ' red range '.[6] From the Welsh *coch*, red, we have CRIB GOCH, the name of the striking peak which overhangs the pass of Llanberis,[7] while MONTE ROSSI, one of the peaks of Etna, and MONTE ROSSO, an outlier of the Bernina, are so called from their characteristic russet or rosy hue.[8]

A very large number of the loftiest mountains in the world derive their names from their white coverings of snow. From the Sanskrit *hima*,[9] snow, and *âlaja*,[10] an abode, we have the name of the majestic HIMÂLAJA, the perpetual 'abode of snow '.[11] HIMAPRASTHA is the snowy head, HIMAWHAT is the snow-covered, and the names of the HAEMUS and the IMAUS are from the same root. DWAJALAGIRI is the ' white mountain ', and CVÊTAGHARA, the second highest peak of Dwajalagiri, is the white castle.[12] The AKHTAG in Bokhara are the white mountains, and from the Hebrew *laban*, white, we deduce the name of LEBANON.[13] The hoary head of DJEBEL ESH SHEIKH,[14] the chief summit of the Lebanon, is covered with snow even

---

[1] Buttmann, *Deutschen Ortsnamen*, p. 79 ; Zeuss, *Die Deutschen*, p. 613.
[2] Buttmann, *Ortsnamen*, pp. 80, 81.   [3] Gibson, *Etym. Geogr.* p. 133.
[4] Drake, *Book of the Indians*, book ii. p. 18.
[5] Root, *morus*.
[6] Prescott, *Ferdinand and Is.* vol. ii. p. 387
[7] Cf. the Latin *coccinus*. The *cock* is the ' red ' bird. Diefenbach, *Celtica*, vol. i. p. 61. [Rather the bird that cries *cok !* as Chaucer says, *Nun's Priest's Tale*, l. 456.]
[8] See p. 160, *supra*.
[9] Cf. the Latin *hiems*, winter, and the Greek χιών, snow.
[10] Cognate with the verbs to *lie*, and *lay*, and the common English suffix, *ley* See p. 255, *supra*.
[11] Lassen, *Ind. Alterth.* vol. i. p. 17 ; Curtius, *Grundzüge*, vol. i. p. 169 ; Charnock, *Local Etymol.* p. 131 ; Welsford, *English Language*, p. 22 ; Cooley, *Hist. Discov.* vol. i. p. 42 ; Pott, *Etymologischen Forschungen*, p. lxxiv. ; Pictet, *Orig. Indo-Europ.* part i. p. 90.
[12] Lassen, *Ind. Alterth.*, vol. i. p. 55.
[13] See Robinson, *Bibl. Researches*, vol. iii. p. 439 ; Stanley, *Sinai and Pal.* p. 403 ; Charnock, *Local Etym.* p. 154.
[14] This Arabic word seems to have been adopted from the Persian *shah*, a king. [*Sheikh*, meaning an old man or elder, is quite a distinct word.] The name of Xerxes (Khshay-oarsha) is the ' venerable king ' ; that of Artaxerxes is the ' great venerable king '. The English ramifications of this root are curious to trace. We received the game of *chess* from the Persians through the Arabs. The name of the game is a corruption of shah or sheikh. We cry *check* (king , to give notice that the king is attacked ; check mate means ' the king is dead '. The verb *mata* = he is dead, we have in the name of the Spanish matador, who kills the bull. The word *checkered* describes the appearance of the board on which the game is played. In the Court of Exchequer the public accounts were kept by means of tallies placed on the squares of a chequered cloth. Hence the phrase to *check* an account, and the other uses of the verb to check. See Forbes, *History of Chess*, pp. 207, 208 ; Schafarik, *Slaw. Alterth.* vol. i. p. 283 ; Yonge, *Christian Names*, vol. i. p. 133 ; Ménage, *Origines*, pp. 279–286, 702.

during a Syrian summer. Graucasus,[1] the old Scythian word from which we derive the name of the CAUCASUS, means *nive candidus*, as we are told by Pliny. The Mustagh are the ice mountains.[2] The name of the APPENNINES has been explained by a reference to the Welsh *y-pen-ghwin*, the white head.[3] The BIELOUKA, the giant of the Altai, is the white mountain ; and a range in China is called SIUÈ-LING, or the snow mountain. More obvious are the etymologies of Mont Blanc, the Sierra Nevada in Spain, the Nevado in Mexico, Ben Nevis in Scotland [?], Snowdon in Wales, Sneehattan in Norway, and Sneeuwbergen in the Cape Colony, two Snafells in Iceland, Sneefell in the Isle of Man ; Schneekoppe, the highest peak of the Riesen Gebirge ; Sneeberg, Sneekopf, and the Eisthaler Spitze, in the Carpathians ; and the Weisshorn, Weissmies, Dent Blanche, and many other peaks in Switzerland.[4] The names of the Swiss mountains are often admirably picturesque and descriptive.[5] How well do the words Dent, Horn, and Aiguille describe the rocky teeth, spires, and pinnacles of rock which shoot up into the clouds. How appropriate, too, are the names of the SCHRECKHORN, or ' Peak of Terror ' ; the WETTERHORN, or Peak of Storms ', which gather round his head and reverberate from his fearful precipices ; the EIGHER, who uprears his ' giant ' head ; the MÖNCH, with his smooth-shaven crown ; the JUNGFRAU, or ' Maiden ', clad in a low descending vesture of spotless white ; the glittering SILBERHORN ; the soft disintegrating rock of the ill-conditioned FAULHORN ; the DENT DU MIDI, or ' the Peak of Noon ', over whose riven summits the midday sun streams down the long Rhone valley to the lake. PILATUS, the outlier of the Bernese chain, takes his name from the ' cap ' of cloud which he wears during western winds. On the other hand, the MATTERHORN, the most marvellous obelisk of rock which the world contains, takes its name, not from its cloud-piercing peak, but from the scanty patches of green meadow which hang around its base ; and which also give their name to ZERMATT—the village ' on the meadow '.[6]

The root *alp*, or *alb*, is widely diffused throughout the Aryan languages. The Gaelic and Welsh word, *alp*, means a height, a hill, or a craggy rock.[7] Alp, Owen says, is common in Glamorganshire as a name of hills. It is, no doubt, connected with the root of *albus*,[8] though in Switzerland the ALPS are now the green pasturages between the forests and the snow line.[9] ALBANIA, as seen from Corfu, appears as a long snowy range. We may refer the name ALBION to the same root ; it may have been bestowed on the land lying behind the white cliffs visible from the coast of Gaul. ALBANY

---

[1] Evidently from the Sanskrit *grâva-kasas*. The former part of the name seems to be related to the Greek κρύος, and the latter to the Latin *castus*. See Grimm, *Gesch, d. Deut. Spr.* p. 234 ; Pictet, *Orig. Indo-Europ.* part i. p. 73 ; Donaldson, *Varronianus.* p. 53.

[2] Lassen, *Ind. Alterth.* vol. i. p. 16.

[3] Keferstein, *Kelt. Alterth.* vol. ii. p. 186 ; Morris, in *Gentleman's Mag.* for 1789, p. 905. Cf. *Church of England Quarterly*, No. 73, p. 148.

[4] See p. 4, *supra*.

[5] See Stanley, *Sinai and Pal.* p. 18.

[6] Cf. Andermat.

[7] *Al*, high, is common in Shropshire names, e.g. Ercal, Shiffnal, Pecknall, etc. ; Hartshorne, *Sal. Ant.* p. 240.

[8] On this root in river-names, see p. 152, *supra*. The *elves* are the white beings. [? See Kluge *s. v. Alp*.]

[9] The Alps, as well as the Albis in Zurich, seem to have received their names before the meaning of the root was thus restricted. See Meyer, *Ortsnamen*, p. 81.

(Duke of Albany), the old name of Scotland, means probably the hilly land.[1]

The name of the PYRENEES is probably from the Basque word *pyrge*, high ; [2] that of the URAL is from a Tatarian word meaning a belt or girdle.[3] The name of the CARPATHIANS comes, we have seen, from the Sclavonic *gora*, a mountain [?], or *chrbat*, a mountain range.[4] HOR means the mountain ; [5] PISGAH is the height ; [6] SION is the upraised ; HERMON, the lofty peak ; [7] GIBEAH, the hill ; [8] and SAMOS, the lofty.[9]

[1] On the root *alp*, see Pott, *Etym. Forsch.* vol. ii. p. 525 ; Latham, *Germania*, p. 18 ; Diefenbach, *Celtica*, i. p. 19 ; *Orig. Europ.* p. 224 ; Owen, *Welsh Dictionary*, s. v. *alp* ; Davies, *Celtic Researches*, p. 207 ; De Belloguet, *Ethnog.* vol. i. p. 96 ; Duncker, *Orig. Germ.* p. 44 ; Adelung, *Mithridates*, vol. ii. p. 43 ; Arndt, *Europ. Spr.* pp. 241, 242 ; Radlof, *Neue Untersuch*, p. 287 ; Sparschuh, *Berichtigungen*, p. 28.

[2] Arndt, *Europ. Spr.* p. 233. Cf. the Zend *pur*, a mountain.

[3] Müller, *Ugrische Volkstamm*, vol. i. p. 18.

[4] See p. 60, *supra* ; Knobel, *Völkertafel*, p. 44.

[5] Compare the Sclavonic *gora*, and the Greek ὄρος. Stanley, *Sinai and Pal.* p. 494.

[6] *Ibid*, p. 496.

[7] *Ibid*, p. 403.

[8] *Ibid*, pp. 41, 497.

[9] Curtius, *Die Ionier*, p. 28 ; and p. 65, *supra*.

W.P.   Z

LIST OF SOME OF THE
CHIEF SUBSTANTIVAL COMPONENTS OF
LOCAL NAMES

I. NAMES OF MOUNTAINS AND HILLS

PEN ; Welsh ;
CENN ; Gadhelic ; } a head, hence a mountain. *E.g.* Pennigant, Ben
BEN ; Gadhelic ; } Nevis, Kenmore, Kent, Cantal. p. 157.

BRYN ; Welsh ; a brow, hence a ridge. *E.g.* Brandon. p. 159.

DRUM ; From the Erse *druim*, a back or ridge. *E.g.* Dromore, Dundrum.

CEFN ; Cymric ; a back, hence a ridge. *E.g.* Les Cevennes. p. 157.

ARD ; Celtic ; a height. *E.g.* Ardrossan. p. 160.

TOR ; Celtic ; a tower-like rock. *E.g.* Mam Tor. p. 160.

PEAK ; England ;
PIKE ; England ; } allied to the words beak, spike, spit, etc.
PIC ; Pyrenees ; } Spithead is at the end of a long spit
BEC ; Piedmont ; } of sand. *E.g.* Peak of Derbyshire,
PIZ ; Eastern Switzerland ; } Pike o'Stickle, Pic du Midi, Beca di
SPITZ ; Germany ; } Nona, Piz Mortiratsch, Oertler Spitz,
PUY ; Auverne ; } Spitzbergen, Puy de Cantal.

GEBEL ; Arabic ; a mountain. *E.g.* Gibraltar, Gebel Mousa. p. 70

BARROW ;
BOROUGH ; } Anglo-Saxon *beorh*, a hill. Liable to be confused with
BERG ; } names from *burh*, an earthwork. Common in Ger-
} many, rare in England. *E.g.* Spitzbergen, Erzberg,
} Ingleborough in Yorkshire, Brownberg Hill in West-
} moreland, Queensberry in Dumfriesshire. p. 123. Leo,
} *Rectitudines*, p. 65 ; *Codex Dipl.* vol. iii. p. xviii.

GORA ; Sclavonic ; a mountain. *E.g.* Görlitz, Carpathians. p. 60.

CARRICK ; Ireland ;
CRAIG ; Wales ; } Gadhelic, *carraig* ; Cymric, *craig*, a rock or crag.
CRICK ; England ; } *E.g.* Craigruigh, Carrickfergus, Cricklade, p. 160.
CRAU ; Savoy ;

CHLUM ; Sclavonic ; an isolated hill. There are forty-seven places in
Bohemia alone which go by this name, or by its diminutive Chlumetz.
Buttmann, *Ortsnamen*, p. 76.

DAGH or TAGH ; Turkish ; a mountain. *E.g.* Altai, Agridagh, Belurtagh
(the cloud mountains), Mustagh (the ice mountains). Lassen,
Indische Alterth. vol. i. p. 16.

TELL ; Arabic ; a heap, a small hill. Stanley, *Sinai and Pal.* p. 119.

LOW ; England ;
LAW ; Scotch border ; { Anglo-Saxon *hlaw*, a mound, a rising ground. *E.g.* Houndslow, Ludlow, Marlow, Broadlaw. p. 150.

HOW ; Lake district ;
HAUGH ; Northumberland ; { Norse *haugr*, a mound. Old High German *houc*, of which the German *hügel* is a diminutive. *E.g.* Fox How, Silver How. Ferguson, *Northmen*, pp. 54–56 ; Förstemann, *Ortsnamen*, p. 42. p. 122.

HILL ; Anglo-Sax. *hyl*, Norse *holl.* Leo, *Anglo-Saxon Names*, p. 73.

KNOTT ; a small round hill. *E.g.* Ling Knott, Amside Knott.

SLIABH or SLIEVH ; Erse ;
SLIEU ; Manx ; { p. 175. a mountain. *E. g.* Slievh Beg.

KOM ; Arabic ; a high mound.

FELL ; Norse *fjeld* ; a hill-side. *E.g.* Goatfell in Arran. pp. 112, 131.
FELS ; German ; a rock. *E.g.* Drachenfels.

HAGAR ; Arabic ; a stone. p. 67.

KAMEN ; Sclavonic ; a stone.

STONE ; England ;
STEIN ; Germany ;
STEEN ; Netherlands ; { Anglo-Saxon *stan*, a stone. Old German *stain.* *E.g.* Godstone, Ehrenbreitstein, Brunsteen.

DUN ; Celto-Saxon ; a hill fort. *E.g.* London, Dunstable. pp. 157–168.

HERMON ; Hebrew ; lofty.

SION ; Hebrew ; upraised.

RUDGE
RIDGE
RIGGE ; { a back or ridge. Anglo-Saxon *hrycg* ; German *rücken*, a back ; and English *rick*-yard [?]. *E.g.* Reigate, Rugeley, Rudge.

SIERRA ; Arabic. Not, as is usually supposed, from the Latin *serra*, a saw, but from the Arabic *sehrah*, an uncultivated tract. *E.g.* Sierra Nevada. Gayangos, *Dynasties*, vol. i. p. 546. [No doubt the word is the old Spanish *Sierra*, a mountain, a saw (Minsheu, 1623), with reference to the jagged or serrated outline of a ridge. The Greek πείων, a saw, is used similarly in the Septuagint.]

CORDILLERA ; Spanish ; a chain.

HORN ; German ; a peak. *E.g.* Matterhorn, Schreckhorn, Finsteraarhorn, Wetterhorn.

DODD ; Lake district ; a mountain with a round summit. *E.g.* Dodd Fell, Great Dodd.

MONADH ; Gaelic ;
MYNYDD ; Welsh ; { a bald head. *E.g.* Monadh liadh, Inverness. Mynydd-Mawr, Carnarvonshire.

MULL ; Scotland ; Gaelic *maol* ; a headland. *E.g.* Mull of Cantyre.
MOEL ; Wales ; a round hill. *E.g.* Moel Siabod.

ROG ; Sclavonic ; a horn. Buttmann, *Ortsnamen*, p. 61.

DENT ; French, a tooth. *E.g.* Dent du Midi.

BLUFF ; American. A bluff, as distinguished from a hill, is the escarpment formed by a river running through a table-land.

MONT ; France ;
MONTE ; Italy ; { a mountain. Latin *mons.* *E.g.* Mont Blanc, Montmartre, Monte Rosa.

KNOCK ; Gadhelic ; a hill. *E.g.* Knocknows, Knockduff.

BALM ; Celtic ; an overhanging wall of rock ; a cave : not uncommon in Switzerland and France. *E.g.* Col de Balm. Meyer, *Ortsnamen*,

p. 81 ; Adelung, *Mithridates*, vol. ii.   p. 45 ; Diefenbach, *Celtica*, i. p. 192.

SCAR ; Norse ; a cliff.   *E.g.* Scarborough   p. 114.
GOURNA ; Arabic ; a mountain promontory.
NESS ; Norse ; a nose or headland.   *E.g.* Wrabness, Sheerness.   p. 114.
HOO ; England ; Anglo-Saxon *ho*.   A hoo or heal is a spit of land running into the sea.   *Codex Diplom.* vol. iii. p. xxxi.
RAS ; Arabic ; a cape.   p. 72.
ROSS ; Celtic ; a promontory.   *E.g.* Rossberg, Kinross, Roseneath, Melrose, Ross.   p. 159.

II. PLAINS

GWENT ; Celtic ; a plain.   *E.g.* Winchester.   p. 164.
CON ; Ireland ; from the Erse *cluain*, a plain surrounded by bog or water.   *E.g.* Clonmel, Cloyne. It occurs four times in Shropshire. *E.g.* Clunn, Clunbury.
PLUN ; Sclavonic ; ⎫ a plain.   *E.g.* Plöner See, in Holstein.
PLON ; Sclavonic ; ⎭   Buttmann, *Ortsnamen*, p. 79.
LAN ; Celtic ; ⎫ a plain.
LAND ; English ; ⎭   p. 163
DOL ; Celtic ; a plain.   *E.g.* Toulouse, Dolberry.   p. 159.
BLAIR ; Gadhelic ; a plain clear of wood.   *E.g.* Blair Atholl.
SHARON ; Hebrew ; a plain.
TIR ; Welsh ; land.   *E.g.* Cantire.   p. 146.
BELED ; Arabic ; a district.
GAU ; Teutonic ; a district. Cf. the Greek γυία.   *E.g.* Spengay in Cambridgeshire, Wormegay in Norfolk. Pictet, *Orig. Indo-Europ.* part ii. pp. 15, 505.   pp. 84, 94.
MAN ; Celtic ; a district.   *E.g.* Maine, Manchester.   p. 163.
MAT ; Swiss ; ⎫
MAES ; Welsh ; ⎪ a field.   *E.g.* Andermat, Masham, Armagh, Maynooth,
MAGH ; Erse ; ⎬   Marmagen.   pp. 165, 166.
MAG ; Gaulish ; ⎭
ING ; Anglo-Saxon ; a meadow.   *E.g.* Deeping.   p. 94.
SAVANNAH ; Spanish ; a meadow.
AGH ; Ireland ; ⎫ From Erse *achadh*, a field,   *E.g.* Ardagh, Auchin-
AUCH ; Scotland ; ⎭ leek. See Sullivan, *Dict. of Derivations*, p. 282.
AC ; sometimes a corruption of *agh* ; sometimes of the Celtic *ach* or *axe* water ; sometimes of the Teutonic *aha* or *ahi* ; more often the Celtic derivative particle. Nine out of ten of the village-names of Western and Central France exhibit this derivative suffix. See Zeuss, *Gramm. Celt.* vol. ii. p. 771 ; Förstemann, *Ortsnamen*, p. 29.

III. FORESTS

HOLZ ; German ; ⎫ a copse.   *E.g.* Bagshot, Sparsholt,   p. 254.
HOLT ; Anglo-Saxon ; ⎭   *Codex. Dipl.* vol. iii. p. xxxii.
HURST ; England ; ⎫ thick wood. Anglo-Saxon *hyrst*.   *E.g.* Lyndhurst,
HORST ; Germany ; ⎭   Penshurst. Ingram, *Sax. Chron,* p. 427.   p. 255.

HART ; Germany ; ⎫
CHART ; England ; ⎭ a forest. *E.g.* Hunhart, ˙Seal Chart. p. 255.

BOR ; Sclavonic ; a forest. *E.g.* Bohrau. Buttmann, *Ortsnamen*, p. 83.

DROWO ; Sclavonic ; a wood. *E.g.* Drewitz.

GOLA ; Sclavonic ; a wood. *E.g.* Gollwitz.

WEALD ; England ; ⎫
WOLD ; England ; ⎪ woodland ; related to *holt.* Anglo-Saxon *wudu,*
WALD ; Germany ; ⎬ and *weald* ; Old High German, *witu.* *E.g.*
WOOD ; England ; ⎪ Waltham, Walden, The Cotswolds, Wootton,
WOUDE ; Netherlands ; ⎭ Schwarzwald, Emswoude. pp. 256, 255.

COED ; Welsh ; a wood. *E.g.* Bettws y Coed, Cotswold Hills, Catlow. p. 362·

LEY ; England ; ⎧ an open place in a wood. Anglo-Saxon *leah,* *E.g.*
LOO ; Belgium ; ⎨ Leighton, Hadleigh ; Waterloo, Venloo. pp. 255.
⎩ 360 ; Leo, *Rectitudines,* p. 86 ; Morris, *Local Names,*
p. 46.

DEN ; Celto-Saxon ; a deep wooded valley. *Den* and *dun* are from the
same root, but the meanings are converse, like those of *dike* and
ditch.

MONEY ; Ireland ; from Erse *muine,* a brake or shaw. *E.g.* Moneyrea,
Moneymore.

ACRE ; a field. Latin *ager,* Low Latin *acra.* *E.g.* Longacre.

SHAW ; England ; a shady place, a wood. Anglo-Saxon *sceaga* ; Norse
skogr. *E.g.* Bagshaw. Liable to be confused with *haw.*
pp. 133, 254.

HAW ; German *gehaw,* a place where the trees have been *hewn.* Nearly
the same as field. See Vilmar, *Ortsnamen,* p. 265 ; Förstemann,
Ortsnamen, p. 79. Cf. Leo, *Anglo-Saxon Names,* p. 115.

FIELD ; Anglo-Saxon *feld,* a forest clearing, where the trees have been
felled. *E.g.* Sheffield, Enfiéld. pp. 112, 255.

ROYD ; Teutonic. Probably land that has been *ridded* of trees. Low
Latin *terra rodata.* *E.g.* Huntroyd, Holroyd, Ormeroyd. Names
in *rod, rode,* or *roth* are very common in Hesse ; liable to be confused with *rithe,* running water, and *rhyd,* a ford, q.v. See Förstemann, *Ortsnamen,* p. 79 ; Vilmar, *Ortsnamen,* pp. 278, 279 ; Charnock, *Local Etymol.* p. 229.

LUND ; Norse ; a sacred grove. *E.g.* Lundgarth. p. 234.

NEMET ; Celtic, a sacred grove. *E.g.* Nismes, Nymet Rowland. p. 234.

IV. VALLEYS

NANT ; Cymric ; a valley. *E.g.* Nant-frangon. p. 163

GLYN ; Wales ; ⎫
GLEN ; Gaelic ; ⎭ a narrow valley. *E.g.* Glynneath, Glencoe.

STRATH ; Gaelic ; a broad valley. *E.g.* Strathclyde, Stratherne.

THAL ; German ; ⎫ a valley. *E.g.* Lonsdale, Arundel, Frankenthal.
DALE ; Northumbrian ; ⎪ Names in *dol* are very common in Bohemia
DELL ; Southumbrian ; ⎬ and Moravia. p. 160. Buttmann, *Orts-*
DOL ; Sclavonic ; ⎭ *namen,* p. 79.

VYED ; Malta ; ⎰ Arabic *wadi,* a ravine, valley, or river. *E.g.* Guadal-
GUAD ; Spain ; ⎱ quiver. p. 75.

COMBE ; Celto-Saxon ;) a bowl-shaped valley. *E.g.* Wycombe, Cwm
CWM ; Welsh ; ∫   Bechan.   p. 161.
KOTL ; Sclavonic ; a kettle or combe. Buttmann, *Ortsnamen*, p. 79.
COP ; Celtic ; a hollow or *cup. E.g.* Warcop.
DEN ; from Celto-Saxon *denu*, a deep-wooded valley. *E.g.* Tenterden.
                                               pp. 161, 255.
GILL ; Lake District ; a ravine. *E.g.* Aygill.

V. RIVERS AND WATERS

A ; Anglo-Saxon *ea* ; Norse *a* ; Old High German *aha* ; Gothic *ahva*,
    water. Cognate with Latin *aqua. E.g.* Greta, Werra.   p. 120.
AVON ; Celtic ; a river.   p. 139.
DWR ; Cymric ; water.   p. 141.
ESK ; Celtic ; water.   p. 144.
BURN ; Anglo-Saxon ; ⎫
BRUNNEN ; German ; ⎬ a stream. *E.g.* Blackburn, Tyburn, Hachborn.
BORN ; in Hesse ;[1] ⎭
BROOK ; from Anglo-Saxon *bróc*, a rushing stream.
                     ⎫ a ⠂ small stream. *E.g.* Welbeck, Holbeck,
BECK ; Northumbria ; ⎪ Caudebec. There are fifty names in *batch*
BACH ; Germany ; ⎬ in Shropshire, as Comberbatch, Coldbatch,
BATCH ; Mercia ; ⎪ and Snailbatch (*i.e.* Schnell-bach).
BEC ; Normandy ; ⎭ p. 132 ; Hartshorne, *Salopia Antiqua*, p. 240 ;
                           Notes and Queries, vol. i. p. 267.
REKA ; Sclavonic ; river. *E.g.* River Regen. p. 147.
WODA ; Sclavonic ; water. *E.g.* River Oder. Buttmann, *Ortsnamen*, p. 114.
RUN ; Anglo-American ; a brook. *E.g.* Bull's Run.
CREEK ; Anglo-American ; a small river. *E.g.* Salt Creek, p. 20, *supra.*
FORK ; Anglo-American ; a large affluent. *E.g.* North Fork.
PARA ; Brazilian ; a river. *E.g.* Parahiba, Paraguay, Parana, Parany-
    buna.
RITHE ; Anglo-Saxon ; running water. *E.g.* Meldrith, Shepreth, etc., in
    Cambridgeshire. See ROYD, p. 341, *supra.*
FORCE ; Northumbria ;) a waterfall. *E.g.* Airy Force, Skogar Foss, p.
FOSS ; Iceland ; ∫   160.
FLEET ; England ; ⎫ Anglo-Saxon *fleót*, a flowing stream. *E.g.* North-
FLEUR ; Normandy ; ⎬ fleet, Byfleet, Harfleur. See pp. 132, 193.
VLEY ; Cape ; ⎭ Leo, *Rectitudines*, p. 81 ; Ingram, *Sax. Chron.*
                   p. 426 ; Förstemann, *Ortsnamen*, p. 36.
GANGA ; India ; a river. In Ceylon most of the river-names terminate in
    ganga. The Ganges is the river ["goer"].
BIRKET ; Arabic ; a lake.
LINN ; Celtic ; a deep pool. *E.g.* Lincoln, Linlithgow, Dublin, Lynn.
                                                 p. 153.
VAT ; Hebrides ; a small lake. Norse *vatn*, water. *E.g.* Ollevat, p. 172.
TARN ; Lake District ; a small mountain lake, lying like a tear on the
    face of the hill. [?] Norse *tiörn*, a tear. *E.g.* Blentarn.
KELL ; England ; ⎫
WELL ; England ; ⎬ a place whence water flows forth. Cf. the Wel-
QUELLE ; Germany ; ⎭ land, which is a tidal stream.

AIN ; Arabic ; a fountain. *E.g.* Engedi, the fountain of the kid ; Enrogel, the fountain of the foot. pp. 71, 80.

HAMMAM ; Turkish ; hot springs.

BEER ; Hebrew ; } a well. *E.g.* Beersheba, Beyrout. Dr. Stanley says
BIR ; Arabic ; } it is something *bored* [!]. *Sinai and Pal.* pp. 147, 512. p. 72.

BAHR ; Arabic, a canal.

BALA ; Welsh ; effluence of a river from a lake.

ABER ; Welsh ; } a confluence of two rivers, or of a river and the
INVER ; Gadhelic ; } sea. *E.g.* Abergavenny, Inverness. p. 174.

CONDATE ; Old Celtic ; confluence of two rivers. *E.g.* Condé, Ghent. Zeuss, *Gram. Celt.* p. 994 ; Adelung, *Mithridates*, vol. ii. p. 54.

WICK ; Norse ; a bay. *E.g.* Sandwich. p. 113.

FORD ; England ; } Norse *fiord*, an arm of the sea. *E.g.* Orford, Haver-
FJORD ; Iceland ; } ford, Faxa Fjord. p. 112.

OVER ; Anglo-Saxon, *ofer* ; German, *ufer* ; a shore. *E.g.* Hanover, Overyssel, Over near Cambridge, Wendover. Andover is not from the root *ofer*, but *waere*. See *Sax. Chron.* ; *Cod. Dipl.* vol. iii. p. xxxiv. ; Morris, *Local Names*, p. 38, Förstemann, *Ortsnamen*, p. 39. p. 97, *supra.*

POOL ; } Welsh *pwl*, an inlet, or pool. *E.g.* Pill in Somerset, Poole in
PILL ; } Dorset, Bradpole, Pwlhelli, Liverpool.

SHORE ; *e.g.* Shoreham.

OR ; Anglo-Saxon *ora*, the shore of a river or sea. *E.g.* Bognor, Cumnor, Oare near Hastings, Elsinore. Windsor was anciently Windlesora, the winding shore. *Ore* in Iceland denotes a narrow strip of land between two waters. Leo, *Rectitudines*, p. 79 ; Laing, *Heimskringla*, vol. i. p. 119 ; Ingram. *Sax. Chron.* v. 428 ; Charnock, *Local Etymol.* p. 298.

TRA ; Erse ; a strand. *E.g.* Tralee, Ballintra.

MERE ; Anglo-Saxon ; } a lake, a marsh. *E.g.* Foulmire, Mersey, Morton,
MOOR ; Anglo-Saxon ; } Blackmore.

JASOR ; Sclavonic ; a marsh. Buttmann, *Ortsnamen*, p. 107.

RUIMNE ; Celtic ; a marsh. *E.g.* Romney. pp. 152, 248.

RHOS ; Celtic ; a moor. *E.g.* Rossall, Rusholme. p. 159.

VI. ISLANDS

YNYS ; Welsh ; } an island. *E.g.* Inchiquin and Inchkeith in Scot-
INNIS ; Gadhelic ; } land ; Enniskillen, Ennismore, Ennis, and at least
ENNIS ; Irish ; } 100 names in Ireland, as well, perhaps, as Erin
INCH ; Scotch ; } and Albion. pp. 119, 250.

EY ; } an island. From the Anglo-Saxon, *ea*, Norse *oe*. Eyot is the
A ; } diminutive of *ey*, and ait the contraction of *eyot*. *E.g.* Ey in
OE ; } Suffolk, Sheppey, Rona, Faroe, Colonsay. pp. 114, 120, 247.
AY ; }

AIRE ; }
AYRE ; } a small river-island of shingle or sand. *E.g.* Saltaire, Stonaire.
EYRE ; }

HOLM ; Norse ; an island in a river. *E.g.* Flatholm in the Severn. p. 114.

JEZIRAH ; Arabic ; an island. *E.g.* Algiers, Algeziras. p. 72.

VII. ROADS, BRIDGES, FORDS

GATE ; England ; ⎫
GUT ; Kent ; ⎬ a passage, a road or street. *E.g.* Reigate, Gatton,
GHAT ; India ; ⎭ Ramsgate, Calcutta. pp. 178, 179.
GHAUT ; India

ATH ; Erse ; a ford. *E.g.* Athlone.

RHYD ; Welsh ; a ford.

WATH ; Northumbria ; a ford. Related to the verb to *wade.*   p. 179.

FORD ; England ;   *E.g.* Oxford, Frankfurt, Lemförde.   p. 180.
FUHRT ; Germany ;   Buttmann, *Ortsnamen,* p. 17 ; Bender, *Ortsna-*
FÖRDE ; Hanover ;   *men,* p. 118 ; Ingram, *Saxon Chron.* p. 426 ;
                        Förstemann, *Ortsnamen,* p. 38.

PONT ; Welsh and French ; a bridge. *E.g.* Pontaberglaslyn.   p. 180.

MOST ; Sclavonic ; a bridge. *E.g.* Babimost, Motzen, Maust. Buttmann,
Ortsnamen, p. 135.

BRIDGE ; England ;   ⎧ *E.g.* Brixton, Bruges, Innsprück, Weybridge,
BRÜCKE ; Germany ; ⎨ See p. 254 ; Bender, *Ortsnamen,* p. 119 ; In-
                  ⎩ gram, *Sax. Chron.* p. 425.

BRIVA ; Old Celtic ; a bridge.

BAB ; Arabic ; a gate ; *E.g.* Babelmandeb.   p. 180.

STREET ; Latin and Saxon ; a road. *E.g.* Stretton, Stratford. p. 177.

SARN ; Welsh ; a road. *E.g.* Sarn Helen.

VIII. BOUNDARIES

TWISTLE ; Northumbria ; a boundary. *E.g.* Entwistle, Birchtwistle,
Extwistle. Whitaker, *History of Whalley,* p. 377.

GILL ; Northumbria ; Norse, *gil,* a ravine. *E.g.* Dungeon Gill.

STONE ; Anglo-Saxon and Norse, *stan.* *E.g.* Stanton, Godstone. Staines
is so called from the Stones bounding the river jurisdiction of the
Lord Mayor.

KAMEN ; Sclavonic ; a stone. *E.g.* Chemnitz. Buttmann, *Ortsnamen,*
pp. 61, 103.

HAGAR ; Arabic ; a stone.

GISR ; Arabic ; a dyke.

DYKE ; Anglo-Saxon ; a ditch. *E.g.* Wansdyke.   p. 181.

HATCH ; England ; a *hitch*-gate. Cf. the French, *hèche.* This is a common suffix in the neighbourhood of ancient forests. *E.g.* Westhatch
in Somerset, Pilgrims' Hatch in Essex ; Colney Hatch in Middlesex
was the gate at the southern extremity of Enfield Chase. See *Notes
and Queries,* vol. x. pp. 107, 197, 238, 316.

CLOUGH ; Erse *cloch,* a stone. *E.g.* Cloghan, Claughton in Yorkshire.

MARK ; Indo-European ; a boundary. *E.g.* Denmark, Altmark. p. 186-7.

IX. HABITATIONS AND INCLOSURES

HEIM ; Germany ; ⎫
HAM ; England ; ⎪ a home. *E.g.* Hocheim, Buckingham, Rysum,
HEN ; Picardy ; ⎬ Hamburg.   pp. 87, 94, 110.
UM ; Friesland ; ⎭

TON ; Anglo-Saxon *tun*, an inclosure. Hence a village.   pp. 84, 94.

WICK ; Anglo-Saxon *vîc*, an abode. Related to the Latin *vicus*. p. 113.
WAS ; Sclavonic ; a village. *E.g.* Weska, Wasowetz. Buttmann,
   Ortsnamen, p. 145.

WIKI ; Sclavonic ; a market. *E.g.* Fourteen places called Wieck. Buttmann, *Ortsnamen*, p. 139.

WEILER ; Germany ; ⎫
VILLIERS ; France ; ⎪ an abode, a house. *E.g.* Berweiler, Hardivil-
VILLE ; Normandy ; ⎬ liers, Haconville, Chiswill, Kettlewell.
WILL ; ⎫ ⎪
WELL ; ⎬ England ; ⎭   pp. 112, 115.

BALLY ; ⎫ Gadhelic *baile*, an abode. Equivalent to the Cymric *tre* and
BAL ; ⎬ the Norse *by*. *E.g.* Balleymena, Balbriggan. pp. 175, 193.
BALLA ; ⎭ Sullivan, *Dict. of Der.* p. 283.

ABAD ; India ; an abode. *E.g.* Allahabad.
BY ; England ; ⎫
BŒUF ; Normandy ; ⎬ Norse, *byr*, an abode. *E.g.* Derby, Elbœuf,
BÜREN ; Germany ; ⎭ Amelsburen.   pp. 110, 125.

BOTTLE ; ⎫ England ; ⎫ Anglo-Saxon and Norse, *botl*, a house, from
BOLD ; ⎬ ⎪ *bytlian*, to build. Rare in Anglo-Saxon
BÜTTEL ; Germany ; ⎬ names. *E.g.* Newbottle, Wolfenbüttel,
BLOD ; Friesland ; ⎭ Bothwell. *Cod. Dipl.* vol. iii. p. xviii ;
   Bender, *Ortsnamen*, p. 132.

BUS ; Sclavonic ; a dwelling. *Bus* is very common in Sclavonic districts. *E.g.* Trebus, Lebbus, Putbus. Buttmann, *Ortsnamen*, p. 130.

BUDA ; Sclavonic ; a hut. *E.g.* Buda, Budin, Budan, Budkowitz. Buttmann, *Ortsnamen*, p. 129.

BOD ; ⎫
BOS ; ⎬ Cymric ; a house. *E.g.* Bodmin, Bodwrog, Boscawen, p. 163.

STAN ; Persian ; a place. *E.g.* Kurdistan, Hindostan, Beloochistan, Affghanistan.

STEAD ; England ; ⎫ Anglo-Saxon *stede*, a place. *E.g.* Hampstead,
STADT ; Germany ; ⎬ Darmstadt.

STOKE ; ⎫ Anglo-Saxon *stoc*, a stockaded place. *E.g.* Bristow or Bristol,
STOW ; ⎬ Chepstow, Tavistock, Stockholm, p. 121 ; Ingram, *Sax. Chron.* p. 428.

SET ; from Anglo-Saxon *seta*, a settlement. *E.g.* Dorset.   p. 50.
SETER ; Norse ; ⎫ a seat or dwelling. *E.g.* Ellanseter, Seatollar,
STER ; Norse ; ⎬ Ulster.   pp. 119, 127.
SSEDLO ; Sclavonic ; a possession. *E.g.* Sedlitz. Buttmann, *Ortsnamen*, p. 144.

PATAM ; India ; a city. *E.g.* Patra, Seringapatam.

HAGEN ; Germany ; ⎫ a place surrounded by a hedge ; a park. *E.g.*
HAY ; ⎬ England ; ⎬ Hagendorn, La Haye Sainte. p. 122. Bender,
HAIGH ; ⎭ *Ortsnamen*, p. 128.

PARK ; Celto-Saxon, p. 　. Diefenbach, *Celtica*, i. p. 146.

TRE ; Cymric ; a village. 　*E.g.* Tredegar, Treves. 　　　　　p. 162.

HOUSE ; England ;　　　　⎧ A house. *E.g.* the portage at the falls of the
HAUS ;　　　⎫ Germany ;⎨ Rhine is Schaffhausen, ' at the ship-houses '.
HAUSEN ;　　⎬　　　　　　The dative plural *hausen* is the commonest
HUUS ; Norway ;　　　　　 suffix in German names. Förstemann,
　　　　　　　　　　　　⎩ *Ortsnamen*, p. 84 ; Vilmar, *Ortsnamen*, pp.
　　　　　　　　　　　　　264, 273.

TY ; Welsh ; a house. 　　　　　　　　　　　　　　　　　p. 163.

JAZA ; Sclavonic ; a house. 　*E.g.* Jäschen, Jäschwitz. Buttmann, *Ortsnamen*, p. 131.

DOM ; Sclavonic ; a house.

BETH ; Hebrew ; a house. 　*E.g.* Bethany (house of dates), Bethlehem
(house of bread), Bethsaida (house of fish), Bethel (house of God),
Bethharon (house of caves), Bethphage (house of figs).

COTE ; Anglo-Saxon ; a mud cottage. Coton is the plural of cote. *E.g.*
Fosscot, Coton Hill in Shropshire. 　　　　　　　　　p. 257.

SELL ; Anglo-Saxon ; a cottage, a little superior to *cote*. Leo, *Anglo-
Sax. Names*, p. 54.

HALL ; Anglo-Saxon ;⎧ a stone house. *E.g.* Coggeshall, Mildenhall,
SALL ; Anglo-Saxon ;⎨ Kensal, Walsall. Leo, *Anglo-Saxon Names*,
　　　　　　　　　　⎩ pp. 52, 54.

CLERE ; Anglo-Norman ; a royal or episcopal residence on a lofty hill.
Almost the only Anglo-Norman suffix. *E.g.* Highclere, Burghclere,
Kingsclere. See *Notes and Queries*, vol. i. p. 400.

SCALE ; Norse ; a shepherd's hut. Cf. the Scotch, a *shealing*. *E.g.*
Portinscale, Scalloway. 　　　　　　　　　　　　　p. 209.

FOLD ; Anglo-Saxon ; an inclosure made of *felled* trees. 　　　p. 86.

WORTH ; Anglo-Saxon and German ; an inclosure. *E.g.* Tamworth,
Königsworth. 　　　　　　　p. 86. Leo, *Rectitudines*, p. 52.

GADIR ; Phœnician ; an inclosure. *E.g.* Cadiz. 　　　　　　p. 67.

CARTHA ; Phœnician ; an inclosed place, a city. *E.g.* Carthage. p. 66.

GARTH ; Norse ;　　　⎧ an inclosed place. *E.g.* Fishguard, Apple-
YARD ; Anglo-Saxon ;⎨ garth. pp. 121, 159, 185. Bender, *Orts-
　　　　　　　　　　⎩ namen*, p. 134.

GOROD ; Russian ;⎫　　　　⎫ Related to *gora*, a mountain, just as *burg*
GROD ; Polish ;　　⎬ a burgh⎮ is related to *berg*. *E.g.* Grätz in Styria,
GRATZ ; Sclavonic ; a town ;⎬ Königsgrätz in Bohemia, Novgorod
HRAD ; Bohemian ; a castle ;⎮ (new town), Belgrade (white castle),
　　　　　　　　　　　　　　⎭ Stargard (Aldborough). 　　p. 86.

BARROW ;⎫
BURG ;　　⎮ From the Anglo-Saxon *burh, buruh*, and *byrig*, an earth-
BOROUGH ;⎮ work, hence a fortified town. Related to the Celtic
BURY ;　　⎬ *briga* and the Sclavonic *gorod*. See p. 87 *supra*.
BURGH ;　⎮ Bender, *Ortsnamen*, p. 135 ; Leo, *Rectitudines*, p. 34 ;
BROUGH ;⎭ Ingram, *Sax. Chron.* p. 425.

CHESTER ; Saxon ;　⎫
CESTER ; Mercian ;⎬ From the Latin *castra*. *E.g.* Winchester, Leicester,
CASTER ; Anglian ;⎭ Doncaster. 　　　　　　　　　　pp. 177, 183.

CAER ; Welsh ;　　⎫ Either related to the preceding, or to the Erse
CAR ; Welsh ;　　⎬ *cat̃air*, a fortress. *E.g.* Caermarthen, Carlise,
KER ; Brezonec ;　⎭ p. 184.

DON ; Celto-Saxon ; a hill fort. *E.g.* London, Dunmow. p. 157.

LIS ; Gadhelic ; an earthen fort ; equivalent to *bury*. *E.g.* Lismore, Listowel, and 300 names in Ireland.

RATH ; Erse ; an earthen fort, or mound. *E.g.* Rathboyne, Rathlin. See Sullivan, *Dict. of Deriv.* p. 293.

KASR ; Arabic ; a fort.

KALAT ; Arabic ; a castle. *E.g.* Calatagirone, Alcala. See pp. 70, 76.

PEEL ; Celtic ; a stronghold.

CIVITA ; Italy ; }
CIUDAD ; Spain ; } Latin, *civitas.* *E.g.* Civita Vecchia, Ciudad Rodrigo.

MEDINA ; Arabic ; a chief city. *E.g.* Medina Sidonia. p. 76.

POOR ; India ; a city ; Sanskrit, *pura,* related to πόλις. *E.g.* Singapoor.

POLIS ; Greek ; a city. *E.g.* Constantinople, Grenoble, Naples. p. 272.

BEN I ; Arabic ; sons of. Common prefix to the names of Arab villages *E.g.* Benihassan. p. 76, *supra* ; Wilton, *Negeb,* p. 140.

ING ; England ; }
INGEN ; Germany ; } sons of. *E.g.* Reading, Tübingen. pp. 88–103.

MENZIL ; Arabic ; a station. p. 71.

RAHL ; Arabic ; a village, or house. pp. 73, 74.

KAFR ; Arabic ; a village.

BENDER ; Arabic ; a market-town.

COLN ; Latin, *colonia.* *E.g.* Lincoln, Cologne. p. 185.

HIPPO ; Phœnician ; a walled town. p. 68.

HAZOR ; Arabic and Hebrew ; an inclosure for cattle in the desert. A common prefix in the names of the settlements of the fixed Arabs. *E.g.* Hazar-Ithman, Hazar-Aman. Wilton, *Negeb,* pp. 75, 99.

RUP ; Holstein ; }
THORPE ; } }
THROP ; } England ; } Norse ; a village. *E.g.* Althorp, Ibthrop,
TROP ; } } Rorup, Wanderup, Dusseldorf. Buttmann,
DORF ; Germany ; } *Ortsnamen,* p. 21. pp. 111, 115, 121, 131, *supra*

TOFT ; Danelagh ; } Norse ; an inclosure ; related to turf. *E.g.* Lowestoft,
TOT ; Normandy ; } Plumetot. pp. 111, 131.

THWAITE ; Norse ; a forest clearing. *E.g.* Finsthwaite. p. 111.

LEBEN ; Germany ; a place to live in. This suffix is very prevalent north of the Hartz. See Gerland, in Kühn's *Zeitschrift,* vol. x ; Förstemann, *Ortsnamen,* p. 107 ; Latham, *English Language,* vol. i. p. 125.

STAPLE ; England ; a market. *E.g.* Dunstable, Etaples. p. 265.

KAHN ; Arabic ; a market.

MULLEN ; Gadhelic ; a mill. *E.g.* Mullingar, Mulintra.

MLYN ; Sclavonic ; a mill. *E.g.* Mlinek. Buttmann, *Ortsnamen,* p. 133.

MASARA ; Arabic ; a mill.

CHURCH ; Southumbria. }
KIRK ; Northumbria. } *E.g.* Church Stretton, Kircudbright, p. 239.

KIL ; Gadhelic ; a cell ; a church. *E.g.* Killin. p. 238.

LLAN ; Cymric ; an inclosure ; a church. *E.g.* Llanberis. pp. 163, 238.

MOUTIERS ; France ; }
MINSTER ; England ; } a monastery. *E.g.* Westminster, Mo-
MONASTER ; Ireland, Greece ; } nasterevin in Ireland. p. 244.

DEIR ; Arabic ; a house ; a monastery. p. 72.

GHAR ; Arabic ; a grotto. *E.g.* Trafalgar.   pp. 72, 78.
HITHE ; Anglo-Saxon ; ⎱ a wharf. *E.g.* Greenhithe, Erith, Lambeth,
HAFEN ; Norse ;   ⎰   Copenhagen, Kurische Haf. pp. 132, 248.
WERP ; from the Danish *hverve*, to turn, a word which appears in the
       name of Cape Wrath. *E.g.* Antwerp. See pp. 276, 278, *supra* ;
       Wedgwood, in *Philolog. Proc.* vol. vi. p. 89.
MARSA ; Arabic ; a port. *E.g.* Marsala.   pp. 72, 291.
DAM ; an embankment. *E.g.* Rotterdam, Amsterdam.

APPENDIX A

List *of* Names *of* Ancent Tribes *preserved in the* Names *of* Modern Cities *and* Provinces.

(See p. 52.)

Ancient Names.	Modern Cities and Provinces.
Abrincatui,	Avranches.
Ambiani,	Amiens.
Andecavi,	Angers in Anjou.
Arverni,	Auverne.
Atrebates,	Arras in Artois.
Ausci,	Auch.
Bajucasses,	Bayeux ?
Bellovaci,	Beauvais.
Bigerrones,	Bagnères de Bigorre
Bituriges-Vivisci,[1]	Bordeaux ?
Bituriges-Cubi,	Bourges ? Berri.
Boii,	Buch.
Brannovices,	Briennois.
Brixantes,	Bregentz.
Cadurci,	Cahors in Quercy.
Caletes,	Caux.
Carnutes,	Chartres.
Cassii,	Cashiobury.
Catalauni,	Chalons.
Caturiges,[1]	Chorgres.
Cenomani,	Le Mans.
Centrones,	Centron.
Cimbri,	Cambrilla, Quimper.
Conembricæ,	Coimbra.
Consorranni,	Conserans.
Convenæ,	Comminge.
Curosolites,	Corseult.
Damnonii,	Devon.
Diablintes,	Jubleins.
Durocasses,	Dreux.
Durotriges,	Dorchester in Dorset.
Eburovices,	Evreux.
Elusates,	Eause.

[1] The second portion of this name is the Celtic *rix*, a king, which is found in the names of Ambiorix, Dumnorix, Orgetorix, Rigomagus, etc. See Zeuss, *Gram. Celt.* vol. i. p. 25, Rajah, rex, reich, and rich, and th. names Austria, Richard, are cognate words.

Ancient Names.	*Modern Cities and Provinces.*
Gabali,	Javaux in Gévaudan.
Huicii,	Worcester.
Iberi,	Ebro.
Iceni,	Iken, Ickborough, Ickworth.
Lexovii,	Lisieux.
Lemovices,	Limoges in Limousin.
Lingones,	Langres.
Mediomatrici,	Metz.
Meldi,	Meaux.
Namnetes,	Nantes.
Nantuates.	Nantueil.
Parisii,	Paris.
Petrocorii,	Perigueux in Perigord.
Pictones,	Poictiers in Poitou.
Remi,	Rheims.[1]
Rhedones,	Rennes.
Rothomagi,	Rouen.
Ruteni,	Rhodez in Rovergne.
Santones,	Saintes in Saintonge.
Scoti,	Scotland.
Seduni,	Sion or Sitten.
Selgovæ,	Solway.
Senones,	Sens.
Sesavii, or Saji,	Séez.
Silvanectes,	Senlis.
Suessiones,	Soissons.
Taurini,	Turin, or Torino.
Tolosates,	Toulouse.
Treviri,	Trêves, or Trier.
Tricasses,	Troyes.
Tungri,	Tongres.
Turones,	Tours in Touraine.
Vassates, or Vasarii,	Bazas.
Velavii,	Velay.
Veliocasses,	Vexin.
Veneti,	Vannes in La Vendée.
Veneti,	Venice.
Veromandui,	Vermand.
Viducasses,	Vieux, near Caen.

On these and other more doubtful names of the same class, see Contzen *Die Wanderungen der Kelten,* pp. 9–18 ; Zeuss, *Die Deutschen,* pp. 204–206 ; Glück, *Die bei Caius Julius Cæsar vorkommende keltischen Namen.*

[1] Dean Milman states that Rheims took its name from St. Remigius. A strange ὕστερον πρότερον. See *History of Latin Christianity,* vol. i. p. 257.

APPENDIX B

See p. 95.

Family Names.	French Villages.	English Villages.
Æblings	Eblinghem	Ablington, *Glouc. and Wilts.*
Æclings	Aeclinghen	Acklington, *Northumberland.*
Ælings	{ Alencthun. { Alenthun	{ Allington, *Kent, Hants, Dorset,* { *Devon, Wilts, Lincoln.*
Æscings, the royal race of Kent	{ Assinghen. { Azincourt (the { battle-field)	{ Essington, *Staff.* { Essentona (*Exon' Domesday*). { Æscingas (*Codex Diplomaticus,* { *Surrey.* No. 111).
Æslings	Eslinghen	{ Ashlingham, *Kent.* { Esselingaforda (*Exon' Domesday*). { Æslingaham (*Cod. Dipl.* No. 111).
Aldrings	Audrehem.	Aldrington, *Sussex.*
Adings	{ Autingues. { Audinghen { Audincthun	} Addington, *Northants.* } Adingtone (*Kent, Domesday*).
Bafings	{ Bayenghem { Baincthun. { Bainghen (2)	{ Bavington, *Northumberland.* { Bevington, *Warwick.* { Bevingford, *Sussex.*
Basings	{ Bazinghen { Bezinghen	{ Bassingham, *Lincoln.* { Basing, *Hants.* { Bessingham, *Norfolk.* { Besingas (*Cod. Dipl.* No. 994). { Basingeham (*Domesday, Sussex* { *and Lincoln*).
Bælings	Balinghem	{ Ballingham, *Hereford.* { Ballingdon, *Essex.* { Belingham (*Sussex, Domesday*). { Belintona (*Hertfordshire, Dom.*).
Beorlings	Barlinghem	{ Barling, *Kent and Essex.* { Bœrlingas (*Codex Dipl. Kent,* No. { 152).
Berlings	Berlinghen	{ Birlingham, *Worcestershire.* { Berling, *Sussex.* { Birling, *Kent and Northumberland.*

Family Names.	French Villages.	English Villages.
Bonnings . . .	Bonningues .	Boningale, *Salop.* Boninghall, *Salop.* Bonnington, *Kent and Notts.* Bonintone (*Kent, Domesday*).
Bosings . . .	Boeseghem .	Bossingham, *Kent.* Bossington, *Hants and Somerset.* Bossingden, *Kent.* Bosintuna (*Exon' Domesday*).
Bucings . . .	Bouquinghen .	Buckingham, *Bucks.* Bocking, *Essex and Suffolk.* Boccingas (*Cod. Dipl. Essex,* No. 698). Buccingas (*Chron. Sax.* A.D. 918).
Boflings . . .	Bouvelinghem.	Bowling, *Kent.*
Collings . . .	Colincthun (2) .	Collington, *Sussex and Hereford.* Collingham, *Notts, Yorkshire.* Colingas (*Cod. Dipl. Wilts,* No. 336).
Ellings . . .	Ellingehen .	Ellingham, *Hants, Norfolk, North-umberland.* Ellington, *Kent, Hants, Yorks, Northumberland.* Ellinge, *Kent.*
Eorings . . .	Eringhem . .	Eringham, *Sussex.* Eringden, *Yorkshire.*
Frescings. . .	Fersinghem .	Fressingfield, *Suffolk.*
Frelings . . .	Frelinghien .	Frillinghurst, *Surrey.*
Garlings . . .	Garlinghem .	Garlinge, *Kent.*
Gystlings. . .	Guslinghem .	Guestling, *Sussex.* Gyrslingas (*Cod. Dipl.* No. 967).
Hallings . . .	Halinghen . .	Halling, *Kent.* Hallington, *Linc. Northum.* Halinga Hailinegai }(*Exon' Domesday*). Halingas (*Cod. Dipl. Kent,* No. 160).
Heardings . .	Hardinghem . Hardinghen . Hardenthun .	Hardingham, *Norfolk.* Hardingstone, *Northamptonshire.* Hardington, *Somerset.* Hardinctona (*York. Domesday*).
Hæferings . .	Hauvringhen .	Haveringham, *Suffolk.* Havering, *Essex.*
Helvelings . .	Helvelinghem	Elvington, *Yorkshire.*
Hircelings . .	Herquelinghen	Hecklinge, *Kent.*
Horings . . .	Heuringhen .	Horrington, *Somerset.* Herington, *Dorset.* Herringe, *Kent.*
Hundings . .	Hondeghem .	Huntingdon, *Hunts.* Hunningham, *Warwickshire.* Hodingas (*Cod. Dipl.* No. 983).
Islings . . .	Islinghem . .	Islington, *Norfolk and Middlesex*
Lecings . . .	Ledinghem .	Liddington, *Rutland and Wilts.* Leding (*Domesday, Somerset*).

Family Names.	French Villages.	English Villages.
Ledrings . . .	Ledringhem .	Litheringham, *Suffolk.* Ledrincgeham (*Domesday, Inquisit' Eliensis*).
Lings	Linghem . .	Lingham, *Chesh.* Lingen, *Hereford.* Lingas (*Cod. Dipl. Mid.* No. 159).
Locings . . .	Locquinghen .	Locking, *Somerset.* Lockinge, *Berks.* Lockington, *Leic. and Yorks.*
Lodings . . .	Lottinghen .	Loddington, *Kent. Leic. Northamp.*
Leasings . . .	Lozinghem .	Lossingham, *Kent.*
Lullings, or Lilings . . .	Leulinghem . Leulinghen . Leulingue .	Lullington, *Sussex, Derby, Somerset.* Lillington, *Dors. Oxford. Warwick.* Loligtona (*Exon' Domesday*).
Mannings . .	Maninghem . Maninghen .	Manningham, *Norfolk.* Manningtree, *Essex.* Mannington, *Dors. and Norfolk.*
Mærings, Merovingians of France	Moringhem .	Marington, *Salop.* Mering, *Notts.*
Mæssings . .	Masinghen . Mazinghem . Mazingarbe .	Massingham, *Norfolk.* Messingham, *Lincoln.* Messing, *Essex.* Mæsingas (*Cod. Dipl.* No. 953).
Mæcsings . . .	Macquinghen .	Matching, *Essex.*
Myrcings . . .	Merkeghem .	Markington, *Yorkshire.*
Mellings . . .	Melingue-dal .	Melling, *Lancashire.* Millington, *Chesh. and Yorkshire.*
Mollings . . .	Molinghem .	Molington, *Chesh. Oxford. Warw.* Malling, *Kent and Sussex.* Molintona (*Cheshire, Domesday*).
Ulings . . .	Olincthun . .	Ullingswick, *Herefordshire.*
Pællings . . .	Pelincthun .	Pallington, *Dorset.* Pallingham, *Sussex.* Pilling, *Lancashire.* Palingas (*Cod. Dipl. Sussex,* No. 432).
Rædings . . .	Radinghem (2)	Raddington, *Somersetshire.* Reading, *Berkshire.* Radingetuna (*Exon' Domesday*). Readingas (*Cod. Dipl. Berks,* No. 685).
Ricings . . .	Racquinghem .	Rickinhall, *Suffolk.* Ragintona (*Dorset, Domesday*).
Riclings . . .	Recklinghem .	Rickling, *Essex.*
Sinnings . . .	Senninghem .	Sennington, *Yorkshire.* Senendone (*Exon' Domesday*).
Tætings . . .	Tatinghem .	Tattingstone, *Suffolk.* Taddington, *Gloucester. Derby.* Tatintune (*Hereford. Domesday*). Tatintone (*Gloucester. Domesday*).

Family Names.	French Villages.	English Villages.
Teorlings . .	⎰Terlincthun . ⎱Tourlincthun .	⎱Terling, *Essex.* ⎰Terlingas (*Cod. Dipl. Essex.* No. 907).
Tings . . .	Tinghen . .	Tingeham (*Dorset, Domesday*).
Tortings . . .	⎰Terdinghem . ⎱Tardinghen .	⎱Tortington, *Sussex.*
Todings . . .	Todincthun .	⎰Toddington, *Bedford. Gloucester.* ⎮Tottington, *Lanc. Norfolk.* ⎮Totingas (*Cod. Dipl. Surrey,* Nos. 363, 785).
Trings . . .	Dringem . .	Tring, *Herts.*
Feorlings . .	⎧Verlinghen . ⎨Verlinghem . ⎩Verlincthun .	⎰Farlington, *Hants, Yorkshire.* ⎨Ferlintun (*York. Domesday*). ⎱Ferlingelai (*Kent, Domesday*).
Wiccings . .	⎰Wicquinghem ⎱Wacquinhem .	⎰Witchingham, *Norfolk.* ⎮Wickinghurst, *Kent.* ⎮Wigingas (*Cod. Dipl. Kent,* No. 225 ; *Chron. Sax. Herts,* A.D. 921).
Westings . .	Ouestinghen .	Westington, *Gloucestershire.*
Wealings. . .	Velinghen .	⎧Wellingham, *Sussex.* ⎮Welling, *Kent.* ⎨Wellington,*Wilts,Salop, Som. Herts.* ⎮Welingas (*Cod. Dipl.Wilts.* No.462). ⎩Wellingas (*Cod.Dipl.Herts,*No. 410).
Wadings . . .	Wadenthun .	⎰Waddington, *Lincoln. Yorkshire.* ⎱Waddingham, *Lincoln.*

APPENDIX C

PATRONYMICS IN ENGLAND, GERMANY, AND FRANCE

See pp. 101-108.

⁎ The German names in the third column to which a *W* is appended
are in the Westphalian district. The rest are in Franconia and Swabia,
unless the contrary is expressly stated.

Families.	England.	Germany.	France.
Ecgings	. Eckington, *Dev. Wor.*	Eckingen	
Edings .	. Edington, *Ber. Som.*	Eutingen .	. Autigny, *Cham.* (2),
	Wilts, Nthld.		*Lorr.* Audenge,
			Guienne.
Eadlings	. Edlingham, *Nthld.*	. Aidlingen	
	Edlington, *Lin. York.*	Ettlingen	
		Oetlingen	
Efings .	. Evingar, *Hants.* . .	. Oevinghausen,	Effincourt, *Cham.*
		W.	
	Evington, *Gl. Lan.*	. Ehingen	
	Effingham, *Sus.*	. Oeffingen	
Æfings .	. Avington, *Ber. Hants.*	Auingen	. Auvignac, *Ang.*
Ofings .	. Ovington, *Ess. Hants.*	. . . .	. Offignies, *Pic.*
	Nor. Nthld. York.		
	Ovingham, *York, Nthld*	Offingen	. Offingues, *I. of F.*
Uffings .	. Oving, *Sus. Bucks.*	. Owingen	. Oigny, *Pic., Bur.,*
			Vend.
	Uffington, *Ber. Lin. Sal.*	. . . .	. Euffigneux, *Cham.*
		Uihingen .	. Juvigny, *Nor.*
Eoferings	. Everingham, *York.*	. Effringen .	. Evrange, *Lorr.*
		Erflinghausen,	Avrigny, *Fr. Com.*
		W.	
Eaglings	. Eglingham, *Nthld.*	. Eglingen (2)	
Icelings	. Icklingham, *Suf.* .	. Igglingen	
Ælings .	. Allington, *Dev. Dor.*		Allinges, *Burg.* (2).
	Hants, Kent, Lin.		Alaigne, *Nivern.*
	Wilts. . . .	. . .	. Alligny, *Bur., Berri.*
			Alincourt, *Champ,*
			Alaincourt, *Fr. Com.,*
			Lorr.
Ellings .	. Ellingham, *Ham. Nor.*	Oelinghausen, *W.*	
	Nthld.		
	Ellington, *Hunts,*	Oellingen	
	Kent, Nthld. Yor.		

Families.	England.	Germany.	France.
Illings .	. Illington, *Nor.* . .	. Illingen .	. Iligny, *Burg.*
	Illingworth, *York.*	. Ihlingen	
Ælcings .	. Alkington, *Glo. Sal.*	. . . . .	. Alzing, *Lorr.*
Elcings .	. Elkington, *Nhm. Lin.*	Elchingen .	. Elzange, *Lorr.*
Aldings .	. Aldingham, *Lan.*	. Aldingen	
	Aldington, *Kent,*	Altingen	
	Worc.	. Hailtingen	
		Eltingen	
Ælfings .	. Alphington, *Dev.*	. Alfingen .	. Alvignac, *Quercy.*
		Eilfingerhof	. Elvange, *Lorr.*
Elmings .	. Elmington, *Ntham.*	. Elmingen	
Elrings .	. Ellerington, *Nthld.*	. Ailringen	
Emmings .	. Immingham, *Lin.*	. Imminghausen, *W.*	
		Emmingen	
Annings .	. Anningas (*Cod. Dip.*)	Uninghausen, *W.*	Aniange, *Fr. Com.*
Antings .	. Antingham, *Norf.*	. . . . . .	.Antigny, *Bur.* (2)
			Poit. (2).
			Andigné, *Lorr.*
Eppings .	. Epping, *Ess.* . .	. Eppinghofen, *W.*	Epping, *Lorr.*
		Ebbinghausen,	Epagny, *Bur.*, *Pic.*
		W.	
			Epagne, *Cham.*
Ipings .	. Iping, *Sus.* . . .	. . . . .	Ibigny, *Lorr.*
Æbings .	. Abington, *Cam.* . .	. Appingadam,	Aubigné,*Poit.*, *Anj.*
			(2).
		Groningen .	Aubigny, *Bur.* (3),
			Cham. (3), *Niev.*
			(2), *Berri.* (2), *F.*
			Com.
			Ebbange, *Lorr.*
			Epinac, *Bur.*
Uping .	. Uppingham, *Rut.*.	. Upfingen	
	Uppington, *Sal.* .	. Oppingen	
Arrings .	. Arrington, *Cam.* .	. Ehringen .	. Arrigny, *Champ.*
Eorrings	. Erringden, *York.*.	. Erringhausen,	Eragny, *Bur.*
		W.	
Irings (royal	Erringham, *Sus.* .	. Oehringen	. Erigné, *Anj.*
race of			Eringes, *Bur.*
Avars).			Origny, *Cham.*, *Bur.*,
			Pic. (2).
			Irigny, *Lyon.*
Arlings .	. Arlingham, *Glou.*	. Erligheim	
	Arlington,*Dev.Glo.Sus.*		
Earmings	. Ermington, *Dev.*	. Ermingen	
Eorpings	. Erpingham, *Nor.*	. Erpfingen	
	Orpington, *Kent.*	. . . . . .	. Orbigny, *Cham.* (2),
			Tour.
Ercensings .	Kensington, *Mid.*	. Ergenzingen	
Artings .	. Artington, *Sus.* .	. . . . . .	. Antigny, *Tour.*

Families.	England.	Germany.	France.
Eardings	. Erdington, *War.* . .	. Ertingen	
	Eardington, *Sal.*		
Æscings .	. Assington, *Ess.* . .	. Assinghausen, *W.*	Assigny, *Berri.*
Essings .	. Essington, *Staf.* . .	. Essingen .	. Essigny, *I. of F.*
	Easingtoɔ, *Buc. Dur.*	Oeschingen	
	Glou.Nthld.Ox.York.		
Isings .	. Issington, *Hants.*		. Isigny, *Lorr.*
			Ising, *Lorr.*
Æsclings	. Ashling, *Sus.* . .	. Aislingen	
(*C.D.*)			
Islings .	. Islington, *Nor. Mid.* .	. Esslingen .	. Etzling, *Lorr.*
		Eislingen	
Ætings .	. Attington, *Oxon.* . .	. Atting .	. Attigny, *Lorr., Cham.*
		Aygem, *Belgium*	
		(once Addingem)	
Ettings .	. Ettinghall, *Staf.* . .	. Ettenheim.	. Etting, *Lorr.*
		Oettinger .	. Etigny, *Cham.*
			Etang, *Bur.* (2), *I. of Fr.*
Bæbings.	. Babington, *Som.* . .	. Babing .	. Balbigny, *Bur.*
Bobbings	. Bobinger, *Ess.* . .	. Bobinger .	. Baubigny, *Norm.*
	Bobbing, *Kent.* . .	. Böbingen .	. Beaubigny, *Bur.*
	Bobbington,*Staf.Sal*		. Bobigny, *I. of Fr.*
	Bobbingworth, *Ess.*		
Beccings	. Beckingham, *Ess. Lin.*	Bechingen (2) .	Becquigny, *Pic.*
	Notts.		
	Beckington, *Som.*		
	Begging, *Ess.* . . .	. Bigginghausen, *W.*	
Bocings .	. Bocking, *Ess. Suf.* .	. Böchingen .	. Bouquigny, *Maine.*
	Buckingham, *Berks,*		Bocquegney, *Cham.*
	Essex, Bucks. . .	. . . . .	. Bochange, *Lorr.*
Bædings	Beeding, *Sus.* .	. Betinghof, *W.*	Betting, *Lorr.*
(*Cod. Dip.*)	Beddington, *Sur.* .	. Böttingen .	. Bettigny, *Cham.*
	Beddingham, *Sus.*		Bettagny, *Lorr.*
	Norf.	. Biding .	. Biding, *Lorr.*
		Bietigheim	. Bettange, *Lorr.*
			Bettignies, *Hain.*
Budings .	. Buddington, *Sus.* . .	. Beutingen	. Buding, *Lorr.*
Bædlings	. Bedlington, *Dur.* . .	. Bettlingen	. Budeling, *Lorr.*
		Betlinghausen, *W.*	
Biterings	. Bittering, *Norf.* . .	. Bettringen	
Bofings	. Bovington, *Ess.* . .	. Bopfingen .	. Bouvigny, *Lorr.*
	Bovingdon, *Herts.*	. Boihingen .	. Boigny, *Orl.*
		Böinghausen, *W.*	
Beofings.	. Bevington, *War.* .	. Beihingen.	
Bellings .	. Bellinger, *Hants.*	. Böllingerhof .	. Belingreville, *Norm.*
	Bellingham, *Nlhld.*	. Belinghausen .	. Belligne, *Anjou.*
	Bellingdon, *Bucks.* .	. . . . . .	. Belligneux, *Burg.*
			Belange, *Lorr.*

Families.	England.	Germany.	France.
Bælings	Ballingham, *Here.*	. . . . . .	Balagny, *I. of. F.* (2)
	Balingdon, *Ess.*	. . . . . .	Blagny, *Burg.*
Billings	Billing, *Nthld.*	. . Billenhausen	. Billanges, *Marche.*
	Billinge, *Lan.*	. . Billingsbach	. Bligny, *Burg.* (3),
	Billingham, *Dur.* .	. Billinghausen,	Champ. (3).
	Billingside, *Dur.*	W.	
	Billingley, *York.*		
Bolings	Bolingbroke, *Lin.*	. Bollingen .	. Bolligney, *Fr. Com.*
	Bollington, *Ess. Ches.*	. . . . .	. Bolligneux, *Bur.*
	Bowling, *Kent.*	. . . . . .	. Bologne, *Champ.*
Bullings	Bullingdon, *Oxon.*	. Buhlingen.	. Bulligny, *Lorr.*
	Bullingham, *Here.*		
Blæcings	Bletchingley, *Sur.*	. Blöchingen	. Blessignac, *Guienne.*
	Bletchington, *Oxon.*		
Beltings	Belting, *Kent.* . .	. Baldingen	
Bennings	Bennington,*Herts.Lin.*	Benningen.	. Bening, *Lorr.* (2).
	Benningworth, *Lin.*	. Benninghausen,	Benigne, *Burg.*
		W.	
	Benningbrough, *York.*	Bönnigheim	
	Bonnington, *Kent.Ess.*	Beuningen,	
	Notts.	*Limburg.*	
Bings	Bing, *Suff.* . .	. Bingen .	. Binges, *Burg.*
	Bingham, *Nthamp.*	. . . . .	. Buigny, *Champ.*
	Bingley, *York.*		
Bondings	Bondington, *Som.*	. . . . .	. Bontigny, *Lorr.*
Beorings	Barrington, *Som. Ess.*	Bähringen	. Berigny, *Norm.*
	Glo. Cam. Berks.	Bieringen	. Berengeville, *Norm.*
Berrings	Berrington, *Dur. Gl.*	Beringen, *Limburg.*	
	Sal. Wor. . . .	Beringen,	
		(*Charters*)	
Burrings	Burrington,*Dev. Here.*	Böhringen	
	Som.		
	Burringham, *Lin.*		
Eberdings	Birdingbury. *War.*	. Eberdingen	
Birlings	Berling, *Sus.* . . .	Bierlingen.	. Berlingen, *Alsace.*
	Birling, *Kent, Nthld.*	Berlinghausen, W.	
Bermarings	Birmingham, *War.*	. Bermaringen	
	Barming, *Kent*		
Beornings	Barningham, *Suf.*	Berninghausen,	
	York. Notts.	W.	
Brantings	Brantingham, *York.*	. . . . .	. Brantigny, *Champ.*
Brahcings	Braughin, *Herts.*	. Bröckingen	
(*C.D.*)			
Bressings	Bressingham, *Nor.*	. Bretzingen	
Brimings	Brimington, *Derby*	. Breimingsweiler	
Brislings	Brislington, *Som.*	. Börslingen (2)	
Britings	Brittenton, *Ox.* .	. Breitingen	. Bretegny, *Fr. C.* (2),
			Nor., Bur., I. of Fr.
Basings	Basing, *Hants.* .	. Baisingen .	. Bazegny, Cham.,
			Fr. C.

Families.	England.	Germany.	France.
	Bassingham, *Lin.*	. Ecisinghausen,*W*.	
Bessings	. Bessingby, *York*.	. Bissingen (2)	. Bissines, *Lim.*
	Bessingham, *Nor.*	. Bessigheim	. Bezing, *Bearn.*
		Betzingen .	. Bezange, *Lorr.*
Buslings	. Buslingthorpe. *Lin.*	. Börslingen.	. Bousselange, *Bur.*
Cidings .	. Keddington, *Lin.*	. Kedding-	Quetigny, *Burg.*
		hausen, *W*.	
	Kedington, *Ess. Suf.*	Köttinghausen, *W*.	
Geddings	. Gedding, *Suf.*	. . Jettingen	
	Yeading, *Mid.*		
Cædings	. Caddington,*Bed.Herts.*	. . . . .	. Catigny, *I. of F.*
Godings	. Goddington, *Oxon.*	. Göttingen	
Ceadlinge	Gedling, *Notts.*	. . Gültlingen	
or Cycelings		Gögglingen	
	Cucklington,*Som.*	. Guglingen	
Gægings.	. Gagingwell, *Oxon.*	. Gechingen	
		Gächingen	
Cofings .	. Covington, *Hunts.*	. Goffingen .	. Cauvigny, *I. of F.,*
			Pic.
			Couvignon, *Champ.*
Cifings .	. Chevington, *Suf.*		Chevigny, *Cham.,Fr.*
	Nthld.	. . . . . .	. Com. (4), *Burg.* (3).
			Chevincourt, *I. of Fr.*
			Chavigny, *Fr. Com.*
			(4), *I. of Fr.* (2),
			Lorr.
Ifings .	. Jevington, *Sus.* . .	. . . . .	. Gevigny, *Fr. Com.*
	Ivinghoe, *Bucks.*	. . . . .	. Juvigné, *Maine.*
			Juvigny, *Champ., I.*
			of Fr. (2), *Lorr.*
			(2), *Norm.* (4), *Pic.*
Callings	. Callington, *Corn.* .	. . . . .	. Caligny, *Norm.*
			Challange, *Burg. Nor.*
			Galinagues, *Lang.*
Cyllings	. Chellington, *Bedf.*	. Kellinghausen,	Challange, *Burg.*
		W.	*Norm.*
	Kelling, *Norf.*		
	Kellington, *York.*	. Kellinghausen,	Chaligny, *Lorr.*
	Chillington, *Som. Dev.*	*Holstein*	
	Chillingham, *Nthld.*	. Gellinghausen,*W.*	
Gillings	Gilling, *York.* .	. . Killingen .	. Julligny, *Burg.*
	Gillingham, *Dor.*	. . . . .	. Jaligny, *Bourb.*
	Kent, Nor.		
	Yelling, *Hunts.*		
Collings .	. Collingham, *Notts, York.*	. . . .	. Collonge, *Burg.*
	Collington, *Here.*	. . . . .	. Coligny, *Burg.*
Cullings .	. Cullingworth, *York.*	. . . . .	. Coulange, *Bur.Bourb.*
Camerings .	Cameringham, *Lin.*	. Gemmrigheim	Chemigny, *I. of F.*
		Gomaringen	

Families.	England.	Germany.	France.
Cennings	Kennington, *Kent,* Surrey, *Berks.*	Gönningen	
Gings	Ginge, *Berks*	Gingen. Giengen	Gigny, *Bur* (2),*Cham* (2), *Lorr., Fr. C.* Jeugny, *Cham.*
Copings	Coppingsyke, *Lin.*	Kuppingen	
Cubings	Cubbington, *War.*		
Gippings	Gipping, *Suf.*	Göppingen	
Cerrings	Carrington, *Ches. Lin.* *Notts* Charing, *Kent* Cherrington, *Wor. Sal..*		Charigny, *Burg.* Guerigny, *Niev.*
Corings	Corringham, *Lin. Ess.*		Corignac, *Guienne.*
Cearlings	Carlingcot, *Som.*		Carling, *Lorr.*
Garlings	Garlinge, *Kent* Yarlington, *Som..*	Gerlingen Gerlinghausen,*W.*	
Cyrtlings	Kirtling, *Cam.*	Körtlinghausen,*W.*	
Cridlings	Cridling Stubbs, *York.*	Creglingen	
Cressings	Cressing, *Ess.* Cressingham, *Norf.*	Griesingen [1] Grözingen	Gressigny, *Burg.*
Cæssings	Cassington, *Oxon.* Chessington, *Sur.* Kessingland, *Suf.*	Kasing. Geisingen Jesingen Kösingen Güssingen	Chassigny, *Burg., Cham.* Chasseigne, *Niev.* Chassange, *Bur., Fr. Com., Niev.* Chessigny, *Burg.*
Cosings	Cossington, *Leic. Som.* Cussington, *Kent*		Jossigny,*I.of F. Bur.* Gussignies, *Flan.* Ghisignies, *Flan.* Ghisignies, *Flan.*
Gislings	Gislingham, *Suf.*	Geislingen	
Gestings	Gestingthorpe, *Ess.*	Justingen	
Tibbings	Tibbington, *Staf.*	Tübingen	
Docings	Docking, *Norf.*	Döchingen	
Dycings	Duckington, *Ches.* Dykings, *Lin.*	Dächingen Deggingen (2)	
Dicelings	Ditchling, *Sus.*	Dusslingen	Desseling, *Lorr.*
Deddings	Deddington, *Oxon.*	Dedinghausen,*W.*	
Diddings	Diddington, *Hunts.*	Dietingen Döttingen Dattingen Dettingen (6) [2] Daiting	Tetting, *Lorr.* Theding, *Lorr.*
Dodings	Doddington, *Cam. Ches. Kent, Lin. Nthld. Ntham.* Dodington, *Glou. Sal. Som.*	Dottingen Dudinghausen, *W.*	

[1] In the Charters Chresinga. Kausler, *Urkund.* vol. i. p. 407.
[2] Teddingen, Tettingen, and Totingen in the Charters. See Kausler.

Families.	England.	Germany.	France.
Todings	. Toddington, *Bed.*		
	Tottington, *Nor. Lan.*		
Dæfings.	. Davington, *Kent*	. Döffingen . .	. Davignac, *Lim.*
			Daigny, *Cham.*
			Digny, *Orl.*
Dillings	. Dillington, *Nor.* . .	. Dehlingen	. Delincourt, *I. of F.*
Dællings	. Dalling, *Norf.*		. Talange, *Lorr.*
	Dallington, *Sus.*		
	Nthmp.		
Demings	. . . .	. Demingen .	. Demigny, *Burg.*
Dinnings	. Dinnington, *Som.*	Deiningen	
	York. *Nthld.*		
Dintings	. Dinting, *Derby* . .	. Dentingen [1]	Denting, *Lorr.*
Durings *or*	Thorington, *Suf.*		. Thorigny, *Poit.* (2),
Thurings.	Thorrington, *Ess.*		*Nor., I. of Fr.*
			Thorigné, *Poit.*
Dartings	. Dartington, *Dev.* . .	. Dertingen.	. Tartigny, *Pic.*
Trings .	. Tring, *Herts*		. Trigny, *Cham.*
			Thrangy, *Lorr.*
Dissings.	. Dissington, *Nthld.*	. Dischingen	. Desaignes, *Lang.*
		Ditzingen	
Finnings	. Finningham, *Suf.*	. Finingen	
Feormings	. Farmington, *Glou.*		. Formigny, *Norm.*
Frestings	. Frestintorp (*York,*	Frestingen	
	Domesday)		
Frings .	. Fring, *Nor.*		. Frignicourt, *Cham.*
			Freigné, *Anj.*
			Vregny, *I. of Fr.*
			Vrigny, *Cham., Orl.,*
			Nor.
Frescings	. Fressingfield, *Suf.*		. Fressines, *Poit.*
			Fressigne, *Marche.*
Frilings.	. Frillinghurst, *Sur.*	. Frilinghausen, *W.*	
Hæcings	. Heckingham, *Nor.*	. Heckingen	. Hickange, *Lor.*
	Heckington, *Lin.*	.	
	Heighington, *Dur.Lin.*		. Heyingen, *Lor.*
Hocings.	. Hucking, *Kent*		. Hocquincourt, *Pic.*(2)
Hædings	. Haddington, *Lin.*		. Hadigny, *Cham.,Lor.*
Heddings	. Heddingham, *Ess.*	. Hedding-	Hettange, *Lorr.* (2).
		hausen, *W.*	
	Heddington, *Wilts*		
Hudings	. Huddington, *Wor.*	. Hütting .	. Hodeng, *Nor.*
			Hodenger, *Nor.*
Heofings	. Hevingham, *Nor.*	. Höfingen	
Hofings .	. Hovingham, *York.*	.	
Hellings	. Hellinghill, *Nthld.*	. Hellinghausen,	Helling, *Lor.*
		W.	
			Hœlling, *Lor.*
			Halignicourt, *Cham.*

[1] Tantiga in Charters.

Families.	England.	Germany.	France.
Holings.	Hollington, *Staff. Sus. Dev.*	. . . .	Holling, *Lor.*
Hemings	Hemington, *Ntham. Som.* . . . . Hemingbrough, *Yor.*	Hemmingen . Hemminghausen, *W.* Hemingstedt, *Holstein.*	Heming, *Lor., Als.*
Hanings	Hannington, *Hants, Ntham. Wilts* . .	Heiningen . Henninghausen, *W.*	Hiening, *Lor.*
Hunings.	Hunningham, *War.* .	. . . . .	Huningue, *Als.*
Hundings	Huntingdon, *Hunts* .	Undingen . .	Hunting, *Lor.*
Hensings	Hensington, *Oxon* Hensingham, *Cum.*	. . . .	Hensing, *Lorr.* Hinsingen, *Als.*
Heorings	Herring, *Kent, Dor.* .	Heringhausen, *W.*	Hareigny, *Pic.*
Hearings	Harrington, *Lin. Nthm.* Hornsey, *Mid.* (anciently Haringsey)	Haringkarspel, *Holland.*	
Horings.	Horrington, *Som.* .	. . . . .	Hurigny, *Burg.* Origny, *Burg., I. of Fr.*
Herelings	Harling, *Norf.* . . Harlington, *Bed. Mid. York.*	Herrlingen Herlingen . Hirrlingen	Hallering, *Lorr.* Hellering, *Lorr.* (2).
Heardings	Hardingham, *Norf.* .	. . . .	Hardancourt, *Lorr.*
Hæssings	Hassingham, *Nor.* .	Hessigheim Hausingen	Hesingue, *Als.*
Hicelings	Hickling, *Nor. Notts.* Hecklinge, *Kent*	Heuchlingen	
Hæslings	Heslington, *York.* .	. . . . .	Hesling, *Lorr.*
Hæstings	Hastings, *Sus. Ber. War. Ntham.*	. . . . .	Hastingues, *Gasc.*
Læcings.	Lackington, *Som.* . Lachingdon, *Ess.*	Laichingen	Lixing, *Lorr.* (2).
Leasings	Leasingham, *Lin.* . Lossingham, *Kent* Lissington, *Lin.* .	Lazingen	Lassigny, *Pic.* Lusigny, *Burg.* Lessigny, *I. of Fr., Poit.* Lezigné, *Anj.*
Ledings.	Leding (*Som. Dom.*). Liddington, *Rut. Wilts.*	. . . .	Leting, *Lorr.* Ladignac, *Lim.* (2), *Gui.*
Lidlings.	Lidlington, *Bed.* . .	Leuglingen	
Ledrings	Ledrincgeham (*Ely Domesday*)	Lütringhausen, *W.*	
Leafings	Lavington, *Kent* . Leavington, *York.* . Levington, *Suf.* .	. . . . . Lauingen	Lavigny, *Fr. C.* (2). Levigny, *Cham.* Leffincourt, *Cham.* Levignac, *Gui.* (2). Levigneu, *I. of Fr.*

Families.	England.	Germany.	France.
Lofings .	. Lovington, Som. Ess.		. Louvagny, Nor.
			Louvigny, Nor.
			Leuvigne, Maine.
Læferings	. Leverington, Cam.	. Leveringhausen,W.	
Lullings.	. Lullington, Dev. Som.	Lollinghausen,	
	Sus.	W.	
Lings .	. Lingham, Ches.		. Ligny, Lorr., Niev.
	Lings, York		(2), Bur., Cham.,
			Orl.
	Lingen, Here..		. Legny, Burg.
			Laigné, Poit. (2),
			Anj., Maine.
Mecings.	. Meeching, Sus. . .	. Maichingen	. Mecquingies, Flan.
			Macquigny, Pic.
Mæglings	. Maudling, Sus. . .	. Mögglingen (2)	
		Mecklinghausen,W.	
Mallings.	. Malling, Kent, Sus.		. Malange, Fr. C.
			Maligné, Orl.
			Maligny, Bur., Cham.
Mellings	. Meling, Lan. . . .	. Meiling . .	. Meligny, Lor. (2).
Millings	. Millington, Ches. York.	Millinghausen,	Melincourt, Fr. C.
		W.	
			Melange, Lorr,
Mollings	. Mollington, Ches. Ox.		Mollincourt, I. of Fr.
	Wor.		. Molinges, Fr. C.
			Molangues, I. of Fr.
Mincings	. Minchingbury, Herts.	Münchingen	
Mintings	. Minting, Lin.. . .	. Mundingen	. Montigny, Fr. Com.
			(3), Norm., I. of
			Fr., Flan. (2).
Myrcings	. Markington, York.	. Merkingen.	. Marcigny, Bur. (2).
	Marchington, Staf.	. Emerkingen	. Marquigny, Cham.
			Marsigne, Niev.
Mærings or	Mering, Notts . .	. Möhringen [1]	. Marigny, Bur. (3),
Myrgings	Merrington, Sal. Dur.	Muhringen [2] .	Cham. (2), Poit.
(Merovin-	Marrington, Sal. .	. Mähringen	(3), Orl., I. of Fr.,
gians, the	. . . .	. Möringen .	Bour., Norm. (2),
royal race	. . . .	. Mehring . .	Fr. C., Neiv. (3).
of France)	. . . . . .	. Emeringen	. Emeringe, Bur.
		Vollmaringen .	Merigny, Poit.
			Meeringes, Cham.
			Maringés, Bur.
			Maragny, Bur.
			Marignac, Gui. (6).
			Mairegne, Lang.
			Marigna, Fr. C. (3).
			Marigné, Anj. (2),
			Maine.
			Merignac, Gui. (3).
			Morigny,Bur.,I.ofFr.

[1] Meringen in Charters.   [2] Mieringen in Charters, *Kausler*, vol. i. p. 34.

Families.	England.	Germany.	France.
Mæssings	. Massingham, *Notts*	. Messinghausen, *W.*	Massigny, *Bur.*
	Messing, *Ess.*	Mössingen.	. Messigny, *Bur.*
	Messingham, *Lin.*	. Metzingen.	. Messignac, *Bur.*
		Mötzingen.	. Metzing, *Lorr.*
		Mussingen.	. Musigny, *Bur.*
Mætings	. Mettingham, *Suf.*	. Mietingen.	. Metting, *Lorr.*
	Mattingley, *Hants*	. . . . .	. Matigny, *I. of Fr.*
Mædings	. Maddington, *Wilts*	. Medingen .	. Medegny, *Champ.*
	Madingley, *Camb.*		
Mottings	. Mottingham, *Kent*	. . . . .	. Mutigny, *Cham.*
Mutlings	. Mudling, *Ess.*. .	. Möttlingen	
Næcings.	. Nedging, *Suf.* .	. Notzingen	
		Nichtinghausen, *W.*	
Nydings.	. Needingworth, *Hun.*	Nettingen .	. Nitting, *Lorr.*
Nollings.	. Nollington, *Sus.* .	. Nellingen (2)	. Nelling, *Lorr.*
		Nellingheim	
Pæccings `.	. Patching, *Ess. Sus.*	. Peiching .	. Picquigny, *Pic.*
			Pussigny, *Tour.*
Pæfings .	. Pavingham, *Bed.*. .	. Pfäffingen	. Pagney, *Fr. C.*
	Pevington, *Kent* .	. . . . .	. Peugny, *Fr. C.*
			Poigny, *Lorr.*
			Pagny, *Cham., Bur.* (2), *Lor.* (3).
Pællings.	. Palling, *Norf.*	. . . . .	. Paligny, *Bur.* (2).
	Pallingham, *Sus.*	. . . . .	. Palignes, *Bur.*
	Pallington, *Dor.*		
Polings .	. Poling, *Sus.* . .	. . . . .	. Poligny, *Cham., Poit., Fr. C.* (2).
	Pollington, *York.*		Pouligny, *Bur., Poit., Berri* (2), *Fr. C.*
			Poulangy, *Cham.*
		Pulling	. Pulligny, *Lorr.*
Pennings	. Pennington, *Hants,* *Lan.*	Pinning	
Porings.	. Poringland, *Norf.*.	. Pöring .	. . Perigny, *Bur.* (7), *Fr. C.* (2), *Poit.*
			Perigne, *Poit. Maine* (3).
			Perignac, *Guin.* (2).
			Parigny, *Bur.* (3), *Nor.*
Pætings.	. Pattingham, *Sal. Staf.*	. . . . .	. Patigny, *Bur.*
	Puddington, *Bed.* *Ches. Dev.*	Putting	. Petignac, *Ang.*
Petlings.	. Peatling, *Leic.* .	. Püttlingen, *W.*	
	Pedling, *Kent*		
Pætrings	. Patrington, *York.*	. . . . .	. Petring, *Lor.*
Rocings.	. Rockingham, *Nham.*	Röckingen.	. Rigny, *Poit., Cham.* (3), Tour., *Fr.C., Burg.*

Families.	England.	Germany.	France.
Riclings.	. Rickling, *Ess.* . .	. Reckling-hausen, *W.*	Richling, *Lorr.*
Rædings	. Reddinge, *Der.* . .	. Rieding . .	Reding, *Lorr.*
	Reddings, *Ess.* . .	. Rödinghausen, *W.*	Redange, *Lorr.*
	Readings, *Ess.*		
	Reading, *Ber.* .	. Röttingen	
Rodings.	. Rodington, *Sal.* . .	. Roding	
	Rottington, *Cum.*		
Rætlings	. Ratlinghope, *Sal.*	. Riedlingen (2)	
	Redlingfield, *Suf.*	. Reutlingen	
		Reutlingdorf	
		Radling	
		Ratlinghausen,*W.*	
Rifings .	. Rivington, *Lan.* . .	. Riffingen . .	Revigny, *Lor.*
			Ruvigny, *Cham.*
			Rouffignac, *Perig.*(2).
			Rouffigny, *Norm.*
Rillings.	. Rillington, *York.*	. Rellinghaus, *W.*	
		Rielingshausen,*W.*	
		Rehlingen.	. Rahling, *Lorr.*
		Rehling	
Rimmings	. Rimmington, *York.*	Remmingheim	Remigny, *Bur.* (2), *Pic.*
		Rammingen	. Rumigny, *Cham.,Pic.*
Rennings	. Rennington, *Nthld.* .	. Renningen	
		Ringingen (2)	
		Rohning	
Riplings.	. Riplingham, *York.* .	. Rüblingen	
	Riplington, *Hants,* *Nthld.*	Rieblingen	
Risings .	. Rising, *Nor.* . . .	. Rissing . .	Resigny, *Pic.*
	Rissington, *Glou.*	. Reissing	
		Rexingen	
		Reixingen	
		Ritzing . .	Ritzing, *Lorr.*
		Ratzing	
		Reseghem, *Belgium.*[1]	
Rustings	. Rustington, *Sus.*	. Reistingen.	. Restigny, *Tour.*
Rowings	. Rowington, *War.*	. Roigheim .	. Rugney, *Cham.*
Secgings	. Seckington, *War.*	. Sickingen	
		Schöckingen	
Sceadings	. Shadingfield, *Suf.*	. Schietingen	
Sceanings	. Shenington, *Glou.*	. Scheningen	
Syclings.	. Sicklinghall, *York.*	. Siglingen	
Sceaclings	. Skeckling, *York.*		
Sydlings.	. Sydling, *Dor.* . .	. Züttlingen	
		Siedlinghausen,*W.*	

[1] Anciently Rassinghem.

Families.	England.	Germany.	France.
Scyllings	. Shellington, *Bed.*	. Schillinger	
	Shillingthorpe, *Lin.*		
Sælings	. Saling, *Ess.*		. Saligny, *Bur.*, *Fr.*
			Com., *Cham.*,
			Bourb., *Poit.*
			Saleigne, *Poit.*
			Salignac, *Gui.* (3).
Sullings	. Sullington, *Sus.*		. Solongy, *Bur.*
			Soulagny, *Nor.*
			Souligny, *Cham.*
			Soulignac, *Gui.*
Sinnings	. Sinnington, *York.*	. Sinning	. Signy, *Cham.*
		Zaininingen	
Sandlings	. Sandling, *Kent*	. Sindlingen	
Syfings .	. Sevington, *Kent* .	. Zöbingen .	. Sevigny, *Cham.*
Sceafings	. Shavington, *Ches.*	. . . . .	. Savigny, *Bur.* (8).
	Shevington, *Lan.*		*Nor.*, *Cham.* (3).
Seafings	. Seavington, *Som.*		*Fr. C.*, *Poit.*, *Lorr.*,
			Berri, *I. of Fr.*
			Savigné, *Poit.*,
			Maine. (2), *Tour.*
			Savigneux, *Bur.* (2).
			Savigna, *Bur.*
			Savignac, *Gui.*
			Savignies, *I. of Fr.*
			Sauvagny, *Fr. Com.*
			Sauvigny, *Bur.* (3),
			Fr. Com. (3), *Fl.*
Sealfings .	. Salvington, *Sus.* . .	. Söflingen .	. Selvigny, *Fland.*
			Silvange, *Lorr.*
Seppings	. Seppingeham, (*Linc.*	Suppingen	
	Domesday)		
Serings .	. Shering, *Ess.*		. Serrigny, *Bur.* (3),
	Sherringham, *Nor.*		*Poit.*
	Sherrington, *Bucks*,		Seringes, *I. of Fr.*
	Wilts		. Serignac, *Gui.* (4).
Scearings	. Sharrington, *Nor.*	. . . . .	. Sarronga, *Bur.*
			Sarregny, *Bur.*
			Sarrigné, *Anj.*
			Sorigny, *Poit.*
Swannings .	. Swannington, *Nor.*	Schwenningen	
	Leic.		
Swefelings	. Sweffling, *Suf.* . .	. Zweiflingen	
Wiccings	. Witchingham, *Nor.* .	. Weiching	
		Weckinghausen, *W.*	
Wiclings	. Witchling, *Kent* .	. Weuchlingen	
Wealings	. Welling, *Kent.* .	. Wellingen	
	Wellington, *Here. Sal.*	Vellinghausen, *W.*	
	Som, Wilts.		

Families.	England.	Germany.	France.
Fylings .	. Fylingthorpe, *York* .	Pfullingen. .	. Fuligny, *Cham.*
	Fylingdales, *York.*	. . . . .	. Foulanges, *I. of Fr.*
			Folligny, *Nor.*
Wealdings .	Waldingfield, *Suf.*	. Weldingsfelden	
	Wildingtree, *Ess* .	. Weiltingen	
		Walding	
		Walting	
Wealdrings .	Waldringfield, *Suff.*	. Waltringhausen, *W.*	
Wælsings .	Walsingham, *Nor.*	. Wilsingen	
Wendlings .	Wendling, *Nor.* .	. Wendlingen	
Wippings .	Whippingham, *Han.* .	. Wippingen	
Wæplings .	Waplington, *York.*	. Waiblingen	
		Wiblingen	
		Waibling	
Ferrings.	. Ferring, *Ess. Sus.*	. Vöhringen [1]	Veiigny, *Lorr.*
			Farincourt, *Cham.*
			Ferrange, *Lorr.*
Wærings	. Werrington, *Dev.*	wehringen	
	Ntham.	. Weringhausen	
	Wereingeurda (*Ex.*	Wieringerwaard,	Varengreville, *Nor.*
	Domesday) . .	*Holland.*	(2).
Wæsings	. Wessington, *Derby*	. Wessingen	
	Wasing, *Berks.* .	. Wasing. .	. Vasincourt, *Lorr.*
	Washington, *Dev. Dur.*		
	Sus.		
Wiscings	. Wissington, *Sal. Suf.*	Wiesing	
		Wissinghausen, *W.*	
Weordings	. Worthing, *Nor. Sus.*	Wörtingen	
Westings	. Westington, *Glou.*	. Oestinghausen, *W.*	
Wittings	. Whittington, *Dev. Gl.*	Wittingen	
	Nthld. Lan. Nor.	Weitingen	
	Sal. Staf. War. Wor.		
	Whittingham, *Lan.*		
	Nthld.		
	Weddington, *War.*	. Weddinghausen	
Wederings .	Wittering, *Sus.* .	. Wittringen	. Vetrigne, *Fr. Com.*
	Witherington, *Wilts.*		
Witlings	. Whitlingham, *Nor.*	. Wittlingen	.

** The English village-names have been taken chiefly from Mr. Kemble's lists, supplemented from the *Ordnance Maps*, the *Codex Diplomaticus* and *Domesday* : the German names from Bender's *Ortsnamen*, and the Government Surveys of Würtemberg and Bavaria : the French names from St. Fargeau's useful *Dictionnaire de toutes les Communes de la France*, and from the great French Survey.

1 Veringen in Charters, *Kausler*, vol. i. p. 315.

[APPENDIX D.—NOTE ON AFRICA.

See p. 56.

It is curious that a matter so important as the naming of a continent should be a matter of doubt. The likelihood seems to be that the name Africa was originally an adjectival form (*sc. terra*), the land of the Afer and was applied at first to a particular region in the north part of the continent in the neighbourhood of Tunis, from which it was extended to the whole, as also happened with the name of Asia. The Romans seem to have borrowed the word Afer from the Phœnician Afir, which has been identified by some with Aphar, a Semitic word for a city or metropolis, whence according to Dr. Peters came the Ophir of the Bible, the emporium of the gold-trade in South Arabia (possibly Moscha or Muza). So Peters, *Land of Ophir*, 44 ; 65 ; *The Eldorado of the Ancients* ; Hall and Neal, *Ancient Ruins of Rhodesia*, viii.–xi. 25–35 ; Peters, *Nach den neuesten Forschungen.* Glaser conjectures that Ophir (Aphar) may be the same word as the Indian Abhîra (and even the Greek Êpeiros, mainland). In that case the word may ultimately be from the Semitic *âbar*, Assyrian *ebêru*, to cross or pass over, whence the names 'Hebrew' and Beth-abara, ' place of passage '. So *aphar* (*afir*), would mean a landing-place to which one passes over, a coast or sea-board. The first ' Hebrew' (*ibrî* Greek περατὴς) was Abraham, when he migrated across the Euphrates. Compare in an Assyrian inscription ' Burat *i-bir*,' ' I crossed the Euphrates ' (Schrader, *Cuneiform Insc. and the O. Test.*, i. 143) ; and Driver, *Genesis*, 138. Asia, primitively a district of Lydia, the Asian mead of Homer (*Il.* ii. 461), seems to have been so called by the Phœnicians as the country to the East of them, being akin to the Assyrian *asū*, to rise (go forth), used of the sun (whence *sît Shamshi*, ' rising of the sun '). Thus Asia would be ' the Orient ' (like Japan, Anatolia, the Levant, etc.). Similarly the land to the West seems to have been named by the same people *Ereb* (compare Ass. *erêb shamshi*, ' the going in or setting of the sun '), the West (*Erebos*), whence Europa, the Occident (Oppert). An inscription of Sargon II says that he conquered ' ishtu sît shamshi adi *erib* Shamshi', from the *rising* of the sun to the *setting* of the sun, or, as we might say, ' from Asia to Europe '. Europa, as the dark region was appropriately the mother of Minos and Rhadamanthys in the nether world. The first syllable of the word, however, is not satisfactorily accounted for. [See *supra*, p. 55].]

[APPENDIX E.—NOTE ON BOZRA.

See p. 278.

The legend of the Carthaginian Byrsa (Semitic *Bozra*, a stronghold, Renan, *Sem. Lang.* 125), getting its name from the ox-hide strips which encircled it, Greek and Latin *bursa*, a hide of leather,

' Facti de nomine Byrsam
Taurino quantum possent circumdare tergo '—*Æneid*, i., 369,

has many widespread analogues in addition to those presented by Thong Caistor (Streatfield, *Linc. and the Danes*, 292), and Tong in Shropshire. Ivar obtains a large grant of land from Ella by the same device (*Saxo-Grammaticus*, Folk-lore Soc., 382), and Bulverhythe in Sussex according to local tradition was gained by William the Conqueror by the crafty extension of a bull's hide, just as St. Brigid with her cloak won an estate from the King of Leinster (P. Kennedy, *Legend. Fictions of Ir. Celts*, 296). An Amazon from the East similarly acquired from the Burmese aborigines as much land as an ox-hide could enclose, and cuts it into strips (' Shway Yoe ', *The Burman*, ii., 161). Harûnu-r-rashid gets a site for a castle in Turkey by the same artifice (*Travels of Evliya*, i., 25), and so does Sultan Mohammed (*id.* ii. 67). For a similar story among the Bechuanas and others see Frazer, *Adonis, Attis, Osiris*, 325–6.]

[APPENDIX F.—NOTE ON TIGRIS.

See p. 322.

The name of this river, not discussed by Dr. Taylor, deserves a note to itself. The earliest name for it, with which we are acquainted, was Diglat, seen in the Assyrian Idiglat, Hidiglat, which is generally analysed as Id-Diglat, ' the river Diglat ' (Lenormant, T.S.B.A. vi., 378), though it is interpreted by Muss-Arnolt as ' River of date-palms ' (*Assyr. Dict.*, *s.v. Idiglat*, p. 22). Hence comes the Hebrew form Hiddeqel in Genesis ii. 14. This Mesopotamian word was adopted and altered by the Persians into Tigrâ, as if ' the rapid ', with reference to the arrow-like swiftness of its current, for (as Strabo notes, xi. 148) ' Tigris with the Medes denotes an arrow ', Old. Pers. *tighri*, an arrow, *tighra*, sharp (Sansk. *tig*, to be sharp, Curtius, *Gk. Et.* i. 265 ; Pictet, *Origines Indo-Europ.* i. 425). The Zoroastrian *Tir Yasht* says ' Tigrish has the swiftness of an arrow and is the swiftest of Aryan rivers ' (Haug, *Essays on the Parsis*, 1878, p. 200). Compare in the *Avesta* ' swift he flew as the arrow ' (*tathra tigrish*—*Yasht*. viii. 6 ; *Drisler vol., Classical Studies*, p. 113).

Pliny speaks of the ' velocitas tremenda ' of the river (*Nat. Hist.* vi. 27), and notes ' a celeritate Tigris incipit vocari. Ita appellant Medi sagittam,' thus Englished by Philemon Holland, ' It is called Tigris for the swiftness thereof, which in the Median's language betokens a shaft '. Similarly Varro, ' et sagitta et vehementissimum flumen dicitur tigris ' (O. Schrader, *Prehistoric Antiquities of the Aryan Peoples*, p. 250 ; Yule, *Hobson Jobson*, *s.v. Tiger*).

' They ly neerer the diapry verges
Of tear-bridge *Tigris* swallow-swifter surges '.
J. Sylvester, *Works*, 1621, p. 276.

W.P.   B B

The modern name *Shat*, 'arrow', which is given to a portion of the river from its rapidity, curiously preserves the ancient meaning (O. H. Parry, *Six Months in a Syrian Monastery*, 1895, p. 265).

The same attribute of swiftness has given its name to the tiger (Lat. and Greek *tigris*), both river and beast sharing it in common ; just as with the Romans impetuous streams were symbolized by the bull (Compare *tauriformis Aufidus*, Hor. *Odes*. iv. 14, 25), and the Nile was sometimes called Aetos, 'Eagle', by the Greeks. 'Tigris is as moche for to seye as fast rennynge ; for he rennethe more faste than ony of the tother. And also there is a Best that is clepid Tigris, that is fast rennynge ' (*Voiage and Travaile of Sir John Maundevile*, ed. Halliwell, 1869, p. 304). Compare for the figurative use Byron's

> ' By the blue rushing of the *arrowy Rhone*'.—*Childe Harold*, iii. 71.

and Jean Ingelow's

> ' Again I hear the Lindis flow
> Swift as an arrow, sharpe and strong '.
> *The Brides of Enderby*.

Arwe or *Arewe*, the ancient name of the Orwell in Suffolk, is thought by some to be the same word as Old Eng. *arewe*, an arrow, but very possibly, like the Arrow in Warwickshire and Herefordshire, it is akin to the Arve, and Arar, and of Celtic origin. Camden says ' Whether this River Arrow tooke name of swiftnesse, as Tigris in Mesopotamia (for Arrow with us, like as *Tigris* among the Persians, betokeneth a shaft), or contrariwise, of the still streame and slow course, which *Ar* in the old French and British tongue implied, let other men looke who have better observed the nature of the River.'—*Brittania*, 1636, p. 565.

One would be tempted to compare Dart, the river in Devon, but that word is known to be a contraction of Darent.]

[APPENDIX G.—NOTE ON LIVERPOOL.

It is strange that the etymology of the names of the two most important cities in England should still be contested. Mr. Henry Harrison, in his *Place-Names of the Liverpool District*, 1898 (pp. 24–31) in a careful investigation of the history of the name, mentions that the earliest recorded spelling he was able to find is Leverpol in a deed of the reign of Richard I (1189–1199), Liverpul in a charter of John, 1207, and Leverepul *temp.* Henry III, 1229. But Litherpol appears almost equally early (*The Moore Charters relating to Liverpool*, part i., 1889). Harrison has ' Lire-poole or as it was called of old Liverpoole haven ' in Holinshed, *Chronicle* 1587, i, 84*b* (ed. Hooker).

The writer himself suggests that the name is from a Norse *hlithar pollr*, ' the pool of the slope', *hlithar* being the genitive of *hlith*, a slope, and compares Litherland in the vicinity as possibly being Norse *hlithar-lönd*, ' the land of the slope ' (p. 30). This has little to recommend it.

An old form of the word is Litherpul, understood to mean the ' stagnant pool,' whence Thomas Carlyle comes to say, ' The Creek of the Mersey . . . is a *Lither*-Pool, a *lazy* or sullen Pool, no monstrous pitchy City.'—*Past and Present*, book ii., ch. 5, *sub fin.*

' Lither-pool, sive *Pigra palus* '.—Baxter, *Glossarium Antiquitatum Britanicarum*, 1733, p. 213. *Lither* is a common word for lazy, sluggish, in the northern dialects.

' The River Mersey spreading abroad . . . entreth into the Irish Sea, where *Litherpoole*, called in the elder ages *Lifer-pole*, commonly *Lirpoole*, is seated, so named, as is thought, of the water spreading it selfe in manner of a Poole. . . . There is no mention extant thereof anywhere in ancient writers '.—*Camden, Britain*, 1637, p. 748.

In all probability the name was originally descriptive of the site as a *pool* infested by *livers*, *liver* being an old word for a water-flag or bulrush, still used in the Isle of Wight and elsewhere (glossed by *Gladiolus* and *Scirpus* in *Cockayne, Leechdoms* i., 382) ; A. Sax. *læfer, lebr*, the yellow flag, cognate with ' leaf ', Lat. *liber* (bark), Lith. *lapas*, leaf, and Greek λέπ-ειν, to scale off (whence ' *leper* '), the flat blade being distinctive of the plant. See Prof. Skeat, *Notes and Queries*, 6th S., ix., 173 ; 10th S., xi., 261. Of the same origin are Livermere in Suffolk and Liversedge in West Yorkshire.

When the right meaning of the word was forgotten some local antiquaries of an heraldic turn invented a bird to bear the name of *liver*, and introduced this fearful wild-fowl into the coat of arms of the city which it now adorns. See *N. and Q.*, 6th S., ix., 268.

' During the last decade the mythical *liver*, descendant by evolution of the eagle of St. John, cannot be said to have folded his wings in somnolent remembrance of the glories of the past '.—*Saturday Review*, vol. xlvi. p. 673.]

INDEX I

LOCAL NAMES

W.P.

C C

INDEX II

MATTERS

₊ Prefixes, suffixes, and roots are distinguished by the absence of an initial capital. English words whose etymology is explained or illustrated are printed in italics.